OLYMPIO

Books by André Maurois

ARIEL

BYRON

CAPTAINS AND KINGS

DISRAELI

MAPE

LYAUTEY

THE SILENCE OF COLONEL BRAMBLE

GENERAL BRAMBLE

DICKENS

PROPHETS AND POETS

THE THOUGHT READING MACHINE

RICOCHETS

THE MIRACLE OF ENGLAND

CHATEAUBRIAND

THE ART OF LIVING

TRAGEDY IN FRANCE

I REMEMBER, I REMEMBER

THE MIRACLE OF AMERICA

WOMAN WITHOUT LOVE

FROM MY JOURNAL

THE MIRACLE OF FRANCE

PROUST: *Portrait of a Genius*

LÉLIA: *The Life of George Sand*

OLYMPIO: *The Life of Victor Hugo*

OLYMPIO

THE LIFE OF VICTOR HUGO

by

ANDRÉ MAUROIS

Translated from the French by Gerard Hopkins

ILLUSTRATED

HARPER & BROTHERS | PUBLISHERS, NEW YORK

Contents

CONTENTS

Illustrations

Author's Foreword

WHY Hugo? I cannot, in his case, invoke the name of any mediator. To George Sand I was led by way of Marcel Proust and Alain: but I can remember no time when Victor Hugo was not for me an object of admiration. Even before I could read, I listened, thrilled, to my mother reciting *Les Pauvres Gens*. When I was fifteen, I was completely bowled over by *Les Misérables*. All my life long I have continually been discovering fresh aspects of his genius. It was only by degrees that I, like many other readers, came fully to understand the beauty of his great philosophic poems, and it was many years before I learned to love the last poems of *Le Vieux Orphée*, and to find in *Toute la Lyre*, *Les Années funestes* and *La Dernière Gerbe* a collection of almost unknown masterpieces.

Why Hugo? Because he is the greatest of all French poets, and because we need to know the story of his life if we are to understand his tormented genius to the full. How came it that this prudent, economical man was also generous? That this chaste adolescent, this model father, grew to be, in his last years, an ageing faun? That this legitimist changed, first into a Bonapartist, only, later still, to be hailed as the grandfather of the Republic? That this pacifist could sing, better than anybody, of the glories of the flags of Wagram? That this bourgeois in the eyes of other bourgeois came to assume the stature of a rebel? These are the questions that every biographer of Victor Hugo must answer. In the course of the last few years many new facts about him have been discovered; many of his letters and diaries have been published. I have tried to make a synthesis of these scattered documents, and out of them to compose the figure of a man.

Though this book contains many unpublished texts (Victor Hugo's letters to Madame Biard, to his daughter-in-law Alice, to his grandchildren, to the Comte de Salvandy and to Colonel Charras; Adèle Hugo's letters to Théophile Gautier; Auguste Vacquerie's letters to Adèle Hugo; extracts from Sainte-Beuve's notebooks; letters from Émile Deschamps to Victor Hugo and from Léopoldine Hugo to her father; letters from James Pradier to Juliette Drouet, etc.), these revelations were not my principal object. Indeed, I have withheld a great number of letters because, though interesting in themselves, they did not seem to me to add anything essential to the story. I had to be careful not to bury my hero under a pile of evidence, and I did not wish to overburden the narrative by introducing discussions on the art of poetry, on politics, on religion, on Hugo's sources, since this work has already been done, and well done, by others. In short, what I have done here is to write a life, nothing more and nothing less, always keeping clearly before me the fact that in the life of a poet his work plays as large a part as the incidents of his career.

I owe much to the researches and commentaries of those scholars who among my contemporaries are most familiar with Victor Hugo: Raymond Escholier, Henri Guillemin, Denis Saurat, M. Jean Sergent, curator of the Victor Hugo House, and his assistant, Mlle Madeleine Dubois, all of whom have been my guides to the contents of the wonderful collections over which they preside. From their catalogues and exhibitions I have acquired much useful and new information. My friends at the Bibliothèque nationale, MM. Julien Cain, Jean Porcher, Jacques Suffel, Marcel Thomas, Jean Prinet, have made available to me the manuscripts, notebooks and papers of Victor Hugo. M. Jean Pommier was so kind as to give me permission to publish certain fragments of Sainte-Beuve's posthumous article now in the Spœlberch de Lovenjoul Collection. M. Marcel Bouteron has, on my account, made researches into the fifth volume (still unpublished) of Balzac's *Lettres à l'Étrangère*.

Many documents have been generously put at my disposal by Mme Andrée Gaveau (before her marriage, Lefèvre-Vacquerie), by Mme Lucienne Delforge, and by MM. Georges Blaizot, Alfred Dupont, Jean Montargis, Philippe Hériat, Francis Ambrière and Gabriel Faure. Pierre de Lacretelle, whose mother was a friend of Alice Lockroy, has been so very kind as to tell me what he knows of the circle in which Victor Hugo spent his last years. Finally, my wife, with all her customary devotion, has collected for my examination many most precious letters. Without her help, this work, the largest in scale and the most difficult that I have undertaken, could never have been brought to a successful conclusion. All that I can say of myself is that I have done my best to reduce to order, with a lively sense of my duty to the cause of truth, all that is now known about the life of this great man.

Translator's Note

I HAVE provided English versions of the more extensive quotations from Victor Hugo's poetry. In a number of cases—alas! too few—I have been able to make use of the translations by the late Mr. Alan Conder, published in *Treasury of French Poetry* (Harper). These appear on pages 465, 470, 472 and 476 and are reprinted by courtesy of Mr. Conder's executrix. For the rest I alone am responsible. I claim to have done no more than provide a *construe* of the poems in question, and to have presented (with a few dishonesties of rhyme) a very rough idea of the metrical pattern of the originals. (All translations are to be found among the numbered notes beginning on page 459.)

G. H.

PART I

The Magic Sources of the Stream

Oh memories! treasures in darkness born!
Murky horizon of our ancient dreams!
Dear brilliance of a past that brightly beams!
Casting a radiance on things dead and gone!

VICTOR HUGO[1]

1

Two Strains in the Blood: Lorraine and Brittany

ROUND about the year 1770 there lived in Nancy a master-carpenter named Joseph Hugo, who enjoyed the privilege of claiming for his own use such timber as was floated down the Moselle. He was a tough character and of ill repute. The son of a farmer of Baudricourt, "hard by those pastures of Lorraine which had seen the birth of Jeanne d'Arc and of Claude Gelée,"[2] he had, in his younger days, served as an ensign in the Light Cavalry. Having first abandoned the plough for the sword, he then turned the sword into a plane. The family name, Germanic in origin, was common in Lorraine. In the sixteenth century a certain Georges Hugo had been a captain in the Guards and subsequently ennobled. Another, Louis Hugo, became Abbot of Estival and, later, Bishop of Ptolémaïs. Whether there was any relationship between the carpenter and the bishop we do not know, but the children of the former liked to believe that there was, and maintained that Françoise Hugo, Comtesse de Graffigny, habitually addressed their father as "cousin." Joseph Hugo had by his first wife, Dieudonnée Béchet, seven daughters, and by his second, Jeanne-Marguerite Michaud, five sons, all of whom served in the armies of the Revolution. Two of them were killed at Wissembourg; the other three became officers. After the fall of the monarchy military promotion assumed new importance as a method of bringing about a mingling of classes, and this particular family seemed instinctively to take to the profession of arms.

The third son, Joseph-Léopold-Sigisbert Hugo, was born in Nancy on November 15th, 1773. He had thick hair growing rather too low on his forehead, a broad nose, full, sensual lips, and a reddish complexion. His general appearance would have been vulgar, had not a good-natured expression, an intelligent gleam in the eyes, and a very sweet smile made him decidedly attractive. He began life as a pupil of the Canons Regular at Nancy, but his school career was cut short when he enlisted at the age of fifteen. He had a knowledge of Latin and of mathematics and could write reasonably well, not only military reports in the style of the day, but also madrigals, songs, letters in imitation of Rousseau and, later, a number of outrageously romantic novels, black

[2] Numbers refer to notes, which are arranged by chapters, beginning page 459.

as ink, and thickly sown with catastrophes. This normally gay young man and charming conversationalist was subject to gloomy moods and, at that time, was fully convinced that he was an object of persecution to his enemies. In 1792, as a junior captain in the Army of the Rhine, he was on terms of friendship with his battalion commander, Kléber, with Lieutenant Desaix, and with General Alexandre de Beauharnais, Joséphine's first husband. His men adored him and regarded him as a "good fellow," capable of terrible outbursts of temper, but also of much kindness. Fundamentally, in spite of his physical strength, he was a man of weak character, except in action, when he shone.

He was a gallant soldier, was wounded more than once, and had two horses killed under him. In 1793 he was sent to put down the insurrection of La Vendée and promoted major, to serve as adjutant to his best friend and commanding officer, Muscar. Hugo was twenty, Muscar thirty-four. The latter was a regular soldier, a Basque by birth, who had risen from the ranks. In 1791, after seventeen years in the king's service, he had not got beyond the rank of sergeant-major. The Revolution and the war gave him his chance. He had all the qualities which in troublous times go to the making of a military tribune. He was a fine figure of a man, with a stentorian voice, a ready flow of language, a gift of speaking to the point, and, it need scarcely be added, great courage. In the course of six months of fighting he was three times promoted. In 1793 the 8th Battalion of the Lower Rhine elected him as their commander.

Muscar and Hugo were naturally equipped to get on together. They had, in common, faith in the principles of 1789, a jovial and dissolute temperament, enthusiasm and loyalty. The task imposed upon them was, as is always the case in civil wars, savage in the extreme. Their orders were to burn down all isolated houses, especially châteaux, to raze all bakehouses and mills to the ground, and, in short, to make a desert of the countryside. Harassed by an enemy with whom they could never get to grips, in thickly wooded country intersected by ditches and hedges, the republicans became panicky. Both "Whites" and "Blues" shot their prisoners out of hand. Léopold Hugo, who owed everything to the Revolution, shared its passions to the point of signing himself "the sans-culotte Brutus Hugo," but remained human at heart. "Charette's brigands" quickly came to realize that this particular "Blue" was far from being incapable of pity. Maybe his reputation for mercy served the republican officer well with a Breton woman, Sophie Trébuchet, who lived at the manor-farm of La Renaudière, at Petit-Auverné, when he asked her to give temporary shelter to his exhausted men.

This handsome, delicate young creature with her brown eyes, her energetic and faintly arrogant air, and the straight line of brow and nose of a classical Greek statue, "abounded in vitality, vigour and animation, and had a magnificent complexion. Her easy carriage, her harmonious movements, combined to give her an appearance that was at once elegant and rustic."[3] She was one of the three daughters of a sea-captain of Nantes who had engaged in the slave-trade, and grand-daughter, on her mother's side, of a judge in the same city, Monsieur Lenormand du Buisson. The Trébuchets and the Lenormands had, like everybody else, been royalists under the monarchy. The national up-heaval brought division into the family. Some of Sophie Trébuchet's relations were "Whites," others "Blues." Her maternal grandfather, Lenormand du Buisson, a lawyer by profession and litigious by nature, had consented to serve on the revolutionary tribunal of Nantes, thereby forfeiting the respect of his granddaughter, who was sickened by the excesses of the Terror.

Left an orphan in childhood, Sophie had been brought up by an aunt, a managing woman of royalist sympathies and Voltairean lean-ings, whose ideas the young girl soon adopted. This Aunt Robin, the widow of a notary, was sixty years old when her niece was entrusted to her care in 1784. In 1789 she had viewed with favour the summoning of the States-General, but in 1793 both aunt and niece, outraged by the activities of the butchers of Nantes and by the execution of those whom they most respected, decided to take refuge in the small town of Châ-teaubriant, where they had relations. Not far from that place, in the very heart of the royalist country, lay the estate of La Renaudière which for two hundred years had belonged to the Trébuchet family.

Strong-minded and independent, like many girls who have grown to womanhood without the care and companionship of a mother, obsti-nate, free-thinking and generous, Sophie Trébuchet galloped along the sunken roads which lay round Châteaubriant, protected from official interference by a civilian identity-card which had been issued to her (thanks, no doubt, to grandfather Lenormand) by Carrier, the terrible Jacobin pro-consul of Nantes. This she used as a talisman in her self-imposed activities of saving refractory priests and helping "Chouans" to escape.

For she had become a "whole-hearted woman of La Vendée, filled with a horror of the despotism exercised by the Convention." In actual fact, the choice before the two ladies at Châteaubriant lay between two forms of terrorism—that of the Jacobin soldiers on the one side, that of the "brigands" or Chouans, on the other: Red Terror or White. And so it was that Sophie came to prefer her simple country establishment to the small market-town the inhabitants of which were rent with hatreds. She loved to wear clogs and to work in her garden. At Petit-Auverné the local bumpkins still called her "our young lady" as in the old days. A free-living young amazon, proud of her connection with the neigh-bouring squirearchy, a woman of stoic temperament, occupied in the tending of flowers and the reading of poetry, dreaming of some vague, heroic husband-to-be, she grew more and more attached, as the days went by, to the mysterious countryside which lay around her home.

The small army of "Blues," short of food, perpetually harried, kept in a constant state of nerves by the general atmosphere of hatred in which it moved, sought revenge in killing and pillaging. The courageous Muscar, a fine and by no means bloodthirsty man, was far from happy: "It is distressing to be in command of troops who bring dishonour on their leaders." But that feeling did not keep him from calling down curses on the "furies, scoundrels and termagants" who were hand in glove with the Chouans and did all they could to get patriots massacred. Sophie Trébuchet was one such, and took sides all the more violently since the "Blues" at La Renaudière indulged in "an orgy of blood and lust."

Nevertheless, when, one summer's day of 1796, riding in the direction of Châteaubriant, she met the gay Captain Hugo, who was beating the coverts for "brigands," she found more than one reason for being friendly. The young officer was not responsible for the massacres. She had heard that his influence over Muscar was considerable, and knew that influence to be good. But what counted most with her was that a peasant had just said to her: "The Blues are upon us. All our priests are nearby. Keep the brutes occupied." She thereby played the coquette, not without success; at once agreed to extend the hospitality of her house to Hugo and his men; and took the whole detachment back with her to La Renaudière.

Conversation followed food and drink. The young captain was decidedly presentable. He was not without education, quoted Livy and Tacitus, recited poems by Voltaire and elegies by Parny, as well as madrigals and acrostics of his own, "composed in a style admirably suited to appeal to the fair." Furthermore, he was the possessor of a crude but pleasing humour, and at all times was as ready to sing as to fight.

To be on good terms with Hugo, the regimental adjutant who exercised great powers in the neighbourhood, suited the young lady's book. She saw him more than once and observed, with no little curiosity, this captain of twenty-three, with the sensual lips and tender glances. Although he took about with him on active service, as did all his fellow-officers, a lady of easy virtue (this one was called Louise Bouin, who "was better equipped in body than in mind," and insisted on being called "Hugo's Lady"), and in spite of the fact that he boasted rather coarsely of his amorous conquests, he was attracted by this young Breton woman who had the courage and the intelligence of a man. She thought it good policy to get him and Muscar invited to her Aunt Robin's. Most of the local houses were closed to the officers of the Republic and these two were touched by the more kindly welcome extended to them. The young woman was clever and the glow of youth made her almost pretty. Very soon they were calling the niece "Sophie," and her Aunt Robin "Aunt." On her side, Sophie, who in temperament was distinctly Spanish, found that her interest in the young captain was growing. He had been responsible for saving the lives of women, hostages and children. She enjoyed going for rides with him along the sunken roads of the Bocage, all the while stoutly maintaining that the war now being waged against the Chouans was unjust. Hugo vigorously defended the Republic, but admired the strength of mind shown by this young woman for whom he felt an urge of desire. He was no less surprised at his own respectful attitude towards her than was she by the fact that she could speak thus freely to an enemy.

This strangely discordant idyll was of short duration. As the result of a quarrel between Muscar and his general, the 8th Battalion of the Regiment of the Lower Rhine was recalled to Paris by the Directory. Brutus Hugo experienced an attack of melancholy when it came to leaving his Breton enchantress. Aunt Robin also regretted the separation. She was sufficiently philosophical to accept the changed times and would have put no difficulties in the way of a marriage between her niece and a republican officer. But when she sounded Sophie on the matter, the girl said that "marriage was not for her." She returned to her way of living at La Renaudière and the cultivation of her garden. Meanwhile Hugo, now in Paris, did not forget his "little Sophie of Châteaubriant" and continued to write to her, though he kept with him, for day-to-day use, his Louise Bouin of the well-equipped body. *Hugo to Muscar*: "I press her often to my heart, and feel through her two pretty spheres the movement that gives life to the world!" Let us draw a veil.[4]

Strange to relate, the high-spirited and lusty captain succumbed to an odd persecution-mania whenever he was thwarted. After Muscar had relinquished the command of the battalion, Hugo exhausted the patience of the High Command with grievances against his new chief, "a rascal who deserves not only to be put in irons but condemned to death," "a muddy-minded scoundrel," "a crocodile spewed up by the Rhine." The complainant was got rid of by being appointed "rapporteur" to the War Council, a position which entitled him to quarters in the Hôtel de Ville on the Place de Grève. There it was impossible for him to keep a concubine. Louise Bouin disappeared with the discreet and rapid indifference usual in those days, and the captain was free to dream of Sophie Trébuchet. She replied to his letters with "an extreme reserve" and a "modesty of feeling" very different from the captain's amusing fluency. Perhaps that very reserve had a stimulating effect upon him. However that may be, he sent her an offer of marriage.

She was alone in the world. She was his senior in age by seventeen months. She needed someone to lean on. Still, she seemed scarcely even tempted by the proposal, and only after her friends in Nantes had brought strong pressure to bear did she make up her mind. She went to Paris in the company of her brother. Hugo's "raptures overwhelmed her," and on November 15th they went through the form of civil marriage at the Mairie on the 19th arrondissement, the Quarter of La Fidélité. The contract shows that the captain, apart from his pay, had a certain amount of property and a private income. His bride brought nothing to the common stock, since the freehold of La Renaudière did not belong to her. The soldier, however, generously accepted an arrangement by which all property acquired by husband or wife should be held in common and, though life under the Directory was very expensive, he never complained. "Money," he said, "is only the sinews of war. All that matters is that I should have enough for us to live on in times of peace. I am free of debts and of worries."

The young couple spent two years in Paris. Hugo was deeply in love with his delicate Breton wife; she was slightly wearied by her husband's burning verbosity and taste for broad humour, and exhausted by her bull-necked companion's amorous propensities. She remained, however, secretive, tenacious and imperious. She long retained unhappy memories of the "gloomy times spent in the old communal dwelling, with its pictures torn to shreds and its walls befouled by the Revolution." The young household had neither linen nor crockery. Sophie regretted La Renaudière with its garden, and the salty air of her native Brittany. Their best friend was the Clerk to the Tribunal, Pierre Foucher, the son of a Nantes cobbler and a friend of the Trébuchet family, who was the same age as Hugo but of a very different temperament, being prudent, chaste and sedentary. The education which Foucher had received from an ecclesiastical uncle was better suited to a monk than a soldier. "There was one point only on which the two friends were at variance— politics. The rapporteur was a republican, the clerk, a royalist."[5] Neither, however, was violent in his views. When the clerk, a few weeks after his friend's marriage, wedded Anne-Victoire Asseline, he asked Hugo to act as his witness. At the wedding-breakfast Hugo filled his glass and said: "You must have a daughter, I a son, and we'll marry 'em. I drink to their future family."

In the Paris of the Directory, with its lascivious draperies and daring talk, the young Hugo couple were constant visitors to places of entertainment. Sophie wore the flimsy garments which, as her husband said in the abstract bawdy of the day, "offered to the curious eye a spectacle of the most secret charms." In the Jardins d'Italie at the corner of the rue de Chaillot and the Champs Élysées, where extremely frank *tableaux vivants* were displayed, such, for instance, as "The Conjunction of Mars and Venus under a Transparency of Clouds," they met a

certain Colonel Lahorie, now Adjutant-General, who had been one of
Sophie Trébuchet's childhood friends. Victor Fanneau Lahorie had
come originally from Mayenne. Though he had rallied to the Revolution, he still retained the aristocratic manners which he had acquired at
Louis-le-Grand at a time when it was still a Jesuit school. He wore a
well-cut blue dress-coat, blue breeches without braid, a "black cocked
hat with a tiny cockade, and white gloves." In short, he looked distinguished in a quiet, classical way. Sophie's pleasure at renewing the
acquaintance was obvious. No doubt she appreciated his noble gravity
the more for being in such glaring contrast with her husband's exuberance. In a period of loose manners, the colonel of the flashing eyes lived
in a condition of celibacy. He was a great reader of the Roman and
French poets, a stoic and a dreamer. "He was a man of highly cultivated
intelligence which he knew how to display to advantage." By temperament he was a proud and exacting man who deserved to be loved. He
became closely attached to the young couple, who set great store by his
friendship. The husband was pleased to have found as protector a man
who was General Moreau's friend and had been entrusted by the Directory with several missions to the Army of Italy. His wife was happy in
the possession of a confidant who was as discreet and secretive as she was
herself.

In 1798 a son, Abel, was born to the Hugos, and in the following year
the major, as he now was, was returned to active service. Since the 20th
Half-Brigade, to which he belonged, had been detailed to form part of
the Army of the Rhine—at that time proudly called the Army of the
Danube—he settled his wife at Nancy. Her address was: "Citizeness
Hugo the younger: at his mother's house, rue des Maréchaux, Old
Town, Nancy." The street was melancholy, the house gloomy. The
yellowish façade was as dismal as the courtyard was dark. The Breton
woman, used to an open-air life, could scarcely breathe. She liked
neither her mother-in-law, nor, especially, her sister-in law Marguerite,
more commonly known as Goton, the wife of Martin-Chopine, who
presumed to dictate to her. Sophie wished to suckle her baby, to wash
him, to give him plenty of fresh air. Her in-laws were all for bottle-feed-
ing, and cleansing with the corner of a towel. Like so many heroes
fought over by wife and mother, Léopold Hugo agreed with each in
turn.

Lahorie, the handsome colonel met in the Jardins d'Italie, came to
Nancy. He had not forgotten the serious Sophie. She was his ideal of
what a wife should be and he got into the habit of going to chat with
her. There was no lack of a meeting-ground: severe comments on the
Terror, hopes of peace and genuine liberty, praises of General Moreau
to whom Lahorie was attached for service, nostalgic memories of childhood years spent in Brittany and Normandy. These meetings led to

the birth of a secret love which, at first, was scarcely conscious and certainly was altogether innocent. In December 1799 Moreau was appointed Commander-in-Chief of the Army of the Rhine. Lahorie became his chief-of-staff and, in accordance with an immemorial army tradition, Major Hugo, whose wife was a great favourite with the young general, was now in a position to get everything he wanted, and was seconded for personal duty with Moreau.

At first he left his wife at Nancy. Once more pregnant, and vaguely in love with another man, Sophie was more than ever terrified of her husband's voracious sensuality, begged for a marital holiday, and in letters which the major, himself a correspondent of the Saint-Preux school, found icy, asked to be allowed to have her child in Brittany. *The Major to Madame Léopold Hugo:* "I by no means disapprove of your pleasure at the thought of leaving Nancy, and of seeing once again a family to which you are devoted, but the manner in which it is expressed wrings my heart . . ."[6] She wanted to take little Abel with her to La Renaudière: "I should be vexed in the extreme," she wrote, "were I compelled to leave him in a part of the country to which I am bidding farewell for ever . . . Once back in my own home, I shall not move again. You will be completely free to visit me and your children there at such times as you may wish to be with us."[7]

This hostile attitude drove the young husband to despair: "Can it, indeed, be you, Sophie, who penned those cruel words?" He spoke of suicide, but the threat was no more than literary posturing: "I was about to . . . then I stopped myself, though not from fear . . ." He would not hear of her leaving, and wrote from Augsburg saying that he would come to see her at Nancy: "The picture I conjure up of sitting with you on one knee and Abel on the other, the thought of the pleasure that will be mine when I kiss that darling body already rich with the promise of new happiness . . ."[8] These pictures of domestic and carnal bliss made no appeal to Sophie. In vain did the major insist on the delight that would be his could he only lie beside her and take her in his arms. That was precisely what she most dreaded. Nevertheless, after the birth of a second son, Eugène, on September 16th at Nancy, she had, in duty bound, to rejoin her husband at Lunéville, of which town he had been appointed governor. She found Lahorie there as well, now in high favour, and charged by Joseph Bonaparte with the task of conducting peace negotiations. He acquitted himself with a fine feeling for diplomacy. The distinction of his person, the polished perfection of his language, showed to great advantage by comparison with the vulgarity of those with whom he was associated. "He has," said Ségur, "the manners of a royalist." As to Governor Hugo, he ordered a set of fine uniforms, and showed a pride in the successes of his wife, whose intelligence called forth praise from no less a person than Joseph

Bonaparte. To his former comrade-in-arms, Muscar, now governor of the garrison-town of Ostend, Hugh wrote an enthusiastic letter full of "my adorable Sophie" and of the "excellent Lahorie." The situation was developing along classical lines.

At the Headquarters of the Army of the Rhine Hugo was now hand-in-glove with General Moreau. It turned out to be an unfortunate intimacy, for when, in 1800, Moreau was cast for the part of rival to Bonaparte, his familiars aroused suspicion in the mind of the new master. Though enjoying the warm recommendation of Joseph, Hugo left Lunéville without achieving further promotion. Friends who had his future at heart managed to get him appointed as a battalion commander in the 20th Half-Brigade. "This," he said, "was the beginning for me of a whole new series of troubles and discouragements . . . ,"[9] for the 20th Half-Brigade was commanded by a senior officer with whom he had quarrelled.

In 1801, as a result of an expedition into the mountains during the journey from Lunéville to Besançon, a third Hugo child was conceived, as his father once told him, at Donon, the highest point of the Vosges, among the clouds—which shows that the major's ardour was still imperious and sudden. This third son was born at Besançon on February 26th, 1802, in an old seventeenth-century house. The parents had asked General Victor Lahorie to stand godfather to the child, and Marie Bessirier, wife of Jacques Delelée, Brigade Commander and Governor of Besançon, godmother, whence his name, Victor-Marie. In point of fact there was no baptismal ceremony, and the godparents were no more than witnesses at the civil registration. Lahorie, who by that time had returned to Paris, was represented by General Delelée.

The child was to all appearances so sickly that the doctor was convinced it would not live. It was saved by the sheer "obstinacy" of its mother. *Hugo to Muscar*: "I have three children, my dear Muscar, all of them boys. The conditions of my life are suited to boys. If they follow in my footsteps, I shall be satisfied. If they do better than I have been able to do, I shall bless the days of their birth as truly as I adore the mother who gave them to me . . . My brother has turned up here.[10] He is a strapping young fellow of five foot six who has served throughout the war as a grenadier in the Army of the Sambre-et-Meuse. I have got him a second-lieutenant's commission. There is one left.[11] I have been hard put to it to find him a job, not but what he's a good chap. He did well at school and is the author of a tragedy which is not without merit . . . He has decided to enlist."[12]

These Hugo brothers were a fine lot, soldiers or poets, all of them. But Léopold was ill served by his love of plain speaking. In the 20th, this tiresome habit had involved him in an unequal tussle with his commanding officer, a certain Colonel Guestard, who had a way of keeping the regimental accounts undisclosed. Hugo charged him with this and was accused of fomenting mutiny among the officers. It was an unfortunate business, since no friend of Moreau could rely on support in high places. The colonel complained of the violent, quarrelsome character of this "coarse-grained major who sports the blue uniform coat of the Spartiates in the Army of the Rhine." *Hugo to Muscar*: "He had the impudence to say that I had seen no active service! . . . The scoundrel judges me by himself."[13] In the black books of the War Ministry, Hugo now figured as a "schemer." The First Consul had a horror of mischief-makers. Six weeks after the birth of his third son, the "coarse-grained major" was ordered to report to Marseille to take over command of a battalion due to leave for Santo Domingo.

Convinced that he was a victim of persecution and, as such, in imminent danger, he was foolish enough to send his wife to Paris, there to beg Joseph Bonaparte, General Clarke and Lahorie to snatch him from the clutches of his enemies by getting him a change of appointment. Sophie, though saddened by the thought of having to leave her three sons, agreed to make the journey; she had always had a weakness for difficult missions. But to apply for help to Lahorie was, to say the least, imprudent, and it was not difficult to see what would happen.

The general now had fanned-out whiskers, and wore his hair *à la* Titus. He painted a far from encouraging picture of the situation. For some considerable time he had been acting as intermediary between his patron Moreau and the First Consul who, though he did not trust the former Commander of the Army of the Rhine, was still handling him with kid gloves. Bonaparte could easily have won Lahorie to his cause by offering him an embassy, but this he did not do. The other had, as a result, been forced to fall back on Moreau, though he was well aware of his weakness. The Consul refused to have Lahorie promoted to the rank of divisional general, a decision which was tantamount to condemning him to retirement at the age of thirty-seven and, almost certainly, to disgrace. The general was far from well. His complexion had taken on a yellowish tinge. The flashing eyes were sunken. Sophie, a fighter by nature, urged him to accept the First Consul's challenge. Royalist emissaries were paying court to Moreau. This daughter of La Vendée came out strongly in favour of such an alliance, at least in so far as it might lead to the overthrow of Bonaparte. Her advice was lacking in prudence: but she had an aggressive temperament, and her feelings were nothing if not ardent.

Meanwhile, at Marseille, the young Victor, prematurely weaned, had been handed over to the care of the batman's wife. Major Hugo, promoted to the position of nursing-father, watched over his three sons, did all he could for them, and was loud in protestations of conjugal love. "I made them kiss your letter, and gave them sweets which I pretended had been sent by their adored mother . . . Have no fear of my youth, nor of the temptations of which this town is full . . . You will find, when we next see one another, that I have remained worthy of your chaste endearments."[14] True to his role of the Eternal Husband, he attempted to overcome any misgivings he might have at her unexpectedly prolonged absence: "no wife, and I should be profoundly unhappy were I proved wrong in this belief, could be more devoted to her husband."[15] The very wording, however, proves that he was not without a certain amount of uneasiness. On January 1st, 1803, he sent news of the boys to their mother: "Today, Abel came in to wish me a Happy New Year, with fat Eugène at his heels, who repeated it: they made a comic little couple. If you have reason to believe that your efforts will be unavailing, shorten my widowerhood, I beg of you, and return hither to console me. If unhappiness is to be my lot, I shall feel it less keenly when I am once more your lord and master."[16]

In June 1803 Victor, then sixteen months old, loudly demanded, according to the major, his "mamaman." In strict truth, he scarcely knew her. Madame Hugo was just then at the Château of Saint-Just, near Vernon, with Lahorie, now fallen into disfavour. The "Moreau club" was continuing its imprudent attacks on Bonaparte, who struck back with thunderbolts at his presumptuous enemies. In spite of Sophie's representations to Joseph Bonaparte, Major Hugo was dispatched to Corsica. With his three small children he took ship for Bastia, an ancient town of tall, gloomy houses. "Come back, my dear Sophie, to the arms of your faithful Hugo. Rest assured of my fidelity. Apart from the fact that laying siege to the ladies of this place is fraught with danger—not only of disease, but of stiletto thrusts—the ever-present memory of you, and the constant vision of your dear face, would in themselves be enough to keep me from inflicting upon you pains and sorrows, your possible reprisals for which cause me to die of misery."[17]

Reprisals, in this case, had anticipated offence. Madame Hugo scarcely troubled to reply, and the neglected father was kept busy with three small urchins who were cutting their teeth. "One might compare him," said Sainte-Beuve, "to a warrior of gigantic stature carrying in his helmet three chubby tots with the faces of young cherubs, on each day's march, with a mother's tender care."[18]

Abel was sent to school; Eugène, fat and pink-cheeked, with fair, curly hair, was a favourite with the women; Victor remained frail and melancholy. With his enormous head, seemingly too big for his body, he looked like a deformed dwarf. "He was to be found crying quietly to himself in corners, though no one ever knew the reason for his tears."[19] His father entrusted him to a woman who took him for walks, but from the very first Victor conceived an intense dislike of her. He resented her inability to speak French and called her *cattiva,* nasty. It is not difficult to imagine the attitude of this sickly junior to a couple of vigorous brothers now that he was deprived of his mother. It was in this way that he developed an underlying melancholy which all through his life from time to time broke through the surface of his prodigious vitality.

In 1803 the battalion was moved to the isle of Elba, and it was there, at Porto-Ferrajo, that Madame Hugo at last rejoined her family. Her husband had insisted on her coming. "Everybody here thinks it a mighty strange thing that you do not put in an appearance, and that I should be left with the children. The situation is giving rise to tittle-tattle . . ." When she did come she was quite certain in her own mind what it was she wanted—to take back to Paris the three sons whom she adored, and there to rejoin Lahorie. She took the major's consent for granted. From her knowledge of him she thought it more than likely that he was conducting some amorous intrigue and that he was probably longing to be free. And indeed, almost as soon as she arrived, certain kindly souls informed her that the major was deep in a liaison with a local woman, Catherine Thomas, whose father, the almoner of the hospital, had just been dismissed for malversation of funds. Sophie, though she, too, was far from guiltless, adopted an attitude of injured innocence, rejected the advances of the amorous major, and left again in November 1803. Her stay at Porto-Ferrajo had lasted for less than four months.

She later maintained that her husband had not pressed her to stay, and was concerned only to be free so that he might live openly with his mistress. It is no use pretending that Major Hugo was not weak where bodily appetites were concerned. All the same, he would have preferred to keep the mother of his children with him if she had been willing to make their life together tolerable. But husband and wife were temperamentally ill-suited. *The Major to Madame Hugo, March 8th, 1804:* "Farewell, Sophie. Always remember that there is a worm for ever gnawing at me—the desire to possess you; that I am at that period of a man's life when passions are at the strongest, and that, though I may gird at you, I feel an imperious need to press you to my heart."[20] Had she returned to him sooner, he would never, so he asserted, have been unfaithful. "Yes, I want to remain true to you, and to you alone. But, if that is to be possible, I must not be treated with coldness and snubs. If you cannot give me that assurance, then we had far better live apart."[21] The rupture was not complete. He loved his sons; he admitted his misdoings, but placed the responsibility for them on his wife:

It is but natural that a man of my age, and one endowed, as I am, with excessive ardour, should occasionally have forgotten himself. But the fault has lain always with you. I am too young to live alone, too healthy not to be attracted by women. I love, nay, I will go further and say that I am still prepared to *adore*, my own dear one, provided that my own dear one will bring herself to recognize that I need her love and kindness. Only when my wife is with me can I be sane and sensible. Consequently, my dear Sophie, I think it better that I should give you a child the more, rather than neglect you for another, and see them grow up far from the eyes of a fond father. I have, I believe, a sufficiently good heart to ensure the happiness of any woman who will judge me fairly and without prejudice. Physically speaking—and this I would say to none but you—I have never been better than I am at this present. In the matter of education, I have made a deal of progress during your absence. . . .[22]

Such disarming frankness might, in different circumstances, have had its effect on Sophie, but her heart was elsewhere. In the course of her long and difficult return journey she found pleasure in the thought of presenting her three sons to Lahorie—the sturdy Abel, Eugène with his golden curls, and little Victor, so delicate and sensitive. When their conveyance drew up at the coach-office in the rue Notre-Dame-des-Victoires, she was surprised that Lahorie was not there to meet her, for she had notified him of her arrival. She hastened to the general's lodging. Two notices were affixed to the door. They stated that royalist brigands had made an attempt on the life of the First Consul, and urged the people of Paris to denounce their accomplices, that they might be brought to justice. There followed a list of suspects. Among them she read: "Victor-Claude-Alexandre Fanneau Lahorie."

She was overwhelmed, though not surprised. That Moreau had conspired against Bonaparte; that he had regarded the Concordat as nothing more than a meaningless formula; that he had refused to accept the Légion d'Honneur; that he was surrounded by foreigners, émigrés and political visionaries; that his wife and his mother-in-law had been openly plotting—these had been facts well known to her before she left Paris. She knew also—who better?—that Lahorie had played a part in rousing Moreau against the First Consul, and that, republican though he was, he had been in favour of a temporary alliance with the royalists. Moreau who, at one time, had been a genuine Jacobin, and still smelled of his past, had long held back. He was Lord of the Manor of Grosbois; he had grown fat, and remained libidinous. He was the type of man who would lead his troops to the bank of the Rubicon . . . and then give a party.

The only one of his familiars who had any energy was Lahorie. The police of the Consulate, therefore, attached particular importance to laying their hands on him. His description was circulated to all prefects: *Height, five foot two; hair, black and worn* à la *Titus; eyes, black, rather wide-open, though sunken—the whites yellowish; face, marked*

with small-pox. Has a sardonic laugh. A further distinguishing mark
was that he had bandy legs as the result of much riding. The police
looked for him far and wide, in Mayenne, at the Château of Saint-Just,
at a friend's house, No. 19 rue de Clichy. He was nowhere to be found.
Actually, he was living opposite, at No. 24, under the protection of
Madame Hugo, who had taken up her residence there, with her sons,
a few days earlier. He stayed there for only four days and then, not
wishing to endanger his friend, resumed the life of a hunted man.
Napoleon Bonaparte, inclined to clemency by nature as well as by
political considerations, would have been only too glad for the young
general to have got away to the United States, there to live forgotten.
But Lahorie stayed on in France and from time to time, now in this
disguise, now in that, put in an appearance at the rue de Clichy, where
he was always welcomed with kindness.

2

I Had Dreams of War

IT WAS with this house in the rue de Clichy that Victor Hugo's earliest memories were connected. He recalled that it had a courtyard in which there was a well, next to the well a trough, and, shading the trough, a willow; that his mother sent him to school in the rue Mont-Blanc; that, because he was very small, he was given more attention than the other children; that every morning he was taken into the room of Mademoiselle Rose, the headmaster's daughter; that Mademoiselle Rose, not yet up, would seat him on the bed beside her; that while she was dressing he used to watch her putting on her stockings.[1] The earliest stirrings of sensuality leave deep scars, and the grown man is for ever trying to recover the emotions of childhood. This particular man was to be obsessed, all his life long, by "unshod idylls," by women's legs, their white or black stockings, their naked feet.

Meanwhile, Léopold Hugo had been transferred to Italy. The easygoing Joseph Bonaparte, a man of the study, transformed against his will by an illustrious brother into a man of war, had been ordered to conquer the Kingdom of Naples. Major Hugo was known to the new monarch, having served under him at Lunéville, and Joseph felt well disposed towards him; but the authorities in Paris long set their faces against granting advancement to an officer who had been compromised by his association with Moreau and Lahorie. Sophie no longer gave a thought to her distant husband, except when she wanted money. For all she cared, he might have ceased to exist. He sent her half his pay, not without a good deal of grumbling. When this allowance fell into arrears, Lahorie, who still possessed secret reserves of cash, provided for the needs of the family.

At last Hugo got his chance to win distinction. After the occupation of Naples, bands of cut-throats, part patriots, part brigands, began to appear all over Calabria. The most daring of their leaders, Michel Pezza, known as "Fra Diavolo," an irregular rather than a bandit, since he was in arms against the Occupying Power, was captured by the major after a desperate battle. This incident gained for Hugo a "gigantic reputation." He was appointed governor of the province of Avellino by Joseph, and promoted colonel of the Royal-Corse.

About this time (1807) Lahorie's position had taken a turn for the worse. What money he had was exhausted. The life of a hunted man had given to his face a secretive look. His jaws moved incessantly in an aimless way, like "those of a man who is suffering from lockjaw." Feverish and restless, he thought with regret of the days when the soldiers of Liberty had blithely entered the cities of Bavaria and the Tyrol, and he cursed the "tyrant" who, this time, was not Louis XVI, but the Emperor. When Sophie realized that her friend, spied upon by Fouché, could no longer come to Paris, and that money for her children would be lacking, she at last decided to obey her husband and again return to him. This, however, he no longer wanted. "I have no intention of asking you to come to me. You have killed all desire in me for a life in common with you, until such time as I have some fixed and definite employment."[2] But necessity is a hard task-master. Sophie ignored her husband's protests, and in October 1807 started for Italy without notifying him of her intention.

Little Victor was no more than five, but a sensitive and observant child. Until the end of his life he remembered that journey across France by diligence: Mont Cenis, and the way the ice crackled under the runners of the sledge; an eagle brought down in the mountains, and then eaten; but, above all, gobbets of human flesh, still raw and bleeding, hanging from trees, and seen by him and his brothers through the glass of the windows on which, to pass the time, they had stuck little crosses made of straw. Horror of the death-penalty, an obsession with torture and hanging, the antithesis of Cross and Gallows, all of them ideas by which he was haunted all through his life, had their roots in these violent impressions of childhood. Madame Hugo, who infinitely preferred Breton gardens to the vivid colours of the South, had no thoughts to spare for anything but lodgings. The children, however, were enchanted by Naples "glittering in the sun, and wearing a garment of white, fringed with blue."[3] How proud they felt, too, when they were welcomed at their journey's end by the colonel in his gorgeous uniform. It was wonderful to be the children of the governor, and members of the winning side.

In point of fact, the colonel, who had been living in Government House with the woman Thomas, was flabbergasted at his wife's arrival. But he had decent feelings, and was fond of his sons. He lodged the family in Naples and, having evacuated Catherine Thomas, even opened the house at Avellino for their temporary reception.

Every child lives in a fairy land, but the fairy land in which Victor Hugo's early years were spent was more than usually glittering. During the time of their residence in Italy the three brothers lived in a palace of cracked marble, close to which was a deep ravine overshadowed by hazels. No longer did they have to go to school, but enjoyed unhampered freedom, a sort of holiday atmosphere, the thought of which Victor relished until the day of his death. Their father was all-powerful, but they saw very little of him. From time to time he would put in an appearance, straddling his great sabre to amuse the boys, though there were always cavalrymen in shining helmets in respectful attendance on him in the great court. He was the friend of the King of Naples, who was no less a person than the Emperor's brother, and had had little Victor entered on the role of the Royal-Corse. From that moment the boy thought of himself as a soldier. The children, filled with admiration, played with their father's gold epaulettes. In his letters the colonel spoke of them with affection: "Victor, the youngest, shows great aptitude for his studies. He is as staid as his eldest brother, and very thoughtful. I have been more than once struck by the things he says. There is great gentleness in the expression of his face. All three are good lads and devoted to one another. The two older ones are extremely fond of their small brother. Not to have them still with me makes me very sad. But there are no educational facilities here. It is essential that they go back to Paris."[4]

That, however, was not the real reason. There had been no reconciliation between the colonel and his wife. The woman Thomas, and Victor Lahorie, bulked too largely on the horizon. The mistress insisted that the wife should be sent packing: the wife refused to be treated as though she were a mistress. The boys felt that some mysterious struggle was going on, though they had a very imperfect knowledge of its causes. They were proud of their father, yet fully conscious of any injury done by him to their adored mother. It was with sadness in their hearts that they left the lovely marble palace. In Italy they had renewed acquaintance with the two children of Pierre Foucher, their father's friend. The Clerk of the Court had had himself temporarily appointed as Inspector of Supplies in Italy. There had been a diminution of litigation, and the clerk's source of income in Paris had dwindled. He dreamed now of military contracting, in which fortunes were being made. Victor Foucher was five; Adèle, four. She was a dreamy, absent-minded little girl "with a brow already golden, and bronzed shoulders . . ."[5] The three Hugo boys adopted her. There were games of "boule" with oranges. But Madame Foucher, insensible to the charms of Naples, was homesick for the rue du Cherche-Midi and the shady garden of the Hôtel de Toulouse. The Foucher family left Italy at almost the same time as Madame Hugo and her sons.

In any case, they would not have remained long in Naples, for soon after their departure Colonel Hugo was summoned to Madrid by Joseph Bonaparte, now elevated to the position of "King of Spain and the Indies." The Emperor moved kings about as others move colonels. Léopold Hugo had given up all thought of recapturing his wife's affection, though not of remaining the protector of his children. "You are very much convinced in the matter of your own conscience. In nothing does mine reproach me, and to decide which of us two is more in the right would mean loading all the wrongs into one scale. Let us leave it to time to calm the memory of our most unfortunate situation. Bring up your children to show the respect they owe to us, and give them an education suited to their abilities. So conduct matters that, in time to come, they may even be in a position to render good service. Let us stick to them, since we have found how difficult it is to stick to one another."[6] The letter in which these words occur is not without dignity. There is in it even a certain kindliness. The man with the big sabre had a tender heart.

Paris, February 1809: Madame Hugo, who could now count on an allowance of three thousand, shortly to be increased to four thousand, francs, found for herself a vast apartment on the ground floor of what had once been a convent founded by Anne of Austria, at 12 Impasse des Feuillantines. The drawing-room of almost feudal proportions, "filled with light and birdsong," had a fine air about it. Above the garden wall could be seen the graceful dome of the Val-de Grâce, "a tiara terminating in a carbuncle." The garden itself was immense— "a park, a wood, a stretch of open country . . . an avenue of chestnuts with room for a swing, and a dry quarry in which to play at soldiers . . . all the flowers one could possibly want, and what, to a child's eyes, was a virgin forest . . ."[7] The boys were constantly making discoveries: "D'you know what I've found?" "Oh, that's nothing: come over here!" Happiness took on a new lease when, on the following Sunday, Abel came home from the Lycée and his brothers introduced him to their paradise. "I have a vision of myself, a young and laughing schoolboy, playing, running and joking with my brothers in the great green avenue of the garden in which my earliest years were spent, once the walled pleasaunce of a community of nuns, overlooked by the dark dome of the Val-de-Grâce with its leaden crown."[8]

> J'eus dans ma blonde enfance, hélas! trop éphémère,
> Trois maîtres: un jardin, un vieux prêtre et ma mère.[9]

As a matter of fact the "old priest," Father Larivière (more properly, de la Rivière), was an unfrocked Oratorian who, in the days of the Revolution, had married his housekeeper, preferring, as he said, "to give away his hand rather than his head." With his wife, he conducted a small school in the rue Saint-Jacques. As soon as he set about teaching Victor to read, it became apparent that the boy had already performed that task for himself. But Father Larivière, "bred up on Tacitus and Homer," was well equipped to instruct his pupil in Latin and Greek. Together they translated the Epitome, the De Viris, Quintus Curtius and Virgil. The tight shape of the Latin sentence imposed itself on the boy's mind. He was instinctively drawn to this compact and forceful language.

But his real master was the garden. It was there that Victor Hugo learned to know nature in its varying aspects of beauty and terror; there that he came to love buttercups, daisies, periwinkles; there, too, that he saw rats preying on birds, birds on insects, and insects on each other. He indulged in cruel amusements, "catching bumble-bees in the holly-hocks by suddenly closing the flower upon them with one's fingers."[10] This world of universal slaughter set the precocious child thinking. The three brothers were by temperament inquisitive and restless, an easy prey to enthusiasm and fear. "What they found loveliest in the garden was what it did not contain."[11] They had inherited from their father an imaginative power which at times could be excessive. In the dry quarry they lay in wait for "Old Deafy," a monster invented by themselves, black, hairy, sticky and covered with warts. They had never seen "Old Deafy"; they knew they never would see him, but they loved giving themselves a fright. Victor would say to Eugène: "Let's go and look for Old Deafy."

Terror and mystery fascinated Victor. The name "Black Forest" awakened in him "one of those complete ideas such as children love. I imagined a huge, impenetrable and terrifying forest, a dense expanse of trees, a dark and foggy place . . ."[12] Above his bed hung an engraving in black and white of an old ruined tower on the bank of a river, a haunt of terrors. This image, imprinted on his mind in childhood, contributed, no doubt, to give him a taste for violent effects of light and dark. The tower was the Mäuserthurm, the river was the Rhine.

At the Feuillantines, "one could see on the garden walls, among the worm-eaten espaliers which had broken away from their nails, traces of ancient objects of devotion, niches in which Madonnas once had stood, the remains of crosses, and, here and there, a notice saying, 'National Property.' "[13] At the far end of the garden stood an old and ruined chapel, now invaded by weeds and birds. For some time Madame Hugo forbade her sons to go near it. She was using it as a hiding-place for Lahorie, who was still being hunted by the police as one who had been involved in Moreau's conspiracy. By sheltering him she was risking her head; but this courageous young Breton woman, who had been brought up in the midst of plots, laughed at danger. Having been thus discovered, "Monsieur de Courlandais" (his assumed name) took to having his meals with the family. The boys had seen him in the old rue-de-Clichy days, but since then he had greatly changed. The man they saw now was of middle height, with glittering eyes, a pock-marked face, black hair and black whiskers. He was deserving of respect, and they duly respected him. He had a camp-bed behind the altar, his pistols in a corner, and a Tacitus which he set his godson to translate. One day he took Victor on his knee, opened the parchment-bound octavo volume, and read aloud the words: *Urbem Romanam a principio reges habuere.* Then he stopped and said: "Had Rome kept her kings, she would not have been Rome." Then, looking fondly at the child: "My boy," he said, "remember liberty ranks higher than anything else." He had had so long to carry a burden of tyranny that he now professed the religion of Liberty with an almost mystical fervour. The boys grew to be devoted to this man whose praises their mother was for ever singing. They understood, though vaguely, that the Emperor was persecuting him, and felt that they were on the side of the proscribed against the powerful.

On Sundays, in addition to Abel, two other children came to play in the Feuillantines garden: Victor and Adèle Foucher. The boys were still of an age to treat girls with contempt. Victor Hugo, who had set up a swing under the chestnuts, condescended to let Adèle make use of it, and she, proud but scared, begged him each time not to push her as high as the last. A favourite game with the boys was to put her into an old, broken-down wheelbarrow, with her eyes blindfolded, and then push her along the paths. She had to guess where she was. If they caught her cheating, they tightened the handkerchief "till it made a mark on her face," and then asked sternly: "Where are you now?" When the young gentlemen had grown tired of playing with a little girl, they pulled up the vine-props and fought each other, using them as lances.

For eighteen months Lahorie lived at the Feuillantines, invisible and unsuspected. His face became once more placid. He held the view that the Emperor, now on the point of marrying an archduchess, would soon feel himself strong enough to forget the resentment which had gnawed at him when he was First Consul. The general was sick of living a hole-and-corner existence. He indulged in every kind of extravagant hope. Perhaps the Emperor still remembered the services he once had rendered and, now that there were fewer men of talent available, would consider giving him employment. In June 1810 Savary replaced Fouché at the Police Ministry. He was one of Lahorie's former friends. They had been on intimate terms. Why should the outlaw not pluck up courage and go to see the Minister? Sophie Hugo, to whom he spoke frankly of what was in his mind, strongly discouraged him. One could never trust people like that. All the same on December 29th, 1810, Lahorie, without saying a word to her, went to see Savary.

He returned to the Feuillantines in a mood of high hope. The Minister had shaken him warmly by the hand, saying: "We shall meet again before long!" Madame Hugo trembled. Next morning, just as the family was sitting down to early breakfast, Monsieur de Courlandais in his dressing-gown, Madame Hugo in a quilted jacket and morning cap, there came a ring at the bell. Claudine, the maid, came into the room, saying that two men were asking for Monsieur de Courlandais. He went out. Snow was falling. A sound of carriage-wheels was heard. Claudine came back, crying out: "Oh! madame, they have taken him away!" He was imprisoned in the stronghold of Vincennes. A small boy with a high forehead had been an observer of this dramatic scene, and the emotion produced by it remained stored away in his memory. Did he know what Lahorie was to his mother? Children do not know things; they only confusedly feel them. By the time they learned the truth, their love for their mother was such that they did their best never to break silence on this aspect of her life.

At Vincennes, Lahorie was kept in solitary confinement, and Sophie Hugo was unable to communicate with him. By the time he was granted permission to see visitors, in June 1811, she was in Spain. How that came about has now to be explained.

Léopold-Sigisbert Hugo had become a general in the army of King Joseph, occupied a high court post, and had been created Count of Siguenza (a Spanish title). The king lavished honour and money on him. The general's brother, Louis Hugo, a cheerful, eloquent and charming man, paid a visit to the Feuillantines for the purpose of suggesting to his sister-in-law that she should be reconciled with her husband. His glittering sabre, his stories of Spain, the prestige which attached to all things military in the eyes of the boys, had the effect of making them see this uncle as a sort of "archangel Michael." What he had to tell them was both dazzling and terrifying. The wife of the governor of three provinces would enjoy a high position in Spain. She would be a countess; she would be rich. King Joseph had settled a million réals on the general, on condition that he should settle in Spain and buy an estate. This meant that the future of his family would be assured. But Uncle Louis also described the shooting of prisoners, the burning of convents, brigand ambushes. The children and their mother could make the journey only under protection of a convoy.

Louis Hugo had failed to convince his sister-in-law. A little later, however, the banking house of Ternaux advised her that her husband had transmitted the sum of fifty-one thousand francs to enable her to buy a house in France. Matters were really becoming serious. If the boys' father had genuinely attained to such high honours, had she the right to deprive them of a fortune? The arrival of emissaries from the king decided her. Joseph knew Sophie well. In the old Lunéville days he had thought her a woman of distinction. To see one of his court dignitaries compromising himself with an adventuress, the woman Thomas, who now insisted on being addressed as the "Comtesse de Salcano," made him uneasy and out of temper. He now begged the legitimate wife to claim her rightful position.

Joseph, the king, was prodigal of assurances. Sophie Hugo yielded. Next day she presented Eugène and Victor with a Spanish dictionary and a Spanish grammar. "In the course of six weeks these two gifted boys had learned enough of the language to make themselves under stood in it." In the spring of 1811 Madame Hugo was informed that a convoy was being made up and that she should join it at Bayonne. She withdrew from the Ternaux Bank twelve thousand francs journey-money, took out a passport in the name of Madame Hugo, formerly Mademoiselle Trébuchet of La Renaudière, and booked a complete diligence for the use of herself and her family. She hated journeys. For her sons, this one was intoxicating. They fell in love with their convey-ance and with the cities through which they passed. So keen an eye had Victor, and so retentive a memory, that twenty years later he was able to draw the two beautiful towers of Angoulême Cathedral, of which he had had the merest glimpse. All his life long he remembered Bayonne, where they had to wait for a whole month before the convoy arrived: the theatre where, seated in a box hung with red calico, he had wit-nessed on seven separate occasions a melodrama called *Les Ruines de Babylone;* the evenings on which the three boys, with much messing about with water-colours, set themselves to decorate, in a most ferocious style, a copy of the *Arabian Nights* which Lahorie had given them. Above all, he never forgot a young girl of fourteen with an angelic expression and a classical profile, who read aloud to them in the Bayonne garden. Standing behind her, he heard nothing, so absorbed was he in looking at the reader's smooth, transparent skin. As her tucker rose and fell, he saw, with mingled embarrassment and fascination, a white and rounded breast which stirred with the movement of her breathing, while the warm sunlight touched the shadows to fleeting gold.

It sometimes happened, on those occasions, that she suddenly raised her large blue eyes and said to me: "Are you listening, Victor?" I was so taken aback that I blushed and trembled. I never kissed her of my own accord: it was she who called me to her, and said: "Give me a kiss." When the time came to leave, I had two great sorrows, the thought that I should not see her again, and having to release my pet birds.

Bayonne has remained in my memory as a pink and smiling town. It was there that my heart was thrilled for the first time. Oh! simple days of inno-cence, though already marked by a sweet unrest! It was there that I saw for the first time, gleaming in the darkest corner of my being, that indescribable light which is the divine breaking of the dawn of love.[14]

The general's wife and Comtesse de Siguenza was treated with re-spect throughout the journey. Her equipage, an immense rococo travelling-coach, drawn by six horses or mules, and hired for the journey at a cost of two thousand four hundred francs, was so large that even Spanish duchesses had to give it pride of place. This made the three young men feel extremely proud. Victor at once fell in love with Spain, that land of contrasts, with landscapes now smiling, now gloomy; the Gulf of Fuenterrabia glittering in the distance like a huge precious stone; the first town they came to, Ernani, noble, haughty, severe; the Castilian shepherds in whose hands simple crooks had the look of sceptres. Wonder began at the frontier. Irun, with its black houses, narrow streets, wooden balconies and embattled doorways, astonished this little French boy brought up in a world of Empire mahogany. His eyes, used to star-spangled beds, swan-necked chairs, fire-dogs in the form of sphinxes, and a wealth of gilded bronze, gazed with what almost amounted to terror at the great canopied beds, the squat, contorted objects of silver-ware, the leaded windows. But there was something delicious in the terror. Even the agonizing squeaking of the Spanish carts was so odd and violent as to seem almost pleasant. He was never to forget the rough, solemn tongue of Spain, the words of which "evoke instinctively, one might almost say automatically, men of imposing presence, violent emotions, brilliance, colour and passion."[15]

In the churches he saw strange statues, some bleeding, some dressed in golden robes, and clocks adorned with farcical, fantastic figures. Monsters, in Spain, are part of life. Goya's beggars, the dwarfs of Velasquez, throng the streets. All around the convoy swarmed a miraculous life. His memory was packed full with "parti-coloured caricatures," with disquieting forms silhouetted on high rocks against the sky, shot bandits beside the road. Terrible sights. The stories he heard put the finishing touch to the things he saw. It was said that General Hugo had had Spanish deserters flung from a window and sent crashing to the ground; that in one monastery, his men had massacred all the monks. As to the insurgents, men told how they tortured women and children, disembowelled them, and burned them alive. Hidden in the deep defiles, guerrillas watched the passing of the convoy. Dreams of war and death haunted the children.

At Madrid, with its houses and green vegetation, which they loved after the barren uplands of Castile, there was no sign of their father. Knowing nothing of this journey which had been undertaken in response to King Joseph's request, the general was in his Government, with the woman Thomas, whom he had brought from Naples disguised as a man. The general's wife and sons were honourably accommodated at the Masserano Palace, in a magnificent suite of rooms, furnished with red damask, brocade, Bohemian glass, Chinese vases, Venetian lustres, and drawings by Raphael and Giulio Romano. Victor had a charming bedroom hung with yellow brocade. From his bed he could see an image of Notre-Dame-des-Sept-Douleurs, dressed in a robe embroidered with more than one layer of gold and with seven swords piercing her heart. The steward addressed his mother as Madame la Comtesse, but the child could feel the presence of rebellion in the hearts that beat around him. In the Masserano Palace there was a gallery of portraits. Victor was often to be found alone there, seated in a corner, silently contemplating the many proud grandees in arrogant poses, confusedly guessing at their pride of family, their pride of country. He moved through the great rooms as the son of a conqueror, but it was as a foreigner, an intruder, that he gazed at the baroque altars, at the pictures of men in great starched ruffs. He knew that the Spaniards had nicknamed Napoleon "Napoladron" (Napoleon the robber).

About the Emperor he was himself in two minds. Like every French child, he admired the hero, but, along with his mother and Lahorie, he hated the tyrant. His attitude to his father was similarly ambiguous: there was pride in the thought that he was the son of General Count Hugo, the governor of three provinces, and that, thanks to the name he bore, he was living in a fine palace. But there was also a growing sense of resentment against the father who was making "mamma" so unhappy, as well as an obscure embarrassment in his knowledge that the general was hunting down in Spain, as he had formerly done in Italy, patriots to whom he gave the name of *bandits*. When in the Galerie des Ancêtres Victor told himself stories, he best liked to think of himself as a proscribed outlaw who would one day return in triumph.

He came, too, to feel that there was a strong bond between Spain and sexual love. In the great painted rooms of the Masserano Palace he had come across a young girl of fourteen, Pepita, the daughter of the Marquise de Monte-Hermoso, one of King Joseph's mistresses. She had found it amusing to make this boy fall in love with her.

It was now June 1811. King Joseph had gone to Paris for the christening of the King of Rome. Who should tell the general of his family's arrival? Once again Madame Hugo had recourse to her charming brother-in-law Louis. There was a violent scene, and the Governor of Guadalajara very nearly had a stroke. What? A woman who was no longer willing to behave as his wife pursue him into Spain! He at once instituted divorce proceedings on the ground of grave offences against the obligations of marriage. He insisted, while judgment was in abeyance, on having custody of his sons. Their "perpetual holidays," he said, had lasted long enough. Abel was to be enrolled among the king's pages. He would have a handsome uniform of royal blue, with silver shoulder-knots. Eugène and Victor were to be sent to the Collège des Nobles (the Monastery of San Antonio Abad), to which his father's Spanish title gave them right of entry. The building was gloomy, and scarcely less so the masters. A thin, pale, sinister-looking monk, Don Bazile, was put in charge of the two French boys. Left alone in the inner court, they burst into tears. A hunchback, dressed in a red woollen jacket, blue breeches and yellow stockings, a real court fool, supervised a dormitory of a hundred and fifty beds. The Spaniards called him "Corcovita."

The pupils were all supposed to serve Mass in turn, but Sophie Hugo, an unbeliever and a follower of Voltaire, had told Don Bazile that her sons were Protestants. They were, however, treated with respect because their father was not a man to be trifled with, and because they turned out, much to the astonishment of the monks, to have a remarkable knowledge of Latin. In what class should these little *Frances* be put? They regarded the *Epitome* and the *De Viris* as child's-play. They could get on, quite well enough, with Virgil and Lucretius. "What were you translating at the age of eight?" asked the dumbfounded monk. "Tacitus," replied Victor. Their Spanish fellow-pupils all openly prayed for the defeat of Napoleon. Eugène had a fight with the young Comte de Belverana; Victor had another with a hideous oaf with crimped hair, called Elesperu. School became for them a hell.

Meanwhile, matters between their parents were going from bad to worse. When Joseph returned to Madrid he found numerous petitions addressed to him by the Comtesse Hugo. He summoned her to his presence, listened to what she had to say, and at once issued instructions that the general-governor should come immediately to Madrid. The general hastened to obey and, faced by an ultimatum from the king, yielded on all points. He would accept a post in Madrid; he would live in the Masserano Palace; he would remove his sons from school; he would at once make over three thousand francs to his wife who, by this time, had not a *maravédis* to bless herself with. *The General to the Comtesse Hugo:* "This evening, after dining with His Majesty, I will come to see you. I send you a box of candles. Farewell, my friend: do not doubt my devotion. . . ."[16]

The reconciliation did not last long. Some mischievous friend brought up the whole Lahorie story, and pointed out how dangerous it was to have as wife the mistress of a conspirator. The general again waxed furious. Joseph had no argument to advance now that the situation was placed on this basis. Léopold-Sigisbert left the Masserano Palace, installed his mistress in a charming house in Madrid, and compelled Eugène and Victor to show themselves driving on the Prado with himself and the "Comtesse de Salcano." Sophie Hugo, now quite alone and abandoned by all, did however manage to stage a come-back. She exercised considerable influence over the king's mind, and convinced him that her relations with Lahorie had been innocent. It was her husband, she asserted, who had owed his advancement in the army to that "worthy man." How, she asked, after such loyal devotion, could she refuse shelter to her husband's protector? Once again, Joseph released his thunders against the governor: "I must make it perfectly clear that I will not have you giving rise to scandal by refusing to live with Madame Hugo."[17]

At long last, in desperation, she obtained permission to return to France with her two younger sons. Abel was to remain one of the royal pages. The sum due to the general as majordomo of the royal palace, twelve thousand francs a year, would, in future, be paid direct to his wife. There must be no further talk of divorce. It was a victory for her.

The return journey, again made in an escorted convoy, was long and excruciating. The boys witnessed a number of abominable scenes: scaffolds; a man about to be garrotted—in other words, strangled; a cross on which were nailed the bleeding limbs of a condemned criminal who had been cut in pieces. It was an ill-omened journey. Nevertheless, Victor took back with him from Spain pictures of another kind which seemed to him to be noble and beautiful. Obscurely he could understand why this people should refuse to accept the French invaders. "Remember, my boy, liberty ranks higher than anything else," Lahorie had told him. He loved the mixture of grotesque and sublime, the somewhat theatrical haughtiness which he had noticed in the ancestral portraits of the Masserano Palace, as well as on the faces of his schoolfellows.

Spain has always attracted Frenchmen, because she has conserved, in a primitive state, passions which, in their own country, have been weakened by community living. We find there "the strange, sour smell of Latin blood."[18] Corneille, when he borrowed *Le Cid* from the Spaniards, struck straight to the hearts of Frenchmen in the time of Louis XIII. Ever after this journey, the young Victor Hugo was haunted by those vague and, as yet, nameless figures who afterwards became Hernani, Ruy Gomez de Silva, Don Salluste and Ruy Blas; by images of blood and gold; by "a little Spanish girl with large eyes and a mane of hair, brown, gold-dusted hair, red lips and pink cheeks, Pepa, the fourteen-year-old Andalusian."[19] From this brief but close contact with Spain, he retained a liking for sonorous words and emphatic sentiments. "One might say, with a considerable amount of truth, that the mind of Victor Hugo was naturalized by the first impressions to which it was subjected."[20] We may accept that as true enough, with the single reserve that his passion for Spain was soon counterbalanced by a latent Germanism.

3

The End of Childhood

WHAT joy to see the Feuillantines again! Thanks to the faithful Madame Larivière the garden was in good heart, there was a joint on the spit, and the beds were made. Soon old Larivière had resumed his Latin lessons, and the garden its teaching of poetry. Victor and Eugène were no longer sent to school; a tutor came to them. The headmaster of the Lycée Napoléon, who was anxious to enlist them among his boys, was coldly received by Madame Hugo. She shared the horror felt by her sons for boarding-schools. Her whole existence now was dedicated to them and to her imprisoned friend. She lived in complete retirement in her cul-de-sac. She took out a library subscription and sent her children to choose books for her. The two boys, eight and ten respectively, were free to rummage on the library shelves. The proprietor was an odd creature who wore knee-breeches dating from the days of Louis XVI, and mottled stockings. In the basement, to which were relegated the more extreme philosophical works and the too indecent novels, Eugène and Victor would lie at full length for hours on end, making acquaintance with Rousseau, Voltaire, Diderot, Restif de la Bretonne, *Faublas,* and the *Voyages of Captain Cook.* When good old Royol pointed out the danger of giving such young boys the run of licentious works of fiction, their mother replied that "books had never yet harmed anybody." In this view she was wrong. The violently sensual temperament of her youngest son was still further stimulated, but he also acquired a more healthy appetite for strange and unusual reading which was later to suggest to him many subjects for plays and novels.

Abel, Eugène and Victor all tried their hands at writing verse. Victor filled many notebooks with his early efforts. In poetry he inclined naturally to the more classical rhythms. "It goes without saying that the verses he wrote at this time were very imperfect. They neither rhymed nor scanned. The boy had nobody to instruct him, and knew nothing of prosody. He read aloud what he had written, took notice of what was wrong, and began again correcting the lines until his ear was satisfied. By a process of hit and miss, he taught himself the elements of metre, caesura, rhyme, and the alternation of masculine and feminine rhyme endings. , , ."[1]

Madame Hugo exercised an effortless control over the minds of her sons. She demanded, and obtained, unquestioning and punctual obedience. "An austere and reserved tenderness, a regular and insistent discipline, little familiarity, no mysticism, logical and instructive conversation at a serious level well above that of childhood—such were the main characteristics of a mother-love which was deep, devoted and vigilant."[2] Sophie's authority was more a man's than a woman's. In her liaison with Lahorie, it was she, rather than he, who had stood for political ambition. In 1812 she was obstinately determined to make a conspirator of him. After her return from Spain she went to see him in the visitors' room as Vincennes. She found him bent and emaciated, yellow in the face, and continually chewing away on nothing. He was now better treated than he had been in the early days of his confinement. His supply of clothes and linen had been renewed. Most important of all, he once more had access to his favourite books: Virgil, Horace, Sallust, and a great number of works on mathematics, chemistry and the art of war. Before Sophie Hugo's arrival he had seemed to be resigned to his fate, and Savary had spoken of banishment, which is the clemency of tyrants. But with the coming of that strong-minded woman all this was changed.

In April 1812 she made contact with a certain Abbé Lafon who was planning to unite royalists and republicans in one vast conspiracy against the Emperor. She managed (through the medium of a director of police who had been a school-friend of Lahorie at Louis-le-Grand) to have her lover transferred to the prison of La Force. There discipline was relaxed, and he would be free to receive visitors and even to give dinner-parties. Next, she entered into relations with General Malet, "a fanatical republican," who, though he swore by Brutus and Leonidas, was willing to work for a "good and just" king. The Emperor was in Russia. What more simple than to spread a rumour that he was dead, and to set up a provisional government?

Lahorie distrusted Malet, whom he regarded as a scatterbrain. "What we need is a wise leader, and all we've got is a blusterer." The disillusioned prisoner read Sallust, and admired Catiline's energy, but thought: "It would be madness to play a similar part! The rumour has only to be seen for what it is, for the whole plan to collapse!" Sophie, all passion, had eyes only for results: the infamous Savary arrested and put in irons; the master conquered; liberty re-established. On the morning of October 23rd, 1812, Malet, in uniform, appeared and broke the news of the Emperor's death to a credulous gaoler, who at once set Lahorie at liberty. The latter, with a company of soldiers, went straight to the Police Ministry, where he arrested Savary, Duke of Rovigo. Sophie Hugo had gone to the house of her friend Pierre Foucher, now a clerk in the War Ministry, who would be certain to have had information from his brother-in-law Asseline, Registrar to the War Council. Very soon she learned that the news of the Emperor's death had been contradicted, that the conspirators had all been arrested, and that preparations were being made to bring them to trial. She hurried back to the Feuillantines where she found her sons crazy with anxiety at her long absence and scared by the talk of revolution. "It is nothing," she told them; "one should never give way to anxiety. Still less should one cry."

This stoical woman, the better to be in a position to follow the proceedings of the Court, went to the home of the Fouchers, who were still occupying their official lodgings in the War Council building situated in the rue du Cherche-Midi. Nothing but the width of a corridor separated the room in which she installed herself from the Court. An unceasing stream of officers arrived bringing news. Malet, in reply to the President, who had asked him for the names of his accomplices, said: "The whole of France, sir, and you, too, had I been successful!" Sophie Hugo, when this was told her, repeated the words with ardour: "Yes! yes indeed, the whole of France!" At two o'clock in the morning Foucher, "with that look he had of a neat and frightened mouse," came to tell her that all twelve had been sentenced to death. She asked him: "Is the execution fixed for today?" "Yes, at four o'clock on the Plain of Grenelle." Informed by him of the route to be followed by the carts bearing the condemned men, she waited for them at the barrier, after the sentence had been carried out, and accompanied to the paupers' grave the body of the only man whom she had ever loved.

In 1813, after the fall of Joseph Bonaparte, General Hugo had no alternative but to return to France. In September he was at Pau with Abel and the person whom Madame Hugo called, sometimes, the "woman Thomas," sometimes the "alleged Comtesse de Salcano." *Madame Hugo to her son Abel, September 24th, 1813:* "I do not suppose that your father can forbid you [to write to me], though, if he should do so, that will be behaviour truly in keeping with the many reprehensible things that he has done, and your duty will be to obey him no longer, just as it would be the duty of your brothers not to obey me if I so far forgot the sacred claims of a natural bond as to forbid them to write to their father. Should he, in fact, have issued such an injunction, then, in order to avoid the vexatious arguments to which your father's blind passions might give rise between you and him, you must write to me without his knowledge. I realize, my poor dear, what you must have had to suffer at the hands of that woman. I have shed many tears over your lot, and even over that of your unfortunate father. He has done us much harm, but he has done himself, and still is doing, a great deal more. Let us look forward, my dear Abel, to a happier future, and may our common misfortunes teach you a lesson, and show you whither lack of principle, and the indulgence of extravagant passions, can lead a man."[3]

Léopold-Sigisbert Hugo might be a general in Spain, but he was no more than a battalion commander in France. The allowance promised to his wife was not paid. Lahorie was no longer there to help. How were they to live? "No more playing the great lady." The garden of the Feuillantines had been taken over by the City of Paris, with a view to prolonging the rue d'Ulm. Sophie took rooms at No. 2 rue des Vieilles-Thuileries,[4] next door to the Fouchers, that she might have the benefit of their garden. They had remained, through thick and thin, the most faithful of friends. Victor had renewed acquaintance with Adèle Foucher at the Feuillantines. Already they had ceased to be children. Passionate dreamer that he was, he fancied that in her "look of an Infanta," in her great blue eyes and golden-brown skin, he could see again the Pepita of Madrid. They were told to run and play; instead, they walked and talked. They sauntered slowly, and spoke in low voices. When their hands touched, they trembled. The little girl had become a young woman.

A childish thought had flitted through his brain. Pepa had become Pepita. She said to me: "Let us run!" and started to run ahead of me, with her little bee-slim waist, and her tiny shoes tossing her frock knee-high. I pursued; she fled. At moments the wind of her passage lifted the black tippet she was wearing, and afforded me a glimpse of her brown young back.

I was beside myself. Close to the old abandoned quarry I came up with her. I took her round the waist by right of conquest, and made her sit down upon a grassy bank. She did not resist. She was out of breath and laughing. But I was serious, and gazed into her black eyes behind the curtain of her dark lashes.

"Sit down over there," she said. It was still broad daylight. "Let us read something: have you a book with you?"

I had the second volume of Spallanzani's *Voyages*. I opened it at random, and drew close to her. She leaned her shoulder against mine, and we began to read, each separately, the same page, murmuring the words to ourselves.

"Have you reached the bottom?" she asked, but I had scarce as yet begun it.

Our heads touched, our hair was intertwined, our breathing, little by little, merged. All of a sudden our lips met. By the time we were ready to go on with our book the stars were shining.

"You should have seen us running, mamma!"

I was careful to say nothing.

"You are very silent," said my mother: "you look sad."

I had paradise within my heart. I should remember that evening all my life.

All my life. . . .[5]

This love of theirs remained absolutely chaste. Adèle Foucher was a virtuous and pious young woman. Her mother scarcely ever left her side. Madame Foucher was always to be seen with her baby, little Paul, in her arms, and Adèle close beside her. Each evening she combed her daughter's beautiful black hair "and the operation was one long endearment." The mother, who was an excellent manager, set herself to train Adèle in household duties. From the age of six the child had cut out her own clothes. One of their neighbours, Madame Delon, had got her to mark her son's linen. The Fouchers suspected this woman of being inquisitive, and when, each month, the civil servant received his pay, they would shut the door so that she might not hear the chink of coins. The family of the one-time registrar lived, in spite of the abnormal times, the traditional existence of the French lower-middle class: secretive, limited, austere and affectionate.

General Hugo asked that his name might be restored to the active list. On January 9th, 1814, he was appointed commander of the fortified town of Thionville. He defended it bravely against the invading forces, and surrendered only when news reached him of Napoleon's abdication. Abel had joined his mother in Paris. She was proud of the handsome, broad-shouldered lad and, straitened though she was financially, had a dress-coat made for him of green Louviers cloth, trousers of light grey cashmere, and a riding-coat of a mixed weave. Very soon Russians and Prussians were in occupation of the capital. One part of the population looked on them as liberators, and referred to them, not as "the enemy" but as "our allies." Madame Hugo made no secret of her pleasure when the Bourbons were restored. Her royalism had been very intermittent. So long as her husband had needed Bonaparte, she had been careful not to show her feelings. Besides, Lahorie had been more a republican than a monarchist. Since the violent death of her friend, however, she had entertained a livelier hatred of the usurper. She denied that he had possessed any genius at all, remembered that she was a daughter of La Vendée, was careful not to miss a single public celebration, and attended all of them dressed in white cambric, with green shoes, "so that she might tread the colours of the Empire under foot with each step she took." Her sons had too great a respect for her not to share her opinions. Tacitus had taught them to execrate the Caesars, and Victor now always used the name Bonaparte, as did his mother and their Foucher friends. It gave him a feeling of pride to go to Notre-Dame for the Thanksgiving Mass and, more especially, to offer on that occasion his arm to Mademoiselle Adèle.

General Hugo remained at his post in Thionville until May 1814. He had sent a letter to the king assuring him of his loyalty, his view being that it was "a soldier's duty to stand by his country," no matter what its form of government—an attitude at once noble and convenient.

His wife went to Thionville, accompanied by Abel, for the purpose of claiming her allowance. Eugène and Victor took advantage of their mother's absence to spend what spare time they had with the Fouchers.

To Madame La Comtesse Hugo, at Thionville, May 23rd, 1814: My dear mamma—since you went away we have all been very bored here. We go often to Monsieur Foucher's house as you told us to do. He suggested that we might like to attend the lessons he was giving to his son. We thanked him. We work every morning at Latin and mathematics . . . Monsieur Foucher was so kind as to take us to the Museum. Come back soon. Without you we do not know what to talk about nor what to do. We are all at a loose end. We never cease thinking of you. Mamma! mamma!

Your obedient son
VICTOR[6]

The Comtesse Hugo found installed in the general's lodgings, where she ruled the household, the woman Thomas, who now called herself the Lady Anaclet d'Almet (or d'Almé), giving out that she was the wife of a colonel. Sophie Hugo, whom her husband addressed as Madame Trébuchet, was put to sleep in a dressing-room, while the Lady d'Almé locked herself into the bedroom with the general. The legal wife went to law, demanding restitution of conjugal rights, and a sum in alimony. The general, who had leased the Château d'Hus, just outside Thionville, in his mistress's name, brought a counter-action for divorce. The wise and gentle Pierre Foucher was fearful lest the publicity given to the law-suit might evoke the blood-stained ghost of Lahorie. He wrote two urgent letters to the general in which he begged him to avoid a scandal which might recoil upon the heads of his children.

Under the influence of his mistress and of his own resentment, incompatibility had turned to hatred. The general wished to tear his sons away from his "detested" wife. He had had them already separated by his sister from the Foucher family. When he went to Paris in September 1814 he boarded them out, as, being their father, he was perfectly entitled to do, with Cordier and Decotte, in the rue Sainte-Marguerite, "a gloomy thoroughfare running between the Abbaye Prison and the Passage du Dragon." When, in March 1815, he was recalled to Thionville, in order, once again, to defend the town against a new invasion, it was not to Sophie, but to the shrewish widow of Martin-Chopine that he delegated his authority. "I entrust to your care my two young children, who are attending the school of Monsieur Cordier. I do not intend that under any circumstances they should be restored to their mother, or placed under her supervision."[7] The two boys were soon in open rebellion against this woman. They called her Madame instead of Aunt. They complained with the dignity of Spanish grandees of her "unbecoming behaviour," of her "coarse insults," and of the "disgusting scenes" to which she exposed them. Both of them remained unshakably devoted to the mother from whom they had been separated. Both judged their father with respectful severity. They blamed him for his irregular life, and for the way he treated them as pig-headed bandits.

General Hugo to the Widow of Martin-Chopine, October 16, 1815: These young gentlemen, it seems, consider that they would be dishonoured should they give you the title of aunt or write to you with affection and respect. The conduct of my children is wholly attributable to their cursed mother.[8]

This combination of boarding-house-prison and gaoler-father spelled the end of childhood. In spite of set-backs, in spite of the black cloud which the disagreement of their parents had suspended above their heads, it had been for them a lovely and poetic time. The Feuillantines garden with its mystery and its secret woodlands; the shadowy ravine of Avellino; bivouac fires; the gilded baroque galleries of the Masserano Palace; the charming, shadowy forms of beings half-women and half-children; the unknown girl of Bayonne, Adéle, Pepita, and, as background, the victories of France, the flash of breastplates and the rolling of drums—what a scene to dream on!

How free, too, they had been to indulge their dreaming in a system of education which knew no rules! Everything had combined, for thirteen years, to make Victor free of the constraints which formed part of conventional schooling. Frequent journeys had made regular classes impossible. The savage moods of a mother with no home to call her own had kept the world at bay. A secret love-affair, at once noble and dangerous, had served to thicken round them a wall of greenery and silence. The singular respect for books and poetry exhibited by a little product of the middle class who, under her apparent severity, was systematically liberal-minded"[9] had allowed the happy development of natural genius. Like all the children of those heroic days, Victor had, at first, "in his restless heart," dreamed of military glory. Then the conflict of his parents and the fall of the Empire had set his desires moving in a different direction. But whatever he was to be, it must be on a grand scale. "When I was small I had before my eyes the spectacle of somebody who was great." Unconscious rival both of his father and the Emperor, men whom in spite of himself he had admired, he longed to cut a figure in the imagination of mankind. But how? That he did not know, and "dreamed upon the future."

> Je revins, rapportant de mes courses lointaines,
> Comme un vague faisceau des lueurs incertaines.
> Je rêvais comme si j'avais, durant mes jours,
> Rencontré sur mes pas les magiques fontaines
>   Dont l'onde enivre pour toujours.

> Mes souvenirs germaient dans mon âme échauffée,
> J'allais, chantant des vers d'un voix étouffée,
> Et ma mère, en secret observant tous mes pas,
> Pleurait et souriait, disant: "C'est une fée
>   Qui lui parle, et qu'on ne voit pas!"[10]

Rarely was a mind so divided. Within it struggled for mastery the temperament of a faun; his father's bizarre imagination, ever seeking what was strange; the severe stoicism and classic taste of Sophie Trébuchet; the love of glory and a hatred of tyranny; high poetry with always a touch of madness in it; and those middle-class virtues which were the more valuable, seeing that his instincts had so severely suffered from the violence done them by those of his own flesh and blood. He was a mass of contrasts. If ever a writer was formed by life to create new and beautiful antitheses, it was he. It is important that we should have a clear view of him during those early years when he was just emerging into conscious existence. "It is not in the palaces it will adorn that the pearl takes shape, but under an embryonic polypary, hundreds of leagues beneath the sea."[11] We have taken a plunge into the blue-grey depths of this childhood's magic sources. In those liquid profundities, to which little light drifts down from above, we have caught a glimpse of shattered wrecks and the green tentacles of nightmare, but also of white sirens, of drowned cathedrals, of the submerged palaces of Andalusian cities. "The better part of genius is made up of memories." It is from those that we shall see slowly taking form the pearly colours, luminous, inimitable and changing, which, out of a grain of matter, make a precious stone, and, out of a man, a genius.

PART II

The Fires of Dawn

The fires of dawn are not so sweet as the first
rays of glory.

VAUVENARGUES

Caged Birds

AFTER the paradise of the Feuillantines, and the leafy chestnuts of the Hôtel de Toulouse, the boarding-school kept by Decotte and Cordier, a dark and treeless place, seemed like a dismal purgatory. Cordier was an unfrocked priest, ailing and old. Out of respect for his beloved Rousseau, he wore a greatcoat and skull-cap, which gave him the look of an Armenian. It was his habit to rap the pupils' heads with a metal snuff-box. Emmanuel de Cotte, who had changed his name to Decotte, showered impositions upon the boarders, and picked the locks of their drawers. Eugène and Victor, rebel angels both of them, were not disposed to cringe. *General Hugo to Madame Martin-Chopine, August 7th, 1817:* "It is my considered opinion that if they remain any longer under the cruel influence of their mother, they will be for ever lost. In their behaviour to you there is nothing unusual; but their attitude to Monsieur de Cotte is truly shocking. They have even come within an ace of striking their head master."[1]

From the very first, their prestige among the other boys was high, because their father had insisted that they should have a room to themselves. The school was soon divided into two groups, one with Victor as its king, the other with Eugène. In the evenings the two sovereigns met in their room where they carried on negotiations. One is reminded of the Bonaparte brothers sharing out Europe between them, and doubtless the Hugo brothers were not unaware of the parallel. Trained from an early age in the virtues of ancient Rome, and brought up in the shadow of French victories, they had a healthy appetite for glory. They organized dramatic performances in the school. Victor wrote the plays and took the part of Napoleon, surrounded by marshals resplendent in stars of gold paper; but that was no more than theatrical pretence. In real life his political enthusiasms remained the same as ever: hatred of the Revolution; horror of Bonaparte; love of the Bourbons who, so he believed, had with the Charter brought back liberty.

That was what their mother told them, and she was still their idol. To Madame Martin-Chopine, and to their father, they stood up with a degree of authority and dignity which seems almost incredible. The general, who as a result of the Restoration was placed on half-pay, had retired to Blois with Madame d'Almé, Comtesse de Salcano, in other words, the woman Thomas, whose influence over him was absolute. The odious widow Martin doled out to the two boys their meagre allowance of pocket-money, and transmitted the general's orders. It was his intention that they should enter the École Polytechnique, and to this end he wished them to devote themselves to the study of drawing and mathematics. Politely but firmly his sons asked for the means which would enable them to carry out his instructions.

Victor Hugo to His Father, June 22nd, 1816: Madame Martin waited a whole month before finding out our requirements and for the last two months has deducted the amount from our two sous a day. She also had the wise foresight not to tell us of this until June 1st. When we politely pointed out to her that, counting on this money, we had found it necessary to borrow, not only to pay for our chairs at church, but also to have our penknives sharpened, our books bound, and also to buy mathematical instruments, she replied that she would not listen to us, and told us haughtily to leave the room. That, my dear father, she will not do twice! We would rather give up our weekly outing than have any more to do with her. If it is your intention that we should pay our debts and not be entirely deprived of money, please be so good as to let Abel carry out your wishes, and nobody else.[2]

Again, on November 12th, 1816:

We have given careful consideration to what you propose: we trust that you will permit us to speak frankly, as we have done, and will reply only after weighing our arguments. Realizing that we are of an age to judge the value of money, you have offered us twenty-five louis a year for our upkeep. This offer we accept, on condition that the money is paid directly to us. For, in that case, with the experience we have been able to acquire, and, above all, with the help and advice of mamma who, whatever anyone may say, does understand financial matters, we feel certain that, with this modest sum at our disposal, we can keep ourselves far more decently than we have been able to do so far, and, at the same time, that we shall be less of an expense to you. But if the money is to reach us through other hands, we shall have no such certainty. We can no longer consent to make use of the means through which the money would be remitted to us, nor can we, like you, *adjust our expenses to our income, and so be easier in our minds as a result of keeping our affairs in good order, and spending our money sensibly* . . . As to the last part of your letter, we cannot conceal from you how excessively painful it is to us to see our mother referred to as a *worthless person*, and that, too, in an open letter which was delivered to us after having been read by others . . . We have seen your correspondence with mamma. What would you have done to anyone who had dared use such language to her in the days when you first knew her, when it was your delight to find happiness in her company? She is still, and always has been, the same, and we shall ever think of her as you thought of her then. Such are the reflexions to which your letter has given rise in us. Deign to give some thought to what we say, and rest assured of the love which your obedient and respectful sons will always feel for you.

E. HUGO—V. HUGO[3]

This letter shows both maturity of mind and a vigorous style. There are no repetitions; the writing never flags. Which of the two had inspired this collective epistle? The hand is Eugène's, but that matters little. The two brothers had had the same upbringing; both were disciples of their mother; both were soaked in the classics; both were athirst for poetry. Such time as they could steal from mathematics they gave to the writing of verse. Translations of Virgil and Lucretius, elegies, epigrams, songs, tragedies—all was grist to their mill.

At that time, it is true, a great deal of verse was being written in France, and the school was chock-a-block with poets. Even the gloomy Decotte dabbled in rhyming, and grew quickly jealous of the two geniuses who were his pupils. An intelligent young usher, with a pock-marked face but a gay and loyal disposition, Félix Biscarrat, had a great fondness for Eugène and Victor, and a greater still for Mademoiselle Rosalie, the school laundress, for whom he composed a number of odes. When Biscarrat took his two favourites, the Hugo brothers, to the top of the towers of Notre-Dame, Victor, who was immediately behind Mademoiselle Rosalie, had a good look at her legs.

It was but natural that, at an age when "all the little angel faces—are trying to peep into bathing-places," an adolescent who had inherited a lascivious temperament, who was impregnated, through Horace and Martial, with erotic verse, should be obsessed by the female form. Never, all through his life, did he outgrow the pleasure of glimpsing a bare shoulder, a naked breast, a rosy leg. Faun, or woodland god, he spied upon the untamed women of the woods or the washers at the stream. As a poor student in an attic room he peered through nearby windows or, with his eye to a crack in the wall, watched some little servant-girl getting ready for bed.

Virgil for him supplied a double need—the sense of mystery and clean, precise, definite expression. When Biscarrat had read through five hundred lines by his pupil on the subject of "The Flood," he found that thirty-two were good, fifteen very good, and five passable. Victor, more exacting, burned each year the note-book which contained his poetic efforts over that period. They were cheap little note-books which he "bound together with a piece of knotted string."

He was getting only two sous a day, and every purchase had to be carefully weighed and considered. Only from the eleventh note-book on did he begin to keep the works of his boyhood. Modest, biddable and a furious worker, he was eager for criticism. Eugène, who had more pride, was only too ready to blow his own trumpet. Both dedicated their poems to their mother, who, since she could not have her sons under her own roof, went to visit them at school. In all their labours, and when success came to them, they thought only of the "pleasure it might give to mamma." Victor, when he was fourteen, dedicated to her a tragedy in verse: *Irtamère*. Its subject, naturally enough, was the triumph of a legitimate king over a usurper. "When one hates tyrants," was the author's conclusion, "then one must needs love kings." In other words, if one hated Bonaparte, one ought to love Louis XVIII. On the cover of the note-book containing *Miscellaneous Poems* (1816-17), he wrote, under the date September 1817: "I am fifteen. What I have done is bad. I can do a great deal better"; and, elsewhere: "The follies I committed before my birth." True, the poems were not masterpieces, but no less true that much might be expected of a youth capable of so sustained and so admirable an effort.

For the note-books which have come down to us are filled with thousands of lines: a complete *opéra comique;* a melodrama in prose, *Inez de Castro;* the first draft of a poetic tragedy in five acts, *Athélie ou les Scandinaves;* an epic poem, *Le Déluge;* all of them illustrated in the margins with drawings which, in their tentative daring, are reminiscent of Rembrandt. It should be added that all this writing had been done while Victor was working for the École Polytechnique; that at the same period he had compiled an excellent series of notes on scientific subjects; and that, after the end of 1816, he was, in company with Eugène, his senior by two years, attending the regular lectures at Louis-le-Grand from eight o'clock every morning until five in the evening. In order to write poetry he had to cut into the night hours and work by candle-light in his attic—a furnace in June, an ice-house in December—from which he could see the semaphore on the towers of Saint-Sulpice. An injury to his knee, which kept him for some weeks in bed, allowed him to devote himself still more to what he loved. The good Biscarrat became uneasy: "It is with grief that I see how your health is deteriorating. Like you, I attribute this to late hours. By all that is sacred, and in the name of our friendship, do take care of yourself . . ." But work that one loves is stimulating, not exhausting.

1817. "The French Army was dressed in white uniforms, after the Austrian fashion . . . Napoleon was at St. Helena, and, since the

English refused to supply him with green material, was having his old clothes turned . . . At the Navy Office an inquiry had been opened into the fate of the *Medusa* frigate . . . The leading newspapers were all of small size . . . Divorce was abolished . . . The Lycées were renamed Colleges . . . Standing each morning in front of his window at No. 27 rue Saint-Dominique, Chateaubriand, in long trousers and slippers, with his grey hair bound in a bandana handkerchief, his eyes focused on the looking-glass, and a complete set of dentist's instruments open before him, was attending to his beautiful teeth, and dictating variants for *La Monarchie selon la Charte* to Monsieur Pilorge, his secretary."[4]

The Académie Française had set, as the subject for its poetry prize, "The happiness to be derived from Study in all the Circumstances of Life." To himself Victor said: "What if I entered?" With him, to think of action was to act. He sat down and wrote three hundred and thirty-four lines.

The poem finished, it remained to submit it to the Secretary of the Institute. The boarders at Cordier's establishment were prisoners. Victor took Biscarrat into his confidence and the good fellow, who was in charge of the boys' walks, managed to lead his little procession past the Palais Mazarin. There, while the others stood looking at the cupola and the lions, the master and his pupil hastened to the office of the Secretary of the Académie Française, where they left the poem with an official wearing a skull-cap. On their way out, they ran into Abel who, older than his brothers and, at that time, his father's favourite, enjoyed more liberty than they did. He had to be made privy to the whole business. This done, the schoolboy rejoined his comrades and returned to his algebra.

Some weeks later, when he was playing at prisoner's base in the school yard, Abel suddenly appeared, and called to him: "Come over here, you ass!" He had been an officer and exercised a sort of affectionate protection over his brothers, whom he looked upon as children. Victor went across to him. "Who was it asked you your age?" said Abel. "The members of the Academy are firmly convinced that you are trying to mystify them. If it hadn't been for that you would have got the prize. What an idiot you are! As it is, you've been awarded an Honourable Mention." The reason given by Abel for his having missed the prize was not quite accurate. Victor's entry had been put ninth, and the Permanent Secretary, Raynouard, author of *Les Templiers,* had written in the margin of his report: "If this really is his age, the Academy ought to encourage so young a poet." One part of the poem was read aloud in public session. The ladies applauded, and Raynouard, to whom Victor had sent his birth certificate, asked him to come and see him in a letter which contained a gross solecism:

"Je *fairais* avec plaisir votre connaissance." It was said of this Raynouard that he most certainly knew *one* language, but that it was Romance, not French.

Old Cordier, seeing the light of fame beating upon his school, suddenly became all honey, and gave Victor the necessary permission. Raynouard, donnish and brusque, received the boy with a degree of insolence which led the latter to say that "his knowledge of manners was about on a level with his spelling."[5] But others among the Academicians made a pet of him, especially the Dean, François de Neufchâteau, who had received a prize at fifteen, in the reign of Louis XV. Voltaire had anointed him poet, and had written a letter in which he had said: "Somebody must needs succeed me, and to you, as my heir, I extend affectionate greetings." He liked to think that he, in his turn, was playing the Voltaire to somebody else. Like many people, this kindly old gentleman had been, in turn, royalist and Jacobin, a minister under the Directory, and a count of the Empire. In 1804 he had said to the Pope: "I congratulate Your Holiness in that Providence has seen fit to lay upon you the task of anointing Napoleon." In 1816 he was naïvely astonished that Louis XVIII did not create him a peer of France. Rivarol had described his work as "prose into which a little poetry has crept." At the time when the young Hugo got to know him, Neufchâteau had turned his back on the epic, whether lived or written, and was modestly cultivating potatoes. This meeting with a man who had attained to some degree of celebrity caused the schoolboy no little surprise. Neufchâteau gave him an account of the 18th Brumaire, in which he spoke only of himself. This was his first revelation of the extent to which egotism in literary men can go.

The newspapers took an interest in the infant prodigy. At school, his "party" grew in numbers at the expense of that led by Eugène, who grew jealous. It is always painful to be outdistanced, more especially by one's junior in age.

Victor began to keep a journal. On July 10th, 1816, he wrote in it: "I must be Chateaubriand or nothing." It is not difficult to understand the choice. Ever since 1789 France, drunk with Roman rhetoric, had been searching for grandeur. After Vergniaud, Desmoulins and Robespierre, youth's chosen prince had been Bonaparte. After the fall of Napoleon, the appetite for glory had to seek other food. There was nothing particularly exciting about the old king with his swollen legs. Religious faith among the spiritual sons of Voltaire was no longer strong. The young enthusiasts who shed sentimental tears over Louis XVIII's gaiters had uneasy consciences. Brought up "when the thunder of the miracles of the Empire was in all men's ears,"[6] and "fed on the Emperor's communiqués,"[7] they could not forget the time when

France had been the mistress of Europe. Yet they needs must love this new world of theirs. Who better than Chateaubriand could, in poetry, rally the new generation round the standard of greatness? Who had more of it than this man of genius, with his noble and disdainful bearing, who was for ever painting a picture of himself facing the storms of Destiny and the Western Ocean, who had adorned Christianity with all the beauties of art, and monarchy with all the prestige of loyalty? Napoleon gone, the young were still suffering from a nostalgia for spectacular attitudes. The splendid isolation of Chateaubriand was truly one.

On this point Victor, for the first time, found himself at variance with his mother. He admired *Atala*, while she, as a woman of the eighteenth century, was amused by a stupid parody: *Ah! là là!* It is unlikely that Chateaubriand was acquainted with Victor Hugo's early efforts. He rarely attended the Academy and found his favourite reading in the Ancients, a sound preference. But ever since the famous Honourable Mention, the young Hugos had been living in a condition of feverish excitement and happiness. François de Neufchâteau asked Victor to dine, and some time later employed him in making some researches into *Gil Blas*, which he needed, at the Bibliothèque royale. In this work Victor sought the assistance of Abel, who knew more Spanish than he did. The school porter was instructed to let the peerless pair come and go as they wished.

The summer holidays of 1817 were, for Victor "one long festival." All his friends were busy celebrating his success. Abel, now realizing that it was hopeless to look for any advancement in a military career, had taken to business, though he still continued to write. Being blessed with a little money, he established a monthly literary banquet, at which the guests, all of them young, were supposed to read aloud their latest productions. Victor never failed to attend. Eugène, an odd, capricious creature (Biscarrat had nick-named him "The Fanatic"), refused most of the invitations and shut himself away in the school buildings. It was for one of these readings that Victor roughed out, in the space of three weeks, a long short-story, "Bug-Jargal," which dealt with the Santo Domingo revolt. The solidity of its narrative and the restraint with which it makes its effects are astonishing. In many places it is equal to Mérimée's best tales. It is clear evidence that the boy was a born writer and already a natural master of his medium. Meanwhile, the three brothers were dreaming of starting a literary weekly—*Les Lettres bretonnes*—but two of them were still at school and a publisher had still to be found.

All through the year 1817 there had been open warfare between Eugène and Victor on the one side and Madame Martin-Chopine on the other. Their wicked fairy had gone so far as to forbid them to spend New Year's Day with their mother. The boys wrote her several sarcastic letters:

May 21st, 1817: Madame: may we be permitted to remind you that we have been without money since the 1st. Seeing that our needs have remained as they have ever been, we have found ourselves under the necessity of borrowing. Consequently, we should be glad if you would let us have the six francs still due to us: namely, three francs which we ought to have received on May 1st, and three on the 15th. Also, will you be so good as to send us a barber, and to speak to Madame Dejarrier about our shoes and hats.

With such esteem and affection as you deserve, we remain your very humble and obedient servants—

VICTOR HUGO—EUGÈNE HUGO[8]

Abel who, up till then, had been the general's favourite, bravely took up the cudgels on his brothers' behalf, thereby risking a battle royal.

August 26th, 1817, Abel Hugo to General Hugo: Any other man than you would have taken pride in having such sons, but you treat them as wretches and scoundrels likely to bring into dishonour a name on which you have brought distinction in your career as a soldier. . . . This, father, I find it hard to understand. I know you too well. That you wrote that miserable letter I will not deny, but your heart was not in it. An evil genius, a demon from Hell, to whom, rather than to our excellent mother, you should attribute all your misfortunes, has bewitched your eyes, and what you take for proofs of love are but the signs of hatred which she displays whenever you venture to draw nigh to the hearts of those who feel real affection for you . . . A day will come when you will see in her true colours the infernal creature to whom I refer. When that happens the moment of our vengeance will be at hand, and we shall once more recover our real father.[9]

Catherine Thomas, or Madame, as he called her in his correspondence, was infuriated by this letter and prevailed upon her lover not to answer it. Between the general and his sons the gap widened. On February 3rd, 1818, an event of capital importance occurred: the separation of the Hugo husband and wife was made official. "Madame Trébuchet" was given the custody of the children, and awarded an allowance of three thousand francs. Eugène and Victor remained at Cordier's until August, when they wrote a dutiful letter to their father in which they asked to be allowed to embark upon their law studies, which would open for them the shortest road to lucrative employment.

July 20th, 1818: You must be fully aware, dear Papa, that it is not possible for us to stay on at Monsieur Decotte's now that our school work is finished. We suggest that you should give us eight hundred francs each for our expenses. We would gladly ask for less, but you will realize that we cannot, when you remember that you already give us three hundred for our upkeep, and that, even with an additional five hundred, we shall not be able, without exercising the strictest economy, to meet the cost of our food, the purchase of books, our entrance and diploma fees, etc. . . .[10]

The general's reaction, if we consider that he, too, was short of money, was generous. "What you ask does not seem to me excessive. Go ahead and study law. I will have paid to each of you, in twelve monthly instalments, the sum of eight hundred francs a year."[11]

In August the two brothers rapturously took their leave of the Cordier and Decotte school and went to live with their mother at 18 rue des Petits-Augustins.[12] The apartment, on the third floor, was smaller than the one they had known in the rue du Cherche-Midi. The allowance provided by the half-pay general made it impossible any longer to have a garden. From their window they could see the courtyard of a museum littered with tombstones, which were those of the kings of France, removed violently from Saint-Denis by the revolutionaries. At the age of sixteen Victor wrote "Adieux à l'Enfance":

> Ô temps! Qu'as-tu fait de cette age?
> Ou plutôt qu'as-tu fait de moi?
> Je me cherche, hélas! et ne vois
> Qu'un fou qui gémit d'être sage. . . .[13]

To console himself for "growing old," he called on Fame, the thought of which was now his constant companion:

> Ô Gloire, ô Déité puissante,
> Accorde à celui qui te chante
> Une place dans l'avenir;
> Gloire, c'est à toi j'aspire;
> Ah! fais que ton grand nom m'inspire
> Et mes vers pourront t'obtenir.[14]

That fame would come, one person at least did not doubt—the wife of General Hugo.

Heaving Sighs

THERE is nothing more beautiful than a woman's belief in the genius of her children. It never so much as occurred to Madame Hugo to press her sons' noses to the grindstone of the law. Their agreement to take that line was no more than a "scrap of paper" between them and the general. In point of fact, though for two whole years Eugène and Victor kept their names on the books, they attended no lectures and passed no examination. Already proud, by anticipation, of their future triumphs, she wished to make of her sons neither advocates nor civil servants, but great writers. Nothing less would satisfy her. Day after day she left them free to work as they deemed fit in the little closet which looked on to the courtyard peopled by the mementoes of the illustrious dead. Each day, after dinner, they went out with her, and there is something moving in the thought of Sophie Hugo, looking rather stiff, rather like the Mother of the Gracchi, in her purple dress and cashmere shawl with its pattern of palm leaves, accompanied by her two young, submissive and affectionate hopefuls. Every evening they would walk as far as the rue du Cherche-Midi, where Pierre Foucher, now a departmental head at the War Ministry, still lived in the Hôtel de Toulouse. There they would find Madame Foucher, a sweet-natured, pious woman, with something of the lingering freshness of youth about her, and her daughter Adèle, a beauty of the Spanish school, who once had played games with the three Hugo boys. *Tres para una.* They found it difficult to believe that, ten years earlier at the Feuillantines, they had trundled this delectable young woman in a wheelbarrow, and pushed her to and fro in a swing. Madame Hugo would take her sewing from her bag and silently ply her needle, together with Madame Foucher and Adèle, while the thin, ascetic-looking Pierre, with a skull-cap on his head, and cotton sleeves fastened about his arms, worked away at his files by the light of a candle. Eugène and Victor had been taught by their mother never to speak unless spoken to, but neither of them felt bored by these evenings spent at the crackling fire, so fully occupied were they in watching Mademoiselle Adèle bending over her work, "eyebrows arched, mouth pursed in a cherry pout, and eyelids touched with gold."[1] Both were in love with her. If, now and again, she stole a sidelong glance at one of them, it was always at Victor who, with his long fair hair, his high forehead, and his frank, deep-probing eyes, produced an impression of sovereign power and, in their little world, was already something of a celebrity. There was a note almost of respect in the letters which the faithful Biscarrat, who had left Paris for Nantes, wrote to him: "A day is coming when you will take your place among the greatest of our poets. I seem to catch in your work something of Racine's choruses"; and, on another occasion: "What you write is always good: this time it is more than good."[2] But Victor Hugo realized that true fame would be hard to come by.

Soon he was in communication with the Académie des Jeux Floraux, with its memory of ancient glories in the days of the troubadours and of "Clémence Isaure," which crowned poets, fêted them to the sound of flutes, and rewarded their labours with gifts of violets and amaranth and lilies of gold or silver. Eugène had submitted to this body an "Ode sur la Mort du duc d'Enghien," for which he had been given a special prize. The young poets felt that there was a warmer welcome awaiting them in the Capitol of Toulouse than in the Palais Mazarin. Victor, in his turn, offered an "Ode sur les Vierges de Verdun," who had been sent to the scaffold during the Revolution for having attended a ball given by the Prussians, and also entered for a prize poem, the subject of which was "On the replacing of the Statue of Henri IV." Up to the last day, so much occupied had he been in nursing his mother through an attack of bronchitis that not a line was on paper, but, seeing how miserable she was at the idea of his missing this chance, he composed the whole ode in a single night.

It was an academic exercise, but such undoubted mastery did the young writer show in the balance between content and form, and in the verse itself, that he was awarded the Golden Lily—in other words, the first prize—thus defeating a large number of entrants, including Alphonse de Lamartine who was ten years his senior. One of the members of the Toulouse Academy, Alexandre Soumet, wrote to Victor, praising his "high talent," and speaking of the "prodigious hopes for our literature" to which this new author gave rise. "If the Academy shares my feelings, Isaure will have insufficient crowns for the two brothers. All here are struck with wonderment at your seventeen years; indeed, are well-nigh sceptical. You are for us a riddle to which only the Muses hold the key."[3] These somewhat self-conscious words of praise came from a writer already well known in Toulouse, and even in Paris, as "our Alexander the Great." Soumet adopted an affable attitude towards the young. "He was compact of poetry . . . affection seemed to overflow from a brimming heart." In 1811, when he was twenty-five, he had been awarded the great golden amaranth for an "Ode on the Birth of the King of Rome." The matter of his verse changed with the changing régimes. When the King of France came into his own again, he thought it wise to withdraw to Toulouse for a while, and there to occupy his time in the composition of a "Eulogy of Louis XVI." "It may be regarded," he said, "as one of the outcomes of events in the world of politics." It most certainly may!

Soumet, still in the running-in period of monarchism, was at that time an infrequent visitor to Paris, but he had friends there whom he made known to Victor Hugo. He introduced him to a high-ranking official in the Department of Crown Lands, Jacques Deschamps de Saint-Amant, a venerable and cultivated old gentleman, whose two sons, both of them poets, lived with him—Émile and Antoni Deschamps. They had built up a group of men in their thirties, all writers, the main link between whom was that they were all middle class by extraction, all catholic and all monarchist. Traditional though this little society was, there was much talk in it of Goethe, Byron, Schiller and Chateaubriand. Germany and England seemed at that time to be providing the advance-guard of European literature, because France, between 1789 and 1815, had been too busy making war to have time or energy for anything else. These kindred spirits dreamed of a "new movement in poetry." The posthumous works of André Chénier, recently given to the world by Henri de Latouche, were causing no little excitement. It was amazing to find in them turns of verse which were entirely new, and a simplicity of tone which seemed to hark back to a genuine antiquity. Victor, still a golden-haired boy, found himself being taken seriously, and treated as a "dear colleague" by men who had already "arrived." Not that he was particularly astonished, because he had that calm self-confidence which gives a sense of power. In September 1819, because Chateaubriand had written in his journal, *Le Conservateur,* a fine article on La Vendée, the young Hugo, who derived from La Vendée on his mother's side, composed an ode on "Les Destins de La Vendée" which he ventured to dedicate to Chateaubriand. Abel, always generous, put him in touch with a printer friend. The ode was published. Its sale was not altogether negligible, and it became the talk of Paris.

There was a young girl with black eyes who watched with emotion the soaring arrow-flight of her friend. This girl was Adèle Foucher. One day, when she found herself alone with Victor under the chestnuts, she said: "You must have secrets: have you not one that is greater than the rest? He agreed that he had. "So have I," she said: "tell me your great secret, and I will tell you mine." "My great secret," replied Victor, "is that I love you." "And mine, that I love you," said she. This happened on April 26th, 1819. They were both of them shy and sensible young people, he serious and ardent, she extremely pious.

Their love remained completely innocent and, for that reason, grew stronger. "Hearing you say that, dear Adèle, has given me the courage of a lion."[4]

The Foucher family spent the summer at Issy, near Paris. Victor sometimes went there with his mother and, for the rest of the time, thought about his absent love. "The sweet fondness became a fire that could not be subdued." During the winter of 1819-20 they exchanged letters. Victor, a great reader of *Werther* and *René,* of Tibullus and Catullus and translator of Horace's *Priapus,* was burning with desires which he did not put into words. Adèle, a little middle-class girl of seventeen, who had been strictly brought up, was ashamed of her "sin." She was proud to know that she was loved by a young man whose hands had already touched the skirts of fame, but fearful, too, of writing to him in secret, nervous all the time of her parents and her confessor. When, in December 1819, Victor gave her a poem which he had written for her, "Premier Soupir," and asked for twelve kisses in return, she promised them, but later haggled and gave him only four.

> Ces vers pour qui ton jeune amour
> M'a promis des baisers que ta pudeur craintive
> Me refuse de jour en jour . . .[5]

Victor had been trained by his mother to take life seriously. From this moment he thought only of marriage, and would not compromise his fiancée. "For the lover fain would keep in trust the husband's purity." He prostrated himself at the young girl's feet. "Is it really true that you love me, Adèle? Tell me so, that I may pin my faith to that entrancing thought . . . How happy you make me! Goodbye, goodbye. I shall spend a truly blessed night dreaming of you. Sleep well, and let your husband take the twelve kisses which you promised."[6] Adèle replied, sometimes in the language of a woman in love, more often like a model little girl who had been scolded by her mother. Madame Foucher had declared that she was "much dissatisfied" at the preference shown by her daughter for a young man. *Adèle to Victor:* "It is miserable, Victor, to desire one's mother's absence . . . It makes me very unhappy, when I say my prayers, to be able to give God lip-service only, and to feel that my whole being is taking flight to you. That, certainly, is a matter for great sadness. When my poor mother has her back turned, I secretly take up my pen, and so deceive her."[7] She begged Victor to be cautious, and he, much against the grain, consented.

Victor Hugo to Adèle Foucher, 19th February, 1820: It seems to me that from now on we must show in public an extreme reserve towards one another: it is only after much struggling that I have brought myself to the point of advising you to be cold to me, your husband, your Victor, the man who would give everything to spare you a moment's pain. I must needs condemn myself never to sit beside you, and, Oh! my dear love, I beg you to have pity on my wretched jealousy, and avoid all other men as you must avoid me. I will never approach you; but let me, at least, have the consolation of never seeing others enjoy that happiness which only on your account I have renounced. Stay with your mother: sit with other women. You can have no idea, my Adèle, how much I love you. If I so much as see another man draw near to you, I tremble with longing and impatience: my muscles grow tense, my breast swells, it is all that I can do to keep a hold upon myself. . . .[8]

On December 28th, however, they were allowed to go, chaperoned by Adèle's young brother (Paul Foucher), to see a performance of *Hamlet* at the Théâtre Français. "Tell me, dear friend, have you retained any memory of that lovely evening? Do you recollect how we waited a long time for your brother in the street close by the theatre, how you said that *women are more true in love than men*? Have you forgotten how, all through the performance, your arm was pressed to mine, and how I told you of the unhappiness in store which, only too soon, has struck at us?"[9]

One day, when Adèle had a letter hidden in her bodice, she bent down to put on her shoes. The letter fell out. "What's that?" asked Madame Foucher. "Tell me at once." The girl told her of Victor's love, and how they had agreed to get married. Monsieur and Madame Foucher talked the matter over together, and came to the conclusion that there were only two possible solutions. Either the young people must be officially betrothed, or they must be separated. Pierre Foucher did not set his face against such a marriage. In his eyes, a general of the Empire, even on half pay, was a desirable father-in-law. He believed in Victor's future, and knew that men of intelligence thought well of him. But some sort of decision must be reached, because people were beginning to gossip. Adèle wrote to Victor: "All the old tittle-tattlers of the Quarter are making fun of me, and saying things which, though they may not destroy my reputation, certainly do me a great deal of harm. And there is another thing, too: I cannot help reproaching myself for the way I am behaving to mamma. I love her, and would do anything she asked . . . Oh! dear Victor, how very much to blame I am! After the way in which I have been acting, I should not be at all surprised to learn that you hold me in contempt. . . ."[10]

He was far from doing any such thing, but he did play the schoolmaster with her, and already used the tone of a husband when advising her. "You are now General Hugo's daughter. You must never act in a manner unworthy of yourself, nor allow others to be lacking in respect towards you. Mamma attaches great importance to such matters. . . ."[11]

And so did he, and to an even greater extent. "A pin the less in my tucker made him angry," said Adèle. "The slightest hint of licence in my talk shocked him, and it is not hard to realize how mild such 'licence' must have been in a family so strict that my mother refused to admit that anyone could even hint at a lover in connection with a married woman—she did not believe that such a thing was possible! He saw dangers everywhere, and took offence in many things in which I could see no cause for offence at all . . . His mind could go to extravagant lengths, and I could never foresee what he would think."[12]

Victor Hugo to Adèle Foucher, March 4th, 1822: I have something, my dearest Adèle, to say to you which causes me the most acute embarrassment. I cannot keep silent about it, yet, at the same time, do not know how to speak of it . . . I could wish, Adèle, that you were less fearful of dirtying your skirts when walking in the street. Only yesterday I noticed, with feelings of distress, the precautions that you take . . . It seems to me that modesty is something more precious than clothes . . . I cannot describe to you, dear friend, the agonies I went through yesterday in the rue des Saints-Pères at seeing the woman whom I respect making herself a target for impudent glances. I should have liked to warn you about this, dear Adèle, but did not dare, because I had no words with which to express to you what I meant . . . Pay attention to what I have said in this letter unless you wish me to be put in the position of having to chastise the first insolent puppy who ventures to stare at you. . . .[13]

These letters to his fiancée are curious effusions, all filled with "respectable truisms," and written with the "sincerity of a choirboy in love," and in a tone of "virtuous exaltation." The vocabulary is "terribly reminiscent of the ornaments to be seen on French Restoration clocks."[14] But how could this young man help being of his age and world? How could he have dared tell a young, pure and pious girl of the thoughts that were passing through his mind? Their mixture of desire and respect caused him to feel embarrassed whenever he was near her. She noticed this, and put an entirely wrong interpretation on his attitude of constraint. "As though I have not enough troubles and sorrows of my own," moaned the unhappy Adèle, "without being made to realize that I vex you during the few moments which we have together!"[15] "I can see from the expression of your face, and hear in the least thing you say, that you are vexed."[16] What agonies! What torments! And then, he has an idea of the true Werther vintage: why should he not marry her, be her husband for one night, and then kill himself next morning? "Nobody could reproach you. You would be my widow . . . One day of happiness is worth a life-time of misery."[17]

Adèle refused to follow him into such rarefied regions, and brought the discussion back to the subject of local gossip. Her mother had been saying to her: "Adèle, if you do not cease from behaving in this manner, if people go on talking about you as they are doing, I shall find myself compelled to speak to Monsieur Victor, or, rather, to his mother, and, because of you, to break with one of whom I am fond, and of whom I think with respect."[18]

This was why he felt terrified when, on the morning of April 26th, 1820, the anniversary of their mutual declaration, he saw Monsieur and Madame Foucher arrive with an air of great solemnity at Madame Hugo's door, and heard them ask to see her. Sophie Hugo was a possessive mother, both jealous and proud of her son. She *knew* beyond any possibility of doubt that Victor was destined for a brilliant future. Furthermore, he was the son of General Count Hugo. Was he, a youth of eighteen, to ruin his life by marrying this trivial little Foucher girl? Never, so long as there was life in her body, should such a marriage take place! This aggressive attitude on her part inevitably led to a coldness which was "not far removed from a complete breach" between the two families. Victor was summoned to the drawing-room, where the nature of the quarrel was explained to him. In the presence of the Fouchers, he kept a tight hold on himself, but openly declared that he was in love with their daughter. After they had left: "My mother saw me pale and silent. She redoubled her usual tenderness and tried to console me: I took to my heels, and, as soon as I was alone, wept long and bitterly."[19] The idea that he might be able to make his mother change her mind did not so much as occur to him. He knew that she was "unshakable, inexorable, as intolerant in her hatreds as she was ardent in her affections." As to poor Adèle, as soon as her parents reached home, they told her quite simply that she would never again see the general's countess, nor Victor. Did he still love her? She did not know. Her parents maintained that he had *refused* to visit them. A curtain of silence fell between the lovers.

6

"Le Conservateur Littéraire"

Hugo, like every true poet, is also a critic of
the first rank.

PAUL VALÉRY

LOVE had slipped through his fingers, and he tried to find consolation in work. Abel had decided that the three brothers
Hugo should, at long last, have their magazine. The periodical sponsored by their master Chateaubriand was called *Le Conservateur*;
theirs should be *Le Conservateur Littéraire*. It appeared regularly from
December 1819 till March 1821, and was edited by Victor. Abel
contributed a few articles; Eugène, ever quick to take offence, held
aloof, and was represented only by some items of verse. Biscarrat wrote
from Nantes urging Victor to make his brother get down to work:
"otherwise, I see no hope for the young man."[1] The main nourishment
provided by the paper was supplied by the overflowing zest of the
youngest of the trio who, under eleven different pseudonyms, published in the space of sixteen months a hundred and twelve articles
and twenty-two poems.

Reading this collection one cannot help but be staggered by the
intelligence and erudition shown by this young man who was little
more than a boy. Literary criticism, dramatic criticism, foreign literature—in every subject that he touched there was a wealth of references
which betokened genuine culture, especially in Latin and Greek.
Voltaire, whom at that time he admired, was the object of an adverse
criticism: "a great genius who wrote history for the purpose of embarking on a long campaign of sarcasm at the expense of the human
race . . . There is some lack of a sense of justice in one who can find
in the annals of mankind only the record of crime and horrors . . ."[2]
Yet he, too, is frequently moved to a display of harsh cynicism by
the events of history: "The Roman Senate declared that it would
not ransom the prisoners. What does that prove? That the Senate was
short of money . . . The Senate went out to meet Varro, who had
made good his escape from the battle, and thanked him for not
having despaired of the Republic. What does that prove? That the

55

faction which had had Varro appointed general was still sufficiently strong to save him from being punished."[3] The power of this young man's thought, the firmness of his style, the extent of his knowledge, gave promise of a great writer.

In 1820 Victor Hugo took to carrying about with him a note-book in which he jotted down his occasional thoughts: "One walks as heavily through life as one does through mud." "Chateaubriand translates Tacitus as Tacitus would have translated him." "Ministers say what one wants them to say, so that one may do what they want one to do."[4] The young man who wrote like this was eighteen years old. Here is another entry: "De Vigny says that when Soumet becomes animated, his soul shows itself at the window."[5] Soumet and his Toulouse friends—the volcanic Alexandre Guiraud, the Comte Jules de Rességuier—played a prominent role in the *Conservateur Littéraire*. In appearance he was every inch a poet. He was liked for his long dark lashes, for the seraphic expression of his face, for the effrontery with which he could communicate the wild and shattering effects of inspiration. He was capable of great devotion, provided he was put to the test *at once*. "With him," said Virginie Ancelot, "one must never put anything off till the morrow." Guiraud was "a vivacious creature with something of the squirrel in him. One got the impression that he was for ever running round in his cage."[6]

Victor could call himself one of the group, having been named *maître des Jeux Floraux*. Other valuable contributors were the Deschamps brothers, whose father entertained this swarm of youth in his handsome apartment: Antoni, slightly eccentric; Émile, an ardent son and faithful husband of a wife who had no claims to beauty—"a charming fellow, perhaps a little too charming." "Call that poet a star? You're wrong, he's a candle," he has said of Jules de Rességuier. The epigram was turned against himself.

Émile Deschamps had been a childhood friend of Alfred de Vigny, and in 1820 introduced the handsome sub-lieutenant of the Royal Guards, a poet who so far had published nothing, to Victor Hugo. At first the relationship between the two men was extremely ceremonious. They addressed one another as "Monsieur Alfred" and "Monsieur Victor." Vigny, who was on garrison duty at Courbevoie, was invited to the home of the Hugos: "When you feel so inclined I hope you will come, expecting boredom, and bringing pleasure." Was this a deliberate display of humility? Undoubtedly, but also a confession of nervousness at the idea of receiving into the family circle this senior by five years, an officer and a man who was very much conscious of his ancestral glories. Needless nervousness, however, for Vigny, who was growing bored of his gold epaulettes and his great sabre, soon became the friend, not only of Victor, but of Abel and Eugène, whom he called Harold the intrepid. "I am, you see, greedy for the three of you," he wrote. "Come, that we may have one of those long sessions in which time passes only too quickly."

Through the Deschamps, again, Hugo got to know Madame Sophie Gay and her ravishing daughter Delphine, who, scarcely more than a child, herself wrote verses which her beauty made admirable; and, through Vigny, his two best friends, Gaspard de Pons and Taylor, both of them officers in his regiment, the first a poet, the second a man mad about literature. The writer he most wanted to meet, however, was obviously Chateaubriand. The *Génie de Christianisme,* "by the music and colour of which he had been dazzled," had revealed to him a poetical catholicism which "merged itself with the architecture of the cathedrals and the great pictured scenes of the Bible."[7] He passed rapidly from his mother's royalism *à la* Voltaire, to Chateaubriand's Christian royalism which, he hoped, would to some extent bridge the gulf between him and the Fouchers, both of whom were devout Catholics. When the Duc de Berry was assassinated, Victor Hugo wrote an ode on the event which produced a great effect. One stanza of it drew tears from the old Louis XVIII, who gave instructions that a gratuity of five hundred francs should be sent to the young poet. A deputy of the Right, Agier, published an article on the ode in *Le Drapeau Blanc,* and quoted Chateaubriand as having referred to the author as a "sublime child." There is nothing to prove that the words were ever uttered. The vicomte always pulled a face when he was reminded of them. One evening in 1841, at Madame Récamier's, the Comte de Salvandy, who was to make the speech of welcome at Hugo's reception into the Academy, said to Chateaubriand: "I shall confine myself to expanding that fine phrase of yours about a *'sublime child.'* " "But I never said anything so nonsensical!" said Chateaubriand irritably.

However that may be, Agier introduced Victor Hugo at 27 rue Saint-Dominique, where the welcome extended to the young man ran strictly to form. Madame de Chateaubriand, with her pointed nose, was installed on a small settee. She made no movement and spoke not a word. Chateaubriand, dressed in a black frock-coat, was leaning against the mantelpiece, and straightened his small, bent body. René, now an old man, was sparing of praise. "There was, however, in his attitude, in the inflexions of his voice, in the way he had of assigning to those who were introduced to him what he considered to be their due place in the hierarchy of fame, something so regal that Victor Hugo felt reduced rather than raised in importance. He stammered out a few embarrassed words, and longed to get away . . ."[8] He returned more than once, because his mother wanted him to, but the subsequent visits were no more exciting, except on one occasion, when the vicomte left his bed, and had himself sponged down and massaged, stark-naked, in the presence of his surprised disciple. The

Old Magician had a frightening way of breaking off a conversation, and indicating with icy politeness that he was bored. "One felt more of respect than liking . . . one felt that one was in the presence of a genius, not of a man."[9]

Literature is sometimes, for a writer, a means of making known to those he loves things which he cannot tell them directly. Victor, who sent a copy of the *Conservateur Littéraire* each month to Monsieur Foucher and reviewed the latter's insignificant Official Reports as though they were works of major importance, hoped that the paper would be seen by Adèle. He therefore published in one of the numbers an elegy—"Le Jeune Banni"—in which one of Petrarch's disciples, Raymond d'Ascoli, driven from home by his father because of his love for a young girl, announces that he is about to commit suicide:

> J'ose t'écrire. Hélas! à nos ardeurs naissantes
> Qu'eut servi jusqu'ici ce pénible secours?
> Les doux aveux de nos amours
> A peine ont effleuré nos lèvres innocents;
> Un mot faisait tous nos discours. . . .[10]

The last line was not unworthy of La Fontaine. But would Adèle read it? Victor tried, too, to give expression to his love by writing a wildly romantic story, *Han d'Islande,* in which he painted a portrait of himself as Ordener, and of Adèle as Ethel. "I had a soul that brimmed with love and misery and youth. But to no living creature could I breathe its secrets: instead, I chose a silent confidant, a sheet of paper. . . ."[11]

The unfinished *Han d'Islande* could not appear in the *Conservateur Littéraire,* which had ceased publication in March 1821 or, more accurately, had been merged with *Les Annales de la Littérature et des Arts.* Mergers of this kind are, for literary reviews, a respectable form of suicide. *Le Conservateur Littéraire* had provided useful experience for the sublime child. "The years devoted to journalism (1819 and 1820) mark a decisive period in his life: love, politics, independence, chivalry and religion, poverty and fame, a stubborn pursuit of knowledge, an iron will at odds with destiny—all these things played their part in him, and grew to a stature which alone is consonant with genius. His every experience burned and writhed and fused in the volcanic heat of his passions, under the dog-days' sun of embittered youth, and this mysterious alloy, created by bubbling lava beneath a granite surface, produced a solid, white-hot, and protective armour . . ."[12] There was in this young man something other, and something more, than a great journalist, but he possessed, and would retain all his life long, one precious gift: the power to give to the events of every day a dramatic intensity.

7

Betrothal

I learned, from a strong-minded mother, that
one can be the master of events.

VICTOR HUGO

FEBRUARY 1821. The two lovers had not seen one another for
ten months. Madame Hugo had done everything in her power
to make her son forget Adèle: "She tried to lure me into worldly
dissipations . . . Poor mother! for it was she who had planted in my
heart a contempt for the world and a scorn of false pride."[1] He never
spoke to her of his love, but, from the look in his eyes, she knew that
he was thinking of nothing else. There was no possibility of direct
communication with the fiancée. Victor knew, however, that she was
taking drawing lessons at the house of a friend, Julie Duvidal de Montferrier, and that she went there unaccompanied. He took to spending
his mornings in loitering nearby. When his fiancée appeared he
intercepted her and started to talk. At first she seemed pleased, but
later grew frightened of what people might say if she were seen with
a young man. She still had a grudge against Victor. Was it not he
who, as an obedient son, had agreed not to see her again? He swore
that he asked nothing better than to present himself in the rue du
Cherche-Midi, if that were "honourably possible." Adèle detested that
honourably. True love, she thought, takes no heed of such conditions.
"You most skilfully managed to elude the request I made that you
should come to our house."[2]

Could anything be more teasing than for two lovers to have to
take into consideration the wounded pride of their respective families?
Victor grew bitter: "For your sake I would have jumped over a
precipice: you held me back, but the hand that did so was as cold
as ice."[3] Adèle took offence: "I should really *like* mamma to see me
talking to you. She would shut me away in a convent, and I should
be completely happy."[4] Lovers' quarrels, these, in the true Molière
manner, sharpened by spiteful sarcasm, but carefully conducted so
as not to produce a definite breach. "Goodbye," said he; "I shall write
to you no more, I shall see you no more. Now, at last, you can be

happy."[5] But, two days later: "If, impossible though it may seem, you still have something you want to say to me, you can send a letter to this address: à Monsieur Hugo, de l'Académie des Jeux Floraux, Poste Restante, au bureau général, à Paris."[6] Of course she wrote again, and resumed her position of "adored Adèle." Victor's diary for the winter of 1820-21 is filled with mysterious entries: meeting-places— "rue du Dragon; rue de l'Échaudée; rue du Vieux-Colombier; at the Luxembourg (R); Chambre-sourire (X); Mainadieu (lux g). . . ."[7]

April 26th, 1821. Twin anniversary of their happiness and their despair. *Victor to Adèle*: "Today begins our second year of misery. Shall I survive to see the third? Goodbye for the present, Adèle mine. It is late. You are sleeping and do not dream of a certain curl of your hair which, every night before going to sleep, your husband presses religiously to his lips . . ."[8] *Adèle to Victor*: "This is the last time I shall write. I am scribbling this in haste because I have the whole Duvidal family on my back. I shan't see you again. It is impossible— and I shall hear from you no more. I can deceive mamma no longer, but whether she will feel the more beholden to me on that account, I do not know."[9]

It was at this moment that events took a sensational turn. Madame Hugo suddenly fell dangerously ill. Unable to go on living in a third-floor apartment, without a garden, she had moved in January 1821 to a ground floor, rented by Abel, at 10 rue de Mézières. Her sons, whom she had brought up to work with their hands (they had inherited a family tradition of craftsmanship), took on the jobs of carpenters, painters, upholsterers and dyers, because their mother had no money to spare for a new installation. She and her children dug, planted, grafted, raked. She overtaxed her strength, got too hot, caught a cold, and was laid low with a serious attack of pneumonia. Her sons spent whole nights at her bedside. On June 27th, at three o'clock in the morning, she died in their arms.[10]

Abel, summoned by his two younger brothers, helped them with the mournful duties which now fell upon them. The three sons, to-gether with a few friends, including a young priest, the Duc de Rohan, who was an admirer of Hugo's earliest ventures into poetry, accom-panied her to the Vaugirard cemetery. Victor spent that evening in aimless wandering. He had lost all taste for life. How lonely he was now! She who had been his all was dead. His father was living at Blois, hostile, or at least indifferent, to him. His fiancée had been taken from him. Between Eugène and himself two shadows stood: Adèle and Success. Already in the days of the Feuillantines' swing, the two brothers had been competing for the favours of "beauty in the bud." Since Victor's triumph, Eugène had been conscious of a rising tide of hatred which he had made little attempt to stem; while Victor, though he felt some pity for his elder, could not help but be pleased at the thought that he had been the stronger. The younger had his revenge, but a revenge which soon grew painful. For a long time now Eugène had had periods of black depression which had frightened the members of his family. His mother's death very nearly sent him out of his mind. Seeking desperately for some hope to which he might cling, Victor hurried through the rain to the Hôtel de Toulouse.

He was staggered, on this night of mourning, to see the Fouchers' windows blazing with light. Gusts of music, bursts of laughter, reached him where he stood in the shadowed garden. By paths long known to him he approached the house, peered through the windowpane, and saw Adèle in a white dress and with flowers in her hair, dancing and laughing. It was a shock which he never forgot. If later he understood so well the feelings of poor folk who, with their noses glued to the windows of the rich, saw with bitterness in their hearts the merrymaking in which they would never share, it was because of this memory. Next morning Adèle, walking in the garden, saw Victor running towards her. His presence there, and the pallor of his face, must mean that something terrible had happened. "What is the matter?" "My mother is dead; we buried her yesterday." "And to think that I was dancing!" They mingled their sobs, and in this way plighted their troth.

Monsieur Foucher went to the rue de Mézières to express his sympathy, and urged Victor to leave Paris. Life there was expensive, and the young men appeared to be without resources. Victor had written to his father informing him of the terrible news.

The three brothers would have liked their father to come to Paris and settle the family affairs. They felt like shipwrecked sailors, and still clung to this piece of flotsam even now adorned with the pathetic relics of a figurehead. But the general's financial position showed no signs of improving. The first thought that had come to him on finding himself a widower was to marry "the Lady Marie-Catherine Thomas y Sactoin, thirty-seven years of age, widow of Anaclet d'Almé, landowner." Those were the names entered at the Registrar's Office. The letters, however, sent out by the general announced his marriage to "Madame d'Almé, widow, Comtesse de Salcano." She had been his mistress for eighteen years, and for two such old "married persons" all that was required was the municipal sanction. There were no wedding bells. Colonel Louis Hugo, now living at Tulle, wrote an indignant letter to his Goton sister, complaining that the general had not so much as informed his brothers of his wife's death. "Such thoughtlessness proves how little he cares for us . . ."[11] The second marriage had taken place on July 20th, 1821, at Chabris (Indre). Louis Hugo learned of it only in January 1822. He immediately informed the widow of Martin-Chopine: "If the news be true, we had better resign ourselves to the inevitable, and put the best face we can on the matter."[12]

For some months the sons pretended to know nothing of the fact that their father had regularized his position. What protest could they have made? They were entirely dependent on the general. Their mother had left nothing but debts, and, except for Abel, they were none of them making any money.

The Fouchers decided that if they followed their usual custom, and took a house near Paris for the summer, sooner or later the youngest Hugo would be sure to turn up there. They picked, therefore, on Dreux. The fare to that place from Paris was twenty-five francs, and Victor had not got twenty-five francs. But they forgot that he possessed two things a good deal more valuable than money: a will of iron, and a taste for adventure. They set off by carriage with their daughter on July 15th. Victor followed on the 16th.

Victor Hugo to Alfred de Vigny, July 20th, 1821: I did the whole journey on foot under a blazing sun and along roads without a shadow of shade. I am pretty well exhausted, but bursting with pride at having covered twenty leagues (about fifty miles) on my two feet. I look at wheeled traffic with feelings of pity. If you were with me now you would have before your eyes the spectacle of as insolent a biped as you could hope to see . . . I owe a lot to this trip, Alfred: it has helped to take my mind off things. I was sick and tired of that gloomy house.[13]

On the 19th he was at Dreux, climbing old towers on a hill that fell sharply to the plain, "the funerary chapel of the Orléans family . . . This white, unfinished chapel stands out in contrast to the black, dilapidated fortress: it is a tomb reared on a crumbling palace . . ."[14] Already his tastes were strongly marked: "Ruins and greenery, black and white, the symbolic interpretation of past and future."[15]

He was determined to take walks in the neighbourhood until such time as he should meet Adèle and her father. Dreux is not a large place, and sure enough the meeting took place. *Adèle to Victor* (in pencil): "My friend, what are you doing here? I could scarcely believe my eyes. There is no way in which I can talk to you. I am writing this secretly to beg you to be prudent, and to tell you that I am still your wife. . . ."[16]

Victor Hugo to Pierre Foucher, July 20th, 1821: Sir: I had the pleasure actually to see you here, today, in Dreux, and I am still wondering whether I was dreaming. I do not think that you saw me: I, at least, took great care that you should not do so. Nevertheless, since it is quite possible that you may run across me by some chance or other in the course of the next few days, and since my presence here might be variously interpreted, I think it only polite and loyal on my part to warn you . . . We can only be surprised at this oddest of all odd chances . . . My intentions are pure. I should not be honest if I did not inform you that the unexpected sight of your daughter gave me great pleasure.[17]

The lie was ingenuous and transparent, but calculated, all the same, to touch the heart of so decent a fellow as Pierre Foucher. He had known young Victor in the days when he was "a puny, sickly little chap, without, it seemed, any will to live."[18] He saw before him now a youth in robust health, entirely self-assured, and capable of expressing his love vigorously and with eloquence. It was quite impossible, he thought, to refuse to have a talk with this son of his old friends, and at a time, too, when he was plunged in grief. He therefore received Victor in the presence of Adèle and Madame Foucher. He asked the young man's intentions. Victor had only one—to marry his beloved. He declared that he had confidence in his future, that he had started on a long novel *à la* Walter Scott, *Han d'Islande,* which would certainly have a large sale; that the king's government ought surely to grant a pension to a poet of monarchist leanings; that he would obtain General Hugo's consent to the marriage. All this was pretty nebulous, but the two young people were in love. Pierre Foucher decided that there should be no public announcement of the betrothal; that, for the present, Victor should not have the free run of his house, but that Adèle and her wooer-designate should be allowed to correspond.

With joy in his heart Victor went off to spend the first fortnight of August at Montfort-l'Amaury with his friend Saint-Valry, yet another poet, one of the Deschamps group, a good-natured giant of whom Alexandre Dumas said: "When he gets a cold in his feet it takes a year for it to reach his head." Saint-Valry, filled with admiration for Victor, offered him the freedom of his family house. From Montfort-l'Amaury and later from La Roche-Guyon, where he was staying with the Duc de Rohan, Victor wrote several letters to his father-in-law presumptive:

Victor Hugo to Pierre Foucher, August 3rd, 1821: Whatever the future may have in store, however events turn out, we must not lose hope. Hope is a virtue. Let us then do all in our power to be nobly happy. If we fail we need reproach nobody but the Good God. Don't be frightened at the exaltation of my ideas. Remember that I have just experienced a grievous sorrow, that my whole future is in question, that I do not lack serenity. It might have been better for your daughter had she been attached to some man who was nimble-witted and docile, and could at any moment have stretched a hand to fortune. Still, could she have loved such a man as she deserves to love? Is there any true tenderness without energy? I ask these questions with considerable uneasiness, because I realize that I am offering her no guarantee of happiness save a desire, beyond my power to express, to make her happy.[19]

Pierre Foucher replied: "a docile man is a bad guest to have in any family," which sounded encouraging.

The Duc de Rohan, who had followed Madame Hugo to the grave, was a man of thirty who exercised a certain amount of influence in Brittany where he owned two properties, Josselin and Pontivy. In January 1815 an appalling accident had turned his whole life topsy-turvy. His young wife, who was dressing for a ball, had approached too close to the fire. The flames had caught the lace trimmings of her gown and she had died of burns, showing an heroic resignation to the end. The duke had entered Saint-Sulpice, though the austere rule of that community must have tried hard a man of delicate physique and almost feminine sensitiveness. The Abbé de Rohan had an innate feeling for the good and the beautiful. From the first publication of Lamartine's verses, he had let their author know that he would esteem it an honour to be his friend. A similar admiration had drawn him to Victor Hugo who, after Madame Hugo's funeral, had lost no time in going to thank him, and had been received with warm-hearted simplicity. The duke explained to him that he had no ambition beyond becoming the curé of his village, a statement which gave the poet much pleasure. Rohan, guessing that he had to do with one who was temperamentally religious but knew little of the religion he professed, set about finding him a confessor. "You stand in need of one, and I will make it my business to find him." He took him to the Abbé Frayssinous. This worldly cleric, who was very much the fashion at that time and a welcome figure at Court, explained to the young man that his duty was to succeed, and to employ his success in the service of the Faith. This comfortable form of religion was extremely displeasing to the neophyte who, on leaving, told Rohan that the Abbé Frayssinous should never be his director. Rohan next introduced him to Lamennais, whose shabby coat, coarse stockings of blue wool and peasant's clogs produced a greater impression. Lamennais became for Victor, not only a confessor but a friend, whose rough frankness he liked. The man he first knew was a kindly, tender-hearted Lamennais, for whom a long experience of persecution soon substituted the "nervous and irascible" man of the 'thirties.

La Roche-Guyon was a Renaissance château on the bank of the Seine. The walls were covered with beautiful panelling and Gobelins tapestries. The host seemed "divinely" charming. An obvious beauty of mind was added to his other seductive qualities, but there was about him still something of the prince. When he looked in the glass at his black, silky hair, he could not repress a smiling and coquettish glance. A bishop out of Stendhal. Victor, who had been given a magnificent room, was served by an army of obsequious lackeys. How brutal was the contrast when, on his return to Paris, he had to leave the apartment in the rue de Mézières and take up his quarters in an attic at 30 rue du Dragon, with one of his cousins from Nantes, Adolphe Trébuchet. The three brothers, in their isolation, tried to make contact with their mother's side of the family. Abel, Eugène and Victor wrote a collective letter to their Trébuchet uncle: "My dear uncle: I trust that you will allow your family in Paris to join their congratulations to those of your relatives in Nantes, on the occasion of your birthday, like all your other children. We, who know you in Adolphe, miss you badly from all our pleasures . . . Adolphe is good, gay and friendly . . . Happy are the fathers who, like you, can be praised for the good qualities in their children . . ."[20]

Victor and his cousin jointly leased the attic which was divided in two. One portion was the "drawing-room" in which they received their guests. Its sole magnificence was a marble mantelpiece above which was suspended the Golden Lily of the Jeux Floraux. The other half was an ill-lit passage in which two beds had, with great difficulty, been accommodated. This was more than enough for Victor, who owned but three shirts.[21]

Later he painted, in Marius, a portrait of himself, in the rue du Dragon days:

A high and intellectual forehead, wide, ardent nostrils, a calm and sincere expression, and in his face a something that told of pride, thought and innocence . . . His manners were reserved, cold, polished, and not very forthcoming. He made his meals off such food as he could find. There was a time in his life when he swept his own landing, and bought a pennyworth of Brie at the grocer's . . . He would live for three days on a cutlet which he cooked himself. On the first day he ate the meat, on the second, the fat, and, on the third, he gnawed the bone. . . . [22]

But in this life he retained a sovereign dignity. He respected himself, and saw to it that others should respect him. He did not hesitate, monarchist though he was, to give shelter to a young republican friend who was wanted by the police, a man called Delon. From his mother he had learned always to protect the proscribed.

All this would have been easy to bear had love gone smoothly, but the quarrels *à la* Molière had started again. Adèle, for no reason at all, decided that she had been "scorned." Victor went up in smoke as soon as his jealousy took fire. He now began to attack Julie Duvidal de Montferrier, Adèle's friend and a talented teacher of drawing, with a violence of prejudice which he had inherited from his mother:

Victor Hugo to Adèle Foucher, February 3rd, 1822: It is quite enough to ruin that young woman's reputation that she should have turned herself into an artist. A woman has only to belong to the public in one way, for that public to believe that she belongs to it entirely. How can a young woman keep her imagination chaste, and, consequently, her behaviour pure, after embarking on studies connected with the art of painting, studies which demand the abjuring of all modesty? . . . Is it fitting that a woman should lower herself to the level of artists, where she will find herself cheek by jowl with actresses and dancers? . . .[23]

Poor Adèle felt herself completely crushed by such a weight of severity. "I cry you mercy!" she wrote: "love me, I beg, with that peace and tranquillity which, of necessity, you owe to your wife." And, again: "Such passion is excessive: it cannot last, or so, at least, I have always been led to suppose."[24]

This was charming and comic, but Victor had no sense of humour. Serious and solemn, he replied with a lecture on the passion of love:

Victor Hugo to Adèle Foucher, October 20th, 1821: Love, for the world at large, is nothing but a carnal appetite, or a vague tendency which possession extinguishes and absence destroys. That is why you have heard it said, by a strange abuse of words, that *passion does not last*. Alas! Adèle, are you aware that *passion* means *suffering*? Do you really believe that there is any suffering in the love experienced by the common run of mankind, so seemingly violent, but, in reality, so feeble? No, immaterial love is eternal, because he who feels it cannot die. It is our souls, then, that love, and not our bodies. But I would point out that nothing should be pushed to extremes. I don't go so far as to say that the body has nothing to do with this greatest of all affections, for, in that case, what point would there be in difference of sex, and what should prevent two men from being in love? . . .[25]

In her heart she was pleased to think that she was adored in this way, but she was uneasy about the future. Could she play the part of the great lover for which he had cast her? "I must tell you, Victor, that you are wrong in thinking me superior to all other women . . ."[26] It is the fault of passionate men to set the women they love upon a pedestal. To be placed so high produces dizziness, and dizziness leads to a fall. The Foucher parents, too, were at times terrified by the young man's violence. One evening, in the rue du Cherche-Midi, where Adèle, after much begging, had got her parents to invite him, the talk turned on the subject of adultery. He became positively ferocious, arguing that in such a case the husband should either kill or commit suicide. Adèle rounded on him: "How intolerant you are! You would turn executioner if there were not one already. What sort of a life am I going to have, I wonder? There are times when you frighten my family, and it is no use pretending that you do not. One of these days I shall stand before you, trembling . . ."[27] He stuck to his point of view. "I have wondered, sometimes, whether, perhaps, I am wrong, and have found it impossible to blame my easily aroused jealousy. Indeed, I have actually come to see that jealousy of that kind is the very essence of the chaste, exclusive and pure love which I feel for you. I am reduced to misery when I think that I have been unable to inspire the same in you. I would have you know that it is those who love all women indiscriminately who never feel jealousy of one in particular."[28]

There was a further cause of friction between them. The only thing that counted for Hugo, his love apart, was his work, and he now tried to get his beloved to take an interest in it. She confessed that she just could not understand poetry. "It is not, and I admit it, your mind and the talent you may possess—which I cannot, unfortunately, appreciate— that have made an impression on me."[29] This made him smile. "You say, Adèle, that a day will come when I shall realize how little you know, and that then your ignorance will leave me with a feeling of emptiness . . . You once told me, with charming simplicity, that you could not understand poetry . . ."[30] "Let me tell you, quite briefly, Adèle, that poetry is virtue expressed. High character and a great talent for poetry are almost always inseparable, so, you see, you *must* be able to understand poetry, which comes only from the soul, and can be made manifest just as truly in fine actions as in fine verse."[31] He did not want her, by underrating herself, to force him into the position of having to champion his wife against his wife. "You tell me that I *do* understand poetry," she wrote, "though I have never been able to invent a line of verse. Surely, verses *are* poetry?"[32] To this he patiently replied: "When I told you that you have an understanding of poetry in your soul, all I was doing was to reveal to you one of its divine faculties. *Surely verses are poetry?* you ask. *Mere* verses are not. Poetry resides in ideas, and ideas come from the soul. Verse is no more than the beautiful dress in which a beautiful body is clothed. Poetry can be expressed in prose; only, it is more perfect when decked out in the grace and majesty of verse . . ."[33] What a vista of instruction for future fireside domesticity!

On the altar of his love he did offer one great sacrifice. He would be reconciled with his father. It seemed to him that, in taking this step, he was betraying his adored mother. "I am proud and timid, yet I beg for favours. My wish is to ennoble literature, yet I work in order to make money. I love and respect my mother's memory, yet, in writing to my father, I condemn my mother to oblivion."[34] Closer acquaintance, however, showed that the father was a much pleasanter person than "Madame Trébuchet," in her resentment, had allowed him to be. The general was a very good sort of fellow, with a genuine love of poetry. He wrote short stories, and was modest enough to judge them as unworthy of publication. Realizing that his sons, contrary to the promise they had made, were not pursuing the law, he made no difficulties about accepting the idea of a purely literary career for them.

General Hugo to his son, Victor, November 19th, 1821: I knew only too well that you and your brother would never put your hearts into this business of studying for the law, and have been daily expecting to hear from you the reason for this change in your plans. I do not think it is altogether explained by the excuse you give, worthy of respect though it may be. I think it must be sought, rather, in that taste for literature which is your birthright: in your feeling for poetry, a feeling which led me more than once to scold your uncle Juste, because it led him to neglect his duties. That feeling has often led me astray, too, but, in your case, it has been justified by a deal of truly excellent verse. Conceived as you were, not on the Pindus, but on one of the highest peaks of the Vosges, in the course of a journey from Lunéville to Besançon, you seem to be conscious of your almost aerial origins. Your Muse, so far as I can see, shows herself to be consistently sublime. . . .[35]

Victor had got into the habit of sending him his odes. The general was full of praise for them, though he criticized them in a somewhat simple-minded and schoolmasterly fashion. In the matter of money he showed himself to be open-handed, mourning his castles in Spain and the settlement he could no longer make, but helping his sons as best he could, according to his means. These would have been greater, he explained, if only the government would give him the promotion to which he was entitled, and Victor, a friend of Chateaubriand, whose influence was at that time very great, ought, he pointed out, to put in a word for him. In this way, Victor became his own father's patron, and the relationship between them soon became so affectionate that the general invited the poet to come and work at Blois, where, jointly with his second wife, he had bought a vast country mansion, the Priory of Saint-Lazare. But such a visit would have implied recognition of the new Madame Hugo, and the sons of the first were not, as yet, prepared to accord it.

Another bond between Victor and his father was a shared anxiety about Eugène's health. The boy was as unbalanced as Abel was calm and staid. There can be little doubt that violence, a morbid love of horrors and a visionary outlook were family failings; but with Eugène, and more than ever since his mother's death, this inherited violence had begun to assume disquieting forms. He criticized Victor's poems with a jealous display of ill-temper which shocked Biscarrat. He would disappear for days on end, no longer showed the slightest affection towards his brothers, and wrote hateful letters to the general for which Victor did his best to find excuses. "We must suspend judgment, my dear father. Eugène has a good heart, and will, I am sure, admit that he is in the wrong."[36] The truth of the matter was that Eugène was madly jealous, and sought refuge in something not far removed from insanity. He could not face the thought that his brother would almost certainly marry Adèle, and went so far as to say the most horrible things to Victor about his fiancée.

Victor Hugo to Adèle Foucher, November 30th, 1821: A hideous light has been cast upon the character of one to whom, only yesterday, I would have devoted myself, to whose future I have already sacrificed part of my own, for whose sake I have used the products of long nights of work which I should, by rights, have regarded as belonging to you. Until now I have forgiven him every wrong that he has done me: I have seen in his vulgar envy, in his cowardly spite, only the unfortunate results of a moody temperament . . . God! if I told you . . . no, I won't tell you, I don't even want to tell myself. You don't really understand me, Adèle mine: you are amazed that your Victor should be so violent in his indignation, so implacable when he considers the wrong that has been done him. You don't know what he has done to me, Adèle. I *did* forgive him everything, I *would* have forgiven him still more—except this. Why did he not stab me to death in my sleep? There is but one being *in the whole world* whom I cannot forgive for even the tiniest wrong done to me, even if it be only a wrong of intention, and that being is not, oh, most certainly is not, myself! Why should this wretch dare to touch what is to me the dearest and most sacred thing in all the world? Why should he take from me my goods, my life, my only treasure? Why is he not a stranger to my heart?[37]

But he did forgive. His sense of justice forbade him to treat as a responsible person a brother who, at moments, seemed not, himself, to know what he was saying.

8

Where There's a Will...

Oh! days of reverie and strength and grace
... To be pure, and strong, and sublime, to believe
In all purity. . . .

VICTOR HUGO

MORE than six months had passed since the young people had plighted their troth at Dreux, and a cloud of tittle-tattle was again gathering about the Fouchers. Uncle Asseline, who had more than his due share of spitefulness; the elder brother, Victor Foucher; the friends, the gossips—all were saying that Adèle was dangerously compromising herself with a young man who was doing nothing to earn a living, or even to obtain his father's consent. The young fiancée was becoming sceptical and urgent: "I see, my dear Victor, at such times as I don't deceive myself, how little likely it is that all this planning to get married will ever come to anything. You must try to understand my parents' position. They see nothing definite, nothing certain in our future."[1] Adèle's complaining was gentle, and such as might have been expected from the daughter of a respectable middle-class family. The natural thing for Victor to do in such a case was to play the Spanish lover—"I will go to your parents and will say to them: *Farewell, you shall see no more of me until I have won my independence and got my father's consent ...*"[2] Then he went on to describe with bitterness what would happen. He would die of grief, and a day would come when "you will find yourself the wife of another. When it does, you must burn all my letters that no trace may remain of my spirit's passage on this earth."[3] At once, Adèle, all common sense and obstinacy, brought him back to solid ground. "Our love presents immense difficulties, especially when you are in a mood to let matters take their course":[4] and, on another occasion: "Yes, my friend, I am happy in the knowledge that you have been working. Perhaps I should be still happier if I knew you to be working with greater regularity. It seems to me that, except in things where one cannot look ahead, one ought not to begin something before one has finished what one already has in hand. You see, I am being severe with you."[5]

These doubts of hers provoked in him an uprush of pride.

Victor Hugo to Adèle Foucher, January 8th, 1822: Do not ask, Adèle mine, how it is that I am sure of being able to achieve an independent existence, for, if you do, you will force me to speak of a *Victor Hugo* of whom you know nothing, and with whom *your Victor* is not anxious to make you acquainted. The Victor Hugo I mean is a man who has both friends and enemies; to whom his father's military rank gives the right to appear in any society as an equal; who owes to some rather feeble attempts the advantages and drawbacks of a precocious reputation; whom the haunters of those salons where he but rarely shows his cold and melancholy visage believe to be occupied with some grave and solemn contemplation, whereas, in fact, he is only dreaming of a young girl who is sweet, charming, virtuous, and, fortunately for her, a stranger to all salons.

I am often told, was told, indeed, only a few days ago rather too crudely, that I am destined for something vaguely described as a *dazzling celebrity* (I repeat the hyperbole in the very words that were used to me). Personally, I consider that I am suited for nothing but domestic happiness. If, however, I must pass through the fire of fame before reaching that goal, I shall look on the fame only as a means and not as an end. I shall live outside any such fame, merely showing it that attitude of respect which all men owe to fame. Should it come to me, as many foretell, I shall neither have hoped for it nor desired it, for I have neither hope nor desire for anything but you. . . .[6]

Why should their marriage be impossible, or even distant? A pension? He had the promise of a Minister for that: "It is quite likely, my dear friend, that in a very few months I shall obtain a position worth two or three thousand francs. Then, with what my writing brings me, why should we not live quietly and at peace in the assurance that our income will increase step by step with our family? The general's consent? Tell me this, why should my father, when he sees that I am independent, refuse to make me happy? . . . My father is a weak man, but, fundamentally, he is a good one. By showing that they regard him with affection, his sons can bring much influence to bear. My hope is that, having made my mother miserable, he will not wish to make me so, too. Some day, Adèle, we shall live together under the same roof, in the same room, and you will sleep in my arms . . . Our pleasures then will be our duty and our right. . . ."[7]

Enchanting visions, those, for a young man with all his senses on fire, who read and wrote the poetry of love while living in a state of rigorous chastity. Of that, too, he wished to make a merit in the eyes of his fiancée: "I should consider a woman very ordinary (that is to say, as somebody of no very great value) who married a man without being morally certain, from what she knew of his principles and character,

not only that he had *sound good sense* but also was, and I use the word
in the strictest sense, *virgin,* as wholly virgin as she herself. . . ."[8]

But Adèle's reaction was surprising. Surely one didn't talk of "such
extraordinary things" to a well-brought-up young girl? *Certainly* one
did, replied her impetuous betrothed: "I was showing you how great a
power you exercise over me, since the mere image of you when conjured up is stronger than all the sappy effervescence of my years. What
I meant was that should any man have the effrontery, himself soiled
and impure, to join himself to a being pure and without blemish, he
would deserve only contempt and indignation . . . If I were a woman,
and the man of my choice were to say to me: *You are the woman who
has stood defensive between me and all other women; you are the first
whom I have ever pressed in my arms, the only one whom I ever shall
so press; the more I draw you to me with delight, the more shall I drive
from me with horror and disgust all who are not you* . . . it seems to me,
Adèle, that if I were a woman, such confidences made to me by the man
I loved would be far from unpleasing to me. Can it be that you do not
love me?"[9] No, only that she loved him in the Foucher manner, which
was simpler.

On March 8th, spurred on by her, he decided to ask the general for
his consent. The letter was shown to Adèle, who quarrelled with nothing in it except its portrait of her as an angelic being. "There is nothing
of the angel about me. You must get that out of your head. I am *earthy.*"
How magnificently realistic women are! She went on to explain to him
that happiness meant a great deal more to her than fame. "How *can*
you say that the one thing which might make me see marriage with
you in an advantageous light is *your father's rank?* What a mistake you
are making! I care nothing about rank or honours. I tell you plainly
that what you rate so highly is what matters least to me. Why should
I care about being the wife of an Academician if I were not yours . . .
or the daughter-in-law of a general?"[10]

Several anxious days of waiting followed. They discussed the possibility, should his father refuse, of running away together and getting
married in some foreign country. This time it was the well-brought-up
young lady of the rue du Cherche-Midi who roused herself almost to
passion. But they need not have worried, for the general's reply was a
model of good sense, and conveyed an unconditional consent. He was
far from blaming his son for being in love with Mademoiselle Foucher.
As for the "social position" of her parents, it was quite enough that
they were old friends. If only he had the millions of *réals* promised
him by Joseph Bonaparte! But he had nothing: "Whence it results that,
before even thinking of marriage, you ought to have a definite position
or employment, and I cannot regard a literary career as such, no matter
how brilliantly you may have embarked upon it. As soon as you have

the one or the other you can rely upon me to do everything in my power to forward a plan to which I am by no means opposed . . ."[11] There was only one cloud on the horizon. The general repeatedly referred in his letter to "my present wife." If his favour were to be retained, it was essential that his son should recognize his second marriage, and to this condition Victor agreed with exemplary tact, and that dignity in which he was never lacking.

The summer came and with it the Fouchers' annual holiday. It was decided that they should take a house at Gentilly. Thither Victor, now Adèle's official fiancé, was invited, though, for reasons of propriety, he was given quarters in an outbuilding which contained a dovecot. Madame Foucher, in her fourth pregnancy, was going through a difficult time, and the "late-comer" was causing her a considerable amount of inconvenience.

In spite of the long hours he had to spend of an evening in the family circle, "suffering the torments of perpetual embarrassment," he revelled in the "happy atmosphere" of Gentilly. The days were filled with a sense of intoxication and mystery. Sometimes Adèle would visit him secretly in his tower and grant him a kiss, a caress. Why could not two beings who loved live ever in each other's arms? But, if the happiness of Gentilly were to be made permanent, it was first necessary that he should achieve success. He did his best to press forward with the publication of a volume of his *Odes*. It was the generous Abel who had them printed and put on sale at Pélicier's bookshop in the Place du Palais-Royal. He had sent his brother the proofs as a pleasant surprise. The book appeared in June, an edition of fifteen hundred copies bound in grey-green paper. The author received fifty centimes per copy, in other words, seven hundred and fifty francs. The first copy went, as was proper, to *"My best-beloved Adèle, the Angel who is my sole glory, as she is my only happiness*—Victor."

The sales were encouraging, and brought the marriage closer. Adèle now plucked up courage to visit her fiancé when he was lying ill in Paris. "I care not what anybody says . . . There are circumstances in which I am prepared to disobey all parental injunctions without the faintest feeling of remorse . . ."[12] But not till the marriage was an accomplished fact could they give themselves to one another. *Adèle to Victor*: "Still three months to wait before I shall be with you for ever . . . How much the happier we shall be knowing that we have done nothing unworthy of our love, and that, though we might have been together sooner, we have set self-respect higher than happiness."[13]

Three months . . . She faced the delay bravely, because the only thing now lacking was official confirmation of the pension. The promise had been definite, but there were delays in ministerial quarters. "They treat this business of my pension as though it were just another piece of routine. It does not occur to them that they are dealing with a matter involving human happiness."[14] A charming way of putting it! At last the Abbé-Duc de Rohan intervened, enlisted the support of the Duchesse de Berry, and, on July 18th, 1822, Victor was in a position to write to the general that everything was settled: twelve hundred francs a year from the Privy Purse. That was the amount promised by the Ministry of the Interior; with an equal amount from Victor's literary labours it would be possible for them to set up house; the more easily, since the kindly Fouchers offered to take their daughter and their son-in-law to live with them. The general at once wrote a letter in form: "Victor has charged me with the duty of requesting the hand of this young lady whose happiness he feels he can assure in addition to his own . . ."[15] Monsieur Foucher replied in the friendliest fashion. He praised Victor's serious and orderly mind, said how pleased he was to renew his former intimacy with the general, and regretted that he could not give his daughter a bigger dowry. She would have "furniture, clothes and cash to the value of two thousand francs," and the young people would be welcome to live in the Hôtel de Toulouse until such time as they could set up house for themselves.

All that now remained to be done was to produce the bridegroom's certificate of baptism. It could not be found. The general's memory of what had happened so far back was faulty, but he was inclined to think that his son had never been baptized at all, unless his wife had had the ceremony carried out unknown to him, a possibility which, in view of her life-long attachment to the writings of Voltaire, seemed to be in the highest degree improbable. "Victor held religious beliefs, but was not an adherent of any *specific* religion."[16]

A suggested solution came from the general. "I have been assured that it is necessary only to make a declaration to the Parish Priest of Saint-Sulpice to the effect that, in the absence of your father, your mother had you baptized abroad—though you do not know where—for that dignitary to carry out a second baptism in the presence of any godfather and godmother you may like to name. You can then make your First Communion, and there will be no further difficulty about your being married in church . . ."[17] To have recourse to a subterfuge of this nature was not very pleasant. It did not, however, seem possible to admit to Monsieur Foucher that Sophie Hugo had failed to have administered to her son "the Sacrament which makes a child a member of the Christian community." On the advice of his "illustrious friend, Monsieur de Lamennais," Victor asked the general to make a statement to the effect that the child had been baptized in Italy. This was done, and Lamennais supplied a certificate of confession. The nuptial blessing was given at Saint-Sulpice on October 12th, 1822, by the Abbé-Duc de Rohan. The groom's witnesses were Alfred de Vigny and Félix Biscarrat, who came from Nantes for the purpose, overjoyed at the opportunity of once again seeing his two favourite pupils; the bride's were uncle Jean-Baptiste Asseline and the Marquis Duvidal de Montferrier. General Hugo was not present at the wedding.

The Fouchers provided the wedding-breakfast, which was followed by a ball in the State Apartment of the War Council's building, the very room in which General Lahorie, Victor's godfather, had been condemned to death. In the course of the evening, Biscarrat, the young pock-marked schoolmaster, noticed that Eugène was in a state of ab-normal agitation. He seemed to be quite beside himself, and made a number of very strange remarks. Carefully, so as not to attract atten-tion, Biscarrat explained matters to Abel, and the two of them led the unfortunate young man away. That night he went raving mad. Always melancholic, convinced that he was a victim of persecution, in love with Adèle, and suffering from wild and long-standing jealousy, he had been unable to bear the sight of his brother's happiness.

The young couple mercifully knew nothing, that evening, of the tragedy which had occurred. At last, what they had so long desired had come to pass, and they spent the night under the same roof, in each other's arms. For Victor, so chaste in fact, so ardent in imagination, it was an intoxicating experience to possess the young woman who, in his eyes, was the very perfection of beauty, and to know that he had be-come a member of the family living in that Hôtel de Toulouse, through the windows of which, twelve months previously, he had watched his fiancée, with flowers in her hair, dancing with another. From a strong-minded mother he had learned that a man may be the master of his fate. What a long road he had travelled in a single year! At twenty he was well on the way to fame: the old king and the members of the rising generation read his works; the Government had given him a pension; he stood high in the esteem of his fellow poets. By sheer force of arms he had won the woman of his choice, regained his father's affection, achieved a victory in his choice of a career. After so much unhappiness it all seemed a lovely dream, filled with shade and peace and love. A magician had made the longings of the boy come true. But the magi-cian was himself. *Ego Hugo.*

He had earned his night of bliss. That there was in him a faunlike potency of desire cannot be doubted (in his old age he maintained that he had had knowledge of his wife nine separate times in the course of that first night of marriage),[18] but he felt it necessary to combine with the delights of the flesh the highest of all possible human values. "In true marriage," he once said, "that is to say, where love is present, there is always a mingling of the ideal. The marriage-bed is a patch of day-break in the surrounding darkness . . . Such felicity alone is worthy of the name. Only in it is true joy possible . . . To love, or to have loved, is the sole essential. We should ask nothing more. No other pearl remains to be found in the dark turns and twists of life."[19] By the time he came to write those words the young bride, so deeply loved, had become a sad and disenchanted woman, who no longer wished to be his wife, except in name. All the same, even in that disappointing future, when Adèle had turned into an *Eve whom no fruit can tempt,* Hugo never forgot that once, in the distant long-ago, they had together tasted an almost superhuman happiness. This little Foucher daughter had then been just a young girl among other young girls, but simple-minded, rather obstinate, an artist (her drawings prove it) and far from stupid. Herself indifferent to poetry, Adèle had brought a poet to birth.

Let us take one last look at the young man, with the high forehead and the "formidable gift of virginity," as he crosses the threshold of the wedding chamber. A true knight upon the threshold of life, he could face the world with confidence. He lived in expectation of fame, being perfectly sure that it would come to him. Though only twenty, he had already, more than once, known what it was to despair. "What does one call it," asks one of Giraudoux's characters, "when in the new light of early day, as now, everything seems botched and spoiled, when all around is violence and ruin, though there is a sense of breathing in the air; when one has lost all and the city burns, when the innocent slaughter one another, but the guilty lie dying in a corner of the broadening morning?" And a beggar answers: "That, oh wife of Narses, has a lovely name: one calls it dawn."

What does one call it when the senses are on fire and the heart is pure; when genius asks only to leap like a fountain above the quiet pool, and a man knows not how to reach that liquid and refreshing surface; when he feels stronger than all the world, but powerless to prove his strength; when life, scarcely as yet begun, is already littered with strange memories, and the heart sings in the breast; when he is impatient and despairing, yet overflowing with hope? That has a lovely name, oh wife of Hugo: one calls it Youth.

PART III

Male Triumphant

One has long to live, and one will see all things
—and their opposites.

9

The Aftermath of Marriage

"THE immediate aftermath of marriage is solitude. The world respects the privacy of the happy—and, to some extent, the need to make up for lost sleep. . . ."[1] Adèle and Victor Hugo had no such calm awakening. On the very morning after the wedding, Biscarrat, in a terrible state, knocked at their bedroom door. Eugène's condition was giving rise to extreme anxiety. Victor hurried off with his friend, and found the "poor companion of his childhood raving." Eugène had filled his room with lights, as for a wedding feast, and had then chopped the furniture to pieces with a military sabre. For a whole month, Abel and Victor, Paul Foucher and one of the Trébuchet cousins, took turns in watching by the sick man. It was necessary to inform the general, who at once undertook the journey from Blois to Paris. "He had not come expecting to share happiness; he wished to share their grief." Victor and Adèle welcomed affectionately the "dear papa" to whom they owed their union. "Like white frost in the sun, all bitterness evaporated in the rays of the good man's kindliness."[2]

It was heartbreaking for the father to find in a state of delirium the handsome Eugène whom, in Corsica and Italy, he had known as a fair-haired, strapping, cheerful lad and later, in Madrid, as a promising schoolboy. He decided, and it is much to his credit that he did so, to take him back to Blois where, for a while, Eugène seemed to recover his reason, and even sent to Victor his good wishes for the marriage. He expatiated on the goodness of his father, and of "Madame our stepmother." But, alas, he had another crisis, this time so serious that he had to be brought back to Paris and sent for treatment to the clinic presided over by Doctor Esquirol. The fees there amounted to four hundred francs a month, and this sum the family could not possibly pay. Victor intervened, and arranged that his brother should be cared for by Doctor Royer-Collard, at Saint-Maurice, at government expense. The medical verdict was that the case was incurable. Poor Eugène became a sort of living corpse whom even his brothers visited but rarely. *Eugène Hugo to Victor, December 12th, 1823:* "I have been here for almost seven months, and in all that time I have seen you only once, and my brother Abel, twice . . . You must, surely, have some wish to see me, and easy ways of realizing that wish"[3]—words which carry the implication of tragic reproach.

This terrible fate was, for Victor, a permanent cause of sadness and of vague remorse. Was it not he who, by triumphing over his brother alike in the fields of poetry and love, had reduced him to despair? He had committed neither crime nor fault, but it is a fact that the theme of brothers at enmity became one of his obsessions. It returns again and again in all his writings—drama, poetry, prose fiction. Sometimes Cain is self-dubbed Satan; Claude Frollo in *Notre-Dame de Paris;* Job in *Les Burgraves*: sometimes he appears under his real name, as in *La Conscience* and *La Fin de Satan*. That his other brother was called Abel may have given strength to this *idée fixe*.[4] Yet Victor had done no harm; rather was it Eugène who, by reason of his jealousy, had played the part of Cain. But always, in his nightmares, Victor Hugo was haunted by the figure of a man buried alive, the dungeon of the Man in the Iron Mask, the tomb of Torquemada. He was for ever seeing in imagination some poor wretch squatting in darkness in a low-roofed cell. *"Oh! genius! Oh! madness! How terribly close to one another they are!"*

Of this truth he was fully conscious. Every dreamer—and Victor Hugo was fond of referring to himself as the Dreamer—carries within himself an imaginary world: with some, a dream, with others, madness. "This somnambulism is human; a certain tendency of the personality, momentarily, or partially, irrational is no rare occurrence . . . but such venturing on the borders of darkness is not without danger. Dreaming has its victims, and those are the persons we call mad . . . In those depths disasters happen. There are explosions due to fire-damp . . . never forget that. The dreamer must be stronger than his dream; otherwise there is danger. All dreaming is a struggle. The possible does not make contact with the real without some mysterious outburst of rage of which we know nothing. The brain can be gnawed away by a chimera. . . ."[5] In the case of Victor Hugo, the Dreamer was always stronger than the dream. He was saved because he sublimated his delusive agonies in poetry. He had solid roots in reality; but in Eugène he saw what he might have been.

There was no outward sign of these dark fires within. All those who knew him in these first months of his marriage remarked on his conquering look, on his bearing, which was that of a "cavalry officer who has just taken a post by storm." That was due to the feeling of strength which his many victories had given him: to the intoxication that came with the possession of the woman he had chosen; to the sense he now had that he was on terms again with his father, with a military greatness in which, strangely enough, he believed himself to share. His admirers, when they saw him for the first time, were struck by the seriousness of his face, and surprised, when he received them at the top of the stairs, by the rather solemn dignity of his youth garbed in ingenuous integrity and a black coat.

"Nothing could be more interesting than the spectacle of this young couple," wrote Saint-Valry to Rességuier. "Theirs is the love of the angels, and more poetic than anything presented by the pen of Thomas Moore . . ."[6] Adèle had dark, gleaming hair and fine Andalusian eyes. But what was most noticeable in her was a curious combination of calmness and passion, something that "wanted to break free but seemed to be held in check." On a first acquaintance, the general composition of her temperament lacked charm. It took time for it to make its effect, but, sooner or later, it did so. In a very short while she became pregnant. Victor was overjoyed at the prospect of so precocious a fatherhood. Young though he was, he felt a strong desire to live the life of a husband and a father. "An atmosphere at once idyllic and sublime, formed spontaneously about him." From now on he would have to provide for three persons, for Léopold Hugo the Second was born almost precisely nine months after the marriage, on July 16th, 1823.

Work, work, work . . . above the great chestnuts of the rue du Cherche-Midi. New odes saw the light; *Han d'Islande* was no sooner finished than sent to Persan, the marquis turned publisher, who promised, in accordance with his contract, to reprint the *Odes* and to issue an edition of one thousand copies of *Han d'Islande*. But the only royalties that Victor touched amounted to five hundred francs, for Persan went bankrupt and, being unable to pay Hugo, took to slandering him, as is usual in such cases. The young man's apprenticeship in the more sordid side of the trade of letters had begun. Once again he had to have recourse to the general. Fortunately, the Minister of the Interior granted a second pension of two thousand francs a year, and the good Monsieur Foucher took the young family in at Gentilly for the summer. This time, Victor was lodged not in the Gothic dovecote, but in his Adèle's own room.

Han d'Islande had appeared in four volumes, printed on coarse paper and bound in grey. "This remarkable work," said Persan in his advertisement, "is, we are given to understand, the first of its kind to be written by a young man who has already made a brilliant success in the field of poetry." The book, inspired by the "novels of horror" so popular in England (Maturin, Lewis, Mrs. Radcliffe), had been undertaken originally in the hope of making money and also to express in the persons of its two leading characters, Ethel and Ordener, the author's love for Adèle Foucher. It is important to realize that there is a deal of leg-pulling and parody in this accumulation of murders and monsters, of gibbets, executioners and tortures. It is an exercise in virtuosity, a deliberate exploiting of the rage for the "Horrid," and it shows "mastery in the handling of nightmare fantasy."[7] There was something of deliberate mystification in the author's claims to scholarship. He had read, in a haphazard fashion, a number of little-known books, ranging from Fabricius's *Voyage en Norvège* to *L'Héritier du Danemark,* by P-H. Mallet, and had poured into his own work, undigested, all the pseudo-erudite information thus obtained: "Odin's real name is Frigge, son of Fridulph."[8] This kind of pedantry commanded respect though, in fact, Hugo had made no serious study of the world he set out to describe. This he admits ironically in the Preface. The author would "merely point out that the picturesque aspects of his novel have been the object of his particular care: that Ks and Ys, Hs and Ws will frequently be found in its pages, though he has made use of these romantic characters only with extreme moderation . . . that there are several instances, too, of numerous diphthongs which he has varied with taste and elegance; that, finally, all the chapters are preceded by strange and mysterious quotations which add greatly to the interest."[9] One might be reading Sterne or Swift rather than Walter Scott or Monk Lewis.

Nevertheless, he succeeded in arousing feelings of horror and interest. He was well served by a bizarre imagination. His father and his brothers shared his taste for the macabre and fantastic. Like Byron, he was unsparing in his supply of skulls from which his heroes drank. He claimed that he had worked in his Gentilly tower in the company of a bat. Not all his friends took the book seriously. Lamartine wrote to him from Saint-Point, on June 8th, 1823: "We are re-reading your enchanting poetry, and your terrible *Han*. Let me say, in passing, that I find it a little bit too terrible. You must modify your palette. Imagination, like music, should woo and charm the mind. You strike too hard. This I tell you with your future in view, for you have a future, whereas I have none. . . ."[10]

Undoubtedly, *Han d'Islande* was, as Lamartine had said, "too terrible," and was easily parodied. But what vigour it has, and what imagination! In an article written for *La Quotidienne,* Charles Nodier, though expressing regret that the young author should have shouldered the task of searching out all life's infirmities, all its disgusting anomalies, admitted that it was given to very few men to begin their careers with errors of that kind, and praised the lively style, the picturesque qualities of the book, as well as the delicacy of many of the sentiments contained in it. Such an article was likely to go to the head of any young writer when signed with so famous a name.

Charles Nodier, critic and novelist, was twenty-two years older than Victor Hugo. He had had a more than usually strange life. The son of an unfrocked Oratorian turned revolutionary leader at Besançon, he had been entrusted by his sans-culotte father, for his education, to a ci-devant noble, Girod de Chantrans. The child spent all his time reading, and developed an enthusiastic fondness for Amyot, Ronsard and Montaigne. He could read Homer at sight. His master made running translations for him of Goethe and Shakespeare. At Dole, Nodier had married a woman with neither faults nor money. He became a librarian at Besançon, then secretary to a mad Englishman, Sir Herbert Croft, and, finally, librarian at Laibach in Illyria, a country which furnished him with material for a number of stories: "Jean Sbogar," "Smarra," "Trilby ou le Lutin d'Argail."

He was by nature charming and adventurous. There was in him something of Hoffmann *plus* a botanist, an entomologist, a painter, a traveller and an archaeologist with a passion for the Gothic. There was nothing he did not know. Appointed to the staff of *Le Journal des Débats* and, later, of *La Quotidienne,* he gave his support to young writers, first as a comrade, then as an elder brother, and became more and more of a personage. Hugo hurried round to the rue de Provence to express his thanks, but failed to find the critic. Nodier, with his "bony face, his tired but lively eyes, his odd but pensive gait," went to see the Hugos, who invited him with his wife and his daughter, Marie (twelve years old, but with the shrewdness of a grown woman). Thus began a happy friendship.

"Dear Alfred" (Vigny) praised *Han d'Islande*: "My friend, let me tell you—you are the hundredth person I have told, though I am at Orléans—that this book of yours is fine, is great, and will live. You have laid in France the foundations of a Walter Scott. Take another step forward; naturalize the genius you have expended on Norway, change the names and the scenery, and we shall soon be prouder than the Scots. The story drives ahead, it is thrilling. I almost stopped breathing until I had come to the last word. In the name of France, I thank you."[11] In this letter, Vigny spoke of his "miseries of the heart." He had confessed to Hugo that he was in love with Delphine Gay. The passion was reciprocated. Delphine's affection had been stirred by "the nicest of the lot," as her mother, Sophie Gay, put it. But the Comtesse Léon de Vigny wanted her son to make a rich marriage, and vetoed the connection. Vigny had sadly obeyed her, and Delphine had accepted the verdict with resignation.

Relations with General Hugo became more and more affectionate. Father and son corresponded on the subject of Eugène, and about the general's wish to be again employed as a soldier and given promotion. Victor took an active interest in the matter and went so far as to say that he might get Chateaubriand to offer his father an embassy. He also took upon himself to have the older man's *Mémoires* published by the bookseller Ladvocat. Interest went hand in hand with sentiment. General Hugo had two objects: to gain the support of this son of his who was so "well in" with the party in power, and to persuade his children to accept the new Madame Hugo who was, he said, "a second mother to you all." In the event, when Victor's first son was born after a difficult lying-in, and it was thought that the "poor little angel" would not survive, the general and his wife installed him and his nurse at Blois, in the large white house which they had just bought. The woman Thomas was never now called anything but "Léopold's grandmother." Adèle embroidered a bonnet for her mother-in-law. It was barely two years since the first Madame Hugo had been buried.

On October 9th, the little Léopold died. Vigny, who was on garrison-duty at Pau, wrote: "Your sorrows as a father have trodden hard on the heels of those you have had to bear as a son and a brother. You are crushed under the weight of griefs, all of them connected with the family, that natural community which is supposed to be the source of all good things. Dear God! my friend, how sad life is!"[12] Of Eugène, Vigny wrote in noble terms, referring to those "great scourges which physical nature lays upon us when, suddenly, it falls into ruin long before death comes, when the mind leaves it, and all that remains is a body, upright and smiling, like those horrible corpses found at Herculaneum . . ."[13] But Hugo, in spite of so many misfortunes (mother, brother, son), did not see life as sad. He was too much occupied with living and working and making love. Once more, Adèle became pregnant. "Victor," said Émile Deschamps, "turns out odes and children without pausing. He never gives himself a moment's rest."

10

"La Muse Française"

> That admirable period of the Restoration, when men combined a romantic spirit with a classic discipline.
>
> MAURICE BARRÈS

"FROM 1819 to 1824, under the double and direct influence of André Chénier and the *Méditations*,[1] against the echoing background of masterpieces by Byron and Scott, to the sound of Greece crying for aid, in the thick of the religious and monarchical illusions of the Restoration, a group of preludes took form, to which a vague and idealistic melancholy, a marked leaning towards the chivalry of the Middle Ages, and a grace—not seldom exquisite—in matter of detail, gave the tone."[2] It was the men of Toulouse—the gentle Soumet, the petulant, red-headed Guiraud with his Gascon accent, who sounded the first notes. Émile Deschamps proposed that a small society should be established, and a magazine founded. In this way there came into being *La Muse française*. The members consisted of distinguished—somewhat over-distinguished—young men, lovers of poetry and royalists by tradition, who were also "Christians for reasons of good manners and vague sentiment."[3]

Its programme was: in religion, the Christian mysteries according to Chateaubriand in place of the pagan licentiousness of the Empire; in politics, the monarchy *selon la Charte*; in love, the platonism of medieval chivalry. There was something "soft, aromatic, caressing and magical" about the whole movement. Initiation was a ceremony of mutual praise. An aspirant for membership was recognized as a poet, and duly welcomed, in virtue of some sort of mysterious sign . . . The golden age of chivalry, the lovely medievalism of chatelaines, pages and fair ladies, the Christianity of chapels and hermits, poor orphans and humble beggars were all the rage and between them supplied most of the subject-matter—to say nothing of innumerable cases of individual melancholy. The initiates called each other by their first names: Alfred, Émile, Gaspard, Victor. Several women belonged to this sentimental free-masonry. The lovely Delphine Gay was Delphine to all and sundry.

85

But when Jules de Rességuier, the out-and-out troubadour of all this company of troubadours, asked Victor, in his strong local guttural, for permission to address his wife as Adèle, the "serious young poet" refused. Familiarity was not his strong suit.

It had been Émile Deschamps's proposal that each member should contribute a thousand francs towards the founding of the *Muse*. This was too great a sum for the Hugo household. Lamartine, who was already taking a high line and preferred to live the life of a country gentleman far from the noise and turmoil of the literary world, refused to join the group, but offered to pay Hugo's subscription. "I should like you to be a founder-member, though, personally, I do not wish to lend my name or my gifts to the undertaking. I shall, however, be most happy to supply the thousand francs agreed upon. That will be a private transaction between the two of us."[4] Victor Hugo, offended by this pretence of a loan, refused membership on these terms, but continued to play a preponderant part in the movement, as much by reason of his articles and poems as by his natural authority.

The real centre of the *cénacle de la Muse française,* was the good Nodier, and the meeting-place was the *salon* which he maintained, at first in the rue de Provence, and, after January 1st, 1824, in the Library of the Arsenal, the post of Director there having been presented to him as a New Year's gift by a minister friend, with the backing of the Comte d'Artois. Airy nonchalance is a supreme form of astuteness, and not seldom the highest rewards go to the childlike and irresponsible. The great enjoy protecting the scatterbrains, for the simple reason that they seem to stand in need of protection. Nodier suddenly found himself residing in a palace, at the heart of a populous quarter. From his window he could see the sun setting behind Notre-Dame. The curator of a library is a sort of lay-canon. Delighting in domestic peace and quiet routine, Nodier thoroughly enjoyed this comfortable existence which had come to him late in life. His wife, a simple-minded creature, soon gave a thoroughly middle-class look to what had been a royal pavilion, and her bright face, "dazzling as a bouquet of flowers," brought a note of gaiety to this somewhat severe setting. Their daughter, Marie, grew in beauty, and all the poets were her friends.

On Sundays, the *salon de l'Arsenal* was filled with festal lights. Everybody came and went at will. Among the constant visitors were Séverin Taylor, born in Brussels of English parents, a French officer, a friend of Vigny and much in favour with the party in power; Sophie and Delphine Gay, the latter as radiant as the sun in his splendour, and generally known as "la Muse française"; Soumet who had just had two resounding successes in the theatre with "the finest tragedies of the day," according to Hugo, and was more than ever "our Alexander the Great"; Guiraud, who had attained celebrity with his *Petit Savoyard*;

Alfred de Vigny and Gaspard de Pons in their uniforms of royal blue; and, of course, the Deschamps brothers, as well as Adolphe de Saint-Valry, the co-editor of *La Muse française*.

From eight till ten, conversation was the rule. Nodier would open the proceedings, standing in front of the fireplace, with memories of his childhood, or with some fantastic tale. On these occasions, emerging from his habitual indolence, he would wax eloquent. Then a literary discussion would begin. "André Chénier went too far," said Victor Hugo, "because of his alternation of short and overrunning lines, he produced verse that was no longer musical, and poetry is primarily a form of singing." Nodier protested: "Chénier was romantic in his own way, and a very good way it was . . . art knows nothing of fixed rules." Émile Deschamps, with a smile parting his finely chiselled lips to reveal his beautiful teeth, intervened: "You will come back to him, my dear Victor."[5] On the stroke of ten, Marie Nodier would go to the piano, and all general conversation stopped. The chairs were pushed against the walls and the company danced. Nodier, a passionate gambler, took his seat at the écarté table. Vigny, pale and delicate-looking, waltzed with Delphine Gay. The serious-minded, among whom was the young Hugo, withdrew into a corner and continued their discussion in low voices. Madame Victor Hugo, her Spanish eyes showing a sudden gleam, danced and, from time to time, her husband looked uneasily at her.

Though all the men present were colleagues, they were, all the same, good friends. To the reign of wit, said Émile Deschamps, had succeeded that of a warm heart. They all praised one another generously. The warmest approval went to "Alexander the Great":

> La France attend tes vers; et ton siècle enchanté
> Les lègue avec orgeuil a la postérité . . .[6]

But each had his turn, and Rességuier burned incense before Hugo:

> La gloire est à Bouvines ainsi qu'à Marengo:
> Immortalisez-vous par une ode superbe.
> N'importe après cela, qu'on se nomme Malherbe,
> Jean-Baptiste ou Victor Hugo.[7]

This mutual-admiration society irritated beyond bearing the bitter Henri de Latouche, who denounced its excesses in the *Mercure*: "An agreement seems to have been reached between Messieurs Alexandre S . . ., Alexandre G . . ., Gaspard de P . . ., Saint-V . . ., Alfred de V . . ., Émile D . . ., Victor H . . ., and several more, to quote one another, turn and turn about, as examples of excellence. And why, indeed, should not these petty princes of poetry have entered into an alliance?" The petty princes, by the hand of Hugo, delivered a vigorous reply:

"The writer insults the enthusiasm with which a poet's song inspires
another poet, and seems to wish that those who have talent should be
judged only by those who have none . . . It would appear that we have
become accustomed only to literary jealousies; that our envious generation merely mocks at that brotherhood of poetry which, when it is
composed of rivals, is so noble and so sweet."[8]

Most of the contributors to *La Muse française* hoped that, while injecting new blood into poetry, they might be spared the necessity of
taking sides in the quarrel between the romantics and the classicists.
In lines of unbelievable flatness, Jules de Rességuier had given expression to this prudent attitude of eclecticism:

> Des deux écoles, donc, quelle est la différence?
> Ce sont d'aimables sœurs, leur âge n'y fait rien.
> L'une est le souvenir et l'autre l'espérance.
> Leur intérêt commun est de s'entendre bien.[9]

What was it all about? What reality lay behind those words, *romantic*
and *classic*? Madame de Staël had professed to see a clear line of
demarcation: on the one side, "writing which imitates that of the
ancients, and, on the other, that which springs from the outlook of the
Middle Ages; two forms of writing, in short; one having its origins in
paganism, the other stimulated by, and developing out of, the religious
spirit."[10] If those two definitions are correct, then the gentlemen of
La Muse were closer to the romantics. They were Christians and Troubadours, ousting the old Nymphs and Furies in favour of the Sprites
and Vampires of the North. They read Schiller (those few, that is, who
knew enough German to enable them to make his acquaintance). The
liberal opponents of *La Muse française* reproached it for being more
German and more English than French; for offering a dose of mystery
to a nation which had seen mystery only as a subject for joking; for
having given nebulous poetry to a people whose special genius was for
the positive; for having confronted the philosophic reader with works
in which superstitious beliefs were treated seriously. The contrast resolved itself into a battle between the attitude of the eighteenth century
and that of the nineteenth. At the Académie Française which, by reason
of the age of its members, is often out of step with the times and, at that
particular moment of history, was a stronghold of the classical and
philosophical, Auger, the permanent secretary, thundered against the
cénacle de l'Arsenal, which he called a collection of literary schismatics:
"the sect is new, and at present contains only a small number of declared adherents. But they are young; they are fervent. With them,
enthusiasm and activity supply the lack of strength and numbers . . ."[11]
He called Madame de Staël to order for the manner in which she had
set the classic and the romantic at odds, had "introduced a breach into

the literatures of all lands, and has cut in two our own in a manner of which, hitherto, it has been in blissful ignorance . . ."[12] He blamed the romantics for seeking to destroy the rules on which the whole of French drama and poetry was based, for holding gaiety in abhorrence, and finding poetry only in suffering. All this, said Auger, was merely literary posturing which was powerless to affect the glowing health of the national tradition. In short, romanticism had no genuine life of its own; it was a phantom which vanished away as soon as the hand was laid upon it.

The strange thing is that this violent enemy of the romantic was, not long afterwards, to kill himself like any simple-minded Werther, but nobody could foresee his suicide, and the gentlemen of *La Muse* were not a little embarrassed by the attack. "Alexander the Great" had hopes of one day being himself an academician, and the other Alexandre—Guiraud—was also thinking seriously about the body housed on the Quai Conti. Besides, the members of the *cénacle* did not think of themselves as being romantics, and less and less understood what the word meant. "Romanticism has been so often defined," said Émile Deschamps, "that the whole issue has become quite confused enough as it is, without my making darkness darker still with any new attempt at illumination."[13] What all these young people had in common was an uneasy feeling about the mysteries which had been neglected and held in contempt by the philosophers of the eighteenth century, an instinct to revolt against the frigid poetry of the Empire, and a strong impulsion towards the throne and the altar. Was that romanticism? The truth of the matter was that "it is impossible to think seriously if one uses words like *classic* and *romantic*. Nobody can get drunk, or quench his thirst, on labels. . . ."[14]

"If the Academy is determined to separate literature into two camps," wrote Émile Deschamps in *La Muse française,* "then we, for our part, would like to point out that among those writers of many nations who, for the last twenty years, have been regarded as *romantics* can be numbered: Monsieur de Chateaubriand, Lord Byron, Madame de Staël, Schiller, Monti, Monsieur de Maistre, Goethe, Thomas Moore, Walter Scott, the Abbé de Lamennais, etc. etc. It is not for us, after mentioning such distinguished names, to speak of younger men. In the opposite camp, over the same period, will be found Messieurs ———. I leave the names blank. Let the *classicists* fill them in for themselves. In the long run, Europe—or a child—will decide between us. . . ."[15]

This was all very fine, but "Alexander the Great" still kept his eyes firmly fixed on the Palais Mazarin, and went in fear of the permanent secretary. "We scarcely dare breathe under the oppression of this literary Terror,"[16] sighed Émile Deschamps. Guiraud and Rességuier, animated by a sense of loyalty as men of Toulouse, were prepared to cover Soumet's retreat. The defection of this splinter-group would not have been fatal to *La Muse,* had the rest of the team been in complete agreement. That, however, was not the case. An article on Lamartine's *Nouvelles Méditations,* not so much hostile as reticent, had been designed to punish this literary "elder" for having refused to play a part in *La Muse.* He had struck back in a sharply worded letter to Hugo: "Everyone in this world does his best with such small gifts as have been given him. Birds sing and serpents hiss. They are not to be blamed on that account . . ." This was a disagreeable lesson to receive. Vigny, who was a passionate admirer of Lamartine, wrote to Hugo: "What a disgusting business literature is! That is the first thing I want to say, and my reason for saying it is that I am constantly hearing all around me the things that are being said about Monsieur de Lamartine. . . ."

On July 20th, Soumet was elected to the Académie Française. Did this mean that romanticism, in his person, had made its entry into that august assembly, or was it that Soumet had bowed himself out of the romantic camp?

Blois, Rheims, Chamonix

All beautiful works are the daughters of their
form, which is born before they are.

PAUL VALÉRY

THE family's financial position was improving. Ladvocat paid two
thousand francs for a two-year licence to publish *Nouvelles Odes*.
The general was contributing a small monthly allowance, and Victor,
who was now in possession of two royal pensions, told his father that he
must "primarily consult his own convenience before making the pay-
ments." In 1824, the young Hugos were able to move into a small
apartment at 90 rue de Vaugirard, over a carpenter's shop. The rent was
625 francs a year. Léopoldine Hugo was born there on August 28th.
"Our Didine is charming, and resembles both her mother and her
grandfather. . . ."[1]

The general's "countess" was asked to stand godmother, a politic
stroke.

The rue de Vaugirard became, for many young writers, a rallying-
point. In their eyes, the Hugo family was the model of what a family
should be. Madame Victor diffused the radiance of her beauty over the
quiet interior which was entirely dedicated to work. The *Odes* seemed
to the *cénacle* to be the very echo, sweet and solemn, of the couple's
"chaste and solitary" existence. *Hugo to Vigny:* "I stay at home, where
I am happy. I dandle my daughter, and have as a companion the angel
who is my wife . . ."[2] He wanted to "hold first place"[3] as husband and
father, as well as poet. His friends remained faithful. Alfred, now in
garrison at Oloron, had at first been indignant at the scuttling of the
Muse: "I don't begin to understand the letters I am getting, dear friend,
but here, in my mountain fastness, I cannot help feeling that we are
being very foolish. Is the *Muse* really to stop publication just when it
has become a power? . . . you must save it at no matter what cost . . . to
abandon it now is nothing less than cowardice . . ."[4] He expressed
indignation at the idea of Soumet hankering after "a dilapidated arm-
chair." But Oloron was far away and, when the officer-poet wrote this
letter, the *Muse* was already dead and Soumet among the immortals.

This incident in no way damaged the Hugo-Vigny friendship. "Let us leave to others these petty defections and childish terrors. Continue to love me, and send me a letter. That always does me good.—ALFRED."[5]

Lamartine went occasionally to dine in the rue de Vaugirard, a man now getting on in age, rather distant in manner, remote and noble. He was a candidate for election to the Académie, and the business was telling on his nerves. *Lamartine to Hugo, November 16th, 1824:* "Certainly, my dear Hugo, I will dine with you on Wednesday. But please do not ask Monsieur Soumet. You can have no conception of the odious manner in which these ex-officio electors treat us. I am indignant and exasperated. I know perfectly well that Monsieur Soumet is not a willing accessory to all this, but he and others are being *used*. The great thing is to be self-sufficient. If ever, once this affair is over and done with, you should see me standing again for the Académie, then you can rest assured that I have lost both heart and head . . ."[6] Lamartine adored the young family: *December 23rd, 1824:* "You have never done a foolish thing in your life; my own, up to the age of twenty-seven, was all faults and profligacy . . . Your heart belongs to the Golden Age, your wife to the Earthly Paradise. With what you have got, a man may still live in this Age of Iron . . ."[7] In the summer, when Lamartine was living at Saint-Point, the two poets exchanged letters. To Hugo, who had written in defence of grammar, Lamartine replied: "Grammar is a weight that crushes poetry. Grammar was never made for men like us . . ."[8] The difference between the two men was that Hugo knew his grammar. But they remained good friends, and Lamartine invited Hugo to Saint-Point—in verse.

Eugène's illness had kept the general in Paris and, as a result, had brought about between Victor and his father a degree of intimacy which was based on more than mere family affection. Once, when the father had been triumphant and severe, he had aroused antagonism; but now, as a parent in retirement, leaning upon a celebrated son, he inspired tolerance, filial piety and also a sense of pride in his past exploits, about which Abel and Victor loved to hear him talk.

As a consequence of his knowing his father better, and loving him more, Victor became almost reconciled to the Emperor. Napoleon, during his life-time, had been the "tyrant" whom his mother hated. After the tragedy of Saint Helena he had become a persecuted hero and Hugo in his heart of hearts felt that, for a French poet, it was a finer thing to do honour to the "men of Friedland and of Rivoli" than to turn out odes on commission to celebrate the ephemeral doings of the Royal Family.

Now that Chateaubriand was a minister, Victor had hopes of getting his father raised to the "summit of all military dignities." But Chateaubriand in power was becoming difficult of access. *Victor to General*

Hugo, June 27th, 1824: "Should my illustrious friend return to the Foreign Office, our chances will increase threefold. My relations with him have grown closer since his disgrace. While he was in favour, the bond grew slacker . . ."[9] *July 29th, 1824:* "The condition of our poor, dear Eugène still remains the same. This stagnation drives one to despair . . ."[10] With the ex-Comtesse de Salcano things were going better and better. "Please convey my thanks to your excellent wife for her kind thought on my birthday. I cannot tell you how deeply touched I was, as was Adèle, too. Thank her also for promising to send us some butter; it will come in very useful this winter. . . ."

The general, delighted by his son's new Bonapartist sympathies, was insistent that the young family should go and stay with him at Blois. So far this had been impossible because of Adèle's two difficult pregnancies, but at last, in April 1825, the visit took place. Victor Hugo who, in spite of the death of Louis XVIII, was still in favour at Court, had managed, through the good offices of the Postmaster General, to reserve the *coupé* in the mail coach, and this he occupied with his wife and small daughter. The general met them, florid and smiling, delighted to be able to show them his fine house, "white and square-built . . . with walls of stone and all with slate-work roofed," and still more so when, after his arrival, his son received a letter from the Vicomte de Rochefoucauld, "Supervisor of the Arts in so far as they concern the King's household," informing him that Charles X, "with charming graciousness," had just made Messieurs Hugo and Lamartine Chevaliers of the Légion d'Honneur. As a matter of fact, they had both applied for this decoration. His Majesty expressed himself courteously at having been distressed at an oversight which, very naturally, had caused a feeling of surprise in the world of letters. He invited the young poet to be present at his Coronation. One can well imagine what happiness it was to the father to see his son decorated with an order which was so dear to his heart, and at the age of twenty-three.

For Victor, who revelled in emotions on the grand scale, and had long grown to think of himself as an orphan, it was a very special joy to be living under the paternal roof. In the old days he had defied the general, and it now brought him peace of mind to find himself again a child in his presence, but this time a respected child, and to visit in his father's company the lovely countryside. He considered Blois to be "the most delicious town one could see anywhere . . . The whole place is set, for the delight of the eye, on the two banks of this beautiful Loire. On one side there is an amphitheatre of gardens and ruins, on the other, a plain flooded with verdure. At every step some memory is evoked. . . ."[11] He loved the châteaux, so rich in history and legend.

Victor Hugo to Adolphe de Saint-Valry, May 7th, 1825: I have visited

Chambord. You cannot imagine how strangely beautiful it is. Every variation of magic, poetry, and even extravagant fancy is represented in the whimsical perfection of this palace of knights and fairies. I scratched my name on the summit of the highest turret, and took from it a fragment of stone and moss, as well as a piece of the frame of the window on which François I wrote these two lines:

> Souvent femme varie,
> Bien fol est qui s'y fie!

These two relics are very precious to me. . . .[12]

He felt, too, a love for la Militière, a property which the general had bought in Sologne, a few miles from Blois.

Victor Hugo to Paul Foucher, May 10th, 1825: I am just now sitting in a green arbour at la Militière. The ivy rioting over the walls is casting a silhouetted pattern of shadows on my paper. I enclose a rough sketch of it, since you have expressed a wish that my letter should contain a pictured something. Don't laugh at the crude jottings which I have scribbled on the back of this sheet. Use your imagination. Think what it must all look like in terms of sunlight and shadow. That will give you some idea of the charming effect produced. This is the kind of thing that lunatic poets do. . . .[13]

This quotation is important as showing the mood of happy freedom in which Hugo began to draw, and sometimes to write. Limpid ponds under the oaks, a group of ancient buildings, will-o'-the-wisps flickering in the crutched arms of trees, made la Militière for him "a very special haunt of mystery."

His stay there seemed too short. Which of us does not yearn for the honours that have been refused us, and grumble at those that are accorded? When the moment of his departure for Rheims to attend the Coronation approached, the young poet-laureate became depressed at the thought of leaving Blois, his father and, for the first time since their marriage, his adored Adèle; but the die was cast. Victor had promised to make the journey from Paris to Rheims with Nodier, and had begged his parents-in-law to provide him with the necessary court dress—knee-breeches, silk stockings, buckled shoes and sword. He set off on May 19th, rather pleased than otherwise to see Adèle in tears. The few days he would have to spend away from her seemed to him an eternity. "What a source of sadness all these honours are! There are many who envy me this trip, not realizing how melancholy a piece of good fortune makes me which rouses jealousy in others . . ."[14] But he was twenty-three years old, he loved renown, and took no little pride in displaying the red ribbon in his buttonhole to his fellow-travellers in the diligence. "Tell father that I have more than once been asked whether *I am rejoining my regiment*, etc., and all because of the ribbon!"—a sentence which reveals the presence in him of a secret love of military glory. He asked Adèle to open any letters that might arrive for him, and to tell him briefly what they contained. How artless the trust of married couples who have nothing to hide!

At the rue de Vaugirard he slept, as was natural, in the bridal chamber, and this brought him a harsh reminder of his state of grass-widowerhood. Paris without Adèle was like a foreign city: "it is you who are my native land..."[15] He lunched with his parents-in-law, and Monsieur Foucher regaled him with lobster sauce. He paid a visit to his tailor who showed him his new dress-coat, all very smart and very ugly. He went to see Soumet, the "Immortal," who, good and kind as ever, offered him the loan of his knee-breeches for the occasion. Then, since both he and Nodier were short of money, he had an interview with Ladvocat who, being already eager to obtain the "Ode sur le Sacre de Charles X" (to be), advanced him the necessary funds. For dinner he went to Julie Duvidal de Montferrier, who combined the role of artist with that of a pretty woman. There had been a time when Victor detested her, but now she was a friend of the family, and much admired by the young husband. "We drank your health, my beloved Adèle . . . I kissed your letter a thousand times. How beautiful it is! So eloquent of grief and tenderness."[16]

The journey to Rheims began well. Charles Nodier and Victor Hugo had combined with two other friends to hire a sort of large-sized cab at a cost of one hundred francs a day, since it would have been impossible to get places in the diligence. The main road, raked and sanded until its surface resembled that of an avenue in a private park, was crowded with traffic and all the inns were full. At each stopping-place Hugo hurried off to see the monuments, while Nodier visited the second-hand bookshops. At Rheims they had to sleep four in a room, but Nodier turned out to be a charming companion, full of erudite knowledge, who talked extremely well about Gothic cathedrals. Hugo loved the art that had gone to their making: "true child of nature, and infinite as she is, on a scale both great and small; at once microscopic and immense. . . ."[17] Chateaubriand had awakened his admiration. Nodier, an excellent antiquarian, taught him how to people a great fane with the ghosts of those who had sanctified it, and made it live again with his tales of all that it had witnessed in the past. "This land of Champagne swarms with stories . . . Rheims is the very home of fancy . . ."[18] It was Nodier who told the stories and awakened the fancies. The streets of Rheims were crowded with people waiting to see Charles X drive by. Hugo said to Nodier: "Let us rather go and see His Majesty the Cathedral." Charles laughed: "You've got the demon Ogive in your blood." "And you," replied Victor, "the devil Elzevir."[19]

Charles and Victor, dressed in the French fashion, with swords at their sides, attended the Coronation ceremony in a concourse of fat men and women loaded with jewels. "The church was aglow with the light of May. The archbishop was a mass of gold, and the altar of sunbursts. . . ."[20] In the course of the proceedings, a Deputy from the Doubs, named Émonin, made a present to Nodier of a book he was carrying. "I've just bought it for six sous," he said. It was an odd volume of Shakespeare, in English. That evening Nodier gave a running translation of *King John*. This, for Hugo, was a revelation. "I found it tremendous," he said. In 1823 Lamennais had advised him to undergo a "Shakespeare cure," but Hugo had not wanted to read the dramatist in Letourneur's detestable translation. Victor, in his turn, treated Nodier to a running version, this time of the *Romancero* which they had picked up in a second-hand bookshop in the course of their drive from Paris. It was in Spanish. The night at Rheims when, in a hotel bedroom, Victor Hugo discovered Shakespeare was a coronation of a different kind—that of a sovereign poet.

Chateaubriand was at Rheims. Hugo went to pay his respects, and found him in a furious temper. "I," he said, "should have interpreted the Coronation ceremony very differently: the church undraped and bare; the King on horseback; two books displayed open—the Charter and the Gospels—religion linked with liberty . . ."[21] The Vicomte de Chateaubriand's feeling for stage-management was greater than his respect for ritual. The "sublime child" conducted the great man to his carriage, and found no one else there. Fallen ministers are seldom courted. Victor himself was in a hurry to get back to Blois. Adèle's letters were causing him uneasiness. She complained of the coldness with which, since Victor's departure, she was being treated by the general's "countess." "I have learned certain matters with sorrow. They prove to me that Madame Hugo puts up with us much against her will, and that she regards our presence here as a grievance . . . You really must write saying that unexpected business makes it essential that you should return at once to Paris . . ."[22] She begged him to fetch her as soon as possible: "We could leave two days after you got here; I would reserve our places in the diligence. We could always find some excuse to explain our departure . . ." Now Victor had hoped to spend six weeks with his father. The next letter was even more urgent. The situation had become intolerable. Victor, much upset, counselled a cool head. "Don't worry. We will make everything come right. Your Victor, your husband, your protector, is on his way back, and what more can you want?"[23] But she could not wait, and left with Didine and the nurse for Paris where her mother met her.

Lamartine had invited Hugo and Nodier to pay him a visit at Saint-Point. "Let us go," said Nodier, "and take our wives with us. The trip will cost us nothing." "How d'you make that out?" "We'll push on as

far as the Alps, write up our journey, and sell it to a publisher." All
went well. The publisher, Urbain Canel, commissioned, for the use of
tourists, *Un Voyage poétique et pittoresque au Mont Blanc et à la vallée
de Chamonix.* Nodier was to supply the text, for which he would
receive two thousand two hundred and fifty francs; Hugo was to get
the same amount for "four shocking bad odes"—as he wrote to his
father—"which is pretty good pay."[24]

Even Didine was included in the party. Hugo, dressed in grey duck
and running up and down the roadside banks, was like a schoolboy on
holiday. Nodier was a delightful conversationalist. His sleepy, drawling
voice was in happy contrast to the liveliness of his wit—and such a
conversation is the very recipe for humour. Good Madame Nodier, too,
played an amusing role, and added to the laughter by denying with
her good, solid French common sense that there was any truth in her
husband's outrageous stories. The Saint-Point interlude was not the
pleasantest part of the trip. "Monsieur Alphonse's" house was very
different from what they had been led to suppose from his poems, and
they were disappointed. There were no *embattled towers,* no *clumps
of tangled ivy,* and the *colour of old time* turned out to be a yellowish
distemper. "Ruins are all very fine when it comes to description, but
not suited to living in," said Lamartine with prosaic good sense. His
wife, who was English,[25] always dressed for dinner, a habit which the
travellers found extremely embarrassing. "She was all low-neck and
ribbons," wrote Adèle Hugo. "Our poor high-necked silk dresses
seemed very much out of place in all that splendour . . ."[26] Hugo and
Lamartine held one another in high esteem, but were not really twin
souls.

The Alps, and especially Mont Blanc, rising "royally with its crown
of ice and its mantle of snow," moved Hugo to enthusiasm. In those
vast masses, alternately dazzling and sombre, green and white, he found
a spectacle cut to his measure. To the antitheses within himself (mother-
father, Christianity-Voltaire, beauty-cruelty in the world at large, joys-
nightmares, angel-faun) he needed one that should be complementary
and objective. He loved the contrast afforded by the gleam of sun on
snow, and the blackness of a precipice. "At this moment, a gap was torn
in the clouds over our heads, and through it we saw, not sky, but a
chalet, a green meadow, and a few barely perceptible goats browsing
above the level of the clouds. I have never had so strange an experience.
At our feet there flowed what could be described as one of the rivers of
Hell; above our heads there stood one of the islands of Paradise . . ."[27]
His instinctive love of mythology transformed mountains, rocks and
torrents into Monsters, Spirits and Demons: "Let me confess to an
infirmity of mind; there would have been something lacking for me in
the horrid beauty of this savage scene had not some folk-tradition set

on it the print of the marvellous. I have lingered over these details with a sense of pleasure, because I have a love of superstitions. They are the daughters of religion, and the mothers of poetry. . . ."[28]

In the evenings, at the inn, they would laugh together over the dangers they had run. Hugo never forgot "that lovely trip to Switzerland . . . one of the brightest memories of my life."

12

Mastery

Hugo's extraordinary craftsmanship put no
brake upon his genius.

JULES RENARD

BETWEEN 1826 and 1829 Hugo worked hard, learned much, discovered a great deal. It would be a mistake, in measuring the
gigantic strides he was making at that time in his art, to pay too much
attention to the dates at which his works were published: *Odes et
Ballades* (end of 1826); *Cromwell* (1827); *Les Orientales* (1829). He
would sometimes hold back a manuscript for two or three years. *Les
Orientales* contains poems written in 1826. The lovely "Madman's
Song" from *Cromwell* had already appeared as an epigraph in *Odes et
Ballades*. It is more worth while to indicate the general lines along
which his mind was moving.

The period with which we are here dealing was one in which poetry
had become for him a pleasing pastime, and a form in which he knew
himself to be a master. The official *Odes* had given him all they had
to give. He was now assured of a public. Ladvocat had just paid him
four thousand francs for a volume of *Poésies diverses*. His journeys,
Nodier's conversations, the study of the poets of the sixteenth century,
had done much to inspire him, as had his taste for Scottish and German ballads, whence had come "La Fiancée du Timbalier," "Les Deux
Archers," etc. But a great deal was due to sheer virtuosity. He composed many fantasies, or, as he called them, *guitares*. The political or
religious content of what he wrote counted for little with him. He had
already moved far from the theory he had maintained in 1824, that all
poetry must be monarchist or Christian. All that, he now felt, was a
mere mirage.

Coming after the processional *Odes*, this evolution is surprising.
When *Odes et Ballades* appeared in 1826, Lamartine wrote to him
from Florence: "There is one piece of severe criticism which I must,
in all friendliness, repeat: never try to be original! Think this over,
and then decide whether I am right or wrong. Originality is little
more than a form of wit, and not at all what you ought to be bothering

about . . ."[1] *Le Globe,* an intelligent and serious-minded journal, had so far not been very favourable to Victor Hugo. It was a liberal paper concerned with international culture, and had been annoyed, sometimes exasperated, by the brand of fashionable catholicism affected by *La Muse française.* Its editor, however, Paul-François Dubois, a dictatorial and somewhat irascible journalist, had been introduced to the "angel Victor," as Sophie Gay called him, and admitted that he had been charmed by the young couple. "In the rue de Vaugirard, over a carpenter's shop, I saw before me, in a tiny drawing-room, a young poet and a young mother carrying in her arms a child of only a few months, and teaching him how to join his hands in prayer before a number of engravings of Raphael's Madonnas and infant Christs. Though the scene had something slightly self-conscious about it, it was so naïve and sincere that I was touched and enchanted . . ."[2]

Hugo, for his part, assured Dubois that "in the short time we have been together, you have awakened in me a feeling of genuine friendship."

When *Odes et Ballades* was published, Dubois, who retained affectionate feelings for the Holy Family of the rue de Vaugirard, sent the volume for review to one of his former pupils at the Collège Bourbon, Charles-Augustin Sainte-Beuve, whom he had appointed as one of the critics of *Le Globe,* with the following words: "It is by that young barbarian Victor Hugo, who has a good deal of talent. I know him personally, and we sometimes meet." Sainte-Beuve wrote about the book at length. He praised it, but wisely warned the author against certain excesses of which he was guilty. "In poetry, as in other things, nothing is so dangerous as the forceful. If one lets it have its head it runs away with one. Because of it, what was no more than original and new comes perilously near to being eccentric. A brilliant contrast deteriorates into a mannered antithesis. The author aims at grace and simplicity, only to fall into the mincing and the artless; when he attempts the gigantic, he fails to avoid the puerile . . ."[3]

The critic was even younger—by at least two years—than the poet, but he was the possessor of a vast culture and a feeling for fine shades, and had at his disposition one of the most penetrating intelligences of the day. An exquisite taste and a sure judgment were, with him, natural gifts. A few remaining dregs of Christian faith warred in him against a realistic and sceptical outlook which was the result of his scientific studies. Both lyrical and positivist, he had only one dream of happiness—love—and suffered from his inability to inspire it. A writer's inner life was of more interest to him than word-painting. He expressed admiration of Hugo's style, "which is all fire, glittering images, and leaping harmonies"; but what he found most worthy of praise in *Odes et Ballades* were the not very frequent poems which the author, surmounting mere virtuosity, had written for the woman he loved, telling of what lay nearest to his heart. "If one imagines, as intensely as one can, all that love contains of purity and chastity within the bonds of marriage, all that God can find most sacred in the union of two souls; if, in short, one sets oneself dreaming of ecstatic pleasure swept heavenwards upon the wings of prayer, it will be as nothing to what Monsieur Hugo has realized and perfected in such delicious pieces as 'Encore à toi' and 'Son Nom'; merely to quote them comes very near to tarnishing the delicate surface of their modesty . . ."[4] They were, indeed, extremely intimate and most tender:

> Je t'aime comme un être au dessus de ma vie,
> Comme un antique aïeul au prévoyants discours,
> Comme une sœur craintive, à mes maux asservie,
> Comme un dernier enfant qu'on a dans ses vieux jours.
> Hélas! je t'aime tant qu'à ton nom seul je pleure. . . .[5]

It is not difficult to imagine the joy felt by the young couple when, on January 2nd, 1827, they read such praise of lines most precious to them, in the pages of a journal notorious for its rough handling of authors. The critic's reservations mattered little. The tone of his article was friendly, not to say respectful. Goethe, who read it, had no doubts. On January 4th, he said to Eckermann: "Victor Hugo is a man of genuine talent, and one who has been influenced by German literature. His poetic youthfulness has, unfortunately, been denigrated by the pedantic, fault-finding classicists; but now here's someone who has championed him in *Le Globe*. He has come through . . ."[6] This was, indeed, genius recognizing genius.

The *Globe* article was signed S. B. Victor wrote to Dubois asking for the critic's address. Dubois replied: "He lives close to you, at No. 94 rue de Vaugirard." Hugo lost no time in ringing at his neighbour's door. Sainte-Beuve was out, but next day paid a visit to the poet and his wife. They saw a shy, frail, badly built young man, with a slight stammer and a long nose. He had red hair and a globular head which was too big for his body; but it would have been a mistake to call him ugly. There was nothing positively displeasing about his face; on the contrary it was rather pleasant than otherwise. The mind within irradiated it and when Sainte-Beuve felt at his ease his conversation was inimitable. He had a way of leaving his sentences unfinished: "it was as though he flung them from him in disgust before bringing them to an end"; but his ideas were deep and closely reasoned.

On this occasion, however, it was chiefly Hugo who did the talking. Sainte-Beuve listened, "enthralled by the flash of genius," and stole sidelong glances at Madame Hugo who was present at the interview, looking very beautiful.

En sarrau du matin, éclatante sans art,
M'embarrassant d'abord de son fixe regard.
Et moi qui, d'elle à lui, détournais ma paupière,
Moi, pudique et troublé, le front dans la lumière,
J'étais tout au poète et son vaste discours,
A peine commencé, se déroulant toujours.

Debout, la jeune épouse écoutait, enchaînée;
Et je me demandais quel merveilleux accord
Liait ces flots grondants à ce palmier du bord.
Puis elle se lassa bientôt d'être attentive;
Sa pensée oublieuse échappa sur la rive;
Ses mains, en apparence, au ménage avaient soin,
Mais quelque char ailé promenait l'âme au loin
Et je la saluait, trois fois, à ma sortie . . .
Elle n'entendait rien s'il ne l'eût avertie. . . .[7]

Sainte-Beuve came again. All that Hugo said about rhyme, colour, fancy, rhythm and his own poetic theory opened new vistas to the young critic's dazzled eyes. He was just then working on a survey of sixteenth-century poetry, and what he heard gave him illuminating glimpses into such matters as the style and technique of verse. When he made his second visit, he left with Hugo some of the poetry which he had been writing in secret. Compared with Victor's fireworks it seemed almost drab. It was not, however, without merit. He had a natural gift, and could express with grace the more intimate impressions which things had made upon him. Hugo was able to praise the best of his work: "Come soon that I may thank you for the beautiful poems which you have confided to me . . ."[8] "From that moment," said Sainte-Beuve, "I was won over to the romantic movement of which he was the leader. He had entered the house as a critic, he left it as a disciple. Hugo had read everything and remembered all he had read . . . There was something of ostentation in the way in which he displayed his erudition . . ."[9] But he knew so well how to distribute his praise that a whole group accepted him as its patron. "Literature," he wrote in *Le Globe,* stands on the brink of an 18th Brumaire; but God knows where its Bonaparte will be found . . ." God did know.

Victor Hugo had been working for the past year on a drama, *Cromwell.* He had always had a liking for the theatre and, from childhood on, had written plays. He had read everything he could lay hands on which had to do with the life of Oliver Cromwell, nearly a hundred volumes, and in August 1826 had embarked upon his task. When Vigny's friend, Taylor, who had been ennobled by Charles X, and was now Commissaire Royal at the Comédie-Française, asked why he had never produced anything for the stage, Hugo told him about his *Cromwell*. Taylor asked him to luncheon to meet Talma, to whom the poet explained what he had in mind—to substitute drama for tragedy, Shakespeare for Racine; the style to have every sort of appeal, ranging from the heroic to the farcical. He would do away entirely with declamatory passages and set poetic speeches. "Splendid!" said Talma, "no high-falutin stuff!"

But Talma died that same year. The play had become inordinately long. It seemed impossible that it should ever find its way into a theatre, or not for a very considerable time. Victor Hugo decided to give a reading of *Cromwell* to his friends. Such readings were then very much in the fashion. The listeners would swoon with rapture, as in the days of *les Précieuses*. Madame Ancelot tells how, at the end of an Ode, someone had approached the poet, his face working with emotion: "He took his hand and raised his eyes to heaven." There was a moment's silence, after which the words could be heard; "Cathédrae! Ogive! Pyramide!" after which the room relapsed into a profound meditation.[10] After a partial reading of *Cromwell* at the house of Madame Tastu, Hugo invited "Monsieur Sainte-Beuve" to the Fouchers, in the rue du Cherche-Midi, where he was to give a reading of the whole drama on March 12th, 1827. "Everyone will be charmed to see him, I in particular. He is one of those listeners whom I would always choose to have about me, because I enjoy hearing them talk."[11]

The reading, like all such readings, was a success, but with this difference, that it deserved to be. The high-spirited comedy of certain scenes, the "newness" of the vocabulary, the Shakespearean gaiety of the Four Fools, all combined to make of *Cromwell* an original and major work which, quite clearly, ought to be seen upon the stage. "*Cromwell*," said Vigny to the author, "makes all the tragedies of our day look like old, wrinkled faces. When it takes the theatre by storm it will cause a revolution, and there will be no more arguing." Next morning, March 13th, Sainte-Beuve wrote Hugo a letter which is a document of capital importance. He had admired the beauties of this "tragi-comedy," but had a number of criticisms to make.

My criticisms all come back to the same thing, a weakness in your talent which I have already mentioned to you—excess; forcefulness carried to extremes, and, if you will pardon the word, *exaggeration*. The serious portions of your drama are admirable. No matter to what extent you have let yourself go, have spread yourself, you have managed never to carry your subject beyond the sublime. The scenes in which the ambassadors are received, the two that follow upon them in the second act, Cromwell's monologue after his interview with Sir Robert Willis, the Privy Council scene in the third act, the one in which Milton throws himself at Cromwell's feet—all fine, very fine. Nearly every line makes one want to shout one's enthusiasm aloud. My reservations are chiefly concerned with the comic parts. Your idea of mixing them, of intermingling them, with the main action—all of which is conceived in a mood of terror—gives you possibilities of beauty which you have exploited to the full. But the greater the effect which this contrast is capable of producing, the more soberly should it be employed, and, to my mind, you have overstepped the limits, especially in the *asides*, which are very long, and more frequent than is necessary. More, I think, should have been left to the imagination; the note of parody should have been less stressed, should have been hinted rather than stated . . . It is this *abuse* of your powers, it is the *details*, and the details only, to which I take exception, and I don't mind telling you that there were moments yesterday to which I very much took exception. I don't want you to think that they *bored* me; nothing that you write can ever bore, but they irritated me, made me impatient. I was tempted to say, as Cromwell says to his Fools when he is out of humour: "Stop! A truce to that! Have done!" Forgive, dear sir, the freedom with which I write to you; but the more honest I am in this matter, the more easily shall I be excused . . . I feel that it is impertinent on my part thus to assail you with my criticisms; they are a poor return for the beauties with which you have overpowered me. Let me, however, say one word about your style. It is very beautiful, especially in the serious passages; elsewhere it is not always free from a rather too obtrusive use of images, some of them odd and somewhat too thickly sown. You have set yourself the task of achieving two different effects—Corneille at some moments, Molière at others. So far as Corneille is concerned, you have succeeded, but in the Molière part you have failed. It reminds one more of Regnard, perhaps even more of Beaumarchais. There is a great deal of *Le Mariage de Figaro* in your play. . . .[12]

These comments shed a bright light on the difference in temperament of the two men. Hugo, endowed with overwhelming vigour, could not, nor should he, turn his back on the heights. Sainte-Beuve, sensitive and fragile, could breathe freely only on "moderate slopes." He had understood romanticism, as he understood everything, but, in his view, the great play was harnessed to a "lightweight skit." He brought a severe and lucid gaze to bear upon his own ecstasies. "I am a classic," he once said, "in the sense that unreason, extravagance, ridicule or bad taste, carried beyond a certain point, are enough to 'put me off' a work of literature permanently, and to cause me to discontinue my applause abruptly." Hugo, a born poet, was strongly susceptible to ideas suggested by rhyme, just as Michelangelo was susceptible to the forms suggested by a block of marble. Sainte-Beuve, a writer of prose, held that there should always be some logical link between ideas. Consequently, whenever he tried his hand at verse, it never acquired that regulated extravagance which is the life-blood of poetry. Hugo, a more complete and rounded character, could obey, when he wished to, the exigencies of prose, as the Preface to *Cromwell* shows.

It was written after the play, and was received, especially by the young, with quite extraordinary enthusiasm. For Hugo it was a deliberate act, a burning of his boats. Goaded by cantankerous and stupid adherents of the classic school, he put himself at the head of the rebels. He no longer said, as he had done in 1824: "Romantic? Classic? What do names matter?" He created his own brand of romanticism and gave it a dogma. Language must be injected with a new *youth*; the "free, unfettered methods of the ancients" must be restored; the writer must eliminate Delille and go back to Mathurin Régnier. Drama should be a struggle between two opposing principles, because on that contrast all reality is based. The beautiful and the ugly, the comic and the tragic, the grotesque and the sublime, should be at grips with one another, and from their opposition great emotions should be produced: light and shade, Heaven and Hell. Hugo was obsessed by the Manichaean dualism. His mistake, which was that of peoples in their infancy, was to incarnate the sublime and the grotesque in different characters. He could see only in terms of black and white, whence his monsters. A certain simple-mindedness, analogous to that of *Han d'Islande*, is still noticeable in *Cromwell*, but the sweep and power of its poetry are wholly admirable.

The times had an appetite for power. How could it be otherwise? How could a generation brought up on the roll of the drums of the Empire be expected to remain satisfied with respectable odes and neo-classic tragedies? A young colonel once said to Stendhal: "After the Russian campaign, I can't help feeling that *Iphigénie en Aulide* is an indifferent tragedy." The public was no longer composed of "good society." A new class had arisen which was not terrified by violence, and felt an ever-increasing craving for "strong emotions."[13] It had been possible in 1816 to believe that Louis XVIII was the embodiment of liberty; in 1827 nobody really thought that the spirit of the century was incarnate in Charles X. Victor began to realize that, under the influence of his mother and the Fouchers, he had reached a dead-end in politics; that he had embraced, in religion, a theology which was not that of his imagination. Sainte-Beuve, and his new friends of *Le Globe*, preached, for his benefit, an anti-dynastic liberalism. General Hugo, by revealing to him the other side of the medal, so far as history was concerned, had turned him into a Bonapartist. How should he, a lover of giants, not have felt the poetry of such a life as Napoleon's?

In 1827 a ball was given at the Austrian Embassy. Several marshals of the Empire were invited. One of them, when asked for his name, replied "Duc de Tarente"; the major-domo announced him as "Marshal Macdonald"; another, "Duc de Dalmatie," was announced as "Marshal Soult"; "Duc de Trévise" as "Marshal Mortier"; "Duc de Reggio" as "Marshal Oudinot." Europe wanted to erase the French victories from the map. The marshals called for their carriages, and the scandal in Paris was great. The son of General Count Hugo rightly felt affronted, and at once wrote an "Ode à la Colonne de la Place Vendôme":

> Prenez garde! La France, où grandit un autre âge,
> N'est pas si morte encore qu'elle souffre un outrage!
> Les partis, pour un temps, voileront leur tableau.
> Contre une injure, ici, tout s'unit, tout se lève,
> Tout s'arme, et la Vendée aiguisera son glaive
> Sur la pierre de Waterloo!
>
> . . . .
>
> C'est moi qui me tairais! Moi qu'enivrait naguère
> Mon nom saxon, mêlé parmis les cris de guerre!
> Moi qui suivait le vol d'un drapeau triomphant!
> Qui, joignant aux clairons ma voix entrecoupée,
> Eus pour premier hochet le nœud, d'or d'une épée!
> Moi, qui fus un soldat quant j'étais un enfant![14]

As a matter of strict truth he had never been a soldier except as figuring on the parade-state of the Royal-Corse, and then as a joke, but the part pleased him. Youth trembled with excitement; half-pay warriors applauded; Bonapartists and Liberals were triumphant. "We speak his language now, and his religion has become our own. His blood boils at Austrian insults, and he grows bitter at the sound of foreign threats. Standing before the Column he declaims a sacred hymn which recalls to the men of our day the swing, refrain and choruses sung by our soldiers on the field of Jemmapes."[15] The Preface to Cromwell had turned him into the doctrinal leader of the romantic school: the "Ode à la Colonne" rallied the *globistes* to him. In the kingdom of letters the reign of Nodier was over, and in the triumvirate Lamartine-Vigny-Hugo it was he who stood out as First Consul. The son of General Hugo had taken over the command of Young France.

13

The "Orientales" of Vaugirard

> Victor Hugo is a form that one day went in
> search of its content, and found it at last.
>
> CLAUDE ROY

IF HUGO ever had the appearance of a happy man it was in 1827 and 1828. A son, Charles, had been born to him in 1826. The first floor in the rue de Vaugirard became too cramped, and he rented a whole house at 11 rue Notre-Dame-des-Champs, "a place of monastic calm, suited to a poet, hidden away at the far end of a shady avenue,"[1] behind which there was a romantic garden with a patch of ornamental water and a rustic bridge. A door at the far end gave access to the Luxembourg, while the main carriage-entrance put Hugo within reach of the *barrières* of Montparnasse, Maine and Vaugirard. There he found the open country almost at his door; windmills standing high above fields of lucerne and stretches of gorse. The main street of Vaugirard was lined with arboured pleasure-gardens, the haunt of half-pay military men, loafers and *grisettes*.

Sainte-Beuve, who could not do without the Hugos now, moved into an apartment almost next door, at No. 19, where he lived with his mother. Lamartine went to visit him there, and was loud in his praises of "the peace, your mother, the garden and the doves . . . It reminds me of the presbyteries, and the kindly country priests to whom I was so devoted in my childhood." Hugo saw Sainte-Beuve every day, and took an interest in the work he was doing on the poets of the Pléiade. Ronsard, Belleau, Du Bellay gave him a taste for literary forms that were old and, therefore, new—as well as for the loosely constructed *ballade* in which his virtuosity was more completely at home than in the full-dress ode.

Every man sees nature through the prism of a temperament. Hugo had a real passion for this Vaugirard of the common people, for its songs, its sounds, its uninhibited love-making. The sensitive Sainte-Beuve sighed his distaste: "Oh! how dreary all this flat land is that stretches all round the fortifications!" Consequently, it was not often in his company that Victor Hugo, of an evening, when his eyes were tired from work, set off on foot towards the hamlet of Plaisance and the setting sun. There was always a small "court" about him, his brother Abel, his brother-in-law Paul Foucher, and a crowd of poets and artists.

There was a constant succession of them. Hugo had a genius for, among other things, enlisting young men. Whenever an admirer wrote to him, he replied by return: "I don't at all know whether I am a poet, but I am quite sure that you are." A youth from Angers, Victor Pavie, wrote a few enthusiastic lines about *Odes et Ballades*. He got not one letter back, but a whole sequence of letters. "An article which the great names of our literature would not be ashamed to have set their names to . . . Is not the principal merit of my book that it has furnished matter for admirable articles in the *Feuilleton et Affiches d'Angers*? . . ."[2] Praise can never go too far. Even the most hyperbolical never quite comes up to the author's expectations. Pavie came to Paris and was received in such a way that he sobbed from sheer happiness. Twenty years later he was still agog with the memory: "It was enough to make a man go nearly out of his mind."[3]

Pavie put Victor Hugo in touch with the sculptor, David d'Angers, who was already famous, and "stood for" a living, modern art. Several painters and lithographers had already been enlisted among the poet's following: Achille and Eugène Devéria, two handsome young fellows with proud looks, who shared a studio with Louis Boulanger and, by a miraculous turn of fortune, also lived in the rue Notre-Dame-des-Champs. Boulanger, who was four years younger than Hugo, clung to him like his shadow. He produced illustrations for some of Hugo's poems—"Mazeppa," "La Ronde du Sabbat"—and painted portraits of both Victor and Adèle. It was not long before he became intimate with Sainte-Beuve, and Hugo always addressed them as "my painter and my poet." Eugène Delacroix and Paul Huet were also in the habit of joining in the evening walks. Thanks to Victor Hugo, many writers and painters of the younger generation got to know one another in this way.

On summer evenings there was a sort of group exodus. They ate pastries at the Moulin de Beurre, and then went on to dine at a wooden table in one of the garden restaurants, where there would be much singing and argument. On one occasion, Abel Hugo, having caught the distant sound of "old ma Saguet's fiddles," started off to spy out the land, went into a garden, dined in an arbour, and expressed himself favourably on the subject of the cooking. For twenty sous one could get two fried eggs, chicken *sauté*, cheese and unlimited white wine. On Sundays, Adèle made one in these expeditions, admired and respected by all the young men. Théodore Pavie thought her "welcoming but absent-minded."[4] She would sit lost in her own thoughts while the others talked and, on the occasions when she joined in, usually said something wholly irrelevant. But that happened very seldom. She was terrified of her husband's withering glance, and rarely uttered a word. Her mother, Madame Foucher, had died on October 6th, 1827, and her younger sister, who was only two years older than Didine, had been sent away to school at a convent.

Victor Pavie, on the occasion of his first visit, was struck by the fact that Hugo spoke to him not about poetry but painting. The reason was that, in those days, poetry was very close to painting. When Victor led his party to the foot of the Moulin de Beurre

> . . . précisément à l'heure
> Où quand par le brouillard la chatte rôle et pleure,
> Monsieur Hugo va voir mourir Phœbus le blond.[5]

He watched night fall upon the gardens of Grenelle and made notes of forms and colours. Next day, observing in the distance the "archipelagoes of blood-red cloud," he would recite to his disciples seated round him on the grass a "Soleil couchant":

> J'aime les soirs sereins et beaux, j'aime les soirs,
> Soit qu'ils dorent le front des antiques manoirs
>   Ensevelis dans les feuillages;
> Soit que la brume au loin s'allonge en bancs de feu
> Soit que mille rayons brisent dans un ciel bleu
>   A des archipels de nuages.[6]

Often, too, he read to them extracts from *Les Orientales*. Whence had come to him the idea of painting a conventionalized picture of the East? It was the fashion. Greece was fighting for her freedom. Byron had just died in her service. All over the world liberals were rising in her defence, and Hugo's artist friends were liberals to a man. Delphine Gay, Lamartine, Casimir Delavigne were all writing poems in praise of Greece; but they were uninspired compositions. Hugo, on the other hand, had a feeling for drama, and now tried to make an *Orientale* a living scene. He loved the rattle of words, and found it amusing to make them dance a wild *zapatéado*: *Trébizonde* and *blonde*, *sultane* and *tartane*, *guitare* and *tartare*, *mahométane* and *capitane*—always, miraculously, the rhyme fell pat, and always the harmony of the verse was perfect. As background decoration he used his Grenelle sunsets. From them he drew his gold and his flames. His Orient was the rue Notre-Dame-des-Champs.

Perhaps the loveliest of those songs was the one that snatched the poet away from East and West alike, out of time, out of space: "Ecstasy":

> J'étais seul près des flots, par une nuit d'étoiles,
> Pas un nuage aux cieux, sur les mers pas de voiles,
> Mes yeux plongeaient plus loin que le monde réel.

> Et les bois, et les monts, et toute la nature,
> Semblaient interroger dans un confus murmure
>   Les flots des mers, les feux du ciel.
>
> Et les étoiles d'or, légions infinies,
> A voix haute, à voix basse, avec mille harmonies,
> Disaient, en inclinant leurs couronnes de feu;
> Et les flots bleus, que rien ne gouverne et n'arrête,
> Disaient, en recourbant l'écume de leur crête;
>   "C'est le Seigneur, le Seigneur Dieu!"[7]

Here was born the Hugo of *Les Contemplations*, skilled, like Beethoven, in making thought and feeling alike mount to the repeated affirmation of the final chord.

With *Les Orientales* Hugo achieved "the unity of romanticism." The young men were intoxicated: "Victor is for ever performing wonders, with unimaginable speed . . . and, from time to time, slams down on us an *Orientale* like a paving-stone on a swarm of ants." Victor Pavie was filled with admiration, and begged for mercy: "Victor read us some of his incredible, his doubly incredible, *Orientales* . . . not a single weak line! He fairly bludgeons one!"[8] The painters, the sculptors, praised to high heaven the poet who had brought them subjects and colours, who had rushed to arms in defence of freedom for the artist. But the "good Nodier's" reaction was not so good. Ever since the Arsenal days he had longed to be the leader of the movement, and now, with the coming of Hugo, promoted to the rank of Prince of Youth, found that his power had been undermined. He published an article, entitled "Byron et Moore," which was hostile to *Les Orientales*. The modern school of French poetry, he said, had failed to produce anything capable of competing with the charming compositions of the two English geniuses. "There are those who think that great talents are formed by rubbing shoulders with their like, and that innate genius, with all its richness, can be developed in the give and take of polite conversation without other stimulant than the need to be famous, and the emulation of the successful. . . ."[9]

This was a clear case of lampooning Hugo's Vaugirard "court." Hugo, always quick to take offence, was saddened by the defection of the companion of his earliest days of happiness. *Victor Hugo to Charles Nodier*: "You, too, Charles! I would give much not to have read yesterday's *Quotidienne*. There is no more violent shock in life than that caused by the uprooting from the heart of an old and fervent friendship . . ."[10] Nodier made his submission: "My whole literary life is wrapped up in you. If ever I am remembered, it will be because you have made up your mind that I shall be . . ." The fragments of their old friendship were stuck together again, but never more was there between them that fond and utter confidence which is the very heart of friendship.

The good Émile Deschamps, whom jealousy never touched, had become a kindly familiar in the rue Notre-Dame-des-Champs. "I love and admire you more and more," he wrote after each visit. *Émile Deschamps to Victor Hugo*: "I left behind me yesterday in your house many regrets and an umbrella. Send back the umbrella and keep the regrets. You will find the umbrella in your dining-room, close to the door; the regrets are everywhere where you were not. Madame Victor, I think, was even sweeter than she usually is. She showed us the whole of your palace, not excepting the gardens. You are admirably housed, and your gallery is marvellous. Nowhere could one see more, or better, pictures."[11]

Émile Deschamps to Victor Hugo, October 13th, 1828: It is quite impossible that you should not come to dine, next Saturday, October 18th, at rue de la Ville-l'Évêque, No. 10 (*bis*) along with Lamartine and Alfred. I regard that as settled. I've just *got* to consult you about the whole of my poem, "Rodriguez," and fully intend to give you a reading of it. Forgive me, won't you? It is essential that I regard you as the *nègre plus ultra* of friends . . . Lamartine had not seen your wonderful Preface to *Cromwell*, so I lent it him. Needless to say, he is madly enthusiastic, and can't now read any other prose. Send me news of Madame Victor. We must know how she is in order to know how we are ourselves . . . Do please answer this question—three vowels will do.[12]

Alfred de Vigny remained, to all appearances, fairly faithful. In February 1825 he had married, at Pau, an Englishwoman from India, a Miss Lydia Bunbury, whom he believed to be very rich. Vigny loved all Englishwomen. Those "fair complexions, straight out of Ossian," strongly appealed to him. "If only you knew how poetic that nation is!"[13] He had informed Victor of his marriage: "Between our wives there will be the same bond of affection as between you and me, and the four of us will be as one . . . I have promised my wife that your dear Adèle will be her friend. We want to live as you live, and as near to you as possible."[14] Lydia's attitude was somewhat more distant. If her nation was poetic, *this* representative of it constituted an exception. She was cold, haughty and frequently ailing, as a result of "certain accidents of maternity." In the interval between two miscarriages she dragged Vigny off on visits to the Duchesse de la Trémoille, the Princess de Ligne, the Duchesse de Maillé, a great deal more readily than to the house in the rue Notre-Dame-des-Champs.

Nevertheless, the two poets remained on terms of intimacy, each providing the other with those rations of praise so necessary for the maintenance of friendship. Victor sent Vigny all his new books: "I feel a strong need to give you *Les Orientales* and the *Condamné*; I feel a strong need that you should not be angry with me; I feel a strong need that you shall not say 'Victor is neglecting me'; because I admire you and love you with more than most men have of love and admiration."[15] Vigny was eloquent in praise of "all those perfumes of the Orient brought together in a golden censer," and kissed Victor on both cheeks, "one for the Oriental, the other for the Occidental, side of your head which is a whole world in itself . . . I have had and held you, dear friend, for a very long while, and never leave you; you follow me all day long until night comes, and next morning I find you again. I move from you to you, from low to high, from the *Orientales* to the *Condamné*, from the Hôtel de Ville to the Tower of Babel. Wherever I am, you are there with me, always you, always your glittering colours, always your deep emotion, always your true, your wholly satisfying expression, always your poetry."[16]

This was the Holy Water of the *cénacle*. In the intimacy of his *Journal* Vigny used harsh words about his old friend. *May 23rd, 1829*: "I have just seen Victor Hugo: he was with Sainte-Beuve, a small, rather ugly man with a commonplace appearance and a back that is more than bent, who, when he talks pulls obsequious and flattering grimaces like an old woman . . . Victor Hugo is . . . dominated, politically, by this intelligent young man who has succeeded, as a result of being with him daily and using his influence, in making him completely, and quite suddenly, change all his opinions . . . He has just told me that, after thinking matters over, he has decided to leave the Right . . . The Victor whom I once loved is no more. *That* Victor was a bit of a fanatic for religion and royalism, as chaste as a young girl, and a bit of a wild man of the woods. But it suited him, and we liked him as he was. Now he has taken a fancy to bawdy talk, and has become a Liberal. The new suit sits badly on him. It can't be helped—he began life as a mature man, and is only now entering on adolescence. He started by writing, and only after that began to live, whereas the proper sequence is to live first and write afterwards."[17]

Le Dernier Jour d'un Condamné, which Vigny praised, was a short and extremely moving prose work which Hugo had published without his name on the title-page, one month after *Les Orientales*. It was presented as a piece of writing found in a prison cell, and written by a man under sentence of death in the last few hours before going to the guillotine. For some considerable time he had been morbidly obsessed by the problem of capital punishment. He had seen corpses for the first time in Italy and Spain. On the Place de Grève he had averted his eyes from the horrible engine of execution. In order to write this book he had worked seriously at the subject, had gone to Bicêtre and there watched the convicts being put in irons before leaving for the penal settlement. A powerful imagination breeds a sense of pity. Hugo was quite sincere in his wish to abolish the death sentence, which he thought more cruel than useful. Perhaps, too, he thought that by setting *Le Dernier Jour* side by side with *Les Orientales*, he might succeed, by publishing this first essay on social problems, in reducing to silence those who had reproached him on the grounds of an insolent virtuosity. "He is a good planner," said Vigny with haughty disdain. But this was being unfair to Hugo, who felt a great deal more than he "planned."

On one point, however, Vigny showed a shrewd insight. Like many who have had a strict upbringing, Hugo, at twenty-seven, had only just begun to live. His greed for happiness was still unappeased, and he took a voluptuous delight in his success. "One might search in vain through all Europe," wrote Jules Janin, "before finding a prince, a king, a military leader more deserving of envy, or happier, than the author of *Les Orientales*"[18]—and again: "I know of nobody anywhere who could laugh like Monsieur Victor Hugo, when in good humour, over the success of *Les Orientales*." It is probable that, about this time, he was living through his own personal drama. A man does not change sides without much tearing up of roots and, at another level, the young husband was being exposed to a great deal of temptation in the company of young painters and their models. The moral standards of the Plain of Vaugirard were very different from those of the rue du Cherche-Midi.

Adèle, almost always either pregnant or nursing, was very tired, and in no condition to share the sensual transports of this "drunken treader of the grapes." It may be that, in spite of himself, he let his thoughts turn to other women. He had, for a brief while, engaged in a mild flirtation with Julie Duvidal de Montferrier, but the latter's brother, a captain of Light Horse, had intervened in no uncertain fashion, whereupon Abel Hugo had proposed to and, on December 20th, 1827, married the former drawing-mistress. The Hugo brothers had a strong family affection for one another. Victor, easily consoled, composed an epithalamium:

> Tu devais être à nous, et c'était ton destin,
> Et rien ne pouvait t'y soustraire . . .[19]

A short time after this marriage, on January 28th, 1828, General Hugo had had an apoplectic stroke. It had come upon him with the "suddenness of a cannon-ball," in Abel's house, and he had died immediately. *Victor Hugo to Victor Pavie, February 29th, 1828:* "I have lost the man who in all the world most loved me, a being of goodness and nobility whose gift to me was something of pride and much of love . . ."[20] That same year, on October 21st, a second son was born in the rue Notre-Dame-des-Champs.[21]

Happiness seemed once again to have descended upon the family circle.

Happiness, fulfilment, gaiety—those three words are used by all who have described Hugo at the approach of his thirtieth year. There were times when he suffered from doubts, both political and religious, which had followed hard on the heels of his adolescent faith. "We carry in our hearts a rotting corpse—the corpse of that religion which was a living presence in the lives of our fathers," but certainties, in him, were stronger than doubts. Certainty of his physical vigour: no trace was left of the weakness from which he had suffered in childhood; "shark's teeth which could crunch a peach-stone"; the strength of a wild animal. In his poems of 1829 one can feel something of the general's full-blooded sensuality. In his talk, the chaste author of the *Odes* had momentary fits of licentiousness. In *Les Orientales,* cheek by jowl with *Premier Soupir* was to be found a *"Péri éblouissante, chaque jour en train de s'embellir."* In the strong, desire is a manifestation of strength.

Certainty of worldly success: he lived in a fine house with a large garden; his work provided for everything. From the first edition of *Les Orientales,* published by Bossange, he received three thousand six hundred francs. Gosselin, another of his publishers, paid him seven thousand two hundred francs for a duodecimo edition of *Les Orientales, Bug-Jargal, Le Dernier Jour d'un Condamné,* and a novel still to be written, *Notre-Dame de Paris.* Having spent his youth in a condition of financial stringency, he attached great importance to those easy circumstances which alone, he thought, can guarantee a writer's independence. To Fontaney he said: "I want to make, and spend, fifteen thousand francs a year." This was an ambition worthy of Balzac, but Balzac was burdened with debts. Hugo had a horror of owing. He made up his accounts every evening to the last centime, and insisted on Adèle, whom he regarded as a spendthrift, doing the same.

Finally, certainty of fame: from 1829 he was the "Master" to all the young men of the rising generation. "Victor Hugo," said Baudelaire, "was the one man to whom everybody turned for the watchword of the day. Never was royalty more legitimate, more natural, more whole-heartedly acclaimed, more confirmed in its occupancy of the throne by the powerlessness of rebellion . . ."[22] Not that he was without enemies. Success always breeds enemies, and only a great man can endure with equanimity the glory of others. He even had adversaries who were sincere and disinterested. Stendhal and Mérimée found him boring; libertines of their stamp did not believe that the father of a family could be a poet. Musset laughed at him, though not ill-naturedly. Why

Victor Hugo in 1829, an etching by Achille Deveria
(*Bibliothèque Nationale*)

"The birth of Victor Hugo"
Painting by Marie (*Musée Victor Hugo
—Photo Bulloz*)

Victor Hugo in his boyhood
Painting by Eugène Legenisel
(*Musée Victor Hugo*)

Adèle Foucher, wife of Victor Hugo,
in her early thirties
Portrait by Louis Boulanger
(*Musée Victor Hugo—Photo Bulloz*)

Victor Hugo with his youngest son,
François-Victor Hugo, in 1835
Portrait by Auguste de Châtillon
(*Musée Victor Hugo*)

Léopoldine Hugo,
eldest daughter of Victor Hugo,
when eleven years old
Portrait by Auguste de Châtillon (*Musée Victor Hugo*)

Mademoiselle Juliette in 1832
Lithography by Léon Noël
(*Bibliothèque Nationale*)

Sarah Bernhardt as Maria,
Queen of Spain, in *Ruy Blas*
Portrait by Georges Clairin
(*Petit Palais des Beaux-Arts*)

Juliette Drouet
at the age of seventy-six
Portrait by Jules Bastien-
Lepage (*Musée Victor Hugo*)

Juliette Drouet
Bust by Victor Vilain
(*Musée Victor Hugo*)

Madame Victor Hugo
Bust by Victor Vilain
(*Musée Victor Hugo*)

An ink drawing by Victor Hugo of Vianden, his house in the
Grand Duchy of Luxemburg
(*Musée Victor Hugo*)

Victor Hugo with his family at Guernsey
(*Musée Victor Hugo—Photo Bulloz*)

The blue drawing room in Hauteville House, Victor Hugo's residence on
Guernsey
(*Picture Post Library*)

Victor Hugo in 1872
(*Collection of Simone André-Maurois*)

should he care? He knew himself to be the leader of the new school, and the champion of a free literature. It was at his house in the rue Notre-Dame-des-Champs that the men of his generation came together. He kept a box crammed with rough drafts and projects for the future. One notebook, "Dramas I've got to get to work on," contained sketches for what would ultimately become, or had become already, *Marion de Lorme, Les Jumeaux, Lucrèce Borgia,* and others never pursued, *Louis XI, La Mort du duc d'Enghien, Néron.* At the bottom of one page, filled with titles, appears this note: "When they're done, we'll see." Power of such magnitude engenders a prodigious self-confidence. The Preface to *Les Orientales* in 1829 is aggressive. "Art's concern is not to burden itself with leading-strings, handcuffs and gags; it says 'Go!' and looses you into the great garden of poetry where there is no forbidden fruit." The author knows that there are some who "have taxed him with presumption, cocksureness, pride, etc.; have represented him as a sort of young Louis XIV, dashing head-on into all manner of serious questions, booted, spurred and brandishing a hunting-crop. He ventures to assert that those who see him thus have bad sight. . . ."[23]

Undoubtedly that was so. He was more Imperial than Royal. Like the young Bonaparte, he dominated, not by right of birth, not by divine right, but by right of conquest and by right of genius. With high sublimity, he cried aloud in his joy: "The future is mine!—the future!—the future!" But it was he, too, who soon would answer: "The future is nobody's, sire." It was he who would paint the portrait of the eagle hovering above the eternal depths "when a great blast of wind broke both his wings." It was he who was, in a short while, to fall into the bottomless pit of moral suffering, but who, through suffering, was to find that secret place of which he stood in need in order to become the greatest of all French poets.

For, no matter what he had said of it in the Preface to *Cromwell,* romanticism was not just the mingling of tragic and grotesque, or the giving of new blood to an old vocabulary, or the freedom to cut his coat according to his cloth, but something that went far deeper. It was the Spirit of the Age; it was an anguish, a discontent, a conflict between man and the world in which he lived. This was something the classics had known nothing of. "The feeling that life is no longer enough, that it is strangely, incredibly empty if one does not stray beyond its frontiers: the strange movement of a human soul never at rest, sometimes on the heights, sometimes groaning in captivity . . ."[24] The heart all filled with self-disgust, except when it is revelling voluptuously "in its own misery accepted as a challenge," was what Goethe and Byron had given to the generation after Rousseau. It was that which a whole section of French youth was seeking, round about 1830, delivered over to melancholy because, suddenly, it had been deprived of glory. It was that which the too happy Hugo of the Plain of Vaugirard, the Hugo of *Les Orientales,* could not, as yet, supply.

Yet he, and only he, possessed the instrument. No other poet, not even Lamartine, not even Vigny, was capable of enlisting in the service of the times so great a mastery of language and of rhythm. All that Hugo needed to bring his genius to maturity was the anxiety, the uncertainty, the melancholy which would make him one with his Age. He was far from suspecting that the deepening processes of sorrow would come to him from the silent young woman with whom he had so closely bound his life, and from the friend with the red hair and repellent face who said about his work such fine and useful things. At the very moment when, in complete security, he was taking joy of his triumphs, he was standing on the very brink of dire catastrophe. But it was needful that we should see him in the brief years of his utter happiness, a husband as yet unshaken on his throne, a father of the Golden Age, a master with a gay crowd of disciples at his heels, looking on the giant city sleeping at his feet, with the lovely mist clinging to its towers, and spreading in great waves—

> Sur des œuvres de grâce et d'amour courronnées
> Le frais enchantement de ses jeunes années.

PART IV

Precocious Autumn

Whom on this earth would one not pity if one
knew everything about everybody?

SAINTE-BEUVE

14

The Faithful Achates

VIGNY, within the secret pages of his *Journal*, analysed, without kindliness, the relationship between Hugo and Sainte-Beuve. The latter, said Vigny, "has turned himself into Victor Hugo's faithful henchman, and by him has been led to poetry: but Victor Hugo who, all his life, has spent his time in going from man to man, skimming the best of each one's cream, has acquired from him a deal of knowledge which he had not got before; it is all very well for him to play the master; actually, he is the pupil . . ."[1] There speaks the voice of resentment. Hugo did not "skim" Sainte-Beuve. He most certainly did learn a great deal from him, but only a very stupid man would fail to add to his own stock whatever he might happen to pick up and, besides, the influence was reciprocal. Hugo, a past master in the music of language, paid insufficient attention to the inner life; Sainte-Beuve, endowed with the sensitivity of a poet, failed when he tried to write poetry, because of the clumsiness and flabbiness of his poetic form.

"The reason was that his temperament was itself clumsy, insecure, impotent, and, as it were, tied up in knots, being both exquisite and vile at one and the same time. When in the company of his friends of the *cénacle*, he had the uneasy, constrained manners of the 'backward.' So far as intelligence went, so far, even, as genius went, he knew that he was their equal, but he desperately admired, and with scarcely a trace of jealousy—so great was the influence upon him of its fascination—their bursting virility, which he found terribly attractive, fundamentally healthy . . . A cherub, less pink than pallid, as wrinkled as an old man, and for ever biting his nails; a schoolboy who had read Laclos, and would have liked, though he did not dare, did not know how, to live the life that Laclos painted; an ingenuous chorister crying his eyes out behind the altar; an angel, a beast, but never a man. . . ."[2]

It is impossible not to feel pity for this melancholic, studious and subtle-minded young man, whom an ailment of which he could never speak (he was sexually malformed) made even more timid than he would otherwise have been; who, marked out by a natural sensitiveness for the most delicately amorous experiences, was reduced to finding satisfaction only in the company of mercenary women, and in wooing the Venus of the streets. "You cannot possibly know what it is like," he once said in a fit of black depression, "to feel that one will never be loved, because for a man like me to be loved is impossible, is beyond hoping for." What he found under the Hugos' roof seemed to him quite wonderful. It was everything he had not got: a home, friends, children to love. *Sainte-Beuve to Victor Hugo, October 11th, 1829:* "Such little talent as I have I owe to your example, to the advice you have given me in the guise of praise. What I have done, I have done because of what I have seen you doing, because you have believed me capable of doing it, too. But my real, my basic, self is so poor a thing that my talent has emerged wholly in you, as a stream, after a long journey, emerges into a river or a sea. I can draw inspiration only from you, and from the atmosphere about you. Finally, such domestic life as I have is in you alone, and I never feel truly at home except when I am lying on your sofa, or sitting by your fire . . ."[3] That is scarcely the language of a man who has been "skimmed."

He painted a portrait of himself, of all his utter desolation, in a book which appeared without his name: *Vie, Pensées et Poésies de Joseph Delorme.* Joseph Delorme longed to become a great poet, but inspiration fled from him. "What agonizing tremors he experienced at each new triumph of his young contemporaries!" Joseph Delorme was without a master, without friends, without religion. "His spirit showed nothing but an inconceivable chaos in which monstrous images, recent memories, criminal fantasies, great thoughts miscarried, wise foresight followed by lunatic actions, pious yearnings after outbursts of blasphemy, moved confusedly against a background of despair . . ."[4] He described himself as pure, "sick, and devoured by the torment of never having loved."

At the end of 1828, Sainte-Beuve had made Hugo privy to these "miserable pages," and had asked him whether he did not think it would be unseemly and absurd to make public such "spiritual nudities." Hugo had replied in a note couched in the warmest terms. He spoke of "the emotion which your grave and lovely verse, your masculine, simple and melancholy prose, have given me, and your *Joseph Delorme,* which is you. That short, austere tale, that cunning dissection which strips bare a human soul, almost made me shed tears."[5] It was a happy day for poor Sainte-Beuve. For a moment he believed himself to be a great poet. In January 1829 *Les Orientales* appeared; in March of the same year, *Joseph Delorme. Les Orientales* made the greater sensation, but their diligent author studied with care the lesson of Joseph Delorme, and learned from it that an intimate and personal form of poetry is possible.

His friend's success made Sainte-Beuve feel humble rather than jealous. In his writings he stood forth as a champion of Hugoesque romanticism, making up by the warmth of his language for the weakness of his convictions. For he had never been a true romantic. Joseph Delorme was only one aspect of himself, born of Werther. Deeper down, there was in Sainte-Beuve a sceptic who laughed at Joseph Delorme. But he liked to understand, and that anyone should have as much colour and force as Victor Hugo puzzled him. When he followed up his *Tableau de la poésie française au XVme siècle* with a selection from the works of Ronsard, he gave Victor Hugo the beautiful folio volume, in which the extracts figured, with this dedication: "To the greatest inventor in lyrical poetry whom France has had since Ronsard, from Ronsard's very humble commentator, SAINTE-BEUVE."[6] Victor and Adèle put this beautiful Ronsard, bound in white vellum, stamped with heraldic bearings, on the table in their drawing-room where already reposed the Golden Lily of the Jeux Floraux, and, one by one, all the friends, Lamartine, Vigny, Guttinguer, Dumas the elder, enriched it with their autographs. Sainte-Beuve himself in his small, spindly handwriting had inscribed a sonnet which was not without a certain grace and delicacy.

It would seem that this sensitive soul, "a poplar with white and fragile leaves" trembling in all the winds of heaven, had been fulfilled by the presence in his life of a virile, attentive and indulgent friendship. For the first time, thanks to his intimacy with the Hugos, he was one of a group, and believed that at last he had been saved from his prolonged and sterile introspection.

15

Way for the Theatre

It was not a red waistcoat that I wore at *Hernani*,
but a rose-coloured doublet. That is very important.

THÉOPHILE GAUTIER

VICTOR HUGO was always a great worker, but 1829 was one of the most laborious years that he had ever known. He had begun *Notre-Dame de Paris*, was writing a great deal of poetry, but, first and foremost, was making a determined effort to conquer the theatre. There had been no production of *Cromwell*, but the *cénacle* of the romantics believed, with reason, that the playgoing public was now demanding something different from pseudo-classical tragedies. Only fanatics denied that Corneille and Racine had been great, but their genius had given excessive prestige to the conventions—the three unities, subjects drawn from the ancient world or Oriental sources, dreams or visions, and noble language—all of them things which, in the eighteenth century, and in less powerful hands had bred platitude and monotony. All that so far had been thought necessary was a spectacle "in which," said Vigny, "in a setting of vestibules opening on to nothing, characters, going nowhere in particular and talking of nothing very important, with undefined ideas in their heads, and vague metaphors on their lips, faintly agitated by moderate emotions and peaceable passions, died gracefully or ended on a fabricated sigh. Oh! pageants of emptiness! Shadows of men and women in a world that was all shadow! Vacant kingdoms! . . ."[1]

Against the tedium of this pasteboard stage the public had reacted by developing a taste for melodrama. Pixérécourt, the Shakespeare of the boulevards, had worked out a formula: a hero, a heroine, a villain, a clown and, long before the Preface to *Cromwell*, had brought together the grotesque and the tragic. The great Talma himself had said to Lamartine: "No more tragedies: what they want is drama," and, to Dumas: "Hurry up, and try to make a go of it while I am still alive."

In 1822, a certain enterprising theatrical manager named Jean-Toussaint Merle had brought to Paris a company of English players to give performances of Shakespeare's plays. He had found himself

up against fierce liberal opposition. Louis XVIII was thought to harbour pro-English feelings, and this was enough to cause *Macbeth* to be
greeted with cat-calls. Merle had been tactless in the wording of his
bills, one of which ran as follows: *OTHELLO, by the greatly renowned
Shakespeare performed by the very humble servants of His Britannic
Majesty*. There were cries from the Pit of "No more foreigners! Down
with Shakespeare! Just one of Wellington's toadies!" Merle threw in his
hand, and it was not until 1828 that an English company again appeared in the French capital. By that time the atmosphere had completely changed. The company was an excellent one, containing, as it
did, Kean Kemble and the adorable Harriet Smithson. So great was
the success that more than one author set about providing renderings
of Shakespeare in French verse. Émile Deschamps and Vigny collabo-
rated in *Roméo et Juliette*, and Vigny, unaided, started on a *More de
Venise*, based upon *Othello*. No doubt he was helped by his English
wife in the labour of translation.

As early as 1822, Hugo had turned Walter Scott's *Kenilworth* into a
play, entitled *Amy Robsart*. This he had kept in a drawer and, later,
revised, though he had no very great belief in it. When at last he
brought it to the stage at the Odéon in 1828, he refused to acknowledge
its authorship, and used the name of his brother-in-law, Paul Foucher,
at that time a young man of barely seventeen who showed no enthusiasm for the venture. *Paul Foucher to Victor Hugo, January 1828:* "In
a few days' time that ill-starred *Amy Robsart* is to make its bow. The
only thing I shall get out of it will be to appear as the man-of-straw, or
dummy. Some people never have any luck."[2] The piece could scarcely
have had a worse reception at the hands of the public, and Hugo had
been wise to dissociate himself from it. *Victor Hugo to Victor Pavie,
February 29th, 1828:* "I expect you have heard of the small misfortune
which has befallen Paul. It's not, really, a very serious matter . . . I had
to do my best to cover him. After all *I* was the cause of the trouble. The
truth of the matter is that what the gutter-curs had in mind when booing *Amy Robsart* was to get in a side-blow at *Cromwell*. The whole
thing was a classic example of low-class rigging, and is not worth talking
about."[3] It might, perhaps, have been better if he had not talked about
it at all.

He decided to play high, this time under his own name, with a drama
on a quite different subject: *Marion de Lorme* (originally called *Un
Duel sous Richelieu*). The action is set in the time of Louis XIII, and
the plot, a sufficiently trite affair, deals with a courtesan who finds salvation through her love for a chaste and high-minded young man, named
Didier, who is wrapped in Byronic gloom, brings disaster upon himself
and others, and is a political outlaw—a sure claim to the sympathy of
the author, whose sensibility had been deeply marked by the fate of

Lahorie. Victor Hugo had read a number of pamphlets, memoirs and historical works dealing with the period. Vigny's *Cinq-Mars* provided him with the portrait of a romantic Richelieu, "the omnipresent man in red." He had caught to a nicety the "tone" of the *Précieuses*. Much of the poetry was fine. In short, the play had great merits, and was an example of a strongly drawn, solid piece of work packed full of all that Hugo had it in him to do at that stage of his development.

Baron Taylor (ennobled in 1825) asked to hear the play. A reading was arranged for July 10th, 1829, and was held in the "Golden Lily room" before an audience of all the poet's friends—Vigny, Dumas, Musset, Balzac, Mérimée, Sainte-Beuve, the two Deschamps, Villemain, and the regular painter-members of the circle. "Victor Hugo was himself the reader, and he read well. No one who did not see that pale and remarkable face, and, above all, the stare in the rather wild eyes which, in moments of high passion, flashed as though with lightning can realize the full effect produced on his listeners . . . The play was interesting, and there was much to admire in it, but in those days admiration was not enough. What was demanded was exaltation, was shuddering and quivers, was to be able to cry with Philamante: 'On n'en peut plus, on pâme, on se meurt de plaisir!' There was nothing to be heard but vague interjections, ecstatic outbursts. So much for the general scene. The details were no less gay. The diminutive Sainte-Beuve kept trotting round the massive Victor . . . The illustrious Alexandre Dumas—this was before the breach—waved his enormous arms in a frenzy of enthusiasm. I even remember that, when the reading was finished, he seized the poet and, lifting him off his feet with a herculean effort, shouted—'we will carry you to glory!' . . . As to Émile Deschamps, he applauded even before he had heard. Always one for the fair sex, he shot sly glances at all the ladies present. Refreshments were served. I can still see the immense Dumas stuffing himself with cakes, and roaring out, with his mouth full: 'Superb! superb!' This scene of comedy, falling so hilariously hard upon the heels of the lugubrious drama, did not end until two o'clock in the morning."[4]

On July 14th the play was accepted with rapturous applause by the Théâtre-Français. Three days later, Vigny read his *More de Venise* before an audience of the same men of letters with the addition of a great number of listeners from the world of fashion. "The air," said Turquety, "rang with the names of counts and barons." At the Hugos' the atmosphere had been romantic and domestic; at the Vignys' it was romantic and heraldic. *Vigny to Sainte-Beuve, July 14th, 1829:* "On Friday, the 17th, at half-past seven P.M. precisely, *Le More de Venise* will live and die before your eyes, my friend. If you would like the ghost of Joseph Delorme to be present at this funeral feast, a place for him, as once for Banquo, has been reserved . . ."[5] The welcome was no less tumultuous than that accorded to *Marion de Lorme*.

The censorship, at that time very powerful, authorized *Le More* but prohibited *Marion*. The prime minister of the day, the Vicomte de Martignac, approved the censor's ruling. He decided that the portrait of Louis XIII drawn by the poet constituted a threat to the monarchy. Victor Hugo, convinced that it was historically correct, appealed from the minister to the king, Charles X, and was at once granted an audience at Saint-Cloud. An account of this interview, at which the prince showed himself to be kindly disposed, and the poet frank and respectful, was printed in the *Revue de Paris* over the signature of the editor, Louis Véron. Actually, it was from the pen of Sainte-Beuve, and inspired by Victor Hugo. The latter stated that he had told the sovereign that times had changed since the *Mariage de Figaro*. Under an absolute monarchy, the opposition, reduced to silence, had tried to make itself heard through the medium of the theatre. Under a Constitutional régime, with the Charter, the press had become a safety-valve. The king, he said, had promised to read the "offending passage," which was in Act IV. This he did, and upheld the prohibition. But, since Hugo had always shown himself, as a writer, to be a well-wisher to the throne, an attempt was made to soothe his indignation with royal favours, and he was offered a further pension of two thousand francs. This Hugo refused in a very dignified letter:

Victor Hugo to the Comte de la Bourdonnaye, Minister of the Interior, August 14th, 1829: Monseigneur, it is my earnest desire that you should tell the King of my wish to be allowed to remain in the situation in which I find myself at the moment of receiving this new evidence of his signal graciousness. Come what may, I need not, I think, repeat my assurances that nothing hostile to the throne could ever be within my intentions. From Victor Hugo the King may expect nothing but continued proofs of fidelity, loyalty and devotion. . . .[6]

At once, with a power of concentrated work which was little short of miraculous, he started work on another play, *Hernani*. The hero's name (with the addition of an H) was that of a Spanish town through which he had passed in 1811. The theme recalls that of *Marion de Lorme*. The motto on the title-page is *Tres para una*, three men for one woman. The first, young, ardent and, as is only to be expected, proscribed, is Hernani (a replica of Didier); the second, a ruthless old man, is Don Ruy Gomez de Silva; the third is Charles V, emperor and king. The sources on which he drew are not known with any certainty; the *Romancero*, undoubtedly, was one, Corneille another, and a number of Spanish tragedies. Beyond doubt, the poet made use of his own *Lettres à la Fiancée* for much of the love interest. *Hernani* is the drama of his relations with Adèle. The struggle of two young lovers with fate brought back to him memories of a peculiarly personal nature. The intimacy of Uncle Asseline, a middle-class version of the imperial despot, with a pretty niece who had been the object of certain liberties had several times given rise to bursts of Hugoesque jealousy. The offer to submit to death after a single night of love was one which the young Hugo had actually made. The setting chosen for the drama allowed Hugo to give expression to his pro-Spanish leanings. *Hernani* has often been compared with *Le Cid*—and quite rightly. The dramatic conventions of the two plays are different, but the same heroic climate broods over both. But in Hugo there are greater emphasis and an "excessive use of zoomorphic metaphors,"[7] lion, eagle, tiger, dove.

The play was written with incredible speed. It was begun on August 29th, finished on September 25th, read to his friends on the 30th, produced at the Théâtre-Français on October 5th, and greeted with enthusiastic applause. The censor's office gave its approval—not without a certain amount of resistance—and the word went round that, to make up for the affront offered to *Marion de Lorme*, it was to be given priority over *Le More de Venise*. Vigny was furious. Already within the *cénacle* there was talk of a breach, when a letter from Hugo, very Spanish-Hidalgo in tone, was published in *Le Globe*. "I can well understand that always, and irrespective of dates of acceptance, *Othello* should come before *Hernani*; but *Hernani* before *Othello*—that I will never countenance!"[8]

What had happened? The members of the Comédie-Française, cut to the quick by Vigny's arrogant attitude at rehearsal, had, unprompted and unasked, extended to Hugo this unexpectedly favourable treatment. Still, he knew that he was an object of envy to opponents who were merely biding their time. To Sainte-Beuve he wrote: "There is a terrible storm brewing over my head, and so swollen is the hatred of the gutter-press that no one, now, will pay the slightest attention to anything I say or do . . ."[9] Actually, in the "subterranean caverns of Grub Street," Janin and Latouche were busy putting an edge on weapons to be used indiscriminately against both *Othello* and *Hernani*. This solidarity of the newspapers was something that Vigny would not admit. Nevertheless, a critic of the stamp of Viennet included in one blanket condemnation "these two young lunatics whose preposterous theories are pointing the way to an utterly meaningless literature," and the irascible classicist quoted, as an example of this "happy-go-lucky and destructive attitude which will leave nothing standing," three lines from *Le More de Venise*:

Demain soir, ou mardi matin sur le midi,
Ou bien mardi, dans la soirée, ou mercredi
Matin, fixe avec moi le moment, je te prie . . .[10]

Othello reached the stage first, but it was round *Hernani* that the great battle was to rage.

16

And Lead Us Not . . .

My being thrust itself upon the brambles of
desire. . . .

SAINTE-BEUVE

DURING the whole of that year, 1829, Hugo was hard at work,
from morning till night, and sometimes from night till morning, either writing, or rushing round unavoidably to theatre managers
and newspaper editors, or exploring old Paris in the neighbourhood
of Notre-Dame, or composing poetry as he walked in the Luxembourg
Gardens. Sainte-Beuve had formed the pleasing habit of dropping in
on the house in the rue Notre-Dame-des-Champs every afternoon and,
occasionally, twice a day. It was alone now that he found Madame
Hugo, by the rustic bridge in the garden, with the children playing
near her on the grass. In the friendship of the two writers Adèle had,
at first, played only a secondary role. The birth of François-Victor,
and then the months during which she was feeding him, had plunged
her into that condition of physical torpor to which many women at
such times are subject. For a long while Sainte-Beuve had been in a
"state of considerable indecision about her," due to his "wire-drawn
attitude of respect" where she was concerned. Alone with her, he found
that, freed from the presence of her illustrious husband, she was
inclined to slip easily into confidences. Sainte-Beuve, who loved to
spend his time perched on the edge of other people's nests, had a
natural taste for playing the confessor. "He was born to be a priest,"
said Pavie, "and I remember his saying to us one day: In an earlier
age I should have been in Holy Orders. I should have loved to be a
cardinal."[1] But this abbé with the warped mind was for ever hesitating
between La Trappe and Thelema. No one has, better than himself,
analysed this aspect of his general attitude:

I had a natural taste for intimacies and privacies, for the thousand and
one little details of domestic interiors. I found it always emotionally satisfying to explore a new relationship. From the first moment I was conscious
of an inner thrill. In a trice, assuming that the atmosphere was favourable,
I made myself master of the main features, and could then construct within

them every detail of the relationships involved. But, instead of controlling this natural aptitude, keeping it on a straight course, and holding the ship to its compass-bearing, I let myself wander off in search of incompatible goals, to sharpen my perceptions on futilities and glooms, and so would spend a great portion of my days and nights in slinking round garden walls, like a thief, playing the Peeping-Tom.[2]

Sometimes he would find Adèle in tears. Why? Because all women cry; because it is pleasant to arouse sympathy; because being married to a man of genius did, sometimes, hang like a weight upon her; because this illustrious husband of hers was a potent and insatiable lover; because she had already had four children, and dreaded the possibility of having more; because, in a confused sort of way, she felt crushed. Sainte-Beuve was careful never to utter an imprudent word. He sang the praises of Victor, but hinted that he was one with his fair companion in a "shared unhappiness," and allowed himself to be gently "led back by her to the Lord."

At a later date he wrote to Hortense Allart: "I have done a bit of Christian mythology-making in my time, but it all evaporated. It provided me, after the fashion of Leda's swan, with a means of approaching the fair, and developing a more tender love. . . ."[3]

In 1829 he was far removed from such a degree of cynicism. Still attached by a few threads to the faith of his childhood, he enjoyed letting himself be "reconverted" by this woman whose beauty he found disturbing. They talked together of God and immortality. Sainte-Beuve quoted Saint Augustine and Joseph Delorme: "Gladly I would, oh Lord: I want to, why can I not?" Adèle Hugo was proud at being taken seriously by a man whom the members of the *cénacle* regarded as highly intelligent. She had her merits, could draw with no little skill, was not at all bad with her pen, and the life she led in the company of a super-egotist had led to her being at times unfairly humiliated. Sainte-Beuve laid balm to her wounded pride. Now and again, mother of a family though she was, she gave hints of coquetry, though barely conscious that she was doing so. When winter made sitting in the garden no longer possible, she received her friend in her own room. "She was indifferent to outward things" and seemed unmindful of her morning négligé. Sometimes, too, of an evening, when Hugo was absent elsewhere, the two "waifs" sat until very late before the dying fire: "Oh! those moments were the loveliest of my life at that time, and the best . . . That memory, at least, brings no blush to my cheek."[4]

When he was away travelling, Sainte-Beuve used to write to Victor, savouring the pleasure, so familiar to lovers, of sending, through him, messages to Madame. "All this is for you, my dear Victor, and for

Madame Victor, too, who cannot be separated from you in my heart.
Tell her how much I miss her, and that I will write to her from
Besançon. . . ."[5]

Sainte-Beuve to Adèle Hugo, October 16th, 1829: In very truth, Madame,
was it not a mad idea, this of mine, to leave for no good purpose your
hospitable fireside, Victor's fruitful and encouraging talk, and my two daily
visits, one of which was for you? I am unceasingly restless because I have an
emptiness within, because I have no object in life, because I lack perseverance, and work to do. My life is a prey to every wind that blows, and I
seek outside myself, like a child, what can come only from within. There
is but one fixed and solid point to which, in my moods of desperate boredom,
and my never-ending shiftlessness, I cling—and that is you, Victor, your
family and your home. . . .[6]

She took it upon herself to answer, because Victor was suffering
from eye-strain. With his help, therefore, she composed a letter. It
never occurred to him to be jealous. Sainte-Beuve was *his* friend, and
the least fascinating of men. Sainte-Beuve himself, and Adèle, believed that their friendship was perfectly pure, but the Devil cannot
have been very far distant on the day when Adèle so arranged matters
that her friend, arriving at three o'clock, found her doing her hair.
Such games are dangerous, even, and more especially, for an honest
woman. "The tide of emotion is at the flood, the agitation of the
heart is contagious; her every word and every gesture seem to take on
the nature of a favour. It is as though her hair, piled high upon her
head, were about to break free from its bonds at the least sigh, and
drown one to the eyes; a delicious fragrance exhales from all her
person as from a flower. . . ."[7]
On January 1st, 1830, Sainte-Beuve went to the rue Notre-Dame-
des-Champs with a present of toys for the children, and the intention
of reading to his friends the Preface to *Les Contemplations.* It was
addressed to Victor Hugo, and dedicated to friendship, which should
be the union of souls in God, for any other friendship than that is
trivial, deceitful and soon exhausted. More than one phrase, expressive
of these pure and pious sentiments, though inscribed to the husband,
was intended for the wife. Two of the poems, extremely intimate in
tone, and not without beauty, were dedicated to Madame Victor Hugo.
Hugo, completely trusting, saw no great harm in that and Sainte-
Beuve was sincere. "*Les Consolations* belonged to but one season of
my spiritual life, six months, divine but fugitive . . ."[8] True enough.
For the last half-year he had been in a world of lovely fiction, had
been living a novel which he had thought was innocent, and now
he melted into self-pity. "Why, when I was young, did I not have an
angel in my life?" If only, like his friend, he had had beside him

a white-skinned beauty, then he would never have been seen "aimless and thoughtless, setting out each day with hanging head" to prowl the streets, shamefully bearing the load of his abortive genius; would never have been seen, when night fell, going with Musset to haunts of vice, seeking in vain to forget his bitterness and melancholy in dissipation—which often came to nothing, for Sainte-Beuve was no great trencherman at the feast of sex.

That New Year's Day of 1830 marked, alas! the end of those divine but fugitive moments. In January Hugo was living through a period of storm. *Hernani* was in rehearsal at the Comédie-Française, and the rehearsals became one long succession of battles between author and interpreters. The actors knew, of course, that the play was awaited as a literary event. The young and handsome poet was, of course, in their eyes, infinitely attractive—"aflame with genius, glowing with glory." But they were frightened by the play's familiar language, by the violence of its passions, by so many deaths in full view of the audience. The all-powerful Mademoiselle Mars, never anything less than conscientious at rehearsal, let scarcely a day pass without inflicting some humiliation on the author. Hugo, cold, calm, polite, severe, was sharply observant of this exasperating goddess. His anger, though he kept it under control, was mounting. A day came when he had had all that he could stand, and asked Mademoiselle Mars to surrender the part of Doña Sol. "Madame," he said, "you are an extremely talented woman, but there is something you do not seem to realize, of which, therefore, I must inform you—I, too, am an extremely talented man. I should like that to be quite clearly understood. In future you will treat me as I deserve to be treated." There was something military, something authoritative, about this young man. Mademoiselle Mars bowed to the gale.

Victor Hugo, absorbed in the business of rehearsal, now scarcely lived at home at all. To his friends he wrote: "You know how involved I am, how crushed, burdened, stifled. The Comédie-Française, *Hernani* rehearsals, back-stage jealousies of actors and actresses, newspaper squabbles, and continual police intervention. And, as though that were not enough, the confusion of my private affairs: my father's estate still not wound up; our Sologne sandpits still unsold after twenty months; the houses at Blois which our stepmother is contesting; nothing, or next to nothing left from the remnants of a great fortune but law-suits and vexations. That is my life. How can you expect me to be at the disposal of my friends, when I am not even at my own?"[9]

He, who had prided himself on being a model husband and father, no longer belonged to his family. At all costs, *Hernani* must be a success, for litigation and claims had eaten up what little money had been put by. Adèle, without a penny, flung herself wholeheartedly into the crusade at her husband's side. The set-back of *Amy Robsart* had proved to them what power was wielded by the factions, and Hugo had made up his mind that on the first night the Comédie-Française should be occupied by his own troops. There was no lack of man-power. Not a student from the art-schools but was on fire with a desire to fight for the greatest poet in France against the classical fogies. "What simpler than to set youth against decrepitude, waving locks against bald-pates, enthusiasm against stick-in-the-mud, the future against the past?" Gérard de Nerval, charged with the duty of enlisting the legions, had his pockets stuffed with little squares of red paper, bearing a word of mystery: *Hierro.* This was the warcry of the Almo-gavares: *Hierro despierta te!* (Steel flash forth!)

Now, when Sainte-Beuve arrived at three o'clock on his daily visit, he found Madame Hugo, surrounded by hirsute young men, busy studying a plan of the auditorium. Women have a liking for heroes, and this particular woman was deeply concerned about the issue of a battle on which depended her husband's reputation and the family fortunes. Adèle was no more than twenty-five. She seemed to have been suddenly shaken out of her habitual state of dreaming and brooding by these youthful fanatics. Naturally, the Young Guard welcomed the "faithful Achates," the Master's lieutenant. "Is that you, Sainte-Beuve?" Adèle would say: "Good-day to you. Sit down. As you can see, we're in the thick of things . . ."[10] He was exasperated at being no longer able to see her alone, jealous of the handsome young men, and vaguely irritated against Hugo, who was counting on him with complete confidence to praise in the public press a drama full of bombast which Sainte-Beuve, in his heart of hearts, detested. He felt that he would have been incapable of the torrential passion of *Hernani*—a piece of self-knowledge which humiliated him—and that he would not have wanted to be capable of it, which set him against the whole enterprise: whence his melancholy and dejection at seeing his nest-by-adoption "so full of din and filth. What?—no more to be alone with those one loves so well? That is indeed sad, very, very sad!"[11]

A sense of irritation which can no longer evaporate in confidences increases pressure to bursting-point. A few days before the first performance, he sent to Hugo a letter of quite incredible harshness, to excuse himself for not writing an article on the subject of *Hernani*:

Truth to tell, seeing, as I have been doing for some time now, what is happening—your life turned to a thing for all to prey upon, your leisure lost, hatreds redoubling about your head, old and noble friendships vanishing, to be replaced by fools and lunatics; seeing your face grow lined and shadowed as a result of things other than the working of great thoughts within you—I can only grieve, regret the past, wave a hand to you in greeting, and find some spot in which to hide. The Consul Bonaparte was, to me, a far more sympathetic figure than the Emperor Napoleon.

It is quite impossible for me now to give my mind for five minutes to *Hernani* without all these gloomy thoughts crowding in upon me; without being forced to think of all this business of eternal fighting and bargaining in which you have become involved, of your integrity as a poet compromised, of the tactical considerations which must now determine everything you say or do, of the squalid creatures you have got to see, with whom you must be for ever shaking hands. I am not saying all this in the hope of making you alter your course, because temperaments such as yours are unyielding, must indeed be so, since they bear in themselves the mark of their vocation. What I say, I say for myself alone, and in order to explain to you my silence, which I would not have you misunderstand, and my uselessness. . . .

Tear this up, forget what I have written. I do not want this letter to be a care the more added to the only too obvious cares which now beset you. But I felt I had to write, since it is no longer possible to talk to you in any sort of privacy, and your home is like a battlefield. Your sad but ever faithful

SAINTE-BEUVE

And what of Madame? What of her whose *name* should never sound upon your lyre save when one can hear your songs devoutly kneeling; she, even she, made a show, all day long, to sacrilegious eyes, handing out tickets to more than eighty young fellows of whom but yesterday she had barely heard; this chaste and charming intimacy, true prize of friendship, for ever ravished by the mob; the word *devotion* become a prostituted thing, only the *useful* now valued above all else, practical schemings and considerations determining all! ! ! ![12]

The postscript is written lengthways in the margin. The very handwriting is expressive of a mad fury. This insane explosion on the subject of "Madame" resembled, more than anything, the outburst of a jealous lover, and it seems surprising that Victor Hugo put up with it. He could scarcely any longer doubt the nature of Sainte-Beuve's feelings; but he was in the thick of the fight, and a quarrel with his own group would have weakened his position. The two men continued to work side by side. Sainte-Beuve, in the name of his friend, "who is snowed under with urgent business," sent pit-seats to admirers. On the opening night (February 25th, 1830) he went with Hugo, eight hours before the rise of the curtain, to watch the faithful crowding into the auditorium before the lamps had even been lit. Young Théophile Gautier, who was in command of a whole platoon of red tickets, was wearing his famous rose-pink doublet, trousers of a very pale sea-green and a dress-coat with facings of black velvet. The great thing was to give the bourgeois goose-flesh! The boxes took note, with feelings of horror, of the extraordinary hair-cuts sported by the modern school, while the art-students, staring hard at the array of "classical" heads exhibited in the circle, shouted "Off with the bald-pates!" These writers, painters and sculptors who formed the "Ironsides" of Hugo's army were by no means a casual collection of "gutter-snipes." Crammed into every corner where a heckler might be hiding, they were out to champion the freedom of art. Their zeal was the outward and audible sign of their vigour. It was a fine, exuberant and stormy moment in social history, with royalists and liberals, romantics and classicists, facing one another in the theatre as a preliminary to fighting on the barricades.

At last came the "three thumps," and the curtain rose. From the very first words, battle was joined. "L'escalier-Dérobé," and "Quelle heure est-il—Minuit bientôt," everything shocked one side, intoxicated the other. But for the terror inspired by Hugo's troops the murmurs of the disgruntled might have turned into ear-splitting protests. Two armies, each with eyes fixed on the other. *"Oui, de ta suite ô roi! de ta suite j'ens suis"* became, for the "immense tribe of the beardless, a pretext for intolerable cries and hisses." But the Hernanian knights permitted no movement, no gesture, no sound save those of admiration and enthusiasm. Outside, on the Place du Théâtre-Français, during one of the intervals, Mame, the publisher, offered Hugo five thousand francs for the book-rights.[13] "You don't know what you are buying! The success may be less than you think." "But it may be greater! At the end of the second act I had it in mind to offer you two thousand; at the end of the third, four; I'm now prepared to pay five thousand . . . After the fifth, I might be shy of offering you ten!"[14] Hugo hesitated. Mame held out five one-thousand-franc notes. At that precise moment fifty francs were all that remained in the rue Notre-Dame-des-Champs house. Hugo took the notes.

When the final ovation broke out, "every face in the audience was turned towards the ravishing young woman whose pallor showed the effects of the morning's labours and the evening's emotion. The author's triumph was reflected in the dearest half of himself."[15]

When the play was over, the members of the staff of *Le Globe* met at the paper's printing-house. Sainte-Beuve was present, together with Charles Magnin, who was to write the notice. "There was argument, there were expressions of admiration, there were reservations. In the very joy of triumph mixed feelings were voiced, and a considerable amount of astonishment. To precisely what extent would *Le Globe* commit itself? Would it go all out in blazoning the success of a work in which, after all, it found only one-half of its theories expressed? There was a moment of hesitation. I was not feeling altogether easy in my mind when, from across the room, one of the most intelligent of the staff (he afterwards became a minister of finance, and was no other than Monsieur Duchâtel) shouted, "Come on, Magnin, *plump* for it!"[16] *Le Globe* duly published a bulletin of victory. *Le National,* on the other hand, was hostile and complained of the conduct of the author's friends, saying that they had shown "neither restraint nor common decency." The faithful, on duty, must be warned not to express their applause by slapping their neighbours' faces. The later performances were organized by Hugo with the same meticulous care. Opposition was vocal always at the same passages. Émile Deschamps advised that the line: "Vieillard stupide, il l'aime!" should be cut. Joanny (who had created the part of Ruy Gomez) wrote in his *Journal:* "Bare-faced log-rolling . . . Women of high birth taking part in it . . . House always crowded, and always the same uproar, which does no good to anybody except the Box-Office . . . *March 5th, 1830:* House Full, and interruptions noisier than ever; there is something contradictory in all this. If the play is so bad, why do they come? If they are so eager to come, why the interruptions?"[17] *Journal* of Viennet the Academician: "A tissue of improbabilities, nonsense, and absurdities . . . Of such a conglomeration is the play which a literary clique has the effrontery to substitute for *Athalie* and *Mérope* . . . under the mysterious patronage of a certain Baron Taylor who was formerly introduced into this beargarden by the minister Corbière, with instructions to destroy the French theatre. . . ."[18]

The receipts exceeded all expectations. *Hernani* got the young couple afloat again. Thousand-franc banknotes, hitherto a rarity in their home, now piled up in Adèle's drawer. Victor, at sea on a high tide of triumph, grew accustomed to adoration. "He flies into a tantrum whenever a bad article appears," said Turquety. "He looks upon himself as a man in a great official position. You'd scarcely believe it, but just because *La Quotidienne* published a few unfavourable comments, he threatened to thrash the critic to within an inch of his life. Sainte-Beuve went about cursing and swearing and brandishing a monkey-wrench. . . ."

Sainte-Beuve to Adolphe de Saint-Valry, March 8th, 1830: My dear Saint-Valry—*Hernani* had its seventh performance this evening, and a little light is beginning to show in all this murky business—which wasn't always the case. The three first performances, supported by friends and by the *romantic* section of the audience, went off very well; the fourth was stormy, though victory lay with the tough lads; the fifth, so-so—the gangs pretty well in hand, the general public indifferent, inclined to mock, but in the long run responsive. The receipts are excellent and, with a little more help from our friends, the Cape of Good Hope is well in the way to being rounded. Well, that is how matters stand; and at the very heart of everything Victor, calm, with an eye to the future, trying to find a quiet spot in all this hurly-burly so as to sit down and write another play, a true Caesar or Napoleon, *nil actum reputans,* etc. The play appears in print tomorrow. He has made a good deal with the publisher: fifteen thousand francs; three printings, each of two thousand copies. We are all completely knocked-up, because there are scarcely enough troops for each successive battle, and we must be always on the offensive—as in the campaign of 1814. . . .[19]

The voice was the voice of the loyal lieutenant, but, in his heart of hearts, Sainte-Beuve was fuming. He had just learned that the Hugos were going to move, in May, to the only house so far built in the new rue Jean-Goujon. Their landlord in the rue Notre-Dame-des-Champs, frightened by the hirsute and disreputable art-students of *Hernani* fame, had given them notice; but the Comte de Mortemart had leased them the second floor of the house he had just put up. Their brand-new fortune permitted them to live now in the Champs-Élysées Quarter. Adèle was expecting her fifth child, and Hugo was by no means averse to putting a little distance between their home and Sainte-Beuve. There would be an end at last to the daily senti-mental visits. In any case, it was an open question whether they could have been continued. The mixture of hatred and admiration which "Joseph Delorme" felt for Hugo was making the atmosphere difficult to breathe. He knew now that what he felt for Adèle was not just loving-kindness, but a less muted passion. There are some who think that he spoke about his scruples to Victor Hugo, who at once warned his wife; others who believe that this scene of confession took place at a later date. That it did take place seems certain. Sainte-Beuve used it in *Volupté.* The poems that Hugo was writing from May 1830 onwards make it clear that he had serious cause for bitterness. All the same, to Sainte-Beuve, who was staying with his friend, Guttinguer, at Rouen, he wrote still in the old language of affection: "I wish you knew how much you have been missed recently, what an emptiness, what a sense of sadness, has oppressed us, even in our close domestic circle, even with our children around us, here, in this deserted city of François I, without you; how, at every moment, we have felt the need of your advice, your company in the evenings, your conversation, and, at every moment of the day, your friendship! All that is over now, but our hearts have caught the habit. Never again, I hope, will you be so unkind as to leave us, to desert us, like this . . ."[20] But in this very same month of May he was writing poems of disenchantment very different from the triumphant *Orientales.* Reading over again his *Lettres à la Fiancée,* he thought sadly of the days when "l'espérance en chantant le berçait de mensonges."

Adèle cried a great deal, and the sight of her tears made her husband miserable.

Sainte-Beuve was in Rouen with the romantic Ulric Guttinguer, among the hortensias and the rhododendrons. In a moment of indiscreet pride, he made him privy to the love he felt for Adèle. The confessor was in turn confessed, and Guttinguer, who in the circle of the Romantics had a reputation for being a great expert in matters of love, encouraged these guilty thoughts, friend though he claimed to be of the Hugos. This visit was unhealthy for Sainte-Beuve; Don-Juanism is contagious. Back in Paris, he saw the Hugos again, but not without a certain sense of embarrassment. *Sainte-Beuve to Victor Hugo, May 31st, 1830:* "I feel I must write to you, because yesterday we were so sad, so cold, we parted on so wrong a note, that the whole incident has left me with a pain in my heart. All the way home I suffered from the memory, and again at night. I told myself that it would be impossible for me to see you often if the price I had to pay was to be so high, since I cannot see you all the time. What is there left for us to talk about, to tell one another? Nothing, since not now, as formerly, can we have all in common . . . But you must believe that if I do not come to see you, I feel as warm an affection for you, and for Madame, as ever I did. . . ."[21]

Sainte-Beuve to Victor Hugo, July 5th, 1830: Oh! do not think of me with blame, my dear, my great, great friend: do you, at least, keep of me a memory single-hearted and entire, as lively as it ever was, imperishable, that I may count upon it in my bitterness. I have horrible and evil thoughts: hatred, jealousies, misanthropy. I can no longer shed tears; I analyse everything in a mood of treachery and sourness. When one is in such a state as I am in now, it is better to hide, to try to achieve peace of mind, to let the gall drip away, to do one's best not to stir too much mud, to accuse oneself at the bar of one's own conscience, at the judgment-seat of a friend like you, as I am doing at this moment. Do not answer this, dear friend; do not ask me to come and see you; I could not do it. Tell Madame Hugo to give me her pity and her tears . . .[22]

Sincerity or strategy? A mixture of the two, no doubt. He had loved and admired Hugo too much, and saw him now too generous towards him, to have so soon forgotten the old affection. But it was also true that there were times when he hated him, and then he tried to find reasons for hating him still more, for no better reason than that he once had loved him. To compensate himself for lacking the powers that Hugo had, he called them, in the intimacy of his notebooks, "at once puerile and titanic." He reproached him for knowing, among the Greek orders, only the "cyclopean," and painted a picture of him in his mind as Polyphemus hurling at random his monstrous slabs of rock. He noted that, in *Le Dernier Jour d'un Condamné,* he had "preached compassion in a tone of arrogance." In short, he found him heavy, oppressive, a Goth back from Spain; Hugo was a young barbarian king. "At the time of *Les Consolations* I tried to civilize him, but with small success"—and concluded: "a fig for Cyclops!"[23] Then, in an attempt to establish a parallel between his rival and himself: "Hugo has grandeur but also coarseness: Sainte-Beuve has delicacy but also rashness."[24] He might have added—Hugo has genius; Sainte-Beuve, talent.

17

An Alternation of Odes

> After all, it is a fallen monarchy: and many
> others in their turn will fall.
>
> CHATEAUBRIAND

ON JULY 21st, 1830, Juste Olivier, a young Swiss who was mad about literature, and had been introduced by Vigny and Sainte-Beuve, entered the door of No. 9 rue Jean-Goujon, and rang the bell of the second floor. The servant said to him: "Will you be so good, sir, as to go into the master's study? . . ." There he saw medallions by David d'Angers, lithographs by Boulanger—wizards and phantoms, vampires and massacres. The window of the room gave on to gardens and trees with, in the distance, the dome of the Invalides. At length Victor Hugo appeared. Olivier explained that he was the young man who had been sent by Sainte-Beuve. Hugo at first seemed to know nothing whatever about him, and then said: "It had gone completely out of my head." They talked of Chillon, of Geneva, of old houses. A lady entered, tall, handsome, and far gone in pregnancy. With her were two children, one of whom, a girl, the poet called "my little kitten," a charming creature with a tanned, expressive face. This was Léopoldine, alias Didine, alias the Doll. It was the visitor's opinion that Hugo was not at all like his portraits. Black hair (in fact, the colour of his hair had become dark-brown) "rather damp looking," with a curious wave in it; high forehead, white and unlined though by no means immense; lively brown eyes; a gracious and natural expression. Coat and stock, both black; shirt and stockings, white.[1]

That evening, at the Vignys', Olivier spoke of his visit. He said he found Hugo looking slimmer than the pictures of him had led him to expect. "You don't say so," was Sainte-Beuve's acid comment; "actually he is putting on fat." Then the conversation turned to *Hernani*. The actors, left to their own devices, were introducing a number of changes. In Charles V's monologue, instead of "Ces deux moitiés de Dieu: la Pape et l'Empereur," Michelot was now saying: "Ces deux moitiés du monde: le peuple et l'Empereur"—which produced a false quantity. "In that way," was the rather simple-minded view of the public, "the play isn't so absurd," a comment which produced much laughter among the faithful. Sainte-Beuve described how Firmin got out of the difficulty presented by the line: "Oui, de ta suite, ô roi! de ta suite, j'en suis!" by saying, ". . . de ta suite," dancing about like a cat on hot bricks, striding across the stage, and then coming down to the footlights with a ". . . j'en suis" spoken in a conspiratorial whisper. Certain lines still provoked hisses, and Vacher, head of the Théâtre-Français *claque,* declared: "With six more men on the left, I could get even that one across!" In short, the talk on that evening was typically Parisian, in which those taking part, like playful young animals, sharpened their claws on masters and friends alike.

The young Swiss left the house with Sainte-Beuve, whom he found garrulous and acrimonious. "A poisonous age," said Sainte-Beuve, "the only way to forget it is to live withdrawn on a comfortable fortune, with plenty of distractions. One doesn't commit suicide, because suicide is an absurdity . . . But life! . . . the best thing to do, I think, would be to retire into the country, go to Mass and do one's Easter duty quietly and in peace." "Is Monsieur Hugo of that opinion?" "Oh, Victor is not a man to let himself be upset by that sort of thing! His talent assures him a continual flow of wonderfully fine, wonderfully pure, wonderfully delicate delights! Everything he does is so superb, so perfect! He is so enormously prolific. He lives happily in the bosom of his family. He is gay—perhaps too gay. Victor is a happy man . . ."[2] It is worth remarking that this "happy man" had just written on the subject of happiness, a poem full of resignation, gloom and disenchantment.[3] But Sainte-Beuve scarcely ever saw the Hugos now. His chair at their fireside remained empty and, before the month was out, the critic of *Le Globe* had taken himself off to Rouen.

On July 25th, 1830, Polignac's lunatic attempts to curb the liberties of the subject set Paris in a turmoil of indignation. "Yet another government," said Chateaubriand, "flinging itself from the towers of Notre-Dame." On the 27th, barricades went up in the streets. Gustave Planche, who had been on a visit to the Hugos, said he would take Didine to the Palais Royal for an ice. They started out in his gig, but met such crowds and so many soldiers that Planche felt nervous about the child and drove her home again. On the 28th, the temperature reached 90° in the shade. The Champs-Élysées, a dismal stretch of flat land, given over at ordinary times to market-gardening, were thick with troops. In this remote quarter of the city the inhabitants were completely isolated and without news. Bullets were whistling over the Hugos' garden. The night before, Adèle had given birth to a second plump and chubby replica of herself. The sound of artillery could be heard in the distance. On the 29th a tricolour flag was broken from the roof of the Tuileries. What should be done? A Republic?

Lafayette, who might have assumed the Presidency, was as frightened of responsibility as he was avid of popularity. He handed the republican flag to the Duke of Orleans. There was no longer a king of France, but, instead, a king of the French. Verbal subtleties often carry the day over principles.

Victor Hugo at once accepted the new régime. Since the banning of *Marion de Lorme* he had been out of favour at Court, but it was his opinion that France was not yet ripe for a republic. "What we need," he said, "is a republic in fact, but a monarchy in name."[4] He was opposed to violence. His mother had given him a description of the sordid side of all mob risings. "We don't want to call in the surgeons, but the doctors." Very soon he was shocked by the antics of the profiteers of the revolution, of those who sought jobs and of those who gave them. "It is sickening to see all these creatures sporting tricolour cockades." In spite of the odes he had written to the dethroned family, he had nothing to fear for himself. Had he not just accomplished a literary revolution with the help of the same young men who were acclaiming Chateaubriand at the barricades? "Revolutions, like wolves, don't eat one another." He bowed his head before the fallen monarch. "Oh, laissez-moi pleurer sur cette race morte, Que rapporta l'exil, et que l'exil remporte."[5] He accepted the July monarchy; it remained for the July monarchy to accept him. He put his ship about with perfect skill—with odes but not with palinodes. His *Ode to Young France* was, from a literary point of view, better than his earlier legitimist efforts—an indication of his sincerity. He wanted the poem to appear in the Liberal *Globe*. Sainte-Beuve, back from Normandy, acted as midwife to this conversion. Hugo went to see him at the paper's printing-house, to ask him to stand godfather to his daughter. Sainte-Beuve at first hesitated, but at last consented, after being assured that it was Adèle's wish. It was he who piloted the Ode through the still narrow fairway of triumphant liberalism. On the occasion of its appearance in the *Globe,* he wrote a generous "leader." "He has succeeded with perfect tact," he said of Victor Hugo, "in reconciling the glow of his patriotism with the decorum due to misfortune. He has remained a citizen of the new France without blushing for the memory of the old."[6] That was well said—and good tactics. Sainte-Beuve was pleased with himself. "I championed the poet in the name of the régime just beginning, in the name of the new France. I deroyalized him. . . ."[7]

As for Hugo, he felt perfectly at home in his new role which, as a matter of fact, he had begun to play with his *Ode à la Colonne*. "It is ill praise to give a man," he said, "that his politics have never changed for forty years . . . That is no more than to praise water for being stagnant, a tree for being dead."[8] To the *Journal* of the *Jeune Jacobite de 1819* succeeded that of the *Révolutionnaire de 1830*. "Charters must sometimes be raped if they are to bear children." Everything was going well for him. He was a National Guardsman in the 4th Battalion of the 1st Legion, and Secretary of the Disciplinary Council, which meant that he did not have to take his turn at guard duty. With his play running, and his adhesion to the new régime accepted, he could now at last get back to work on *Notre-Dame de Paris*.

It was of the first importance that he should get the book finished. Gosselin, who had published *Les Orientales*, had a contract in which the novel was promised for 1829. Now, it so happened that Gosselin had already got on the wrong side of Hugo for having suggested an alteration in *Le Dernier Jour d'un Condamné*, and, later still, had been very badly treated by Madame Hugo when, after the first perform- ance of *Hernani*, he had gone to the rue Notre-Dame-des-Champs in the hope of acquiring the book-rights in the play. On that occasion, Adèle, very much the "Spanish Infanta," and looking at Gosselin with a "hawk-like stare," had described, in tones of extreme hauteur, the inci- dent of Mame and his five thousand francs. Gosselin, not unnaturally annoyed, had specified a date for the delivery of *Notre-Dame de Paris* and had inserted a clause in the agreement according to which the author should be subject to a forfeit of one thousand francs for each week in excess of the date named. Realizing the position, Hugo had been about to set to work in earnest, when the July Revolution broke out. A further respite was granted by the publisher until February, 1831. But this time there could be no hope of any further reprieve. Victor Hugo "bought himself a bottle of ink and a thick, knitted shawl of grey wool in which he could wrap himself from head to heel, locked away his clothes so as to be safe from any temptation to leave the house, and walked into his novel as though it had been a prison."[9]

Since he now never left his work-table, Adèle found herself again very lonely. This constituted an irresistible temptation for Sainte- Beuve, who confessed as much. *To Victor Pavie, September 17th, 1830:* "Pray for me, dear friend, and think kindly of me, for I am a prey to terrible agonies of conscience. My poetry is in a state of frustration; my love is imprisoned in a dead-end, and the result of all this is that I am becoming embittered and obsessed. Once again I am feeling spiteful and ill-natured. . . ."[10] The great advantage in calling oneself vicious is that it permits one to be vicious. At the *Globe* there was an open quarrel. Dubois wanted to get rid of Pierre Leroux, whose Saint-Simonian divagations were getting on his nerves. Sainte-Beuve showed for Leroux, on this occasion, something of that surprising weakness which sceptics have a way of feeling for fanatics. Dubois boxed Sainte-Beuve's ears and a duel took place between the latter and his sometime master. The meeting was bloodless, but Madame Hugo gave signs of being excessively uneasy. Sainte-Beuve, who had seen Adèle again at the christening of the youngest Adèle, now, in order to make clear the state of his heart, employed the same methods as her fiancé had done in the days of the *Conservateur littéraire*. Finding himself under the necessity of writing an article on the correspondence between Diderot and Mademoiselle Volland, he included a number of very fine quotations which he deliberately aimed at the object of his affections:

Let us so act, my dear friend, that our lives may be free of subterfuge. The more I respect you, the dearer will you be to me. The more virtue I can show in my relations with you, the greater will be your love for me. In the midst of all these matters I sometimes let my thoughts wander to the places where you are, and so find distraction. With you I love, listen, look, caress and can enjoy that species of existence which I prize above all others. It is four years now that I first found you beautiful. Today you are even more beautiful. That is the magic of constancy, the rarest, the most difficult of a man's virtues. Oh! my dear friend, let us do nothing wrong, but love, that we may make each other better. Let us be as we have always been, the censors, one of the other. . . .[11]

This was an adroit combination of adoration and respect. Then, on November 4th, 1830, in another article written on the occasion of a reprint of *Joseph Delorme,* he once more, behind the façade of that poor devil, indulged in an orgy of self-pity. "He was awkward, shy, a miserable wretch, and proud. He revelled in his unhappiness, and told it over to himself without shame." Sainte-Beuve made himself the mouthpiece of the future glory of his friends: Hugo, Vigny. "As for poor Joseph, he would see nothing of all that; he lacked the strength to come through these many crises; he had grown too soft in the water of his own tears."[12] In short, the reader was given to understand that Delorme, like Chatterton, had taken his own life. This suicide by proxy badly shook Victor Hugo who, giving himself a day off from *Notre-Dame de Paris,* wrote an honest, tender-hearted letter to his friend:

Victor Hugo to Sainte-Beuve, November 4th, 1830: I have just read your article about yourself, and it brought tears to my eyes. For pity's sake, my friend, do not abandon yourself to such despair. Think of those who love you, of the one, in particular, who is writing this letter. You know what you are to him, the trust he reposed in you in days now past, the trust he will repose in you in days to come. You know that your poisoned happiness injects poison into his own, because he needs to know that you are happy. Do not grow discouraged. Do not despise what makes you great, your genius, your life, your virtue. Think only that you belong to us, and that there are two hearts here of which you are the dearest and continuing concern . . . Come and see us. . . .[13]

Sainte-Beuve went to thank Hugo. Victor talked to him like a brother, and begged him to renounce a love which was ruining two friendships. Victor Hugo, like George Sand, like all the romantics, respected the "rights of passion." No doubt he thought of Sainte-Beuve as Don Ruy Gomez thought of Hernani: "This then is hospitality's reward!" But it would have horrified him to give to another the part of the magnanimous hero, while himself playing that of the jealous husband. He suggested to Sainte-Beuve that he should leave Adèle to choose between them, and, quite honestly, thought this attitude sublime. The incident would have made a telling scene in one of his own dramas, but in spite of genuine greatness of heart, Hugo on this occasion acted clumsily. How could Sainte-Beuve, given his state of infatuation, have accepted such an offer? Adèle had four children by her husband. Sainte-Beuve could barely earn a living for himself. The impression he received was that the offer was more cruel than generous. Noble posturings may reduce an interlocutor to silence: they do not transform him. In the novel where he describes this scene, Sainte-Beuve makes Amaury say: "I had been made too uneasy by what had occurred, was too greatly moved by so great a tenderness in so strong a man, to reply at length. I should have been afraid, had I raised my eyes, of seeing a blush upon his stern, chaste cheek. I quickly shook his hand, murmuring that I would give way to him, and we changed the subject. . . ."[14]

Sainte-Beuve had promised that he would make an effort to forget, that he would return to the fold as the friend he had been in the past. But he had gone away humiliated, and on December 7th he wrote a heartrending letter:

Sainte-Beuve to Victor Hugo: My friend, I cannot go on. If you knew what my days and nights are like, to what contradictory passions I am a prey, you would feel pity for one who has been a cause of offence to you, might wish me dead, but would not blame me, would maintain about all that concerns me an eternal silence . . . There is despair in me, and rage. At moments I could gladly kill you, murder you—and for those horrible thoughts you must extend to me your forgiveness. But do you, whose mind teems with so many thoughts, just think for an instant how a man must feel in whom a friendship such as ours has left so vast an emptiness. Lost to one another for ever? Is that what inevitably comes to your mind? I can no longer visit you. Never again can I set foot across your threshold—that has become impossible. But the cause of that impossibility is, at least, no feeling of indifference. If I come to see you no more from this time on, the reason is that friendship such as ours has been cannot suffer diminution: either it lives, or one kills it. How could I sit beside your fire now that I have betrayed your trust, now that suspicion makes a third between us, now that you bend on me a watchful and uneasy eye, now that Madame Hugo can no longer meet my gaze without first taking note of yours? The only thing for me to do is to withdraw, and abstention has become to me something amounting to religious scruple. . . .[15]

Hugo replied to this next day with gentleness: "Let us treat one another with indulgence, my friend. I have my wound, and you have yours. The pain of the shock will pass. Time will heal all, and we must hope that a day will come when we shall find in all this only a reason the more for loving one another. My wife has read your letter. Come and see me often. Write to me regularly . . ."[16] But what he had said was "Come and see *me*," not "Come and see *us*," and Sainte-Beuve did not come.[17] Meanwhile, Hugo had told his wife about the tragic interview, the offer he had made to Sainte-Beuve, the challenge which had not been taken up. He showed her, too, the letters which had passed between them in December. That was not the action of an astute reader of the human heart. How should she not have been moved by the feverish tones of Sainte-Beuve's misery? How could she have kept herself from regretting the absence of a friend, a confidant, who had also, as she believed, been her convert? Can we wonder that she should have found it easier to forgive Sainte-Beuve for having rejected so manifestly absurd an offer than her husband for having even admitted the idea that he might lose her? But all this remained still hidden in the proud, bewildered little head.

On January 1st Sainte-Beuve sent some toys to the children, and received a note from Hugo: "You have shown great kindness to my little ones, and my wife and I feel that we must thank you. Come and take dinner with us the day after tomorrow, Tuesday. 1830 is over and done with. Your dear friend, Victor."[18] To this there was no answer.

Sainte-Beuve tried to deaden his pain by embracing a politico-religious system—Saint-Simonism. "My heart was sick," he wrote; "my heart was suffering, and a prey to passion. To find distraction I played at every game available to the intelligence."[19] Hugo went back to *Notre-Dame de Paris*, and Adèle, left to herself, relapsed into dreams.

18

Anankè

Notre-Dame is very old; but maybe she will
attend the funeral of that Paris which saw her
birth.

GÉRARD DE NERVAL

HUGO finished *Notre-Dame de Paris* at the beginning of January
1831. He had written the whole of this long novel in six months,
bringing it to conclusion at the very end of the time-limit set by
Gosselin. It had been, as a matter of fact, merely a question of the actual
writing and composition. The documentary material had been accumulated over a period of three years: histories, chronicles, charters, in-
ventories. Hugo had read widely. He had explored the Paris of Louis
XI, and examined what remained of its old houses. In particular, he
had made himself familiar with every nook and cranny of the cathedral
—its spiral staircases, its mysterious closets hollowed out of the stones,
its inscriptions, both ancient and modern. Everything about the book,
he hoped, would be historically correct: the scene-painting, the persons, the language. "But that is what matters least in it. Its sole
merit, if it has one, lies in the fact that it is a work of imagination,
whim and fancy."[1] In strict truth, if the erudition is real, the characters seem to be more than real, larger than life. The archdeacon
Claude Frollo is a monster; Quasimodo, one of those hideous, bulbous-
headed dwarfs with which Hugo's imagination teemed; Esmeralda, a
vision of grace rather than a woman.

Nevertheless, these characters have achieved a life of their own in
the minds of readers in all countries and of all races. They have
about them the primitive grandeur of epic myths, and that inner
truth bred of their author's private phantoms. There is something
of Victor Hugo, though but vaguely adumbrated, in Claude Frollo,
a man torn between desire and his vow of chastity; there is something of Pepita (and of Adèle as a young girl) in Esmeralda, with her
dark, gold-flecked, Andalusian skin, her great black eyes and slender
figure; there is the basic, Hugoesque theme of a tripartite rivalry in
the fight waged between the archdeacon, the hunchback bell-ringer

and Captain Phœbus de Châteaupers for the gipsy girl. *Tres para una*. Finally, there is, in Claude Frollo's acceptance of fatality, something of Hugo's own mental confusion in 1830. Not that there is any direct confession. The umbilical cord had been cut. But throughout the long period of its gestation the work had fed upon the life-blood of the author. The reader can feel, without ever coming to grips with, these secret correspondences. Powerful, though invisible, they give life to the novel.

But most of all, that life comes from the living reality of *things*. The book's true heroine is the "immense church of Notre-Dame which, with the black silhouette of its twin towers, of its stone flanks and monstrous rump, seen against the star-spangled sky, looked like some immense, two-headed sphinx squatting in the middle of the city . . ."[2] In his descriptions, as in his drawings, Hugo had the gift of focusing a brilliant beam upon his models, of setting against a light background a series of strange, black silhouettes. "He could see a whole period in terms of the play of light on roofs and ramparts, on rocks and plains and stretches of water, on swarming crowds and compact armies, revealing here a white veil, there a costume, and, still farther off, a stained-glass window . . ."[3] Capable, as he was, of loving or hating inanimate objects, he could give a quite extraordinary sense of life to a cathedral, a city, a gallows. This book of his had a marked influence on French architecture. Buildings dating from before the Renaissance, which, till then, had been looked upon as barbarous, now came to be revered as Bibles in stone. A Comité des monuments historiques was established. Hugo, himself influenced by Nodier, was the starting-point, in 1831, of a revolution in taste.

Notre-Dame de Paris is not a Catholic, or even a Christian, book. Many of its first readers were shocked by this story of a priest eaten up by desire, and sensually enslaved by a gipsy girl. Hugo was breaking free from his quite recent, and fragile, faith. At the beginning of the book he inscribed the one word *Anankè* . . . Fatality, not Providence . . . "Vulture fatality, is it you that holds the human race in thrall?" Tormented by hatreds, wounded by the deceptions of friendship, the author was ready to answer "Yes." It is a cruel Power that rules the world. Fatality, the drama of a fly entangled in a spider's web; fatality, the drama of Esmeralda, a pure and innocent young girl, caught in the tangle of ecclesiastical courts; and behind it all, the fundamental *Anankè*, the inner fatality of the human heart. Not Adèle, not Sainte-Beuve himself, poor flies struggling in vain in the web laid for them by Destiny, were strangers to this philosophy. Maybe he was echoing the murmur of the times in his yielding to an all-pervading anti-clericalism. "This will kill that . . . The printing-press

will kill the Church . . . All civilizations begin in theocracy and end
in democracy . . ."⁴ A contemporary view.

Lamennais, who read the novel, blamed it for being insufficiently
Catholic, but praised its picturesque imagination. Gautier lauded its
"granite" style, as indestructible as the great cathedrals. Lamartine
wrote: "It is a colossal work; a piece of antediluvian rock. It is the
Shakespeare of prose fiction, it is epic of the Middle Ages . . . But
it is immoral because it contains no sufficient indication of the workings of Providence. There is everything in this temple of yours except
a trace of religion . . ."⁵ Hugo expected that "in spite of everything"
Sainte-Beuve would write *the* really important article on *Notre-Dame
de Paris,* and felt that he had deserved, by reason of his behaviour
in December 1830, to see literary friendship, and even friendship pure
and simple, outliving domestic crises. He had tried to see Sainte-
Beuve's love for Adèle as a guilty passion, but pure and without hope,
after the manner of *Werther,* and after all Werther *had* respected
Charlotte's husband, Albert. In short, though three months had passed
in silence, he felt sure that he could set Sainte-Beuve's feet once more
upon the path of duty and admiration. In this he was wrong. During
that time of silence Sainte-Beuve had greatly changed. From the
celestial vapourings of *Les Consolations* he had returned to the sceptical
and bitter tone of *Joseph Delorme.* He talked quite shamelessly about
Adèle to his friends, and even to certain priests, such as the Abbé
Barbe and Lamennais. Guttinguer wrote to him: "I have been hearing
much about your love affair." In fact, it was the tittle-tattle of Paris.
When, in March, Sainte-Beuve received a letter from Hugo in which
the writer said that he had recommended him to François Buloz,
who was busy just then with "resuscitating" the *Revue des Deux
Mondes,* and also, that he had sent him a copy of *Notre-Dame de Paris,*
the critic thought it coarse-grained in the novelist to hint that a service
for which he had not asked should be paid for in advance by an
obliging notice. This was foolish of him. The service had been rendered to Buloz rather than to Sainte-Beuve, but this the latter failed
to understand. Once more he felt staggered by Hugo's "monstrous
egotism," and left the letter unanswered. Hugo, uneasy, returned to
the charge, and suggested that he should go round to see his friend,
that they might "talk at length, seriously and affectionately"—adverbs
calculated to exasperate so distrustful a nature—and received back,
on March 14th, 1831, a letter which, though not harsh in form, for it
was couched in indirect terms, was in essence extremely so. Affection?
Admiration? Yes, nothing was changed so far as those feelings were
concerned, wrote Sainte-Beuve, "but to say that my affection is the
same now as it once was, to say that my admiration has retained the
nature of a private, domestic and family cult, would be to lie, and if

I told you twenty times that that is the truth, you would still not believe it . . ."[6] How very unexpected! It was *he* now who was playing at being the aggrieved party!

However blameworthy I may have been towards you, and must have seemed to you to have been, I felt, my friend, that given the intimate nature of our friendship I had reason to complain of your lack of openness, of confidence, of frankness. It is not my intention to stir the mud of all this miserable unhappiness. But the wound remains. Your conduct would appear, in the eyes of the world, if it were made public, to have been beyond reproach. It was dignified, firm and noble. But I do not find it anything like so tender, so good, so rare, so *unique*, as it might have been, considering the nature of the friendship which once ruled our lives. . . .[7]

We are all of us apt to be amazed by what others think of us. Hugo was staggered. Not until five days had passed did he answer this letter, on March 18th, 1831:

I did not want to write to you while I was still suffering under the impact of your letter. It was too sad, and too bitter. I might, in my turn, have been unjust. I thought it better to wait for a few days. Now I am at least calmer, and can re-read your letter without tearing open again the deep wound which it left in me. But this I must say—I did not think that what had passed between us, *what is known only to us two, and to nobody else,* could ever have been forgotten . . . You should have recollected what occurred between us on that most painful occasion of my whole life, when I had to make a choice between her and you. Think back to what I said to you then, *to the offer I made, to the suggestion I put forward,* with the fixed determination to keep my promise, and *to act as you might wish me to do.* Think back to all that, and then reflect upon what you said in writing to me, that in the whole of this affair I had behaved to you with a lack of *openness, confidence* and *frankness!* Three months scarcely have gone by, and you can write like that! I forgive you for it now, but a day may come when you will not forgive yourself.[8]

In the margin of this letter, opposite the words *what is known only to us two,* Sainte-Beuve wrote (doubtless for the eyes of posterity): "FALSE! *he made use of it with Her, attributing to me things I never said.*" Opposite, "*think back to the offer I made,*" he commented furiously: "*He lied to me even while making it, and was being double-faced.*" On the envelope he scribbled: "*He was playing a double game. He expressed magnificent sentiments in words, but his actions gave them the lie. From then on, for years, there was concealed warfare between us.*"

Concealed warfare: two men fighting for Adèle, and she, as these marginal notes seem to prove, in part responsible. That she had

ceased at some time during the summer of 1831 to love her illustrious
husband cannot be denied. He himself, deeply suffering, confessed
as much to no less a person than his rival. Why this alienation of
feeling? No doubt, like his father, Hugo had made physical demands
far in excess of the normal. Adèle was longing for a rest and, knowing
nothing of sensuality herself, held aloof. Besides, a famous husband
is not necessarily an agreeable presence in the home. Indeed, the contrary is usually the case. As a mother gives all of herself to her child,
so does the poet give all of himself to his work. He becomes exigent,
overbearing, dictatorial. Adèle found in Victor a tyrannical master.
She had known how it would be in the days of their engagement.
She regretted the shy and humble confidant. It is certain that she had
secret meetings with Sainte-Beuve; that she saw him alone; that she
imprudently repeated to him things that her husband had said; and
even that the clandestine couple got into the habit, when "Cyclops"
was away, of criticizing him mercilessly.

It took several months for conjugal trust to turn into a treachery of
the heart and mind. In April, after that harsh exchange of letters, Adèle
brought pressure on the two men to be reconciled. The fact that their
quarrel had made her ill had an effect upon both of them. Sainte-Beuve
wrote to Hugo: "May I come and shake you by the hand?" Hugo replied: "You will, won't you, come one of these days and dine with *us*?"
We should remember that Sainte-Beuve had by this time read *Notre-
Dame de Paris;* that, in spite of dishing out a seasoning of praises, he did
not like the book well enough to write about it; that Hugo knew this,
and that, therefore, the invitation was wholly disinterested. This re-
sumption of a semi-friendship did not make for happiness. There was
an absence of trust on both sides. When his wife and his friend were
together, Hugo was constantly on the watch. When he was alone with
Adèle, he made scenes. At first she tried by sweetness of manner to
bring him to his senses. Then she lost patience. "Is it my fault that I
love you less when you torture me?"[9] She threw herself at his feet and,
later, wrote to him: "Forgive me." In order to reassure him, she begged
him to be always present when Sainte-Beuve came, which may have
been no more than a woman's guile, and most certainly had the effect
of increasing Victor's fears.

Towards the end of June Hugo had a gleam of hope. For one thing
Adèle and the children went to spend the summer near Paris, with the
Bertins, at the Château des Roches. This lovely house, set in a great
park close to the village of Bièvre, was built high above the valley, and
the view "was one to bring delight to the eyes." Louis-François Bertin,
known as Bertin the Elder, the founder of the *Journal des Débats*, of
whom Ingres has left a powerful portrait, had made of it his favourite
refuge. Many friends lived within easy reach: the Lenormants; the Dol-

fusses, who had established in the district their factory for the production of *toiles de Jouy*; and two sons, Édouard Bertin, the painter, and
Armand Bertin, a journalist. A daughter, Louise, who was musical,
played operas based on the novels of Walter Scott to the assembled
family. All these persons combined to make a hospitable and cultivated
little group. Hugo had got to know them in 1827. After the publication
in the *Débats* of an article on *Odes et Ballades* he had gone to express
his gratitude to Monsieur Bertin who, like Dubois, had been charmed
by the poet's Holy Family. An affectionate friendship had grown up
between the Hugos and the Bertins. Mademoiselle Louise in particular,
a woman without beauty, who was so plump as to come perilously near
to being stout, but who possessed a majestic serenity, "a person with
a man's brain and a woman's heart," the "good fairy of the happy
valley," became at one and the same time Victor Hugo's confidante,
and the second mother of his children.

At Les Roches, Victor Hugo laid aside his sceptre. He forgot that he
was the leader of a school, dropped his romantic mask, and became once
more just a simple man, a paterfamilias, a Parisian bourgeois, a man of
genuine feeling. Each year it was a real pleasure to see again, instead
of the dusty boulevards with their grey elms, the lawns and wooded
slopes. "I would give the rest of the world in exchange for Les Roches,
and all mankind for your family," he write to Mademoiselle Louise;
and again: "All the pines of the Black Forest count as nothing in comparison with the acacia which stands in the courtyard at Les Roches."
There, Dédé renewed acquaintance with her cows; there Toto and
Charlot played with the pasteboard carriages which their father made
for them, and there the serious Didine, known as Poupée, begged
Mademoiselle Louise to play the piano for her. *Victor Hugo to Louise
Bertin, May 14th, 1840:* "Could one bring back the years that are gone,
I would choose to be at the beginning of one of those enchanted sum-
mers when we spent such delicious evenings by your piano, with the
children playing all about us, and your good father providing warmth
and light for all of us."[10] When the time came to go back to Paris, all
the children wrote to Mademoiselle Louise, or begged Victor Hugo to
write for them, and scolded him when they found that no letter had
been sent: "Papa did not write as I told him to," added Didine in a
postscript.

In that year of 1831, so full of storms for him, the calming influence
of the Bertins worked wonders. The poet went for walks in the moonlight, "under the pensive willows weeping above the stream." All he
heard now was music and the voices of his children. Buried in nature,
he forgot the "fatal city." His wife, too, seemed to have been completely
won over by the charm of this country existence. News came that the
Belgians had offered Sainte-Beuve a professorial chair at Liége, and

that he had accepted. So the rival was going to make himself scarce! But, alas! early in July Hugo was so foolish as to write telling him that everything was going marvellously well, and that Adèle seemed once more to be very happy. At once Sainte-Beuve, now on his mettle, decided to refuse the Liége post. Then, regardless alike of pride and prudence—which shows how shrewdly the blow had struck home—Hugo put his fears into words:

Victor Hugo to Sainte-Beuve, July 6th, 1831: What I have to say to you, dear friend, causes me deep pain, but it must be said. Your going to Liége would have been a great relief to me, and that is why I have sometimes seemed to you to want something which at any other time would have made me genuinely unhappy—your removal from the scene. Since, however, you are not going, and I admit that there may be good reasons for your decision, I cannot, my friend, refrain from opening my heart to you, even though it may be for the last time! I can no longer endure a state of affairs which, so long as you remain in Paris, must continue indefinitely. For the time being, therefore, let us see no more of one another, so that one day, and may it be soon! we may meet again and be together for life . . . Send me a line. With that request I conclude this letter. Burn it, that nobody, not even you, may read it again. Good-bye: Your friend, your brother, Victor—I have shown this letter to the one person who ought to see it before you do.[11]

Sainte-Beuve's reply was honeyed and disingenuous. The roles of the two men were now reversed. In his secret heart he felt triumphant, and played the innocent to his friend. Why should Hugo feel hurt? And was he really hurt? He, Sainte-Beuve, had attributed his friend's increasing gloom to the difficulties of the times; his silence to the fact that they knew one another so thoroughly that all they had to say to one another had been said already. As to "the other person," he had never again seen her alone. "Furthermore, my friend, your letter, though it has stunned and saddened me, has in no way acted as an irritant. I feel a sharp regret, a secret sorrow at the thought that I have become a stone of stumbling in the way of a friendship such as yours, a deposit of gravel in your system, a blade broken off short in the wound. Only by resigning myself to the operations of Fate can I find absolution for having thus become the deadly instrument which is furrowing your great heart. Beware, my friend—and this I say without a trace of bitterness—beware, poet that you are, of filling reality too tightly with your fantasies, of letting your sun bring forth a weed-growth of suspicions, of lending your all-too-sensitive ear to what are really no more than the echoes of your own voice."[12]

To which, poor Hugo: "You are right in everything you say; your conduct has been loyal and perfect, you have not wounded, nor could wound, anybody . . . My poor, unhappy head is alone responsible, my friend! I love you better at this moment than I have ever done, and hate myself—without the least exaggeration I can say that I hate myself —for having let my sickness and my madness reach such a pitch. If a day ever comes when my life can be of service to you, it is yours for the asking, and I shall count the gift as but the most trivial of sacrifices. You see, the truth of the matter is—and this I say *for your ears alone*— that I am no longer happy. I realize now with absolute certainty that it is possible for one who had all my love to love me no longer; and that, perhaps, you had actually very little to do with the change in her attitude. It is all very well for me to repeat what you have said to me, that the mere thought that this change has indeed taken place is sheer madness, that there is enough of poison in it to infect my whole life. Pity me, yes, I say, pity me for I am truly miserable. I no longer know how I stand with the two beings whom I most love in this world. You are one of them. Pity me, love me, write to me . . ."[13] What delicious reading this must have made for Sainte-Beuve's vanity! The god, on his own confession, had forfeited the favour of his handmaiden. With the facile serenity of a man who has won his cause, Sainte-Beuve offered his advice:

Sainte-Beuve to Victor Hugo, July 8th, 1831: Allow me to say again: are you sure that, under the influence of that fatal imagination of yours, you are not injecting into your relations with one so frail, so dear to you, a degree of emotion so excessive that it frightens her, and, to your own hurt, shuts her heart to you, with the result that you, yourself, by the very fact of your suspicion, force her into a moral position which reflects back that suspicion, and makes it burn you with a fiercer fire? You are so strong, my friend, so emphatic, so much a stranger to our common measure, our scarcely perceptible shades of feeling, that, especially when you are in the grip of passion, you impart to, and see in, the objects on which you gaze, the colour only that you give to them, and make of them the embodiment of phantoms which are of your own creating. Try, my friend, to let that limpid stream run once more at your feet, and do not muddy it. Do that, and very soon you will see again, reflected in its surface, the image of your-self. I will not say: "Be merciful, be kind," for that, praise God, you are; but, instead, "Be kind in the ordinary way of men, and accommodating in small things." I have always thought that a woman married to a genius resembles Semele. The God's mercy consists in laying aside his burning rays, in modulating his fierce heat. Often, when he thinks he is doing no more than let his beams dance and play, he is wounding her he loves, and burning her to ashes. . . .[14]

Could sanctimoniousness go further? During all this while he was corresponding with Adèle, who received his letters, *poste restante*, in the name of "Madame Simon," sometimes through the good offices of Martine Hugo, a relation of poor Victor, whose hospitality she now repaid by betraying him. Sainte-Beuve wrote, for the captive loved one, poems in which the lyrical familiarity of address accentuated the intimate nature of their content. He considered these amorous elegies to be his best work. She replied with letters (delivered by Aunt Martine) in which she called him "My dear angel," "Dear treasure." Poor Adèle! The little Foucher girl, daughter of a neat, mousy civil servant, was formed by nature neither for romantic drama nor for the comedy of love. She was essentially domesticated, a perfect mother, affectionate. Her senses had remained wholly unawakened. What she would have liked would have been to keep husband and lover in a joint relationship of chastity. "Love him, then, too," said the friend with consenting magnanimity, and went on to reassure her: "The purity of our intentions is written on our faces . . ." Purity was relatively easy for a man accustomed to associate the carnal with the venal, who, when he left his heart's idol, made tracks for a drab. Nevertheless, there was desire in his feelings for Adèle, and his revenge on Hugo would be complete only when she gave herself to him.

19

Les Feuilles d'Automne

It is good that men should know what another
man has suffered.

GOETHE

I dislike hearing severe views being expressed on
the subject of women: they have so much to
suffer.

MADAME FOUCHER

IN ORDER to pacify Victor, and to distract his attention, Sainte-Beuve did his best, as of old, to serve him in the field of literature.
He got the *Revue des Deux Mondes* to publish, on August 1st, a highly
flattering biography of the poet. Hugo's time was now completely occupied with rehearsals of *Marion de Lorme* at the Porte-Saint-Martin.
The July monarchy had licensed the work which Charles X had, earlier,
forbidden. Marie Dorval was to play Marion. She was mad about the
part, but wanted Didier to pardon the girl at the end of the last act.
Hugo was all for an implacable Didier, but gave way. Somebody told
him that Sainte-Beuve had said: "Didier is another Hugo, more passionate than sensitive." Sainte-Beuve denied ever having made such a
remark, and offered to do what he could for *Marion*: "I should dearly
like to be of some use in this business, my friend . . ."[1] Meanwhile, he
went on writing elegies for Adèle. He conjured up for himself a picture
of the loved one in confinement, watched over by the "moody husband," dreaming of the "timid conqueror" who would never possess
"more of her than her heart." To Charles Magnin, one of his colleagues
on the *Globe*, he solemnly entrusted, in the event of his death, a large
sealed packet which no doubt contained their letters and his poems.

In September, he prevailed upon her to meet him, first in some convenient church where they could converse in low voices behind a pillar,
and later in her room. How had he managed to induce this religious-minded and scrupulous wife to be so imprudent? By working on her
jealousy. He had pretended—or perhaps he really had tried—to find
peace in another's arms, and she, suddenly overwhelmed by the fear of
losing him, had given . . . little enough in all conscience, but enough

to make him feel sure that he had conquered, for the first time in his life, a woman whom everybody else regarded as unapproachable, a woman who told him that she loved him.

> Plus qu'un premier enfant ou qu'un suprême adieu—
> Que l'époux dans sa gloire, et ta fille, et ton Dieu!
> Tu me redis, le front contre mon sein qui bout:
> "Ami, j'ai tout senti, mais toi, tu passes tout."

Strange declaration addressed to a man so unsuited for love, who himself confessed:

> Tu n'as jamais connu, dans nos oublis extrêmes,
> Caresse ni discours qui n'ait tout respecté;
> Je n'ai jamais tiré de l'amour dont tu m'aimes
> Ni vanité, ni volupté.[2]

Casuistry for the scrupulous mistress, because a "sein qui bout"—a seething breast—beneath a woman's eyes must feel some sort of "volupté," and, as to "vanité," that must be satisfied, since all Paris was chattering about his conquest. Sainte-Beuve told Fontaney that Victor Hugo was a wretch who had shut away his wife out of jealousy and had made her ill. To Lamennais, who wanted to take him to Rome, he said: "It is what I should like more than anything else in the world, but urgent and persistent reasons keep me here," and to the Abbé Barbe: "Passion, which I had but glimpsed and desired, I have now felt; it is something that will endure, it is fixed and certain, and has thrust into my life many necessities, bitterness mingled with sweetness, and the duty of sacrifice which will have its good effects, but costs human nature high. . . ."[3]

And what of Victor Hugo? Some rumour of what was going on must have reached him. He spoke to his friends of a journey he was planning to Italy, Sicily, Egypt and Spain. Would he have entertained the idea of leaving France, by himself, for a whole year, if he had not been very unhappy? He had staked the whole of his life on this one love. He had fought hard for three years to win the woman of his choice. For eight years he had lived in the illusory conviction that he was for her the object of a religious adoration. He had dreamed of creating an ideal home-life, at once romantic, sensual and pure. Buried in his work, absorbed in his battle, he had never so much as guessed the presence by his side of a disappointed heart. The awakening, when it came, was hideous. "Woe to him who loves and is not loved! Ah! that is a frightful thing! Look on this woman. She is a being endowed with charm. She is soft and white and artless. She is the joy and the love of your home. But she does not love you. Nor does she hate you. She just does not love you, that is all. Sound, if you have the courage, the depths of that despair. Look at her—she does not understand your looks. Speak to her —she does not hear. All your thoughts of love have settled upon her. She lets them fly away, as she has let them come, without pursuing them, without holding them fast. The rock in the midst of the Ocean is not more indifferent, more unmoved, or more immovable than her heart's insensibility. You love her, do you? Then, alas, you are lost. Never have I read anything more freezing, more terrible, than those words of the Bible: *Harmless as a dove . . .*"[4] It was enough to drive a man mad! But a poet can, by some mysterious act of sublimation, change his sorrow into song. In November 1831 *Les Feuilles d'Automne* appeared.

This collection went far beyond *Odes et Ballades* and *Les Orientales*. Sainte-Beuve had been an evil guest but a good master. The intimate poetry of Joseph Delorme, passing through the magician's crucible, had attained to a perfection of form without losing that "plaintive note which it is so difficult to define." As the author wrote in his Preface: "To the adolescent this poetry speaks of love; to the father, of the family; to the old man, of the past." For that reason it may claim immortality, "for there will always be children, mothers, young girls, old men, human beings, in short, who must love, rejoice and suffer . . . There is not here the poetry of noise and tumult; but verses telling of serenity and peace, verses such as all the world makes, or dreams, verses of family life, of the domestic hearth, of the deep life of privacy; verses of the secret places of the heart. They look upon the world with eyes of melancholy and resignation, with eyes which take in all that is, and especially all that has been. . . ."[5]

To feel as all men feel, and to express tactfully better than any other man could, was what Hugo wanted now. He succeeded in doing what he wanted. In *Les Feuilles d'Automne* are to be found some of the loveliest poems ever written on children, on charity, on the family. The fact that "Lorsque l'enfant paraît . . ." or "Donnez, riches; l'aumône est sœur de la prière" are poems stored in all French memories has taken from them the violence of their initial impact. But, like those statues of the saints which have been worn smooth by the lips of the faithful, they have become defaced only because they have been so deeply venerated. The tone of melancholy resignation which runs all through the book came as a surprise to the readers of 1831 and touched them profoundly. These pieces were, indeed, autumn leaves, leaves ready to fall—such, for instance, as the disenchanted lines in which the poet weeps over himself: "Voilà que ses beaux ans s'envolent tour à tour, Emportant l'un sa joie et l'autre son amour." What, not yet thirty, and already a prey to such dismal broodings?

Le soleil s'est couché ce soir dans les nuées.
Demain viendra l'orage, et le soir, et la nuit;
Puis l'aube, et ses clartés de vapeurs obstruées;
Puis les nuits, puis les jours, pas du temps qui s'enfuit![6]

The religious beliefs which once, for a few years, had sustained him grew weak as he looked upon the world around him. He meditates upon the mountain-top:

Et je me demandai pourquoi l'on est ici,
Quel peut être après tout le bout de tout ceci,
Que fait l'âme, lequel vaut mieux d'être ou de vivre,
Et pourquoi le Seigneur, qui seul lit à son livre,
Mêle éternellement, dans un fatal hymen,
Le chant de la nature au cri du genre humain.[7]

Only the thought of his daughter Léopoldine held him to his faith, of the solemn little girl with the wasted face, for whom he wrote his "Prière pour tous."

Leaves of autumn, and withered before their time. The process of living wears out the spirit. "By dint of walking, man wanders from his route— We all of us leave something round about— Upon the thorns and bushes— Lambs their fleeces new— And man his flimsy covering of virtue." No one has better expressed than Sainte-Beuve the thrilling beauty and painful scepticism of these poems. "To the green confidence of early youth, to the ardent faith and simple prayer of a stoic and a Christian soul, to the mystic idolizing of one veiled and only Being, to facile tears and vigorous words, controlled and firmly etched so that they resembled the sharp and forceful profile of an adolescent, have here succeeded a feeling for the bitter truth of nothingness; a farewell, barely to be expressed, to fleeting youth, to an enchanted loveliness which nothing can replace; fatherhood following on the heels of love; new, clamorous charms of childhood dancing before the entranced gaze, yet causing anxious lines to seam the brow, and fond anxieties to weight the father's heart; tears (but never now a prayer for himself, or almost never, for how should he dare pray whose faith is now so faint?); the dizziness of dreams, and, if he lose his hold, a bottomless abyss; a distance that grows dark the higher he climbs; a sort of deep depression in his resignation, which seems to yield the fight to Destiny; already a thick press of urgent words, as of an old man telling tales beside the fire; and, in the tone and in the rhythms, a thousand variations, a thousand flowers of speech, a thousand taut and virile phrases with which the practised hand still plays, though never is the deep, essential lamentation lessened."[8]

Of this monotonous and persistent lamentation Sainte-Beuve well knew the secret cause, and was surprised, perhaps envious, to see the poet accept anguish and doubt while all the time maintaining an attitude of high and darkly toned philosophy. "How strange a spiritual vitality does that imply!" he said; "there is nothing like it outside the wisdom of the Jewish King." That is truly observed. In this serenity, with nothing in it either of hope or of revolt, we find an echo of Ecclesiastes; but here the mainspring of resignation is poetic genius. As the celestial harmonies of a requiem release men's hearts from the imprisonment of grief by imposing purity and measure on the raw cries of suffering, so did Victor Hugo, now that he had lost his greatest love and his greatest friendship, dominate his bitterness by giving it a form of perfect simplicity. Nor is it less deserving of admiration that Sainte-Beuve, too, should have been capable of setting aside resentment, and of recognizing the high achievement of a work of art. After treading in these poems of sadness, not without a sense of melancholy, upon the husks of dead friendship and decaying love, it is well that we should see how much richer are these autumn colours than those of spring, and realize that art, like nature, can make immortal what dies and passes.

Hugo dedicated a copy of the poems to his "fond and faithful friend, Sainte-Beuve, in spite of a silence which has settled, like a sundering flood, between us."

PART V

The Love and Sadness of Olympio

20

Place Royale

Hatred is spilled upon me from a brimming
mouth.

VICTOR HUGO

1832: Victor was no more than thirty, but struggle and sadness had
left their marks upon him. His body and his face had grown
coarser. Gone was the angelic charm of his eighteenth year, gone the
air of triumph which he had shown as a young married man. There
was an imperious quality now about the authority which once had sat
so easily upon him. Frequently he had a brooding look, as of one who
is always gazing inwards. All the same, in his constantly recurring
moods of gaiety there was a pleasing sense of the jovial. Hugo once
wrote that he had four selves: "Olympio," the lyric poet; "Hermann,"
the lover; "Maglia," laughter; "Hierro," the combative spirit. There
can be no denying that he loved a fight, but he needed, when he fought,
to feel himself supported. True friends were becoming rare. Sainte-
Beuve was ever observant, ever watchful, and showed an absence of
goodwill. Lamartine had always held aloof, and was now on a journey
to the East which lasted from 1832 to 1834. The *cénacle* was conscious
of being outmoded, and its members had grown a little bitter in that
knowledge. Saint-Valry and Gaspard de Pons, who had once rallied
round Hugo in the days of his young poverty, complained that they
were being sacrificed upon the altar of new friendships. Alfred de
Vigny, whom Sainte-Beuve and Hugo had ironically nicknamed "the
gentleman," found it hard to endure the success of a man who once had
been "dear Victor." When the *Revue des Deux Mondes*, speaking of
Hugo, said: "Drama, novels, poetry, every form of literature, now
bring fresh laurels to this writer's brow," "dear Alfred" protested, and
demanded that the paper should publish a recantation. Sainte-Beuve
swore to Hugo that Vigny's name should never again figure in any
article written by him, an undertaking which he did not honour, and
should never have given.

If friends were withdrawing, enemies were becoming more and more
numerous. Gustave Planche, who had formerly shown himself in a

sympathetic light, now adopted a hostile attitude. Nisard and Janin went for Hugo tooth and nail. This is a matter for some surprise, because he was always a conscientious writer and a loyal colleague, ready to serve the cause of his fellow-authors. But his recent triumphs had gone far beyond what his rivals' vanity could stomach. Since the appearance of *Hernani, Notre-Dame de Paris,* and *Les Feuilles d'Automne,* Byron had died, and both Goethe and Walter Scott were near the end of their lives. Chateaubriand and Lamartine had relapsed into silence, and there could be little doubt that he was now the greatest living writer anywhere. This was not a pleasing thought. "All poetry at that time looked dull and faded by comparison with his." Whether in verse or in prose there was a "boldness" in his use of words, the "shapeliness of a cut diamond."[1] Before his appearance on the literary scene, language had gone flat. He had given it a new incisiveness, had, by his vivid manipulation of light and dark, brought to it a fresh beauty. The trouble was that he was rather too much aware of what he had done. His pride, his self-confidence, were over-obvious. It was as though he were conscious of a "divine mission." He looked upon himself as being a "living temple."

In the Preface to *Marion de Lorme,* he openly mocked at those who maintained that the age was incapable of producing genius. "Let them talk, young man! Had anybody said, at the end of the eighteenth century, that new Charlemagnes might yet appear, all the sceptics of that time would have shrugged their shoulders and laughed. Nevertheless, the nineteenth century, while still in its early years, produced an Empire and an Emperor. Why should a poet not now appear who would be to Shakespeare what Napoleon was to Charlemagne?"[2]

It is not hard to guess at the poet of whom he was thinking, and he had every right to think of him. But his contemporaries condemned such a vainglorious attitude. Young Antoine Fontaney, who had a great respect for Hugo, was surprised to hear him say that "if he had any doubt of his ability to take the foremost place, and to rank above all his rivals, he would give up writing, and become a lawyer tomorrow."[3] That is no more than his "my ambition is to be Chateaubriand or nothing," but when he wrote those words at the age of fifteen, it had been in the secret recesses of a private diary. Now he was crying it aloud in the market-place, where such statements are circulated and put on record. "He, whom I had taken for a friend, was a man eaten up with envy, who felt for me a hostility born of long-standing intimacy, which, consequently, is armed to the teeth . . ."[4] The case of Sainte-Beuve was curious. On the literary level he was still, officially, an ally, though not without reservations. On the level of human relationships, he was a traitor who pleaded passion as an excuse for his treachery. He was no longer on visiting terms with the Hugos, and confined himself to asking for news of "the dear family," as when, for instance, in the spring of 1832 little Charlot had, or was thought to have, the cholera. He was, however, still seeing Adèle secretly:

Sainte-Beuve to Madame Victor Hugo: My dearest Adèle, how sweet you were yesterday, and how beautiful! What eternal and delicious memories that half-hour in the corner of the chapel will leave in me! My dear, it is fourteen years since I was last in that place. Fourteen years ago I went there, with, as yesterday, strong and tender feelings in my heart. I was very pious in those days. The occasion to which I am referring dates back to the first years of my residence in Paris . . . Oh! my dear! How little lost for me is now that interval of fourteen years, since, after all that while, I could find myself again sitting on the same chair, almost at the same corner of the same pillar, still with a pious and a tender heart, and now so sweetly loved. . . .[5]

Was it this year, or only the next, that Sainte-Beuve took to receiving Adèle under his own roof? It is impossible to say. Though his official address was that of his mother, at first in the rue Notre-Dame-des-Champs, and later in the rue du Montparnasse, he was in fact living, in order to escape his National Guard duties, and also to enjoy greater freedom, in a down-at-heels hotel in the Cour du Commerce, the Hôtel de Rouen, where he had taken, under a false name, a room for which he paid twenty-three francs a month.

The Hugos spent the summer, as they had done that of the previous year, at the Château des Roches. Mademoiselle Louise Bertin played to them, and sang "Jamais dans ces beaux lieux," or "Phœbus, l'heure t'appelle." She composed an opera based on *Notre-Dame de Paris*, called *La Esmeralda*, for which she induced Hugo to write some dog-gerel verses. Didine, sweet-tempered, studious and vivacious, delighted her parents and their hosts. They all lived in a world of Elysian bright-ness. "No sound reached them from the city, no hint of human voices."[6] Such silence was pleasing to the poet who, at that time, was avoiding his fellows, "because of a love of solitude, and a naturally melancholy temperament." And Adèle? "My wife," he wrote, "walks two leagues every day, and is visibly putting on fat . . ."[7] A woman who covers five miles a day and feels well on it has sentimental reasons for the exercise. It is probable that these expeditions, which appeared to do her good, led Adèle to the small romanesque church of Bièvre, where she met Sainte-Beuve.

In an article on the "Intimate Novel" the latter wrote: "Every woman with the gift of loving is always susceptible to a second love when the first has flowered within her at an early age. Her first love, that which comes when she is eighteen, no matter how lively it may be, and surrounded with no matter what favourable circumstances, never lasts beyond the age of twenty-four, after which there comes an interval when the heart sleeps, and new passions are coming to maturity."[8] For Adèle, meanwhile, he continued to write flattering articles on Victor, and corresponded with him for the purpose of organizing a protest against the government, which had declared a state of siege, ending his letters with "affectionately yours." Hugo signed his "Your brother, Victor." Both knew perfectly well what they were doing, and took this small change of friendship at its face-value.

In October 1832 the Hugos moved once again. In July they had taken a lease of a large apartment at No. 6 Place Royale, on the second floor of the Hôtel de Guéménée, a magnificent house, built in about the year 1604, giving on to one of the finest squares in Paris:[9] greenery, red brick, and slated mansard roofs. The rent was high, fifteen hundred francs, but the rooms were of immense size, and when Hugo, always a passionate collector of bric-à-brac, had hung them with red damask, and filled them with Gothic and renaissance furniture, cracked plates and vases, Venetian chandeliers, and the pictures of his painters-in-ordinary, they had a royal look.

During the following summer the Hugos entertained their friends and their enemies (often the same persons). The brightly lit rooms, the open windows, in the embrasures of which young women in low-necked dresses laughed and chattered, offered a ravishing spectacle. The *salon* of the Place Royale outshone that of the Arsenal. Adèle, a proud and decorative beauty, received better than Madame Nodier, and made up with her flashing eyes for the poverty of her refreshments. Those who went there had to be "all soul, and leave their stomachs in the cloak-room."[10] But what matter? Hugo had nine persons to provide for. In food alone the family cost him five hundred francs a month. In addition, he made Eugène an allowance, and only by his pen could he accumulate the necessary money. Since Sainte-Beuve, poor though he was, took another room not far off in the Hôtel Saint-Paul, Adèle could go to see him on foot without tiring herself.

If the square and the rooms were of baronial splendour, the district was a working-class one. "We poor workers of the Faubourg Saint-Antoine," Hugo liked to say. Affectation, perhaps, but also prompted by genuine affection. Having himself known poverty, he could understand and pity those who suffered from it. Success had left him with an uneasy conscience. In 1828 he had published *Le Dernier Jour d'un Condamné*, and he followed this up, in 1832, with *Claude Gueux*. The theme of the two books was the same—an unjust penal system. Both contained the same attacks on a society made for the rich and powerful. The many outlaws he had come across in his childhood still haunted him. He dreamed of writing a long novel, *Les Misères*, which was to deal especially with a criminal hunted by the law, in whose case there should be mitigating circumstances. About this time, too, he was pondering, as a possible character, the type of the lofty prelate, and, for this purpose, began to make notes on Monsignor Miollis, Bishop of Dignes, who was a man of great saintliness. He wanted to become a sociological writer and a champion of the poor. The strange thing is that, at the same time, he was intent on making a fortune, and drove hard bargains with his publishers. But is it so strange, after all? He needed money in order to assure the future of his four children. It was poverty, in the old days, that had taught him to keep his accounts with scrupulous exactitude. Everything he did was meticulously ordered. Fontaney, who was once present while he was dressing, was exasperated by the way in which he shaved. "It is extraordinary to see the incredible amount of time he takes over stropping his razor, the way he leaves it standing for a quarter of an hour in a mug so as to get it properly warmed, then washing his face in rose-water, and finally emptying a whole jug of it over his head. . . ."[11]

Writing for the theatre seemed, at that time, the shortest way to amassing a fortune with the pen. A play which reached fifty perform- ances with nightly takings of two thousand francs "made" a box office total of a hundred thousand francs, say twelve thousand for the author, who could also count on a further five thousand for the book-rights (he had received fifteen thousand for the first three editions of *Her- nani*). *Notre-Dame de Paris* had brought him in no more than a quarter of this sum. On the other hand, Hugo knew that the theatre could— and should—exercise a moral and political influence. "The theatre is a tribune. The theatre is a pulpit." His favourite subject for drama was still the championing of a social outcast, of an exile, against his oppres- sors. A vague memory, this, perhaps, of a childhood which had been thickly sown with such dramas. Now, of all the outlawries, the most unjust is that which results from the circumstances of birth (the bastard), as in the case of Didier in *Marion de Lorme*, or of deformity (the dwarf Triboulet in *Le Roi s'amuse*).

The idea for this last had come to him at Blois. Triboulet, the court fool of François I, had been born not far from General Hugo's house. Victor had made the acquaintance of this personage in the pages of a *History of Blois* which he had found on his father's shelves. Of the actual incident he retained nothing, but constructed round the figure of François I a melodrama in which Triboulet, procurer for the royal profligate, found himself punished in his feelings as a father. The plot was a tissue of improbable coincidences, redeemed by a lively sense of dramatic effect and, occasionally, by a vein of robust comedy. A few fine tirades gave light and fire to the whole. Sainte-Beuve, who was present at the Comédie-Française when the play was read, made a num- ber of sub-acid notes: "I have certain personal opinions about this kind of play-writing, and on the degree of truth to human nature involved, but I have no doubt whatever about the impression likely to be made upon the public, or about the immense talent shown in the construction of this work, which glitters with fine lines . . ."[12] In the intimacy of his private journal he wrote: "Once upon a time Hugo gave birth to a phrase so turgid and high-flown that it turned into a balloon which carried him off. At first he was caught in his own bombast, duped by his own rhetoric: now he is sincere. . . ."[13]

The first performance of *Le Roi s'amuse* took place on November 22nd. Though all the "big mouths," all of Young France, all Théophile's boys and Deveria's, were on duty, there seemed to be no warmth in the audience. All the same, Saint-Vallier's tirade won a triumph for the first act, and the pit was already stamping and singing *"L'Académie est morte . . . Mironton ton ton mirontaine"* . . . But the scene at the close of the second act, in which the gentlemen of the bedchamber are helped by the fool to carry off his daughter Blanche in a half-naked condition, gave an opportunity to the boxes, already roused to fury by attacks on the Cossés, the Montmorencys, and other noble families, to raise a cry of immorality. *"Vos mères aux laquais se sont prostituées— Vous êtes tous bâtards!"* shouts Triboulet, which they liked not at all. So great was the uproar at the fall of the final curtain that the actor Ligier had the greatest difficulty in getting the author to take his call. Next day the minister, the Comte d'Agout, "in view of the fact that several passages constitute an outrage on public manners," banned all further performances. The real reason was that the Court could not bear to see the monarchy, even in the person of François I, held up to ridicule on the public stage.

Victor Hugo lodged an appeal, and was strongly backed by Eugène Renduel, the play's publisher. *Victor Hugo to Eugène Renduel:* "I think, my dear publisher, that it is important for you, for me, for the success of the printed text and the whole business, that there should be a big publicity campaign in the newspapers on the eve of publication. I enclose seven short paragraphs, and beg you to use your influence to see that they appear in the seven leading Opposition journals . . ."[14] Among other great gifts he had the ability to turn even a fall from favour into advantageous advertisement. Fontaney's *Journal:* "*Le Roi s'amuse* has been suspended by Government order. No better service could have been rendered to Victor! I went to see him. He is playing his part to perfection: 'They have filched twenty thousand francs from my pocket . . .' "[15]

The Commercial Court declared the case to be outside its competence. The plaintiff had, at the bar, made a violent indictment of the July Government, accusing it of whittling away, one after the other, all the rights of the citizen established by the Revolution. But was it not a fact that Napoleon had shown no more respect than his successors for public liberties? Yes, but he had not stolen them. "The lion," said Hugo, "had not the habits of the fox. In his day, it is true, our liberties were taken from us, but in return we were given a sublime spectacle ... Napoleon set up a censorship; the bills announcing our plays were torn from the public hoardings, but there was one unfailing answer to our grievances: 'Marengo! Jéna! Austerlitz!' . . ."[16]

It should, perhaps, be pointed out that the speaker was, at that time, in correspondence with Joseph Bonaparte, to whom he wrote that, should the Duc de Reichstadt guarantee the liberties of the citizen, he would have no more fervent supporter than Victor Hugo.

21

Princess Negroni

There was about Hugo something of the lay
evangelical which made him grow maudlin over
what Juliette told him of her past . . . He was
in some ways a precursor of Tolstoy.

PIERRE LIÈVRE

THE son of General Hugo had never been afraid to fight. The ban
imposed upon *Le Roi s'amuse*, far from bringing him to his knees,
filled him with a desire for immediate vengeance. He had another play
ready: *Le Souper de Ferrare*, three acts in prose, suggested by a reading
of Marchangy's *Gaule poétique*. There he had come across the story of
a number of great lords gleefully dining at the table of an enemy who
has sworn to have them done to death, and of the entrance, with the
final course, of a company of monks ordered to hear their confessions.
The idea of horror knocking at the door of the banqueting hall, of
prayers for the dying treading hard upon the heels of drinking-songs,
of contrasted black and white—all this struck a chord in him. More
than once in his life (when the police arrested Lahorie at dinner, when
Eugène was seized with madness at the wedding-feast) he had heard the
terrible tread of the Commander. He transposed Marchangy's anecdote,
and made Lucrezia Borgia his heroine. He would portray her with all
her vices, then rehabilitate her through mother-love, as he had already
redeemed Triboulet through his feelings as a father. He must have
found the theme a tempting one, and in fifteen days the play was finished. In point of fact, he said nothing new in it. *Marion de Lorme,
Le Roi s'amuse, Lucrèce Borgia* are three versions of the same subject:
vice redeemed by tremendous emotion. Hugo's dramas had nothing
like the quality of his lyric poetry; but the stage has its own peculiar
aesthetic standards. At this moment in French theatrical history, melodrama had won the day over tragedy, and it was natural that *Lucrèce
Borgia* should see the light on the very stage that had presented *La
Tour de Nesle*.

The theatre was the Porte-Saint-Martin, the director of which, Harel,
had as mistress Mademoiselle George, a famous actress who had de-

serted from the Comédie-Française. She glowed with a nimbus of Imperial favours (she had been Napoleon's mistress) and, though now approaching her fiftieth year, still longed for roles of passionate love, which she was well equipped to play, not only on the stage but in real life. Victor Hugo gave the first reading of his play at her house, and with her in view. A second reading, designed to enlist the interest of Frédérick Lemaître, took place in the greenroom of the Porte-Saint-Martin. A young and beautiful actress, Juliette Drouet, who had been only too glad to accept the minor role of the Princess Negroni, was present on this latter occasion. "There is no such thing as a minor role in a play by Monsieur Victor Hugo," she wrote to Harel. The poet's knowledge of her was confined to a glimpse he had caught at a ball in May 1832: "white-skinned and black-eyed, young, tall and dazzling," ablaze with jewels, one of the most radiant beauties of all Paris. He had not ventured to speak to her.

In the course of the reading, he more than once found her looking at him, and guessed that she was attracted and would put up no great show of resistance should he pay court to her. At that time his heart was sad and empty. Their feelings were mutual and immediate. He talked a lot about her, and inquired into the details of her life. This is what he discovered. Mademoiselle Juliette was twenty-six years old. She had been born at Fougères in 1806. Her father was a tailor, a certain Julien Gauvain, who had "gone underground" and fought with the Chouans in '93. Orphaned from babyhood, Julienne (known as Juliette) had been entrusted to an uncle, Second-Lieutenant René Drouet, at that time serving with the coastal artillery in Brittany. He was a decent fellow, and while she was in his charge she had led a wild and undisciplined existence of shifts and dangers. At the age of ten she had been sent to a boarding-school in Paris kept by the Benedictine Nuns of the Perpetual Adoration, among whom were two of Drouet's female relatives. There, Juliette had been a favourite of the good sisters, thoroughly spoiled, and extremely well brought up. There was grave danger that she might, in a rash moment, take the veil, and would have done, but for the intervention of the very wise Archbishop of Paris, Monsignor de Quélen, who, on the occasion of a visit to the convent, noticed the charming young creature, questioned her, decided that she was not at all suited to the life of the cloister, and gave her her freedom.

Her astonishing beauty, "that fatal gift of the gods," and her perfect figure brought her in 1825, when she was nineteen, by stages of which we know nothing, to the studio of the sculptor James Pradier. When Juliette first met him he was thirty-six. By birth he was a Huguenot from Geneva, but by temperament, and as a result of his way of life, had developed into a romantic rake, sombre-eyed, long-haired, with a weakness for challenging sartorial elegancies—doublet, tasselled top-boots, skin-tight trousers, and military cap. In his studio there was a deal of fencing and music. He was a kindly, well-meaning man, but sensual and inconstant. Juliette sat for him in the nude, adopted poses that were something more than daring, and between sittings bore him a child, Claire, whom, though he never acknowledged her, he never abandoned. In 1827 he became a member of the Institute, and since his ideal was to make a solid middle-class marriage, he encouraged Juliette to take up the theatre as a career, giving her, at the same time, much intelligent advice on the art of acting, and a deal of cynical comment on how to seduce men and keep them faithful to her. "My counsel to you is by no means influenced by passion, but is wholly disinterested. My affection for you will never grow less so long as you show yourself to be *worthy* of it . . ."[1] It is not quite clear how he meant that word to be understood.

Juliette had played a few small parts in Brussels, and later in Paris, and had been rewarded by a number of successes, due more to her beauty than her talents. As an actress she had neither training nor gifts, and obtained, as she wrote to Pradier, no more than "beggarly" engagements. She had shed a great many tears, and feared that she would get nowhere.[2] "Damme!" Pradier replied, "pull yourself together, get it firmly fixed in your head that you are tremendous, and you will be. Above all, get on the right side of your fellow-actresses, who are devils the world over. Never stop playing a part, even when you're not in the theatre." He signed himself "Your devoted friend, lover and father."[3]

Corrupted by the cynicism of the studios, she gave herself to many lovers, and her experiences with them by no means increased her respect for the masculine sex. They included an Italian fop of fifty-three, Bartolomeo Pinelli; an insolvent scenic designer, Charles Sechan; Alphonse Karr, a cocksure journalist, who spoke of marriage and borrowed money from her; and finally an enormously rich idler, Prince Anatole Demidoff, a handsome, violent creature, somewhat too much inclined to make use of his riding-crop, who in 1833 set her up in a luxurious apartment in the rue de l'Échiquier. In spite of living the life of a kept woman, Juliette retained a genuine freshness of feeling, a Breton dreaminess, a passionate love of her daughter, a soft and velvety look in her eyes, "which at times gave one a glimpse of her angelic nature," and a gay intelligence which was altogether charming. Much later, Victor wrote in Juliette's commonplace-book: "That day when your eyes met mine for the first time, a beam of light struck from your heart on mine, like the radiance of dawn striking upon a ruin." Truth to tell, each of them, without knowing it, had come upon a being in deep distress. Having lost Adèle, Hugo was feeling a need, not only for love, but for renewed self-confidence. Juliette had so far known only sensuality, but since the age of sixteen had longed to be the "passionate

companion of a decent man." When Alphonse Karr, a lover with depraved tastes, had wanted to have her trained in a brothel, "It seems to
me," she had replied, "that my spirit has desires no less than my body,
and a thousand times more ardent. The pleasure you give me is followed by weariness and a sense of shame. I, on the other hand, dream
of calm, unbroken happiness. Listen to me: I am far too proud to tell
lies. I will leave, will abandon, you, this earth, and even life itself,
if I find a man whose spirit can caress my spirit, as you love and caress
my body."[4]

During the rehearsals of *Lucrèce Borgia* she was lavish of advances
and coquetries. But Hugo remained on the defensive. Had he always
been a faithful husband? On that point we have no evidence. But his
attitude, the poetry in which he had vaunted the joys of fatherhood
and conjugal love, demanded that he should have been. He was terrified of actresses, of "back-stage intrigues," and he treated the women of
the theatre with "cautious respect." The uproar which had greeted
Le Roi s'amuse had taught him a lesson, and he was giving to the preparations for his new first night all the careful attention to detail of a
great general planning an operation. Delegates representing the "Heroes of *Hernani*" were summoned to a reading. As a result of all the
foresight given to the presentation of the play to the public, the occasion was a resounding success.

A great part of it was due to the high abilities of Mademoiselle
George and Frédérick Lemaître; but Juliette, too, brief though her
appearance on the stage was, entranced the audience. She had, said
Théophile Gautier, "but two words to speak, and little more to do than
move across the stage. With so little time at her disposal, and so little to
say, she managed to produce a ravishing effect, to give the impression
of a genuine Italian princess with death in her lovely smile . . ."[5] As to
the author, it was a delight for him to put on record the verdict of the
audience, which was also his own: "How pretty she is! How beautiful!
What a figure, what shoulders, how delicious a profile! What a charming actress, what modesty and distinction in her bearing! She knows
exactly what she has to express, and does it to a nicety. Her emotions
are profound. She has a lively gift of feeling. There is in her voice and
her manner something of Madame Dorval, but how much more natural
and intelligent she is! After another year of experience she will be perfect! So far as style goes, she will be our leading actress. What sensitiveness, what meaning, in her silences. . . ."[6]

He was wrong—not about the actress's adorable beauty, but about
her talent. Mademoiselle Juliette was a clumsy performer because she
invariably "over-acted." But love is blind, and Hugo was in love. Evening after evening he went to the Porte-Saint-Martin to watch while
one little scene was turned to a shining brightness by those lovely eyes

which never left his own. He was terribly tempted. For a long while now Adèle had been obstinately refusing herself to him. Under the mask of a young conqueror he concealed a secret and devouring sorrow.

Each evening he called on Juliette in her dressing-room, gave her advice, sunned himself in the heady warmth of her proffered beauty. Four days after the first performance, on February 6th, he said to her: "I love you!" That was precisely what she had been waiting for, and hoping. On the night of February 16th-17th, the Saturday in Easter week (all their lives long they thought it had been a Tuesday, but they were wrong, either about the date or the day of the week), author and actress were to go on together, after the performance, to a theatrical ball. They decided to spend that night in Juliette's apartment. She was still living in the boulevard Saint-Denis, until such time as her "nest" in the rue de l'Échiquier should be ready for occupation. *Juliette to Victor*: "Monsieur Victor, come to me this evening to the house of Madame K[raft]. Till then I will love you, and so contain myself in patience. Until this evening! Ah! when it comes it will bring everything. I will give myself to you completely, without reservation . . ."[7] Eight years later he recalled the occasion to her:

Do you remember it, my best beloved? Our first night was a night of carnival, Shrove Tuesday, 1833. There was, in some theatre or other, I can't remember which, something in the nature of a ball (I can't remember what) at which we were both of us expected. (I break off for a moment to kiss your lovely mouth. Ah! now I can go on.) Nothing, I am sure, not even death, will ever wipe that memory away. In my mind I still go over all the hours of that night, one by one. They are like stars moving before the eyes of my heart. Yes, you were due to go to that ball: but you didn't go, you waited for me! Poor angel! What beauty and what love you lavished on me. Your little room was filled with an adorable silence. Outside, we could hear Paris laughing and singing, and could see masked figures shouting as they passed. In the midst of that general festival, we had set aside, and hidden in the darkness, our own particular celebration. The drunkenness of Paris was a make-believe: ours was true. Never forget, my angel, that hour of mystery which changed the course of all your life. That night of February 17th, 1833, was a symbol, the outward and visible sign of the great and solemn thing that was taking place within you. On that night you had left outside, and far from you, the tumult and the noise, the false glitter and the crowds, to enter into mystery, and solitude, and love. . . .[8]

Victor Hugo was like a drunken man. Adèle, once so eagerly desired, had been able to give him only the shy docility of a young bride. Now, suddenly, he had entered into possession of a woman who knew how to love, and was beautiful as few are beautiful: "eyes diamond-bright and limpid, a brow serene and smooth . . . neck, shoulders, arms, all with the perfection of an antique statue. She was worthy to inspire sculptors, and to rank in beauty with the young Athenian maidens who let fall their veils before Praxiteles when he planned his Venus."[9] That body, with its firm little Breton breasts, comparable to any statue of the ancient world, responded with practised skill to every fantasy of love. Juliette, on that "holy night," revealed the secrets of physical pleasure to a man of thirty, himself marvellously equipped to savour it, and to give it in return; a man who, married at twenty, had probably known no bed but his wife's. The ritual of love, like poetry, is an art; and in that art Juliette was deeply skilled.

To talk with Juliette was yet another enchantment. She had so much to speak of: Brittany, the bare-foot schoolgirl, the convent, the years of poverty; and so much to hear from him. Her life had been difficult and venturesome, and her stories satisfied many of the writer's curiosities. "I am of the people," she said with pride. Now, there had been in the "Baron Hugo," in spite of occasional spurts of a somewhat simple-minded upper-class vanity, a warm-hearted desire to know the people. Besides, a poet needs to be understood. Whenever he wrote poems for Juliette, she received them with a far livelier pleasure than ever Adèle had been able to show. The apathetic wife had seemed to take no interest in manuscripts or drafts. Juliette, a "natural hoarder," kept everything with a devoted care. She gave a savour to success which, by itself, is flat!

For Hugo, this love, after twelve humiliating months, meant resurrection. The idea of taking a mistress, of spending whole nights away from home, had at first frightened one who was the poet of domesticity. But he came to find a cause for pride in this new way of living. He talked to everyone about his conquest, even to Sainte-Beuve, who poked fun at him: "Hugo represents himself to me as a man with only one fault—an over-fondness for women. He pretends that fame means nothing to him. Every man has two weaknesses: to one he will admit, the other he conceals . . ."[10] Of course the adventure became the talk of Paris, and some of the poet's faithful friends, Victor Pavie, for instance, grew uneasy. But Victor wanted to believe that so much happiness must be innocent. *Victor Hugo to Victor Pavie:* "I have never committed more faults than during this past year, and never have I felt better. I am worth a great deal more now than I was in the days of my *innocence* which you regret. Once I was indeed innocent: now I can make allowances. That, God knows, is to have made considerable progress. I have at my side a good and sweet friend, and she knows it, too: one whom you worship, as do I, who pardons me and loves me. . . ."[11]

This Angel of Pardon was Adèle. It was easy for her to play the angelic part. How should she not have pardoned him? How, since she no longer wanted to be his wife, could she demand fidelity? Besides, there was no break in her domestic existence. Didine wrote to Louise Bertin: "Louise mine, it is a very long time since I saw you . . . My little aunt, Julie [Foucher], has come from the convent . . . Toto and Dédé have had their hair cut . . . Julie says she has no liking for usurpers: she detests Louis-Philippe"; and Hugo, the sinner, added: "I must apologize for making use of such white paper as the Doll has left me . . . This poor Paris of ours is still very boring . . . One finds oneself almost regretting the summer of political disturbance, and the cholera year . . . I spend my days gleaning from among old odds and ends enough material to make two volumes of *Littérature mêlèe* (and what a mêlèe it will be!) . . . In the evenings my wife and I go walking over towards la Rapée, along the river bank . . ."[12] An idyllic picture. Family life *à la* Greuze.

When, as every summer, Adèle settled down with the children at Les Roches, Sainte-Beuve came nosing round the valley.

While Hugo was absent from Bièvre, Adèle set out on foot, and at some point on the road picked up Sainte-Beuve, who had hired a carriage. They were as happy together as it was in them to be, which is not saying a great deal. Their love-affair had, since its dawning, been tinged with twilight colours. "It merges," wrote Sainte-Beuve to Madame Victor Hugo, "with the delicate fall of evening in the churches where we go together. It has grown used to mourning even in the lap of happiness. I have ever been but mildly gifted with the power to hope. Always, in everything, I have been conscious of absence and obstacle. In my feelings there has always been a lack of sunlight when things were going well . . ."[13] Meanwhile in Paris Victor had taken Juliette to see the apartment in the Place Royale. Next day she wrote to him:

Do you realize how charming it was of you to throw open the doors of your home to me? You have done more than satisfy my curiosity, and I thank you for having shown me the place where you live, love and think. But, if I am to be sincere with you, my dear darling, I must admit that I carried away from that visit a terrible sense of sadness and depression! I feel now, much more than I ever felt previously, how completely separated from you I am, and the extent to which we are strangers. That is no fault of yours, my poor love, nor is it mine. It is just that things are like that. It would be stupid in me to hold you responsible for more of my unhappiness than you are; still, the fact remains, beloved, that I am the most wretched of women. If you have any feelings of compassion for me, my dear love, you will help me to free myself from the humiliating and crouching posture in which I now find myself. It torments my spirit no less than my body. Help me, my good angel, to stand up straight again, and have faith in you and in the future! Please do that, I beg of you: please do that! . . .[14]

This humility was sincere. The drama of Juliette's life was that, in the days of her innocence, she had become a courtesan, and had thought it natural, having found in men only cynicism and brutality, to look at least for luxury from a Prince Demidoff or his fellows. And now, here she was, in love with an exigent master who was contemptuous of all venality; who could not bear the thought of sharing her with another; who had suffered too much from jealousy not to demand certainty. Because the love he felt for her was "complete, profound, tender and burning, inexhaustible and infinite," he wanted her to be as pure as she was beautiful. But she could depend for a livelihood only on her rich protectors. In the theatre she made no more than a pittance. She was wholly responsible for her daughter, Claire. Deeply in love though she was, she hesitated before turning her life upside down. She had just moved into the handsome apartment in the rue de l'Échiquier, and would, no doubt, continue to put up with the visits of the rich man who had provided her with its splendours, Demidoff the backwoods-man, and his friends. Victor was treating her as a lost woman, just as Didier had treated Marion de Lorme. A man of the type of Balzac would have dismissed the whole business with a laugh, but for Hugo it constituted a personal drama. There were times when, wounded by "outrageous suspicions" (which were only too legitimate), Juliette would have liked to break off the connection altogether. She ran away, only to return and ask her terrible judge and marvellous lover to "give her absolution, and revive in her all that was good and virtuous."

He was prepared to forgive her on condition that she broke with the past. To this, eventually, she consented, and found herself suddenly in a state of extreme poverty. In January 1834 she had in pawn "48 em-broidered cambric chemises, 36 plain cambric chemises, 25 dresses, two of them without sleeves, 31 embroidered petticoats, 12 embroidered camisoles, 25 wrappers, 1 striped and flounced cashmere dress, 1 shawl of Indian cashmere, etc."[15]

This scrupulous and lamentable inventory puts one in mind of the leavings of the dead. Princess Negroni *was* dead, and Juliette was fight-ing for survival. Creditors were besieging her door, and their coming increased Victor Hugo's jealousy. When she was compelled to admit to him the extent of some small part of her anxieties, the nail-paring bourgeois in him grew indignant, while the romantic hero declared that he would make himself responsible for her debts.

Victor Hugo to Juliette Drouet: This money is for you. I have just made it for you to have. It is what remains of the night which I wanted to give entirely to you. I had to deliver what I had undertaken to deliver this morn-ing or not at all. The pen dropped from my fingers at least twenty times, but the work I was doing was for you. Therefore I gave myself to it. I am not like other men. I accept the activities of Fate. Even in your degradation I look on you as the most generous, the worthiest and the noblest of all the creatures struck down by misfortune. Never shall I join with others in crushing a poor prostrate woman. Nobody but I shall have the right to cast the first stone at you. If anyone dares to do it, my body shall be your shield. . . .[16]

Then, since he had separated her from all those who had known her in the old days, and could not live with her, he provided her with work. The natural thing for a writer to do is to turn the woman he loves into a secretary. *Juliette to Hugo:* "It is not yet quite six o'clock. I have just finished copying the poems you gave me yesterday . . ." She had to account to him for everything she did. "I came home yesterday; I read your poems; I had dinner; I did my accounts, then I went to bed. I read through your journals; I went to sleep; I dreamed of you; I awoke this morning at eight, and got up almost at once; I did part of the house-work, and mended the dress I wore yesterday . . . At half-past-two I sat down to my copying, and when it was finished, I wrote to you. That, sir, is my routine report. Are you satisfied?—the corporal of the guard is. After dinner I will hear the children their lessons and count the number of lines in *Les Feuilles d'Automne*."[17]

But she had her compensations. He had bought for her a note-book bound in black horn encrusted with gold: an "Engagement Book" in which, each evening, before returning to the Place Royale he wrote some commonplace and tender thought: "On the first day of the year I will write—I love you; on the last, I adore you . . ."—"Your kisses make me in love with the earth; your eyes make me understand Heaven . . ." —"I will define you in a phrase, my poor love—an angel in hell . . ." —"Beauty you have, intelligence you have. If society had treated you as well as nature, you would stand high indeed. But have no regrets. Society could have done no more than make you a queen; nature has made you a goddess . . ."[18] The lover, though greatly enamoured, was still very much a Didier, and continued to think of this Marion de Lorme as a fallen angel. She herself was filled with self-contempt. Victor's serious and solemn sentiments, which bored Adèle, delighted Juliette, the more so since they alternated with periods of student gaiety which she found charming.

She still hoped to make a career in the theatre. Hugo, after a deal of quarrelling, had promised Félix Harel a new play for the Porte-Saint-Martin: *Marie Tudor*. It contained two women's parts of almost equal importance, and these he intended for Mademoiselle George and Mademoiselle Juliette. The first was to play the Queen of England, the second, Jane, a poor girl, guilty and touching, forgiven by her lover. The rehearsals were stormy. The imperious, and imperial, Mademoiselle George was not the type of woman to endure a rival. Though she was not herself in love with Hugo, she took it in ill part that an author should do homage to a mere "extra." Acid and arrogant, she complained at having to play opposite so mediocre an actress. The handsome Pierre Bocage, spurred on by her, threw up the part of Gilbert after treating Juliette with impertinence at rehearsal. As an intimate friend of Alexandre Dumas, he did not want Hugo to have a success, because, in the eyes of the public, the two romantic authors, no matter what they personally might think, ranked as rivals. As a result of the machinations of Bocage, of Sainte-Beuve, and even of Harel, the preliminary paragraphs in the press were unfriendly. It was said that the play was full of crimes and horrors, that the executioner was to appear in person on the stage, and, in particular, that Juliette was excruciatingly bad.

On the eve of the first performance the director said to the author: "Mademoiselle Juliette is impossible; Mademoiselle Ida[19] [Dumas's mistress] knows the part and is prepared to take it on." Hugo was too much in love, and too fair-minded, to give way. Harel was furious, and at the last moment refused to let him have the seats due to him. Dumas chivalrously surrendered his own to his rival. The evening began in an atmosphere of gathering storm. The first two acts got by, but in the third the scenes in which Juliette appeared were booed. Put out of her stride by the hostility of her fellow-actors and of the audience, she unfortunately justified the fears of the director, and the aspersions of the critics. Next day, under pressure from Adèle, Sainte-Beuve and the "veterans of *Hernani*," Hugo, grieved and angry, was compelled to agree that the unhappy Juliette should plead indisposition (she really was ill and had to take to her bed) and give up the part.

Hugo to Juliette: Not once, not for a moment, did you miss the true and passionate note, the note of feeling. Those who were not listening now complain that they could not hear. Don't pay any attention, but let them say what they choose. At the climax you looked beautiful and were deeply moving, as, earlier on, you had looked beautiful and were charming. All that you had to say, you said without once losing the delicate shades of meaning—and that, in moments of passion, is a very difficult achievement. You faced the Queen with dignity in the great scene at the end, and it was a real triumph not to fall down over that. It is not enough to show just two women fighting; what has to be made clear is that it is Jane against Marie, the gazelle against the panther. Don't worry; one day you will get your deserts. . . .[20]

As a result of the cruel reception given her by the public, Juliette was so much upset that she lost what small talent she had. "My courage is all gone," she said: "they have undermined my self-confidence. I can't face another rehearsal; I feel paralysed." The whole incident was wretched in the extreme, and most unfair.

22

The Year 1834

> If two persons quarrel, it is because they have
> been rather too much together.
>
> PAUL VALÉRY

ONE of Sainte-Beuve's notes, not for publication, contains the following comment: "How all, I say to myself, that a few years ago was fine, flourishing, and still endowed with the principle of growth, has now withered! Lamennais reduced to silence, ruined and without disciples; Lamartine, in *l'Orient désert,* cut off from the world of the living by the death of his daughter; all our poets blighted, our angels fallen! Hugo, who once wrote 'Son Nom' and 'A toi,' at Juliette's feet; 'Eloa'[1] the slave and scapegoat of Madame Dorval; Antony mad, and Émile become a dandy;[2] only we two, my Adèle, have followed the path of our Destiny, and kept to it strictly. Let us cling to one another, dear angel, and stay together till death, and after death! I love you!"[3] This disenchantment was to strike deeper still, for even that love was later to be vulnerable. The year 1834 saw a complete severance between Sainte-Beuve and the Hugos. It was also the year in which the worst of many storms broke over poor Juliette's head.

The breach between the old friends was due, not to sentimental reasons, but to a literary squabble. At the beginning of 1834 Victor Hugo published an "Étude sur Mirabeau." Why Mirabeau? Because the subject was one which enabled him, indirectly, to explain his own position. Balzac has painted his portrait during these disastrous years as that of a man who was "both unhappy and an object of detestation." That is perfectly true. In and out of season he was treated with snarling injustice. Sainte-Beuve, even, unctuously expressed surprise at the extent of this severity. "The critics had, for some months, been raising a quite incredible and unanimous outcry against his work and his person . . ."[4] Now Mirabeau, in his day, had suffered similarly from unjust attacks. He had been compared unfavourably with Barnave, who shared his political ideas, though not his genius, much as in 1798 Moreau had been lauded at the expense of Bonaparte. In 1834 there were those who professed to see in the elder Dumas a better writer than Hugo.

180

"Nevertheless," wrote Hugo, "the people, who are not envious because they are great, stood for Mirabeau . . ."[5] Hugo was beginning to hope that these same "people" would one day give him his revenge on those "men of exemplary behaviour, though in fact they are the very men whose behaviour should never be taken as an example by anybody." As once he had written, "we must have a Shakespeare of our own," so now he said: "After the great revolutionary figures, we need a figure that shall stand for progress . . . The French Revolution started an immense book in which there was a place for every variant of social theory, a sort of Great Testament. Mirabeau made his contribution to it, so did Robespierre. Louis XVIII erased much of what had been written. Charles X tore out a page. The Chamber of August 7th stuck it in again, more or less, but that is all. The book is still there; the pen is there. Who will dare to take it up and write?"[6] That question he answered with a whispered "You!" He was looking beyond literary fame to a political future. Sainte-Beuve published an article on "Mirabeau." It was full of praise for the writer, but Victor Hugo had good reason to think that it dealt treacherously with the man. *Victor Hugo to Sainte-Beuve:* "I have found in it, my poor friend (and the effect has been precisely the same on *two of us*), passages of tremendous praise, but, at bottom, and this profoundly saddens me, no real kindliness . . . I should have preferred less of praise and more of sympathy . . . Victor Hugo has been overwhelmed with honours, but Victor, your old Victor, has been made very unhappy . . ."[7] Sainte-Beuve made protestations of a friendship "which, after all, is my chief claim to consideration as a man of letters, and was the first great emotional experience of my life . . ."[8] But these feline compliments were multiplied in vain. Hostile comments, things said in private and repeated in public, poisoned the relationship between the two men, and made complete reconciliation impossible. The break, when it came, was sharp and sudden. *Sainte-Beuve to Victor Hugo, March 30th, 1834:* "I think, if you don't mind, we had better leave it at that. There has been more than enough talk of, not, as you put it, *unworthy persons,* but certainly of an unworthy subject. Give us good poetry and I will do my best to provide conscientious articles. Let us both get back, you to your work, I to my trade. I do not dwell in a temple, and am contemptuous of nobody. You do, so be careful to avoid all scandal. . . ."[9]

Victor Hugo to Sainte-Beuve, April 1st, 1834: Those who take my part have, just now, to endure so many hatreds, so many cowardly attacks, that I find it easy to understand why friends, even of long standing and proved loyalty, throw up the sponge and take to their heels. Therefore, let it be goodbye, my friend. Let us each silently bury what is already dead in you and has been killed in me as a result of your letter. . . .[10]

After these farewells the two men continued to shake hands whenever their professional obligations made meetings necessary. Each
January 1st Sainte-Beuve sent a present to his god-daughter. But the
friendship was ended.

For Victor Hugo and Juliette Drouet 1834 was a chaotic year. There
were heights of sublimity, but also deep and dark abysses. The one
stable element in their changing life together was a mutual love of heart
and body. "If happiness could be bought with life, all mine would long
ago have been spent . . ."[11] February 20th, 1834: "Good-day to you,
my dearest and my best beloved; good-day to you, my great poet; good-
day to you, God of my life. Here is a beautiful morning of love and sunlight, worthy in every respect to recall the day when you were born
. . ."[12] "My Toto, I love you. You made me very happy last night. If
only it could have lasted as long as my life, I should have no regret, no
other desire . . ."[13] Juliette Drouet's enemies maintained that she was
lacking in intelligence. What nonsense! One may smile at her often
fantastic spelling, but not at her style. She had a charming sense of fun,
would head her letters with parodies of her poet's romantic epigraphs,
and could devote an incredible amount of ingenuity to inventing a
thousand variants on the words "I love you." "I write as my heart dic-
tates. I love you as might a woman in the fields of Heaven, but the
words I use to tell you so are those of a kitchen wench . . . My heart is
full of love; your head of wits."[14] She could use language worthy of the
Portuguese Nun. Hugo had been no laggard in recognizing the existence in her of this lyrical gift, and he treasured all her letters.

But no one can live on love and intelligence alone, and she was a
poor young woman loaded with debts. Twelve thousand francs were
owing to Janisset the jeweller; two thousand five hundred to Mesdames
Lebreton and Gérard, who dealt in cashmeres; a thousand francs to
Poivin for gloves; four hundred francs to Vilian who supplied her with
rouge . . . in all, twenty thousand francs (between five and six million
at today's rates). At first, terrified of her suspicious lord and master, she
had tried to come to terms with her creditors, to pawn her under-
clothing, to raise a loan through the good offices of Jacques-Firmin
Lanvin and his wife.[15] This had led to mysteries, concealments, suspicious goings-on, and jealousy on the part of Hugo, who assumed his
"Grand-Inquisitorial" air. More than once, in the course of the year,
they came within an ace of parting. *Victor Hugo's Diary: January 13th,
1834, 11.30 p.m.:* "Today a lover still. Tomorrow . . ." Juliette, who
had sacrificed everything, and in order to keep her lover had faced poverty, could scarcely help feeling hurt by the severity with which he
judged her. "Nothing I have done seems to find favour in your eyes.
Today I am still, for you, what a year ago I was for everyone—a woman
whom sheer necessity could fling into the arms of the first rich man who

came her way. There lies the hard, the irresistible reason for our separation. These are the things which I can no longer endure."[16]

There were other things, too, to cause her unhappiness: Place Royale, for one, where Victor Hugo was living a brilliant life from which she was excluded. (It sometimes happened that, tired of waiting for him, she would wander up and down beneath his windows, and as he in the old days had done in front of the Hôtel de Toulouse, look at the lights and listen to the laughter.) Then there was the ease with which he accepted the calumnies, or truths, about her past, told him by Ida Ferrier and the mature Mademoiselle George, who asked with hypocritical solicitude why he had picked on "that false, vain, coquettish and dissolute woman." Finally, the lack of all interest, seemingly, in her career as an actress. In 1834 he got her taken on at a salary of three thousand francs a year by the Théâtre-Français. This enabled her to pay the rent of the apartment at 35 rue de l'Échiquier, for which, naturally enough, Demidoff no longer considered himself to be responsible. But no parts came her way, and she began to think that her lover took as poor a view of her professional abilities as the audience of *Marie Tudor* had done. To what sort of a future could she look forward? Must she remain for ever a poor young woman, with no career, no home of her own, the mistress of a jealous man who despised her? When her creditors distrained upon her, and seized the furniture, she seriously contemplated suicide.

Victor, you spent last night throwing in my teeth the infamous calumnies of the woman George, and the wretchedness of my former life. You laughed at the fifteen months of love and suffering which I have spent with you. Do not, I beg, spurn the truth of the pure and ardent love I have felt for you. Do not behave like those children who, seeing an old man pass by, cannot believe that he has ever been young and strong. Here are all your letters, and the handkerchief you returned to me. It is not mine. . . .[17]

Then, since Hugo's body and heart were wiser than his pride, he returned to her, repentant. Watching her as she slept, he wrote:

You will find this little letter when you wake, folded in four upon your bed, and you will smile at me, will you not? I long for a smile from those poor, lovely eyes which have shed so many tears. Sleep, Juliette mine— dream that I love you; dream that I am at your feet; dream that you are mine; dream that I am yours; dream that I cannot live without you; dream that I am thinking of you; dream that I am writing to you. When you wake you will find that dream is true. I kiss your tiny feet and your great eyes. . . .[18]

He took her into the country round Paris, and showed her his dear valley of the Bièvre, brimming with laziness and green growing things. On July 3rd they spent a night at the Hôtel de l'Écu de France, at Jouy-en-Josas. It was an unforgettable occasion.

Victor, my love, I am still all shaken by the memory of yesterday night. Yesterday, July 3rd, 1834, at half past ten, at the Inn of the Écu de France, I, Juliette, was the happiest and proudest woman in all the world. I tell you again that, until then, I had not felt in all its fullness the joy of loving you and of being loved by you. This letter, which has all the appearance of an Official Report, is in very truth a legal instrument defining the state of my heart. This document, drawn up this day, must serve for the rest of my life here below. That day, hour and minute when it shall be presented to me, I solemnly engage to surrender the said heart in the same state in which it is today, in other words, filled with one only love, which is yours, and with one only thought, which is of you. Given at Paris, this 4th July, 1834, at three o'clock of the afternoon. Signed, JULIETTE—the thousand kisses with which I have covered this letter serving as witnesses. . . .[19]

When the time came for the summer migration to Les Roches, they looked for a room where she could stay, not too far from the Bertins. They found what they were seeking in the hamlet of Metz, on the top of a wooded hill, in a low-built, white-walled cottage with green shutters, half buried in wild vines. The name of the family that lived there was Labussière, and the rent was ninety-two francs a year, which Victor paid in advance. Then, all arrangements made, they returned to Paris. *Victor Hugo to Juliette Drouet, July 9th, 1834:* "My love, my angel! There is nothing more intoxicating than the song which comes from your lips, unless it be the kiss I gather from them. Never forget that I am writing these lines in your bed, with you, naked and adorable in my arms, while you sing my songs in a voice that steals my heart away. Poor songs, which you have rendered charming! The lines are mine, the poetry all yours!"[20] On July 19th she left the rue de l'Échiquier, treasuring "an eternal memory of a place where we have been so happy and so unhappy, too," and moved into a tiny lodging at 4 bis, rue de Paradis. "Oh! my Juliette, that street is well named! Heaven is in it for us, in the house, in the room, in the bed!"[21]

In the month of August (1834) this paradise became a hell. The pack of creditors had found the scent, and was baying so loudly that Juliette was finally compelled to confess the total of her debts to her lover. Twenty thousand francs! The son of General Hugo, who as a boy had had nothing for a long while but two sous a day, became terrifyingly angry. He said that he would pay off every penny, little by little, even at the risk of putting his health, and even his life, in danger. But his promises were mingled with harsh reproaches. What had she been doing? The very violence of her remorse led him to imagine the existence of yet graver faults. *Juliette to Victor:* "Oh! go! go! Never will you be loved with a love more pure than mine, a truer or more lasting love, and yet, I am the most miserable of women. What atonement, what expiation do you demand for a crime which is not mine, which comes I know not whence, for which neither my body nor my heart is responsible? Speak! pronounce judgment. I will submit to any punishment short of the death of our love!"[22]

She fled with her young daughter to Brittany, where her sister Renée (Madame Koch) was living at Saint-Renan. The lovers, now separated, took stock of their folly. What did money, what did debts, matter compared with such wealth of love? Hugo fought "tooth and nail" to bring temporary relief to Juliette. He even went so far as to beg Pradier (whom he called the Prince of Furstenberg from the name of the street in which the sculptor was living) to shoulder at least the expenses of his daughter's upkeep, but Pradier refused. He could not manage it, he said, unless Hugo could get him appointed chief of one of the groups working on the Arc de Triomphe: a cynical piece of bargaining. From all the stages on her journey, Juliette sent letter after letter. "Victor, this separation will be my death. Is it true you hate me, that I am odious to you, that you despise me? I will do all you wish, dear God!—all! Do you still want me? Say you do!"[23] He wanted her so badly that he did everything he could to help. "I have just been to see Monsieur Pradier, I appealed to his better feelings. He behaved very well, and it has been agreed between us that the father of your child and I shall do all in our power to save you. If necessary, we will both of us pledge ourselves, but in that case it will be essential to have you here in Paris. He agrees with me. Your presence is indispensable if the situation is to be disentangled, and affairs put on the right road. I, on my side, have just managed to scrape together a thousand francs. See what love can do! I am just off to the coach-office. If there is a vacant seat I shall start on Tuesday, and you will see me on Friday . . . For the last thirty hours I have not eaten a mouthful—but I love you. . . ."[24]

Leaving Adèle and the children at Les Roches, he took wing for Brittany. The lovers met at Brest. There was blue sky and blue sea, fine days after a period of mist. They swore that never again would they hurt one another.

While pursuing his mistress, Hugo found time to pacify his wife. *Victor Hugo to Adèle Hugo: Rennes. August 7th, 1834:* "Farewell, Adèle mine, I love you. Till we meet again. Write to me often, and at length. You are the joy and the honour of my life. I kiss your lovely brow and your lovely eyes . . ."[25] Adèle, in this month of August, was free to go walking with Sainte-Beuve in the tree-shaded alleys at Bièvre. It cost her little to reply to these expressions of complacent resignation, and her merit was small. "I do not want to say anything," she wrote, "which might cause you sadness now that you are far from me, since I cannot be at hand to give you consolation. I do believe that, in spite of everything, you love me, and that you are enjoying yourself, since you are in no hurry to return. Truth to tell, these two certainties make me happy . . ."[26] Indulgence is the child of indifference.

Juliette and Victor returned by short stages, she, sleeping with her head on his shoulder in the diligence, he, seeing the convicts at Brest, the menhirs at Carnac, churches everywhere, and *Lucrèce Borgia* at Tours. Then, on September 2nd, Juliette settled once more into her little room at Metz, while Victor went back to Les Roches. There followed six weeks of a simple, matchless existence. Juliette had to live with old mother Labussière (whither Antoinette Lanvin, the friend who acted as intermediary between her and Pradier, frequently brought her daughter, Claire), doing her own housework, eating in the kitchen, and making do with two dresses, one of wool, the other of a white-and-pink-striped muslin. But her very poverty, her tin spoons, her heavy shoes, and the absence of all amusements, gave evidence of her submission and of her love. Hugo, in whom this asceticism, imposed by himself, satisfied a strange appetite for domination, wrote in a copy of *Claude Gueux* which he gave to his mistress: "To my Angel, whose wings are putting forth new feathers: Metz, September 2nd, 1834."[27] Each day Hugo arrived on foot, having walked through the woods. Adèle was an accessory, Louise Bertin a confidante. Old maids, when they are kindly disposed, enjoy sniffing at love. As a rule, Juliette went to meet her lover, and waited for him in the forest, perched in the fork of an old chestnut tree. "With pouter-pigeon breast, pink cheeks, lips parted, and an expression of charming playfulness, she looked like a flower growing out of the tree's rough bark."[28] She jumped down when she saw him, kissed away the forest damp from his cheeks, and led him to one of the many thickets densely carpeted with moss.

Love and Nature in combination produce celestial harmonies. "The happy sound of nesting birds comes from the shadowed woods," and mingles deliciously with lovers' sighs. They were happy. Hugo, who enjoyed explaining the world, God and everything under the sun, found in his lovely penitent a docile and admiring pupil. A storm, during which they took shelter in the forked chestnut, became for her a precious memory. She shivered with cold, and he did his best to warm her. Raindrops fell from the man's hair on to the woman's neck, and he never stopped talking. "All my life long I shall hear your tender words of solicitude and instruction." She was one of those women who are grateful to the men who praise not only their beauty, but their nobility of soul. She must have been very happy and truly proud when on September 25th he left for her, in the old chestnut which was their letter-box, whither she took as many as five notes a day, a poem with the following dedication: "To You whom I respect: to Thee whom I love—V." The poem was entitled: "Dans l'église de. . . ." It had been written on the evening of a day when, after a walk together, they had spent some time in the little church at Bièvre:

> C'était une humble église au cintre surbaissé,
>   L'église où nous entrâmes,
> Où, depuis trois cents ans, avaient déja passé
>   Et pleuré bien des âmes.
>
> Elle était triste et calme à la chute du jour,
>   L'église où nous entrâmes,
> L'autel sans serviteur, comme un cœur sans amour,
>   Avait éteint ses flammes. . . .[29]

There, doubtless, she had prayed, telling a God in whom she believed with all her being of the despair she felt as a woman who had about her "neither a happy home, nor tender family," who "was a stranger in this hard, metallic world"; and there her lover had given her comfort and reassurance, "finding her solemn-sweet, and worthy of that sacred spot." In the simplicity of its feeling, in its use of plain, unliterary language, in the flow of its verses, and the perfect matching of thought and rhythm which seemed the result of nature rather than of art, this poem was one of the loveliest he had written. But Juliette's lamentation, which he had set himself so tunefully to interpret, proved that, in spite of mutual love, there was no happiness in their relationship.

23

Olympio

Nothing more redounds to the credit of Victor
Hugo than the calm and tender devotion given
to him by that wonderful creature, Juliette
Drouet.

PAUL CLAUDEL

IT WAS now that there began the most astonishing life of penitence
and confinement ever willingly entered upon by any woman outside a conventual order. Victor Hugo had promised to forgive the
past, but he had laid down conditions, and they were hard. Juliette,
who only yesterday had been one of the most widely admired women
in Paris, adorned with lace and jewels, had now to live for nobody
but him, go out only with him, abandon all coquetry, all ways of
luxury—in short, lead the life of a penitent. She accepted, because
she was caught up in a kind of mystic intoxication, because she had
become a believer in the doctrine of "redemption through love." Her
master and lover gave her, every month, in various small sums, about
800 francs, for which she solemnly accounted:

Date		Francs	Sous
1st	Money made by my adored:	400	
4th	Money made by my adored:	53	
6th	Money for Toto's food:	50	
10th	Money made by my darling man:	100	
11th	Money for my darling's food:	55	
12th	Money made by my beloved:	50	
14th	Pocket-money from my adored:	6	4
24th	Pocket-money from my dear adored:	11	
30th	Pocket-money from dearest Toto:	3^1	

Out of what he gave her she had first of all to lay aside the sums
due to her creditors, the amount of her rent, and her daughter's
allowance. There was little enough left over for her day-to-day requirements. For most of the time she had no fire in her room and,
when the cold was intense, stayed in bed, day-dreaming, reading, or

doing the accounts which her lord and master demanded from her every evening, and carefully checked. She lived on milk, cheese and eggs. In the evening she ate an apple. No new clothes. She "made over" her old ones, with a famous author telling her, day after day, that "what a pretty woman wears adds nothing to her charms." If she bought a box of tooth-powder, she had to explain the purchase. She had to account to him for the presence of a new apron which she had "run up" from an old shawl. The miracle is that she consented to endure this existence of a recluse slave, not only gaily, but gratefully. "I would sooner anything than run into debt! Dear God! what a hateful and degrading thing it is to owe money, and how noble and great you are, my dear one, to love me in spite of my past!"

In such spare time as she had, she copied her lover's manuscripts and darned his clothes. Even that was sweet to her. What she found hard to bear was that, since he did not allow her to go out alone, she had to wait for him, sometimes for days on end, looking at the blue sky like a bird in a cage. When Hugo happened to be free, he went with her to Saint-Mandé, where Claire Pradier was at school, or to the Invalides, where her Uncle Drouet was dying, or on a stroll round the second-hand shops. He loved the young Claire, and wrote to her: "Since, my poor little Claire, you sometimes think of your old friend Monsieur Toto, I send you this line to say good-morning. Work hard, grow into a great big sensible girl, so that you may become like your mother, a noble and a worthy woman."[2] If he delayed too long in coming, the sense of confinement became a torment for Juliette, who no longer had even her "fun in the playground," by which she meant a walk on the boulevard. She allowed herself to relapse into self-pity. "I have been stupid enough to let myself be treated like a farm-dog. A bowl of food, a kennel and a chain—that is my lot! There *are* dogs that their masters take about with them, but for me, no such luck! My chain is so strongly riveted that you clearly have no intention of undoing it. . . ."[3]

The theatre was her only hope of achieving independence, and in spite of her many disappointments she still clung to it tenaciously. Victor had completed a new prose play: *Angelo, tyran de Padoue.* It was a melodrama in the manner of *Lucrèce Borgia*: a courtesan redeemed by a good heart (Tisbé); a sweet and rescued woman (Catarina): the whole bag of tricks, complete with visions, secret passages, phials of poison, and a cross belonging to a beloved mother; but well constructed, and accepted with enthusiasm by the Comédie-Française. Now, Juliette was a *pensionnaire* of that institution. Surely she might hope for one of the two female parts? She guessed that Victor Hugo was nervous about entrusting the fortunes of his play to an actress whose talent had been the subject of so much argument, who was jealously spied upon by a hostile faction, and dared not ask him for his help. Generously, she effaced herself. "It is best that we should keep our two futures in the theatre separate," she said to him, which meant that she must renounce any prospect of one for herself. She left the Théâtre-Français without ever having played upon its stage. The two parts were given to Mademoiselle Mars and Madame Dorval.

As an actress, this was her supreme humiliation, and, as a lover, it gave her cause for fear. The disturbing coquetry and fatal charm of Marie Dorval were matters of common knowledge. Dorval had had Vigny, "the gentleman," and had not remained faithful to him. Juliette felt positive that she would not be able to resist "having a shot" at a young and handsome poet. *Juliette to Hugo:* "I am jealous, not just in general, but of a definite flesh-and-blood woman with as concupiscent a temperament as one could find anywhere, who spends all day and every day in your company, looks at you, talks to you, touches you. Yes, of her I am jealous! So jealous that I am suffering the torments of the damned! . . ."[4] The first night of *Angelo* (applause, enthusiasm, frenzy—thanks, mainly, to the actresses, both of whom were popular favourites) was agony for Juliette, but her loyalty carried the day. "If you knew how sincerely I applauded Madame Dorval, you would make it a point of honour to say nothing and do nothing tonight which could wound my poor heart, which is already slightly saddened by the thought that someone other than myself has been allowed to interpret your most noble thoughts. Shame on me! I am slipping back into a gloomy and suspicious mood, in spite of all my good resolutions, simply because I know that you are with her . . ."[5] The enthusiastic applause she interpreted as evidence that there existed "a sort of marriage of intelligence between actress and author," while he was feeling bitterly resentful that it was not she who had "communicated such sublimities to the public."

She deserved some compensation. It came to her first in a set of beautiful verses:

> Puisque j'ai mis ma lèvre à ta coupe encore pleine,
> Puisque j'ai dans tes mains posé mon front pâli,
> Puisque j'ai respiré parfois la douce haleine
> De ton âme, parfum dans l'Ombre enseveli,
>
> Puisqu'il me fut donné de t'entendre me dire
> Les mots où se répand le cœur mystérieux,
> Puisque j'ai vu pleurer, puisque j'ai vu sourire
> Ta bouche sur ma bouche et tes yeux sur mes yeux . . .
>
> Je puis maintenant dire aux rapides années:
> "Passez! passez toujours! Je n'ai plus à vieillir!

Allez-vous-en, avec vos fleurs toutes fanées;
J'ai dans l'âme une fleur que nul peut cueillir.

"Votre aile, en le heurtant, ne fera rien répandre
Du vase où je m'abreuve et que j'ai bien rempli.
Mon âme a plus de feu que vous n'avez de cendre!
Mon cœur a plus d'amour que vous n'avez d'oubli!"[6]

and, later, in the form of a trip which she took with him in the following summer. Though his two establishments constituted a heavy charge, Victor Hugo was managing to stem the current. *Angelo* was played on sixty-two occasions, at an average of 2250 francs a performance. Renduel, the publisher, bought the manuscript. In 1835 he paid nine thousand francs over a period of eighteen months for the right to reprint *Odes et Ballades*, *Les Orientales* and *Les Feuilles d'Automne*; then eleven thousand francs for a new edition of *Les Chants du Crépuscule*, and a new collection, *Les Voix intérieures*. In three years (1835-1838) Renduel disbursed forty-three thousand francs.[7] From the bookshops, as from the theatres, a flood of money set in— a broad current flowing towards the Place Royale, a rivulet towards the rue de Paradis.

At the end of July Adèle wanted to go to Anjou for their friend Victor Pavie's marriage. Hugo was invited, but knew that Sainte-Beuve would be there, and wished to avoid a meeting. Wanting to be at complete liberty to travel with Juliette, he sent his wife to the wedding in the care of her father, Pierre Foucher. All through the period of this separation, husband and wife, now on a brotherly-and-sisterly, rather than a conjugal, footing, maintained a continual flow of affectionate letters. *Victor to Adèle, Montereau, July 26th, 1835:* "Good day to you, my poor angel: good day to you, Adèle mine. How are you after the journey? . . ." *La Fère, August 1st:* "I trust you are enjoying yourself . . ." *Amiens, August 3rd:* "Where are you? What are you doing? How are you feeling? . . ." *Le Tréport, August 6th:* "The sea is a very lovely thing, Adèle mine: one of these days we must visit it together . . ." *Montvilliers, August 10th:* "I hope this little trip has done you good, and that you are still plump and blooming . . ." *Adèle to Victor:* "I have been thinking a great deal about you, my dear, good Victor: I wish you could have been with me . . ."[8] "My poor friend, I cannot tell you what emotions all this has awakened in me. I hope that you will understand, and share, them . . ." *August 19th:* "Provided you are enjoying yourself, I bear no resentment. It would be most unfair of me to complain of one who writes me such kind and charming letters. . . ."[9]

The sweet-natured and simple-minded Pierre Foucher, who was

accompanying his daughter, confessed to being somewhat "knocked of a heap" by this unexpected friendliness. "On our way through Angers," he wrote, "Adèle found a number of letters from her husband. He is travelling in Brie and Champagne. He expresses himself in the most kindly fashion to Adèle. He tells her to enjoy herself, and to think of him, to love him, and finishes thus: 'I can wish for Pavie no better fortune than a wife like you. If he gets her, he can render thanks to God . . .' "[10] The Angevin marriage festivities were "Pantagruelic" in character. There were feasting and junketing, lasting for four days, first in a marquee, and then on a number of steamboats. Adèle, the wife of a great man, and a very handsome woman into the bargain, "was the admiration of all the wedding-guests." Sainte-Beuve, with tears in his eyes, read an excessively long epithalamium, which was received with every sign of polite boredom. *Adèle to Victor:* "When you get back to Paris, I beg you, dear friend, to write him a few lines thanking him for all the care he took of us. . . ."[11]

The sun shone, the countryside was all grace and welcome, the banks of the Loire were alive with laughter, but melancholy weighed upon Adèle. The eager attentions of her friend with the thinning red hair no longer consoled her for the absence of her husband. *Adèle to Victor:* "Seeing the Loire, I told myself that ten years ago I looked at it with you. When shall we again travel together? . . ."[12] "I have grown old in my habits, and feel sad, though there is nothing to distress me . . ."[13] She was tired of Sainte-Beuve, tired of life, tired of everything. Jealousy had awakened a semblance of love. Didine (eleven) gently chid her father. "Mamma cries sometimes at the thought that she is not with you . . . Do not forget your little girl, my little father, leave all those carved stones, and come with us, who love you so. . . ."[14]

Meanwhile, Victor and Juliette were thoroughly enjoying the poetic atmosphere of their trip. *Juliette to Victor:* "Do you remember our moments of setting out, and how we snuggled up under the hood of the diligence? With clasped hands and shared hearts we lost all feeling for everything that was not our love. And when we arrived at the end of the stage, when we visited cathedrals and museums, we looked wonderingly at everything through the mist of love that filled our hearts. At how many masterpieces did I gaze with enthusiasm simply because you loved them, and because your words threw light for me upon the mystery! How many steps did I climb to the summits of interminable towers, simply because you were climbing them in front of me!"[15] There speaks the language of unadulterated passion. For Juliette the trip created the illusion of marriage. For Victor it held something of fantasy, of renewal, of a return to the wild freedoms of childhood. He loved to travel without any fixed itinerary, without luggage; to clamber about ruins, to draw, to hoard up flowers and images. Juliette, who fell in with all his plans, was an ideal companion. Far from Paris, Victor no longer played the part of prophet or inquisitor, but was as light-hearted as a student on holiday.

When they got back, the routine of the two establishments resumed its sway: Adèle at Les Roches, Juliette at Metz. The escapade faded into a tradition. The months of September and October 1835 were rainy and windy. Juliette often sat alone in her room at the house of old mother Labussière, looking at the storm, worrying about her poor little daughter, "whom we too much forget," sewing at a wrap, or re-reading the works of her "dear little man." She never grew tired of them. "I know all your books by heart. Nevertheless, whenever I read them over, I find more pleasure in them than I did the first time. It is just as it is with your handsome face. I know every detail of it. There is not a hair of your head, not a hair of your beard, that I do not know by name—but that does not prevent me from being always surprised and ravished by the sight of so much beauty."[16] When, in spite of the rain, she ventured as far as the great chestnut, she was often disappointed at finding neither lover nor letter: "Short of the heavens dissolving in water, I shall continue to go to our *great tree*, which, this year, has been sadly sterile for me. Not yet has it brought me the tiniest letter, and thereby shows ingratitude, since I prefer it to all the others which are so much younger, and so much more charming. Ingratitude is the root principle of men and trees . . ."[17] But from time to time she received a marvellous page which consoled her for everything.

Victor to Juliette: Let us, all our lives, remember yesterday. Let us never forget the terrible storm of September 24th, 1835, which, for us, was so full of sweetness. The rain fell in torrents, the leaves of the tree served only to send it cascading more coldly on our heads, the sky was a world of thunder. You lay naked in my arms, your lovely face hidden between my knees, never looking at me except to smile, and your drenched shift sticking to your beautiful shoulders. For all the time the tempest raged, for an hour and a half, not a word was spoken that was not a word of love. You are enchanting! I love you more than I have words to tell, my Juliette. What a frightful tumult all about us, and, in ourselves, what delicious harmony! Let that day be a golden memory to shine upon the days that still remain to us. . . .[18]

Her unrestrained admiration, bred of devotion, was a dangerous encouragement to the poet to think himself a god. The Romantics, the better to flee from their earthly destiny, created for themselves doubles, whom they saddled with their torments, their ambitions.[19] Byron had led the way with *Childe Harold*. With Vigny it was *Stello*; with Musset, *Fortunio* and *Fantasio*; with George Sand, *Lélia*; with

Sainte-Beuve, *Joseph Delorme*; with Chateaubriand, *René*; with Stendhal, *Julien Sorel*; with Goethe, *Wilhelm Meister;* with Benjamin Constant, *Adolphe.* Hugo made of *Olympio* his incarnation, "who was as like him as a brother, a demi-god born in solitude among the mingled murmurings of pride, nature and love."[20]

The choice of the name was a stroke of genius. Olympian, a blasted Titan still mindful of his proud origins, a super-human being who could see farther than men into the dark depths of life, at once a god and a victim of the gods—as such had Juliette's adoration accustomed Hugo to regard himself. He was, just then, going through a difficult period. He knew that he was hated, and saw himself as a prey to calumny. "Almost all his old friends," wrote Heinrich Heine, "have abandoned him, and, to tell the truth, it is through his own fault that they have done so, because it is his egotism that has affronted them." Hugo, therefore, felt it necessary to address a worthy consolation to his double:

> Jeune homme, on vénérait jadis ton œil sévère,
>   Ton front calme et tonnant:
> Ton nom était de ceux qu'on craint et qu'on révère,
>   Hélas! et maintenant
>
> Les méchants accourus pour déchirer ta vie,
>   L'ont prise entre leurs dents
> Et les hommes alors se sont, avec envie,
>   Pencher pour voir dedans . . . ![21]

Passion, in the full and tragic meaning of the word, had achieved the making of a poet who had progressed far beyond, not only the poet of *Odes et Ballades*, but him, too, of *Les Feuilles d'Automne. Les Chants du Crépuscule,* published at the end of October by Renduel, was a collection of masterpieces. The promise made by the title was of a muted light, and, indeed, after the fireworks of *Les Orientales* these new poems showed a truly wonderful marriage of verbal sim- plicity and austere modelling.

More than anything else, the subject of his outpourings in *Les Chants du Crépuscule* was his union, spiritual as well as bodily, with Juliette Drouet. Thirteen of the pieces were, more or less secretly, dedicated to her.[22] Those who, avid of scandal, read the book as judges rather than as friends were surprised to find that many of the poems were inspired by his wife and his children. "Date Lilia" was an act of homage to the virtues of Adèle Hugo, an attempt to give the lie to the many rumours in circulation about a rift in the domestic lute, a gesture of gratitude for the past, and a mark of present affection. This piece, put last as though to crown and consecrate the volume, so exasperated Sainte-Beuve that he could not keep silent. His review of *Les Chants du Crépuscule*, unjust from beginning to end, ended with an attack on this domestic item. "One is driven to the conclusion that the author wanted, at the last moment, to throw a pinch of lily-dust in the reader's eyes. We regret that he should have found this necessary. It spoils the unity of his volume, the title of which, *Les Chants du Crépuscule*, by no means demanded this duality of mood. The same lack of literary tact (embedded in such a wealth of brilliance and power) has led him to introduce into the composition of these poems two colours which quarrel with one another, two pinches of incense which are hopelessly at odds. He seems not to have realized that the impression left upon the reader will be that an object of respect would have been more honoured and better praised by being entirely omitted. . . ."[23]

Adèle was deeply hurt by such indiscreet comment. If the many hymns to Juliette had given her offence, she had been touched by lines like the following:

> Toi! sois bénie à jamais,
> Éve qu'aucun fruit ne tente!
> Qui, de la vertu contente,
> Habites les purs sommets . . .[24]

Eve whom no fruit can tempt . . . In those words her husband gave her a part she was by no means unwilling to play. The love in which Victor Hugo was now involved inspired his wife with the desire of a new relationship which should be affectionate but not sensual. She had never been a passionate woman, and now willingly accepted the position of companion *emerita*.

Adèle to Victor Hugo: I don't want you to deprive yourself of anything. I, for my part, feel no need of pleasures; all I want is peace and quiet. I am very much the old lady.[25] I have but one wish, that those whom I love shall be happy. The joy of life is for me a thing of the past. I seek it only in satisfying others. There is, in spite of everything, much sweetness to be found in their contentment. You speak very truly when you say that I have an *indulgent smile*. Heaven knows I don't mind what you do. So long as you are happy I shall be so, too. I would not have you think that this attitude of mine is due to indifference. No, it is the form that devotion takes in me, and it makes it possible for me to live detached from life . . . I shall never take advantage, where you are concerned, of the rights bestowed upon me by marriage. It is my wish that you should feel yourself as free of all constraint as a bachelor; you, my dear friend, who entered on matrimony at the age of twenty! I do not wish you to be bound to a poor woman like me. What you give me, you will at least give freely and frankly. . . .[26]

After *Les Chants du Crépuscule* she gradually shut Sainte-Beuve completely out of her life. She resented not only that indecorous article, but also the fact that he lost no opportunity of talking about the immorality of the poems. Hugo seriously thought of challenging his old friend to a duel, and Renduel, the publisher, had to intervene. "A duel between two men like you—two poets?—why the very idea is fantastic!" he said. *Sainte-Beuve to Victor Pavie:* "We have, I regret to say, had a serious difference, which looks like lasting. I, at least, see no possibility of a reconciliation. There are *articles* between us, articles which can be neither cancelled nor withdrawn. . . ."[27]

It comes as something of a surprise that Juliette, on whose head resplendent a crown had been set, displayed far more of jealousy than did Adèle. It upset her to find that the critics were interpreting the final piece, "Date Lilia," as indicating a return to domesticity. *Juliette to Victor, December 2nd, 1835:* "I am not alone in noticing that, in the course of the year just past, your habits and your feelings have changed, though I may be alone in dying from grief because of it. Still, what does it matter so long as the domestic hearth is *gay*, and the domestic circle *happy*? . . ."[28] What gave her most cause for complaint was that he was showing less desire for her. "Joking apart, my dear little Toto, we really are behaving in the most absurd way. It is time we put an end to the scandal of two lovers living in a state of positively atrocious chastity . . ."[29] What she wanted was not a *devoted* Victor, but a *passionate* Victor. "It has never been my wish to live with you on any standing other than that of a *beloved mistress*—certainly not on that of a woman kept on because of a love that *has been*. I neither ask, nor want, to be retired on a pension . . ."[30] With the clear-sightedness of a woman in love, she guessed that, having achieved perfect mastery in his art, he was beginning to dream of success in other fields, of becoming a man of affairs, a social reformer, a prophet.

PART VI

Ambitions Realized

When, later, she saw that he was becoming a fop,
she one day said to him sadly,
"Benjamin, you are taking trouble over your
clothes, you no longer love me."

SAINTE-BEUVE, *Madame de Charrière*

24

"Les Rayons et les Ombres"

THE writing of love poems is a natural occupation for a young man. The poet within sight of maturity looks to his genius to produce other fruits. Between 1836 and 1840, Victor Hugo grew worried because he was playing no part in public affairs. It was all very well to sing songs to the woods and the sun and Juliette, but they could scarcely fill the whole life of a man who wanted to be a "leading spirit."

> Malheur à qui prend ses sandales
> Quand les haines et les scandales
> Tourmentent le peuple agité!
> Honte au penseur qui se mutile
> Et s'en va, chanteur inutile,
> Par la porte de la cité. . . .[1]

The volumes of verse belonging to this period, *Les Voix intérieures* (1837), *Les Rayons et les Ombres* (1840), probe more deeply into the nature of things. On mountain tops and ocean promontories, the poet gazes into the depths, and questions God:

> Que faites-vous, Seigneur? A quoi bon votre ouvrage?
> A quoi bon l'eau du fleuve et l'éclair de l'orage
> —A quoi bon incliner sur ses axes mobiles
> Ce globe monstrueux, avec toutes ses villes,
> Et ses monts, et les mers qui flottent alentours,
> A quoi bon, Ô Seigneur! l'incliner tour à tour,
> Pour que l'Ombre l'éteigne ou que le jour le dore
> Tantôt vers la nuit sombre et tantôt vers l'aurore?[2]

But answer comes there none. *Pensar, dudar*: to think is to doubt. Behind the sublime spectacles of nature the poet divines the presence of a God whose countenance is the world. But this God, silent, invisible, never shows Himself.

Action demands no metaphysic certainties. "Ce siècle est grand et forte, un noble instinct mène." Hugo wanted to be one of those who were giving shape to the nations. Chateaubriand, his model, was a peer of France, an Ambassador, a Foreign Minister. That was the royal road he meant to follow from now on. But before a writer could hope to obtain a peerage, it was necessary for him, under Louis-Philippe, to be a member of the Académie Française. If, in the days of *Cromwell* and *Hernani,* Hugo and his friends had handled that august body somewhat roughly, he knew the world of letters too well to think that the Academy would have a lasting grudge against men of talent for having attacked it. Would they have been so violent in their hate had they not loved it? After 1834 Hugo had decided that the first objective of his ambition should be the Quai Conti, and had put all his powerful determination into the assault. "Hugo is set on the Academy," noted Sainte-Beuve, sourly: "he is concentrating upon it; he talks about it with the greatest seriousness, and bores one for hours together with discussion of his chances. It has become such an obsession with him that he can think of nothing else, and will drag you all the way from the Boulevard Saint-Antoine to the Madeleine, discoursing on the subject the whole time. When Hugo gets an idea into his head he brings all his powers to bear on it in a massive concentration. One hears, from afar off, the thunder of his mind's heavy cavalry, artillery, supply-train, an army of metaphors bearing down on the point of attack."[3]

Both his mistress and his daughter, Juliette and Didine, were hostile to the green uniform. They had been brought up to hold these gew-gaws in abhorrence. Their minds were fixed. Juliette was afraid that his candidature, and the social duties it would involve, might come between her and her lover. Whenever he let her accompany him on his round of courtesy calls, she would wait for him, curled up in a corner of the cab, while he tugged at doorbells. It was a wonderful way, she found, of "picking up a few scraps of him" between addresses. Jealously she added: "In that way I shall find out how much time you spend with the wives and daughters of Academicians."[4] Then she began to develop a taste for the business. "It is such a lovely day for picking *immortels* that it would be the greatest pity not to take advantage of it."

But when in February 1836 election-day came round (it was a question of filling the chair left vacant by the Vicomte de Laine) she foretold his failure with unconcealed delight. "In about three hours, my dear little Toto, you will *not* be an Academician, and that'll be something to brag about. I, who care nothing about political advantages when they are dressed in Academic garb, have the same hopes as Mademoiselle Didine, and rejoice, by anticipation, in the thought that I can keep you fresh without any sprigs of parsley."[5] And so it turned out. Mercier Dupaty, a writer of ephemeral farces, was elected. Hugo's bitter comment was: "I thought one reached the Academy by the Pont des Arts. I was mistaken. The right way, it seems, is across the Pont-Neuf . . ."[6] Dupaty, on the other hand, did the handsome thing, and left a card at the Place Royale. He had scribbled on it:

> Avant vous, je monte à l'autel.
> Mon âge seul y peut prétendre.
> Déja vous êtes immortel
> Et vous avez le temps d'attendre.[7]

In November 1836 the visits had to begin all over again. In a letter to Victor Pavie, his brother Théodore expressed himself as being pessimistic about the outcome of this second attempt. "Lamartine has hurt his knee, and in all probability will not be back. Guizot, who is putting Hugo forward as a candidate in opposition to Mignet—Thiers's man—has not yet been 'received,' and therefore cannot vote. Guiraud is at Limoux, busy about his vines. The only certainties are Chateaubriand and Soumet, because Nodier, turncoat and infirm of purpose, has deserted to the classical camp . . ."[8] As things turned out, Lamartine and Chateaubriand, the two geniuses of the Academy, voted for Hugo, but Mignet beat him. "If quality had counted," said Delphine Gay, "Hugo would have got in; unfortunately, the only thing that counted was quantity." This friend of his youth was beginning to wield great influence, having married a cynical, insolent, but well-born journalist, Émile de Girardin. After wallowing in the romantic, she had made a beeline for the other extreme, and had exchanged Stello for Rastignac. Delphine admired her husband, who had just founded *La Presse*, to which she contributed a number of brilliant articles over the pen-name of "Vicomte de Launay." Girardin had commissioned from Hugo an article for the first number, which was to take the form of a manifesto drawn up by the poet, a political programme at once conservative and true to the principles of 1789.[9] He was, therefore, one of the paper's contributors, and his friend Delphine saw to it that there should be published in its columns a denunciation of the "week's great scandal," which treated the Academicians pretty roughly. "France, gentlemen, demands that you should honour what it admires, and crown a talent which has spread our country's fame in foreign parts . . ."[10] She was right, but assemblies are large, clumsy and simple-minded animals which react to stimulus very slowly.

The defeated candidate was not, however, discouraged, and resumed the normal tenor of his days. He was devoting himself more and more to his children. Didine was rapidly assuming the position of confidante. She was charming, wise, sensitive and discreet. In an atmosphere of domestic tension, she had come to seem older than her age, and was now a serious young person. Her mother, who was not without talent, made a number of quite delightful pencil-drawings of her. Thanks to several reprints and new editions the finances of the Hugo family were in a healthy state. Each year a considerable sum was being invested in State Bonds, but this did not prevent Victor from insisting that his wife should keep the most careful accounts. He had given her a set of notebooks carefully ruled in several columns: Food, Maintenance (children), Education, Clothes, Miscellaneous Expenses, Wages, Carriages, Loans. Nothing was omitted, not even fr. 0.12 for an omnibus fare, and fr. 2 to Monsieur Émery, the hairdresser, at 31 rue Saint-Antoine. It is possible to see from the entries that in 1839 Madame Victor Hugo had her hair done eighteen times. She had not improved as a housewife with the passage of the years. The house in the Place Royale, though snug, was ill-kept. Victor Hugo worked in a "little ice-box," his mattresses were stuffed, seemingly, with nails, there were buttons missing from his shirts, and his clothes were never mended. That, at least, was the opinion of Juliette Drouet—but then she is scarcely an impartial witness.

Adèle still corresponded, at long intervals, with Sainte-Beuve, but it was his opinion that their "love" was now, for her, little more than a dream that was over, and in this view he was not far wrong. "She felt that she was growing old; her health was causing her anxiety, and it may well have been that this good, Christian woman thought it her duty to discontinue a guilty relationship which no longer had the excuse of irresistible attraction . . ."[11] Made irritable by discomfiture, Sainte-Beuve filled his notebooks with cruel comments on Victor Hugo: "Hugo, the dramatist, is Caliban posing as Shakespeare . . ."[12] "When Hugo girds at me for being interested only in trivial subjects, does he perhaps mean that I am no longer interested in him? . . ." "Hugo: a glaring example of sophistry . . ." and even on Adèle: "It is easy enough when one is young to dispense with intelligence in the beauty one loves, and with judgment in the talent one admires (I have proved the truth of this in the case of the Hugos—both male and female)."[13] So much lucidity is a sharp-edged weapon, dangerous even for him who wields it, and Sainte-Beuve suffered.

Madame Victor Hugo and the children spent the whole of the summer of 1836, from May till October, not as formerly at Les Roches, but at Fourqueux (in the Forest of Marly) with Monsieur Foucher, who was now an old man. In the month of August, Fontaney spent a day with them there, and enjoyed it immensely: "The gayest dinner I have known for a long time. Victor, coatless, in his shirtsleeves, or, rather, in one of his wife's wrappers, was in the highest of high spirits . . . Heaps of beefsteaks . . . A visit from the curé. Monsieur Foucher and his caterpillars . . ."[14] For the children the presence of their father was a glorious treat. When he left them to go on a trip with Juliette, Didine wrote to him: "I am so sorry, my dear Papa, that you have to cover so many miles on foot with only bad suppers to make up for your weariness. But I am not angry, because I hope that what you are going through will bring you back soon to your little Fourqueux where you will find none but those who love you with all their hearts."[15] When he returned to the Place Royale, his wife joined him there, but the children stayed on at Fourqueux. *Léopoldine to Adèle Hugo:* "We get up at eight, go to Mass, have breakfast. Then I practice the piano ... Dédé plays ... Monsieur le curé comes every day to instruct me in my religious duties, dines here, and spends the evening ... Do ask my darling father whether he wouldn't like to give me a story called *Les Laveuses du Couvent*. It is very pretty. If he won't, please buy it all the same; he'll have to pay for it ..."[16] She was being prepared for her First Communion by the Abbé Roussel, the parish priest of Fourqueux, and by her pious grandfather, who composed a number of hymns for her use. There still exists the Diary of Didine's Retreat, ninety-two pages of "Analyses des instructions préparatoires à ma Première Communion." Victor Hugo, Robelin and Théophile Gautier were present at the ceremony, which took place on Sunday, September 9th, the Feast of the Nativity of the Blessed Virgin, in the parish church of Fourqueux. Léopoldine, the only communicant, was an edifying spectacle for all those in the congregation. In the presence of so much innocence and artless charm, even unbelievers felt deeply moved. Auguste de Châtillon painted a picture of the scene. On August 20th Madame Victor Hugo had sent to the parish priest of Fourqueux a complete bound set of her husband's works in twenty volumes (price: forty francs) and had asked the publisher, Renduel, to deduct the sum "unobtrusively" from the author's royalty account.

The white Communion dress had—oh! shades of romanticism!—been made by Juliette Drouet from one of her old organdie gowns, a filmy relic of the days of her guilty splendour. After the Mass, Hugo returned to Paris, much to the disappointment of the guests invited to the banquet to which Pierre Foucher and his daughter had asked all the clergy of the neighbourhood. Madame Hugo, always nervous where accounts were concerned, wrote to Victor: "The expenses in connection with Didine's First Communion do not come to more than two hundred francs. That is dear enough, I know, but as soon as Châtillon has finished his picture he will leave, and then *I shall shut up the house*."[17] Order reigned at Fourqueux.

On April 16th, 1837, Hugo and Sainte-Beuve both attended the funeral service of Gabrielle Dorval, Fontaney's mistress, Marie Dorval's eldest daughter, and "the perfection of feminine beauty," who had died at the age of twenty-one. The meeting was an awkward one. *Sainte-Beuve to Ulric Guttinguer, April 28th, 1837:* "There were five of us all in one cab, among others, Hugo, Barbier, I, Bonnaire (of the

Revue des Deux Mondes); it needed only Vigny to have made the party complete! Three of the company, Hugo and I, on the one side, Bonnaire and I on the other, did not exchange a word or give the slightest sign of recognition—three out of five in a cab. What a funeral!"[18] The friendship in their hearts was more dead than the young woman in her coffin . . . "Hugo, calm, impassive, talked with the poor husband;[19] Sainte-Beuve, all nerves and uneasiness, said not a word, but sat looking out of the window. Had he had wings he would doubtless have flown away. . . ."[20]

For some while yet he tried to persuade himself that Adèle might come back to him. *To Guttinguer, June 20th, 1837:* "She keeps to her room and can bear neither to drive nor walk. It is only with the greatest difficulty, and at long intervals, that I can get direct and accurate news of her. Alas! An evening or two back, in this lovely summer weather, I took my way through the happy crowds, whimpering and weeping like a wounded stag . . ."[21] In an attempt to win her over, he published in the *Revue des Deux Mondes* a long short story, "Madame de Pontivy," which was only too transparent. In it, he painted his love, in the person of the hero, Murçay—endowed with "all the author's sensibility" —who falls in love with a woman who is unhappily married, disappointed, lonely, and, because of her harsh shyness, misunderstood. "Her life must have been like one of those valleys which are almost completely shut in, and never see the sun except at noon, when its heat is already intense . . ."[22] At last, Madame de Pontivy awakens to passion and, though not fully roused, gratifies her friend's desires, not that she shares them, but because she wants him to be completely happy. Soon, however, their love appears to die from its own inertia. Murçay wanders through the loneliest places he can find, unable to do anything but repeat over and over to himself: "Laissez moi, tout a fui!" In the story, harmony is re-established at the last moment, as the result of a tender approach on the part of Murçay, and the lovers together enter on the happy evening of their days.

But life does not always imitate art. In the real world Madame Victor Hugo was all the more irritated by a story only too obviously aimed at her; too obviously, because some time before its appearance she had received from Sainte-Beuve a set of verses containing the very same moan which he later put into the mouth of Murçay:

> Laissez-moi! tout a fui! Le printemps recommence;
> L'été s'anime et le désir à lui;
> Les sillons et les cœurs agitent leur semence.
> Laissez-moi! tout a fui!

Victor Hugo, too, read "Madame de Pontivy" in the pages of the magazine. He learned that Sainte-Beuve was putting it about that the tale had been written for the sole purpose of reassuring "someone very dear to me," and flew into a fury. It appears that, by common agreement between husband and wife, the indiscreet author was summoned to the Place Royale, and there given his definite dismissal. This violent scene must have taken place round about October 1837. Almost immediately afterwards Sainte-Beuve left for Switzerland where he was to deliver a course of lectures, in Lausanne, on *Port-Royal*. Never was foreign travel more opportune. *Sainte-Beuve to Guttinguer:* "Humanly speaking, my life has been wasted—of that I am only too well aware. There is nothing left for me but to find salvation in literature . . .": and on May 18th, 1838: "When I left Paris in October, I was under a triple curtain of gloom . . . I had every reason to be. So far as the Place Royale is concerned, I had had an experience which only a brief talk between us could make clear: on the one hand, a crude and murky bit of scheming in which I could smell the Cyclops; on the other, an incredible piece of stupid credulity which gave me the measure of an intelligence no longer transformed by the light of love . . ."[23] He went so far, out of sheer spite, as to pass judgment on poor Adèle in the most savage and unfair way. When he returned to Paris, he noted: "Saw A. again. Have I proved that maxim of La Rochefoucauld—'On pardonne tant que l'on aime?' I feel that love, for me, is a thing of the past, so far, at least, as *she* is concerned." Three years later he wrote in his journal: *"I hate her!"* But he always remembered with pride the one and only conquest of his life which really flattered his self-esteem, and, with anger, the humiliating way in which it had been terminated. He never altogether gave up seeing Adèle, or from time to time corresponding with her. In 1845 he wrote to George Sand: "Nothing will ever console me for no longer loving nor being loved; for no longer having, to my present sorrow and my eternal despair, a morrow of hope —as I always did have in that good time when I was so unhappy. . . ."[24]

For Victor Hugo, this rupture carried with it the implication that it was his duty now to establish a system of fair shares between wife and mistress. Where Juliette was concerned, all was love, and nothing but love, though hedged about with storms and poverty. He had set her up in the Marais, at 13 rue Sainte-Anastase, within a stone's throw of the Place Royale. The tiny apartment was plastered all over with pictures of, and drawings by, the god of the house. The two lovers filled it with such objects as luck and the second-hand dealers brought their way—Gothic statuettes and scraps of old fabric. In Juliette's bedroom, between the bed and the hearth, with its "good crackling fire," she had established a corner where her poet could work, with well-sharpened goose-quills, a lamp always trimmed, and a supply of ruled paper. From her bed she would gaze in silence at that "dear head" busy giving life and shape to its sublime thoughts. "As I looked at you a while back, I was overcome with admiration of your face, so beautiful, so noble, so visibly inspired . . ."[25] Those hours repaid her for all her past humiliations.

He was fully alive to the sweetness of being thus adored. Not that the adoration was blind. Juliette had her full share of grudges and jealousies, both of them legitimate, for there was in the Place Royale a secret staircase which led directly to Victor Hugo's study, and she, who had often been received in that room, knew perfectly well that many other women had there surrendered to the master's charms. *Juliette to Victor Hugo:* "You are handsome, too handsome, and I am jealous even when you are with me. I leave you to imagine my feelings when you are not! I want to be the only person in the world who loves you, because my heart is capable of providing you with all the love of all the women in the world . . ."[26] Her lover's chastity could no doubt be explained in terms of his secret pleasures. She often caught him out in a piece of flagrant lying. He said to her: "I have to go into the country to see my family," and she discovered that his family was still in the Place Royale. What secret escapades was he concealing?

Juliette, after having been jealous of Mademoiselle George and of Marie Dorval, was now beginning to live in fear of her own dress-maker, and of Mademoiselle Lison, a dancer at the Opéra. Temptresses fell tooth and nail upon a man who seldom resisted them. Actresses in search of an engagement, ardent and flirtatious young women of the world, 'prentice female novelists—all and sundry pulled at the door-bell of the secret staircase. The divan was a fine place on which to discuss poetry! "If I were a queen," said Juliette, "you should never be allowed out without an iron mask of which only I held the key." But it was she who wore the fetters, and the Unfaithful One still forbade her to go abroad without him. "Why this life of a prisoner?" she asked: "I love you, my Toto, and that is the strongest bolt you could possibly want . . ."[27] She could not grow used to this tyranny: "For very nearly four years, during which your love has smothered me, I have been forced into a position where I can neither move nor breathe. There is danger that my faith in you may be buried under the ruins of our *liaison*. . . ."[28]

Perhaps she would not have put up with his demands had it not been for the holidays they took together. Each summer she had these marvellous interludes. "Someone" (that is to say, Adèle) settled down with the four children in the country, at Fourqueux or Boulogne-sur-Seine, and for six weeks the lovers, temporarily transformed into husband and wife, left for Fougères, the town in which Juliette Gauvain had been born, or for Belgium with its carillons, its belfries, and its old houses, which so completely enthralled him.

Adèle, now that she no longer had for her thin rivulet of sentiment the outlet formerly provided by Sainte-Beuve, could no longer accept these disappearances of her husband with the old high nobility of soul. "You must not again go travelling without me next year. *On that I am resolved.* I am, I hope, acting within my rights. What I am saying to you, I mean. If it is impossible for *us* to go travelling, I will take a house where I shall be a great deal better off with my father and Julie[29] than when left at a loose end. Under those conditions, I merely set her a bad example. You can perfectly well arrange not to have to go to Paris every day, and can take temporary roots in the country. Communications are so easy. In that way, you will be able, my friend, to let me have a happy year, for that I know you can do. When you tell me that such a thing is *not possible* I often pretend to believe what you say so as not to be a plague to you. But I am not convinced. . . ."[30]

Victor, in a very vague reply, appeared to be in agreement with her. *Dieppe, September 8th, 1837:* "Travel is nothing but a form of dizziness, quickly come and quickly gone. It is in one's own home that happiness is to be found . . ."[31] Men who are inconstant but soft-hearted always find themselves driven into a position where they say more than they mean, and make promises which they cannot keep.

There was further compensation for Juliette in the Red Book of Special Occasions which she kept always under her pillow. In this, February 17th, May 26th and other dates of high festival were marked by verses contributed every year by Hugo. Her thanks for these were expressed in ecstatic language: "I believe that should God ever manifest Himself to me, it would be in your shape, for you are my faith, my religion, and my hope. Nothing can be more certain than that it is you whom God has made in His own image. Therefore, it is you whom I love in Him, and Him whom I adore in you. . . ."[32]

This deification revived in Hugo the spirit of Olympio. She would have loved passionately to make with him a pilgrimage to Metz, where they had been so happy, but he chose to go there without her, in October 1837, in order to be alone with their shared memories. Both Lamartine and Musset had, from such "returns," produced masterpieces, and he hoped to compete with them on their own ground.

> Il voulait tout revoir, l'étang près de la source,
> La masure ou l'aumône avait vidé leur bourse,
>   Le vieux frêne plié,
> Les retraites d'amour au fond des bois perdus,
> L'arbre où, dans les baisers, leurs âmes confondues
>   Avaient tout oublié!
>
> Il chercha le jardin, la maison isolée,
> La grille d'où l'œil plonge en une oblique allée,
>   Les vergers en talus.

Pâle, il marchait. Au bruit de son pas grave et sombre,
Il voyait à chaque arbre, hélas! se dresser à l'ombre
Des jours qui ne sont plus! . . .[33]

The fruit of those days, spent in dreamy wanderings about the countryside which had been the scene of the sweetest episode that he had ever known, was a poem: "Tristesse d'Olympio." Why *tristesse* after so much joy? Because the contrast between nature's eternal beauty and man's fugitive happiness is ever painful to the romantic heart:

Que peu de temps suffit pour changer toutes choses!
Nature au front serein, comme vous oubliez!
Et comme vous brisez, dans vos métamorphoses,
Les fils mystérieux où nos cœurs sont liés!

D'autres vont maintenant passer où nous passâmes.
Nous y sommes venus; d'autres vont y venir;
Et le songe qu'avaient ébauché nos deux âmes,
Ils le continueront, sans pouvoir le finir . . .

Eh bien, oubliez-nous, maison, jardin, ombrages!
Herbe, use notre seuil! Ronce, cache nos pas!
Chantez, oiseaux! Ruisseaux, coulez! Croissez, feuillages!
Ceux que vous oubliez ne vous oublieront pas.

Car vous êtes pour nous l'ombre et l'amour même!
Vous êtes l'oasis qu'on rencontre en chemin.
Vous êtes, ô vallon! la retraite suprême
Où nous avons pleuré, nous tenant par la main!

Toutes les passions s'éloignent avec l'âge,
L'une emportant son masque et l'autre son couteau,
Comme un essaim chantant d'histrions en voyage
Dont le groupe décroît derrière le coteau. . . .[34]

Such poetry sets Time at defiance. Thought takes on form and substance, in simple country scenes and human memories, to stir the imagination. "Le Lac" had been very beautiful, this poem was so no less. Juliette, who copied it, used to refer to it artlessly as "those verses about the walks we once took," and, a rare occurrence with her, did not praise as much as she should have done the marvellous gift he had made her. Perhaps it was that she felt sad at seeing thrust back into the past what, in her eyes, was timeless. All she asked was to return to that dear valley, so certain did she feel that she could find, even more unerringly than he could, the spots in which they had once been happy.

Such precise actuality is peculiar to women. Talk of them of eternity, and they will reply with topographical detail.

Poor Eugène died on March 5th, 1837. In the early days of his mental sickness he had had occasional lucid intervals. Fontaney, visiting the Saint-Maurice asylum, had run into him by chance. *April 3rd, 1832:* "Visit to Charenton . . . the yard where the violent lunatics are kept . . . Victor's brother. He got up; remembered about poetry, and the Toulouse Prize . . ."[35] Then the poor fellow's mind had begun to wander, and he had relapsed into forgetfulness. His brothers went to see him, but not very often, because Saint-Maurice (Charenton) was a long way off, life in Paris a tyrannical master, and the doctors uncommunicative. Victor had never freed himself from a sense of remorse. He felt guilty towards this living corpse, this man buried alive in his own private world. To the importunate ghost he offered a libation in the form of a poem: "À Eugène, vicomte H . . ." In it he evoked the memory of their childhood games: "Tu dois te souvenir de nos jeunes années— Tu dois te souvenir des vertes Feuillantines . . ." They had known happiness together and together had discovered the beauty of the world, together, they had taken their first country walks. All that was ended now, for him who lived on as for him who was dead; for both the innocent dreams of boyhood were over.

> Tu vas dormir là-haut sur la colline verte
> Qui, livrée à l'hiver, à tous les vents ouverte,
> À le ciel pour plafond;
> Tu vas dormir, poussière, au fond d'un lit d'argile;
> Er moi je resterai parmi ceux de la ville
> Qui parlent et qui vont!
>
> Et moi je vais rester, souffrir, agir et vivre,
> Voir mon nom se grossir dans les bouches de cuivre
> De la célébrité;
> Et cacher, comme à Sparte, en riant quand on entre,
> Le renard envieux qui me ronge le ventre,
> Sous ma robe abrité.[36]

One way of appeasing the dead is to complain of life. "Regret nothing, you are at rest," say the living. It gives them the right to forget. Abel Hugo sent in the bill:

Paid, for carriage and miscellaneous funeral expenses	17.60
Balance still due for Eugène's keep	165
TOTAL	Fr.182.60
Victor's half:	91.30[37]

Mournful arithmetic, but the Hugo brothers had been trained to count pennies. Eugène's death, for he had been the eldest boy, transformed Victor, if the Spanish title be taken in strict seriousness, into *le vicomte* Hugo. A first step, this, to the peerage. Henceforward, Adèle, whenever she was writing to an intimate friend, always signed her letters—*La Vicomtesse Victor Hugo*. Conjugal long-suffering was not without its compensations.

25

Juliette Among the Immortals

Most celebrated men live in a condition of
prostitution.

SAINTE-BEUVE, Notebooks

Fame is a species of ailment which one catches
as a result of cohabiting with one's thoughts.

PAUL VALÉRY

IN 1837 the Duc d'Orléans married Princess Hélène of Mecklenburg.
Victor Hugo was on better terms with the heir to the throne than he
was with Louis Philippe. Quite apart from personal grievances (such
as the banning of *Le Roi s'amuse*) he reproached the Government with
being false to its origins. Born of a revolution, it was now favouring
reaction. More and more Hugo was becoming conscious of a poet's
duty towards the humble and oppressed.

The republican opponents of the regime, the men of *Le National*,
had had great hopes of winning Victor Hugo to their way of thinking,
but he was still of the opinion that France was not yet ripe for a
republic. What would most have attracted him would have been a
socially-minded Bonapartist movement. But where was a new Bonaparte to be found? The Duc de Reichstadt was dead. Hugo saw the
regime of July growing daily stronger. The journal edited by his friend
Émile de Girardin, a professed opportunist, was adopting a completely
pro-Government line, and hoped to find in Victor Hugo a valuable
recruit. "Girardin," said Sainte-Beuve, "gives me the impression that
he is out to land a big whale; and he'll do it, right enough." In default
of a king whom he found too cautious, and, where he was concerned,
too little enthusiastic, he was establishing ever closer relations with the
Duc d'Orléans, the hope of all who were working for a programme of
political liberalism. Help solicited, not without a little playful self-
deprecation for an old professor ("Prince, may I hope that Your Royal
Highness will deign to listen to the prayer of one unknown for another?"), and immediately granted, and a poem of thanks, had led to
the establishment of a steady friendship between the prince and the

poet. When Louis Philippe, on the occasion of the marriage of his eldest son, gave a great banquet at Versailles, in the Hall of Mirrors, Hugo was invited. His first instinct was to refuse. To make one of a company of fifteen hundred guests seemed to him to be a meagre and a boring honour. Furthermore, the king, with whom Alexandre Dumas had, for some time, been out of favour, had refused to allow the drama- tist to be asked. Hugo declared that he would not attend without Dumas. The Duc d'Orléans intervened in person, managed to have Dumas restored to grace, brought pressure to bear, and finally had his way. Hugo and Dumas, both wearing National Guard uniform (they had no court dress), went to Versailles, where they met Balzac in all his splendour.

Victor Hugo had no reason to regret his acceptance of the invitation. He was placed at table next to the Duc d'Aumale. The king lavished compliments on him. The Duchesse d'Orléans, a princess of vast culture and high nobility of mind, and the possessor of a frank and handsome countenance, told him how pleased she was to make his acquaintance, that she had often spoken of him to Monsieur de Gœthe, that she knew his poems by heart, and was especially fond of the one beginning "C'était une humble église au cintre surbaisse." This was no more than the truth. From the age of sixteen this young German girl had taken a passionate interest in the literary life of France. "Her dream was Paris; her poet Victor Hugo." She told him, too: "I have visited *your* Notre-Dame." It seemed obvious that there was a general wish to please the illustrious guest; and pleased he was. Three weeks after the marriage he received his promotion to the rank of Officer of the Legion of Honour. Lackeys appeared at the Place Royale bearing a romantic picture, "Inez de Castro," a gift from *Le Duc et la Duchesse d'Orléans à Monsieur Victor Hugo, June 27, 1837*. He became *the* poet of the future queen of the French. No reception at the Pavillon de Marsan was complete without him, not only the official Tuesdays, but the more intimate gatherings which were generally known as *la Cheminée*. Those of the inner circle would ask one another: "Are you going to *la Cheminée?*" There they would find Victor Hugo explaining to the Duke, "eight years his junior, the view he held that the poet is God's messenger to the Princes of this world."[1]

Had he a feeling of tenderness for his future queen? No doubt a mingling of admiration as a man, and the chivalrous devotion which a young, beautiful and romantic woman, destined to wear a crown, can inspire, came naturally to the author of *Ruy Blas*, "an earthworm in love with a star." But any feeling of this kind which he may have had remained respectful and secret. There is, however, in existence the draft of a curious letter from the poet to the Duchess. In January 1838 the Vicomte and Vicomtesse Hugo entertained the princely couple under their own roof in the Place Royale. Louise Bertin organized a choir of young girls to sing a chorus from *La Esmeralda*. It was a brilliant occasion which served to establish the dynastic position of the Hugos.

The Duc d'Orléans expressed surprise that Victor Hugo had abandoned the stage. The poet replied that the theatre was a thing of the past, now that "the Comédie-Française is given over to the dead, and the Porte-Saint-Martin abandoned to fools." The Prince caused Monsieur Guizot to offer the poet the rare privilege of establishing a new playhouse. This was the Renaissance, the direction of which Dumas and Hugo entrusted to a newspaper editor named Anténor Joly. It was to be inaugurated with a new drama in verse by Hugo.

Where did he find the subject of *Ruy Blas*? The sources were many and various—a melodrama by Latouche (*La Reine d'Espagne*), a novel by Léon de Wailly which tells how the painter Reynolds arranged for Angelica Kauffmann, whom he had cast off, to be married to an English lackey. For the setting he had recourse to the *Rélation du voyage d'Espagne* by Madame d'Aulnoy. The play, in its mixture of poetry, farce, fantasy and politics, was essentially a Hugoesque production. Ruy Blas, the dreamer, finds himself promoted to a position of power by his genius and by his queen. Dream of accomplishment. "There is, in *Ruy Blas*, something of a fairy-tale, and also something of a political manifesto." Ruy Blas himself "stands for the people, who have the future in their hands, but not the present . . . a man who, in his poverty, falls in love with the only person in whom he sees the divine fire" —the queen.

The play, written in a single month, is his best. The heroic verse has the beat and fullness of the classics of the great period. The rhyme, rich and sonorous, drives home many oratorical passages, one at least of which (the speech in the third act) is a masterpiece of poetry and history. Frédérick Lemaître played Ruy Blas. Victor Hugo was well aware how deeply Juliette felt the total interruption of her career as an actress, and could not ignore the fact that the responsibility for this was his. But for the glare, the excessive glare, cast upon her by the love of a great man, she would, like many others, have gone on filling small roles. Anxious to give her some compensation, he offered her the part of Queen Maria de Neuburg. Dumas had prevailed upon the Renaissance to engage his mistress Ida Ferrier (who, in 1840, was to become his wife), and Hugo had a right to demand a similar favour for Juliette. She was beside herself with delight. "Ever since you have let me see that there might be a chance for me to act in your entrancing play, I have been like a poor sleepwalker who has been given a lot of champagne to drink . . ."[2] But it was too good to be true. She had a feeling that she would be disappointed. "I shall die before I appear at the

Théâtre de la Renaissance. Those folk will make my passage into eternity easy." However, since to this promise he had added the offer of a week's jaunt with him to Montmirail, Rheims, Varennes and Vouziers, the poor woman found herself suddenly caught up into a blaze of happiness: "I love you, my Toto; I adore you, my little man: you are my sun and my life. . . ."[3]

But eclipse soon hid the sun. Adèle Hugo took advantage of her husband's absence to act in a way which was effective, cruel and deserving of the most severe condemnation. From Boulogne, where she was staying with the children, she wrote to Anténor Joly:

> You will no doubt be surprised to find me interfering in a matter which, in the last resort, concerns only you and my husband. All the same, sir, I feel that I have some right to do what I am doing, when I see the success of one of Victor's plays compromised, and deliberately compromised at that. This is what I fear, because the part of the queen has been given to a person who was in part responsible for the disturbances which occurred on the first night of *Marie Tudor* . . . Rightly or wrongly, the talent of Mademoiselle Juliette is much disputed. I hope that you will find some way of entrusting the role to another actress. I need hardly tell you that I am concerned only for the success of the play. That is why I am so insistent. It is but natural that my husband, who takes a great interest in the lady, should have supported her in her attempt to be engaged by your theatre. But I cannot allow his feelings to compromise the success of this very fine composition. . . .[4]

Adèle was laying to the account of artistic anxiety what, in fact, was nothing but jealousy. She had asked Anténor Joly to maintain complete secrecy about her letter to him, and by so doing sinned against conjugal loyalty. The director was duly impressed and, as soon as Hugo got back, told him that he had given the part of the queen to Atala Beau-chêne (who, for this auspicious occasion, would resume her real name of Louise Beaudoin). She had every claim to consideration, being the mistress of Frédérick Lemaître. Hugo knew nothing of Adèle's letter, but since, in his heart of hearts, he shared the nervousness about which Joly had spoken, he gave way. He broke the news to Juliette as diplomatically as he could, explaining that the change was due, not to any lack of talent on her part, but to back-stage intrigue and prejudice. The blow was a hard one. "You have been good and kind to me, my poor darling. I know the efforts you have made to keep me in ignorance of affronts, and to spare me pain. I deeply appreciate those efforts— what must be must be . . ."[5] The successful run of *Ruy Blas* was, for her, one long martyrdom. "I am feeling terribly sad, my best beloved, Secretly, I am in mourning for a beautiful and splendid role which, so far as I am concerned, is now dead for ever. Maria de Neuburg will never live *through* me and *for* me. I grieve more than you can possibly

imagine. The loss of this one last hope has struck me to the ground."
Then, resigned and devoted, she had a new dress made for the opening
night, and split her gloves with the violence of her applause. With
Ruy Blas her last chance of getting back into the theatre, and of earning
a living for herself and Claire, had vanished. What would happen
should Hugo leave her? And, even if he remained faithful, what would
become of her pride? All her life long, she would be nothing but a kept
woman.

Throughout that year the thought grew in her that unless she could
make herself independent all hope of salvation would, in the absence
of legitimate union, be impossible. What she needed was the "moral
consecration of their marriage of love." To be *his wife* in spirit and in
heart, that was what she demanded. Upon the physical fidelity of her
faun with his hundred nymphs she could scarcely rely. Her lover's care
for his personal appearance, his skin-tight trousers, the attention he
paid to the way in which his hair was done—these things were tantamount to a confession, as was his too frequent absence from the bed
in the rue Saint-Anastase. "Verily I say unto you, every man who keeps
not his promise shall be deemed to be a bad lover, and he who, at
evening, looks to see whether his nightdress is laid out at the foot of
the bed, knowing full well that he will not return until the daylight
hours, shall be regarded as a beast. And it came to pass that in those
days Jugu said to her Toto—'You have no common sense: you let the
beautiful fruits of the soul fall to the ground and be devoured of
worms, instead of gathering them up with love and savouring them
with delight as beautiful fruits come straight from the Garden of
Paradise.' "[6] At the very least she wanted the certainty that her relationship with him would last, that she would be able to follow him
wherever he went, and have an absolute right to stand between him
and other women.

To these demands and outpourings which went on all through the
year 1839 he replied with a peevish air. *Ruy Blas* had been no more
than a partial success. He was discontented and harried. Romantic
drama was beginning to be out of favour. The severe Gustave Planche
had said some very hard things: "A challenge to good sense and good
taste . . . revolting cynicism . . . a childish piling up of impossible scenes
. . . Monsieur Hugo came by his success too early . . . He is imprisoned
in self-adoration as in a citadel . . . From pride so excessive as to be
scarcely sane there is but one step, and Monsieur Hugo has just taken
it by writing *Ruy Blas* . . ."[7] If there was anything "scarcely sane" in
this clash, the critic and not the author was responsible for it. It is
perfectly permissible for a man to dislike the melodramatic aspects of
this kind of stage writing, but he should not turn a blind eye to its
manifest beauties. The truth of the matter was that the new generation

was, Sainte-Beuve among them, growing to hate "these great rubri-
cated capitals slashed with gold like the lackeys he brings on to the
stage."

Meanwhile, Hugo was working on a new drama, *Les Jumeaux,* and
explained to Juliette that he was completely exhausted. She wondered
anxiously whether work alone could account for such complete lassitude. "Good-day to you, rhinoceros, good-day to you, royal tiger," she
said to this lover with a sore head. When she complained, he swore that
she was the only woman for whom he had ever felt *genuine love.* Was
that merely one of the things men say when they want to be left in
peace? She would not let herself believe this, and longed for the unique
character of their love to be attested by an oath taken not to men but
to God. On the night of November 17th-18th, 1839, he agreed to the
suggestion. He swore that he would never abandon either Juliette or
Claire. In return, Juliette undertook to give up the stage for ever. This
was not a bargain, but a mystic marriage, and, for Claire Pradier, the
equivalent of a deed of adoption.

Juliette Drouet to Victor Hugo, November 18th, 1839: That nothing
might be lacking to our marriage, I had all the emotions suitable to a bride
on her first day—ineffable happiness—divine ecstasy—sleeplessness—amazement . . . All those things I felt last night. I slept scarcely at all, only a
few hours in fact, although I lay late in bed. And so it was, my poor object
of adoration, my *all-but husband*—and the all-but really does not matter—
that my uprising and my morning prayer were those of a new-made wife.
O yes—I am your wife, am I not, my dear darling? You can acknowledge
me without a blush, and yet my first title, the one I wish to keep among all
others, above all others, is that of your mistress. . . .[8]

And what of him? What were his feelings? He admired such a wealth
of proffered beauty, a creature so noble and so generous, a love so
humble and so passionate. He was grateful to Juliette for having given
him seven years of happiness, for having restored his self-confidence.
He gravely undertook, and honestly, to be as a father to the little Claire
who was being made miserable because of the false position in which
she was compelled to live. Nevertheless, he continued to impose upon
his "mystic bride" a ridiculously cloistered life, without a garden in
which to take the air, without a yard in which to walk. An existence
in which she had, for tree, only her stove-pipe, and for sun, only her
Carcel lamp, was becoming for this Breton girl, bred in the open air,
a veritable torment. "Toto, Toto, you are not being kind to me!"—
less than kind, indeed, since he allowed himself the free enjoyment of
every whim and every infidelity. But rules are not made for genius.
Ego Hugo. And then, in 1840, she had two months of travel with him,
from Belgium to Cologne and Mainz. It was on this occasion that he

made discovery of the Black Forest, the name of which had evoked in his child's mind dark woodland glades. They went as far as the Rhine. Wan skies seen through Gothic tracery. Bushes growing on the ruins of ancient towers. Throughout their trip he was, as ever, "adorably good and sweet." Nothing better suited their love than change of scene.

She had also, in 1839, and again in 1840, more academic calls, more stolen moments in a cab. Hugo still felt an urgent desire for the Académie Française, and he was used to getting what he wanted. In 1839 the death of Michaud, the historian of the Crusades, had made a vacancy. Hugo was looked upon as the Court candidate, and though he denied the imputation that, in fact, was what he was. He had been flirting with Louis-Philippe ever since the evening at Versailles. When Armand Barbès had been condemned to death for making an armed attack on the Conciergerie, the commander of which had been killed in the subsequent affray, Hugo had taken the following lines to the Tuileries:

> Par votre ange envolée ainsi qu'une colombe!
> Par ce royal enfant, doux et frêle roseau!
> Grâce encore une fois! Grâce au nom de la tombe!
> Grâce au nom du berceau![9]

The king's reply was gracious—and constitutional. "My thought had anticipated yours. At the very moment you were asking for mercy, mercy was in my heart. It merely remains for me now to obtain it—Louis-Philippe."[10] It was this incident that led the poet to write at a later date: "Louis-Philippe was as gentle as Louis IX, and as good as Henri IV . . . one of the best princes who has sat upon the throne. . . ."[11]

On this occasion Victor Hugo's rival for the Academy was Berryer. The government censorship authorities, formerly Hugo's enemies, supported him against the legitimist orator. A newspaper which was carrying on a campaign in favour of Berryer wanted to publish a caricature in which the Academy, represented as a dear old soul, was shown, receiving at the door of the Palais Mazarin, Victor Hugo, Balzac and Alexandre Dumas. The legend ran: "You are big, strong men, yet you are asking to be pensioned! Do you wish to steal the bread from the poor and old? Go and work, you good-for-nothing loafers!" The censorship banned it. The election was held on December 19th. The first returns showed: Berryer, ten votes: Hugo, nine: Bonjour, nine: Vatout, two; Lamennais, none. Three blank papers were handed in. After seven ballots, the election was postponed for three months. The votes cast for Casimir Bonjour, a writer of insipid tales for children, were interpreted as in part "against Berryer," in part as "against Hugo."

On December 31st, 1839, a new vacancy was created by the death of Monsignor de Quélen, Archbishop of Paris, the man who had brought about Julienne Gauvain's liberation from the convent. On February 20th, 1840, a double election was held. The Comte Molé, with thirty votes out of thirty-one, succeeded to Quélen's chair, while Flourens won Michaud's, thereby defeating Hugo. Népomucène Lemercier had been one of his most determined opponents, and on one occasion Dumas had said to him: "Monsieur Lemercier, you have refused to give your vote to Victor Hugo. But there is one thing that, sooner or later, you will have to give him—your chair."

And so it came about. Lemercier died on June 17th, 1840. Cousin said to Sainte-Beuve: "Hugo's really *got* to be elected. The whole business is becoming a bore, and it's time it was finished." On January 7th, 1841, Hugo defeated Ancelot, a third-rate dramatist, by seventeen votes to fifteen. Chateaubriand, Lamartine, Villemain, Nodier, Cousin and Mignet all voted for him, as did also a number of the political members—Thiers, Molé, Salvandy, Royer-Collard—which, so he thought, showed the direction in which the wind was blowing. It might even, perhaps, be interpreted as a definite invitation. Guizot, who was one of Hugo's supporters, arrived late and was debarred from voting. Sainte-Beuve in his notebooks expressed approval of the outcome: "After all, it's no bad thing; the Academy needs deflowering from time to time. . . ."[12]

Juliette had been strongly opposed to this fifth candidature: "I wish there were no such things as Academies, Theatres and Bookshops. I wish the world consisted only of Main-Roads, Diligences, and Juju and Toto adoring one another . . ."[13] But on the evening of the election she flung her arms round his neck, with a "Welcome, Toto: welcome, my Academician. You're seated now until such time as you grow sedate!"[14] For the ceremony of his reception she ordered a fine new dress (the recently elected Academician had to accompany her to her fittings, since he still would not let her go out alone), and arrived at the Quai Conti, so excited was she, well in advance of the presiding officials. The crowd was bigger than had ever been seen before on such an occasion. It included Madame de Girardin, Madame Louise Colet, Madame Thiers, as well as numerous actresses. It also included—and this caused much amusement—both Adèle and Juliette. For the first time in ten years members of the Royal Family were welcomed "sous la Coupole." The Duc and Duchesse d'Orléans (the latter looking very pretty in a white hat with pale pink roses under the brim) were received at the door of the Palais Mazarin by the permanent secretary, Villemain. "This, I believe," he said, "is the first occasion on which your Royal Highness has come to the Institut?" "It will not be the last," replied the heir to the throne.

Hugo's entry was that of an emperor. His brown, smooth, carefully brushed hair was swept back from the pyramidal brow and fell in long curls over the green-embroidered collar of his coat. His black eyes, rather small and sunken, gleamed with suppressed pleasure. His first smile was for Juliette, who, seeing him look so pale and agitated, felt that she was about to faint: "Thank you, my adored, thank you, for sparing a thought for the poor woman who loves you, at so solemn a moment, so *supreme* a moment, I should say, were it not that most of those present were hideous boobies and filthy scoundrels . . ."[15] The recluse was filled with happiness by seeing, on the benches, "all *my* dear little ones, Didine, looking ravishing, Charlot, charming, and my sweet little Toto, the very image of that other who looked so pale and seemed so ill. . . ."[16]

Hugo's speech was something of a surprise. He talked for twenty minutes about Napoleon, referred with expressions of high praise to the Convention, the monarchy, the younger branch of the Royal Family, and France—"it is she," he said, "who has directed the course of universal thought." Of the Academy he remarked: "You are one of the principal centres of intellectual power." In a few brief words he touched on his predecessor, Lemercier, and in conclusion referred to Malesherbes as having been a great man of letters, a great Minister, and a great citizen. "Why Malesherbes?" wondered the disappointed audience. Those in the know, like Sainte-Beuve, replied: "deliberate and obvious spite," or, like Charles Magnin: "the key to that mystery lies in the two words *peerage* and *power*."[17] Sainte-Beuve jotted down in his notebook the following comment: "When Hugo succeeded Lemercier, he might have been succeeding Napoleon!" The President for the occasion, Narcisse-Achille de Salvandy, historian and man of politics, whom Thiers called "an honourable peacock,"[18] spared the new Academician none of the traditional "digs." Juliette's opinion of this boor was that he was "ugly, red-faced, offensive and ignorant." His address opened on a note of irony:

The ancients, when they were awarded a Triumph, surrounded themselves with the statues of their ancestors. Napoleon, Siéyès, Malesherbes, are none of them, sir, your ancestors. But you have others, no less illustrious: Rousseau, Clément Marot, Pindar and the Psalmist. We, here, recognize no finer family tree.

Hugo had reminded his listeners that Napoleon would have included Corneille among his ministers:

No! No! [said Salvandy]: had he done so we should have had fewer immortal dramas, that is certain. Is it equally certain that we should have had one great minister the more? To you we are grateful for having bravely defended your vocation as a poet against all the seductions of political ambition.[19]

These were false-hearted words when addressed to a man whose political ambitions were a matter of public knowledge. The faithful Juliette denounced the speaker's "blundering jealousy," but retained a wonderful memory of her first keen emotion: "from the moment when you entered the Great Hall of the Academy, I was a prey to feelings of delicious emotion, half way between intoxication and ecstasy. It was as though I had been granted a vision of Heaven with God in all His Majesty, Beauty, Splendour and Glory . . ."[20] The audience, which did not happen to be a woman in love, applauded Monsieur de Salvandy.

There exists a curious letter from Victor Hugo to Salvandy. The latter had told the new Academician, after the ceremony, that the king had been displeased by Hugo's referring to him as "Dumouriez's lieutenant," since Dumouriez had an evil reputation. Hugo replied: "The king's wishes shall be observed. The biographies are precise on the point, but I would rather believe the king than the biographers. I shall, therefore, alter the phrase to read 'Kellermann's lieutenant,' and will never again mention Dumouriez. I am sending my speech straight to Didot. Yours I have read in the *Débats,* and I am glad to say that, though it has somewhat wounded me as a man, in what are probably illusions on my part, as a writer, it has charmed me . . ."[21] This was a shrewd and subtle answer. But in the printed version of Hugo's speech, the words complained of appear as "Dumouriez's and Kellermann's lieutenant."

Royer-Collard, a mordant and grumpy doctrinaire, said to Victor Hugo, over his high cravat: "You made, sir, a very great speech to a very diminutive audience." The press, however, was not to be sidetracked; the great speech, no doubt about it, heralded great designs. "It is the first step to a parliamentary career; the utterance of a man who will be a candidate for one of the two Chambers, perhaps for both, which will be better still: the manifesto of a minister to be . . ."[22] *La Mode,* a humorous magazine, announced, as a gossip item, that "the Princesse Hélène, had she been about to assume the Crown of France, would have drawn up her list of Ministers as follows:

Minister of War, and President of the Council:
   Monsieur Victor Hugo
Minister of Foreign Affairs:
   Monsieur Théophile Gautier
Minister of Finance:
   Monsieur Alfred de Musset
Minister for the Navy:
   Monsieur de Lamartine[23]

Said Sainte-Beuve: "One can see him moving that way." Yes, one could see him moving that way, because he wanted to be thus seen, and made no secret of the goal he had in mind: *Chateaubriand or nothing*. After dreams—action. For some years now he had been setting up his aiming-posts: a tightening of his relations with the heir to the throne and his wife; Presidency of the Society of Literature; publication in brochure form of all his poems to the Emperor, on the occasion of the return of the Imperial ashes;[24] numerous receptions in the Place Royale (the Swiss Dairy furnished Madame Victor Hugo with decorative ices at 30 francs per hundred, sandwiches at 20 francs per hundred, iced coffee at 4 francs per bowl, and hot punch at 3 francs per bowl);[25] a tidying-up of the family finances. He granted to Delloye, the publisher, the right to handle all his works so far published, over a period of ten years, for a sum of 250,000 francs, 100,000 of which to be paid down. This meant freedom from money troubles, and also the possession of the necessary property qualification for a peerage. But Victor continued to preach economy to both his households. There must be no inroads on his capital. They must live on income alone.

There was, however, one expensive weakness to be reckoned with: he was becoming a fop. In the days when he had first achieved the conquest of Juliette, he had been too much the other way, and she, trained in the school of Prince Demidoff, had twitted him on his lack of smartness. This she now regretted: "What a fool I was ever to put that idea into your head. But who would have thought that a man like you could possibly be bitten by that bug? It makes me furious to think how well I succeeded. If only I could see you again as you were then, with your far-from-fancy braces, your tousled hair, and your crocodile teeth,"[26]—and, again: "Toto's curls make him look like a tailor's assistant: Toto is every inch a wax doll: Toto is ridiculous: Toto is an Academician."[27] He let her have her say. A future statesman must look the part. Madame Victor Hugo, whom the solidity of his liaison was making uneasy, used his ambitions as a weapon in her attempted offensive against Juliette:

I must admit that I feel uneasy about your future. If you are to succeed in your ambitions, your way of living must be a great deal more seemly than it is at present. You must be in a position to entertain in the same way as you are entertained. I know that our quiet way of life is not a serious obstacle, but it will make everything more difficult, and will keep you from reaching your goal as quickly as you want to. I am afraid that the financial burden which you have assumed may force you, sooner or later, to withdraw part of the money you have invested with such care. I tell you all this because I have an uncomfortable feeling that your efforts may prove fruitless, or else achieve only an inadequate result. Neither you, nor those belonging to you, ought to be reduced to having to scrape. You ought to live in a manner befitting your position. And here I must remind you of something

I have already said: I have, in the privacy of my own mind, abdicated every kind of *right* so far as any fortune you may have is concerned. I regard myself as being only a steward whose duty it is to watch over and run your house in as orderly a manner as possible, and supervise our children. I say *our children*. So far as they are in question I shall continue to exercise my rights to the full. It is, therefore, as regards yourself, my friend, and yourself only, that I beg you to reflect. I speak in your interest—as might a sister or a woman friend. I don't quite know what to say to make you believe in my complete disinterestedness. Think, I beg you, of your future. And try to find some way in which you may diminish your financial responsibilities. . . .[28]

But that would have meant breaking with Juliette. The physical bond was less than it had been in the early days, but Juliette was still everything that Adèle had never known how, nor wished, to be: the courageous travelling companion, the hard-working copyist, the skilled mouthpiece of praise, poetry incarnate. To her it was that hymns of gratitude were still sent: "Juliette—that charming name puts forth shoots within me, and flowers into poetry in the world. You are not only my heart, but all my thought as well . . . If I have any genius, it comes from you."[29] Again, on January 1st:

> Qu'est-ce que cette année emporte sur son aile?
> Je ne suis pas moins tendre et tu n'es pas moins belle;
> Nos deux cœurs, en dix ans, n'ont pas vieilli d'un jour.
> Vas, ne fais pas au temps de plainte et de reproche.
> A mesure qu'il fuit, du ciel il nous rapproche
> Sans nous éloigner de l'amour.[30]

The wife, for her part, made herself responsible for the good management of external relations. Since Sainte-Beuve had withdrawn from the battle, she had been, not without a hint of coquetry, wooing another friend, who after entering the family circle as an intimate at the time of *Hernani* had become a powerful critic in all fields—drama, books, painting: Théophile Gautier, known as the "good Théo."

Adèle Hugo to Théophile Gautier, July 14th, 1838: I should very much like to know why you do not try to come more often to this house, why, indeed, you are not always here. Of two evils, the lesser is preferable, and I would far rather see you every day than not at all! I will go so far as to say that I should like it infinitely better, since for me seeing you is always a festive occasion, and I really do not know why you so often deprive me of that pleasure. One can always, it seems, find the time for writing an article when one wants to, and I, most certainly, could always find time to compose one on *Fortunio*,[31] which I love as being one half of yourself, though the other half is lacking, which cannot be less beautiful. One day you will produce it, won't you? I, who am just a little bit *sentimental*, wait eagerly for that. My sentimentality is something I cannot suppress. I am just like the laundresses, the milliners, the ladies' maids, and even the cooks, for whom you have promised to write a novel. I, who am spiritually one with them, insist on your giving it to us.[32]

Boulogne, September 1st, 1838: It is very tiresome to love one's friends more than they love us. I know how true that is in my own case, no less than do those same friends, even allowing that *they* have numberless considerations which take precedence of the "sacred fires of friendship," whence it follows that the goddess of friendship (is she a goddess?) is of very secondary importance, to you in particular. What I am writing will change nothing in things as they are. I might talk for a hundred years, and write for a hundred years, on this same point, and not change a thing. I should merely become a bore. My intention is to beg you to pay me a visit of *some hours' duration*, to come at noon, and to stay until the evening . . . Come *before* you write. Chance has a way of arranging matters better than one expects. You are not being at all kind to me. But that does not alter the fact that I love you with all my heart, for you have the qualities which love finds necessary. Your very affectionate: Adèle Hugo.[33]

September 26th, 1838: Yes, do come and fetch me, tomorrow, Thursday, at the studio of our friend Boulanger. . . . Come at five, and I will take you to Boulogne, where, no doubt, you will dine with the Great Man. What a deal of contriving just to get a few moments of talk with you! . . .[34]

Undated: I am so much afraid that you will not come tomorrow. That is the reason for this letter. I am so heartbroken at the thought that you might come and not find me that I have decided to write to you, so as to set my mind at rest. It is, perhaps, one way of reminding you that you really *ought* to come to Boulogne, and *spend some hours* with me. Who knows?—But, whatever the motive for this letter may be, I shall not be here tomorrow. I shall expect you on Wednesday. What I want is to have you for myself alone, which is something I would do for you even if I were not a woman who, in addition, is your truly devoted Adèle Hugo.[35]

January 28th, 1839: Yes, come and bring us your book![36] It is quite absurd that everybody but us should have read it! All is over! You no longer spoil me . . . You are so good a hand at keeping secrets that I must tell you one— I have discovered a weakness in the *Great Man*: he is really upset that you have not wanted to talk to him about *Don César*.[37] So, there is something human in him, after all. In matters of friendship, he is touchy.

. . . I believe that you are more *sensitive* than you allow. Whether that is true or not, it is the way I see you in my heart, and I stick to it. I have romanticized you in my mind or so filled out a picture of you which I have. This is what women are reduced to, because they become so stupid and ridiculous when they start dirtying their fingers with pen and ink . . . Rest assured that among all the disenchantments of this life, friendship is something about which I have no doubts, something which I set upon an altar and tend as my most precious treasure. I shall see you soon, shall I not? Adèle.[38]

Undated: I always read your articles with the greatest attention, as you wish me to. I notice today that you have not said a word about my portrait[39] . . . it would be very nice of you to object that it is hung too high . . . That might help in getting it brought lower! I feel ashamed at bothering you in this way about me, for, as a rule, I bother so little about myself. But, if you would do what I ask, it would help the career of a young man who is in need of a little success in order to live.[40]

Undated: I was counting on a little visit from you yesterday evening. It is very bad of you to abandon me like this. If you want to "make it up" come and dine tomorrow at Robelin's Saint-James's house.[41] Try to get there early *so that we may* have time for a walk in the Bois. This time be punctual . . . ![42]

Undated: My dear Monsieur Gautier, if it is your wish to visit the Longchamp Baths next Sunday, they shall be open to Your Lordship for inspection. You will take your dinner with us. Do, if you can, say a word in your article about *this spot.* By doing so you will give much satisfaction to the Place Royale quarter, which was once yours. I don't want ever again to plague you. You must do precisely as you please. All I want is that you shall think with affection of your best and oldest friend—La Vicomtesse Victor Hugo.[43]

She still believed in the possibility of friendship between a man and a woman. She had a horror of burning her fingers, but liked playing with fire. A woman neglected by her husband needs to be reassured.

From May to October 1840 Adèle Hugo was living at Saint-Prix, in a large house called La Terrasse, on the edge of the Montmorency forest, with her father and her two daughters. The boys were at l'Institution Jauffret, in the rue Culture-Saint-Catherine (now the rue de Sévigné), where they were pursuing the programme of the "collège royal de Charlemagne." They were boarders, and wrote to their mother, or to Didine, asking for "four sous to pay my debts (this is very urgent) and a pot of jam . . . [44] "Mamma, I love you," wrote Charles: "I adore you as my angel and my life . . . Tell Didine to send me a pot of jam tomorrow to eat with our dry bread."[45] He cried when he went back to school: "I keep on remembering the butterflies on the drawing-room curtains, the pictures, the canopy, the red table. If you leave me a whole year without seeing you, I shall have a good mind to kill myself." Romanticism seemed to be hereditary, and Charles, who saw himself as a character in a Hugo play, indulged in self-pity because he was "the obscure son of a great and happy father."[46] Hugo had, for a long while, been neglecting his sons, but round about 1840 he began to keep a careful eye on their school work, especially their Latin, to which he attached considerable importance. He was happy and proud when on July 31st, 1840, he learned that the younger boy had won a prize for Latin composition in the general examination. He went to celebrate the happy event in the bosom of his family at Saint-Prix. The covey of young children was turning La Terrasse, as formerly it had turned Les Roches, into a happy paradise. As he helped the boys to build a brushwood hut, Dédé to tend her rabibts and chickens, and looked with loving eyes at Léopoldine, he found himself remembering with emotion the times long past, the happy times when he had wished to be "first in marriage" and in fatherhood, as in poetry. But his life since then had begun to creak on its wheels. Discords had multiplied, and for them there was no remedy. "Our destinies and our wishes are almost always at odds."

26

The Rhine

You know my liking for far travel by short stages,
alone with those old friends of my boyhood,
Virgil and Tacitus.

VICTOR HUGO, *Le Rhin*

IN ADDITION to Virgil and Tacitus, Juliette had been the companion of his three journeys to the Rhine (1838, 1839, 1840) which had turned into the prolonged and imaginative pilgrimage of an antiquary and dreamer. But each evening a journal had been sent off to Adèle, in the form of a letter enriched with drawings, to be kept by her because it might come in useful for a projected book. Hugo "has in Paris a fond and dear friend, who is unable to leave the city because of daily duties which make even living in a country house no more than ten miles from the fortifications impossible."[1] This *friend* was his wife (though now and again, but more rarely, the painter Louis Boulanger). The wanderer kept, in addition, another journal, a more solemn affair, filled with historical and political comments. In 1839, for more than two months, he moved about each day, and spent the greater part of every night in writing, while Juliette sat watching and waiting for her moment—the moment of love—to come.

The great legend-haunted river exercised over Victor Hugo a strange, an almost magical, power of attraction. Night after night, as a child, he had looked at a picture which had hung over his bed at Les Feuillantines. It had shown an old and ruined tower, the source to be of the many similar dilapidated buildings which appeared again and again in his later dreams and drawings. Slight though his knowledge of German literature was, he had like his friends Nerval and Gautier read Hoffmann's beautiful *Tales*. He went so far as to say, in his Preface to "Le Rhin,"[2] the "[author of this book] does not conceal the fact that Germany is one of the lands he loves, one of the nations he admires. He has an almost filial feeling for this noble and sacred country, which is so deeply revered by all thinkers. If he were not a Frenchman, he would like to be a German."

In this desire of his to understand and give expression to the poetry of Germany there may have been a wish to appeal to the Duchesse d'Orléans, who was a German princess. But, chiefly, he thought that in the problem of Franco-German relations he could see a way of making himself useful, and so enter the world of public affairs. With all this in mind he added to the legends, the pictures, the broodings on the past, which went to make up "Le Rhin," in 1841, a political epilogue. In the preceding year it had looked as though a conflict was likely to break out between France and Prussia. The German poet Becker had written *The German Rhine*, to which Musset had replied with the famous "Your German Rhine was ours—it was held within our glass." Hugo, in this long and serious last chapter to his book, proposed a peaceful solution. Prussia should make over to France the left bank of the river "which is very much more French than the Germans think." In return, Prussia should be given Hanover, Hamburg, the Free Cities, and access to the high seas. It would be greatly to the advantage of Prussia to be unified and to have free ports. France and Germany, formed by nature to co-operate, could then work hand in hand for the cause of World Peace. "The Rhine is the river which should bring them together: it has been turned into a river that divides them."

This long essay, in its historical breadth of view, in the firmness of its style and in the daring of its projected solutions, had all the appearance of being a solid political contribution; but was it truly statesmanlike? There was reason to doubt it. A genuine negotiator approaches his task with fewer certainties. The brilliant antitheses and generalizations only thinly disguised a not very profound knowledge of men. Who, in France, really wanted a unified Prussia with access to the high seas? Cuvillier-Fleury hit back hard in the *Journal des Débats:* "Prussia, according to you, *in the form given to it by the Congresses, is a botched piece of work!* How very unfortunate! And now, *you* want to set up Prussia against France; *you* want to give her outlets on the sea; *you* want to incorporate Hanover in her territories, to move her frontiers back, to increase her moral influence ten-fold. And all this for what reason? So that you may be elected Deputy for Mount Pisgah! . . ."[3]

The man of common sense was right as against the man of genius. The poet had tried to find in the lively impressions of his own sensibility the solution to an historical problem: "in the mere appearance of old towns in the Palatinate, he thought he could discover the secrets of the past, and look forward into the enigmas of the future."[4] He had looked upon the Rhine and seen it as something terrible, epic, "Aeschylean." The very beautiful sketches which he brought back with him from that visit were, all of them, bathed in the tragic, supernatural, violent and nightmarish light, which was the contribution of his own temperament rather than of the Rhenish landscape. More and more, he was coming to adopt two distinct styles, one of which, as Sainte-Beuve said, could never shed "his gaudiness, his *pomposo*," while the other (*Choses vues*) remained that of the perfect *reporter*. The good Victor Pavie wrote to David d'Angers: "Have you been up the Rhine, not for once in a boat or on wheels, but in Victor Hugo? It is he, as you will find, who on every two occasions out of three is reflected in the river, a poet endlessly drawing from this a voice, striking from that a spark. He has moulded a world, with that strange despotism of his which compels every landscape to swear only by him! So hard a gauntlet, in the long run, bruises one. One emerges from the reading of him, breathless and battered, like some prey fallen from an eagle's claws. . . ."[5]

"Like some prey fallen from an eagle's claws . . ." wrote Pavie, but the eagle himself could fall as well. Hugo, in his triumph, was "soaring in the great spaces of the eternal—but a blast of wind broke both his wings." In this same year of 1842 his friend, patron and future sovereign, the Duc d'Orléans, was killed in a carriage accident, when his horses bolted in the avenue which, at that time, was called the *Route de la Révolte*.[6] The prince tried to jump from the carriage and fractured his skull on the paving. Hugo, who even at the cost of suffering always had to *see for himself,* hastened to the spot where the duke had fallen, at a point between the twenty-sixth and twenty-seventh tree on the left, coming from the Porte Maillot. He noted that the victim had died "on the unadorned red-brick floor of a wretched green-painted grocer's-shop." A broken-down stove stood immediately behind the head of the dying prince. On the wall were several cheap coloured prints representing "The Wandering Jew," "Fieschi's Attempt on the Life of Louis-Philippe," "Napoleon," and "Louis-Philippe, Duc d'Orléans," in the uniform of Colonel-General of Hussars. The friend mourned *his* friend; the poet, ever in love with contrasts, could not help thinking that the duke, young, carefree and happy, must have passed this green-painted door each time he drove to the Château de Neuilly. If he had ever given it a casual glance he could have seen it as nothing more than a miserable little shop, a hovel, a shanty. But it was fated that there he should die. Driving back to Paris with Juliette, Victor saw upon the walls a large poster, printed in heavy type: FÊTE DE NEUILLY—a precious find, indeed, for one who was ever in search of the ironies of life.

The Duc d'Orléans had been a noble-hearted man, and the hope of all friends of liberty. Plans for the future had now to be constructed afresh. Hugo, who was serving his turn as Director of the Académie Française, was charged with the duty of presenting the condolences of the Institut to the king. He praised the virtues of a prince who had died, alas! so young. "Sire, your blood is the country's blood: your family and France have but one heart. What strikes the one wounds the other. It is with a sympathy beyond the power of words to express that the French people, at this moment, turn their eyes upon your family, and upon you, Sire, who will live a long while yet, for God and France have need of you; upon your queen, that august mother who, of all mothers, is most sorely stricken; upon the princess, French in her feelings, French by adoption, who has given to our country two Frenchmen, to the dynasty two princes, to the future, two hopes. . . ."

Who knew what the future was to hold? Perhaps, one day, there would be a Regency, with the Princesse Hélène a *de facto* queen? Hugo, maybe, her First Minister? But, before that could happen, he must acquire a peerage, and with this in view must strengthen his relations with the old king.

One month after the drama he went to pay a visit to the Duchesse d'Orléans, and had the strange fancy to take with him in the cab Juliette, who waited for him at the door of the Château. *Juliette Drouet to Victor Hugo, August 20th, 1842:* "Everything to me is a matter for fear. Consequently, that visit to the Duchesse d'Orléans, on the occasion of which you paid me, I admit, the charming tribute of taking me with you, was turned into an agony by reason of the time and the circumstances. I, in morning dress and scarcely tidy, she, a woman with all the prestige of a great sorrow, in other words, with something that, next to physical beauty, most works upon your feelings. I must confess that, no matter how brave my love may be, no matter how much confidence I may have in your loyalty, I am uneasy in my mind when forced to fight without a weapon in my hand."[7] Her fears were groundless. The royal widow, swathed in veils of crape, had thoughts only of her loss and for her children. But she continued to receive her poet, and to talk with him about the unforeseeable future.

27

At Villequier

He who has loved knows that. He who has not
loved, knows it not. I pity him, and make to
him no answer.

LACORDAIRE

JANUARY 1843: Juliette was worried at finding her "dear little
man" very gloomy. His "poor face" seemed "quite overclouded."[1]
Was he concealing from her some anxiety, some grief? The year,
however, looked like being full of hope. For the first time in five years
Hugo was to have a play produced, *Les Burgraves*. His daughter,
Léopoldine, was engaged to a young man of whom her family thoroughly approved, Charles Vacquerie. The marriage was to take place
in February. *Les Burgraves* would make its appearance at the Comédie-
Française in March. That summer Juliette and Victor were to travel
in Spain. Altogether, a most satisfying programme.

And yet, "it was as though Victor Hugo could not fight free from
his struggle with ghosts."[2] He was very fond of the Vacquerie family,
the members of which had come into his life as the result of simple
admiration. The two brothers, Charles and Auguste, had been born,
the first at Nantes in 1816, the second at Villequier in 1819. They came
of an ancient line of Seine fishermen and pilots. Their father, Charles-
Isidore, had set up as a shipowner at Le Havre, had made a fortune,
and had built a large, white, family house at Villequier on the bank
of the river. The elder boy, Charles, would carry on the business.
The younger, brought up at the Collège de Rouen, on a diet of
Aeschylus, Shakespeare and Victor Hugo, had had so successful a school
career that the headmaster of an educational establishment in Paris
had offered to complete his scholastic training free of charge, as a "prize
examinee." This ardent and excessively romantic young man, having
entered the Lycée Charlemagne, was charged with the duty, together
with some of his companions, of putting on a play for Saint Charlemagne's day. They chose *Hernani* and asked the author for the necessary permission. Hugo not only gave this, but was himself present at
the performance.

230

Later, at the time of the *Marion de Lorme* lawsuit, the poet had noticed the young Vacquerie on the public benches. "The Master, triumphant, came up to me then—and I touched the hand of the king of men . . ." after which the young Norman and his friend Paul Meurice became faithful members of the Place Royale circle. They were given the task of enlisting "front-line fighters" at the time of the production of *Ruy Blas*. When the young Auguste fell ill Adèle nursed him, and the adolescent long remembered the intoxicating experience of seeing her lovely face bending over him. In 1838, during Victor Hugo's journey to the Rhine, Adèle and the children were invited to Le Havre, where they stayed with Auguste's elder sister, who had married Nicolas Lefèvre, the founder of Le Nouveau-Graville.[3] The four young Hugos had never seen the sea. From Le Havre the whole family migrated to Villequier, where they remained until early October.

Auguste Vacquerie to Madame Victor Hugo, October 9th, 1838: My dear Madame, since you left, the house has seemed empty and sad. We all of us miss you and your children. Silence is a melancholy compensation for noise! I have lost no time in writing to you, for the need to do so was upon me. The days since you left have been long and gloomy. My brother and I, in particular, who have never left your side, have acquired the pleasing habit of the life we led during your visit. We miss you badly just now, and nothing can make up to us for your absence. . . .[4]

The Hugo children retained an enchanting memory of their holiday. In the following year they dragged their father with them to Le Havre and Villequier, whence Olympio promptly set off for Strasbourg. The others, however, spent the whole of the summer in Normandy. Léopoldine was fifteen, Charles Vacquerie twenty-two. He knew that he could count on a brilliant future. "Coastal trading and ocean voyages had put the family in easy circumstances," but, in spite of increasing wealth, "it continued to live modestly, and consequently was held in high esteem."[5] Charles Vacquerie the first, now old and ailing, was anxious to retire. For Charles the second, his successor designate, Léopoldine, with her character of wise simplicity, seemed to be an ideal wife. The idea of marriage was mooted. Madame Hugo approved.

Auguste Vacquerie to Madame Victor Hugo, Thursday, October 17th, 1839: The now deserted house weeps tears for you. We are for ever missing part of the family . . . The family which God has given to us has bound us to it by a thousand secret ties, but the one of them all that one chooses is that dictated by the heart. You have long known how filled with you I am! Never till now have I realized how necessary your friendship is, nor how much I stand in need of your home. In spite of the sixty leagues which separate us, I live with you, and *you* occupy more than three-quarters of my thoughts. . . .[6]

Three successive deaths brought sadness to the tenderly united Vacquerie family. In 1839 and 1840 Madame Nicolas-Lefèvre lost her two sons Charles and Paul, and in 1842 her husband. Her father's health had grown steadily worse.[7] The young engaged couple had not the heart to speak of marriage in the prevailing atmosphere of mortality. Victor Hugo, however, consented to their union. "Poets can offer no great dowries with their daughters, but other gifts they have, more precious: elegance of mind, goodness of heart, and bodily grace."[8] Finally, on February 15th, 1843, the nuptial blessing was pronounced in the privacy of the family circle. None of Hugo's friends had been invited to the ceremony. Juliette, who could not decently be present, had refrained from putting in an appearance at the church, but had asked Didine to send her some small memento of the occasion—"some trifle which will no longer be of any use, but will serve to remind me of a young girl now to be *Madame*." This would be a bond between the two human beings who most loved Hugo—his daughter and his mistress. The father transmitted the strange and touching request. Léopoldine, who for a long time now had understood and accepted the equivocal situation, sent more than a trifle: she gave Juliette her missal. Victor Hugo, during the ceremony in church, composed a short poem for the young bride:

> Aime celui qui t'aime et sois heureuse en lui.
> Adieu! sois son trésor, ô toi qui fus le nôtre!
> Va, mon enfant béni, d'une famille à l'autre.
> Emporte le bonheur et laisse-vous l'ennui.
>
> Ici l'on te retient, là-bas on te désire.
> Fille, épouse, ange, enfant, fais ton double devoir.
> Donne-nous un regret, donne-leur un espoir:
> Sors avec une larme, entre avec un sourir.[9]

It was with a sad heart that the poet saw the departure of his eldest daughter, his favourite, a child precociously serious, and very close to him. "Have no fears for your Didine," Juliette wrote to him; "she will be the happiest of women . . ."[10] All the omens, indeed, seemed good, but it is a fact that Hugo suffered intensely from this separation, and was filled with fears, though of what it is impossible to say. Léopoldine was going to live at Le Havre, and at that time Le Havre was a good two days from Paris, whether by diligence or "water-coach."

The letters that came were radiant with happiness. *Léopoldine Vacquerie to Madame Victor Hugo:* "I have been here for a whole month, but so happy, and so completely surrounded by all that makes for bliss, that there are moments when I catch myself feeling frightened because of that very bliss. It seems to me that it is all too lovely to last for long, and then I am reassured when I think that one thing is missing to the completeness of my joy—my dear, good mother is not here with me . . ."[11] *Juliette Drouet to Victor Hugo:* "I hope, my poor angel, that you will be feeling braver now, that the happiness of your beloved child will no longer be to you a cause of weeping and despair. . . ."[12]

The rehearsals of *Les Burgraves* served to wrench his mind away from these bizarre presentiments. He hoped great things of the play, to which he had tried to give an epic grandeur. It was in the course of his journeys to the Rhine, that, visiting by day and by night the many ruined castles now invaded by trees and wild brambles, he had had a vision of the titanic struggle waged against the Emperor by the "formidable robber barons of the Rhine, living in their embattled eyries, served by kneeling officers . . . predatory bandits, with something about them both of the eagle and the owl . . ."[13] and had conceived the idea of turning it into a drama for the stage. Then to the theme of the Burgraves had been added another, from which Hugo never entirely succeeded in ridding his mind, that of enmity between brothers. It will be remembered that he had once started to write a play in verse, *Les Jumeaux,* on the subject of the Man in the Iron Mask who had been sacrificed that his brother, Louis XIV, might reign with undisputed authority. This play he had abandoned, but once again in *Les Burgraves* Fosco (the Burgrave, Job) gets rid of his brother Donato (the future Emperor Frederick Barbarossa) because both are in love with the same girl, Ginevra. Just as, night after night, the conscience-stricken Count Job visits the secret vault where once he had flung Donato, so did Hugo, in drama after drama, return to his obsession of the man-buried-alive.[14]

When a work of art presses upon a sensitive spot in the author's temperament, it is almost certain to contain much beauty. *Les Burgraves,* a "pre-Wagnerian monster,"[15] with its frowning castle, its four generations of robber-knights, and its struggle between Fate and Providence, was not lacking in grandeur. The Comédie-Française had accepted it with enthusiasm. But the climate of the times was becoming less and less favourable to romantic drama. For several seasons now a young woman of genius, Rachel, had been restoring classic tragedy to favour. The public was growing tired "of what most quickly wears thin—novelty." Victor Hugo, who was hoping for a second *Battle of Hernani,* had sent his new organizers of victory, Vacquerie and Meurice, to ask the painter Célestin Nanteuil to supply three hundred young men to serve the cause, "three hundred young Spartans ready to conquer or to die." Shaking his luxuriant locks, Nanteuil had replied: "Young men, go tell your master that youth is a thing of the past!"[16] More precisely, it was romantic youth that was a thing of the past.

The first night passed without disturbance, for the house was packed with friends. The general opinion was that, in spite of much beautiful poetry, the play was solemn and boring. The line spoken by Job, the ancestor, to the sixty-year-old Magnus—"*Jeune homme, taisez-vous!*"— provoked a storm of laughter. At the second performance there was a good deal of booing. From the fifth onwards, the reception was stormy. Juliette maintained that an organized opposition was at work and declared that she "would like to have expressed her indignation against those responsible with plenty of hard knocks and kicks in the stomach."[17] Buloz, at that time one of the administrators of the Comédie-Française, describes how one night, at two o'clock in the morning, Hugo, walking with him past the Tuileries, exclaimed: "If Napoleon were there now there would be but one great event in France—*Les Burgraves*—and the Emperor would have come to our rehearsals!"[18] But the First Napoleon was no longer there, and grandiloquence was anathema to the Birotteaus and the Camusots from among whom the Louis-Philippe audiences were recruited. Sainte-Beuve, pleased by what was happening, wrote: "The thing is being received with boos. Hugo doesn't like the word, and said in the hearing of the actors: 'my play is being disturbed.' The actors, who are a malicious lot, have taken, since then, to saying *disturbers* instead of *booers* . . ."[19] At the tenth performance the receipts fell to 1666 francs, while Rachel, the interpreter of Racine, was taking 5500 francs each evening. On March 17th a comet swept across the Paris sky, and *Le Charivari* published the following verse:

> Hugo, lorgnant les voûtes bleues,
> Au Seigneur demande tout bas
> Pourquoi les astres ont des queues
> Quand les *Burgraves* n'en ont pas?[20]

Though undeserved, the disaster went from bad to worse. "The trilogy of the *Burgraves*? A boredom trebled!" wrote Heinrich Heine. "Characters of wood—a mournful dangle of marionettes . . . sham passion."[21] In April Paris accorded an hysterical reception to Ponsard's *Lucrèce*, because its neo-classic and provincial author could conveniently be cast for the part of anti-Hugo. Balzac was indignant. "I have been to see *Lucrèce*! What a deliberate piece of mumbo-jumbo served up for the mystification of our Paris audiences . . . nothing could be more childish, more null and void, more of a schoolboy essay in tragedy . . . In five years' time no one will remember even who Ponsard was. Hugo has been guilty of a lot of foolishness, and thoroughly deserves that God should raise up a rival to him in the person of Ponsard . . ."[22] Hugo maintained a calm exterior, but so much hatred, so high a price demanded for success, beat him to the ground. The play was withdrawn after its thirty-third performance, and he ceased to write for the stage. March 7th, 1843, had been the "Waterloo of romantic drama."[23]

In spite of opposition from Adèle, Juliette had her "poor little dose of annual happiness" in the course of the following summer. This time it took the form of a journey into the south-west of France and to Spain, which must have evoked for Victor Hugo many memories of childhood, and consequently have cured him of the melancholy which in Paris, ever since February, had seemed to envelop him. Léopoldine, now three months gone with child, and needlessly anxious, had been insistent that her father should not go away. On Tuesday, July 9th, he had paid a visit to Normandy to say goodbye, and on his return had written: "I wish you knew, dear daughter, what a baby I am when I think of you. My eyes fill with tears, and I want never to leave you . . . The day I spent at Le Havre shines brightly in my thoughts; I shall not forget it for as long as I live. . . ."[24]

All the same, he found the prospect of the journey tempting. Bayonne remained in his recollection as a place all ruby-red and smiling. It was "the scene of his heart's most ancient memory . . ."[25] But he could not recognize the house where once he had caught a glimpse of a white bosom in the opening of a tucker. What had happened to the young girl of long ago? Was she married? Was she a widow? Was she dead? Maybe he saw her and did not know her again. Trailing vapours in the heavens of eternity. However, the first Spanish ox-cart, with its wild music, struck him suddenly with a fierce happiness. The darling memories of childhood had found support in a sensation born of the present. "It seemed to me that between the then and the now there was nothing. Yesterday was there again, those lovely days, the sweet and radiant years! I was a child, I was small, I was loved. Experience I had none, but I had my mother. My fellow-travellers stuck their fingers in their ears; for me, there was enchantment in my heart. . . ."[26]

Irun was a disappointment. It had become just like the Batignolles. "Where is the past? Where is the poem?" Fontarobia had left in him an impression of glowing light, a golden village with a sharp church steeple, at the head of a blue gulf. Now, as previously, Spain entranced him with its language, its lithe women, its untamed nature. "This is a land of poets and smugglers . . ."[27] At Pasages, a village close to Saint-Sébastien, he found in Guipuzcoa a place of magnificence and charm: tall houses painted white and yellow; streets with thousands of strange objects floating from the balconies, red, yellow and blue rags; ravishing *bateleras* (barge-women) too, with great black eyes, and piled, magnificent hair.

He pushed on as far as Pampeluna, Auch, Agen, Périgueux and Angoulême. At the Isle of Oléron, on September 8th, Juliette saw him overcome with melancholy. The island was desolate and dreary. "Not a sail, not a bird. Low down in the sky at sunset the moon was visible, round and enormous, looking through the livid mist like the smudged image of herself, red and tarnished. Death was in my heart. That evening, everything for me was gloomy and funereal. I felt that the island was a vast coffin set upon the sea with the moon as its candle. . . ."[28]

Next day they fled the island, and reached Rochefort on their homeward way. Hugo wanted to go to Le Havre to see the young Vacqueries. Adèle and her three other children were installed nearby at Graville, in a villa which her son-in-law had rented for her, where she spent her time in painting flowers. Soon, now, the family would be complete. This thought restored to Hugo his gaiety of spirit. At the village of Soubise, Juliette suggested going to a café for a bottle of beer, and to look at the newspapers from which they had been separated for several days.

Journal of Juliette Drouet, September 9th, 1843: On a sort of great square we saw, written up in large letters: CAFÉ DE L'EUROPE. We entered. The café was deserted at that hour of the day. There was nobody but a young man seated at the first table on the right-hand side, reading a paper and smoking. Facing him, on the other side, was the woman of the place, behind the bar. We took our places at the far end of the room, almost directly under a spiral staircase hung with red calico. The waiter brought us a bottle of beer and withdrew. Under a table facing us were several newspapers. Toto picked one up at random, while I chose a copy of *Le Charivari*. I had had scarcely time to look at the headlines when my poor darling suddenly leaned towards me and said in a choking voice, holding the paper out to me: "This is horrible!" I looked at him. Never, as long as I live, shall I forget the indescribable expression of despair upon his noble features. A moment back I had seen him smiling and happy, and now, in the space of a second, without the slightest transition, he seemed as though thunderstruck. His poor lips were white; his magnificent eyes were staring in front of him. His face and his hair were wet with tears. His poor hand was pressed to his heart as though to keep it from bursting from his breast. I took the hateful sheet, and this is what I read. . . .[29]

What *Le Siècle* contained was the story of an appalling accident which had occurred on Monday, September 4th, at Villequier. Léopoldine and her husband had left Le Havre two days before, intending to spend the week-end at Villequier. There they had found Uncle Pierre Vacquerie, a former ship's captain, and his son Arthur, a boy of twelve. On the Sunday afternoon a racing dinghy, which Charles had had sent from Le Havre, arrived at the jetty. It was a fancy craft belonging to his uncle, who had had it built in the navy yard to his own specifications. Charles had won a prize with it at the Honfleur regatta. The dinghy carried two fore-and-aft sails which, with a following wind, gave a great turn of speed. But the hull was light, too light for Seine sailing. He proposed to use it the following morning to get to Caude-bec, where he had an appointment with his lawyer, Maître Bazire. . . .[30]

The morning of Monday was fine. Not a trace of breeze, not a ripple on the surface of the water; an early mist. It had been agreed on the previous evening that Léopoldine should accompany her husband, her uncle, and her cousin. But her mother-in-law, who felt uneasy at the extreme lightness of the dinghy, had dissuaded her from taking part in the jaunt. The two men and the boy had started without her, only to return almost immediately. The boat was dancing, and they shipped two large flat stones as ballast. This time, Léopoldine was tempted. She asked them to wait for her, hurriedly changed into a dress of red-checked muslin, and went on board. The short outward journey was uneventful.

The plan was to take Maître Bazire with them to Villequier for *déjeuner*. He suggested that they should make the trip in his carriage, since the idea of sailing in the dinghy did not appeal to him. In order to overcome his nervousness, Charles and Uncle Pierre added weight to the ballast by taking on board a number of sandstone blocks which were lying on the quay at Caudebec. The lawyer, much against his will, accompanied them, but since the dinghy was dancing more than ever had himself put ashore opposite the *Barre-y-va*, saying that he would walk from there. "The party set off again. The wind played in the sails. A few minutes later, without the slightest warning, a gust, blowing down the funnel made by the river and a nearby hill, caused the boat to heel over. The stones which had been loaded for the pur-pose of helping the small craft, began to shift, and produced a still worse state of unbalance. Objects, elements, everything, had betrayed the fair promise of the day. In the twinkling of an eye, the stake was laid and lost. Of all the passengers, Charles Vacquerie, who was an excellent swimmer, circled round the upturned hull in an attempt to save his wife. She clung to the dinghy. All his efforts were in vain. Quite simply he, who had never yet left her, gave up the struggle, and let himself sink, that he might be with her to the end. . . ."[31] It was Auguste Vacquerie who, late that night, broke the terrible news to Madame Victor Hugo. He persuaded her to leave for Paris on Tuesday, "with her three remaining children, and not to stay on at Villequier for the painful ceremony of the funeral."

For sentimental and romantic reasons the young husband and wife were buried in the same coffin. They were carried on men's shoulders from the white house to the little graveyard by the church. *Victor Hugo to Louise Bertin, Saumur, September 10th, 1843:* "I loved that poor child beyond my power to express in words. You remember how charming she was. She was the gentlest and most gracious of women. Oh God! how have I offended against Thee? . . ."[32]—for Hugo was, "where the secrets of the universe were concerned, no less than small sums of money," in the habit of balancing accounts, and could not help wondering "whether the father was not paying for the guilt of the lover who had ceased to watch over his children." And so it was that, for a while, he took an aversion to Juliette Drouet, and "ran to his wife for comfort."[33] From the ill-omened Café de l'Europe, at Soubise, he had written to her: "Poor woman, do not weep. We must resign ourselves. She was an angel. Let us give her back to God. Alas! she was too happy. I am suffering abominably, and long to mingle my tears with yours, and with those of our three much-loved children. Darling Dédé, be brave, and so I say to all of you. I shall soon be with you, and we will weep together, my poor darlings. Only a short while now, my dearest Adèle. May this frightful blow bring our loving hearts closer together. . . ."[34] While travelling by diligence to Paris he jotted down a few isolated lines:

> Je suis, lorsque je pense, un poète, un esprit,
> Mais, sitôt que je souffre, hélas, je suis un homme!
> Quand tu la contemplais, cette Seine si belle,
> Rien ne te disait donc, "Ce sera ton tombeau"?[35]

Meanwhile, Adèle Hugo, anxious to have a few pictures of the "Gothic house" where Didine and Charles had lived for seven months in Le Havre, at 1 rue de la Chaussée, had sent her painter friend Louis Boulanger there.

Auguste Vacquerie to Madame Victor Hugo, October 19th, 1843: I send this reply at once, dear Madame, to set your mind at rest. Boulanger has made a drawing of their room. It is very like, and even those who do not know it would recognize it for what it is. So what you wanted is done. I will bring it with me when I return to Paris. I shall spend this week in making a final statement of your accounts. They are quite simple . . . As for the gardener, who has again put in an appearance with a demand for his 104 francs, in spite of the magistrate's ruling, I showed him the door! . . . While I think of it, did you put the black box which my sister lent you, with the three trunks? It is, I think, the only thing she claims. . . .[36]

Adèle was brave. She held firmly to her religious beliefs. "My soul," she wrote to Victor Pavie, on November 4th, 1843, "has departed from me, if I may put it so, that it may be united with theirs . . ."[37] But the house in the Place Royale was for a long time a place of mourning. All day long the mother sat holding a strand of the drowned girl's hair in her fingers. Hugo, in silence, took the little Dédé on his lap. Grand-papa Foucher had suddenly grown twenty years older. On the walls and tables were portraits of the vanished pair, and on an embroidered bag the words: "The dress my daughter was wearing when she died: a sacred relic." Victor Pavie had suggested to Sainte-Beuve that he should make his peace with the Hugos, and enter into renewed relations with them "through this gaping wound." But Sainte-Beuve refused. Three times since the fatal year (1837) offers of this kind had been made to him; three times reconciliation had, he said, been followed by a further insulting breach. "For me to have gone back, even after this terrible tragedy, it would have been necessary that *she* should have expressed formally her wish to that effect. Had she done so, I should have regarded it as a command. But she has not done anything of the sort. So that is how it is, now and for ever! Horrible to think about, but true . . ."[38] Alfred de Vigny, on the other hand, wrote: "Faced by such a calamity, one can say nothing that would not be either inadequate or cruel." Victor Hugo had been stricken to the heart by his daughter's death, and even in December had not emerged from his state of mental prostration. Balzac, preoccupied by his candidature for the Academy, went to pay the customary visit. When he left the Place Royale he wrote to Madame Hanska: "Dear Angel, Victor looks ten years older. I think it possible that he regards the death of his daughter as punishment for the four children he has had by Juliette. However that may be, he is backing me strongly, and I have the promise of his vote. He is loud in his detestation of Sainte-Beuve and de Vigny. Ah! my dear, what a lesson for us is that love-match which he consummated when he was eighteen! Victor Hugo and his wife are a notable warning . . ."[39]—which goes to show that gossip is no respecter of grief.

Juliette begged Hugo to find some way of distracting his mind from what had occurred, to break free from the agonized brooding into which he had sunk. Incapable of working, he asked her to put in order the notes he had made on the end of their journey to the Pyrenees, that he might wind up the account of an experience which had been begun in the happy mood of memories recovered, only to end in misery. Many times he went to Villequier and the rose-planted grave, seeking *"le lieu noir—Avec l'avidité morne du désés-poir . . . Ô souvenirs! Ô forme horrible des collines!"* For several years, on each September 4th, he wrote a memorial poem. Each was beautiful in its tragic simplicity.

1844

Elle avait dix ans et moi trente;
J'étais pour elle l'univers.
Oh! comme l'herbe est odorante
Sous les arbres profonds et verts . . .

Doux ange aux candides pensées,
Elle était gaie en arrivant . . .
Toutes ces choses sont passées
Comme l'ombre et comme le vent.[40]

1846

Ô souvenirs! printemps! aurore!
Doux rayon triste et réchauffant!
—Lorsqu'elle était petite encore,
Que sa sœur était tout enfant. . . .

Connaissez-vous, sur la colline
Qui joint Montlignon à Saint-Leu,
Une terrasse qui s'incline
Entre un bois sombre et le ciel bleu?

C'est là que nous vivions. Pénètre,
Mon cœur, dans ce passé charmant!
Je l'entendais sous ma fenêtre
Jouer le matin, doucement.[41]

1847

Demain, dès l'aube, à l'heure qui blanchit la campagne,
Je partirai. Vois-tu, je sais que tu m'attends.
J'irai par la forêt, j'irai par la montagne.
Je ne puis demeurer loin de toi plus longtemps.

Je ne regarderai ni l'or du soir qui tombe,
Ni les voiles au loin descendant vers Harfleur,
Et quand j'arriverai, je mettrai sur ta tombe
Un bouquet de houx vert et de bruyère en fleur.[42]

28

Escapades and Ermine

Lead me when evening falls to the queen's
garden.

VICTOR HUGO, *Toute la lyre,* VI

SENSUALITY is a violent state. When a man's mind is tormented
and confused, it is natural for him to seek forgetfulness in the
variety and violence of the senses. Victor Hugo in 1843, desperately
miserable, had to find some passion in which to take refuge. Juliette?
No, Juliette could not any longer suffice him. The poor woman, after
ten years of a cloistered existence, had lost her bloom. Though she
was still only in her thirties, her hair was beginning to go grey. Her
eyes were as beautiful as ever, and she had not lost her tender and
exalted air. But she was no longer that "beauty beyond a painter's
power to express" whom he had known, glittering and brilliant in
lace and diamonds, in the old Princess Negroni days. There were times
when she bored him. Her mind might be charming, but what had
she to talk about? Apart from her month's trip every year, she saw
nothing and nobody. Her innumerable letters were nothing but long
litanies, a hotch-potch of eulogy and complaint. "A moment came
when she was little more than a Stylites perched on a stone column,
her eyes lost in contemplation of the heavens, her lips for ever muttering over and over again the same psalm. It is matter for wonder
that she should have continued to pour out an endless flow of adoration
which must have lacked variety, and for surprise that the god to whom
this homage was addressed should not have grown weary of its monotony . . ."[1] There were times when she doubted whether he even read
her letters.

I am good for nothing, not even to make you happy. For two and a half
years you have scarcely seemed to realize that I am here only to love you and
be loved by you. You do all that the noblest and most generous devotion is
capable of doing. But that is not *loving*: it is merely being loyal and good
beyond the power of words to express. I have no illusions. I love you too
well not to be clear-sighted. I know only too well that for more than two

years you have had no love for me, though you have preserved the appearance of love in the things you say and in the way you act. All that proves is that you are well-mannered. There are scenes of violence which, for a loving heart, are more eloquent and more persuasive than the cold gallantry of words: there is more passion and more tenderness in a *kick* than in certain forms of kissing on brow and lips. For more than two years I have been learning these things by sad experience. . . .[2]

Unfortunately, what she said was only too true. Victor Hugo fully realized the extent of her sacrifices, and of the duties which her self-denial had imposed upon him, but he no longer desired her. Any excuse now was good enough for him to force upon her a chastity which was so little to her taste. She could claim her rights only in respect of her three High Festivals: January 1st; February 17th (the anniversary of their first night together); and May 19th (the Feast of Sainte-Julie). In 1844, to make matters worse, he forgot May 19th! The circumspect and ambling Monsieur Foucher had been taken ill, and Victor replied to the lamentations of his neglected mistress by saying that he must stay at his father-in-law's bedside, because he "owed everything to the good old man!"[3] The truth, which Juliette only too accurately guessed, was that other women were now satisfying her lover's sensual requirements. Numerous were the actresses, or the earnest young female students of literature, who climbed the secret staircase in the Place Royale. *Juliette Drouet to Victor Hugo, January 17th, 1843:* "I have a feeling that the women whose interest in you must be highly flattering to the self-esteem of a poet are rousing in you a good deal of curiosity, and a strong desire to know all about them in considerable detail. I certainly can do nothing to prevent you from acting as you choose, but I do know that your first infidelity will cause my death. That is the long and the short of the matter. . . ."[4]

At the beginning of 1844 the reigning favourite was, though Juliette did not know it, a young fair-haired beauty, with swimming eyes which she often kept lowered with the air of a "timid dove," though, frequently, a flashing and mischievous smile gave the lie to that impression. Her name was Léonie d'Aunet, and she came of an authentic, though unimportant, noble line. She had been brought up as a young lady of fashion, but at eighteen had run away and gone to live with a painter, François-Thérèse-Auguste Biard, in his studio on the Place Vendôme.

Biard was a bad and rather vulgar artist, who had achieved success because the king, Louis Philippe, wanted for his galleries at Versailles the sort of historical and pompous canvases which Biard could produce by the car-load. He had travelled in Norway and Lapland and, for that reason, had gained the sort of romantic prestige which thrilled the susceptible heart of Léonie d'Aunet. In 1839 she had gone with him to Spitzbergen. In the course of this trip she had shown no little courage and a considerable degree of coquetry. On the way home the couple had stopped at the castle of Munckhölm, where Léonie, in a setting full of local colour, had read Victor Hugo's *Han d'Islande*.

In 1840 the painter had married her when she was already six months gone with child. They bought, near Samois, on the banks of the Seine, a house "complete with garden, park, ornamental water, and boat." There, round about 1842, they entertained numerous artists. Since her return from the Far North, Madame Biard had been much in the fashion as the "first Frenchwoman to have reached Spitzbergen," and her autograph album was filled with poems all signed with famous names. The authors had been introduced to her by a woman, at that time sixty-seven years of age, who had formerly, under the Directory, been one of the most celebrated of the "Merveilleuses"—Fortunée Hamelin. Like Joséphine Beauharnais, a Creole, Madame Hamelin was intelligent and refined. Among her friends she numbered Chateaubriand and Victor Hugo. Like Mademoiselle George and many other beauties, she had been one of the meteoric favourites of Napoleon, whom she never ceased to look on as "her star." Hugo, who had written so beautifully about the Emperor, was a man after this impenitent Bonapartist's own heart, while he, for his part, loved to listen to her recollections of five, now vanished, regimes: the Monarchy, the Directory, the Consulate, the Empire and the Restoration.

It was Madame Hamelin's custom to rent, every summer, a shooting-lodge (l'Hermitage de la Madeleine) not far from Les Plâtreries, which was the name of the Biards' estate. A strong friendship sprang up between the younger and the older woman. There is something of the procuress in every handsome and amatory dowager. Fortunée Hamelin brought the poet and the painter's wife together. They liked one another; they met again, though in 1843 the *Burgraves*, the trip to the Pyrenees, and then the death of Léopoldine saved Juliette from an immediate infidelity. In 1844 Hugo, overwhelmed by his loss, was driven to make some sort of an effort to break free of his grief. His intention was to stupefy himself with work and official duties (he was assiduous in his attendances at the Academy and the Court) and, doubtless, was occupied with new love-affairs. Madame Biard was now on very unhappy terms with her painter, by whom she was being ill-treated. With Victor Hugo compassion always gave an edge to desire. Despair on both sides proved to be a bond of union. He had a new companion now for his night-time walks, and served the lady as a guide to *his* Paris, from Notre-Dame to the windmills of La Grenelle. Poems flowed from his pen to an angel who was not Juliette:

C'était la première soirée
    Du mois d'Avril.
Je m'en souviens, mon adorée;
    T'en souvient-il?

Nous errions dans la ville immense,
    Tous deux, sans bruit,
A l'heure où le repos commence
    Avec le nuit. . . .

Notre-Dame, parmi les dômes
    Des vieux faubourgs,
Dressait, comme deux grands fantômes,
    Ses grandes tours.

La Seine, découpant les ombres
    En angles noirs,
Faisait luire sous les ponts sombres
    Des clairs miroirs. . . .

Tu disais: "Je suis calme et fière;
    Je t'aime! Oui!"
Et je rêvais a ta lumière
    Tout ébloui.

Oh! ce fut une heure sacrée,
    T'en souvient-il?
Que cette première soirée
    Du mois d'Avril? . . .[5]

There is something painful at finding the same feelings, the same words, here taking service under alien colours. Once again, the woods, the nesting birds, contribute to the scene, and, as of old, a charming and unstockinged foot is amorously hymned. Not for the first time, a woman is transformed into an angel. Léonie was the recipient of passionate letters:

You are an angel, and I kiss your feet: I kiss your tears. Your adorable letter has reached me. I have barely time enough in which to send this line, for I am little more than a poor galley-slave whose nights and days are given to work, but my heart is filled with you. I adore you, you are the light of my eyes, you are the very beating of my heart . . . I love you—that you must know. I love you beyond the power of words to tell, of spell-bound looks, and kisses . . . The most passionate and tender of caresses is wholly inadequate to express the love which overflows my being. . . .[6]

Wednesday, 3 o'clock in the morning: The kiss you gave me through your veil at our moment of parting was like love felt through absence, sweet, sad, but quite intoxicating. The obstacle was there, but in spite of it our bodies touched and felt. You are not beside me now, yet I have you here and see you. Your charming eyes are fixed on mine. I speak to you: I say: "Do you love me?" and I hear your thrilled voice answer me in a low whisper: "Yes." It is an illusion, yet it is a reality . . . You are indeed here, my heart can feel your presence. My love has set your loved and charming ghost moving about my chair. But, all the same, I miss you. I cannot long deceive myself. I have but to ask that ghost to kiss me, and it vanishes. Only in dreams can I have you by my side. To dream of you is sweet, but sweeter still to have the feel of you, to talk with you, to take you on my knee, to put my arms about you, to cover you with burning kisses, to see you redden and go pale, to feel you trembling in my arms. That is life—life full, entire and real. That is the light of the sun; that is the glow of paradise. . . .[7]

Similar letters, alas! to those he had written to Juliette. The truth is that no man can change completely, that the role of the well-beloved is always the same, that the most he can do is to give it to another actress who is younger and better fitted to play it. The peculiar talent and temperament, however, of each actress will lead to its being played differently when the occasion arises. Léonie Biard was not, like Juliette, passionate and wild. She might describe herself as just another wounded heart (thereby touching the knightly Hugo on a sensitive spot), but there was more of Watteau than of Delacroix in her pouts and smiles, and the literary mode of the moment was all in her favour.

In 1845 Hugo's enemies had the impression that he was writing scarcely anything. In this they were wrong. He was composing a number of beautiful poems on the subject of his daughter, as well as love-songs to Léonie. He was also working at a novel, *Les Misères*. But the apparent frivolity of his life roused malicious hopes in them. Three establishments—and three women, continually complaining—are more than most men can deal with. To Juliette, who reminded him of his promise, he replied: "What do you want me to say? . . . For a long time you were my delight; you are now my consolation. I would have you be as happy as you are blessed. Wipe from your lovely brow and your great heart the small sorrows of the moment, the passing clouds and glooms. You are deserving of Heaven . . ."[8] She would rather have had a little more of the earthly paradise. But he was a familiar figure now, not so much at "Madame Drouet's" as at Madame Girardin's and at Madame Hamelin's, where he could be sure of meeting Madame Biard. Of that lady, Juliette, in her seclusion from the world, fortunately knew nothing. It was against Fortunée Hamelin that she bore a grudge. *December 4th, 1844:* "All I get from you, alas! is proof-correcting and letter-writing . . . Everything else is for others to enjoy . . . which is probably why I dreamed last night that I gave your Creole a sound thrashing.⁹ All I hope is that it won't end there, but that I shall be able to continue that nocturnal chastisement in broad daylight."¹⁰

He was regular in his attendance at the Academy, always with a serious expression, a clouded brow, and a set and solemn jaw, not seldom rebellious, but always dignified. Truth to tell, he brought into play the sense of humour, which in his work he kept concealed under a bushel, in the ironical notes he made on the conversation of his colleagues. There were several newcomers in the Quai Conti building. "The older Academicians," he said, "crowd round the fresh arrivals, who are in the prime of life, as the ghostly figures in the Purgatorio round the living Dante and Aeneas, startled and surprised at the spectacle of flesh and blood." What he himself most wanted was to procure the election of Balzac, Dumas and Vigny, thereby showing that he had a sound judgment and a generous heart, since none of the three had been wholly guiltless in their dealings with him.

There was a still greater call upon his magnanimity when Sainte-Beuve came forward as a candidate, declaring that this particular ambition was, in his case, deliberate and controlled. "I have been inoculated," he said; "I am in no danger of the small-pox; vaccination has saved me from that." Nevertheless, he had caught the infection. Hugo's election had opened the gates to the whole of the romantic gang. But there could be no hope of Sainte-Beuve's election unless Vigny refrained from standing, and that depended upon Hugo, who displayed a noble-hearted good-will in his attitude to two men of whom he had good reason to complain. He gave them his advice, receiving Sainte-Beuve at the Place Royale, "like a great lord forgetful of past injuries,"¹¹ and preaching patience to Vigny. He knew nothing at that time of the existence of the *Livre d'Amour*. At long last Sainte-Beuve was elected on March 14th, 1844. The same evening his mother made an offering of flowers to the Virgin. Hugo, who had been acting as Director when Sainte-Beuve's predecessor, Casimir Delavigne, died, had to extend the welcome of La Coupole to the new Academician. He made no attempt to avoid this duty, being only too glad to overwhelm an enemy with benefactions. Paris, expecting a "spicy" session, flocked to the occasion. They came to smile: they stayed to applaud. Victor Hugo welcomed the Academy's choice with high praise:

As a poet, you have achieved the discovery of a twilit path, and have made it your own . . . Your verses, almost always sorrowful, and often profound, touch the hearts of all who have suffered . . . In order to reach them, you keep your thought veiled, not wishing to disturb the shadowed place in which you go to meet them . . . Whence it comes that you have produced poetry which is at once shy and penetrating, which gently sets its fingers on the mysterious fibres of the heart . . . By reason of a mingled gift of erudition and imagination, behind which the poet never wholly vanishes in the critic, and the critic never wholly lays aside the poet, you recall to this Academy one of its most beloved and most regretted members, the good and charming Nodier, who was at once so highly gifted and so gentle. . . .[12]

Referring to *Volupté* and *Madame de Pontivy*, he hinted, in words which were not altogether without a touch of malice, that Sainte-Beuve, as a novelist, had "explored regions unknown within the limits of any possible life"—a delicate way of saying that those possibles had failed to become realities. On the subject of *Port-Royal*, he delivered a passage on Jansenism and Faith. In short, he found himself regretfully compelled to admire. Sainte-Beuve thanked him. *Hugo to Sainte-Beuve:* "Your letter touched and moved me deeply. From the bottom of my heart I thank you for your thanks."[13] He had the two speeches bound together for Adèle, and dedicated the volume to her: "To my wife, this double homage: of tenderness because she is charming; of respect because she is good." To the first page he pinned Sainte-Beuve's letter. Of such are the miracles performed by the Académie Française.

The ambitious are unhappy. Nothing will satisfy them. Victor Hugo, ever since he had been the possessor of a green coat, had been thinking only of the gold-embroidered robes of a peer of the realm. Juliette did not want a political career for him. "To become an Academician, a peer of France, a Minister—what does that all amount to for one whom the good God has made just Toto . . ."[14] Madame Biard, on the contrary, fanned the flame of his ambition, and poured oil upon the flames. Hugo was assiduous in his attendance on the king, and Louis-Philippe came to be on friendly and intimate terms with him. The poet has left a portrait of the monarch, in an account of an audience he had, which is worthy of a Retz or a Saint-Simon. The king is shown in it as being human, crafty, intelligent, and, at moments, bitter. "Monsieur Hugo, I am wrongly judged . . . It is said that I am shrewd. It is said that I am clever. That is as much as to say I am a traitor. I am hurt by such a view. I am a gentleman—that is the simple truth. I walk straight down the road I see before me. Those who know me know that I am frank . . ."[15] Victor Hugo, to whose hand the king gave a familiar shake, was, now and again, tempted to believe this.

Meanwhile, he was busy manœuvring. There were representations made by the Duchesse d'Orléans to her august father-in-law. There were fine addresses to the Académie Française; "All his big guns," as Sainte-Beuve put it. His tactics finally won the day. By a warrant dated April 13th, 1845, *La Vicomte Hugo (Victor-Marie)* was raised to the

Peerage. The republican papers were sarcastic. Armand Marrast, in *Le National*, described the poet's arrival at the Luxembourg: "A sort of pale radiance streaming through the windows imparted to the dim hangings of the palace a lively red . . . Monsieur Pasquier, wearing his Cap of State, recited the Warrant which raised to the dignity of a peer of France *Monsieur le Vicomte Victor Hugo* . . .Our breasts swelled . . . This we had not known! . . . He was a Vicomte! A little shudder of poetry went down our backs: a heraldic ardour seized upon us . . . Victor Hugo is dead! Long Live Monsieur le Vicomte Hugo, the lyric peer of France! Democracy, which he has insulted, is now entitled to a laugh. It has been well avenged . . ."[16] Charles Maurice, in his *Courrier des Théâtres,* wrote: "Monsieur Victor Hugo has been created a peer of France: *le Roi s'amuse . . .*"[17] Popular gossip had it that he was now hoping to be appointed Ambassador to the Court of Spain. "What is certain is that he has good hope of one day becoming a minister . . ."[18] Juliette, in one of the letters she wrote him twice a day, asked: "Why has the good God who, from all time, intended to make of you an Academician and a peer of France, and of me, your loving mistress, lavished upon you such a wealth of black hair and youthfulness, gifts wholly useless in such superannuated employments, and crowned my head with grey?"[19]

Pierre Foucher lived just long enough to see his daughter a peeress. The self-effacing old man died in May 1845. Death spared him the knowledge of a scandal which would have deeply shocked him, both as a father and as a man of religious principles. On July 5th the Commissary of Police of the Vendôme district, acting on representations made by Auguste Biard, demanded access in the name of the law, and in the early hours of the morning, to a discreet apartment situated in the passage Saint-Roche, and there surprised, *in flagrante delicto,* Victor Hugo and his mistress. Adultery at that time was severely dealt with. The husband showed no mercy. Léonie d'Aunet, "wife of Biard," was arrested and confined in the Saint-Lazare prison. Victor Hugo claimed immunity as a peer, and the Commissary, after some hesitation, released him. But Biard lodged a complaint with the Chancellor Pasquier. Next day *La Patrie, Le National* and *La Quotidienne* referred in guarded terms to a deplorable scandal, and to the duty which would be laid upon the House of Peers to pass judgment on one of its members for adultery. The king in person had to intervene. He summoned the painter Biard to Saint-Cloud in order to induce him to withdraw his complaint. It was said that a series of frescoes (*fresques*), commissioned for the Palace of Versailles, had made him forget his wife's escapade (*frasque*).

Friends and enemies alike laughed a good deal over the incident, the second openly, the first behind their hands. Lamartine was soft-spoken and feline. *Alphonse de Lamartine to the Comte de Circourt:* "I am greatly perturbed. But matters of this kind are quickly forgotten. France is resilient. One can rise again, even from a divan." *To Dargaud:* "The amorous adventure of my friend Hugo grieves me much . . . what, for him, must be heartbreaking is the knowledge that, while he remains at liberty, the poor woman is in prison . . ."[20] The king advised Hugo to leave Paris for a while, instead of which the poet chose to shut himself up in Juliette's apartment, there to work, said Sainte-Beuve, "at some book, though what I don't know, in the hope that a brilliant success may serve to cover up his recent activities."[21] Of those activities Juliette knew nothing. Warned by her sister, Madame Louis Koch, who had written to her from the depths of Brittany, asking "what the articles and paragraphs in *Le National* and *La Patrie* meant," she replied by contradicting them—in perfect good faith. As to the Vicomtesse Victor Hugo, she had heard the confession of the guilty man on the very morning of the fatal discovery, had shown great sweetness, and had even gone to visit Madame Biard in prison.

29

Heights and Depths

Apotheosis has the terrible gift of bringing low.

VICTOR HUGO

THE incident of the passage Saint-Roche did no lasting harm to
Victor Hugo's career. The only victim had been Léonie Biard,
who remained locked away at Saint-Lazare with prostitutes and adulterous wives. Meanwhile, Madame Hamelin intervened with the husband, her neighbour at Samois, and tried to prevail with him to take
steps for her release, or to insist, as he had a perfect right to do, on
her being transferred to the Convent of the Sacred Heart. "My friend,"
she told him gaily, "only kings and cuckolds have the right to pardon.
Why not look on the bright side of this business?" At this he burst
out laughing, and forthwith put a stop to the activities of the law. The
fair Léonie was shut away for several months in an Augustinian
convent in the rue Neuve-de-Berri. Deprived of her poet, who continued to send her beautiful verses, she became extremely bored, but
fascinated the good sisters and made them read Victor Hugo. On
August 14th, 1845, a decree of "separation from bed and board" was
pronounced between husband and wife.

After leaving the convent the beautiful, but not excessively repentant, sinner took refuge with her grandmother. The world, at first,
closed its ranks against her, but Madame Hamelin came to her assistance, and even Madame Victor Hugo consented to "take up" Léonie
d'Aunet, who became one of the constant ornaments of the Place
Royale *salon*. Was this attitude on the part of Adèle dictated by a
wish to show her forgiving nature, by a feeling that, as a wife who
was really no more than a companion, she ought to present a united
front with her husband, by the thought that she was herself a guilty
and repentant partner, by simple good sense, or by the knowledge
that, by so acting, she could take a pleasing revenge on Juliette Drouet?
Whatever the reason, the fact remains that she accepted Léonie as
a friend, and that the latter grew to be her dear adviser on matters
of dress and decoration. Lamartine was right: in France one can rise

250

again from any situation. All that remained to be done was to find some way in which the repudiated wife could make a living. She did a certain amount of writing, published a number of articles, and later a few books. Hugo showed himself generous—less so than she might have wished, more, he said, than he could really afford. "I would gladly give you my blood: but blood is not money. . . ."[1]

Admittedly, his earnings were small, for the simple reason that he was publishing nothing. He had pursued, after the scandal, a policy of silence. Not that he was not working. He had returned to an old project, his novel *Les Misères*, for which he was under contract with Renduel and Gosselin. This book, a piece of sociological fiction in the manner of Eugène Sue, was to be in four parts. It was to contain the story of a saint; the story of a convict; the story of a woman; the story of a doll.

Auguste Vacquerie, who read the "opening pages of this epic," was "reduced almost to tears," so great was his admiration. Such a response is not difficult to understand. In this book Victor Hugo expressed the sincere compassion which he had always felt for the destitute, and his indignation at the crimes of a society which he had seemed to accept, but against which his heart rebelled. Juliette, whom he employed in copying *Jean Tréjean* (for a brief moment this was the title of the novel) was completely overwhelmed by it.

December 23rd, 1845: Send me something to copy: I long to know more about the good Bishop of D . . . *February 3rd, 1848:* I can see everything as though it were going on before my eyes. I can feel all the appalling tortures inflicted on poor Jean Tréjean, and shed tears, in spite of myself, over the fate of that poor martyr. I know nothing more heartrending than poor Fantine, nor more painful than the wretched sot Champmathieu. I live with all these people, and share in their agonies as though they were actual human beings of flesh and blood, such reality have you given to them. I can't express what I mean, but I know that all I possess of intelligence, heart and soul is held by this sublime book, which you have so truly called *Les Misères*. . . .[2]

Juliette was enjoying the benefit, though she did not know it, of the incarceration, and later of the enforced retreat, of Léonie Biard, and was seeing a great deal more than she ordinarily did of her lover and master. In 1846 she found herself drawn very close to him by a loss scarcely less terrible than that occasioned by the Villequier tragedy. Her daughter, Claire Pradier (whom the "Prince of Furstenberg"—now married and the father of a legitimate family—had forbidden to bear his name), had been unofficially adopted by Hugo, who had paid for her education, given her lessons, made her endless presents, and was sincerely attached to her. She had grown into a sad and rather touching young woman, deeply conscious of her undeserved misfortunes, and filled, as a result of deep despair, with a longing for death. *Claire to Victor Hugo:* "Dear Monsieur Toto, goodbye, always take care of my dear mamma, who is so good and so charming, and be sure that your Claire will be truly grateful." After what may have been an attempt at suicide she fell seriously ill. Pradier had had her transferred to a "frightful, ramshackle little room belonging to a shopkeeper in Auteuil," and Victor Hugo had more than once abandoned his work, and gone by 'bus to see her. Though such a degree of devotion was, all things considered, only natural, Juliette looked on these visits as those of a God benevolently manifesting Himself to mortals. She adored her daughter, yet, even when the child was at her last gasp, would still write her daily scrawl: "There is despair in my heart, but I love you. The good God may grind my heart to powder if He will, but the last cry that comes from it will be a cry of love for you, my great, grand well-beloved. . . ."[3]

When Claire Pradier was buried in the cemetery of Saint-Mandé, the Vicomte Victor Hugo, peer of France, walked as chief mourner, with the child's father, who during the last sad days had shown a greater tenderness. To attract so much notice in equivocal circumstances, after so recent a scandal, was not without danger for Hugo, but he accepted the risk courageously and simply, in order to give to the dead girl and her mother this supreme proof of affection. A man of achieved success, with the weaknesses inevitably connected with that condition, he yet retained enough of humanity to ensure his ultimate salvation. For the grieving Juliette, and for Claire's poor ghost, he wrote more than one poem:

> Quoi donc? La vôtre aussi! La vôtre suit la mienne!
> Ô mère au cœur profond, mère, vous avez beau
> Laisser la porte ouverte afin qu'elle revienne,
> Cette pierre, là-bas, dans l'herbe, est un tombeau . . .
>
> Elle s'en est allée à l'aube qui se lève,
> Lueur dans le matin, vertu dans le ciel bleu,
> Bouche qui n'a connu que le baiser de rêve,
> Âme qui n'a dormi que dans le lit de Dieu. . . .[4]

After Claire's death the poet's relations with the "Prince of Furstenberg" remained extremely cordial. Victor Hugo sometimes dined at Pradier's table, with Alphonse Karr, and these parties brought together three men who had all been Juliette Drouet's lovers. In 1845, the year which had seen Hugo taken *in flagrante delicto* with Madame Biard, Pradier had caught his own highly respected wife "in criminal intercourse" with another house-breaker. Having driven her from home, he took to wandering in the woods of Meudon with various young models. Meanwhile Juliette, condemned to her life of seclusion, was brooding on her grievances. "If you did not love me," she said to Victor, "I would not put up with life for more than two hours." She had lost more than she had ever had, for during the twenty years of her existence, Claire had scarcely ever lived under her mother's roof. Pradier had put her out to nurse, and after her education at a boarding-school she had stayed on there as a junior mistress. In Juliette's despair a sense of unexpressed remorse played no small a part.

In the House of Peers where the Vicomte, in June 1845, after the Biard affair, had felt the blowing of an icy wind, he was cautious about trying his wings as a speaker. When one has the reputation of a trouble-maker, it is a shrewd move to seem dull. Victor Hugo's first speech dealt with designs and trade-marks. This was reassuring. On the second occasion he intervened in a debate on the subject of Poland, and was badly received. These haughty ancients still felt a grudge against him for having "dragged their ermine in the mud." Truth to tell, there was no lack of adulterous peers, but they had been careful not to let themselves be caught. That is all that matters. With a mocking eye he watched the pompous creatures, and, as at the Academy, made comic notes about his colleagues. On General Fabvier: "I expected a lion: I saw an old woman"; on the Marquis de Boissy: "He is a cool customer, he is not often caught on the wrong foot; he has an easy gift of speech—all the trimmings, in fact, of a great orator; he lacks only one thing—talent." There is nothing more curious than the contrast between the pure and glacial irony of *Choses vues,* worthy of Stendhal, and the showiness of his antithetical speeches and balanced oratory. Hugo-Maglia must often have laughed at Hugo-Ruy-Blas.

There was one speech, however, which he delivered with whole-hearted pleasure. He made it in support of the petition put forward by Jérôme Bonaparte asking that his family should be allowed to return to France. Hugo evoked the memory of his own father, "one of the Emperor's veterans." It was in obedience to *his* wishes that he now "rose to speak." He painted a glowing picture of Napoleon's universal glory, and asked what crime that great man had committed thus to be struck down for ever in the members of his family. "These are his crimes: religion reinstated; the Civil Code drafted; France aggrandized beyond even her natural frontiers; Marengo, Jéna Wagram, Austerlitz; the greatest gift of power and glory that one great man has ever given to a great nation! . . ."[5] One of the ushers, an old battalion commander, burst into tears at the foot of the tribune. Fortunée Hamelin and Léonie d'Aunet, both Bonapartists, were triumphant.

And what, really, was Hugo? An adorer of the imperial idol? A

courtier of the bourgeois monarchy? A friend of the poor? So long
as a man has not taken a private and binding oath of allegiance, how
can he know what he is? Whether he liked it or not, he was le Vicomte
Hugo, member of the Academy, peer of France; a man with a "well-
fed, full-fleshed face"[6] who dined at the tables of ambassadors and
ministers. There, no doubt, he saw, not very close to him, but at the
far end of the board, Alfred de Vigny, with his fair hair and birdlike
profile, who had once again become friendly because he was a candidate
for admission to the Quai Conti; Sainte-Beuve, bald and undersized;
Pradier, with his flowing locks and his air of a man of forty, though
he was all of sixty; Ingres, "with his chin on a level with the table,
so that the red commander's ribbon round his neck seemed to emerge
from the cloth." He figured as a guest at the great receptions in the
Tuileries, where the vast hall, more faithful than the spectators, still
retained its Empire decorations—lyres, gryphons, palm-leaves and
Greek mouldings. Few pretty women: Adèle, mature and Spanish-
looking, was still the loveliest. Mademoiselle George, once a divine
and triumphant goddess, came up to Hugo, looking very old and very
sad: "What is there left for a fat old woman like me! And where are
the authors? Where are the plays? Where are the parts? . . . Poor
Dorval is acting, heaven knows where, at Toulouse, at Carpentras,
in barns, to make a living! She is reduced, as I am, to making a show
of her bald head, to dragging her wretched old carcase about a stage
of ill-fitting planks, in front of four smoky candles . . ."[7] The princes
treated Hugo as a friend. He was no longer even surprised to find
himself on familiar terms with them. Glory and death were pushing
him into the front rank. Who, in the world of letters, was there to
outclass him? Chateaubriand in 1847 was a paralytic dotard, who had
himself carried every day at three o'clock to the bedside of the blind
Madame Récamier. At the funeral of Mademoiselle Mars, who had
been such a thorn in his side in the days of *Hernani*, "an intelligent
actress, but a fool of a woman," Hugo saw the people of Paris in
their smocks, trying to pick out the poets in the crowd. "This people
needs glory. When they have no Marengo, no Austerlitz, they want, and
they love, the Dumas and the Lamartines"—and the Hugos.

A great life, when all was said. In the space of ten years he had
written, beginning with *Les Feuilles d'Automne,* and ending with *Les
Rayons et les Ombres,* the four most beautiful collections in all French
poetry. *Les Misérables* gave every promise of equalling *Notre-Dame de
Paris.* With any luck he would be a minister. Storms had rumbled
about him, and he had emerged from them with his fame intact.
And yet he was not happy. On his way back from the cemetery where
they had buried little Claire he had meditated on the vanity of tumultuous and worldly lives:

On jette sa parole aux sombres assemblées:
Devant le but qu'on veut et le sort qui vous prend
On se sent faible et fort; on est petit et grand;
On est flot dans la foule, âme dans le tempête;
Tout vient et passe; on est en deuil, on est en fête;
On arrive, on recule, on lutte avec effort . . .
—Puis le vaste et profond silence de la mort.[8]

On his way home from these splendid occasions, with the leaves moving in the soft summer breeze, and lights showing from the Opéra, he looked at the crowd and noted the dark and angry expression with which it gazed at the women with their glittering jewels, at the men in their gold-laced uniforms. The peer of France with his ever-increasing gilt-edged investments tried to silence his conscience. After all, is not luxury a benefit to the community? Does not the rich man who spends his money provide the wages of the many? But he knew, only too well, remembering the days when in his misery he had watched happy folk dancing behind closed windows, that the people demand not only bread, but equality. "When the crowd looks at the rich like that, it is not with thoughts that its heads are full, but with events." But what could be done about it all? The man who has made his mark is caught up in an eternal process. The social machine, so cunningly contrived, passes him from cylinder to cylinder, from roller to roller, from ball to ball, from dinner to dinner, and, with each day that passes flattens him out a little more. Twenty persons there are for whom he is responsible, women, children, hangers-on, for whom he must provide in this world, such as it is. Only resolution can force him out of the current—or revolution. The Victor Hugo who was writing *Les Misérables* thought of both. Oppressed by a sense of guilt, he saw no hope of salvation except in sacrifices imposed upon him by some outbreak of social violence. Within him, the desire to suffer was confused with a desire to grow greater. Masochism and ambition were both at work.

He had lost his way, and sought a refuge in forgetfulness. *Recours à l'abîme.* Surrounded by débutantes and adventuresses, by chamber-maids and courtesans, he seemed, in these years from 1847 to 1850, as though he had become a prey to a sort of gloomy craving for fresh meat. The romantic lover now gave himself the airs of a roué, and adopted the style of a Valmont. To Esther Guimont, "a courtesan of letters"[9] and his friend Émile de Girardin's mistress, he sent this off-hand note: "What date for Heaven? Would Monday be convenient, or Tuesday, or Wednesday? The only thing I dread is delay. V. H." With Théophile Gautier, with the painter Chassériau, and with his own son Charles he competed, successfully, for the loveliest piece of woman's flesh in all Paris—Alice Ozy.

Living in close intimacy with young Charles, who in 1847 was twenty-one years old, this superb and easy-going creature had expressed a wish to have in her autograph album a few lines from the hand of the great poet. Hugo paid her a visit and saw the magnificent bed of rosewood encrusted with medallions of old Sèvres. . . .

Genius won the day over youth, and youth, at last, bowed to the inevitable. *Charles Hugo to Alice Ozy:* "Why did you write that letter to my father? On the one hand was the son with a pure heart, a deep love, an endless devotion: on the other, the father in his glory. *You have chosen father and glory.* I do not blame you. There's not a woman alive but would have done the same. But you must realize that I am not strong enough to endure the miseries that lie ahead for me now that you have decided to *share your love in this manner.*"[10]

But Adèle Hugo, fully cognizant of this drama, as she was of everything that went on, consoled her son, and Juliette Drouet, who had been told only that Charles was suffering as the result of a broken love-affair, suggested that he should be sent for a while to stay with Auguste Vacquerie at Villequier. Once again, in the Hugo family history, "the sins of the father were being visited upon the children."

These various hoppings in and out of bed had now no passion to excuse them. They left a bitter taste behind them. "The numbing of life into insensibility is not the same thing as enjoyment." Once again Hugo wanted to tear himself free from temptation, even though he might have to suffer in the process.

Since the Villequier tragedy, since the deaths of Léopoldine and Claire, he had begun to feel conscious of a new need, the need of some belief which would make it possible for him to hope that a day would come when he would meet his loved ones in another place. "Est-ce qu'il est vraiment impossible, doux ange—De lever cette pierre et de parler un peu?" He meditated on the problem of life after death. He tried to build up for himself some sort of religious philosophy. He studied the works of those who were versed in the occult, who held that, even in this world, it is possible to hold communication with the souls of the departed. It was preoccupations such as these that accounted for the veiled and absent look in the eyes of this still young, healthy and seemingly successful man. On February 19th, 1848, while seated in the House of Peers, as a result of what brooding fit we cannot tell, he jotted down on a piece of paper the following words: "Poverty drives the people to revolution; revolutions drive them back into poverty." For a moment he played with the idea of possible action, then, feeling himself to be isolated, abandoned that line of thought. "Better not to get to one's feet at all, than to get to one's feet alone," he said to the Comte Daru. "I love danger, but detest ridicule . . ."[11] He continued, therefore, to play his part; but his heart was heavy.

PART VII

A Time for Decision

30

Heart or Money-Bags

What we lose on the harvest we recover at the
gathering of the grapes.

VICTOR HUGO

IN FEBRUARY 1848 France, which for eighteen years had known
no change of regime, began to be bored. Liberals and Republicans,
at their banquets, were voicing a demand for electoral reform. Legitimists and Bonapartists were becoming restive. There was talk of revolution. King Louis-Philippe continued to smile. "I am afraid of nothing," he said to the ex-king Jérôme Bonaparte, and then, after a brief
silence, added: "I am a necessity." Victor Hugo looked upon the
troubled waters with the detachment of an artist. Electoral reform
did not interest him. There was more in him of the sociologist than
the parliamentarian. The old king remained on the most friendly
terms with him, and would have liked to set him up as a champion
of the monarchy against Lamartine, who was giving the prestige of
his name to the cause of reform. But Hugo was not a candidate for
such employment. What had he to fear? That the ministry might fall?
That the king might abdicate? In that event his dear Princess Hélèna
would become regent, and he her all-powerful adviser. As to a Republic, his opinion was that it was neither desirable nor possible.

On February 23rd, as he walked down to the Chamber in search
of news, he saw the streets filled with soldiers and workmen in smocks,
who were shouting: "Long Live the People!"—"Down with Guizot!"
The soldiers were chatting and joking. In the lobbies he came upon
groups of scared and fussy deputies. To them he said: "The cabinet
is very much to blame. It has carried government into the danger-
zone. A riot can strengthen a ministry; a revolution can overturn a
dynasty." He was obsessed, that day, by images drawn from the sea.
In his notebook he wrote that, in a riot, the people is the ocean on
which the Ship of State rides. When that ship begins to look like a
very small boat, it means that the riot has become a revolution.

Then, being a brave man, and one who liked to see for himself,
and believed only his own eyes, he went off to mingle with the crowd

on the Place de la Concorde. The troops opened fire; several persons were wounded. He found time to notice, in the middle of a group of "smocks," a very pretty woman wearing a green velvet hat, and lifting her skirts as high as possible to reveal a more than usually charming leg. The Faun of Sirius. Close to the Carrousel Bridge he ran into that hairiest of all bald-pates, Jules Sandeau, who asked: "What's going to be the outcome of all this?" "The riot will be quelled," answered Victor Hugo, "but the revolution will be triumphant."

Great events do not affect the delights of lesser pleasures. On that night of rioting, before returning to the domestic hearth, he supped with the divine Alice Ozy, recently promoted to the position of Chassériau's mistress. The painter adored her, and she tortured him. "She was wearing a necklace of fine pearls, and a shawl of red cashmere, strangely beautiful . . ."[1] In the presence of her lover, she opened her dress and showed him "one of those wonderful breasts which poets hymn and bankers buy," then jumped on to the table, lifted her skirt as high as the knee, and gave him a glimpse of the loveliest leg in all the world, clad in a transparent silk stocking . . .[2] Chassériau fainted. Victor Hugo describes the scene in *Choses vues,* entitling it "D'après nature"; Chassériau appears as "Serio," Alice Ozy as "Zubiri." Meanwhile, on the Boulevard des Capucines, a fusillade had transformed the riot into a revolution. When, an hour later, he returned to the Place Royale, he found a whole battalion concealed under the arcades. Bayonets were showing dimly in the darkness. Next morning, he saw from his balcony the mob forcing its way into the Mairie. The mayor of the arrondissement, Ernest Moreau, sent for him and told him of the massacre on the Boulevard des Capucines. Barricades were going up everywhere. About half-past eight, to the rolling of drums, the mayor announced that Guizot had been dismissed and Odilon Barrot, the friend of reform, was in power. In the Place Royale there were cries of "Long Live Reform!" but on the Place de la Bastille, where he had just repeated the announcement, Ernest Moreau received a bullet through his hat. Always a daring diver, Hugo, with the mayor at his heels, plunged straight into the crowd and, in a storm of noise, reached the Palais Bourbon, where the sour tones of Monsieur Thiers informed him that the Chamber was dissolved, that the king had abdicated, that the Duchesse d'Orléans was now regent. "The tide is rising, rising, rising!" said little Thiers in tones of suppressed joy. Guizot's fall had consoled him for everything. He vehemently urged Hugo and the mayor of the 8th arrondissement to go at once to see Odilon Barrot at the Ministry of the Interior and to come to an agreement with him. "The attitude of your district [the Faubourg Saint-Antoine] may well be decisive at a time like this."

The scenario appeared to be developing just as Hugo had foreseen. He found Odilon Barrot as hesitant as usual, with his hand in his coat-front. He had the pose of the Emperor, but not his firmness. The Regency? "It remains to be seen," he said, "whether it will receive the sanction of the Assemblies. It is essential," he went on, "that the Duchesse d'Orléans should bring the Comte de Paris to the Chamber." "The Chamber is dissolved," replied Hugo: "if the duchess ought to go anywhere, it is to the Hôtel de Ville": whereupon Hugo and the mayor hastened to the Tuileries in order to convince the Princesse Hélène. Unfortunately she had already started for the Chamber.

They hurried back to the Place Royale, with the intention of proclaiming the Regency. It was Hugo who told the crowd from the balcony that the king had abdicated (*general applause*), that the Duchesse d'Orléans had assumed the position of regent (*a good deal of muttering*). "I must now repeat the proclamation on the Place de la Bastille," said Victor Hugo. The mayor was despondent. "Surely you can see it would be useless; they're not standing for the Regency . . . At the Bastille you'll find all the revolutionary elements of the Faubourg, and they'll probably give you a rough time." Hugo replied that he had pledged his word to Barrot and that he intended to keep it. Linking arms with two officers of the National Guard, he mounted the platform which had been put up round the base of the Column of July. As the mayor had foreseen, he was given a bad reception: "No Regency! Down with the Bourbons!" A man in a smock levelled a gun at him: "down with the peer of France!" He replied with a considerable flow of eloquence, but was so imprudent, in an attempt to show that constitutional monarchy was compatible with liberty, as to say: "Look at Queen Victoria in England . . ." "We are Frenchmen! No Regency!" the crowd yelled.

With vain gallantry he was playing a game which was already lost. The poet who, on that day, held Paris in the hollow of his hand was not Victor Hugo, but Lamartine, "who had let fall upon the guillotine a ray of his silver moonlight," and achieved popularity with his *Histoire des Girondins*. Now Lamartine, called upon to declare whether he was *for* or *against* a regency, had, after a few moments of deep thought, said that he was, himself, in favour of a Republic. A slip of paper, to which were appended, after his, the signatures of Ledru-Rollin, Garnier-Pagès, Crémieux, Marie and Dupont de l'Eure, decided the fate of a nation. The die was cast. Hugo could scarcely feel satisfied by the turn of events. To exchange Louis-Philippe, who, though he was not open-minded, was at least intelligent, for "this old Dupont de l'Eure with his frightened look," seemed to him to be a bad bargain. He remembered the things his mother had told him, and feared that a Republic would mean anarchy. But the Provisional Government contained Lamartine and Arago, of both of whom he thought highly, and next morning, February 25th, he felt an irresistible desire to go to the Hôtel de Ville and to fling himself once more into the turmoil of the streets. He set off early with his second son, François-Victor. He was born inquisitive, and loved the roar of crowds no less than the din of tempests. The city now seemed rapturous. Groups with flags and drums were singing *La Marseillaise* and *Mourir pour la Patrie.*

On the Place de l'Hôtel de Ville he was held up by a mob, but the commanding officer of the National Guard, charged with the duty of keeping order, was the goldsmith Froment-Meurice, a brother of Hugo's young disciple Paul Meurice. "Way for Victor Hugo!" he shouted, and Citizen Hugo was able to reach Citizen Lamartine. He found him in a buttoned frock-coat with a tricolour scarf over his shoulder. He was received with open arms. "Ah! Victor Hugo!—you are joining us—the Republic is proud of its recruit!"

Hugo, considerably less forthcoming, said that, though *in principle* a republican, he was nevertheless a peer of France, created by the king, and that, as such, he must maintain a decent reserve. In any case, he added, he considered the Republic to be premature, and would have whole-heartedly given his support to a regency had such a solution been possible. Lamartine told him that the Provisional Government had appointed Victor Hugo to be mayor of his arrondissement, and that if, instead of being a mayor, he would prefer to be a minister . . . "Victor Hugo as Minister of Public Instruction under the Republic— Ah, that would be magnificent!" Hugo held back. He saw no reason why he should replace at the mairie of the 8th arrondissement Ernest Moreau who had behaved so loyally. All the same, he put the warrant in his pocket. At this moment, shots were fired from the Place, and a window was broken. "My friend," said Lamartine, "what a heavy burden is revolutionary power!" He pointed to the surging, eddying thousands. "See there, that is an ocean!" An obscure fraternity of genius had brought together two men little suited to understand one another.

Next day Hugo walked through Paris, wondering at the rapidity with which the look of things had changed. Not for sixty years had the good God shown Himself to be so magnificent a stage-manager.

Meanwhile, his friend Émile de Girardin, an old champion of the Regency but an opportunist by nature, had at once rallied to the Provisional Government, carrying over with him to the cause of the Republic the twenty thousand readers of *La Presse.* This was an indication of how things were moving. Though still remaining, so far as the regime was concerned, perfectly non-committal, Hugo was still of the opinion that he had a part to play, and began to wonder whether, if universal suffrage were to declare the nation's will, it might not, after all, be monarchist. Though at the April elections he did not offer himself as a candidate, he issued a "Letter to the Electors," in which dignity was decently allied with ambition.

Gentlemen, I belong to my country: it can make use of me as it will. I have a feeling of respect, perhaps exaggerated, for freedom of choice. You should be glad that I push that feeling so far as not to offer myself for election . . . Should my fellow-citizens judge it right, in their liberty and their sovereignty, to call upon me to take my seat as their representative in an assembly which will hold the destinies of France and of Europe in its hands, then, with my conscience at rest, I will accept that solemn responsibility. . . .[3]

He was not elected, but was given sixty thousand votes on April 23rd, which in view of his manifesto did honour to the electors of Paris. This half-success enabled him to obtain, in May at the complementary elections, the backing of the *Comité de la rue de Poitiers*, in other words, of the Conservatives. This support was given with no very great enthusiasm. Could one really depend upon a poet, the "solid" folk asked themselves. In his profession of faith, Hugo drew a distinction between two possible forms of republic:

One of them will set the tricolour beneath the red flag, will melt down the *Column* into ha'pence, will remove the statue of Napoleon and erect in its place a statue of Marat, will destroy the Institut, the École Polytechnique, the Legion of Honour, and will add to the noble motto, *Liberté, Égalité, Fraternité,* the sinister alternative—or *Death* . . . The other will be the sacred participation by all Frenchmen now living, and, one day, by all peoples, in the principles of Democracy. It will found liberty without usurpation and without violence, a liberty which will give free play to each man's natural bent. It will be a fraternity, not of monks in a monastery, but of free men . . . Of these two republics, the second goes by the name of Civilization, the first of The Terror. I am prepared to devote my life to the establishment of the one and the checking of the other.[4]

His ideas were sensible, but his position was false. He had no liking for the "Burgraves" of the rue de Poitiers, who patronized him with a mistrustful condescension. He most certainly preferred Lamartine to them. But none of those around Hugo was pushing him towards the Republic. Very much to the contrary.

Juliette Drouet to Victor Hugo, May 3rd, 1848: Nothing gets on my nerves so much as these riotings and upsets into which you don't seem able not to push your nose . . . Provided there are no more revolutions, evolutions or mystifications I am prepared to stand by this government! But, in any case give me a kiss, and do your best to attend the sittings of *my* chamber. You are my representative, unanimously elected. I beg you to perform your functions regularly, and to do honour to the trust I repose in you. You see how abreast of the situation I am, and how little I have to learn from the Republicans of yesterday. I could even teach a lesson to those of tomorrow, if I wanted to—but I don't. All I want is that you should kiss me to death. . . .[5]

June 6th, 1848: The more I think of what is going on in Paris at this moment, the less I want your election to be a success. The only thing to do is to let this popular madness burn itself out, for it has no idea what it wants, and is quite incapable of distinguishing true from false . . . I believe that my heart is at one with the real interests of France. . . .[6]

Victor Hugo was elected. By which party? All he knew was that he was "for the little men against the big ones," and for order against anarchy. But his position, ill-defined as it was, did not satisfy him. In the eyes of this more than moderate Assembly, the one great danger was the policy of National Workshops, financially a source of disaster, and the breeding-ground of agitators. Hugo wanted to speak. His speech was embarrassed because lacking in any clear-cut ideas.

The National Workshops are a fatal expedient . . . We have already experienced idleness bred of opulence: you have created idleness bred of poverty, which is a hundred times more dangerous both for itself and for others. The monarchy had its idlers; the republic will have its loafers. I do not altogether echo this rough and peevish talk: I do not go that far. No, the glorious People of July and February will never become so degenerate . . . No one will ever succeed in turning our self-respecting and intelligent working-class, which reads and thinks, into a lot of *lazzaroni* in time of peace, or into *janissaries* for the purposes of war. . . .[7]

The phrasing was clumsy, in that it allowed his enemies to attribute to him something he had not said. Belonging to no group in the Assembly, he had scarcely any authority. He spoke of ideas, of morale, to listeners who were thinking only in terms of self-interest and majorities. He said that the fundamental question was in the *fact,* democracy, and not in the *word,* republic. He drew a picture of the wretched lot of the unemployed workman—the hovel without windows, the children without shoes, the young girls driven on to the streets, the old men without shelter.

That is the question . . . Do you really believe that for me these sufferings are not heartrending? Do you really believe that they do not awaken in me the tenderest respect, the tenderest love, the most ardent, the most poignant sympathy? . . . If you do, then, how sadly you are deceived! . . .[8]

All he did was to advise the people to take no precipitate action. But it looked as though tub-thumping terrorism would win the day over generous eloquence. Lamartine said to Alphonse Karr: "I shall resign, because if I do not go of my own accord in three days, they will kick me out in four!" *Victor Hugo to Lacretelle, May 24th, 1848:* "Lamartine has committed faults as large as he is, and that is saying a lot. But he has stamped the red flag underfoot, and he has abolished the death-penalty; for fifteen days he has been the one radiant figure in a dark and gloomy revolution. Today we move away from radiant men to flamboyant ones, from Lamartine to Ledru-Rollin, marking time until we take a further step, and move from Ledru-Rollin to Blanqui! God help us! . . ."[9]

The National Workshops, where men were spending their time in playing shove-ha'penny, made this terrific worker seriously uneasy. Because he loved the people, he hated to see them being perverted by a system of organized loafing and odious bills on the public hoardings: "They are a noble and dignified people, and are being misled and cheated . . . When will you stop making them drunk on red republic and rough wine?[10] What a situation! I would far rather the hard work with which they were confronted on February 24th . . . There are moments when I feel choked with sobs . . ."[11] The Place Royale was filled with surging crowds, singing *La Carmagnole* and shouting "Down with Lamartine!"

On June 24th, a combination of poverty and provocative agitation led to an insurrection. "It suddenly assumed hitherto unknown and monstrous forms." It was civil war, but ice-cold and dark with gloom. On one side was the despair of the people: on the other, the despair of Society. With a heavy heart Hugo ranged himself under the banner of Society. To apply the tourniquet to an insurrection is never easy. He was far from sharing the passions of those of his colleagues who, with cynical satisfaction, grasped this opportunity of drowning in blood the whole movement of popular rebellion. Nevertheless, he held the opinion that the rebellion of the populace against the people, "the ignorant recourse to violence at the expense of the very principles of the people's existence," must be repressed. "That must be the concern of every honest man; because he loves the mob, he must fight it. But even while taking this necessary stand against the mob, he can see only too clearly the excuses for its acting as it is doing!"[12] Hugo was one of the very few representatives who walked fearlessly to the barricades, there to read the decrees. He encouraged the defenders of order. "We have got to put an end to all this, boys! This war of sniping is a murderous affair. We shall suffer far fewer losses by marching straight on danger. Forward!"[13] He advanced unarmed to the middle of the street, and intervened in person with the insurgents, exhorting them to surrender. But if he hoped for social peace, and was fighting to re-establish it, he felt no love for Thiers—"a small man, trying with his small hand, to stop the roaring mouth of revolution," nor for Cavaignac, a simple-minded but brutal general, who was "breathing fire and slaughter."

At eleven o'clock in the morning, having done his duty at the barricades, he returned to the Assembly. He had just taken his seat when Belley, a red republican, sat down beside him and said: "Monsieur Hugo, the Place Royale is ablaze; they've set fire to your house; the insurgents got in through the side door in the Guéménée cul-de-sac." "What about my family?" "Safe." "How d'you know that?" "I've just come from there. Being unknown, I managed to get through the barricades and make my way here. Your family first took refuge in the mairie. I was there, too. Seeing that the danger was increasing, I got Madame Victor Hugo to give me her word that she would look for another place of safety. She has found shelter with her children in the house of a chimney-sweep, called Martignoni, who lives in the house next to yours, under the arcades."[14] . . . Hugo hastened to Lamartine, who was completely exhausted, and deathly pale. "What is the position now?" he asked. "We're done for!" said Lamartine. But he was wrong. What politics had lost, the military could still win back. General Cavaignac, who had been voted plenary powers by the Assembly, evacuated the working-class district in the east end of the city and concentrated his troops to the west. The bourgeois National Guard fought furiously. The fanaticism of vested interests provided a counterweight to the frenzy of want. Cavaignac's victory was complete. He made it stink in the nostrils of Paris by demanding savage reprisals. Thousands of insurgents were deported without trial. From then on a blood-bath separated middle-class and workers.

Five months had sufficed to weave the winding-sheet of the February Revolution. The Assembly decreed that Cavaignac had deserved well of his country. That was giving a narrow interpretation to the word "country." Everybody thought that the general would be elected president—everybody, that is, except Lamartine, who was sufficiently simple-minded to believe that he would himself have a good chance if the election took place under universal suffrage. For Hugo this was a confused, gloomy, and heartrending time. Elected by the grace of the rue de Poitiers, it was his duty to vote for Cavaignac, whom he considered to be much to blame. "The generals who govern us—who govern us somewhat too much—are today building their reputation by forcing Liberty to withdraw. It would be a great deal better if they forced the Austrians to withdraw . . . I mistrust this state of siege. A state of siege is a sure preliminary to a coup d'état . . ."[15] Though, contrary to the first rumours, his house had been saved from the flames, his family, terrified by the rioting, did not wish to go on living in the Place Royale (renamed, since February, Place des Vosges). He had had to look for a temporary dwelling, and had found one at No. 5 rue d'Isly in the Madeleine quarter. Adèle complained that the "noise and smoke there made life impossible." Fortunée Hamelin and Léonie d'Aunet, who were both of them living on the sunny slopes of Montmartre, were loud in their praise of the gardens, the quiet hill-top, and the grass-grown streets. They found for the Hugos a magnificent old house, No. 37 rue de La Tour d'Auvergne. The move took place on October 13th. It was a Friday. When a mirror was taken down from over a fireplace, the number 13 was found scrawled in charcoal on the wall. The omens were bad.

Facts bore out the omens. Everything went wrong. The Assembly produced an elaborate, but quite ridiculous, constitution. "Here is what the future holds: France to be governed by a single-chamber Assembly, which is as much as to say, the ocean governed by a hurricane . . . Endless elections . . . We shall be living in a house before the plaster's dry. . . ."[16]

All real power was in the hands of Cavaignac, a republican in name, a brute and a sabre-rattler in fact. What could one do? What could one think? As the father of a family, and a holder of State Bonds, Hugo found himself forced into the position of championing vested interests. As a poet, and a friend of the unfortunate, he hated the over-fed "Burgraves" who surrounded him, and spoke with irony of their dangerous victory.

His ill-humour found expression in a protest against the measures taken by Cavaignac to limit the freedom of the press. Eleven newspapers were suppressed. Émile de Girardin was arrested. The general took great exception to Hugo's speech, and there was a marked coolness between the two men. But already the rue de Poitiers was growing tired of its saviour. If the workers called him "Butcher Cavaignac," the fashionable world regarded him as the enemy of private interests. "Cavaignac?—a raft?" said Montalembert. "Nothing of the sort, he's no more than a rotten plank." And Balzac: "Cavaignac's just a nit-wit, a bumped-up N.C.O., that's the long and the short of it. . . ."[17]

In the Chamber, Hugo interpellated the general: "Allow me to inform you," he said, "you a man of power, I, a man of thought . . ." The Chamber muttered and rumbled. All those present considered themselves to be representatives of thought. Assemblies are touchy. The art of enlightening without irritating them is difficult. Hugo did not possess it.

No doubt he was fully conscious of the weakness of his position, for in July 1848 he had tried to find another means of influencing public opinion by founding a periodical—*L'Évènement*. He intended that it, too, should be regarded as an "organ of thought." Its first leader drew a distinction between ideas, which are everything, and facts, which are nothing. This was to forget that those "nothings" have a way of imposing themselves on thinkers with a quite extraordinary obstinacy. Each number bore the same phrase printed on the title-page: *Untiring hatred of anarchy; a deep and tender love of the People*. Girardin, far from being jealous of this new rival, helped it with technical advice. The banker Charles Mahler, seconded by the goldsmith Froment-Meurice, found the capital. A letter from Victor Hugo wished good-luck to *L'Évènement*. He would, it said, neither write for it, nor even inspire its attitude. No one believed this. The members of the staff, all of them drawn from the family circle, were his two sons Charles and François-Victor—the first a "fat and distressingly flabby young man,"[18] the second a dandy who drifted through life—and his two disciples Paul Meurice and Auguste Vacquerie. The latter had just had a play in verse produced at the Odéon, *Tragaldabas,* an "execrable production in the gay-Hugo manner," said Balzac. The first performance was greeted with boos. "I have never," wrote Balzac to Madame Hanska, "seen anything funnier than Frédérick Lemaître coming before the curtain at the end of an ultra-stormy evening and saying: 'Ladies and Gentlemen [with chivalrous grace], the play which we have had the honour of acting before you is from the pen of Citizen August Vacquerie'—unless it was Hugo expressing disapproval of the author's friends, who black-guarded the booers, and called them a lot of jackasses . . ."[19] Balzac reminded him of the *Hernani* battle.

L'Évènement published some memories of Madame Victor Hugo and two stories by her daughter, Adèle. Sainte-Beuve, at the bottom of an article by "his Adèle" on Nodier—a very pleasing effort which he kept—scribbled in his tiny handwriting: "The marked passages are not by her." These passages, it must be admitted, are rich in Hugoesque images. The Fashion and Society Notes were entrusted to Léonie d'Aunet who wrote, over the name of Thérèse de Blaru, a regular fea-ture article, *Lettres mondaines,* which dealt with such matters as interior decoration, the arranging of flowers, and children's clothes. Here, too, at times, in an occasional phrase, the old lion's paw is clearly visible. It would have been scarcely surprising to find Juliette Drouet doing the dramatic criticism, but Auguste Vacquerie kept that for himself, and carried out his task with no little brilliance. Balzac was asked to contribute. *Balzac to Madame Hanska, July 11th, 1848:* "I was interrupted by Hugo's two young hopefuls who are going to have a paper of their own. We are to be treated to Hugo politics, a Hugo party, etc. I'm giving them four sheets of the *Comédie Humaine* for 400 instead of 2800 francs. The whole of the February revolution is in 'em . . ."[20] A summary judgment.

In spite of his denials, the readers of *l'Évènement* attributed the editorials to Victor Hugo. Not that the style proved anything. The

Hugo manner was contagious, and Vacquerie, no less than Charles Hugo, spent much time producing involuntary parodies of the master. But there can be no doubt that the paper's "general line" was pure Hugo: for the immediate future, hostility to Cavaignac; and, in general, an attempt to reconcile order and justice, private interests and compassion, money-bags and heart.

31

Illusions and Rupture

> To be one of this majority? To prefer party dis-
> cipline to the dictates of conscience? No!
>
> VICTOR HUGO

AS A RESULT of the complementary elections held in June 1848
Prince Louis-Napoleon Bonaparte had entered the Assembly
along with Victor Hugo. This son of Hortense de Beauharnais and
(perhaps) a Dutch Admiral had not a single drop of Bonaparte blood
in his veins, but he bore the magic name, and the crowds on the Boulevards sang *"Po-lé-on, nous-l'aurons!"* A small group of the faithful tried
to put forward this strange candidate for the Presidency. At first the
Assembly laughed. On the rare occasions when he addressed the House,
his half-asleep air, his German accent, his stammering speech, were
reassuring. "An idiot!" yelped little Thiers's shrill voice. But Thiers
also held that an idiot would be easy to control, and the rue de Poitiers,
from hatred of Cavaignac, the out-and-out republican, began to look
with favour on the bogus Bonaparte with his heavy-lidded eyes.

Madame Hamelin, a parlour-Bonapartist, extolled her prince to the
skies. "Everyone is rallying to him," she said. Backed by Léonie
d'Aunet, she did her best to lure Victor Hugo into her camp, and urged
Louis-Napoleon to call upon the poet.

The prince put in an appearance in the rue de La Tour d'Auvergne.
His manner was respectful, his conversation wily.[1] "I have come in
order to put matters between us on a plain footing. Tell me honestly,
do I seem to you to be a hare-brained adventurer? There is a lot of very
unfair nonsense going about in connection with me. People say I want
to be a second Napoleon. Now, as I see it, there are two men who can
serve as models to the ambitious: Napoleon and Washington. One was
a man of genius, the other of virtue . . . If Napoleon was the greater,
Washington had the finer character. As between the guilty hero and the
good citizen, I, personally, prefer the good citizen. That sums up my
ambition."[2]

Hugo found him melancholy and ugly, with the look of a sleepwalker, but distinguished, serious, gentle, a good companion and cau-

tious. Queen Hortense had taught her son never to unmask his batteries until the moment was ripe. He said, very solemnly: "I am a man of liberty, a man of democracy," words which produced upon the poet the intended magical effect. Victor Hugo, a man who always thought in terms of black and white, felt lost in this nebulous grey, and entirely failed to understand the astuteness of an adventurer who was "filled with dreams and appetites." He knew that there had been a time when the prince had flirted with the Carbonarist movement, and had been the author of a brochure on "The Extinction of Poverty." That pleased him. He had a vision of a fourth act to *Hernani,* of a romantic part for himself to play, that of a thinker guiding the steps of a liberal emperor—one of his oldest dreams. Besides, the other Napoleon had always inspired his finest poetry. Behind the great nose and the glazed eyes he saw the Arc de Triomphe, the Dome of the Invalides, and verses yet to be written.

Some days later *L'Évènement* harnessed itself to the prince's chariot, following in this the example of *La Presse.* Until the October meeting the Hugo family journal had been cold. It had acknowledged the prestige of a great name, but had pointed out that the prestige belonged to the uncle, not the nephew. On October 28th its attitude suddenly changed. A long article entrusted to the prince's hands the destinies of France and the glory of the Emperor. In the Chamber the poet from that moment made it his task to remove the obstacles which might have barred the prince's path to the Presidency. He voted for the motion that the presidential elections should be carried out under universal suffrage, an error in which he was supported by Lamartine, who thought that such a policy would play into his own hands. He voted against the presidential oath, and later against the constitution, because he was opposed, in principle, to single-chamber government.

The monarchist Right favoured Louis-Napoleon, feeling quite certain that he could be quickly got rid of. It had been decided that he should not be eligible for a second term. His Presidency, therefore, would be no more than a brief interlude. "We'll see that he gets plenty of women," said Thiers contemptuously, "and in that way we will keep him under our thumb." As to France in general, it was prepared to acquiesce in the adventure. Peasants and bourgeois, frightened by the June outbreaks, saw in this sham Bonaparte a saviour. The workers, ever since the affair of the National Workshops, had been holding sulkily aloof from the Liberals: besides, they were still animated by a deep-seated spirit of Bonapartist chauvinism. *L'Évènement* ran a surprisingly fervid campaign in support of the prince. "We said of Monsieur Cavaignac: *he is to be feared;* of Monsieur de Lamartine: *he is to be admired;* of Louis-Napoleon we say: *"he is awaited . . ."*[3] On the eve of the poll the journal published a single-page supplement which contained nothing but the name Louis-Napoleon Bonaparte, a hundred times repeated. This went further than mere party devotion. When the votes were counted, the prince was found to have secured 5,500,000, Cavaignac 1,500,000, Ledru-Rollin 370,000, and Lamartine 17,940. This final figure produced loud laughter from the Right.

L'Évènement was triumphant: "Napoleon is not dead!" The day of great achievements had dawned. Hugo, in a manifesto drawn up in a spirit of romantic Imperialism, outlined a vast plan of work waiting to be done. It was his political preface to *Cromwell*. In foreign affairs: disarmament; a society of nations, a supreme body which should cut the knot of all international difficulties; the piercing of the isthmuses of Suez and Panama; the civilization of China; the colonization of Algeria. In home affairs: war against poverty; the victory of industry and progress; the glory of art, letters and the sciences. It was a fine dream, even a fine programme. But Hugo was capable only of putting it into words, not of making it actual. The innumerable legions of his enemies declared that he was on the look-out for a ministry. He provided some ground for these attacks by calling on the president to "choose new and illustrious names." But he considered himself to be far above any mere minister. "We will follow nobody to power. That is too high a goal—and too low." What he wanted was to play a leading role—that of spiritual, and secret, adviser to the prince. It never occurred to him that he would have to deal with a man who had only one aim in view—to stay where Fortune had placed him, and, for this purpose, to use all available means.

On December 23rd, the prince-president gave his first official dinner-party at the Élysée. Hugo was invited, and arrived late. The president rose and advanced to meet him. "This," he said, "is a very improvised affair: just a few dear friends. I hoped that you would be of the number, and I thank you for coming." The piercing eye of the great journalist in Hugo took in the common white china of the dinner-service, the heavy, much-used bourgeois silver. The regime was starting in a slightly squalid fashion. After dinner the president took Hugo aside and asked him what he thought of the general situation. Hugo was reticent. He said that the bourgeois must be reassured, and the people provided with work; that France, with three centuries of glory behind her, did not want to decline from her high estate; in short, that what was needed was to make peace into something splendid and renowned. "France is a nation of conquerors. When she is not winning victories with the sword, she must win them in the realm of intelligence. Realize that, and all will be well: ignore it, and you will be lost . . ."[4] He talked big. The president appeared to be lost in thought, and moved away. No doubt he was thinking: "A visionary! Beware of him!" Hugo left the palace with his mind full of this "hasty moving in, this improvised ceremonial, this mixture of the bourgeois, the republican and the imperial. . . ."[5]

At the end of that week (December 30th, 1848) he went to see Lamartine, who received on Saturdays. He found him white, bent, anxious and sad. The last ten months had added ten years to his age, but he was generous and resigned. Girardin criticized the president, who had just constructed a weak ministry with the pompous Odilon Barrot, now resplendent in a frock-coat, at its head. "What we needed," said Girardin, "was a great ministry: Thiers, Molé, Bugeaud, Berryer, Hugo, Lamartine . . ."[6] Lamartine said that he would have accepted. Hugo said nothing.

Next day, January 1st, 1849, he meditated upon the changes brought by the surprising year just past. Louis-Philippe was in London, the Duchesse d'Orléans at Ems, Pope Pius IX at Gaëta. The Church had lost Rome. The bourgeoisie had lost Paris. Alice Ozy had appeared, stark naked, in the part of Eve at the Porte-Saint-Martin. In July 1848 Chateaubriand had died. Hugo was present at the funeral, and felt distressed at the mediocrity of the ceremony. "I would have had for Monsieur de Chateaubriand either a royal burial: Notre-Dame, his peer's robes, his uniform of the Institut, his sword of the *gentilhomme émigré*, his Collar of the Golden Fleece, representatives of all the State authorities, half of the garrison on foot, with muted drums, and the minute-guns firing; or else a poor man's funeral in a country churchyard . . ."[7] He obliterated the burial of Chateaubriand, as Chateaubriand had obliterated the coronation of Charles X.

The five-per-cents stood at 74; potatoes were fetching eight sous a bushel; Louis Bonaparte was giving grand dinners to Monsieur Thiers, who had had him arrested, and to the Comte Molé, who had had him sentenced. Prince Jérôme Bonaparte, ex-king of Westphalia, was governor of the Invalides. He, at least, bore some resemblance to the Emperor. He called his nephew, the president, "Monsieur Beauharnais." Entering the Assembly, Hugo heard with surprise the sentry on duty say "I salute the enemy of sentry-duty." It was the National Guardsman Jules Sandeau. "And I, the friend of men on sentry-go," he replied. At the Academy where voting was taking place for the award of the Poetry Prize Lamartine said to Hugo: "Hugo, if I were a candidate, they certainly would not give the prize to me." "And they certainly would not read me through, Lamartine." Both were right.

On February 17th, 1849, Adèle and Victor Hugo were invited to a ball given by the new president. Adèle wrote an account of it to Jules Janin, who, once an adversary, had become a friend of the family: "I found there almost all the Society of Louis-Philippe reconstituted, and enlarged by the addition of two or three men of the Mountain, and a few legitimists such as the Duc de Guiche, the Duc de Gramont and Berryer,[8] who opposed the late king. But I looked in vain for a single artist, thinker or writer. It shocked me that a representative of power, always so fragile, should have forgotten the only really imperishable source of strength. It is because I am sympathetic towards the illustrious name of Napoleon that I was deeply wounded by this exclusion—I am not here speaking of my husband, who had been asked for quite other reasons . . ."[9] In *L'Évènement* Thérèse de Blaru (Léonie d'Aunet) described the ball in Gautier-Musset style, full of eulogies. Nevertheless, the popularity of Louis-Napoleon was on the wane. His mistresses cost a deal of money, and since the Assembly was niggardly in voting credits he had taken to speculating on the Stock Exchange with Achille Fould. The star of Henri V was beginning to show above the horizon. Marshal Bugeaud was preparing a small book for the press on *Street Fighting*: "Just a few items of practical advice," he said, "of the same general sort as directions about dealing with the cholera." Everywhere people were beginning to ask, some anxiously, some hopefully, "What is in the wind?"

The prudent Sainte-Beuve had gone off to spend these difficult days at Liége. Adèle, who still saw him in secret from time to time, badgered him a good deal. She reproached him for neglecting a friend and for showing too much reserve in his attitude towards her. He hastened to justify his behaviour: "My health is delicate; I am physically in a very nervous condition, and my organs are frequently out of order. You say to me: '*Do not be discouraged, and do not break in pieces what is given to you.*' What exactly do you mean? Because I might have written a letter which would have pleased you less, you are afraid that even our friendship is in danger of being broken—is that it?" He needed, he said, a secure friendship rather than a more ardent, perhaps, but spasmodic, exigent and imperious relationship, as only a different kind of relationship tends to be. "The reason why I so often speak of my increasing age is that I want to make it clear that I have renounced for good and all that particular type of relationship."[10] A strange letter which shows that poor Adèle was losing on every number she backed.

There were fresh elections in May, and Hugo was returned, second in the Paris constituency, with 117,069 votes. This time the reactionaries won in a canter. The "Burgraves" of the rue de Poitiers had with them four hundred and fifty deputies, mostly monarchists, but powerless because their sympathies were divided between the senior and junior branches of the royal family. Hugo had figured on the electoral list of the Right majority. His position was becoming more and more false. The rue de Poitiers issued its instructions, but Hugo maintained that he was answerable only to his own conscience. That conscience had permitted him to adhere to a party for the duration of an election. He still retained, as a matter of fact, a prejudice in favour of democratic monarchy. He was, as he had always been, "a friend of order." But if there was in him something of the National Guardsman, it was a "National Guardsman of the epic type."[11] The idealistic tirades of the heroes in his plays had expressed sentiments which were genuinely his own. Cynicism revolted him. He felt suddenly sickened by the pot-bellied talk which went on all around him, not so much in speeches from the tribune, as in committee, and in the lobbies. As soon as he fully grasped the intentions of Falloux and Montalembert in connection with the problem of working-class conditions, he broke away from them with a feeling "almost of panic."[12]

A decent-minded man, whom his political friends regarded as a lunatic, the Vicomte Armand de Melun had proposed in June 1848 the setting up of a large parliamentary commission to inquire into the moral and material conditions of the people. Consideration of this proposal had been several times adjourned, and the majority thought that it had been buried once and for all, when Melun, to the horror of the "Burgraves," himself laid the motion before the House. The old hands immediately began to manœuvre for position. To have opposed the motion fairly and squarely would have been impolitic. A more sensible way of going about the business seemed to be to whittle away most of its contents. Victor Hugo, before whom "these gentlemen" spoke freely, regarding him as a rather simple-minded but docile confederate, heard them say that "in times of anarchy force is the sovereign remedy," that Melun's proposal was nothing less than disguised Socialism, that it had got to be given a decent burial—and other views of the same charming nature.

He was still, in spite of his investiture by the rue de Poitiers, the man of *Les Misérables*. Prepared to believe only the evidence of his own eyes; he had made a point of going to the Faubourg Saint-Antoine, and also to the slums of Lille, to see what genuine misery meant. Not only did he describe what conditions really were like in those places, but denounced the cruel things he had heard said. There was a general outcry. What! a member of the party of order had actually dared to assert: "I am one of those who believe that poverty can be done away with!" As though that were not enough, he had revealed things that had been said privately! "In this House public statements are for the ears of the people; things said in secret are said with votes in view. All right, then, I want no secret talk when the future of the people is at issue, and the laws of my country. I shall make no bones about revealing those secret confabulations, and unmasking concealed influences. That is my plain duty."[13] There was an angry note in the murmurs with which this statement was received. Everyone knew, of course, that a writer is always a bit dangerous, but this fellow had been allowed into the holy of holies, and now here he was, betraying family secrets!

"We must take advantage of the silence imposed upon anarchic passions to let the claims of the people be heard" (*sensation*). "We must take advantage of the disappearance of the revolutionary spirit to bring once more the spirit of progress into the open. We must take advantage of a period of calm to establish peace, not only peace in the streets, but true peace, definitive peace, peace in men's minds and in men's hearts. In a word, what is necessary is that the defeat of demagogy shall mean the people's victory!"[14]

During the parliamentary recess in August 1849 a Peace Congress assembled in Paris. The principal nations of Europe were represented. Victor Hugo was elected president. For some time he maintained the illusion that he was at one with the Élysée in the struggle he was conducting on two fronts, against the *sans-cœur* and the *sansculottes*. *L'Évènement* expressed the hope that a blue party might be established between the whites and the reds, under the leadership of the president. But in the Chamber Hugo enjoyed less authority than ever. The Conservatives greeted him with sarcasm and boos. The Left gave him no support. He was isolated. His speeches, for all their eloquence, produced very little effect. In an Assembly it is not what a man says that matters, but *why* he says it. Victor Hugo knew nothing of parliamentary strategy. Furthermore, since he never spoke on the spur of the moment, but carefully learned his speeches by heart, he could not adapt himself to sudden changes in the mental atmosphere of the Chamber. He even made allowances, in advance, for expected interruptions, and, when they did not come, struck back at a void, and so lost his poise. Louis-Napoleon was not the type of man to remain faithful to a partner whose presence was becoming a source of weakness. A rupture between the two men was bound to occur. When it came, it was extremely violent.

The president, in the hope of pleasing the Catholic majority, had sent an expedition to help the Pope against Mazzini's Roman Republic. General Oudinot had taken Rome and restored the temporal power of the Holy See. Louis-Napoleon, feeling that the extreme clericalism of the "Burgraves" was not popular, had written to the general's aide-de-camp, Edgar Ney, a letter which was made public. In it he had expressed a wish that the liberties of the Roman people should be secured, and a general amnesty granted. "The French flag," *L'Évènement* assured its readers, "will protect the liberties of Italy." Pius IX, with complete disregard for his protector, replied with a Bull—*Motu proprio* —in which he reaffirmed his absolutism. Thiers advised acquiescence, and was applauded by the Montalembert majority. Hugo, who had voted against Thiers's motion, dined on October 16th (or 17th) at the

Élysée.[15] It was agreed that the prince should substitute for his letter to Edgar Ney (which was unconstitutional, and too imperial in tone) a message to the President of the Council, Odilon Barrot. The latter would read it to the Assembly, and Hugo would give it his support. The prince preferred men of action to men of high principles, politicians to thinkers, but on this occasion he had no choice. None of the orators of the clerical majority would have accepted this dangerous mission. Unfortunately (or, perhaps, fortunately) for Hugo, in the interval which elapsed between the dinner and the session of the Chamber, the president came to a compromise agreement with Barrot and Tocqueville. Barrot would not read the message. He would assert, against all truth and all plausibility, that the president's letter and the Bull *Motu proprio* meant, fundamentally, the same thing. In point of fact they expressed diametrically opposed views. But bad faith knows no limits, and can say anything.

Was Hugo not informed of this change of front, or was he, and did he refuse to accept the new decision? Odilon Barrot, who disliked him, was quite capable of leading him into a trap. "I am not a man of politics," said Hugo: "I am merely a free man." Whatever the truth of the affair, he delivered an extremely impolitic speech. He defended the letter to Edgar Ney, though he added that he could have wished that it had been more carefully thought out (a remark which gave offence to the president). He said that the letter and the Bull were mutually contradictory, that the Pope had been asked to grant an amnesty, instead of which he had decreed "mass proscriptions" (a statement which gravely embarrassed Odilon Barrot), and he advised the Vatican to show some understanding of its people and of the times it was living in (a comment which brought the majority angrily to its feet). "Am I to take it then that you, who sit here under the shadow of the tricolour, are prepared to see the gallows go up in Rome? . . . What is *not* possible is that France should commit her honour, pour out her money—the money of her suffering people—and shed the glorious blood of her soldiers, all for nothing . . . no, I am wrong, I ought rather to say for a policy of shame. . . ."[16]

It was a fine speech, but no speech has ever yet convinced an Assembly once its mind has been made up. The Left applauded; Hugo was bringing grist to its mill. Montalembert declared that this applause was Monsieur Victor Hugo's punishment. Hugo replied: "That punishment I accept. I regard it as bringing me honour." (*Prolonged applause on the Left.*) "There was a time—and I hope that Monsieur Montalembert will believe me when I say that I remind him of this with feelings of profound regret on his behalf—there was a time when he found better employment for his great abilities. He once championed Poland as I am now championing Italy. In those days I was with him; today he is against me. The reason is perfectly simple; he has passed over into the camp of the oppressors, while I remain in the camp of the oppressed. . . ."[17]

In this way did the break with the "Burgraves" come about. The break with the Élysée followed not long afterwards. Louis-Napoleon had too strong a liking for duplicity to approve a policy of blunders. Up to the last moment he had wanted to exercise "a moderating influence." Victor Hugo, by his violence, had disarranged his plans. Of the two men, one had ambitions, the other convictions. There are those who say that hard words passed between the poet and the president. *L'Évènement* declared that "the intrigues with which the men of the Right have, for the last two days, been surrounding the Élysée have completely succeeded . . ." There is another view, according to which Hugo asked to be made a minister, and failing to get what he wanted passed over to the Opposition. "To that I can reply in a very few words. Never, in the whole course of my relations with Monsieur Louis Bonaparte, was there ever any question between us, or between me and anybody speaking in his name, of any such proposal whether for the present moment or for the distant future. I challenge anybody to provide even the shadow of a proof to the contrary."[18] Nobody has ever produced such proof, nor the shadow of one.

In its issue of October 25th, 1849, *L'Évènement* published the following paragraph: "Since Monday evening, when he dined with the president—that is, three days before the debate—Monsieur Victor Hugo has not set foot in the Élysée, nor has he been in communication with the President of the Republic . . ."[19] From this moment the paper took up a strong anti-presidential position. "Does Monsieur Louis-Napoleon not realize that his advisers are bad advisers who have undertaken to stifle all his noble impulses?"[20] It is difficult to find anything blameworthy in this *volte-face*. To have remained loyal to a prince whom he had once supported, after that prince had shown himself to be quite different from what had once been hoped, would have meant that Hugo had been disloyal to himself.

32

Political Battles and Struggles of Sentiment (1850-1851)

> Hugo was one of those rare men who always find
> their way back to liberty as to the source of
> all good.
>
> **ALAIN**

THE two years 1850 and 1851 were for Victor Hugo a period of
political battles and emotional upheaval. Politically, after his breach
with the Élysée, he had lost his bearings. Acclaimed by the Left, which
he supported in a series of brilliant speeches, but which never accepted
him as one of its children; blackguarded by the Right, which pretended
to despise him as a turncoat, and made him the object of insults, calumnies and the most scurvy treatment of every kind, he learned to his cost,
as Lamartine had done before him, that popularity is, of all things in
the world, the most fragile of commodities. *January 1850:* "Five years
ago, I was on the point of becoming the favourite of the king. Today, I
am on the point of becoming the favourite of the people. I shall never
be the one any more than I was the other, for a moment will come when
my feelings of independence will rise to the surface, with the result that
my loyalty to my conscience will exasperate the man in the street no less
than it once shocked the Other in the Tuileries."[1]

Louis-Napoleon was carrying out his plans coldly and methodically.
Objective: to remain in power. *Tactics*: to gain control of the army and
the police, in other words, to substitute for the "Burgraves" a body of
"Mamelukes" entirely devoted to his person. While this operation was
developing he must, in order to keep the majority quiet, make a pretence of supporting that same majority's political aims. "It is necessary,"
said Montalembert, "to make an expedition from Rome into the interior." Put in slightly different terms, the republicans must be driven
from the schools as they had been driven from Rome. Louis-Napoleon
threw this to the "Burgraves" as a bone to gnaw. The Falloux Act, in
fact, established not freedom to teach, but a monopoly of teaching to
the advantage of the clerical party. An alliance of the Congregation

279

and of the middle-of-the-road policy. Victor Hugo voiced his indignation in an excellent speech. His formula was simple: free education at every stage; obligatory education at the lowest; "the heart of the people brought into contact with the brain of France"; separation of Church and State, to the benefit of both.

Not that he wished to forbid religious education. Far from it: "do away with poverty in this world, and turn all eyes to Heaven." But religion was not clericalism. "I am no more confusing you, the clerical party, with the Church, than I am confusing the mistletoe with the oak. You are the parasites of the Church, you are the Church's sickness. You are not the believers, but the sectaries of a religion which you do not understand. You are the stage-managers of sanctity. Do not involve the Church in your business, your intrigues, your strategy, your doctrines and your ambitions. Do not call it your mother, in order to make of it your servant. Do not trouble it under the pretext of teaching it politics. Above all, do not identify it with yourselves. Realize the wrong that you are doing to it. . . ."[2]

In April 1850 the "Mamelukes" of the Élysée put forward a project of law dealing with deportation for political crimes. Imprisonment in exile! This was tantamount to planning a policy of future proscriptions. The Revolution of February had abolished the death penalty for purely political offences. It was now to be replaced by a system of slow death. "Consider the type of man likely to be condemned by the special tribunal . . . a man, such is the wretchedness of the times, who to some will be a criminal, to others a hero. . . ." (*Loud protests from the Right.*)

"When sentence has been pronounced," exclaimed Dupin the elder, president of the Legislative Assembly, "the criminal is a criminal in the eyes of all, and can be a hero only to his accomplices!" (*Hear, hear! from the Right.*)

"I would point out to President Dupin," replied Hugo, "that Marshal Ney, sentenced in 1815, was a declared criminal in the eyes of the law. For me he is a hero, and I am no accomplice of his . . ."[3] (*Prolonged applause from the Left.*)

The reply struck home. President Dupin was reduced to silence. On that day Hugo was, indeed, the voice of the conscience of humanity.

I know, gentlemen, that each time we extract from that word *conscience* all that we think should be extracted from it, we have the misfortune to bring a smile to the lips of certain eminent politicians. At first these eminent persons regard us as not wholly incurable. They take pity upon us: they are willing to apply methods of treatment for the ailment with which we are afflicted—namely, conscience—and in the kindliest way possible counter our statements with *Reasons of State.* If, in spite of this, we persist in our errors— Ah! then they grow angry. They declare that we know nothing of business, that we are completely lacking in political sense, that we are not men to be taken seriously . . . and they enlist in their armoury of attack a very harsh word, a word that conveys the worst insult they can think of: they call us *poets*. . . .[4]

The Republic of 1848 had established universal suffrage. The "Burgraves" regretted the passing of the limited suffrage. The prince-president offered them, as a sop, an electoral law which at a single stroke, by juggling with qualifications of *domicile* and *property*, removed four million electors from the register—workers and intellectuals —and with consummate skill laid the responsibility for its administration on a committee of seventeen "Burgraves." Hugo at once took the bull by the horns and was vehement in his defence of universal suffrage. It was, he said, the only means of regulating popular passions, the only way in which legitimate power could be established, the sole rampart against anarchy, a fixed point in the eddies and turmoils of the storm. He made fun of the prince-president, calling him a Numa with seventeen Egerias. "So be it," he said to the members of the Right, "you will remove four million votes, but what you will not change is the march of time, the temper of the present hour, the movement of the turning globe . . . Carry out your sacrifice: whether you like it or not, the past is the past. Try to patch up its old axle and its old wheels, harness to it seventeen statesmen, if you will. A phalanx of seventeen men of politics! Drag the contraption into the light of day, and what do you gain? It will still be the past. Its decayed condition will be only the more visible. . . ."[5]

Against him the majority employed two methods of defence: mocking laughter, and a reminder of his former opinions. Montalembert said of him that he had patted all causes on the back, and then, in turn, repudiated each. He pressed home his points, and defended himself well. But his attitude was not without danger. In the Assembly sinister rumours were circulating. The majority wanted an outburst of mob violence, if necessary fomented by the police, so that his voice might be drowned in a blood-bath. A stray pistol-shot might easily come the way of a troublesome opponent. "Look out for yourself!" said Colonel Charras (Liberal) to Victor Hugo. "Bah!" he replied: "let them hunt me out in my little hole, if they dare: they'll find nothing but poems, and odds and ends of verse everywhere. I should regard it as a great joke!" He was advised, *out of pure friendship,* not to make any more speeches about the electoral law. "That decides me: I most certainly shall. What happens then is God's will. The spectacle of a big sword brandished by the little men of '93 in this year of grace 1850, or of Thiers being brought to bed of an enormity, would amuse me immensely."[6]

His public attitude would have been stronger had his private life been less chaotic and less open to criticism. Duty, gratitude, love and desire had made him the slave of ancient liaisons and greedy fancies of the moment. Three women—one might almost call them three wives —Adèle, Juliette and Léonie, were all living close to him on the slopes of Montmartre, within the limits of a narrow circle. He had to give to each some part of his time, and was for ever hurrying from one to the other, exposed to the danger of meeting, at any moment, with Juliette on his arm, Adèle or Léonie, who had to some extent entered into an alliance against the best of the three.

Juliette, who always unobtrusively followed in the wake of her lord's removals, was now concealing her "humble person and great love" in the cité Rodier, a gloomy cul-de-sac, where she endured "an existence of unbroken absence and boredom."[7] Her only happiness was, now and again, to accompany her lover to the Assembly or the Academy, to listen to his speeches, to wait for his rare visits, and each morning to go and gaze from a distance at the two windows of her beloved who (in 1845) had at last given her permission to walk alone, provided she *only* walked. She was still ignorant of the part played by Léonie d'Aunet in Victor Hugo's life, and was constantly suspicious of other women; with good reason, since he was less than ever capable of resisting such proffered charms as came his way: an actress, Joséphine Faville; a woman of the world, Madame Roger de Genettes; Hélène Gaussin, who had been sentenced for theft; a poetess, Louise Colet; an ardent unknown, Nathalie Renoux; an adventuress, Laure Desprès; a "so-ciétaire" of the Comédie-Française, Sylvanie Plessy; a self-styled Vi-comtesse du Vallon, of whom Viel-Castel said that she "circulated her three extremely pretty daughters like so many items of commerce";[8] a courtesan, Esther Guimont; and, perhaps, Rachel. Hugo, who in the days of his youth had attached such importance to chastity, now, in the matter of love, paraded theories *à la* Shelley.

> Est-on maître d'aimer? Pourquoi deux êtres s'aiment
> Demande à l'eau qui court, demande à l'air qui fuit,
> Au moucheron qui vole à la flamme de nuit,
> Au rayon d'or qui vient baiser la grappe mûre!
> Demande à ce qui chante, appelle, attend, murmure!
> Demande aux nids profonds qu'avril met en émoi!
> Le cœur éperdu crie: "Est-ce que je sais, moi?"[9]

The heart in bewilderment cried aloud when Fortunée Hamelin died on April 29th, 1851, from an attack of apoplexy. The event brought sadness to Victor Hugo who lost in her a faithful friend. For Léonie d'Aunet who, after a decision of the courts, had separated from her husband, it was a catastrophe. In that highly intelligent woman she had found a confidante with whom she had spent nearly every evening, either alone or at the Opera. Deprived of the counsels of the one-time *Merveilleuse* to whom age had brought something of wisdom, and now left alone to meditate dangerously upon her lot, the ex-Madame Biard began to think that she had wasted her life for the sake of Victor Hugo, and that it was her right to demand of him a more considerable part of his own, that at least he ought to sacrifice Juliette in her interest. More than once she had tried to obtain that sacrifice of him, only to be met with a curt refusal.

On the first occasion, in 1849, she had threatened Hugo. She would, she said, reveal all to Juliette. But he had struck back.

You told me yesterday, and they were harsh words, that I should be guilty of a bad action, and one which would forfeit your esteem, if I did what four years of patience and torment have given me every right to do. That is what you said, and though it was unjust of you, and served to give me proof of the love you feel for another, I drew back before that threat with more terror in my heart than if it had been a threat of death. Well, then, I will not do what I had it in my mind to do. I will have the superhuman courage to respect the happiness and the illusions of one whom I most hate in all the world, of one I would kill with pleasure, even if I had to answer to God for the deed! Of one to whom the whole happiness of my life has been offered as a gift. . . .[10]

She plagued Hugo with breathless questions:

If she has none of the rights of a mistress, what is there left for me to tell her? If, on the contrary, she has those rights, then I cannot act differently than I am doing. Since you will not enlighten her, the reason is that you have accorded to her rights that are properly mine. I will abandon all claim to them, even though it kill me to do so, rather than share them with an-other . . . I would still be willing that you should consider her as a *friend*, and yet you dare to tell me that I should be guilty of a *wicked* action in so speaking to her as to regularize the relations of all three of us! But I have agreed to say nothing, so let us not discuss the question further. For more than four years I have been playing a shameful part, for she has the right to think of herself as the only woman who enjoys your love . . . Have it your own way, and may God be your judge. . . . For me that means that I shall live on in despair, but at least be spared the reproaches that *conscience and honour daily make to me* . . . I have enclosed with this all that belongs to you. You may let her have it.[11]

Two years later the wind of her mood had changed and, instead of abdicating, Léonie d'Aunet struck. On June 29th, 1851, there arrived at the cité Rodier, No. 20, a packet of letters tied with ribbon and sealed with the arms of Victor Hugo, that blazon for which he had himself devised the motto: *Ego Hugo*. The writing was that of the man whom Juliette adored and revered. She opened it with feelings of anxiety, greedily read the contents, and learned with horror that, ever since 1844, her lover had loved another woman, and had been writing to her letters every bit as passionate as those which, for eighteen years, had been her only happiness, her only claim to honour: *"You are an angel, and I kiss your feet . . . You are the light of my eyes . . . , you are the very life of my heart . . ."* Even the images he employed were those he had contrived for Juliette. A note from Léonie accompanied the packet, and in this she made it clear that the liaison was still in being, that it had "assumed in the world at large, and even in Victor Hugo's family circle, a sort of respectability, and suggested that it might, perhaps, be as well if Juliette took the initiative in breaking a bond which the poet no longer desired, and felt as a burden rather than as a pleasure."[12] It is difficult to imagine anything more terrible for a woman who had sacrificed her whole life on the altar of a one and only love than this proof of a day-by-day treachery which had remained concealed from her for seven years! Juliette went out in tears and, in a state bordering on madness, spent the whole day in wandering about Paris. She returned in the evening, healthily exhausted, hoping that Victor would come to her, and with her mind made up to take refuge with her sister at Brest, after the necessary explanations had been given.

Hugo denied nothing, begged Juliette to forgive him, and offered to sacrifice her rival. But this he did while all the time praising the merits of the latter, her beauty, her culture, and making it clear with what sympathy and affection his wife and sons regarded Madame d'Aunet. This merely aggravated Juliette's bitterness. She was too proud to accept a love which was no more than a sacrifice.

Juliette Drouet to Victor Hugo, June 28th, 1851: In the name of all that you hold sacred, in the name of my great grief, beloved, do not show any false generosity to me; do not tear your own heart in pieces merely to spare mine. Such a sacrifice, no matter how complete you might make it, would not long deceive me, and I feel that I could never forgive myself for having been taken in by it at the cost of your happiness . . . And now, dear God, if You think that my crime of having been born into this world without my own consent has been sufficiently expiated, have pity upon me! Have pity upon me, dear God, spare me this last drop of bitterness which I must drink in seeing suffer through my fault the man whom I love better than life, better than happiness, better than the blessed joys of Your paradise. O God! let him be happy with another rather than unhappy with me. I ask that of You with hands clasped in prayer: leave him his full freedom of choice; give him true generosity of heart, a clear sense of his duty; grant him real happiness, and I will bless You, and resign myself uncomplaining to my lot. . . .[13]

Generosity piled on generosity. When Juliette, after long and painful thought, spoke to Hugo of breaking with him, he, as any man in
such a case would do, appealed to her sense of pity. He complained
of sleeplessness, of a sore throat, and also of the anxiety he was feeling
about his sons who were being persecuted by the Government. The
ghost of Léonie, of the *femme fatale* with the face of a child, hovered
above this violent scene of abnegation. *Juliette to Victor Hugo, June
30th, 1851:* "I am grateful to this woman for not having spared me a
single one of the proofs of your treachery. Ruthlessly she has thrust
into my heart, up to the hilt, the *adoration* which you have been giving
her for seven years. It was cynical and savage on her part, but, at least,
it was honest. She is worthy to have been my executioner. All her blows
struck home . . ."[14] Two women in love with the same man may hate
one another, but there may well exist between them a mutual esteem
born of the very fanaticism of their love.

Then, because the poet and his mistress were still romantic at heart;
because he had proclaimed the rights of passion; because he excelled
in transmuting his carnal pleasures into mystical effusions; and because
he could still be, when he wanted, "gay, easy-going, pleasing and ravishing," Juliette, once more under his spell, agreed that there should be
a "testing time" for the three of them, after which he must make his
choice. The period of truce was fixed at four months (dating from the
fatal June 28th), which meant for the hero of this drama an agreeable
respite, during which he would be free to see both women. Léonie made
the most of her rights. Juliette wanted "love to be the only arbiter."

Juliette Drouet to Victor Hugo, September 9th, 1851: Happier now than
the woman who wrote to you yesterday, my dearest, I claim no *rights* in you,
and the nineteen years which you have taken *from the very quick of my life*
weigh as nothing in the scales of your peace of mind, of the consideration
you feel for me, of your happiness. . . .[15]

September 22nd, 1851: So far I have completely failed to understand what
that [the mystery] is which has made you give up a woman whom you find
beautiful, young, intelligent, superior, of whose *love, loyalty* and *devotion*
you are absolutely certain, for the sake of a poor woman so ironically lacking in more than half of those advantages . . . For so little, you, a man
with an essentially just mind, a great heart and supreme intelligence, are
prepared to sacrifice a young creature *who is well nigh dying of love for you,*
has had, for seven years, a claim upon you, and can call upon present and
future to fight her battle, all for the sake of the miserable ruin of a human
being who weeps tears of blood over her past, who now, and for the future,
can rely on nothing but despair . . . ![16]

To adopt such a tone, Juliette must have felt that she was in a fairly
strong position. For Victor Hugo, the tests in this great experiment of

his, which took the form of "making two women cross the suspension-bridge of love, in order to try its solidity," were a pleasing penitence. In the mornings he worked at home, while Juliette, in her nearby room, sat copying *Jean Valjean*. Later, she joined him under the porch of Notre-Dame de Lorette, as a preliminary to accompanying him on his afternoon walks. Dinner was kept sacred to the family, and the evenings to Léonie, about whom, next day, he talked to Juliette with a liveliness and enthusiasm which she must have found extremely trying. But when a test has four months to run, Destiny takes upon itself, long before the day of decision dawns, to impose it by indirect and unforeseeable means. Hugo, on the active side of his life, was passing through a more than difficult period. In February 1851 he had taken up a position which was hostile, not only to the Government, but also to Louis-Napoleon in person. "It was not for Napoleon as Napoleon that we voted. Our voices were given for a man who, matured by political imprisonment, had written in favour of the poorer classes of the community. We had banked our hopes on him, and our hopes have been disappointed. . . ."[17]

He admitted that he had long hesitated before accepting the Republic, but that then, seeing it "treacherously seized, bound, pinioned and gagged," had fallen to his knees in front of it. "Be careful," he was told, "you will share its fate."—"All the more reason, he replied, for my acting as I am doing! Republicans, open your ranks and let me in! I am one of you!" High-falutin? Resentment? To some extent, perhaps, but also horror of the "complacent," eagerness to take risks, and a sacred fury. Already the rattle of bayonets could be heard at the doors of the Palais Bourbon. The Assembly was committing suicide. By tolerating a Ministry of "Mamelukes," it was giving control into the hands of the prince. It knew that the adventurer, since he was not eligible for a second term, would inevitably be driven to try a *coup-d'état,* yet acquiesced in his taking the command of the troops out of the hands of Changarnier, who could alone have protected it. *Deus quos vult perdere* . . . The Assembly had for a long time past already reached the stage of *dementat prius.*

Around the president, the leaders of the gang were hoping to find a solution in force of arms. Louis-Napoleon was by no means hostile to the idea, but was not prepared to take the risk until he had got all the odds on his side. He had got to have *his* Prefect of Police, Maupas; *his* Minister of War, Saint-Arnaud; *his* Governor of Paris, Magnan. Until such time as the necessary forces should be in position he continued to negotiate, for he would have preferred a legal settlement— a revision of the constitution in such a way as to maintain him in power for ten years, with a civil list worthy of a sovereign. That was the road travelled by the uncle. Everyone knew that it had led to the

Empire. But in order to revise the constitution the conspirators would have to obtain two-thirds of the votes in the Assembly. Now, there were not a few royalists who were entertaining vague hopes of 1852. Louis-Napoleon was demanding millions in money and years in time. Thiers replied: "Not a sou, not a day!" A breach was certain.

On July 17th Victor Hugo spoke against revision, and was treated by the Right to an unbelievable display of contempt. Shouts, prolonged laughter, interruptions—the great writer was spared none of these things. It is true that he was lumping together in one general attack the principle of monarchy, or legitimacy, with what the Bonapartists called "the monarchy of glory."

The monarchy of glory, say you! Let us see this glory that you vaunt! I am interested to know what glory there has been under this present government . . . What, because there was once a man who won the battle of Marengo, and thereafter mounted a throne, you, too, want to reign, you, whose only victory was gained at Satory[18] . . . What! after Augustus, Augustulus! What! because we have had a Napoleon the Great must we now have a Napoleon the Little?[19]

Never before had anyone dared to use such language in the Assembly. Its very violence, a sane and healthy violence, was an embarrassment to the shamefaced conspirators, the monarchists, who, like Montalembert, were secretly rallying to the Empire. The Left applauded; the Right howled. The tumult, according to *Le Moniteur*, became indescribable. An interrupter from the Right went up to the tribune, and said:

"We want to hear no more. Bad literature makes bad politics. We protest in the name of the French language and of the French tribune. Take that sort of stuff to the Porte-Saint-Martin, Monsieur Victor Hugo."

"You seem to know my name," cried Hugo: "but I do not know yours: what is it?"

"Bourbousson."

"That is better than I could have hoped." (*Laughter.*)

The motion for revision was defeated. With the legal road now closed to him, Little Napoleon now felt himself spurred on to try force. If he succeeded, he would have on his side, as General Malet had once said, the whole of France, which was sick to death of parliamentary squabbles. Hugo, by rallying to the cause of the Republic which already stood condemned, was courting disaster. Already, justice had unjustly proceeded against the editors of *L'Événement*: nine months' imprisonment for François-Victor Hugo; the same for Paul Meurice; and six months for Auguste Vacquerie. Charles Hugo was already serving a sentence. *L'Événement*, after its suppression, re-appeared under the title of *L'Avènement du Peuple*. Every day Victor Hugo visited his two sons and his two friends in the Conciergerie, and drank with them the rough red wine from the Canteen. Soon, no doubt, his own turn would come. *"Le calvaire est au bout et l'auréole aussi."* He found a bitter pleasure in this thought. On the one hand, it liberated his conscience "from remorse for a state of slavery to which he had submitted only against his better judgment"; on the other, the exile's vocation had long played a part in his private sense of Destiny.[20] A hundred times the *motif* of proscription, sometimes in the minor, sometimes in the major, had dominated the symphony of his life. Lahorie outlawed; Hernani outlawed; Didier outlawed; Frederick Barbarossa outlawed. "Oh! n'exilez personne, oh! l'exil est impie." True enough for the common run of mortals, but, for the Dreamer, was not exile tantamount to liberty, escape? Was it not the solution of a great problem—a great, romantic problem such as was dear to him?

In his private life, too, he had need of a sundering sword. The sentimental test had turned to the advantage of Juliette. Léonie d'Aunet, unhorsed by the check she had suffered in her manœuvring, had lost ground. Juliette's love was the more dramatic: pilgrimages to tombs; oaths of eternal fidelity sworn by the spirits of two Guardian Angels (Didine and Claire); furtive visits by Juliette to the rue de La Tour d'Auvergne; kisses and caresses within hearing-distance of the wife. "I can no longer see your fault; I can feel nothing but my love. I have no wish to discover whether, in your heart, I have suffered mutilation; I know that in mine you are whole and intact . . ."[21] From October 20th to 24th there was an autumn pilgrimage to the forest of Fontainebleau. "My heart is strewn with the dead leaves of my illusions. But I feel within me a rising sap which awaits only your life-giving breath to turn it into flowers and fruit."[22] There was beautiful poetry from Victor to Juliette:

> Laissez entrer en vous, après nos deuils funèbres,
> L'aube, fille des nuits: l'amour, fils des douleurs;
> Tout ce qui luit dans le ténèbres,
> Tout ce qui sourit dans les pleurs.[23]

Then, finally on November 12th, 1851, this letter, worthy of Julie de Lespinasse: *Juliette Drouet to Victor Hugo:* "I have too much of true love to have one single grain of self-love. I gather my happiness where I find it, at every street-corner, and at every milestone. I seek it out and beg for it to be given me in many varying tones of voice, and with the most lamentable perseverance. I stretch my heart and my hand for every crumb your charity may offer, and I say thank you for pity, no matter in what way it may be shown to me. My pride and my vanity are all bound up in loving you more than anybody in this world, and in that, I think, I have succeeded moderately well. My ambition is to die for you . . ."[24] Léonie d'Aunet was mistress of no such music. The greater love had emerged victorious from the Ordeal by Fire. Destiny was now hastening the dénouement.

33

Decent Folk

A country which can be saved only by this or
that especial man will never be saved for long,
even by him: what is more, it would not deserve
so to be saved.

BENJAMIN CONSTANT

BY DECEMBER 1851 a *coup d'état* had become inevitable. Louis-
Napoleon wished to remain in power; his gang had decided to
give him its backing, but not to defend either his ideas or opinions.
The leader and his right-hand men had but one idea: to cut a dash,
and to cut it for as long a time as possible. The Assembly had refused
both a large money-grant and a prolongation of power. The only alternative open to them was force. They possessed the necessary means. An
army is obedient to orders, and the Assembly, in its madness, had allowed the troops of the Paris garrison to be placed under the command
of officers devoted to the president. Who was there left who could
take action in defence of the liberties of the citizen? The monarchists?
They were living in dread of the May elections. The people? The
events of June had cut them off completely from the liberal bourgeoisie.
During the autumn of 1851 the conspirators were able to prepare their
coup with impunity. But Saint-Arnaud was in favour of waiting until
all the members of the Assembly should be gathered in Paris, for it
would be easier then to have the lot of them arrested in their beds.
Moreover, December 2nd, the anniversary of Austerlitz and of the Emperor's coronation, was, for Bonapartists, a day of peculiar significance.
It was decided upon.

Hugo was now living in daily expectation of danger. His sons were
in prison. The faithful Juliette was keeping her ears open for every
rumour, "so as to be ready for the *coup d'état*, and was already
taking steps to prepare for the safety of her beloved. On December
2nd, at eight o'clock in the morning, Hugo, fully awake but still in
bed, was hard at work. His servant came into the room with a scared
face. "There's a representative of the people downstairs asking to see
you, sir." "Show him in." Versigny, an honest and courageous man,

entered and explained what had happened. The Palais Bourbon had been surrounded under cover of darkness; the officials had been arrested; the president, Dupin, had played the coward. Proclamations were up on all the walls announcing the resort to force. Those among the Representatives who had decided to put up a fight were to meet at 70 rue Blanche, at the house of the Baroness Coppens.

While Hugo was hurriedly getting into his clothes one of his protégés arrived, an unemployed cabinet-maker named Girard. He was hot from the streets. "What are the people saying?" Hugo asked him. The people were saying nothing. Men on their way to work were reading the proclamation, and then continuing on their way. Stationed in front of each placard was a member of the conspiracy, explaining what it meant: "the reactionaries' majority had been driven out." The passers-by were shrugging their shoulders. Hugo said: "We shall fight," and went into his wife's room where he found her in bed reading the paper. He explained the situation to her. "What are you going to do?" she asked. "My duty." She embraced him: "Do it!" In saying this she displayed courage. She had two sons in prison, and *coups d'état* are no great respecters of women. But Adèle had never been deficient in bravery.

At 70 rue Blanche, Hugo found Michel (of Bourges) and other Representatives, among them Baudin and Edgar Quinet. Very soon the room was packed. Hugo opened the proceedings by saying that the first blow must be struck at once. Blow for blow. Michel did not agree. "This is not 1830," he said. "The 221 were of the people: the present Assembly is not. The people must be given time in which to understand." Hugo, as usual, would believe only his own eyes. He went out on to the boulevards. Close to the Porte-Saint-Martin there was an enormous crowd. A long column of infantry debouched into the square with drums beating. A workman recognized Hugo and asked what should be done. "Tear down the seditious proclamations announcing the *coup d'état* and shout *'Long Live the Constitution.'*" "And if they open fire?" "Run to arms!" His words were answered by a tremendous cry of "Long Live the Constitution!" A friend who was with him begged him to keep calm and not give the soldiers of Louis-Napoleon an excuse for mowing down the crowd.

He turned to the rue Blanche, gave his friends an account of what he had seen, and proposed the draft of a proclamation. No fine phrases: ten lines in all. He began to dictate: *"To the People:* Louis-Napoleon Bonaparte is a traitor. He has violated the Constitution. He has been false to his sworn word. He is an outlaw. Let the people do their duty. The Representatives of the Republic will march at their head . . ."[1] The police were watching the building. The meeting moved to Lafon's house, Quai de Jemmapes, No. 2. A Committee of the Left was set up:

Carnot, Flotte, Jules Favre, Madier de Montjau, Michel (of Bourges) and Hugo. Someone suggested that it should be called the Committee of Insurrection. "No," said Hugo; "the Committee of Resistance. The insurgent in this case is Louis-Napoleon." A few moments later, out in the street, Hugo met Proudhon, who had sent for him. "I am here as a friend, to warn you. You are making a great mistake. The people have been bamboozled. They won't lift a finger." Hugo insisted on sticking to his plan. Fighting must begin no later than next morning. Midnight sounded. Where should he go? A young man, La Roëllerie by name, offered him shelter. Madame de Roëllerie, who was already in bed, got up to receive him, "a ravishing creature, white skin and fair hair, in a dressing-gown, her hair all loose, beautiful, young, bewildered, but very kind." As soon as a woman appeared on the scene he found something romantic in danger. A bed was made up on a sofa. It was too short for him. He did not sleep. In the small hours he went home. His servant Isidore uttered a cry at sight of him. "Is it really you, sir? They came here last night to arrest you!"

December 3rd was a day of barricades. Baudin was killed, and died with a phrase which became famous: "You shall see how a man can die for twenty-five francs!" Such Representatives as were still at liberty decreed that he had deserved well of his country and should be buried in the Panthéon. It should not be forgotten that these men were carrying their lives in their hands. On the Place de la Bastille Hugo addressed a passionate harangue to a group of officers and police agents. Juliette, who all through these days followed him wherever he went, seized his arm and said: "You'll get yourself shot!"

December 4th was decisive. It was a day of massacre. A liberal and bourgeois resistance had been organized. It was savagely suppressed. The total of killed in Paris amounted to four hundred. Hugo said twelve hundred; Viel-Castel, two thousand. Where censorship is operative there is nothing easier than to doctor figures on the morrow of a riot. As in the days of the White Terror, there were *ultras* who demanded that the prince "should veil the statues of Clemency and Pity, and show himself to be a man of bronze, inflexible and just," striding through the age "with the sword of repression in his hand." In these days of bloody disorder Juliette continued to dog Hugo's footsteps. There is something at once pathetic and sublime in the thought of this woman, still beautiful, though worn, with hair turning grey, shadowing her man at a distance, ready should occasion arise to fling herself between him and the raised rifle. Exposing herself in the midst of slaughter, she frequently lost track of him, only to pick it up later. "Madame Drouet gave up everything, sacrificed everything, for me," wrote Victor Hugo; "it is to her wonderful devotion that I owe my life during those days of December 1851 . . ."[2] Eight years later (1860) he wrote on the set of proofs of *La Légende des Siècles,* in place of a dedication, this:

That I was not captured and subsequently shot, that I am alive at this moment, I owe entirely to Madame Juliette Drouet who, at the peril of her own liberty, and her own life, saved me from every trap, unceasingly watched over me, found me secret hiding-places, and saved me, with what heroic courage God alone knows, and will reward. She was up night and day, wandering alone in darkness through the streets of Paris, deceiving sentries, putting spies off the scent, passing fearlessly under fire along the boulevards, always guessing where I was, and, when it was a question of protecting my life, always finding me. She does not like these things to be talked about, but it is right that they should be known. . . .[3]

On December 6th Juliette found a refuge for him at rue de Navarin, No. 2, in the house of Sarrazin de Montferrier, whom he had known at Metz.[4] The Montferriers, who belonged to the extreme Right, gave shelter to the rebel for five days. Juliette, having found him this excellent hiding-place, brought him a no less excellent supper—and other things as well. *Victor Hugo to Juliette Drouet, December 31st, 1851:* "You have been wonderful, my Juliette, all through these dark and violent days. If I needed love, you brought it to me, bless you! When, in my hiding-places, always dangerous, after a night of waiting, I heard the key of my door trembling in your fingers, peril and darkness were no longer round me—what entered then was light! We must never forget those terrible, but so sweet, hours when you were close to me in the intervals of fighting. Let us remember all our lives that dark little room, the ancient hangings, the two armchairs, side by side, the meal we ate off the corner of the table, the cold chicken you had brought; our sweet converse, your caresses, your anxieties, your devotion. You were surprised to find me calm and serene. Do you know whence came both calmness and serenity? From you. . . ."[5]

Meanwhile, it was necessary to make arrangements for him to leave the country. Jacques-Firmin Lanvin, a devoted admirer of Juliette, applied at the Prefecture of Police for a passport, under the pretext of having to go on business to visit the Luthereau printing-house, in Belgium. It was with this passport that on Thursday, December 11th, Victor Hugo left Paris from the Gare du Nord, under the name of "Lanvin (Jacques-Firmin), printer's compositor, domiciled in Paris, rue des Jeuneurs, No. 4. *Age* 48. *Height* 1m. 70. *Hair* turning grey. *Eyebrows* light brown. *Eyes* light brown. *Beard* greying. *Chin* round. *Face* oval." The traveller was wearing a workman's cap and a black overcoat. Was he unrecognizable, or did the authorities not wish to recognize him? Who can say? That they had wanted to arrest him during the disturbances is certain. The young Adèle, in a letter to her father, spoke of "that terrible night when they came to take you . . ."[6] But his flight was less dangerous for the regime than the necessity of hunting him down.

Madame Victor Hugo, ailing and confined to her bed, had been able to play no part in the struggle. Alone with her daughter, expecting the police to appear at any moment, she watched carefully over everything that had been left in her charge, and never ceased from communicating with "her prisoners": Charles, François-Victor and Auguste Vacquerie. For, strange though it may seem, at the very height of the fighting Vacquerie was able to send her a letter by special messenger, from the Conciergerie:

All is well with us and we live in hope. Send us news of yourselves. It is two o'clock and so far nothing has reached us. Don't hang about the streets. If you go out, go to my house, or somewhere else. Don't send news of your husband by name. If you have any, simply say—*We are all right.* It is impossible to know who reads our letters. We see the papers, but since the only ones that reach us are government sponsored, we do not know what to believe. Send us news very often. You are our only anxiety. So far as we are concerned, fear nothing. Always yours.

4 o'clock: The sound of gunfire has come very close. Fighting is going on all round us. The people are gaining ground. We are perfectly safe behind these thick prison walls. I hope that you are equally safe. Fifty or so prisoners and wounded have been brought in here. They are in the great corridor which leads from the office to our rooms. Whatever you do, don't go out. The only thing likely to worry me would be the knowledge that you are not safe. Try to give a word to the bearer of this, so that we may know what is happening. Yours: A.[7]

Indulgent Conciergerie! On December 12th, Hugo wrote to his wife, giving as his address: M. Lanvin, Poste Restante, Brussels. The letter was addressed, Madame Rivière, 37 rue de la Tour d'Auvergne, Paris. *Adèle to Victor Hugo, December 13, 1851:* "Dear friend: we are all singing *Hosannah!* Your blessed letter has just reached me. No search has been carried out here. There was one in the rue Laferrière, which put *the poor old lady* in a terrible taking. I shall follow all your instructions most carefully. Don't worry, nothing in your house shall be touched so long as *I'm* alive . . ."[8] *The poor old lady* was a code phrase, meaning Léonie d'Aunet. But if Adèle was still keeping a watchful eye on her, it was Juliette, alone in Brussels with the outlaw, who had emerged victorious from the Ordeal by Fire.

Victor Hugo to his wife, December 31st, 1851: The year that ends today has been one of great ordeals for us: our two sons in prison, I in exile! All this is hard, but it has its good side. A touch of frost improves the crop. So far as I, personally, am concerned, I can only thank God. Tomorrow, I shall not be there to give you a New-Year's kiss, my dear ones . . . But all that is in my heart will wing its way to you . . . I am almost as much surrounded here as I was in Paris. This morning there was a gathering of former Representatives and one-time ministers . . . I embrace you tenderly, my poor dear friend, and my dear children, too. I send you much affection. Write on the blank envelope which I enclose—*Madame d'Aunet, post restante, Bordeaux,* and put it in the post.[9]

A confident, an almost exultant, letter. *"Car la joie est le fruit du grand arbre douleur."* During those early days of exile he still had faith in ultimate victory. The new master seemed just then in France to be invincible, but already the poet was declaring his belief that his triumph would be ephemeral:

> Les jours mauvais fuiront sans qu'on sache leur nombre
> Et les peuples joyeux, en se penchant sur l'ombre,
>   Diront: "Cela n'est plus."

PART VIII

Exile and Authorship

As one grows older, one becomes both more mad and wiser.

LA ROCHEFOUCAULD

It takes one a long time to become young.

PICASSO

34

From La Place Royale to Marine Terrace

"NOTHING comes to grief like success." Exile was a shock, but it brought salvation. Victor Hugo, peer of France, doubly adorned with gold lace, intimate friend of an old and sceptical king, a prey to ardent women who were all too ready to succumb, had been in danger of becoming bogged down. The death of his daughter, by awakening in him a grief stripped of all egotism, had first begun to save him from himself. The Revolution of 1848 had given him an opportunity to try his abilities as a poet-legislator. It had proved to him that he was unsuited to a parliamentary career, and without skill in party intrigues. "There is a lordly solitude which both giants and geniuses seem to find essential . . ."[1] In exile he found the means to acquire such a solitude. It was necessary, if he were to recover inner peace, to find a genuine attitude, a part with which he might identify his life. Events had suddenly given him the chance he needed. He became the Great Exile, the Avenger, the Dreamer. "In this moment of time through which we are passing . . . those, among so many whose only moral law is enjoyment, who are preoccupied with the short-term views and misshapen interests of material existence, those who choose exile, would seem to deserve veneration . . ."[2] At last he felt pleased with himself. *Victor Hugo to Auguste Vacquerie, December 19, 1851:* "I am hot from the fight, and have shown something of what it means to be a poet. These bourgeois will learn at last that brains can be as valiant as bellies are cowardly. . . ."[3]

That the role should be nobly played, it was necessary that the banished hero should make a display of proud poverty. When "Firmin Lanvin" descended from the train in Brussels on December 12th, 1851, Laure Luthereau, a friend of Juliette, and forewarned by her,[4] introduced him to several very humble hotels—the Hôtel de Limbourg, and later, the Hôtel de la Porte Verte, 31 rue de la Violette. *Victor to Adèle Hugo:* "I am living the life of a monk. I have a bed which is about a hand's-breadth wide, and two straw-bottomed chairs. My room has no fire. The total cost is three francs five sous a day, all in."[5] There was joy in being able to write like this, a delicious sense of humility. "I am now seated in the lowest place of all. I can go no lower . . ."[6] On December 14th Juliette arrived. Victor Hugo was waiting for her in the Customs shed. She had brought his manuscripts with her. She, too, knew that from now on she carried the aureole of an heroic devotion. She was freed from the presence of a hostile wife. She believed that at last she had won complete redemption. "Now it is indeed true that I am a blest and happy woman, that I have the right to live in the full blaze of love and devotion, is it not?"[7]

No, it was not true. Exile demanded a certain standard of behaviour. A Great Outlaw could not decently live with his mistress, and poor Juliette had to find a lonely lodging in the passage du Prince, close to her friends, the Luthereaus. She felt hurt, but resigned. "I would not have you make any sacrifices for me, if they should cause you a moment's regret or remorse. In life or death I am wholly yours . . . My love is beyond the power of words to express, and I promise you never to indulge in bitter recriminations . . ."[8] She swore to respect the limits laid down by her lover to their relationship, no matter how narrow those limits might be. "I want to be, for you, a sure, a tender and devoted friend, with all the courage of a man, all the solicitude of a mother, all the disinterestedness of one who is dead . . ."[9] Never did conjugal abnegation reach such a height.

From her very first days with him Juliette had copying to do. A sacred fury, "the frenzied enthusiasm of an eye-witness," was at work in Victor Hugo, and sought expression. He was resolved to set the "brazen chord vibrating," to become the stern conscience of France, "the man of duty." Especially was he determined to produce a narrative of December 2nd (later called *l'Histoire d'un Crime*). He began it immediately after his arrival. Outlaws were flooding into Belgium, and all told him their experiences. In the same hotel with himself was Versigny, with whom he had embarked upon resistance. Adèle came to Brussels on December 19th to receive her husband's instructions. She was told to send him from Paris, under cover of false names and addresses, leaflets and documents. Alexandre Dumas the elder had fled to Brussels from his creditors and undertook to forward letters. To his wife and children Hugo preached economy. He liked to think that he was ruined, and declared that he was. The Belgian Prime Minister made him an offer of shirts which he accepted. Since *Monsieur Bonaparte* had had his name included in the official list of outlaws, it might well be that his property, and even his furniture, would be seized. Actually, no steps were taken. Adèle found no difficulty in collecting her husband's royalties from the Society of Authors, as well as his salary as a Member of the Institut, a thousand francs a year. The Government had no intention of making itself ridiculous by persecuting a great poet. His wife was even granted facilities for sending him three hundred thousand francs in French State Bonds, which, as a prudent family man and a shrewd capitalist, he at once transformed into stock of the Banque Royale de Belgique, an institution then in its infancy, on to which he was "put" by the Burgomaster of Brussels, Charles de Brouckère, who went to see him almost every day, and confided to a friend that "he is not so poor as he would have us believe. I happen to know that he did not leave France empty-handed. He has quite a nice little nest-egg."

All the same, Hugo wrote to his wife: "We are poor, and must tread with dignity a road which may end soon, but may be long. I am wearing out my old shoes and my old clothes. That is a simple matter. You, on your side, are putting up with privations, even sufferings—not seldom the extremes of embarrassed circumstances. That is less simple, because you are a woman and a mother; but you are doing it cheerfully and with a high spirit. . . ."[10]

There has been a certain amount of smiling at the expense of all this poverty reared on a pile of gold; of pocket-money dribbled out to his sons (François-Victor was receiving at this time only twenty-five francs a month); of this "penury" of a man with handsome investments. There are three explanations of the attitude he was adopting. (*a*) Hugo had a nostalgia for poverty. He liked to reconstruct round the figure of a famous man the scene of an early life spent in a garret in the rue du Dragon, and to deprive himself of the luxuries the possession of which he had never, in his heart of hearts, been able to square with his conscience. At the end of December he left his hotel and went to live at 16 Grand-Place, where he rented an almost completely unfurnished room containing only a horsehair sofa, a mirror, a cast-iron stove, and six chairs. His rent was a hundred francs a month, and he had no more than one meal a day. Juliette, whose budget was 150 francs a month, thought him undernourished, and sent him a cup of chocolate every morning by her servant Suzanne. (*b*) He wanted to live on his income only, and to preserve his capital intact, so as to provide after his death for the members of his family, who, as he was perfectly well aware, were incapable of earning their own livings. (He would open his purse wider, he said, as soon as he had sold some manuscripts.) (*c*) He thought that he would be in a stronger position, when dealing with Belgian and English publishers, if they were made to realize that he did not need them, and could quite well live on twelve hundred francs a year. Still, taking all these points into consideration, it cannot be denied that he had an instinctive love of economizing, and liked to have a balanced budget and a feeling of security. But that is no reason for regarding his attitude as criminal.

In Paris Adèle bore with dignity her position as an outlaw's wife. She was far more proud of her husband's political activities than she had ever been of his literary fame. Many loyal friends went to see her. They were loud in their praise of the courageous manner in which Victor had

fought in the streets against the *coup d'état*. *Adèle to Victor Hugo:*
"The Republicans are amazed. They used to say: *Hugo, no doubt, is a
very progressive-minded man, an eminent orator, a great spirit, but will
he prove to be a man of action when the moment comes?* There were
certain aspects of your character about which they felt uncertain. But
now that you have been put to the test, and have more than satisfied
them, they are sorry that they ever had reservations about you . . ."[11]
Like him, she found consolation in a noble attitude. "I feel that I am
living under a shadow of inevitable gloom. My heart is heavy because
of your exile, because my sons and my friends are in prison, but my
conscience is completely at rest. What saddens me will pass. What
makes me proud and happy will be mine for ever . . ."[12] Since she was
living in Paris she could send useful information to her lord about the
march of events, and thus acquire, for a time, a pleasing superiority at
the expense of his dominant personality. In point of fact the news she
sent was imperfect and spasmodic. Sometimes she told him that the
regime would be short-lived; sometimes, on the contrary, that Louis-
Napoleon was going to invade Belgium and seize the persons of the
proscribed. "Not a protesting voice would be raised in France, no one
would lift a finger to help you."[13] She advised him, therefore, to go to
London. This was also the view of François-Victor, who wrote from
prison: "Go to England, you will be very well received there . . . Besides, you know Cobden and the men who came as English representatives to the Peace Congress. Should need arise, they will pilot you
round."[14] But both Louis Blanc and Pierre Leroux were living as
refugees in London, and were urging him to join with them in founding a paper. He had no desire to get mixed up with them. "That would
put an end to my present position of isolation . . . and would, to some
extent, diminish the reputation for political purity which I now enjoy."
Furthermore, he did not know English, and therefore suggested as an
alternative the Anglo-Norman islands where, at least, French was
spoken.

Not unnaturally, Adèle was annoyed by the presence of Juliette in
Brussels. On that issue, however, he stood firm. "What Abel has been
saying to Meurice is idiotic. The individual of whom he spoke is here;
I don't deny it. She saved my life—you shall hear all about that later.
But for her I should have been taken, and all would have been up with
me when things were at their worst. The devotion she has shown is
absolute, complete. It is the accumulation of twenty years, and has
never faltered. More than that, it is an expression of utter self-forgetful-
ness and resignation. Without her, and this I say to you as I would say
it before the throne of God, I should now be either dead or deported.
. . ."[15]

Adèle stopped nagging him, but poor Juliette was still the target of her resentment, though she continued to extend her patronage to the bland Léonie d'Aunet. *Victor to Adèle Hugo:* "I thank you a thousand times for all you are doing. Do everything you possibly can for Madame d'Aunet. Where she is concerned I have a duty which I cannot ignore. I have been deeply touched by the delicacy and real goodness of all you say in reference to that business."[16] Victor Hugo was also in direct communication with the ex-Madame Biard, who was another of those who were demanding financial assistance. *Hugo to Léonie d'Aunet:* "The best thing I can do is to make payable to you my three Hachette contracts, amounting in all to seven thousand francs. It will be the easiest thing in the world for you to discount them. You may count on the extra thousand francs of which you stand in immediate need. But where you and I are concerned, please do not use the word *lend*. I give, and I thank you for accepting the gift. Please acknowledge the receipt of this."[17] And so it was that the blonde beauty with the brimming eyes was spared a lecture on economy, and received for herself alone more than went to the three children. The family man may have been a shrewd investor, but he had a very strange way of dealing with his income.

Adèle, promoted to the role of confidante, found herself charged with the duty of finding a discreet hiding-place for his indiscreet odds and ends: "papers of every sort, and a number of intimate miscellanea." In the room that had once been Victor Hugo's, the bed-table contained "so many *personal letters* that the drawer was difficult to open." Indifferent to all these proofs of conjugal infidelity, Adèle merely regretted that the drawer in question was not locked. "I really must scold you," she wrote to her husband; "the servants could have read, and made off with, these letters to their heart's content. I have reason to hope, however, that nothing of the sort has occurred, since that particular drawer is difficult to find. . . ."[18]

She was still very uneasy about her children. For Dédé (Adèle the second), who was reaching the age at which she ought to have been married (twenty-two), the sudden abandonment of the Hugos by a brilliant world, which, true to its traditions, had rallied to the orthodox power and excommunicated the heretics, was painful. She took refuge in music and unhappy reveries. *Victor Hugo to his wife:* "Tell my little Adèle that I don't want her to grow pale and thin. She must be calm. The future is for the good . . ."[19] The *little Adèle* was, at that time, keeping a journal. If her father had had access to it this is one of the passages he would have read: "Monsieur Sainte-Beuve has come back to us. He talks at great length. 'I despise politics,' he says, 'or rather, I don't believe in them.' He has promised to send us Monsieur de Salvandy's article on Jersey."[20]

Plump Charles, released from prison in January 1852, joined his father in Brussels. They lived together in two rooms at No. 27 in the Grand-Place, with a wonderful view of the carved and gilded gables of the nearby houses ("Not a façade but is a date, a poem, a masterpiece"), and of the Hôtel de Ville, "a dazzling poetic fantasy born of an architect's brain. . . ."[21]

Charles Hugo had inherited his mother's languor. He slept too much, did little work, and cost his father a hundred francs a month. In the eyes of the outlaw he was a perpetual scandal. As to François-Victor, he too had just been freed as the result of the intervention of the Prince Napoleon (known as "Plonplon") with the president: "an intervention for which he had not asked," Adèle was at pains to state. But this branch of the Bonaparte family had remained faithful to the Hugos, and King Jérôme, now president of the Senate, even went so far as to invite Adèle to his receptions! "We must not bear a grudge against the poor fellow. He is fond of us. He would like, through me, to achieve a reconciliation. He is happy, and would like everybody to be happy, and to join with him in eating up his millions."[22]

Madame Hugo described herself as being "surrounded by friends." Villemain, "gentle, delicate, excellent," had come to her to propose the good offices of the Académie Française in her favour, and with an offer of money.

Adèle to Victor Hugo, January 18, 1852: "Villemain said: 'Victor is a great and courageous man, devoted to his ideas. As such I admire and envy him. But, as I often told him when we used to walk together arm in arm, the mistake he has made is to believe in the people. A noble mistake, when all is said.' I replied that the future lay with them; that one must not judge the people in the light of recent events; that there had been much confusion, much innuendo, lassitude and the memories of June. Just as he was leaving me, he remarked: 'Allow me, Madame, before I go, to speak to you on a somewhat delicate matter. I have come to make you an offer. I am so old a friend that I am sure the offer will not offend you. Your husband left at a moment's notice. Taken by surprise, he had no time in which to attend to business. I cannot bear the thought that a woman like you should, in addition to her many painful preoccupations, have to face a lack of money. I am putting 2500 francs at your disposal. I trust that you will look on it as being no more than a loan. By accepting it, you will be rendering me a great service. The money is safer in your hands and Hugo's than it would be in mine.' "[23]

She had refused everything. "Since I have a rather fierce little pride, I am afraid that I may have seemed somewhat stiff . . ."[24] Béranger went often to see her, and Abel, who had been too much neglected by his famous brother since the death of Eugène, was "wonderful." The two Adèles were living in a single room with a coke fire, "so as to remain within the narrow limits which you have imposed upon us. We drink prison-canteen wine; never anything better. . . ."[25]

In Brussels Victor Hugo was working with that fury and sense of happiness which are the gift of strong passions. In April a rumour was circulating in Paris to the effect that he was to be given a safe-conduct. He published the following statement: "There was a time when Monsieur Victor Hugo obtained for Monsieur Bonaparte permission to return to France. It is not for him to ask for a similar permission now." In May he gave up all attempts to finish his *Histoire du 2 Decembre.* Too much of the evidence was lacking. He might have issued an incomplete version, but no publisher would have ventured to buy the manuscript, seeing that the Belgian authorities, already uneasy, did not wish to expose themselves to reprisals at the hands of a powerful neighbour. He decided to write and publish as quickly as possible a short pamphlet, *Napoléon le Petit.* This was a piece of vivid improvisation, an indictment in the great Roman tradition: Cicero's sweep, the vigour of Tacitus, the poetry of Juvenal. Its prose was the prose of a poet, rhythmical, broken, with something in it of that controlled madness in which the beauty of poetry lies. The tone was marked, now by the invective of the Prophets, now by the terrible humour of Swift.

The first thing you have to learn, Monsieur Bonaparte, is the nature of the human conscience. There are two things in this world—and this may come to you as something new—which go by the names of Good and Evil. It is necessary that you should be told a number of truths: that to lie is not good; that to betray is evil; that to assassinate is worse. It may be useful, but it is forbidden—yes, monseigneur, it is forbidden. Who says so? Who refuses to countenance it? Monsieur Bonaparte, you may be the master; eight million votes may have been cast for your crimes, and twelve million to provide you generously with pocket money; you may have a Senate, complete with Monsieur Sibour; you may have armies, guns and fortresses; you may have Troplongs squirming on their bellies, and Baroches creeping on their hands and knees; you may be a despot; you may be all-powerful—but someone, from out of the darkness, a passer-by, an unknown, stands up before you, and says: "This you shall not do! . . ."[26]

That he might work without a break, he refused "those dinners, those small private ovations in the family circle" which are the consolations of political minorities in exile. Being an outlaw by destiny and by temperament he was, by and large, reasonably happy. "I have never felt my heart lighter, nor more satisfied." He knew that his misfortunes had increased his stature in French eyes. Jules Janin wrote to him: "You are our leader, and you are our God. You have been for us the Resurrection and the Life! It needed only that you should know misfortune, that you should be removed from us, for you to be seen in all your greatness. Only three days ago Saint-Marc Girardin, lecturing at the Sorbonne, mentioned your name, quite simply, in illustration of some point in connection with rhetoric—and at once it was greeted with unanimous applause, that great name, so rich in glory, so filled with echoes . . ."[27] To another of his correspondents Hugo replied: "It is not I, sir, who have been outlawed, but liberty: it is not I who have been exiled, but France." He saw some of the banished: Schœlcher; Colonel Charras, a man of high character and great military knowledge; Girardin. With Hetzel, an exiled publisher, a militant republican, a charming friend, he made plans: "We must build a citadel of writers and booksellers from which to bombard the Bonaparte." Jules Hetzel, the publisher of Balzac and George Sand, seemed quite capable of assuming the technical control of such an enterprise.[28] Would it be possible in Belgium? That was far from certain. The French Imperial Police were bringing pressure to bear on the Belgian authorities. "If not Brussels, then Jersey. . . ."[29]

Poor Juliette saw very little more of her Victor than she had done in Paris. She sent Suzanne to the Grand-Place with delicious little dishes. She continued with her "scrawls." She faithfully observed her cult of anniversaries, but could not help wondering "what point there is in observing these traditions of first love when first love, alas! exists no longer; when there is nothing left but duties, compassion and human decencies." Would it not be better to renounce for good and all "these children's games of the heart, which are so ill-suited to my white hairs? . . . There are subtleties, there are ways of dressing, which are no longer becoming when a woman has passed a certain age. . . ."[30] At forty-six Juliette was turning prematurely into an unwieldy dowager. She had become heavy and fat. Conscious of her physical deterioration, she made touching efforts at renunciation. Hugo, sacrificing her to the proprieties of exile, made it a strict rule that she should never visit him at his lodgings when he was receiving the curious, the indifferent, the idle: "You do not seem to realize how cruel, how iniquitous, this repudiation of my person is. You are bolstering up your self-esteem at the cost of my poor heart."[31] Her lover was "intensifying the state of chastity," and accentuating, at Brussels, that continence which he had been observing, where she was concerned, "for the last two months, or, should I say, for the last eight years, or nearly . . ."[32] Was he observing it in his relations with younger women, too? She had good reasons to doubt it. "Do at least have the courage, once and for all," she told him, "of your physical and moral infidelity . . . I remember the time when you loved only me, and how, on the day when you excused a state of *physical* separation on grounds of health, you were filled with *adoration* of another . . ."[33] Meanwhile, the mistress-servant copied *Napoléon le*

Petit, darned her "little man's" socks, and watched the clouds drifting by.

He did, at least, spare her the humiliation of seeing the arrival of Léonie d'Aunet, who in the course of January 1852 had announced her intention of joining him in Brussels. He had at once sent out a warning call to his wife and ally.

Victor to Adèle Hugo: She means to start on the 24th! You must go and see her at once and try to make her see reason. An ill-considered move at this moment might have the most serious consequences. All eyes are fixed on me. I live a public and austere existence, an existence of work and privations, whence an attitude to me of general respect, which shows itself even in the streets. This state of affairs must not be disturbed. Tell her all this. Be gentle with her, and treat with tenderness what in her is suffering. She is imprudent. Don't show her this letter. *Burn it at once.* Say that I will write to the address she has given me. Keep an eye on her: she is apt to be impulsive. . . .[34]

Adèle, increasingly proud of the role she was playing, and suddenly puffed up with self-importance, announced that she would see to everything.

Adèle to Victor Hugo: Don't worry. I will go and see Madame d'Aunet. I will *answer for* her not leaving. I have just written to Houssaye, asking for an interview, so that I may talk to him about the *Journey* in question.[35] Gautier, Houssaye and two others have the controlling voices in the *Revue.*[36] I will divert Madame d'Aunet's thoughts to matters of art. I hope it may be a noble and powerful distraction. You, I think, would do well to write her letters of a kind to satisfy, if not her heart, at least her pride. Make of her a *twin-soul.* I know that you have not much spare time, but a few words, now and again, will probably suffice. Dear, great friend, I will keep my eyes open. Work in peace, and keep calm. . . .[37]

What is really difficult is not to conquer young women, but to convince them that one can live without them. Léonie dug her toes in.

Victor Hugo to his wife, January 24th, 1852: This morning I got yet another letter from Madame d'A[unet]. She is set on coming if only, she says, for a few days. It is absolutely essential, dear friend, that you have a talk with her, and get her back into a reasonable state of mind. Any impulsive action on her part might ruin everything. It is precisely this violence in her, which I know so well, that keeps from writing to her. I have, however, made use of the means she indicated to me in such a way as to reassure her completely. What she wants is *letters to her!* But it is just in that habit of hers—which you know so well [of telling everything to everybody]—that a great danger lies . . . In Paris one can say all that one has

a mind to say, but here, in Brussels, my life is public, and people don't talk
about things that in Paris would be matters of common gossip. See Madame
d'A[unet] and keep a sharp watch on her. She wants to come, even though
Charles is here! Make her see how impossible it would be. Her coming would
force me to leave Brussels at once. Prevent the proposed journey—it would
be an act of sheer lunacy. . . .[38]

Madame Victor Hugo's *great friend* was duly reassured, and praised
her to the skies for her skill in negotiation. "Let me begin by saying
that you are a noble and a wonderful woman. Your letters bring tears
to my eyes. Everything in them breathes dignity, strength, simplicity,
courage, good sense, serenity and tenderness. When you speak of politics, you do it well; your views are just; your words are true. When you
discuss family matters, it is a great and good heart that speaks."[39] When
husbands are under a cloud, wives get their chance. Adèle revealed her
true character. As to her husband there was little if any change in his
life from January to April: work, dinner at the table-d'hôte with
Alexandre Dumas, Noël Parfait, Charles Hugo, and sometimes Edgar
Quinet. Girardin, an exile without convictions, was a source of some
uneasiness to them. He was subject to recurring fits of Bonapartism.
He said to Hugo: "My wife is as *red* as you are, and like you she calls
him 'the bandit.'" What it all came to was that he was already of a
mind to "come round" yet again. Coming round is, like exile, a matter
of vocation. The doctor of the Duchesse d'Orléans, Noël Guéneau de
Mussy, paid a visit to Brussels, and had to admit to Hugo that the
princess spoke of him with sorrow: "Is it really possible that he is
friendly towards us?" Hugo replied that he had feelings of great respect
and deep sympathy for Madame la Duchesse d'Orléans, though—he
added—"I belong wholly to the Republic, and between the Orléans
family and me there could not be, and is not, a common future." On
the subject of their common past he said nothing.

It became evident that, once *Napoléon le Petit* was published it
would be dangerous for Hugo to leave his family and his property
in France. The Government announced that legal measures were to
be taken against offensive publications produced in foreign countries
by French subjects, and that such misdemeanours would be punishable
with fines and confiscations. Hence his determination to transport the
whole of his little circle either to Brussels, should the Belgians be
prepared to grant them asylum after this latest scandal, or to Jersey if,
as Brouckère told him, a Belgian law was to be introduced forbidding
attacks against the head of a friendly State, which would lead to Hugo's
expulsion. Victor had, for a moment, played with the idea of having all
his furniture sent from Paris to Jersey. He clung to so many objects
which he had bought with loving care in the antique shops—Venetian

glasses, brass-ware, faïence dishes. Adèle, however, thought the idea ridiculous. Why settle permanently abroad? "We must be ready to dig up our roots at any moment . . . Twice already, events have driven us from our home. It is quite possible that events may do so again . . . If we send our furniture to Jersey, we shall incur considerable expense in packing and transport. Don't forget that last time we moved, we had to have *eighteen removal vans*, and that, since then, our possessions have considerably increased in number . . ."[40] His wife's suggestion was that they should surrender their lease of the house in the rue de la Tour d'Auvergne and dispose at auction of the "magnificent Gothic furniture," the whole of the bric-à-brac (of which she had a horror) and the library, including the *Ronsard*. Even the memory of Sainte-Beuve was not to be spared, so eager was she to liquidate every vestige of the years which, for her, had been so unhappy.

Adèle, acting as temporary head of the family, was given the duty of organizing the sale, of preparing a descriptive catalogue, of issuing the necessary announcements to the press, and of carefully emptying the various pieces of furniture which, deprived of their locks and relegated to a lumber-room, were crammed full, like every other receptacle, with letters of the most intimate nature. This duty carried through, and the sale completed, she was to collect the takings and hastily seek safety with Toto and Dédé (Charles was already with his father) before the conspirator exploded his bomb. He was awaiting that moment with impatience and in a mood of pleasurable anticipation. He knew that his *Napoléon le Petit*—the improvisation of a single month—was a fine pamphlet. In Brussels many of the exiles, among them General Lamoricière, came every day, asking him to read extracts from it, and savoured such expressions of vengeance as *"Hatred, for them, held an ineffable sweetness."*

The auctioning of the family possessions might have been painful. But for Hugo the joy of making a public show of sacrifice gave a blessing to the operation, while, as for Adèle, she tasted the pleasures of revenge. She could discharge a few well-aimed shafts at her husband by pointing out to him the worthlessness of all the chipped plates he had accumulated. "That you have no real understanding of furniture is shown by the fact that you buy, as a rule, nothing but worn and shabby hangings, and chipped, cracked and broken china. There is no worse investment than bric-à-brac . . ."[41] She could now triumphantly demonstrate that economy is bad business. It should be remembered that she detested all the odds and ends which he had bought in the rue de Lappe in Juliette's company. The sale brought in only fifteen thousand francs, even though his friends paid high prices for the various objects which had stood on the poet's work-table. The *Dictionary of the Academy* went for 26 francs, Victor Hugo's seal for 101, and his paper-knife for 24. The *Ronsard* appeared in the catalogue as item No. 26. It was knocked down for 120 francs to Mademoiselle Blaizot, who had a bookshop in the rue de Gramont, No. 6. She resold it for 150 to Charles Giraud, Minister of Public Education.[42]

Jules Janin wrote a courageous article on the subject of the sale, in the *Journal des Débats*:

What purpose [he asked] has been served by all these riches of a poet enamoured of form and colour? What purpose? They have merely furnished a list in an auction-room, to be cried aloud to a roomful of buyers. Fond ornaments, dear adornments of a family home! And now the bills have been splashed on the walls of Paris, the catalogue has been distributed to the bargain-hunters, this museum has been handed over to all who wish to acquire it. Ah! dear friend, all your loving search for beautiful objects gone for nothing! And you are treated like a prodigal, like a dead man who has left no children. . . .[43]

La Presse and Théophile Gautier also behaved well.[44] The Exile was noble in the expression of his thanks: "Dear poet, a misfortune immortalized by you is no misfortune . . ."[45] On the evening of the sale (Tuesday, June 9th, 1852) the good Janin returned, under a clear night sky, to the rue de la Tour d'Auvergne.

Jules Janin to Victor Hugo: A great silence has settled down upon your house! The star, a star peculiarly your own, was shining with a piercing radiance on the little garden into which you used to go of an evening . . . At an open window there was a shadowy figure, a patch of whiteness, calmly, attentively, looking out in silence over the city which must be left next day! It was, I am certain, your daughter thus lost in dreams. At a closed window your wife and your son were talking together in low voices. They were talking about something, quietly, sadly. It was impossible to hear what they were saying, but not difficult to guess. They were saying goodbye to that charming nest in which a father's fame had once been sheltered. Ah! who could have foreseen, in the old days, in those great times of battle, when she was greeted as a queen, and her husband was reigning in triumph, who could have foreseen that we should, in days to come, lose even Madame Victor Hugo; that she would leave us for the life of an exile? . . .[46]

For the decision had been taken. On July 25th Hugo urged his wife to go straight to Saint Helier (Jersey). He, anticipating the Faider Law, under the terms of which he would have been expelled, and not wishing to lay on Belgium the dangerous weight of *Napoléon le Petit*, set off on August 1st, with Charles, after taking the chair at a banquet of exiles. Janin had travelled to Brussels to say goodbye to him. "On the Place . . . there was a gloomy shop with a narrow door. A ladder gave access to the retreat which sheltered this peer of France, this Tribune of the People, this Knight of the Golden Fleece—for the man who gave to the world *Hernani* and *Ruy Blas* was surely a born Knight of the Golden Fleece, and a Grandee of Spain. The door was open; I entered the exile's dwelling as once I had been used to entering the poet's. He was lying on a carpet stretched upon the floor, fast asleep. So deeply was he sleeping that he did not hear me, and I was free to gaze in wonder at the man's great solid limbs, at the tremendous chest in which life and breath took up so large a space, at the huge sweep of the brow, at the hands worthy to wield a fairy's wand—in short, I saw the whole of him there before me; I saw the valiant captain of the sounding battles . . . His sleep was the sleep of a child, so quiet and regular was his breathing. . . ."[47]

It was as the sleep of a man whose conscience was at peace.

35

Marine Terrace

Jersey there on a quiet sea,
With a cloudless sky that can almost woo
The mind with a vision of Sicily
In a torn expanse of the deepest blue.

VICTOR HUGO

AUGUST 1852. On a blazing summer's day three travellers, Madame Victor Hugo, her daughter, Adèle, and her faithful slave Auguste Vacquerie, landed in Jersey. They had come via Southampton, and had hated their first experience of "rosbif." They thought that Saint Helier, with its burned-up air, bore a strong resemblance to Saint Helena. Two days later Hugo and Charles joined forces with them at the Hôtel de la Pomme d'Or. The exiles, of whom there was a considerable number on the island, though of a humbler social class than those at Brussels, went down to the harbour to meet the poet and, mingling with the townsmen, gave him a vociferous welcome. Madame Victor Hugo was of the opinion that both her husband and her son had put on weight. Victor Hugo was dressed with studied negligence, and was greatly changed. The former man of fashion, with curled hair and a smart appearance, now looked like a rough manual worker. His face had a tormented and ravaged expression, and his fixed and burning eyes seemed at times to be those of a visionary. But he quickly recovered his gaiety and his realistic commonsense.

The more they came to know of Jersey the better they liked it. *Victor Hugo to Colonel Charras in Brussels:* "... if there could be such a thing as a lovely exile, Jersey would be a charming place in which to spend it. The wild and the smiling aspects of nature are here closely linked in the midst of the sea, on a nest of verdure twenty miles square. I am living in a white cottage at the sea's edge. From my window I can catch a glimpse of the coast of France in the direction of the rising sun. A good omen, that. I am told that my little book is infiltrating into France, where it is falling, drop by drop, upon the Bonaparte. It may end by making a hole in him ... Since my arrival in this place they have done me the honour of trebling the Customs

312

officials, the police and the plain-clothes informers at Saint-Malo. The
fool has raised a hedge of bayonets against the landing of a mere
book. . . ."[1]

The island was a park-land of vivid green, dotted with neat houses
against a background of sea. From the very start the family was at
cross-purposes on the subject of where to live. Hugo insisted on being
close to the sea; his daughter wanted to be within reach of Saint Helier;
Charles longed to settle on a hill in a wild and savage landscape. The
paterfamilias had his way and rented, close to the sea, a completely
isolated house, Marine Terrace, "a clumsy white cube of a place, with
square corners," he was to say later, "which looks more like a tomb
than anything else." In fact, it was a pretty little villa, with a terrace,
a flower-garden and a kitchen-garden. There was nothing funereal
about it. Juliette, who had arrived on a different boat (the proprieties,
and Abel, had insisted on this), took up her lodgings at first in the local
inn, though she afterwards found an apartment in a cottage with the
pompous name of Nelson Hall. *Juliette Drouet to Victor Hugo, August
10th, 1852:* "Time will show whether the sight of the sea will provide
you with better inspiration than the Grand-Place at Brussels, and
whether my *cottage* will be more honoured than my room in the passage Saint-Hubert. . . ."[2]

The whole of this little world, these two households, depended for
a livelihood on the pen and the brain of one man. Publish he must:
but what? He had a volume of verse ready for the press: *Les Contemplations,* poems of love and of mourning . . . Juliette and Léopoldine.
But was this the moment, with politics blowing a full gale, at which to
offer to the public such personal and private pieces? Neither Hetzel,
who was consulted, nor the author thought so. Far better, in these days
of anger, to work out the vein which had already produced *Napoléon
le Petit.* The book was getting into France, unbound, printed on thin
paper, concealed in the lining of clothes, and sometimes in hollow
plaster busts of Napoleon III, and was arousing great enthusiasm. At
Turin Alexandre Dumas read it aloud: "everyone was ravished, transported." There was an English edition—70,000 copies—*Napoleon the
Little,* and one in Spanish, *Napoleon el Pequeño.* A circulation of a
million copies through all the countries of the globe bore witness to
the victory of mind over brute force. When men are afraid to act, those
who at least dare to put their anger into words bring them a sense of
relief.

The good work must go forward, but in verse. "The wretched
creature has been cooked only on one side, so I will turn the grill."
Day and night the furious man with the eloquent tongue could be seen
wandering along the shore and across the dunes in the direction of the
cliffs of Rozel. All through that autumn indignation inspired him to

write much splendid verse. It was at this time that he produced not only *Toulon, Nox, l'Expiation,* but also *La Conscience* and *Première Rencontre du Christ avec le tombeau.* By December 1852, counting the poems written in Paris against the "respectables," he had accumulated sixteen hundred lines. His aim was three thousand. A riot of sarcasm and insult. All exiles, cut off, as they are, from the possibility of action, lose their sense of proportion, a state of affairs which often produces bad politicians, but now and again a great poet, as witness Dante. Like Dante, Hugo, by giving form to his feelings, purged his soul of anger.[3]

What name should he give to a volume of poems about "The Crime?" He hesitated: *Le Chant du Vengeur, Les Vengeresses, Rimes Vengeresses, Châtiments* (without the article), and, finally, *Les Châtiments.* "I am crowding on sail, so as to finish quickly. I must hurry, because I have a feeling that the Bonaparte is beginning to smell a bit high. He won't last long. The Empire took him a step forward, the Montijo marriage will be his doom . . . so full-speed-ahead's the word . . ."[4] The illusions of exile, always false, always true. In the spring of 1853 he wrote *La Force des Choses, Le Manteau impérial.* Then, having collected his material, he settled down to organize it. The plan of the book was an afterthought. It contained a prodigious variety of tone. Strong feeling, the presence of overwhelming indignation, gave it a unity. No doubt, in speaking of it, one might draw comparisons with Aubigné's *Les Tragiques,* with the *Saturae Menippeae,* with Tacitus, and above all with Juvenal, but in hard-hitting, in rhythmic novelty, in beauty of language, in strength of irony, and especially in epic quality, the palm goes to Hugo. Satire undermines and destroys; epic poetry sweeps the reader along. *Les Châtiments* led the imagination from past glories, through present shame, to the immensities of hope. Hetzel regretted the book's violence. Hugo replied: "Niggling strokes have no effect upon the masses. I may, perhaps, terrify the bourgeois, but what do I care so long as I can rouse the people? . . . Dante, Tacitus, Jeremiah, David, Isaiah, were all violent, weren't they? . . . It will be time for us to be moderate when we have won the victory. . . ."[5]

The themes were not many in number: contrast of uncle with nephew, of hero with bandit; the cowardice of those who accepted the favours of the regime; the breaking of the pledged word; the horrors of repression; women and children massacred; announcement of punishments to come; the poet sending the emperor and his gang to the hulks. In short, a dream of vengeance.

Such was the book that gradually reached completion in the winter of 1852–1853, page by page, in the lovely, close-packed writing. For Victor Hugo who, leaning on the rocks, interrogated the ocean, the great gulf and the abysses; for Victor Hugo, who was working better than ever before, and sublimating his hatred by imposing form upon it, time passed quickly. For the others, exile was less stimulating. Madame Victor Hugo, deprived of the high estate of royalty which she had kept in Paris, joylessly accepted the inglorious household tasks, and tried to write a book: *Victor Hugo raconté par un témoin de sa vie.* Since the days of her *lettres de fiancée*, Adèle, so constantly in contact with writers, had made no little progress. Besides, the central figure of her book was there to give her advice. She had available a manuscript by her father,[6] as well as the unpublished *Mémoires* of General Hugo, certain pages of which she copied word for word, and "improved" others. But she found great difficulty in getting started. "What I am writing about my husband goes slowly. I am not a writer. The notes are nothing, but when it is a matter of, as one says, putting them together, my mind becomes greatly confused. . . ."[7]

Before leaving Paris she had written to Léonie d'Aunet: "Pluck up your courage, and work! It is in work that you will find dignity, strength, I would go almost so far as to say happiness . . . Always yours, with unalterable affection. . . ."[8] From Jersey she continued to keep a watch on her friend, and to send her news of "our dear Exile." Charles Hugo and Auguste Vacquerie, both of them blustering talkers, dazzled the French in Jersey, and devoted themselves enthusiastically to photography. Their daguerreotypes of the master perpetuated the fierce look, the convulsed, slightly puffy appearance, which he had at that time. "An impressive, a baleful, physiognomy," says Claudel. "But a great and suffering spirit looks out from it, and, seeing that, I understand suddenly what it is that stares at me from behind the threatening and gloomy expression."[9] The young Dédé, too, glowering with downcast eyes and drawn face, was hiding a suffering spirit. She made music, dreamed of impossible loves, and endured with difficulty the life of a recluse to which she was condemned.

François-Victor had stayed on in Paris, kept there by his passion for a pretty little vaudeville actress, Anaïs Liévenne. This "affair," in which it was the mistress who was ruining herself, the lover being without money, made his parents very uneasy. Janin wrote that François-Victor was compromising a great name. Dumas the younger had taken to lecturing the young man: "the courtesan in love—just a stock figure of romantic drama!"—not a bad remark, that, coming from the author of *La Dame aux Camélias*! Madame Hugo made a sudden descent on France with the intention of snatching her son from the wiles of a designing woman. Her arrival in Paris was an occasion of high festivity for their friends. "Madame Victor Hugo," wrote Janin to Charles de Lacretelle, "gives me the impression of being rather *too* courageous, rather *too* serene; there is a deal of bravado behind her gaiety."[10] The fair Anaïs pursued her lover to Jersey. Victor Hugo had to drive a bargain with her and bribe her to go away. Fortunately, he knew how to talk to women. He painted a picture of exile in the darkest colours, and so successfully frightened her that she left for Warsaw. François-Victor shed tears, then grew consoled, and like everybody at Marine Terrace adopted the trade of author, his subject being a *History of Jersey*. The house was becoming a book-factory.

As for poor Juliette, the proximity of the "Holy Family" made her more unhappy than ever. She could see her poet from her window, but was forbidden to address a word to him when he was with his wife. Not that the idea of doing so would even have entered her head, for she had an "invincible scruple" in the matter. When she saw Madame Victor Hugo walking in her fine silk dress, leaning on her husband's arm, and compared the other's fine clothes with her own "rags," Juliette suffered. Being a native of Brittany, she found Jersey not unpleasant, for she could look once more at the sea of her childhood. But she would have liked not always to be alone with her "scrawls." "Instead of endlessly posing for a daguerreotype, you could sometimes take me for a walk, if you wanted to."[11] She was jealous of the refugees to whom Hugo gave so much of his time. "What brings all these frightful demagogues here today in this lovely weather? . . ."[12] Why did he want to shut himself up in an ill-smelling hovel, when the spring sunlight was flickering, and to flirt "with a lot of bearded, rapacious, moss-grown, hairy, humpbacked and dismal outlaws?" But Hugo had to handle his fellow-exiles tactfully. They were his brothers and his masters, and difficult to get on with, because some were the victims of 1849, others of 1852, and each group was mistrustful of the others. Among them figured—and this was the worst trial of all—the terrible Pierre Leroux, that impenitent sponger and prophet, that bogus genius who had for a long while been poisoning the existence of George Sand, the man whom Hugo called the "sharposopher," of whom Sainte-Beuve said: "when first I knew Leroux, he was a man of distinction, but he has much deteriorated since those days. I have quite lost sight of him or, rather, we have broken with one another. He has become god, whereas I have become a librarian. We have embraced different careers. . . ."[13]

Hugo did his best to maintain unity among the proscribed. He delivered funeral orations; he provided for the poor; he established a general relief fund. On December 2nd, 1852, the French Government authorized the return, without victimization, of all who would give a solemn undertaking "to do nothing against those whom the country has elected." A few of them weakened. "They are leaving," wrote Hugo, "after signing a statement to the effect that they *have been misled by false counsellors*. I forgive, and pity, them . . ."[14] George Sand urged her friend Hetzel to return to France. "Those who think it humiliating to take even the tiniest step might gain no little merit by swallowing their pride out of love for their families and a sense of their personal and individual duty . . ."[15] But the Hugos, one and all, remained irreconcilable. Charles Hugo, having gone secretly to Caen to buy photographic material, was called upon by a police-inspector who searched his luggage. Even in Jersey and among the exiles there were agents of "Monsieur Bonaparte." Wheresoever is disaffection there will the spies be gathered together.

And so the months passed. The poet accumulated material for a volume of *Nouveaux Châtiments*. The family composed, wrote and ate its heart out. In France the new regime was starting in a climate of laughter and extravagance. But Victor Hugo still did not doubt what the end of it all would be.

36

Spirits Descend, and Tables Talk

Alone and pale, I watch descending slowly
Upon my days phantasmal that shroud, eternity.

VICTOR HUGO

A VISIT of ten days in September 1853 served to transform the life of Marine Terrace. Delphine de Girardin was one of Victor Hugo's oldest women friends. He had known her in the days when she was a fair-haired, radiant ornament of Charles Nodier's *salon*. Less of an opportunist than her husband, she had ever since the poet's exile kept up with him a correspondence in which she showed herself as wildly hostile to "Bonaparte le Petit," whom she called "Boustrapa."

Delphine de Girardin to Victor Hugo, April 6th, 1853: Do you remember the lovely Eugénie whom you met at my house, and talked to so fluently in Spanish? She is now Boustrapa's wife . . . a charming woman who deserved a better fate. What really astonishes me is that when she said *yes*, she had already seen your book,[1] secretly, it is true, and with a thousand precautions, still she *had* seen it. In her position, I should certainly have felt somewhat damped. . . .[2]

Hugo was delighted to see her, but found her much changed. She had just lost a dear friend, and was already, in 1853, suffering from the cancer which carried her off two years later. Pale, dressed in black, and attracted by "everything funereal," she had the appearance of one who had yielded to "the charm of death." She told the exiles about the experiments which, at that time, were thrilling Paris and all Europe—spiritualism, table-turning, communicating with the dead. Victor Hugo at first expressed a good deal of scepticism: but he was temperamentally disposed to welcome this type of revelation. All his life long he had been obsessed by vague visions of such intensity that they had almost the quality of hallucinations. What he had attributed to the hero of *Le Dernier Jour d'un Condamné* he had himself experienced. He maintained that all thinkers have, at some time or another, seen "nameless things" in the darkness of the night. He heard nocturnal rappings on the walls of his room. He was convinced that he had been visited by

318

premonitions—for instance, the overwhelming feeling of sadness which had taken hold of him, without any apparent reason, at Oléron, at the very moment of Léopoldine's death, though his conscious mind had known nothing of the catastrophe. His most constant feeling, says Claudel, "was one of *terror*, of a sort of panic contemplation . . ."[3] For him, the supernatural was natural. Furthermore, he believed in the immortality of souls, in their successive migrations, in a continuous ladder leading from the inanimate to God, from matter to the ideal. Why not, therefore, admit the possibility of immaterial beings seeking to communicate? Last of all, his surroundings and the circumstances of his life were favourable to strange experiences: the mental topsy-turvydom of exile; the ever-present shade of Léopoldine; local legends. Marine Terrace was reputed to have a ghost—*The White Lady*.

The first occasion on which Delphine de Girardin dined with the family she asked whether they indulged in table-turning and suggested a séance. Hugo refused to take part. A four-legged table was pressed into service, but remained silent. Delphine said that what they needed was a small occasional table with a central pillar support terminating in a triple-claw foot. Next day she found just what they wanted in a junk-shop at Saint-Helier. For five days there were no results, and those present began to treat the whole thing as a joke. Delphine de Girardin, nettled by their failure, said: "The spirits are not like cab-horses, obedient to the whim of those who hire them. They are free, and come only when they feel inclined." Besides, the master of the house was deliberately absenting himself from the séances. Finally, just to please his guests, Hugo consented to participate. At once, the table made a cracking sound, quivered, and began to move. "Is there anybody present?" asked Madame de Girardin. A single rap: *Yes*. "Who is it?" "*Léopoldine*." Everybody was much upset. Adèle sobbed. Victor Hugo was deeply moved. The whole night passed in addressing questions to the dear, ghostly presence. "Finally," according to Vacquerie, "she said good-bye, and the table went dead."[4] Victor Hugo, "with a fixed look in his eyes, and his mind in a whirl," stared at the invisible, and sought to probe it.

After that, for more than a year, life at Marine Terrace passed in a swarm of spirits. Madame Hugo found no difficulty in believing. "For a long time," she said, "I have held communion with my dead. The table has come to tell me that I was not suffering from illusions."[5] In addition to the members of the family, several from among the political exiles attended the séances: General le Flô, Hennet de Kesler, Teleki, the Hungarian. Many were the spirits who answered the call: Molière, Shakespeare, Anacreon, Dante, Racine, Marat, Charlotte Corday, Latude, Mahomet, Jesus Christ, Plato, Isaiah; animals, too: the dove of the Ark, Balaam's ass; nameless visitors: the Ghost of the

Sepulchre, the White Lady; as well as abstractions: the Novel, the Drama, Criticism, the Idea. Phantoms, these, suited to literary folk. Many spoke in verse and, strangely enough, in verse which might have been written by Victor Hugo. Meanwhile, Marine Terrace became the centre of an increasing number of odd occurrences. The White Lady announced that she would appear in front of the house at three o'clock in the morning. No one dared to go downstairs, but at three o'clock the door-bell rang. Who could have been responsible, if not the ghost? Charles and François-Victor, coming home one evening, saw the drawing-room lit up. The room, as it happened, was empty and contained no means of illumination. Strange and piercing cries were heard. Now it was Hugo himself who questioned the spirits, while Charles and his mother manipulated the table, and Dédé wrote down the answers. That the visitants possessed considerable talents there could be no doubt. They also, on occasion, showed a high degree of intelligence. But talents and intelligence were invariably typical of Victor Hugo. What was the explanation? It seems that Charles must have been a good medium who transmitted the thoughts of his father and of Auguste Vacquerie, both of them poets with a gift of improvisation. The uniformity of style need cause no surprise, because Vacquerie was, all unconsciously, imitating his master. When Hugo was present, André Chénier talked like Hernani, and the Spirit of Criticism gave vent to comments in the Hugo vein. What *is* astonishing is that the poet should have failed to realize that the manifestations came entirely from himself. He never included in the body of his work a single one of the pieces dictated by the spirits. He did not notice that the presence of a young English army officer, Albert Pinson, was sufficient to make Byron talk in English, or that Pinson alone seemed capable of bringing a degree of animation to the melancholy Dédé.

Juliette Drouet, living outside the radius of the contaminated family, escaped infection. She disliked these devil's games. "I have a feeling that there is something dangerous to reason in this sort of playing about, when it is taken seriously . . . and impious should it contain the least element of fraud . . ."[6] She made fun of the whole business. "Go to bed and sleep, and leave me in peace, the more so since I have no accommodating table to provide me with ready-made subjects for books, chapter by chapter. I would have you believe that I am my own Dante, my own Aesop, my own Shakespeare. As to the rest of you, you are pulling up dead fish which the spirits of the other world have tied to your hooks, a trick known in the Mediterranean long before the days of gossiping furniture . . . I rap you out a most affectionate goodnight. . . ."[7]

Victor Hugo took the revelations with deadly seriousness and, quite unaware of the workings of split personality, was deeply thrilled to find that the spirits spoke his own language, and confirmed his own philosophy. The séances at Marine Terrace played a large part in the evolution of his character. He thought it perfectly natural that disembodied souls should have chosen a table in Jersey as a means of communicating. "He genuinely thought that his philosophy had, in this way, received from the fountain-head of the divine a sort of solemn consecration. It was inspired by this belief that he had himself photographed by Vacquerie with eyes half-closed and an ecstatic expression, and wrote, in his royal hand, on the print: 'Victor Hugo listening to God.' "[8]

Such a state of mind might have been highly dangerous had not Hugo been saved in the first place by his powers of artistic creation (from a fixed idea the artist constructs a work of art), and, in the second, by the possession of a prodigious equilibrium. The Dionysiac virility, which might otherwise have imperilled his mental balance, he expended in bouts of triumphant sensuality; in walking (the *mille passus post prandium*); in riding, sea-bathing and nocturnal expeditions. Body and mind, with him, were never at rest. "What there is of excess in him shows in an unusual superfluity of cerebral activity, and never in lack of balance."[9] His metaphysical broodings never entirely narcotized his practical good sense. After a night spent in communing with the spirits, he could take his pen and "describe to Émile Deschanel the damage done among the beans in his garden by his neighbour's geese," or write to a publisher, with the utmost clear-headedness, about the terms of a contract.

But though he still kept a solid head on his shoulders, he believed in his spirits. They had told him that he was a "Wise Man," chosen to guide humanity. He had hoped for a long time that this was so, and under the influence of the "tables" "passed into the state of mind usual in all prophets . . ."[10] The Ghost of the Sepulchre had warned him to proceed slowly in attempting to initiate humanity into the truths of his philosophy, and this counsel from "the beyond" henceforth determined the whole of his plans for publication. The great cosmogonic poems at which he was working must be kept back until a later date.

For two years the séances at Marine Terrace continued. Then in 1855 the sudden madness of one of the participants, Jules Allix, struck panic into the members of the spiritualist group. Madame Hugo, who remembered poor Eugène, became frightened for her family, for her pensive daughter, and even for her husband, who was inclined to talk rather too much about rappings and nightly apparitions. "You have always been inclined that way,"[11] said Adèle pettishly. She blamed him for his nervous irritability. So the spirits were relegated to limbo, and the tables at last fell silent.

37

O Reservoirs of Darkness

There is a seductive charm in pantheism: one
must feel it before one can get the better of it.

VICTOR HUGO

DAYS of work, days of happiness. Reversal of fortune which had
torn the poet from the world had restored him to himself. Never
had Hugo written with such freedom, such power, such ease. No more
sessions of the Academy, no more debates in the Assembly, no more
women wasting his time and sucking him dry. While in Jersey he
composed, without the slightest sense of effort, a second volume of *Les
Contemplations,* in which philosophic pieces rubbed shoulders with
the lovely verses addressed to his daughter ("Pauca Meae") and to
Juliette. Midnight meditations at the dolmen of Faldouet, the voices
of "the sinister white horses of the sea," had served to complete and
confirm that religion of which he believed himself to be the prophet.

Always, with him, accurate *seeing* of the real had alternated with
confused reveries in which scarcely discernible forms floated before
his eyes. His vocabulary was the imaging forth of this confusion. "A
something monstrous which I cannot define . . . A muffled swarm of
hydras, men and beasts . . ." His favourite adjectives—*effaré, fauve,
sinistre, blême, funèbre, difforme, fantastique, livide, hagard, ténébreux, spectral*[1]—gave its peculiar colour to his universe. In an enveloping darkness he caught glimpses of the ghosts of vanished centuries,
of the walls of cities now no more, of the marching columns of armies
dead and gone; and, still farther back in the past, of prehistoric
monsters and primitive forests, of a world still wet from the Flood,
and beyond that of the first stars and the dazzling suns rising out
of chaos, of God.

For a long time he had been meditating on life and death. He believed in the immortality of the soul. Why? Because, if death were
the end of everything, it would matter little what men did in their
lifetime. The man who had been Napoleon III, and the man who
had been Victor Hugo, would vanish, in precisely the same way, into
the Great All. The wicked in this world would make no expiation.

But they are responsible beings. It follows, therefore, that something must remain to assume responsibility. The freedom of the soul implies its immortality. The proof of this lies in dreaming. A man dreams one thing, then another. When he wakes, he recovers his identity. Is not this true of life? All the earthly lives through which we pass are moments of sleep. The I which persists after death is an I anterior to, and exterior to, life. The living man who dies finds himself again as spirit.

These were the thoughts he had been expressing in 1844, but at that time he had been in search of a body of doctrines which should integrate them. Occultism, and in particular the Cabala, into which the strange and simple-minded Alexandre Weill had initiated him, first in Paris, and later in Brussels, may have furnished him with a frame-work on which to build. It has been pointed out that the phraseology of the *Zohar* is that employed by Hugo in his philosophical thinking.[2] At its centre lies the explanation of "Evil." If God is the I of the infinite, if God is all, why should He have created a finite and imper-fect world? In the credo-poem of *Les Contemplations*—"Ce qui dit la bouche d'ombre"—Hugo's reply is the reply of the *Zohar*. God could not create a perfect world, for such a world, not being distinct from God, could not be a world.

Evil is Matter. In all created beings are to be found both God and Matter, God and Evil. But Evil actually engenders Good, because it is imperfection, which, by separating God from His creatures, gives liberty to the latter. For this Evil, willed by God, there can be no such thing as eternal punishment. *"Car le dedans du masque est encore la figure,"* and Satan is still God. An immense ladder composed of living entities leads from the stone to the tree, from animals to men, from angels to God. *"Cette échelle commence aux mondes de mystère,"* in that infernal abyss, at the very bottom of which is visible, *"un affreux soleil noir d'où rayonne la nuit."* It mounts from a bottom of chained demons to a height of winged souls, *"et, dans les profondeurs, s'évanouit en Dieu."* Matter hangs like a dead weight on the ideal, and drags, *"l'esprit vers l'animal, l'ange vers le satyre."* This is the cause of the double nature in sensuality, which is, in man, the mark of the beast, though it also gives birth to ideal love—orgy consecrated.

The essential characteristic of Hugo's religion is a piece of cosmic theatricality. Suddenly what is damned attains to salvation; what previously was humiliated is exalted. Had not his own life known just such a dramatic reversal? As a youth he had been wretched; fame had lifted him above all men. Since his power of work was limitless, everything to him seemed possible. That was the source of his optimism. He *knew* that the usurper would be conquered, that good would triumph, that God would be the victor. *Ego Hugo.*

38

"Les Contemplations"

Contemplation presupposes mental distress already weakened by the passage of time, and a well-balanced mind.

ALAIN

THE position of a political refugee is difficult. He is tolerated by, but not absorbed into the life of, a community not his own. When the political necessities of the country which shelters him demand that there shall be friendly relations with the country of his origin, then the exile is sacrificed. The authorities in Jersey had never much liked the small group of talkative Frenchmen, the poet who moved from wife to mistress, the pontifical reprimands issued from Marine Terrace to Lord Palmerston. Victor Hugo, faithful to his long-felt horror of the death sentence, had protested with justifiable vehemence against the carrying out of the capital sentence in Guernsey where by reason of the executioner's incompetence a hanging had recently deteriorated into a long-drawn-out torture. He had reason on his side, but it is wrong for a foreigner to have reason on his side. He wrote a bitter letter to Lord Palmerston: "You have hanged this man. So be it. I compliment you on the occurrence. Once, many years ago, I dined with you. The memory of that occasion, I imagine, has gone from your mind. I, on the other hand, retain a vivid memory of it. What most struck me about you was the exquisite way in which your cravat was arranged. I was told that you were famous for your tying of knots. I realize now that you are skilled also in tying knots for other people. . . ."[1]

In the House of Commons Sir Robert Peel in 1854 had admonished Hugo with a scant show of respect. "This individual has some sort of personal quarrel with the distinguished personage whom the French people have chosen to be their sovereign . . ." In 1855 the conflict became acute. The Emperor of the French and the Queen of England, as allies against Russia, became good friends. The "dismal war in the Crimea" was concluded by an official visit paid by Napoleon III to Victoria. The arrangements were admirable, the only false note being

324

a letter from Hugo which the Emperor, on landing at Dover, could not but have seen placarded on the walls of the town. *Victor Hugo to Bonaparte:* "What is your object in coming here? Against whom have you got a grudge? Whom have you come to insult? England, in her people, or France, in her exiles? . . . Leave freedom in peace! Leave the exiles in tranquillity. . . ."[2]

When Queen Victoria paid a return visit to the Emperor, Félix Pyat, a French republican refugee living in London, attacked the sovereign in the grossest terms. With heavy humour he made fun of a trip in the course of which, he said, she had "snubbed Canrobert, drunk champagne, and embraced Jérôme." This open letter from Pyat to the queen was published in Jersey by *L'Homme,* the organ of the refugee element. "You have sacrificed many things—your dignity as a queen, your scruples as a woman, your pride of birth, your patriotic sentiments—rank, race, and sex, even modesty, for love of your ally."[3] Charles Ribeyrolles, editor-in-chief of *L'Homme;* Colonel Piancini, business manager of the paper; and a distributor named Thomas were expelled from the island by order of the English Government.

Victor Hugo had not endorsed the "Letter to the Queen," which he thought was in execrable taste, but he championed the victims, and signed a strong protest against their expulsion. On October 27th the Chief Constable of Saint-Clément called on Victor Hugo and, very politely, informed him and his two sons that "by virtue of a decision of the Crown, they were forbidden to reside in the island any longer." A week was allowed them in which to make their arrangements. By November 4th they must leave. "Sir," said Victor Hugo, "you may now withdraw. You can report to your superior, the Lieutenant-Governor, that you have carried out your duty. He, in his turn, can report to his superior, the English Government, which can then report to its superior, Monsieur Bonaparte . . ."[4] On that day he remembered that he had once written an essay on Mirabeau.

The English Liberals held numerous meetings at which they expressed their indignation. All the same, the Hugos and their friends had to leave Jersey for Guernsey. The move was carried out in several groups. Hugo went first, on October 31st, with François Victor, Juliette Drouet and her maid Suzanne, the servant with the heart of gold. Two days later Charles joined his father. The two Adèles, with Auguste Vacquerie (who was not affected by the order of expulsion, and had to organize the whole of the move), arrived later still, with thirty-five pieces of luggage. A heavy trunk hung, for a moment, dangling above a rough sea before being lowered into a boat. It contained, in manuscript, *Les Contemplations, Les Misérables, La Fin du Satan, Les Chansons des Rues et des Bois.* Never had so many immortal works been in more immediate danger of destruction. *Victor Hugo's Note-*

Book, January 15th, 1856: "To the carrier who saw to the loading of the trunkful of manuscripts: 2 francs."

The island of Guernsey is smaller than Jersey, and its cliffs are steeper. "A rock lost in the sea." But Hugo loved this wildness, and Vacquerie, a Norman by birth, painted an agreeable picture of the place:

> We are living in the capital of the island, St. Peter-Port. Imagine, if you can, Caudebec perched on the shoulders of Honfleur. A Gothic church; old, narrow, irregular, fantastic and amusing streets, intercepted by climbing and stumbling flights of steps; the houses piled one on top of the other, so that they all get a glimpse of the sea. A tiny harbour crowded with shipping, with the yard-arms in constant danger of smashing the windows of the quay where these great sea-birds appear to be nesting among the casements . . . The ships pass quite close to us—fishing-smacks, sloops, brigs, three-masters and steamers—and interweave before my eyes almost as at Villequier. The scene is as lively as the Seine, as wide as the Channel. What we have before us is at once a river and a sea—one of the highways of the ocean. . . .[5]

Apart from the Belgian savings, which he did not want to touch, Victor Hugo's resources were at a low ebb. No author's royalties. *Napoléon le Petit* and *Les Châtiments,* fighting books both of them, had been sold under the counter to the profit of no one but the middle-men. After a few days spent at the Hôtel de l'Europe he rented a house at 20 rue d'Hauteville, on the summit of a rock, by the month. He feared that should Monsieur Bonaparte insist, there might be a further *expioulcheune.* The view was magnificent. "From our windows we can see all the islands of the Channel and the harbour at our feet . . . In the evening, when the moon is up, there is a dreamlike quality about it all . . ."[6] Hugo lost no time in getting back to work. A writer is wholly contented so long as he has a table and a generous supply of blank paper. For the others, to whom he preached an even more stringent economy, life was harder.

Then came the miracle of *Les Contemplations.* He had, in his drawers—or, rather, in his trunks—nearly eleven thousand lines of poetry; some dating from long ago, the poems of vanished happiness; others, more recent, the poems of memory or meditation. Hetzel, the "dear fellow-exile," was longing to undertake their publication. Hugo wanted to strike a major blow, to publish the whole collection in two volumes, and so discharge a volley of masterpieces at his enemies. But would the censorship permit the distribution of the work in France? It so happened that the Director of the Sûreté-Générale, on whom lay the duty of administering the censorship, was Pierre-Hector Collet-Meygret, a former member of the staff of *L'Évènement,* who, when the paper had abandoned the cause of the prince-president, had adroitly

trimmed his sails to the prevailing wind. Paul Meurice went straight
to the office of this adversary, whom he knew to be a man of literary
enthusiasms, and an admirer of Victor Hugo. He was warmly received:
"What can I do for you?" Meurice asked whether France would be
closed to the work of the greatest of French writers, who had published
nothing in his native land since 1845. "In principle, no," said Collet-
Meygret, "but I must know the nature of the work." Meurice declared
that it was a question of poetry pure and simple, but added that the
poet would never consent to submit his book to a process of preliminary censorship. Collet-Meygret, with a courage which is extremely
rare under a dictatorship, said that he was prepared to take Meurice's
word: "Will you swear to me that *Les Contemplations* do not contain
a single line of criticism or condemnation of the regime?" "I swear."
"Good. Then you can start printing." The regime, conscious of its
own strength, could afford to wear the velvet glove.

Paul Meurice spent many anxious days while the proofs were being
corrected. Hugo was exigent as only an author can be who knows
the importance of even the smallest details. The proofreader, a man
who knew the Dictionary of the Academy backwards, changed *lys*, the
author's spelling, to *lis*. Hugo thundered: "I have no little contempt
for the Academy's dictionary. I am an augur and, consequently, can
snap my fingers at Isis . . ."[7] He took a personal interest in everything.
The cover must be blue and glossy. There were to be no ornaments;
just a simple rule: "In the announcements on the verso, print GOD very
large and *par Victor Hugo* very small." This exchange of letters dealing
with technical and personal matters is completely free of the grandiloquence to be found in other letters written by Hugo at the same period.
The man of good sense shows through the public character, Maglia
through Olympio. There is nothing at all strange in this split personality. The man who knows himself to be the cynosure of all eyes
sees himself as others imagine him to be, and makes a deliberate effort
to play the part expected of him. There is an actor in every hero.
When the curtain has been rung down, the actor packs up and goes
home.

Meurice was at great pains to prepare the Press. Clean sheets were
sent to friendly papers, bound copies before publication to reliable
critics. *Victor Hugo to Paul Meurice, April 8th, 1856:* "Get the book
into the shops on the same day as the friendly journals appear: *Revue
de Paris*, etc. (are there any others?). It should be on sale everywhere
on that day, and there should be extracts printed in all the papers (the
sympathetic ones, those that want to help, naturally). I want copies
sent, on the *previous* day, to Jules Janin, Eugène Pelletan, Théophile
Gautier, Matharel, Jourdan, Nefftzer, Girardin, Sacy, Édouard Bertin
(and Mademoiselle Louise Bertin), Laurent Pichat, Maxime du Camp,

Louis Ulbach, Madame Louise Colet, Madame d'Aunet, Lamartine, Michelet, Banville, Paul de Saint-Victor, Paulin Limayrac, Paul Foucher, Béranger, Alexandre Dumas, whose name I ought to have put first, and would have done, had I not been writing this in the din made by the paddles of the steam-packet which is on the point of starting. Add Louis Boulanger, Jules Laurens, and others whose names escape me for the moment. I rely on you to remember them for me— I've obviously omitted several, and those, many of the best. I enclose for some of them—for you, first and foremost—several dedicatory pages (six). Please be so good as to have them inserted in the relevant copies. More will follow. . . ."[8]

The success of *Les Contemplations,* unexpected, because no one knew what sort of a welcome France of the Second Empire would give to the absent and rebellious poet, was prodigious. The first edition was exhausted almost on the day of publication. But this success did not extend to the critics. Lamartine remained silent. Sainte-Beuve wrote nothing and when his aloofness was attributed to his fear of displeasing the Tuileries replied that Hugo was no longer a possible subject of analysis for him. If he made reservations, they would be thought offensive by a man of great talent now under a cloud. On the other hand, if he suppressed all serious criticism, he would be reduced to making a mere generous gesture. "That is not a part I wish to play. I am concerned only to be impartial. As to all this talk about the Tuileries and other such matters, I would have you know, sir, what you may perhaps find surprising, that I have never set foot in the place under any regime—no more under this than under another —and that at the moment of writing I can say with truth that I have never so much as set eyes on the head of the State, *nor ever had the honour of exchanging a word with him* . . ."[9] Gustave Planche showed himself as very unforthcoming, and the Bonapartist press was savage.

All lovers of poetry found in the book some of the most beautiful lines ever written in French. Hugo's intention in bringing together these scattered poems had been to build a shapely construction. With a sound concern for symmetry he had divided the collection into two parts: 1831-1843, and 1843-1856, "Autrefois" and "Aujourd'hui." The death of his daughter marked the dividing line, and the book was designed to pass from an "Autrefois," all tenderness and azure, to a black and lugubrious "Aujourd'hui." In order to produce this effect he had had to antedate some of the poems written in Jersey. Nothing would be more false than to think of him in exile as one who was weighed down by an unbroken mood of gloom and tension. He had needed, as a counterbalance to his apocalyptic broodings, moments of sensuality, of happily remembered times of relaxation. He had deliberately pushed back into the first section all such bright intervals, all such glimpses of blue sky through the storm-clouds. Life is not a work of art.

The material success was no less considerable than the artistic. With the twenty thousand francs produced by the royalties, which Hetzel very soon sent him, Victor Hugo on May 10th bought a property, Hauteville House, which was paid for entirely out of *Les Con- templations*. He was anxious to own land in Guernsey. By doing so he would have to pay the "droit de poulade" to the Crown, and could no longer be expelled. Such was the law of the island. He had little hope, just then, that the situation would change rapidly for the better in France, where people seemed to be far more con- cerned with matters of business than with political liberty. Besides, did he really want to leave Guernsey, where he worked well and was in superbly good health?

For Madame Hugo, and especially for her daughter, this sinking of roots was a cause of much sadness. It meant the establishing of exile as a permanent state. Adèle realized that her husband's self- respect made it impossible for him to return to France so long as the Empire lasted; but could he not have found a place of exile a little less wild—some city, perhaps, where they might have built up a pleasant social circle, and, at long last, have found a husband for Dédé? The young girl was living in a condition of silent apathy, and this was seriously worrying her mother. But no matter how great her concern, she could not speak of these things to Hugo, for in conversations of that sort he could always lay his hand on resounding and irrefutable arguments to which the poor woman was incapable of finding an answer. As in the days of the *lettres de la fiancée*, however, she could pluck up the courage necessary to reply in writing:

The child is, at the moment, leading an existence which, though it may go on reasonably well for a time, is bound sooner or later to become impos- sible. I should like you to give some thought to the problem. I keep a con- stant watch upon my daughter. I can see that her periods of deep depression are becoming more frequent, and I am determined to do whatever my con- science may think necessary in order to preserve her in the days to come . . . You have, all three of you,[10] very busy lives; only my daughter has nothing with which to occupy herself. She is powerless and unarmed. To devote myself to her is a duty. A small garden to look after, and tapestry work to do—these are things that cannot, by themselves, provide sufficient mental stimulus for a young woman of twenty-six. . . .[11]

Hugo was irritated. He accused the young captive of being self- centred.

Adèle to Victor Hugo: This morning, at lunch, you said that your daughter loves nobody but herself. I did not want to take you up on that point before the children . . . Adèle has given you her young womanhood without complaining and without any thought of thanks. Is that what you call being self-centred? That Adèle may be temperamentally cold, may seem to suffer from a sort of dryness, is perfectly possible; but have we any right to expect that a girl to whom the joys of love have been refused, in whose nature there is no harmony, who is *incomplete*, should be like others of her sex? Who knows what she has suffered, may still be suffering, as she sees the future turning its back upon her, as she reckons up the tale of years still to come, knowing full well that every tomorrow will be a replica of every today? To this you reply: "What can we do? Can I change my situation?" Exile is a fact about which it is no use arguing, but the place in which it is to be spent might have been chosen with greater care. I admit that, given your celebrity, your mission, your personality, this rocky fastness provides you with an admirable frame. I realize, too, that your family, which without you would be nothing, must sacrifice itself, not only to your honour, but also to the figure you must cut. I am your wife, and what I do is nothing but my strict duty. Exile, in the conditions you have chosen, may weigh heavily upon your sons, but the results where they are concerned have been so good that I am ready to admit that it has been beneficial to both of them. For Adèle, however, it is highly prejudicial, and it is because, in her case, I feel that some improvement is necessary that I devote myself entirely to the poor child's interests. I, as her mother, am concerned with more than mere justice . . . Should one not do for a daughter what one is prepared to do for a mistress?[12]

She was right, right a hundred times over, but Victor Hugo, absorbed in his work, had no imagination to spare for his family. What he would have liked to say to them was: "You don't hear *me* complaining, do you?" In these last months of 1856 he was busy, and happy, occupied as he was in creating a home for himself. It took time. The local workers were leisurely in their methods. "Tortoises building a house for a bird," wrote Hugo to Hetzel.[13] Hauteville House was very large and very English. Its frontage contained fourteen windows, naturally enough of the sash type. The first floor was occupied by the women, the second by the poet and his sons. On the third floor Hugo had had a look-out constructed, a belvedere, which dominated the sea, and whence, on a clear day, the coast of France was visible. This "prodigious cabinet-maker" had built and furnished his dwelling in his own image. One got the impression in its dark corridors that one was moving in an engraving by Rembrandt. Everything about the place seemed to be either a symbol or a memory.

In the dining-room, filled with hangings, old china and Gothic carvings, an old Saxon arm-chair, dating from the times of Dagobert, its arms linked by a chain, stood as an ancestral reminder. It bore the motto *Absentes Adsunt,* with the names of Georges Hugo, a hypothetical forebear, and of Joseph-Léopold-Sigisbert, 1828 (General Hugo). It was, as it were, the accomplishment of a rite, a gesture of respect towards a world of ghosts. A picture-gallery contained the portrait of Léopoldine by Boulanger and numerous drawings by Victor Hugo. There were Latin mottoes all over the place: *Ede, i, ora* (Eat, walk, pray); *Ama et Crede* (Love and Believe); on an ivory skull, *Nox, Mors, Lux.* The furniture, a confusion of the Middle Ages and the Far East, had come partly from their various Paris homes, partly from the junk-shops of Guernsey, through which Juliette, her "little man," and Charles had happily rummaged their way, "tracking down chests," and partly from the labours of Victor Hugo and of the workmen who had carried out his designs. There were still more mottoes, this time in French: *La vie est un exil—Lever à six, coucher à dix, fait vivre l'homme dix fois dix.* His very woodwork was pretentious. In the red drawing-room a vast canopied bed in carved wood, of Venetian origin, presented the spectacle of a monumental mass of drapery, supported by six life-sized Negroes in painted wood. To all these objects must be added rock-crystals, specimens of Murano glass, gold-embroidered screens, mottoes and symbols. A grandiose and tawdry world, as romantic as Hugo himself had been but was no longer; more Oriental than the Orient had ever been; magnificent, absurd, in which the smallest object bore the stamp of the master.

The look-out, at the highest point of the house and the island, where he did his work, had walls and ceiling of plate glass. This transparent cell resembled a greenhouse or a photographer's studio. It "gave upon the sky, and on immensity." Hugo wrote, standing, at a small, flat-topped desk, in front of a mirror on which he, himself, had painted a flower with strange petals. He slept in one of the two small attics adjacent to his workroom, on a narrow bed with a cylinder of wood which served as a bolster. A serving-maid occupied the room next door, and Booz was not always sleeping. Fanny, Julia, Constance, the fair Eva, Marianne, Rosalie, Coelina ... his intimate diaries are filled with notes, in Spanish and in Latin, relating to these young women: *"Visto y tomado Julia."*[14]

On occasion lines came to him in his sleep. Half awake, he jotted them down, and next morning garnered the nocturnal crop. He rose at dawn, roused by the gunshot from the nearby fort; worked until eleven, in the full blaze of the sun, poured icy water over himself, and rubbed his body with a horsehair glove. The passers-by, who knew the strange habits of the great man, watched the unusual spectacle. At noon the family lunched. Charles and his father indulged in discussion, while

Madame Hugo sat wondering at the genius of "her men." Then they separated, each going about his business. *Madame Hugo to Jules Janin:* "My husband is out walking; Toto is dressing—he is the townsman; Adèle is playing the piano or engaged in her English studies; Charles is lying down on an uncomfortable leather sofa, lost in a pipe-dream. As for me, I embrace these great children of mine, and do my best to see that the dinner shall be not too bad . . . Auguste has shut himself in his room to get some work done."[15] For during this period of exile Auguste Vacquerie lived with the Hugos, in the aura of the only woman he had ever loved, Madame Victor Hugo (his elder by thirteen years) having inspired in him, since boyhood, a platonic and hopeless passion, which took the form of extravagant devotion.

The *mille passus* were still reserved for Juliette. A charming little villa had been found for her, La Fallue, so close to Hauteville House that she could watch her demigod at his toilet on the terrace. Each morning, she watched for his rising, that she might feast her eyes upon that dearly loved body. From afar off Hugo displayed the morning's "scrawl" which he had just found at his door, along with two hard-boiled eggs, and kissed the letter. Then he stripped off his red night-dress, took his shower-bath, and disappeared into the belvedere to work. After luncheon he went to fetch Juliette. More often than not she was told to walk beside him in silence, and this she resented: "Try not to be too much invaded by inspiration, that I may make some slight contact with you, and talk as we pursue our way . . ."[16] There was so much she had to say to him! Upbraidings about the shocking way in which he behaved with the servant-girls; reproachful comments on her exclusion from Hauteville House, which made her suspect in the eyes of the people of Guernsey; requests for drawings with which to adorn the walls of La Fallue; "I, too, must have something of my very own to hang up, castles, moonlit scenes, blazing sunlight, and effects of mist." She was "filled full with wonders," and "happy to the very marrow" of her bones. Victor, having taken her for a nocturnal stroll, showed her the crescent moon and the evening star. "There is the ship of souls with its pinnace," he said.

She had one other consolation. Charles and François-Victor (after May 1859) took to paying her visits. They treated her with affection and deference, happy to find good cheer in her house, some new faces, and their father in a happier mood than at home. There was some-thing sinister about Hauteville House. Their mother was miserable. With all this gilt about him, all these fine fabrics and objects of carved wood, he would, she thought, not easily be uprooted. "Here we are once more, fixed firmly to the walls . . . we are spending a great deal of money," wrote Madame Hugo, "in addition to which my husband loves this island. He bathes endlessly in the sea . . . He has recovered his youth, and is magnificent. . . ."[17]

She superintended the cook Olive, who produced as many tragedies as dishes. She copied what Charles wrote. "I have abandoned *my own writing*, and am nothing now but a shadowy understudy—less than that, for I am growing stupid. Am I tumbling still lower? It would not much matter if I were, for I have not far to fall. The best thing I can do is to be the servant of the minds about me . . ."[18] When she spoke of taking her daughter for a short trip to Paris or London, Madame Hugo was sharply snubbed. "You are tired of exile!" said the Great Outlaw contemptuously. "Rid your head of that wicked thought." She replied to her husband (in writing): "I have shared your days of happiness and triumph. I am proud and happy to share your trials . . ."[19] Poor Adèle! she was sincere and good; she had made a determined effort to become a better housewife; she drew on her "personal allowance" to keep things going; she wanted to make her children happy, and to give hospitality in Guernsey to her "dear little sister," Julie Foucher, who after being educated at Saint-Denis, in the school of the Legion of Honour, had stayed on as a mistress. But all Hugo gave his wife was 450 francs a month and, in spite of all her care, she ran into debt. *Adèle Hugo to Julie Foucher:* "I dare not ask him [to increase my allowance]. I brought him no money, and he has heavy responsibilities . . . Besides, dear friend, I have always treated such matters with the most extreme delicacy . . . I am timid, and this timidity is my form of coquetry . . ."[20] Ah! how distant now were the days when she had been a proud young girl with Spanish eyes, in whose presence the "sublime child" had trembled.

39

"La Légende des Siècles"

THE success of *Les Contemplations* revived many Paris friendships. Praise flowed into Guernsey. Michelet, Dumas, Louise Colet, Père Enfantin and George Sand, one and all gave expression to the degree of their enchantment. Louis Boulanger, formerly the family's Painter in Ordinary, wrote a letter which combined a statement of gratitude with the announcement of his engagement, at fifty years of age, to a young woman. Hugo approved. It pleased him to know that this companion of his best years was still capable of love. "I see us again as we were in those radiant days of *Les Orientales*, both of us young, both of us haunters of the plain of Vaugirard, both gazers on the setting sun behind the dome of the Invalides, two brothers—you the dazzling painter of Mazeppa, I the dreamer destined for the unknown and the infinite . . ."[1] He asked George Sand to visit him in his "hovel," which was not yet furnished, and went by the name of Liberty House. "The honest Guernsey workers, believing me to be rich, think it only fair to exploit this *great French gentleman*, and to keep the work and the pleasure going as long as possible. Sooner or later, however, I imagine that the house really will be finished, and hope that perhaps then the fancy may take you to see it for yourself in time and space, and to sanctify a tiny corner of it with your presence and the memory of your coming . . ."[2] Later Louise Bertin rose again from among silent memories and the charming past became real once more: "Les Roches, flowers, music, your father, our children and our youth. . . ."[3]

Hetzel, after the appearance of *Les Contemplations*, had been begging Hugo to hold back for a while the philosophic poems, "Dieu" and "La Fin de Satan." Hugo's enemies had been living in expectation of an Apocalypse which would send back this Johnny-head-in-air to Patmos. Hetzel, on the other hand, was much taken with the idea of a series of *Brief Epics,* historical frescoes in words, covering a large space of time, from the thirteenth to the nineteenth centuries. That Hugo's talent was epic in its onward surge, its more than life-size quality, its sublimity, could not be denied. He already had, tucked away in his files, "Aymerillot," "Le Mariage de Roland," and several other pieces. The immediate necessity was to complete and organize these poems, to make

334

of them a whole. "What, precisely, shall this whole be? Shall I try to express the meaning of humanity in a sort of cyclical work; to paint it, successively and simultaneously, under all its aspects, history, fable, philosophy, religion, the whole brought together into a single, immense movement of ascension towards the light; to show, as in a mirror, here dark, there bright—which the interruptions caused by earthly tasks would probably break before it had grown to the dimensions dreamed of by the author—that great figure, one and multiple, gloomy and radiant, the plaything of destiny, yet the product of the divine, which goes by the name of Man? That was the thought, the ambition—if the word be preferable—from which *La Légende des Siècles* emerged . . ."[4] for such was the excellent title decided upon after the rejection of many alternatives: *La Légende Humaine—La Légende de l'Humanité.* But this gigantic piece of historical painting did not suffice to exhaust the torrential activity of the years 1856-59. Firmly planted on his Quadriga, he drove a team of differing horses: *La Légende, Les Chansons des Rues et des Bois, Torquemada* (a play) and the decoration of his gigantic dwelling.

The first *Légende des Siècles* was written in its entirety between the years 1857 and 1859. Consequently, it shows a massive unity of inspiration. It develops along a linear pattern of history, but so vast is Hugo's imagination that he can take in, at a single glance, the "wall of the centuries." His vision is that of a demiurge existing outside time and space. A confused crowd of accumulated images mounts and mounts in him until the moment comes when he feels that he himself has been absorbed into each moment of the human legend. He becomes, at one and the same time, all created things, and God. Hetzel had hoped for *brief epics,* narrative purged of metaphysics; what he got was "Booz endormi," was "La Conscience," was "La Rose de l'Infante," was "Les Pauvres Gens." But the "great, mysterious thread on which the book is strung" is the ascension of Man, the emergence of Spirit from Matter. The keypiece is "Le Satyre," an astonishing challenge flung in the faces of the outworn gods of Olympus by an enigmatic, lewd, monstrous, inspired, heroic Faun, who is both Hugo himself and an incarnation of Humanity, stuffed full of faults, desires, weaknesses, yet greater than Jupiter, and capable of one day taming the forces of nature.

La Légende des Siècles was so packed with tremendous beauties that it could not but convince even the most hostile members of the literary world of the poet's greatness. "Victor Hugo alone is capable of speech: by comparison with him other men merely stammer," said Jules Renard. "He is a mountain, a sea, what you will, but he is not to be measured by the standard of other men." And Flaubert: "Until that moment, as a result of thoughtlessness and, perhaps, in order to increase his production, it sometimes happened that he would substitute for himself in the eyes of the public a tremendously solemn, boring and grandiloquent *concierge*, who was so extraordinarily like him that everyone was taken in . . . This 'double,' after the *coup d'état*, was compelled to remain in Paris in pursuance of his duties, and Victor Hugo had, thereafter, to work alone. The result of this separation was *La Légende des Siècles*. . . ."[5]

Around the epic forge life continued with the monotony of a small provincial town. Each Monday Charles Ribeyrolles came to dinner; each Tuesday Hennet de Kesler, the hunchback. On Wednesday the men went to dine with Juliette Drouet; Thursday, tea with Madame Duverdier; Friday, tea with Mademoiselle Allix; Saturday, "cider, enthusiasm and a display of fine dresses" in Madame Victor Hugo's reception rooms.[6] Sunday at Hauteville House was sepulchral. It was Constance's day out (Olive, the warrior's widow, had surrendered her apron); Chougna, Auguste Vacquerie's bitch, would be entertaining a lover; the hens clucked; Adèle would be busy with her crewel work or in writing to her sister Julie Chenay, schoolgirlish letters filled with the most unexpected expressions—"la Mademoiselle" for "La Grande Mademoiselle"; *Requiem in pace* for *Requiescat in pace; les Sixti* for the *soixante* great families of Guernsey. Madame Victor Hugo, though now in her fifties, had changed scarcely at all from the Adèle Foucher of the old days, and it was still a great event for her when Uncle Asseline, so long accustomed to the Faubourg Saint-Germain, abandoned the Left Bank and went to live in the Ternes neighbourhood. "If ever I go back, I shall be completely at a loss. I shan't know a thing about Paris. Who would ever have believed that I should have to go and see my uncle in les Ternes? . . ."[7]

Plump Charles was working away at a fantastic tale about the Universal Spirit, the heroine of which was a drop of water. A dangerous subject. He was by this time over thirty, a man with his grandfather's full-blooded temperament, and sexual exigencies which reached alarming proportions. He was for ever complaining of loneliness, lack of money, and the women of Guernsey. François-Victor had undertaken to translate the whole of Shakespeare, and was acquitting himself honourably of this impossible task. He was, however, growing thoroughly sick of striding about a small island, the prisoner of an empty purse. "It's a hard life, this constant keeping company with My Lord Spleen and My Lady Nostalgia. . . . Deary, deary me, what a set of old fossils we are becoming! Heroism is turning us into a lot of provincials. Here's winter on us, season of mists—six months of imprisonment in a bucket of water . . ." It was not so bad for *Him*: after all, *He* had a brain chock-full of masterpieces, and went out in all weathers, bareheaded, with his cloak and stick. But for his children things were very different, for they had within their skulls nothing but their brains, their desires and their boredom. In 1856 Dédé had had a nervous breakdown, and the doctor had forbidden her even to play the piano. As to Vacquerie, he talked of going back to France, and the master of the house, in order to keep him with them, offered to cancel the sum of fifty francs a month paid by their friend for board and lodging.

Hugo loved the members of his family, but he loved them "for their good," which is a bad way of loving. It bred in them a sense of oppression. Eighteen fifty-eight was the year of revolt. On January 16th the two Adèles returned to Paris with leave of absence for two months, which grew into four. In her efforts to obtain this concession, and the necessary money for their trip, Madame Hugo had taken a strong stand —not unnaturally, in writing: "I love you, my dear friend, and I belong to you. I do not wish to cause you pain. Let us talk the whole thing over quietly, and between ourselves. You chose Jersey as your place of residence. I went there with you. When Jersey became impossible, you changed to Guernsey, without so much as asking me *'could you be happy living there?'* I said nothing, but followed where you led. By buying your house you indicated that Guernsey was to be your permanent home. In the matter of that purchase *I* was never consulted. I settled down in the house with you. I submitted myself to your will, but I cannot be a complete slave . . ."[8] This letter Victor Hugo, writing in his diary, summed up in a single Alexandrine: "Ta maison est à toi. On t'y laissera seul." Madame Hugo had made a little money by selling to Hetzel her book-to-be and some papers. She was fully determined to use the proceeds in taking her poor Dédé travelling, for the girl was rapidly sinking into a state of despair. *Victor Hugo's Diary, January 16th, 1858:* "My wife and daughter set off this morning, at twenty past nine, for Paris. They are going by Southampton and Le Havre. Melancholy . . ."[9] Charles, too, begged for mercy. *Adèle to Victor Hugo:* "Dear friend: two days ago, Charles said to me: 'I am devoted to Papa: there is nothing I dread more than grieving him, but I do wish he could understand that I need a change. I have worked all winter in the hope of being able to give myself a treat. I have some money, and can pay my own expenses, but I shall not enjoy myself unless I feel that what is a pleasure for me will also be one for my father. . . .' "[10]

There were times when even Juliette ventured to complain. Hugo had forbidden her to buy a new hat for Easter Sunday, an occasion on which, according to tradition, all the Guernsey women sported "head-coverings expressive of triumph and aggressiveness." She accused him of parsimony because he refused to have her red Birthday Book rebound, though it was falling to pieces after a quarter of a century of use. Then she humbly begged his pardon for advancing these extravagant requests. "Another time, I will try not to make unreasonable demands. I promise to abide by your decision, even in matters which concern myself alone, such as the binding of my dear and precious manuscript."[11] Because his own life was fiery and prolific, Hugo expected others to draw warmth from its radiating heat.

The two Adèles returned in May, and only just in time, because, in June Hugo, for the first time in his life, fell seriously ill. As the result of a carbuncle his life was in danger. *Charles Hugo to Hetzel, July 22nd, 1858:* "For the last three weeks my father has been suffering severely from a carbuncle which forced him to take to his bed for ten days, and prevented him from writing to you. He was in great pain and has only recently taken a turn for the better. The carbuncle was complicated by the forming of two abscesses. He has had to have them lanced, and as a result of this operation the pressure has been diminished. The bad place is so enormous, and so awkwardly situated—in the very middle of his back—that it made, and still makes, all movement impossible for him . . ."[12] The poet had a great hole in his back, and was compelled to lie on his stomach. Burning with fever, he described his condition in verse: "J'entends, la nuit, mon pouls battre dans mes oreilles." Poor Juliette, who, by reason of the moral code obtaining at Hauteville House, could not go to see him, spent three hideous weeks. She sent him all she could: eggs, "scrawls," lint, flowers, grapes, her Suzanne, and the last three strawberries from her garden. "Poor darling, how I wish that I could be a servant in your house at this moment so as to be able to render you all the little services of which you stand in need, without obtruding myself on any member of your family . . ."[13] "Oh, why cannot your saintly wife see deep into my conscience and my heart? Instead of being hurt by my initiative, she would be touched by it, and grateful . . ."[14] At last he appeared upon the balcony, and she could let her eyes rest upon him. "Poor sweet darling; I can see, even from a distance, how greatly you have suffered! Your beautiful and noble face looked thin to me, and so pale that I feared you were feeling ill there, on your balcony! I only hope that this appearance of yours, and the short cruise you made in your sailing-boat, do not mean that you have been over-tiring yourself, my poor little convalescent. . . ."[15]

For the rest of the year 1858 a veil of sadness and lassitude continued to envelope the exiles. The time was too long, their cares too squalid. *François-Victor Hugo to a friend:* "You cannot imagine the present state of gloom at Hauteville House . . . I am very much afraid that our small, so closely knit, group may go to pieces this time. However that may be we are now in the dark period of exile, and I cannot see the end of the tunnel . . ." Vacquerie could no longer stand the strain and departed for Villequier, leaving his cat, Mouche, stranded. *Victor Hugo to Louise Bertin:* "I should have liked my family to go back to France, for I feel that I have made too great a demand upon their sense of duty and sacrifice. But they would not hear of it. My children have chosen to stay with me, as I have chosen to stay with liberty. Charlot, Toto, Dédé have grown into great and proud spirits. They accept solitude and exile with a serenity that is at once gay and austere. . . ."[16]

That sentence is the finishing touch from the brush of a great artist: neither Charlot, nor Toto, nor Dédé had quite the degree of resigned serenity attributed to them by their father. Certainly they did not wish to abandon him completely, but they did insist on having periods of relaxation, and these became increasingly longer in duration. On May 9th, 1859, Madame Hugo and her daughter left for England, accompanied by Charles, and later joined by François-Victor. In London, Adèle the second, who was rapidly turning into an old maid of uncertain health, could at last live a normal social life, go to theatres, dance, visit the galleries, and, no doubt, renew acquaintance with Lieutenant Pinson of the Jersey days, whom she had not forgotten. Meanwhile, in Guernsey, Juliette was doing her utmost to bring together the father and his two sons, who now dined at her table. Charlot and Toto treated their "good friend, Madame Drouet," with sympathy, and admired her Hugo relics. She, too, had her moments of discouragement, when tired of all her lover's infidelities, she threatened to take flight back to Brittany.

But in the eyes of Victor Hugo, lovers' complaints—mere supplementary dishes on the menu of pleasure—and family quarrels were trivial matters, destined to pass "like drifting shadows and blowing winds." He had never been a man to entertain sentimental regrets, or to analyse the movements of the heart. He was the one "who strides ahead," who is for ever moving on. What, for the moment, counted for him was *La Légende des Siècles* which, published in Paris, extorted expressions of admiration even from unwilling lips. "What a man old Hugo is!" exclaimed Flaubert to Ernest Feydeau, "and, my God! what a poet! I have just swallowed the two volumes at a gulp! You're not here! Bouilhet's not here! There is no intelligent audience to which I can bawl aloud three thousand lines of poetry which have not their equal anywhere . . . Old Hugo has swept the board! . . . What a man!"[17] What mattered to him was to keep up an unweakening resistance. In 1859 the Empire offered an amnesty. Some of the exiles accepted the gesture, but not Hugo. *August 18th, 1859:* "Faithful to that undertaking into which I entered with my conscience, I shall, to the end, remain with liberty in exile. When liberty returns to France, I, too, will return . . ."[18] This attitude exasperated those writers who, like Sainte-Beuve and Mérimée, had become Senators of the Empire. It secretly enchanted the people of France. Finally, what, in the last analysis, counted with him was the search, of which he never tired, for the secrets of a better world. That we are all of us poor, tormented, jealous, unhappy creatures, he knew. He had his own example, and that of those close to him, to teach him that truth: but his knowledge went further; he knew how those same poor creatures, in their moments of lyric ecstasy, can glimpse in a vision both sublime and vague the dawn which already shows bright on the horizon. "Solitude," he wrote, "produces to some extent a divine bewilderment. It is the smoke of the burning bush." This great voice crying in the wilderness kept alive in France a respect for liberty and, also, at a time when the literature of the Second Empire was becoming frivolous and sophisticated, a love of great ideas and great images. Of that the French were well aware and, for them, it was at this moment of his career that he took his place in the legend of the centuries.

PART IX

The Fruits of Exile

40

"And If But One Remain . . ."

Power and wealth are often a stumbling-block
. . . When all is taken away, all is given in return.

VICTOR HUGO

THERE is, in *Les Misérables*, a fine passage on the "magnificent egoists of the infinite" who, distracted from the concerns of their fellow-men by consideration of the cosmos, cannot understand why one should brood over human suffering when there is the blue of heaven for the eye to see. "They compose," says Hugo, "a family of spirits at once trivial and great. Horace was one of them: so was Goethe . . ."[1] Though he did not know it, Hugo himself was sometimes of the number. Not that he hadn't, as much as and more than most, brooded upon the problem of human suffering. But his compassion was diffused rather than brotherly, and in his case charity did not begin at home. Absorbed during the ten years from 1860 to 1870 in works of very great stature, poems, epics, novels, essays and *Les Misérables*, which contains a little of everything, he had found in work a curious happiness which was born of a sense of completeness, of power, of isolation. He felt that "remoteness is an excellent thing for the fame, and the sounding voice, of a living man: Voltaire at Ferney, Hugo in Jersey—two solitudes which hold something of the same significance . . ."[2] Voltaire had defended Calas; Hugo tried, though in vain, to save John Brown. He no longer regretted Paris. "Paris? I have no need of Paris. Paris is the rue de Rivoli, and I detest the rue de Rivoli." His very face and bearing were no longer those of a man who had lived in great cities. Ever since he had been afflicted with an obstinate sore throat, which he had thought to be due to tuberculosis of the larynx, he had let his beard grow, and it was white. To some extent it had the effect of masking and softening the convulsed features of the author of *Les Châtiments*. It was at this time that he assumed that bushiness of aspect which gave him the appearance of a universal grandfather, which is how history sees him. The soft hat, the turned-down collar, the blouse—all these things fitted into the picture of an elderly workman. He felt free, powerful and inspired.

But he did not see that, while he was bursting into flower, the other members of his little circle were dying from lack of air to breathe. Madame Hugo more and more kept herself at a distance from Guernsey. Because she was not happy she stood in need of distraction. In France and in England she enjoyed representing by proxy her husband's glory. A husband's exile gives to his wife, by anticipation, a foretaste of the pleasures of widowhood. In Paris she found again her dear, her so truly devoted, Auguste Vacquerie. She visited *her* family (Fouchers and Asselines), and sometimes secretly climbed Sainte-Beuve's stairs in the rue Montparnasse. He was nearly an old man now, and his bladder was causing him acute suffering. But there was still about him a feline charm; he still had the gift of clever talk, "in which there was elegance and epigram, a gentle purring, and the sharp claw under the velvet pad." His conversation was wholly feminine—a restful change after that of the dominating male of Guernsey. In 1861 Adèle was absent from Hauteville House from March to December; in 1862 and 1863, for much the same length of time. She tried, so far as she could, to take her children with her. She defended them timidly against the reproaches of the "Solitary" who was embittered by these abandonments, and could not understand, so full and rich was his own life, that the lives of others might be poor and empty.

Madame Hugo to Victor Hugo: It is essential, just now, for me to go to Paris, by reason of a sacred trust, my sister . . .[3] Nor am I displeased, since the occasion arises, to give Adèle a change of air at this, the gloomiest season of the year. I see no reason why this determination of mind should wound you. My devotion to you remains as complete as ever.[4] You are Adèle's father and ought to feel, as I do, how necessary it is to bring a little novelty into her life. In the well-nigh cloistral conditions of our present existence she is forced in upon herself. She thinks a great deal, and her ideas—often erroneous, since nothing flows in from the outside to modify them—become like burning lava. I know that travel does not change anybody's essential nature, but it does help to banish, for a time, what I may call her "old maid's habits." . . .

Truth to tell, even the mother no longer really understood her daughter. Adèle, cranky and sullen, was in a constant state of depression, endlessly brooding. Music alone could loosen her moods of black melancholy. *Victor Hugo's Diary, December 1859:* "Adèle played me a piece of her own composition, which is charming . . ." *April 1861:* "I have picked up a piano for Adèle to work on: 114 francs . . ."[5] Ever since her meeting with Lieutenant Pinson in Jersey, in the days of the table-turning séances, she had got it firmly fixed in her mind that she would marry the young Englishman. Numerous suitors had made a bid for her hand, but she had turned them all down. In December 1861 she told her father that she considered herself to be engaged. Victor Hugo, a European in theory, but a Frenchman and a fierce nationalist by temperament, hated the idea of a foreign marriage, and was at first extremely put out by the turn of events. His wife made him realize how dangerous it would be to reduce Adèle to a state of despair. At Christmas, 1861, Albert Pinson was invited to Hauteville House. What happened then between the young couple we cannot say. Maybe his foreignness frightened her. All we know for certain is that they parted. She became plunged in gloom as a result of the incident, and there can be little doubt that she intended to set about reconquering his affections, since her brothers surprised her in the act of doing some surreptitious packing.

On June 18th, 1863, she took advantage of her mother's absence to make the passage to England. From Southampton she wrote to her dumbfounded father, explaining that she was on the point of taking ship for Malta. She was thirty-three years of age, and mistress of her own movements. Madame Hugo was just then enjoying herself in Paris. She was carrying on a campaign against the Emperor's candidature—suggested by certain courtiers—for election to the Académie Française, and had announced, with imprudent courage, that "her husband would register his vote in favour of Louis Napoleon both for bringing him into the Academy and for sending him to the hulks." She was seeing a great deal of old Émile Deschamps, who was as pink, chubby and gallant as ever.

My heart [he wrote] is still in those blessed days when I applauded with enthusiasm the earliest poems of our great Victor, and when we, Aglaé and I,[6] gave an immediate and affectionate welcome to the young and divine companion of his glory. Until the day when God took my poor Aglaé to Himself, we never ceased from talking about you all, remembering each tiny detail of our happy intimacy . . . I was in the Vosges, seeking relief in the waters at Contrexéville, when Antoni received news of the musical album then in course of preparation by your dear and charming Adèle, who had been so good as to think of me as a possible provider of some words for one of the songs—"Chant du Laboureur." On my return I sat down to work, and in the last days of last month Antoni addressed my (I won't say poetic) offering to Guernsey. . . .[7]

No acknowledgment of the verses had been sent, and Émile Deschamps was afraid that they might have been lost. He suggested sending another copy to the musical young lady. Madame Hugo wore, for the first time on New Year's Day, a white muslin dress which, she said, made her look quite like a "young girl." Charles was with his mother, and arranged informal parties. They made a pilgrimage to the Place Royale to see once again the arcades and tall windows of their former home.

Meanwhile, in Guernsey, Victor Hugo was piling masterpiece on masterpiece. He finished Hauteville House, with the help of the cabinetmaker Mauger (whom he got to engrave on two columns the words *Laetitia—Tristitia*, and on the door leading to his suite of private rooms, *Perge—Surge*); continued to take an interest in the servant-girls who slept in the room next his own ("gave 20 francs to Coelina as a reward for not coughing last night"); furnished a new house for Juliette, Hauteville Féerie; and had very little time for thinking about family matters. Nevertheless, Adèle's flight made him feel uneasy:

Victor Hugo to Madame Hugo, June 23rd, 1863: You ought, by this time, to have received a letter from Victor, and probably one from Adèle, too? It seems impossible to me that she should not have written. I even think it likely that she will tell you more about this business than she has told me, and that, almost certainly, she will have sent you her address. If that is so, it seems probable that you will go and fetch her, and bring her back with you. What I can't agree to is that she should try to marry this man against his will. I am afraid that there may be some latent *impossibility* which will come to light. How, otherwise, can Adèle's extraordinary conduct be explained, since so far as we are concerned, everything had been agreed upon, and our consent given? How can Adèle so degrade herself as to run after him? . . . It is a matter of urgent necessity that we should have definite news . . . Perhaps Monsieur Pinson already has an establishment? . . . a mistress? . . . children?—who knows? Write to me and tell me what you know. Inform me of what, if anything, Adèle has written to you. . . .[8]

Madame Hugo returned to Guernsey on July 2nd, and left again for Paris on August 15th. A letter from Adèle, posted from New York on July 14th, reached Hauteville House after her departure. A little later, the fugitive announced to her family that she was at Halifax, Nova Scotia, where Pinson was now in garrison, and that their marriage had taken place.

Madame Hugo to Victor Hugo: Adèle was a free agent; she has offended against no human law by marrying the man she loves. Perhaps she might have shown a little more confidence in us, but if we can reproach her for not doing so has she not a great deal with which to reproach *us*? Has not her life been sacrificed to the rigorous demands of politics? Were not those rigours made worse than they need have been by your choice of a place of exile? While you were fulfilling all your obligations, were we doing anything to fulfil our parental duties to our child? Has not her existence been wretched in the extreme? . . .[9]

The father gave way and, in order to explain his daughter's disappearance, had inserted in the newspapers, during the month of October, an announcement to the effect that a marriage had taken place between Mademoiselle Hugo and Lieutenant Pinson, after which the young couple had left for Canada.

Victor Hugo to Hetzel, October 10th, 1863: You will have seen from the papers why my answer to your letter was delayed. My daughter has become an Englishwoman. Such are the blows of exile! Her husband is a veteran of the Crimea, a young English officer, aristocratic, a stickler for propriety, "gentilhomme," and a gentleman. Our family will now be one in which the father-in-law (old) stands for the future, the son-in-law (young) for the past. This young representative of a bygone age took my daughter's fancy, and the choice was hers. True to my duty as a father, in such a case, I gave her my support.

The young people are now on their way to Halifax. Between my son-in-law and me there lies the temperamental distance which separates the French and the English, and the physical distance which lies between Europe and America. But there is such a thing as a right to happiness. My daughter has claimed it, and I cannot blame her. . . .[10]

Victor Hugo to Émile Deschamps, October 16th, 1863: You know, I suppose, that my daughter has turned English?—so much for exile! . . .[11]

Alas! it was all no more than the mirage of a clouded mind. Pinson had never had the slightest intention of marrying Adèle. When the wretched girl, without announcing her plans, went to Canada to join him, she found that he was already married and, in fact, a father. François-Victor, the English scholar of the family, conducted a searching inquiry. From his sister's landlady he learned that Adèle had led "a cloistered existence, speaking little, and receiving no visitors." There were witnesses to prove that she went every day to the barracks where she waited until he came out. She stared at him, and then followed him home without a word. When she was forced to admit that she was not married, she added that Pinson had "betrayed, dishonoured and abandoned her."

Victor Hugo to Madame Hugo, December 1st, 1863: The man is a ruffian, the lowest of the low! He has set the coping-stone upon a *ten years' lie* by taking a cold and arrogant farewell. A nasty and a stupid fellow. Adèle deserves our congratulations—for it is the greatest good luck imaginable that she has not married *that* . . . I can only hope that she will tear herself free from this fancy, this horrible dream, this nightmare, which was never love at all, but only madness. Work upon her, my dear friend, for yours is a great heart and a noble spirit. That she may quickly return to us is now my only wish. We shall say that the marriage was never registered before the French Consul, that it is null and void in France and, since the man was not acceptable to us, has been cancelled. Victor and I have already set the ball rolling here. In six months' time Adèle will be back at Hauteville. The only difference will be that she will go by the name of *Madame* Adèle. She is of a suitable age to be "belady'd," and we are answerable to nobody . . . She has only to get quit of that scamp, and return to us. Thereafter, I will take charge. She will forget, and she will get well. The poor child has never yet been happy; it is high time that she started. I will give some parties for her at Hauteville House, to which I will invite the most intelligent people I can lay my hands on. *I will dedicate books to Adèle.* I will make of her the crown of my old age. I will glorify her exile. I will make all good. If a fool has the power to dishonour, Victor Hugo will have the power to shed splendour! Later, when she is cured and cheerful, we will find a decent, honourable husband for her. Let us dismiss the memory of this type of the licentious soldiery. . . .[12]

The "licentious soldier," called upon to justify his conduct, replied that he had "never fallen short of the standards of honour, had never encouraged any hopes in Mademoiselle Hugo, had never asked for her hand in marriage," and that, in Halifax, he had refused to see her. He had twice asked her, through a third person, to go away. That she should have no illusions, he had twice shown himself under the windows of the recluse driving in a carriage with Mrs. Pinson. But Adèle refused to leave Halifax. In the long run she had come to believe in her imaginary nuptials, and, night and day, awaited the coming of the bridegroom.

Since the girl had taken nothing with her but her jewels, Hugo decided to make her a small allowance—one hundred and fifty francs a month. For some years Adèle punctually acknowledged receipt of this sum. She did not wish her relatives to look for her, spent scarcely any-thing, and found her way of life "tranquil and satisfactory," her par-ticular variant of insanity being that of illusory fulfilment. On three separate occasions she announced her imminent return, then adjourned it, *sine die.* For the members of her family she became a remote and frightening phantom, dwelling in a mysterious world of her own which recalled to them other tragedies no less near home.

Charles, full-blooded and sensual like his grandfather, General Hugo, could no longer put up with Guernsey, where possible conquests were few and far between, and the best hunting-grounds were reserved for the patriarch. In 1862 he made his "act of secession." In that year his period of "leave" should have ended in October, but instead of returning to Guernsey he settled down in Paris without a word to his father. *Victor Hugo to Madame Hugo:* "It is very wrong in Charles to have opposed my wishes, and, as you say, to have a critical attitude towards me . . ." *Madame Hugo to Victor Hugo:* "Dear friend: Charles said to me, two days ago, 'I am very fond of Papa, and I don't want to hurt his feelings, but I do wish he would realize that I must have a change of surroundings' . . ."[13] Charles was now thirty-six, and accused his father of forcing upon him what almost amounted to "police supervision." He even went so far as to send him a "statement of grievances."

Victor Hugo to Charles Hugo, February 25th, 1862 (Confidential): Your statement, my dear Charles, has reached me. We read it in a family conclave consisting of your mother, Victor and myself. We entirely fail to understand it. My dear boy, you must really rid yourself of a persecution mania which is as unworthy of you as it is of us. The facts you catalogue, and of which you complain, are completely new to me. My one wish is to free your mind of the grotesque illusion under which you are labouring, that you live in an atmosphere of *paternal police supervision.* My love for you goes very deep; I watch over you with affectionate anxiety: my life belongs to you . . . My work leaves me but little leisure. Such as I have I now employ in sending you this hurried note. Your mother is about to spend a month with you. I shall feel full of envy of her. . . .[14]

At the end of 1864 Charles left Paris for Brussels. On October 17th, 1865, at Saint-Josse-ten-Noode, he married the goddaughter of Jules Simon, Alice Lehaene.[15] This pretty, gentle orphan of eighteen was the ward of her paternal uncle, Victor Bois, an eminent engineer and builder of railways.

François-Victor, who was bravely struggling to complete his translation of Shakespeare, and was, therefore, less bored than the others, would have stayed with his father had not a sudden loss compelled his rapid removal from the Anglo-Norman island. He had been engaged for some time to a young Guernsey woman, Emily de Putron, the daughter of an eminent architect who had done some work for Hugo. His father approved of the proposed marriage. Unfortunately Emily was consumptive. Shortly before the date fixed for the wedding, the progress of her ailment became alarmingly rapid. Hugo went to see her. She said to him, with a smile: "I should be so very glad not to die . . ." but die she did on January 14th, 1865, and so violent was François-Victor's grief that his father, in a panic, induced him to leave the island before the funeral, at which he delivered a very beautiful oration. *Victor Hugo's Diary:* "I told the Putron family, who are anxious that part of my address shall be inscribed on Miss Emily's tombstone, that I will make myself responsible for the work, and will have the words cut on a block of Guernsey granite, and filled in with gold."

Madame Hugo accompanied her son to Brussels. This time her absence was to last for two years. From January 1865 to January 1867 she put in no appearance at Hauteville House. The old magician was now

almost alone upon his rock. His sister-in-law came to keep house for
him. Julie Foucher had married an engraver, Paul Chenay, but matters
had not gone smoothly between them. Juliette Drouet stuck faithfully
to her post. The more his own flesh and blood abandoned the *paterfamilias,* the more did the old lover belong to his devoted mistress. "I
would, if I dared, beg Heaven to prolong our stay here until the end
of our lives." From time to time, on dates of especial significance, a few
lovely lines would reach her, and set the mark of eternity upon her love:

> Quand deux cœurs en s'aimant ont doucement vieilli,
> Oh! quel bonheur profond, intime, recueilli!
> Amour, Hymen d'en haut! ô pur lien des âmes!
> Il garde ses rayons même en perdant ses flammes.
> Ces deux cœurs, qu'il a pris jadis, n'en font plus qu'un.
> Il fait des souvenirs de leur passé commun,
> L'impossibilité de vivre l'un sans l'autre.
> —Juliette, n'est-ce pas, cette vie est la nôtre?—
> Il a la paix du soir avec l'éclat du jour
> Et devient l'amitié tout en restant l'amour.[16]

In 1863 the book at which Madame Hugo had for so long been
working appeared: *Victor Hugo raconté par un témoin de sa vie.* What
part had Hugo played in its composition? François-Victor provides an
answer to that question:

Madame Hugo used to ask questions of her husband while they were at
déjeuner, a meal which, both at Marine Terrace and at Hauteville House,
was taken at about eleven o'clock in the morning. Victor Hugo narrated
the facts which Madame Hugo wanted to know, and so detailed was his
reconstruction of the past that he would frequently talk on until the meal
was finished, when Madame Hugo would go up to her room in order to
make a few short notes which should fix in her memory what she had just
heard. Next morning she had herself called early, the thick curtains of her
windows were drawn back, and a desk was brought, which she had placed
upon her bed. Then, while drinking a cup of chocolate, she would read
through the notes she had made, before settling down to write the final
version as it was to appear in the published volume. . . .[17]

Juliette received, as the supreme reward for a lifetime of humble
devotion, a copy of *Victor Hugo raconté,* with the following dedication
in the author's own hand: "A Madame Drouet, écrit dans l'exil, donné
par l'exil—ADÈLE VICTOR-HUGO, Hauteville House, 1863." Since ceas-
ing to live with her "dear, great friend" the official wife had to some
extent relaxed her attitude of disapproval towards the concubine, who,
like herself, was now not far off sixty. On Christmas Day, 1864,
Madame Hugo, who was making a short stay in Guernsey, gave as she

did every year a party for the poor children of the island, and for the first time invited Juliette Drouet to Hauteville House. "Today we are celebrating Christmas, Madame. Christmas is the festival of all children, and, consequently, of our own. It would give us much pleasure if you would join with us in this little solemnity, which marks, too, a feast-day in your heart."[18] Juliette tactfully but proudly refused. "It is you, Madame, who have made this day a festival for me. The sweetness and generosity of your letter are a source of great happiness to me. It has warmed my heart. You know my solitary ways, and will not, I hope, think the worse of me if I confine my happiness on this occasion to the reading of your letter. That happiness is great. Please allow me to remain secluded, that I may bless you all while you go about your work of doing good."[19]

Nor did she accept an invitation, sent her by Victor Hugo in the absence of Adèle, for Tuesday, May 9th, 1865. "Allow me to refuse what would have been a great happiness and a great honour, in the name of thirty years of reserve, discretion and respect, which I have shown towards your home and mine. If ever (which I do not anticipate) I should consent to be your guest, then my presence in your house must be a matter, not of *chance* but of *premeditation* approved by all. Permit me still to adhere to a line of conduct which has influenced the whole of my life, and to retain intact the dignity and sacredness of my love . . ."[20] The Princess Negroni had learned only too well the last part she would ever be called upon to play.

41

"Les Misérables"

I am well aware that Hugo, himself, was, in
stature, less than the blessed Bishop. Nevertheless, out of a conglomeration of mixed and varied
passions, this man, of the earth, earthy, could
create the living person of a saint who lived on
a high level above that of the ordinary run of
mankind.

ALAIN

FOR thirty years Victor Hugo had been pondering and working at a
great sociological novel. The injustice of legal penalties, the rehabilitation of the condemned, poverty, and the influence of a true saint,
these themes were already haunting him in the days when he was
writing "Le Dernier Jour d'un Condamné," "Claude Gueux" and such
poems as "Pour les Pauvres." He had amassed notes about prison conditions, about Monsignor Miollis, Bishop of Digne, about the convict
Pierre Maurin, about the glass industry at Montreuil-sur-Mer, about a
young boor who had stuffed snow down a wretched prostitute's dress.
By 1840 he had got down on paper the first plan of his projected novel:
Les Misères, the story of a saint—the story of a man—the story of a
woman—the story of a doll. It was but one more expression of the spirit
of the times. George Sand, Eugène Sue and even Alexandre Dumas
and Frédéric Soulié were all of them writing novels about the sufferings
of the poor. The success of Les Mystères de Paris undoubtedly influenced the composition of Les Misérables, but the author's natural
instincts were all that he needed for guidance.

From 1845 to 1848 he had devoted himself almost entirely to the
writing of Les Misères, the title of which had, by that time, been
changed to Jean Tréjean. His labours had been interrupted "in the
interests of revolution." The torrential sweep of Les Châtiments had
carried everything before it. Later still, his broodings on matters divine
and Les Petites Épopées had absorbed the whole of his attention. It was
on April 26th, 1860, that, having made up his mind that he would never
again leave his rock, he opened the tin trunk containing the manuscript

and notes of *Les Misères*, which in the course of his journeyings as an exile had more than once been almost irretrievably lost. "I have spent almost seven months in thinking over and clarifying in my mind the whole work as I first conceived it, so that there might be complete unity in what I wrote twelve years ago and in what I am going to write now. Everything, I am glad to say, turns out to have been solidly constructed. *Provisa res.* Today I am about to take up again (never more, I hope, to leave it until the end is reached) the book which was interrupted on February 21st, 1848."[1]

It is a matter of general knowledge that much of the material for *Les Misérables* was based on fact. Monsignor Miollis, a "real" bishop, was all, and more than all, that Monsignore Myriel is in the book. The conditions of poverty in which the saintly prelate lives, his asceticism, his charity, the simple grandeur of his language—all these things had, at Digne, aroused general admiration. A certain Canon Angelin, who had been secretary to Monsignor Miollis, has told how Pierre Maurin, a liberated convict, who after being refused admittance by every inn-keeper because of his yellow passport knocked at the door of the Bishop's palace, was welcomed as a friend, as is Jean Valjean. But Pierre Maurin did not, as did Jean Valjean, steal the silver candlesticks. What actually happened was that the Bishop sent the man to his brother, General de Miollis, who was so satisfied at the way he turned out that he made him his orderly. The actual world supplies only the rough outlines of models; it is the artist who touches in the high-lights and paints the shadows.

At a later stage the novelist drew on his own experiences. The reader of *Les Misérables* comes on many of the author's recollections: the abbé de Rohan, Royol, the bookseller, old mother Saguet, the Feuillantines garden, the young Victor Hugo, under the guise of Marius, and General Hugo under that of Pontmercy. Marius pursues Cosette, as Victor had pursued Adèle. Marius sulks for three days because the wind blowing in the Luxembourg garden had lifted Cosette's skirt as high as her knees. Marius's political development is much the same as was Victor's own. A note of 1860 says: "Marius needs a good deal of modification. He must be made to judge Napoleon *truly*. Three phases: i. Royalist: ii. Bonapartist: iii. Republican . . ."[2] Juliette supplied a number of charming details about Cosette's probable life at the convent, and there exists a notebook belonging to her: *Manuscrit autographe d'une ancienne pensionnaire du couvent de Sainte-Madeleine,* part of which had the honour of somehow getting bound up with the manuscript of the book. While in Guernsey Hugo added a number of chapters: students and grisettes; the story of Waterloo (in which he was greatly helped by a fine book, the work of his friend Colonel Charras); la Thénardier, the spoiler of corpses; the Convent of Petit-Picpus; the escape in a coffin; the year 1817; the friends of the A.B.C.; Louis-Philippe; and some others.

All through this prolonged period of work Juliette was a sure tower of strength. She adored the book, and the copying of it was for her a source of delight. After twelve years' absence she met Cosette again as a friend. "I am all eagerness to renew acquaintance with that poor little girl, and to know what happened to her pretty doll. I am impatient to find out whether the monster Javert loses track of that poor, sublime scoundrel M. le maire."[3] In May 1861 she had the honour to be taken, for two months, to the Hôtel des Colonnes, at Mont-Saint-Jean, where Hugo wanted to write the chapters devoted to the Battle of Waterloo, on the spot. She went with him everywhere, and picked cornflowers, poppies and daisies, with which in a fervour of nationalism she made cockades. Sometimes he left her alone, when he went off to see his family in Brussels, and she occupied the time of his absence in copying, "that panacea for all my ills . . . that darling task which I prefer to everything, after yourself . . ."[4] Then, when Hugo got back, they explored together those terrible orchards, where every apple tree could show its scar of ball or bullet. "The English Guards shot to pieces; twenty French battalions out of Reille's corps of forty decimated; three thousand men, in this one farm-house of Hougoumont, cut to shreds, hacked, slashed, shot and burned—and all so that today a peasant may say to a tourist, 'for three francs, sir, I'll tell you all about Waterloo' . . ."[5]

At last the book was finished. *Victor Hugo to Auguste Vacquerie:* "This morning, June 30th, 1861, at half-past eight o'clock, with a bright sun shining through my windows, I finished *Les Misérables*. I know that this news will be of some little interest to you, and I want you to have it direct from me. I owe you this brief notification. You have entertained a friendly feeling for this work of mine, and have made mention of it in your excellent book *Profils et Grimaces*. I would have you know, therefore, that the child is doing well. I write these few lines with the last drop of ink remaining on my pen after the finishing of my book. . . ."[6]

Victor Hugo knew that the book was good, and that an immense public would read it. He wished to turn it to advantage in assuring the future of his family for all time. Who should be its publisher? He was very fond of his friend Hetzel, but considered him to be a bad businessman. A young Belgian publisher, Albert Lacroix ("a small, willowy man, who never keeps still for a moment, with a passion for literature, and very well educated to boot, possessed by a devil of energy, with a lively face and wicked little eyes hidden behind a pair of pince-nez which he is for ever settling on a sharp and prominent nose, and a mass of red whisker"[7]), made him an offer, and accepted his terms: three hundred thousand francs for exclusive license to print over a period of twelve years.[8] Never before had Hugo received such a sum. Up till then Lamartine, Scribe, Dumas the elder, Eugène Sue, had always made more than he had. Lacroix possessed the necessary courage, but not the capital. The banker Oppenheimer lent him two hundred thousand francs. Several newspapers competed for serial rights. Hugo refused them all so as to give his publisher every chance of success, and because he thought that the cutting up of his text would injure the book as a work of art. Lacroix wanted the philosophical parts to be shortened. Once again, Hugo refused: "The quick-moving surface drama will be a success for twelve months; the deeper drama, for twelve years."

In Paris the faithful Paul Meurice resumed his place at the conductor's desk and took steps to organize the advance publicity for the book, assisted by Madame Victor Hugo, Auguste Vacquerie and Charles Hugo. *Paul Meurice to Victor Hugo, July 8th, 1862:* "For the last six days all Paris has been reading, devouring, *Les Misérables*. It is obvious from the first talk about the book, and such small comments as have as yet appeared in the press, that the first effect, as was easy to forecast, has been immense. Everyone is raving! Everyone is carried away! There is a complete absence of petty objections and pedantic reservations. The crushing weight of so much grandeur, justice and sovereign compassion is all that counts. It is quite irresistible. . . ."[9]

The critics were less enthusiastic. Political passion distorted literary judgment. Cuvillier-Fleury accused Hugo of being the "leading demagogue of France." Barbey-d'Aurevilly described the book as "a long-drawn-out piece of sophistry," the work of "a rambling and humourless Paul de Kock." Hugo's friends Jules Janin, Paul de Saint-Victor, Nefftzer, Louis Ulbach, Schérer, Jules Claretie, reacted as warmly as had been expected. Lamartine was cautious. "My dear and illustrious friend," he wrote to Victor Hugo, "I feel dazzled and staggered by a talent which has outstripped nature. My first feeling was that I wanted to write to you about the book. But the contrast between our two ways of thinking, though not between our hearts, has had a restraining influence upon me. I am afraid that I may hurt you by too sharply attacking your egalitarian socialism, which is the creation of systems which go against nature. I have therefore held back, and say frankly that I will not write my *Entretiens littéraires*, unless Hugo tells me, in so many words: 'Personal feelings apart, I am prepared to let Lamartine say what he likes about my theories.' Don't spare me when you answer this . . . think only of yourself."[10]

Hugo gave him a free hand, and Lamartine produced a bitter article.

He praised the writer, but snubbed the philosopher. "This is a dangerous book . . . The masses can be infected by no more murderous, no more terrible, passion than a passion for the impossible . . ."[11] Hugo, deeply hurt, jotted down: "A swan trying to bite." Baudelaire contributed a hypocritical article on the novel in *Le Boulevard,* where he described it as "edifying, and therefore useful," though he told his mother that he had been guilty of a lie in praising "this unspeakably foul and stupid book . . . Hugo's whole family, and his disciples, fill me with horror . . ."[12] The "Religion of Progress" exasperated Baudelaire. He admired Hugo the poet, but when he received a letter from him: "Forward! that is the Watchword of Progress! It is also the Cry of Art. All Poetry is There! *Ite!* . . ."[13]—the rhetorical capitals, turn and turn about, "according to his mood, made him laugh or rage."[14]

Time has now delivered its verdict. *Les Misérables* has come to be accepted by the whole world as one of the great works of the human imagination. Jean Valjean, Bishop Myriel, Javert, Fantine, la Thénardier, Marius, Cosette, have taken their places in the not very large group of fictional characters with a universal appeal, side by side with Père Grandet, Madame Bovary, Oliver Twist, Natasha Rostow, the Brothers Karamazov, Swann and Charlus. The screen has adapted the novel, and brought Hugo's persons to the masses. Why? Is the book a faultless production? Were Flaubert and Baudelaire wrong when they said, "they are not human beings"?

The truth of the matter is that these men and women are human, but larger than life. Some, by reason of their love and charity, are more than human; others, so hard and so degraded that they are less. In art it is the monsters who live on, provided they are magnificent in their monstrosity. Hugo was by nature inclined to portray the excessive, the theatrical, the gigantic. That gift of his would not, by itself, have sufficed for the production of a masterpiece. But his exaggerated characterization was justified by the truth and nobility of his feelings. He genuinely admired Bishop Myriel, genuinely loved Jean Valjean. He respected, no less genuinely, though his respect was mingled with horror, Javert. Sincerity and sweep of vision are no bad combination for a novelist. There is sufficient truth in *Les Misérables* to provide the degree of credibility which every novel must have. Not only was there a deal of "real life" in the book, but its historical sections were, and are, of the highest order. Victor Hugo had lived through the Empire, the Restoration, the Revolution of 1830. He had observed, with realistic intelligence, the secret springs controlling persons and events. One has only to re-read the chapter on the year 1817, or the "Quelques pages d'histoire" dealing with the Revolution of 1830, to realize this. The thought is as good as the style. He speaks truly when he points out that the Restoration "thought it was strong because it had swept aside the Empire as a painted scene is bundled off the stage. What it did not realize was that it had come into being in much the same way. It did not see that itself, no less than the Empire, was controlled by the same hand that had got rid of Napoleon . . ."[15] The portrait of Louis-Philippe, fair-minded and almost affectionate, is as good as anything in Retz or Saint-Simon.

Contemporary critics condemned the digressions, as the publisher had foreseen that they would. "To much philosophy," they said, "slows down and injures the movement of the narrative." Barbey d'Aurevilly, though hostile to the book as a whole, had to admit that he was quite carried away by the account of the Battle of Waterloo, "which is told, I must confess, with that lyrical power which is the peculiar gift of Monsieur Hugo—the Olympian poet of guns and bugles, of manœuvres, skirmishes and uniforms. The battle, as he presents it, grips our hearts in its every phase . . ."[16] He nevertheless maintained that this passage, like those on the Picpus Convent and the general subject of money, had really nothing to do with the novel as such. It is worth noting that the same charge has been brought against Balzac and Tolstoy, though never against Mérimée. The description of Guérande at the beginning of *Beatrix* may, perhaps, be too long, but without that leisured development, the book would be lacking in density. Suspense, interludes of silence, a feeling of time passing, all such tricks of composition are necessary. The *Préface philosophique* to *Les Misérables* begins with these words: "This is a religious book." Therein lies its secret. Sainte-Beuve, who had too sound a judgment not to recognize a masterpiece when he saw one, refrained from writing publicly about the novel, but confided to the pages of his diary his belief that, at a time when the men of his generation had grown old and were sunning their ancient bones on a bench in the Invalides gardens, Victor Hugo had given a shattering proof of his youthfulness.

At one of the Magny dinners, when Taine had said: "Hugo? . . . there is nothing sincere about Hugo," Sainte-Beuve burst out with: "Do you really mean, Taine, that you rank Musset above Hugo? Hugo is a writer of *books* . . . He has stolen from under the very nose of the Government—and a powerful government at that—the greatest success these times have known . . . He has forced an entry everywhere. The whole world, men, women, the common people, is reading him . . . His books go out of print between eight A.M. and noon . . . When I first read *Odes et Ballades,* I was moved to show him all the verse I had written . . . The chaps on *Le Globe* called him a barbarian. All the same, everything I have done *he* made me do, whereas, in ten years, *Le Globe* taught me nothing. . . ."

"Don't misunderstand me," Taine shot back. "I don't deny that Hugo, in these present days, is a tremendous event, but . . ."

"You'd better not talk about Hugo, Taine," Sainte-Beuve broke in, "you don't know him. Only two of us in this room know him—Gautier and I . . . Hugo's work is magnificent!"[17]

Unto Sainte-Beuve much shall be forgiven, for he did much admit.

4 2

The Burning Mountain

A genius without frontiers.

BAUDELAIRE

THÉOPHILE GAUTIER said of *Les Misérables*: "It is neither good nor bad: it is no handiwork of man but a phenomenon of natural forces." The phrase would be more suitably applied to other works dating from the period of exile, and, conspicuously, to *William Shakespeare*—"an epic essay in criticism, with the surge and depth of the ocean in it . . ."[1] a lava-flow from which emerge titanic statues still glowing with dark fires. There were three reasons why Hugo's mind was now turning his thoughts to Shakespeare. The year 1864 would mark the three-hundredth anniversary of the English dramatist's birth and, for that reason, the subject had a topical interest. François-Victor had asked his father for a Preface which might be printed with his translation. Above all, Hugo was feeling the need, forty years after *Cromwell*, to replace the manifesto of those distant days with something more in the nature of a balance-sheet, the literary testament, not only of the nineteenth century, but of the romantic movement.

Hugo's knowledge of Shakespeare was imperfect. The first "revelation," which had taken place at Rheims in May 1825, is worth remembering. Nodier, on that occasion, had produced an improvised version of *King John*, and the young poet had been bowled over. He had not wanted, and with good reason, to continue with his reading of Letourneur's translation. Nodier and Vigny, however, had introduced him to some of Shakespeare's other plays. On the family's arrival in Jersey, François-Victor had said to his father: "How are you going to occupy the years of exile?" To this question his father had replied: "I shall look at the ocean," and then added, "what about you?" "I," said his son, "am going to translate Shakespeare." Hugo's somewhat grandiose comment had been: "Some men are like oceans."

A theatrical piece of dialogue, perhaps, but, in fairness to François-Victor, who till then had been a thoroughly lazy young man, it should be pointed out that he stuck manfully to his tremendous task: "thirty-six plays: a hundred and twenty thousand lines to render into French."

He needed, to keep him at work, the boredom of life in Guernsey, and also the help of a young woman, Miss Emily de Putron. Hugo followed his son's labours as far as it was possible for a man to do who knew scarcely a word of English, and as a result became plunged in meditation about the nature of genius, about the function of the poet, about art in general. It was a heaven-sent opportunity, by using Shakespeare as an excuse, to clarify the problem of Hugo. Inspiration, however, burst through the original framework of the plan. The Preface became a book. It was only to a very limited extent about Shakespeare. The real subject was genius, or *geniuses*. Those whom he placed on the same level with Shakespeare were Homer, Job, Aeschylus, Isaiah, Ezekiel, Lucretius, Juvenal, Tacitus, Saint John, Dante, Rabelais, Cervantes. Only one Frenchman, only one Greek. The little red-whiskered Belgian publisher, Lacroix, protested against the exclusion of Germany. He suggested Goethe. "Goethe was no more than a man of talent," replied Hugo; "Goethe is restrained, geniuses are extravagant. The whole question is how much of the infinite they have in them. Genius contains an element of the unknown. Euripides, Plato, Virgil, La Fontaine, Voltaire, have, in their work, neither exaggeration, nor darkness, nor the monstrous. That is precisely what they lack."

An answer, this, to those who accused Hugo on just those grounds. The whole book is a speech for the defence. Genius must never be criticized. Its very faults are its merits. Genius can never be outdistanced. "Art, *qua* art, moves neither forward nor backward . . . The Pyramids and the *Iliad* always remain in the foreground. Masterpieces all occupy the same level, the level of the absolute . . . whence comes the sense of certainty which is common to all poets. They have an arrogant confidence in the future," and they look upon their peers in past ages with fraternal eyes. Hugo felt himself to be equal with the greatest. His contemporaries smiled at so huge a conceit: we, on the other hand, find it, on the whole, to be well-founded. "The poet of England judged by the poet of France"—so ran the publisher's advertisement, written by the author.

William Shakespeare was sold to Lacroix, who, as soon as the contract was signed, confessed that, for the tercentenary celebrations, he had also commissioned a *Shakespeare* from Lamartine. "I hope," he wrote, "that you will not mind this." Hugo was furious. "I do more than mind. I regard your conduct as in the highest degree offensive; offensive to my illustrious friend, Lamartine; offensive to me. It turns the whole affair into a point-to-point race. Lamartine and I are compelled to figure as two schoolboys competing for a prize on a given subject. You say: 'The success of your book, of which I am confident, will help the sale of M. de Lamartine's study , , .' I dislike the thought that I am to act as a tugboat to a poet of M. de Lamartine's stature, and I very much doubt whether M. de Lamartine will like being tugged . . ."[2]

Another episode marked the tercentenary. Several French writers set up a Shakespeare Committee. Victor Hugo was appointed president, and since he could not be present at the banquet it was decided by the Committee that his chair should be left empty. In this way Paris should be made to realize, during the progress of the feast, how great was the gap left by the absence of the famous exile. Later in the evening the company was to be transported from the Grand Hotel to the Porte-Saint-Martin, there to witness a performance of Paul Meurice's version of *Hamlet*. Madame Sand had written a rather fatuous letter, designed to be read aloud at the banquet, "short and so-so, reconciling Shakespeare and Voltaire." It seemed more than probable that the Government, fearing a scandal, would ban the banquet altogether, but that, said Meurice to Vacquerie, would be admirable publicity for the book.

The ban was applied, the book appeared, Mallarmé said of it: "Some wonderfully sculptural passages, but also some quite frightful things! . . ."[3] The newspaper notices were noncommittal. That a poet should have wanted to write a work of criticism was considered by some to be blameworthy. "What a strange fancy," said Hugo, "to exclude a poet from the exercise of criticism. Who can know better than a miner what the inside of a mine is like? . . ."[4] Amédée Rolland wrote mockingly in the *Revue de Paris*: "The secret—though ill-concealed—conclusion of the present volume is this: 'the great Pelasgian is Homer; the great Hellene is Aeschylus; the great Hebrew is Isaiah; the great Roman is Juvenal; the great Englishman is Shakespeare; the great German is Beethoven. And what about the great Frenchman? You don't mean to say there isn't one?' Rabelais? No! Molière? No! You *are* difficult to please! Montesquieu? Again, no! Voltaire then? Heavens, no! Who then? Who? . . . why Hugo of course! . . . And what about Shakespeare? I have said no more of him than Hugo has done. That great name is no more than an excuse. . . ."[5]

Meanwhile, in Brussels, the prodigious old man was at work sorting and classifying his manuscripts. "I am sending to Hauteville II[6] one new, medium-sized trunk, complete with metal straps and padlocks, containing (unpublished) the sequel to *La Légende des Siècles*. In the other I have put *La Fin de Satan*; *Mille francs de récompense*, a drama; *L'Intervention* and *La Grand-Mère*, a comedy; and several folders of work in progress: *My Diary*, 1840-48; as well as the manuscripts of the following published works: *Les Misérables, William Shakespeare, La Légende des Siècles, Les Chansons des Rues et des Bois*: also (unpublished) the almost completed manuscripts of *Les Chansons de Gavroche* and *Les Poèmes de Jean Prouvère*; finally, *Actes et Paroles et l'Exil* (for Victor Hugo of the exile period). Suzanne is in charge of this trunk."[7] No matter what might happen, the traveller would not set out for eternity without a proper equipment of baggage.

43

"The Toilers of the Sea"

THERE exists a long account of Hugo between the years 1866 and 1869, ironical in tone, but true to fact, written by Paul Stapfer, a young teacher of French who had joined the staff of a Guernsey school as professor of literature, and was given a kindly welcome by the poet, who at that time was living with his sister-in-law Julie Chenay. Kesler, the hunchbacked exile, was present at meals. The islanders paid little attention to the foreign writer in their midst. They were shocked by his republicanism, and by the things he said about Queen Victoria. The only person who had a love of his poetry, and looked on him as a great man, was Miss Carey, the daughter of the local magistrate. Stapfer was struck by the old man's elegant and noble bearing. Strong and upright, wearing a wide-brimmed felt hat, with a cloak flung round his shoulders when the sky threatened rain, his hands thrust into his pockets, and a highly arched instep, he would have produced an effect of grandeur even if he had appeared in the rags of a tramp.

Very ceremonious, very old-world, he always told the young Stapfer that he considered it an honour "to have him as a companion." His conversation in moments of intimacy was simple, natural and very French. When a large audience was present, he became grandiloquent. The person, on those occasions, vanished behind the Personage. He would, when there were many to hear him, loose his thunders against materialism. He quoted with horror a phrase of Taine: "Vice and virtue are natural products of the same general type as sugar and sulphuric acid." To say that, he maintained, was to deny the difference between good and evil . . . "I would like to be in Paris now, I would like to be present at the Academy, just so as to be able to vote with the Bishop of Orléans against such an oaf!" His other pet abomination was Racine: "He wielded his instrument with no certainty," said Hugo, "and could, on occasion, write exceedingly badly:

> Épargnez votre sang, j'ose vous en prier,
> Épargnez moi l'horreur de *l'entendre crier*."

On the other hand he praised the Boileau of *Lutrin*, the Molière of *l'Étourdi*, the Corneille of the comedies, with all the gusto of a literary

363

gourmet. After dinner he had a way of becoming "sublime." Young Stapfer noted, mischievously, that all the vast problems of the human mind—the immortality of the soul, the essential nature of God, the necessity of prayer, the absurdity of pantheism, the nonsense of positivism, the two infinites—were stated and solved. "Oh! what a poverty-stricken thing is atheism! How petty! How ridiculous! God exists. I am more sure of His existence than of my own. I never let four hours go by without praying . . . If I wake in the night, I pray. What do I ask of God? To give me something of His power. I know well enough what is good and what is evil, but I lack the power to *do* what I *know* to be good . . . We are all in God. He is the author of all things. But it is not true to say that He *created* the world, because he *creates* it eternally. He is the 'I' of the infinite . . . Are you asleep, Adèle?"

For on the evening in question it happened that Madame Hugo was in Guernsey on a brief visit. Now, at sixty-four, she was an imposing presence. Her physical attributes showed to advantage in a heavily trimmed dress, with her head weighed down and crowned with a tremendous adornment of corkscrew curls. Young Stapfer was struck by the solemnity of her speech. "You are from Paris, sir? Ah! Paris is the leading city of the world!" Now and again she would correct her sister on points of grammar: "How can you say *du Médoc*, Julie? You should say *du vin de Médoc*."

On the subject of contemporary writers Hugo expressed himself in no uncertain terms. It was extraordinary, he said, that the critics should set about discovering "greatness" in Musset's poetry. "To my mind, the description of him as *Miss Byron* is no less true than amusing . . . He is much inferior to Lamartine . . . This century can show only one true classic—one, mark you—*me*. I am the one man living who knows most about the French language. After me come Sainte-Beuve and Mérimée . . . But Mérimée is a writer of limited gifts. What he has in the most marked degree, and is praised for having, is *restraint*—a curious word to use in praise of a writer! Thiers is a janitor-writer who attracts janitor-readers . . . Courier is an infernal scamp . . . Chateaubriand is full of magnificent things, but he was a man without any love of humanity, his was an odious nature . . . I am accused of being arrogant. That is perfectly true: my arrogance is the source of my strength."

The year 1867 saw an event which for Juliette was of great importance. Madame Hugo paid a visit to Hauteville Féerie; in other words, she called on Madame Drouet. The good lady had been away from Guernsey for two years, and wanted to thank the person who had been responsible for ensuring the "ease and tranquillity of the interim period." Juliette saw with feelings of sadness the "overturning of her saucepan," and the end of her functions "as cook," but she was pleased by this mark of esteem shown her by the "spouse," and immediately returned the visit, as though she had been the head of a Friendly Power. *Juliette Drouet to Victor Hugo:* "My eagerness to fulfil the requirements of good manners arises from the deference which I have the honour to profess for your excellent lady. . . ."[1]

From this moment she developed the "charming habit of taking her part in all the happier manifestations of family life." Somewhat later, she spent three months in Brussels in the close proximity of her beloved, and was received in the Place des Barricades. She was even invited, with Charles, his wife, and their small son Georges (four months old), to spend a holiday of some weeks in the Bois de Chaudfontaine. She read aloud to Madame Hugo whose eyes were growing weak. *Juliette to Victor Hugo, September 12th, 1867:* "My heart can find no words in which to express what I feel for all of you. I am overjoyed, moved, dazzled, and happier than a poor old woman has any right to be. I am overflowing with gratitude for all the happiness which has come to me from this last fortnight of flowers, childhood delights, sun, family and love. I adore you and bless you . . ."[2] At the age of sixty-one, after a long and hard penitence, she could at last "savour the charm of a discreet and delicate rehabilitation."

Even in Guernsey, the prejudices aroused by this couple, whose relationship, though irregular, had been sanctified by time, were being dispersed. Juliette was permitted, in the absence of Madame Hugo, to stay for a month at Hauteville House! Though of short duration that happiness was sweet. *Juliette Drouet to Victor Hugo:* "I want to take full advantage of every moment and every occasion which the good God, and you, are giving me, and to thank both of you for them with adoration . . ."[3] About this time, a company of strolling players gave a performance of *Hernani* in Guernsey and, much to the surprise of Juliette, who was deeply suspicious of the "Sixty" (the leading families of the island), and of their prejudices, the occasion was a success. There was now on sale in Guernsey a photograph of Victor Hugo with his grandchildren, taken during the Christmas festivities, and even the baker went so far as to buy this portrait of the "paterfamilias of Hauteville House." This was local fame with a vengeance!—always the slowest to be achieved.

A new rhythm of life had now set in. Madame Hugo lived for most of each year in Paris, where Charles's family, now and again, sought her hospitality. François-Victor, with Charles and Alice, kept up the house in Brussels, in the Place des Barricades. Julie Chenay and Juliette saw to the requirements of the Great Exile in Guernsey. In summer the Hugo family was reunited in Brussels. In 1865 Baudelaire had announced to Ancelle that the poet was to settle permanently in Belgium: "It seems that he and the ocean have fallen out! Either he is not strong-minded enough to put up with the ocean, or the ocean has grown bored with him! It seems hardly worth while to have gone to all that trouble to establish a palace on a rock! . . ."[4] But the news was false. Hugo still believed that he owed his enormous capacity for work to Guernsey, and he loved his "palace."

All the same, he found the burden of four establishments heavy to carry: Paris, Brussels, Guernsey and the distant Adèle beyond the seas. He was giving the latter a monthly allowance of a hundred and fifty francs, plus (as a result of her mother's request) two hundred francs twice a year for clothes. All in all, his family was costing him, in allowances and house-rent, about thirty thousand francs. His investments (Belgian Bank bonds and English Consols) had increased in value to 48,000 francs, in addition to which he had, as a member of the Institut, a yearly stipend of 1000 francs. If one takes into account the fact that he had sold *Les Misérables* for more than 300,000 francs; that he was still being paid for new books at the rate of 40,000 francs a volume (and a single novel extended to four volumes); that, furthermore, he could rely on innumerable articles and on reprints; it is clear that he was a very rich man, which makes it rather surprising to find him forever haggling with his dependants.

It is for this reason that he has been called avaricious, and has been criticized for the strange pleasure which he took as an old man in investing each year any surplus left in his hands. Two considerations should serve to modify this judgment. The first is that, quite apart from what he was spending on his family, and on Juliette Drouet, he was making a number of free-will gifts. For instance, having for a long time provided financial aid for his fellow-exile Hennet de Kesler, who insisted on living above his means, he ended by giving him the permanent hospitality of Hauteville House. He also supplied a solid weekly meal to forty Guernsey children. His diaries are full of details about assistance given to unfortunate persons. *March 9th, 1865:* "Soup, meat and bread for Marie Green and her sick child . . ." *March 15th:* "Sent a set of baby-linen to Mrs. Oswald who has just been brought to bed . . ." *March 28th:* "Coal for the O'Quien family . . ." *April 8th:* "Sheets to Victoire Etasse who is lying in, and without bed-linen." At least a third of his household expenses were accounted for by charity. If he was guilty of avarice, it was avarice of a markedly beneficent kind.

The second consideration is that he thought it his duty to save as much as he could in order to leave his family provided for after his death. His sons were making very little money, Adèle nothing at all. Charles had had a son, Georges, on March 31st, 1867. This child died on April 14th, 1868, but its place was quickly taken (August 16th, 1868) by the arrival of Georges II.[5] This child lived, and had a sister, Jeanne.[6] *Victor Hugo to his son Charles:* "I have been racking my brains to find some way of assuring the future of Georges and Jeanne, and that is why I do not want to spend a penny more than my income. So, you see, there is still a flicker of good sense in us old fogeys . . ."[7] Besides, the family, if he had not sometimes read it a cautionary lecture, would have grown prodigal. *To Charles and François-Victor:* "Now a word about 'managing.' I think your wine-merchant is a bit on the expensive side. At the end of March I shall pay 334 francs for wine dispatched to Brussels, bringing the total of money spent on wine since October to 978 francs, that is to say, more than 2000 francs for wine only in a single year. Draw your own conclusions!"[8]

In spite of what he gave them, his wife and son were soon in debt to him, and, from time to time, he had to declare a fiscal amnesty.

This did not prevent Madame Hugo from borrowing money in order to help her children and relations. She was endlessly indulgent to her brother-in-law Paul Chenay, a second-rate artist and a mean-spirited man. She would have liked, too, to spoil poor Dédé in her exile. She herself was far from well. In the Jersey days she had caused her family great uneasiness by losing the sight of one eye. The trouble was traced to a broken blood-vessel in the retina. She also suffered from heart-trouble. She had fits of dizziness, and knew that she was threatened with apoplexy. *Adèle to her sister Julie:* "I did not tell you before, but I have made my Will. I have got to live with the possibility of death always before my eyes, and must learn to come to terms with it as with a friend. I have left to my dear, good Aunt Asseline the prayer-book used by my Didine at her wedding." Her husband liked to think that her ailments were of a benignant type. "What your mother needs," he wrote to his son, "is plenty of red meat and good wine"—a somewhat drastic regime for one suffering from excessive blood-pressure!

He would have liked to look after her himself in Guernsey. To Vacquerie, who was full of tender care for her, he wrote: "Tell my suffering darling—I beg of you, dear Auguste—that if she is not afraid of a sea-crossing, Guernsey awaits her with open arms. Her reader of Chaudfontaine[9] will read aloud as much as she likes. Julie can write to her dictation, and I will do all in my power to provide her with a little gaiety and distraction. The spring weather will soon get her back to health . . ."[10] There was no lack of good-will: "Love me, all you dear ones, because I live for you, and in you. You are my life—far away, perhaps, but very close to my heart. Dear and much-loved wife, your letters are very sweet to me. They exude tenderness like a perfume. I inhale each of them as I do the flowers of this brilliant spring. Oh! yes, indeed, we must be all together again. I clasp you in my arms. . . ."[11]

Meanwhile Hugo was working and creating. In 1886 he published a long novel, *Les Travailleurs de la Mer.* He loved gigantic constructions, and liked to think of this book as forming a stone in a vast building that had to do with *Anankè* (destiny, fatality) . . . *Notre-Dame de*

Paris *(Anankè* of dogmas); *Les Misérables (Anankè* of laws); *Les Travailleurs de la Mer (Anankè* of things). The book contains passages of great beauty. Victor Hugo made use in it of the intimate knowledge which he had acquired during his life in the archipelago, of sea, and ships and sailors, of fogs and monsters, of rocks and storms. The habits of the Guernsey folk, the local folklore, the house which it was popularly believed could be seen beneath the waves, the strange language of these Anglo-Normans, gave to the book a new piquancy.

It was on the island of Sark, where he had been with Juliette and Charles in the summer of 1859, that he had watched the methods used by the fishermen to scale perpendicular cliff-faces; had seen the caves used by the smugglers as hiding-places, and the octopus which was later to furnish him with the material for an intensely dramatic combat. Notes jotted down in his diaries were also to serve the purpose of his book which, at that early stage, was called *Gilliatt le Marin.* Gilliatt's suicide is foreshadowed in the following entry: *Port of Sark: June 10, eleven* A.M. "The man who slipped down between the rocks. Jammed at the narrowest point and unable to climb up. Compelled to wait for the rising tide which fills the whole of this crevasse. A terrible death." Throughout his stay in the islands he was forever making notes about the catastrophes for which the sea was responsible.

If the waves and rocks and monsters of *Les Travailleurs de la Mer* were painted from nature by the hand of a great artist, the figures in the foreground were less successful. Some of them might have stepped straight out of the novels of Dumas, or of Eugène Sue. There are musical-comedy smugglers, and melodramatic traitors. As to the principal characters, Gilliatt and Déruchette, they belong to the author's private mythology. Déruchette is the young fiancée, the idealization of a young girl, unintentionally cruel, Adèle before the fault, Adèle before Adèle, a being projected by childish reverie, who had never ceased to haunt him. Gilliatt is the incarnation of the sublime victim, another Hugoesque phantom. Since the days of the attic in the rue du Dragon he had been for ever begetting on his imagination just such humiliated and rebellious figures. All things considered, with full allowance made for genius and artlessness, the book struck its readers at the time as new and arresting. It deserved to be successful. Hugo was in no hurry to publish. He was all agog to start on another novel. "I have little time left, and several great books to write or to finish . . ."[12] But Lacroix, who had made a fortune out of *Les Misérables,* was pressing. His exuberance won the day. There is a certain kind of torrential eloquence, laudatory and plaintive, which a writer finds it hard to resist. Hugo gave in, and sold to Lacroix the two works which he had ready, *Les Chansons des Rues et des Bois* and *Les Travailleurs de la Mer,* for a hundred and twenty thousand francs. At once two newspaper editors, Millaud (*Le Petit Journal* and *Le Soleil*) and Villemessant (*L'Évènement*) made an offer for first serial rights in the novel. Millaud offered half a million francs (at least a hundred million today) and a quantity of sentimental arguments: "By letting a serial from your pen appear in a paper which sells for ten centimes, you will bring your book within the reach of all, and will be making a truly popular gesture. Everybody will be able to read it, the mother of the family, the honest working man, the ploughman in the fields. Without taking the bread from their children's mouths or depriving the old people of one single log of wood, they will be able to enjoy the light, the consolation, and the pleasure which the reading of your eminent work cannot but afford them . . ."[13] Hugo refused the offer: "All my reasons are drawn from my conscience as a writer. It is that which, regret it though I may, compels me to avert my eyes, with a certain sense of delicacy, from the spectacle of half a million francs. It is in book form that *Les Travailleurs de la Mer* must first see the light. . . ."[14]

And in book form the novel duly appeared. *François-Victor Hugo to his father:* "Your success is immense, universal. Never have I seen such unanimity. This is a greater triumph even than that of *Les Misérables*. This time the Master has found an audience worthy of him. I need say no more than that you have been understood. For understanding of a book like this means admiration. Your name is in all the papers, on every wall, behind the windows of all the book-shops, on every lip . . ."[15] He had made the octopus the talk of the day. The scientists, consulted by the journalists, denied that it could be considered dangerous. This controversy did much to help the book. Milliners launched an "octopus" hat to be worn by *Les Travailleuses de la Mer*, in other words, by the ladies who frequented Dieppe and Trouville. The restaurants included *Octopus à la financière* in their menus. Divers brought up a live octopus which was exhibited in an aquarium at the Maison Domède in the Champs Élysées. Madame Victor Hugo wrote to her sister Julie Chenay from Paris: "Everything here has become octopusized. Why, oh why, is my husband the octopus of Guernsey where my heart is concerned?"

Le Soleil, which republished the novel as a serial, increased its circulation (in spite of the fact that the story had already appeared in book form) from 28,000 to 80,000 copies. The press ventured to express enthusiasm. Here was a book which aroused no political feelings. Man, within its covers, was shown warring only against nature. "Here," wrote the young critic Émile Zola, "one can enjoy freedom of the heart and true imagination. He has stopped preaching, he has stopped arguing . . . We are given the spectacle of the grandiose vision of a powerful mind, which ranges man against the immensities. But, at the last, a puff of wind suffices to lay the man low . . . a light puff from a pair of red lips."[16] In these words he gave neat expression to what had tempted the author: "I wanted," said Hugo, "to glorify man's work, man's will, man's devotion, everything that makes a man great. I wanted to show that the most relentless of all abysses is the human heart, and that he who escapes the sea cannot escape a woman."

Madame Hugo wrote to her husband, on the subject of this book, a letter of extravagant enthusiasm studded with adjectives worthy of Juliette, and was rewarded with praise: "An exquisite production . . . You have a great mind and a great heart. Dear and best-beloved of women, I am happy to know that I have pleased you as an author."[17] Adèle spoke much of her approaching death, which she contemplated with complete serenity. "The only thing that saddens me," she said, "is that my life is ending just as I have come to appreciate great works, that I must die at the moment when intelligence has come alive in me."[18] She had now developed democratic convictions, and spoke with contempt of "former superstitions." O shades of the Fouchers!

44

The Last Survivor of the Battle of "Hernani"

The Abbé, to Madame Teste:
Your husband's faces are beyond counting.

PAUL VALÉRY

SINCE the *coup d'état*, the plays of Victor Hugo, enemy of the regime, had not been seen in the theatres of Paris. Eighteen sixty-seven was the year of the *Exposition universelle*. The purpose of this display was to show the world at large the finest things France had to offer. Lacroix published a *Paris-Guide* for which Victor Hugo wrote a preface. Could the Comédie-Française, at such a time, repudiate one of its great authors? A revival of *Hernani* was suggested. The prospect made Victor Hugo uneasy. Would not the police take steps to have it booed? His representatives in Paris, Vacquerie and Meurice, thought not. Paul Meurice, whose mistress was the actress Jane Essler, would have preferred *Ruy Blas* at the Odéon, with Jane in the part of the queen. But *Hernani* won. It was decided that, in order to minimize the danger of disturbance, certain lines which had originally caused trouble should be altered. Hugo wrote to Vacquerie: "Instead of *Oui, de ta suite, ô roi! de ta suite j'en suis*, we had better have, *Oui, tu dis vrai, j'en suis.*" He would rather that the actor Delaunay should have had the courage to say: *Vieillard stupide! il l'aime*, but since he hadn't, then the least harmful, though foolish, variant "will be: *Ciel! qu'as tu fait? il l'aime!*"[1] But these precautions were wholly unnecessary. What really shocked the public of 1867 were the changes. The pit, which knew the play by heart, rose as one man and shouted the correct words. Hugo had sent from Guernsey "passes" signed by himself, and had asked Vacquerie to see that they were stamped with the famous *Hierro*. The success of the performance was immense: a literary triumph, a political manifestation, maximum receipts (seven thousand gold francs).

Madame Hugo insisted on being present at the revival. Her husband and her sons, knowing the danger, her health being what it was, of all emotion, wanted to spare her at least the dress-rehearsal, which might be stormy. But she would not obey. "I have too little time left not to take advantage of the revival of *Hernani,* which is a reminder for me of my young and lovely years. Do you really want me to miss this great occasion? No, sir; in the first place, *Hernani* will not be booed, and, besides, I can face disturbances. My eyes are bearing up; but even if it meant losing my sight, I would still go to *Hernani,* yes, even if it meant putting my old person in pawn. Unfortunately, no one would give me much for it. . . ."[2]

There is something deeply moving in this attitude of humility, as there is, too, in her longing to live again that battle of *Hernani* which had made glorious the last really happy year of her life. Paris saw her radiant and transfigured. She followed all the rehearsals. She went to them accompanied by Auguste Vacquerie, who, since he was now suffering from rheumatism, could scarcely drag himself to the theatre. The blind and the paralytic. The newspapers announced the presence of Madame Victor Hugo in Paris. That pleased her. "What a sounding name I bear!" The students, just as in the old days, asked for seats and offered their support. One of them said to Paul Meurice: "Monsieur Victor Hugo is our religion."

The success was "unnarratable"—the adjective is Adèle's own. All the same, narrate it she did. "The scene was one of frenzy. People were embracing one another, even outside the theatre. The young persons surpassed in fervour those of 1830. They turned out to be superb, stout-hearted, ready for anything. I am happy . . . I am in the seventh heaven . . ."[3] Among those in the audience were Dumas, Gautier, Banville, Girardin, Jules Simon, Paul Meurice, Adolphe Crémieux, Auguste Vacquerie. The boys from the *lycée* filled the galleries. Gautier, in his newspaper column, wrote: "Alas! few of the fighters of the old romantic legions remain, but all who have survived were there, and we recognized them in their stalls and their boxes with feelings of melancholy pleasure, our minds full of the memory of those good companions who have vanished now for ever. *Hernani* no longer needs the old gang. Nobody now would dream of attacking it. . . ."[4]

The line, *Vous êtes mon lion superbe et généreux,* once the terror of the Restoration, was drowned in applause. Jules Janin declared: "There can be nothing comparable to the festival spirit in which this unhoped-for return has been welcomed."[5]

Sainte-Beuve to Madame Victor Hugo, June 21st, 1867: Dear Madame: from all the congratulations which are pouring in on you, mine must not be missing. This has been a brilliant consecration of the loves and admirations of our youth. Thus genius has its hours, and all the hours that are belong to it. It can claim more than a single blazing noon. One of my most bitter regrets is that, forced as I am never to leave my chair, I could not be present, and was not able even to put in an appearance in the foyer, at this festival, this jubilee of poetry, and so could not hear for myself the sympathetic applause which stirs so many memories in our hearts. I should have liked to show that I am anxious not to lose my place in the ranks of the veterans of *Hernani*. . . .[6]

In April 1868 Alice Hugo's first-born died in Brussels of meningitis. She was, at the time, five months gone with child, and Charles took her to Paris, leaving his brother in charge of the funeral arrangements. *Charles Hugo to François-Victor, April 16th, 1868:* "The poor little chap cannot have felt that he took his departure without us, for you were with him, and you, and I, and Alice make one in grief. He is with us still; his soul has not taken the same road as his body. The brother, now awaited, will in his small person bring him back to us . . . Tell my father that *from now on* he must change the way in which he distributes the money he sends us, and send the *major part to Paris*, because my mother cannot, from her own resources, deal with all these fresh expenses . . ."[7] But Madame Hugo was not to survive this new loss for long. *Charles to François-Victor:* "Mamma is still much the same. Axenfeld has warned me that she is suffering from a serious and deep-seated disorder, and that he can do no more than apply palliatives. She is as well as can be expected. We look after her and provide all we can in the way of distraction. . . ."

Charles would have liked to stay on in Paris and start a paper, but he doubted whether the moment was opportune. The "Old Man," when consulted, said that he would not risk a brass farthing in such an enterprise. Months often went by without his writing. He was busy with a new novel: *Par ordre du Roi.* Meurice took upon himself to pay the various allowances out of the receipts from *Hernani*.

Madame Hugo to Victor Hugo, May 3rd, 1868: You should know, my dear great friend, that Charles and his wife have had the happy thought of descending upon me, and this has given me much pleasure, since I can put them up without any increase in expense. The only additional cost will be for food and other miscellaneous items, now that the household has been trebled. The heaviest expenditure, therefore, as Victor must have told you, is for the moment centred in Paris. Brussels is costing little, because only Victor and one maidservant are there, two persons in all, the cook having, temporarily, been given notice. I expect that Victor has also told you that you ought to *increase our budget* in consequence of all this. In view of such an augmentation, ought Meurice to continue to act as my banker, his resources being somewhat uncertain? Would you, perhaps, rather perform that function yourself, and act for me as you have been doing for the Brussels establishment? You should know what money Meurice has in reserve, and if he is to remain our banker you will no doubt instruct him, knowing whether or no he has exhausted the sums received from *Hernani*. My accounts are in perfect order, and I will send them to you whenever you wish me to. Until the arrival of my children I had been keeping expenses within the limits which are familiar to you. You are, therefore, fully informed about the material side of our existence, which is sad enough, you being so far from us, and we so close to the misfortune that has struck us down. . . .

Postscript by Charles Hugo: Hope to see you soon, my dearly beloved father. Please thank that good Madame Drouet for her tears. She was very fond of our little Georges. I embrace both of you. . . .[8]

Charles did his best to persuade his brother to join him in Paris, where life, he said, was very pleasant.

Charles Hugo to François-Victor, May 10th, 1868: We dine out almost every night . . . Yesterday Madame d'Aunet came to dinner here, with her daughter,[9] who is charming. How happy we should all be in Paris if only you were with us! On that point we are unanimous. You really are difficult to understand! Your stoicism and your conscience are a standing marvel. We could have here in Paris the largest and most charming of *salons*. Just think of it! With what we are spending in Brussels, we could make for ourselves an honoured and most agreeable existence. More than that, we should be a centre, and in a short time could create for ourselves lucrative literary employments. Of that I am certain. As to my father, I think it would be much to his benefit to have, as the result of our settling here, a foothold in Paris, and a place in everybody's mind and thoughts. We should be the *salon* of his rock. But, so long as you go on saying: *if but one remain—I will be that one,* all this is impossible.

Would you like me to give you news of Bonaparte? I have seen him several times in the Champs Élysées and the Bois. He has become very fat and faded in appearance. His pasty face is a mass of wrinkles. His eyes still have the same old dull and vacant look. But he seems to be in pretty good health— unfortunately! His moustache is turning grey. The damned scamp lives too well. He drives everywhere. Very few hats are raised, and nobody cheers. What it all comes to is that he just manages to reign, and no more.

Paris is dazzling. The new Quarters are splendid. The houses now going up are quite charming, and built in many different styles. There is an increasing number of Squares, Gardens, Promenades, Fountains. The degree of luxury is *incredible*. The carriages, horses and pretty women are a feast for the eye at every moment of the day. . . .[10]

But François-Victor was determined to stay faithful to the exile, and Charles, somewhat ironically, could only sigh: "So long as you are *that one*, nothing can be done." He complained of the "Old Man."

June 16th, 1868: "Still no news from my father. He hasn't sent us a penny-piece since we came here[11] and we live on the money supplied by Meurice . . . I am enclosing with this the hundred francs which Mamma is sending for Adèle." *June 26th, 1868:* "Mamma would like to know whether my father has remembered to send three hundred francs to Adèle for summer dresses? If he hasn't, please see that he does. You must *insist.* Mamma is worrying about it! Let us have a line on the subject."[12] But summer was approaching, and with it the time of the annual reunion in Brussels. Madame Hugo was looking forward to seeing her husband again. "As soon as I have you with me, I shall stick to you without asking leave! I shall be so sweet and charming that you will not have the courage to desert me! My only wish now is to die in your arms."[13] Now in her weakness she was clinging to the strength which had so often terrified her.

Her wish was granted. On August 24th, 1868, she went for a drive with her husband in an open carriage. He was all tenderness and high spirits. Next day, about three o'clock in the afternoon, she had an apoplectic seizure: breathing constricted, spasms; one side of her body paralysed. *Victor Hugo's Diary, August 27th, 1868:* "Died at half-past six this morning. I closed her eyes. Into God's hands I commit her. May He receive her great and tender heart. May she be blessed. According to her wish, we shall transport her coffin to Villequier, and lay it beside that of our dear dead daughter. I shall accompany it as far as the frontier . . ." Vacquerie and Meurice came from Paris that same day in order to be present when the body was placed in the coffin. The doctor, Émile Allix, left the face uncovered.

I took some flowers which were there. I laid them round her head with a wreath of white daisies, but in such a way as not to conceal her face. I scattered flowers all over the body, and filled the coffin with them. Then, I kissed her on the forehead, and said in a whisper: "Be thou blessed." I remained on my knees beside her. Charles approached, then Victor. They kissed her with tears running down their cheeks, and remained standing behind me. Paul Meurice, Vacquerie and Allix all wept . . . One after the other they bent down and kissed her. At five o'clock the leaden shell was soldered and the oak coffin screwed down. Before the lid was placed in position I, with a small key which I had in my pocket, scratched on the lead, just over her face, V.H. When the coffin was closed I kissed it . . . Before leaving, I changed into the black clothes which I shall wear for the rest of my life. . . .[14]

Victor Hugo went with the coffin as far as the French frontier. Vacquerie, Meurice and Doctor Allix accompanied it to Villequier. The poet and his sons spent the night at Quiévrain. *August 29th, 1868:* "In my room there was a copy of the illustrated edition of *Les*

Misérables. I wrote my name in it, with the date, as a souvenir for my host. This morning, at half-past nine, we started back for Brussels, where we arrived at noon . . ." *August 30th:* "An offer for my unfinished books from Lacroix. Time to get down to work again."[15] Madame Victor had been photographed on her deathbed[16] in the sad trappings of mortality. On an enlargement of this last portrait, carried out for him alone, Victor Huge wrote: *Chère morte pardonnée. . . .*[17]

On September 1st he received an account of the funeral. Paul Meurice had delivered an admirable address at Villequier. Hugo gave instructions that the tombstone should have carved upon it the words:

ADÈLE
FEMME DE VICTOR HUGO

Adèle, Wife of Victor Hugo—was that inscription dictated by reasons of pride? By a desire to regain in death possession of her who, in life, had at one special moment escaped him? Or as a tribute to the fidelity of his "friend"? It was in that last sense that Juliette interpreted the words. Not only did she make no attempt to persuade the great man, now a widower, to marry her, but was at pains to establish a *cult* of Adèle. *Juliette Drouet to Victor Hugo, Guernsey, October 10th, 1868:* "Since I have resumed my life here, I feel as though my spirit had expanded, and taken upon itself a double nature. I love you now with the great heart of your dear departed as well as with my own. I ask of this illustrious witness of your earthly life that she will stand surety for mine at God's throne. I ask her permission to love you as long as I live, both in this world and the next. I ask of her, too, some little part of that divine gift she had of making you happy, and I hope that she will grant me that request now that she can see deeply into my heart."[18] Had Adèle really made her husband happy? Had she, at least, once the situation was accepted, not made him unhappy? The wife of a man of genius finds herself, at once, very close to and very distant from a form of existence which "seems to reduce every other to unimportance."

Immediately after getting back to Hauteville House he resumed the regular rhythm of his laborious life. Every Monday a dinner for forty poor children. Every evening "to dinner at Hauteville II. From now on, God willing, I shall be there every day of the week . . ."[19] From dawn till dusk—work. He continued to "pile Pelion on Ossa." This man of sixty could still announce a whole series of novels still to come: *L'Homme qui rit* (or England after 1688); *La France avant 1789* (title still to be decided upon); *Quatre-vingt-treize*—Aristocracy,

Monarchy, Democracy. For *L'Homme qui rit* he had, as always, accumulated such documentary material as he could find in the bookshops of Guernsey and Brussels. He went so far as to compile a complete
list of English Peers of the Realm, plans of old London and the House
of Lords. What is really astonishing is that this unmethodical and
motley erudition should have succeeded in producing a coherent picture. Hugo had a passion for amassing thousands of odd and useless
details: but he also had a nose for the essential.

He had been trying for a long time to find the proper title. To
Lacroix, who was to publish the book, he had announced it as *Par
ordre du Roi*. Then, on the advice of friends, he had changed this
to *L'Homme qui rit*. An historical novel? It would, he said, be both
"drama and history. The reader will be presented with an unfamiliar
England. The period in which the story is laid is that extraordinary
stretch of years between 1688 and 1705. This is the preparatory stage
of our own French eighteenth century, the reign of Queen Anne,
about whom so much is said and so little known. I think that this
book will contain revelations, even for the English. Macaulay, after
all, is only a superficial historian. I have tried to go deeper . . ."[20]
Hugo envisaged the historical novel differently from Walter Scott
or Dumas. The great figures of history must be seen only at a distance,
profiles against a background, the invented characters being the only
ones in which the author was interested. More than one personal bond
linked him with this book. His childhood's terror at sight of a gibbet
in the darkness was closely connected with the frightful visions which
had haunted him from his earliest years. The hero, Gwynplaine (later
Lord Clancharlie), is, like Triboulet, like Didier, like Quasimodo, like
Hernani, like Jean Valjean, a victim of society. Disfigured from birth,
this man whose face is marked with a terrible grin is a man who
suffers. Restored to his rightful position, he remains faithful to the
companions of his days of poverty, and delivers in the House of Lords,
to an accompaniment of jeers, a speech which recalls Victor Hugo's
own in the Assembly of 1850.

Another characteristic, thanks to which this story, in many ways
so baroque and extravagant, remains human, is the confrontation of
the virgin Gwynplaine with the flesh. There had always been in Hugo,
since his adolescent years, which had been at one and the same time
chaste and haunted with desires, a mingling of obsession and of fear
at the spectacle of the female body—"so full of promise for the senses,
of danger for the spirit." Gwynplaine, seeing Josiane asleep, trembles.
"Nudity in its formidable concision. A sort of mysterious challenge
brazenly evocative of Eden. A calling forth of man's darker side. Eve
worse than Satan . . . a disturbing ecstasy, ending in the brute triumph
of instinct over duty. . . ."[21]

L'Homme qui rit was less successful than the novels which had preceded it. This was in part due to Lacroix, who used it as an occasion for launching a rather too commercial campaign of publicity, but also to the fact that the novelists of the realist or naturalist school had accustomed their public to find emotional satisfaction in the events of every day. "There can be no doubt," wrote Hugo, "that a great gulf is opening between me and my contemporaries . . . If the writer is to write for his own time only, then I might as well break my pen and throw it away."[22] Nevertheless, at the very same moment he was composing poetry worthy of being admired by his own time and by all times, but he stuffed it away in his files, not being over-anxious to publish it. Besides, can it be truly said that he still had any real contemporaries? Lamartine had just died. *March 4th, 1869:* "Lamartine is dead. He was the greatest of all the race of Racine, not even excepting Racine. . . ."[23] "Poor Baudelaire," a much younger man, had disappeared in 1867. Vigny had died in 1863. Dumas was fast going downhill. Mérimée was dying of heart trouble, Sainte-Beuve of more long-standing ailments. Hugo alone remained strong, productive, prodigious. *To Auguste Vacquerie, January 7th, 1869:* "I know only too well that I am not ageing, that on the contrary I am still in the stage of growth, and for that very reason I feel that death cannot be far off. What a proof of the existence of the soul! My body is declining, my powers of thought increasing. Beneath my weight of years a process of blossoming is taking place . . ."[24] A Titan? "No," said Michelet to the Goncourts, "a Vulcan, a powerful gnome, hammering away at iron in a great forge deep within the earth."

A copy of *L'Homme qui rit* was sent to Madame Léonie d'Aunet with this prudent dedication: *Hommage*—V. H.

4 5

The End of Exile

IN 1869 France was filled with the sound of cracking which heralded the end of the regime. Military disaster in Mexico and diplomatic defeat in Europe had exasperated and humiliated the French. The Emperor, worn-out and sick, gave ground, and spoke of "black patches darkening the horizon." He hoped to be able still to transform what he could not maintain. A young journalist, Henri Rochefort, who, Marquis de Rochefort-Luçay by birth, had turned his back on his class, and the better to strengthen his authority had started *La Lanterne*, a disrespectful, witty weekly broadsheet, wrote for the first number an article which contained the famous phrase: "France holds thirty-six million subjects, not counting subjects of complaint." A hundred thousand copies were sold every Thursday. Encouraged by this example, the former editors of *L'Évènement* (the two Hugo sons, Paul Meurice and Auguste Vacquerie) decided that the moment had come to launch a journal the object of which should be to attack the Second Empire. They enlisted the help of two brilliant pamphleteers— Henri Rochefort himself and Édouard Lockroy, the son of the actor. The first need was to find a title. Victor Hugo suggested *L'Appel au Peuple*. *Le Rappel* was thought to be better, and was duly adopted. It appeared for the first time on May 8th, 1869, and from the very first fifty thousand copies were printed.

The journal was a success. It was amusing and non-conformist. Victor Hugo cheered the fighters on from Guernsey. *To François-Victor, May 14th, 1869:* "I want, Victor my boy, to send a cry of joy to you, as well as to Charles. Your first article is a model of strength and high-mindedness. Set your minds at rest, both of you—I am not going to play the fond parent and write like this whenever you set pen to paper. Instead of that, I send you in advance a sheaf of blank cheques on applause."[1] As was only to be expected, both paper and contributors were hounded. Fines, searches, prosecutions. *Victor Hugo's Diary, December 10th, 1869:* "Charles comes up for sentence today. He has the honour of having made the scoundrel squeal. Well done!"[2] His own activities were confined to finishing *L'Homme qui rit*, and starting to write again for the stage, with *Torquemada*. As was his custom

379

he went to Brussels for the summer months of 1869. *To Charles and François-Victor, July 23rd, 1869:* "I am glad, my dear boys, to know that you are in Brussels. I shall be with you some time between July 31st and August 5th. I am just finishing something. I shall try to make a few trips. So long as you are in Brussels, I shall expect you to provide me with a morning meal (coffee and cutlet), and I, in return, will give you dinner, by which I mean that I invite all four of you (including Georges who has six teeth) to dine every day at the Hôtel de la Poste. That will simplify the business of domestic service. Don't forget that I must have one of the maids to sleep in the room next to mine (in the back premises): I still have my choking fits at night."[3] He thought of everything. *Victor Hugo's Diary, August 8th, 1869:* "I have found in the Place des Barricades a new serving-wench, Thérèse, who sleeps in the room next to mine. She is plain, Flemish and fair. I have no idea of her age. Rather think she must be thirty-three. I asked her whether she was married. Her reply was quite Parisian: 'What a hideous thought!' " *August 10th, 1869:* "Five o'clock this morning. Thérèse. . . ."[4]

In September he accepted an invitation to attend a Peace Congress in Lausanne. During the whole journey the train was welcomed by crowds, shouting: "Vive Victor Hugo! Vive la République!" He made a speech to his "fellow citizens of the United States of Europe." It was meant to be about peace, but was, in fact, pretty bellicose. "What is it we want? Peace . . . But in what form do we want that peace? Do we want peace at any price? . . . No! we do not want peace under a despotism . . . The first condition of peace must be liberation. For this liberation to become an accomplished fact, it is very certain that we must have a revolution, a revolution to end revolutions, and perhaps, alas! a war that will end all wars . . ."[5] This was to be the first of the wars "to end wars." A month earlier the Emperor, who now called himself a Liberal, had made another offer of an amnesty. Hugo had replied: "In *Cromwell* you will find this line:

> Allez, je vous fais grâce—Et de quel droit, tyran?"

He decided, on his way home, to see something of Switzerland with Juliette. At Schaffhausen he was delighted to visit again, after thirty years, the Falls of the Rhine. *Victor Hugo's Diary, September 27th, 1869:* "Splendid spectacle of falling waters. When God sets the waters moving, He is not exhausted and out of breath, like Louis XIV. His fountains last for millions of centuries . . . On the edge of abyss I picked a little green leaf which I gave to J. J.,[6] as well as two flowers, on our way up the rock staircase . . ."[7] *October 1st:* On arrival [in Brussels] I found Alice brought to bed. A pretty little girl—an eight months' child. *October 4th, 1869:* "The new servant, who has replaced

Thérèse, is sleeping tonight in the room next to mine. She is called
Élise. Peasant girl. Very dark. Skin almost black." *October 10th:* "When
little Jeanne was being given suck this morning she clasped my finger
in her little fist."[8] In November he left again for Guernsey: "For the
thinker his workshop." The hunchback exile Hennet de Kesler, of
whom he had been very fond, died on April 6th, 1870. The circle
of solitude was growing tighter. In June his grandchildren came to
keep him company. Juliette constituted herself poet-laureate of "our
sweet Georges," and composed the following verse, to be sun to the
tune of *La Carmagnole*:

> Le petit Georges avait promis (*bis*)
> De venir voir ses bons amis (*bis*)
> Il vient à Guernsey
> Pour se faire baisé![9]

The grandfather's heart was warmed. He had the pond and the
terrace enclosed with a wall, and a bowl filled with breadcrumbs set
on the children's balcony. On it he wrote:

> Passereaux et rouges-gorges,
> Venez des airs et des eaux,
> Venez tous faire vos orges,
> Messieurs les petits oiseaux,
> Chez monsieur le petit Georges.[10]

He was still, in the matter of work, keeping to an inflexible time-
table, but his present activity was like that which fills the last few
days before starting on a journey, when one hurriedly finishes work
in progress, and already feels separated from the world one has known.
There was a vague feeling about that something was going to happen.
"Liberty was crowning the edifice at the very moment at which the
foundations were collapsing." In May 1870 the programme of reforms
was submitted to a plebiscite, and with seven million five hundred
thousand "Yes" returns, it looked as though the liberal Empire was
firmly consolidated: "but," said Hugo, "thousands of snowflakes make
but a paltry avalanche."

> Soit. Que restera-t-il de toute cette neige,
> Voile froid de la terre au suaire pareil,
> Demain, une heure après le lever du soleil?[11]

In Europe Bismarck was busy engineering a war. *Victor Hugo's
Diary, July 17th, 1870:* "Three days ago, on July 14th, at the very
moment that in my garden at Hauteville House I was planting the
oak tree of the United States of Europe, war broke out in Europe,
and the dogma of the infallibility of the Pope was promulgated in

Rome. In a hundred years there will be no more wars, no more Popes, and the oak will be a large tree.[12] Of these three prophecies, one only has been realized. The oak is a large tree.

The war confronted Hugo with a problem of conscience. If the Empire were to be victorious, then the power of the man of December 2nd would stand on a firm foundation. If the Empire were to be defeated, it would mean humiliation for France. Should he return as a National Guardsman, forget about the Empire, and let himself be killed for France? Helped by Juliette he packed and strapped his portmanteau. In any case he would go to Brussels. On August 9th it became clear that the war was turning into a catastrophe. Three battles lost in quick succession. *Victor Hugo's Diary, August 9th, 1870:* "I am locking all my manuscripts in the three trunks, and am now prepared to move as duty, and the turn of events, may decide. . . ."[13]

On August 15th he took ship with Juliette, Charles, Alice, the children, their nurse and three maid-servants (Suzanne, Mariette, and Philomène). Georges's name for Victor Hugo was neither "grand-père" nor "grand-papa," but "Papapa." On August 18th they were back again in the Place des Barricades. "I have resumed my old habits. I take a cold bath. I work until *déjeuner*. Just as Charles sat down to table I put on his plate a packet containing a thousand gold francs and this note: 'Charles, my boy, please allow me to pay little Jeanne's passage!—Papapa, August 18th, 1870.' "[14]

On the 19th he paid a visit to the Chancellery of the French Embassy, and requested a passport for Paris. He told Antoine de Laboulaye, the chargé d'affaires, that he was returning to France in order to do his duty as a citizen, but that he did not recognize the Empire. "I want to be nothing in France but one National Guardsman the more." *Victor Hugo's Diary, August 19th, 1870:* "He was very polite. 'Before I go any further,' he said to me, *'let me salute the century's one great poet!'* Then, he asked me to wait until the evening when he would have the passport delivered to my house. . . ."[15]

Louis Koch, Juliette Drouet's nephew, started for Paris. It was agreed that he should see Meurice, Vacquerie and other friends, and that if they thought it advisable for Hugo to return he was to send a telegram to Philomène containing the following message: "Bring the children." Already the Brussels papers were circulating the news that Hugo was going to enlist, and were referring to him as "the Conscript Father."

Victor Hugo to François-Victor, August 26th, 1870: It makes me sad to think that you are not here with me, or that I am not there with you. Matters look like coming to a head. We are watching and waiting, ready to leave at a moment's notice, but on this condition only, that nobody shall say we are going to the help of the Empire. To save France, to save Paris, to get rid of the Empire, that is what we want to do. To *that* cause I will gladly and wholeheartedly devote myself . . . I have just been told that if I show my face in Paris I shall be arrested. I don't believe a word of it, and in any case the threat won't prevent me from going to Paris if Paris finds itself confronted with the consequences of a second Waterloo, and in danger of death. To share death with Paris would be, for me, glory. It would be a fine end, but I fear that all these hideous events will have but a petty one. If that be so, I do not wish to share: Prussia halting her armies, a shameful peace, dismemberment, whether with Bonaparte in power or the House of Orléans—such possibilities fill me with horror, and if the people do not lift a finger I shall go back into exile. . . .[16]

On September 3rd the Emperor capitulated, and on the 4th a Republic was proclaimed. The telegram arrived from Paris: "Bring the children at once." On the 5th Victor Hugo, at the booking-office of the Brussels terminus, asked in a voice trembling with emotion for "a ticket to Paris." He was wearing a soft felt hat, and had a leather satchel slung from his shoulder with a strap. He looked at the time, the time which marked the termination of his exile, and, very pale in the face, said to Jules Claretie, a young writer who was with him: "I have been awaiting this moment for nineteen years." Charles and Alice, Antonin Proust, Jules Claretie and Juliette Drouet travelled in the same compartment with him. At Landrecies they had their first sight of French troops. They were retreating down the permanent way, and looked worn-out and discouraged. They wore blue greatcoats and red trousers. Hugo, with tears in his eyes, called out to them: *"Vive la France! Vive l'armée française!"* They stared glumly and without interest at the white-bearded old gentleman with the tears running down his cheeks. "Oh! to see them again like this!—the soldiers of my country—beaten!"

The son of General Hugo had known a day when the dear name of France had made the foreigner tremble. He had a confused hope that he might live to see a revival, and even share in promoting it. Had he not predicted what would happen? Had he not been the last bastion of liberty? Who could guide the young Republic better than he, the old man who for nineteen years had never been wrong? The moon was high and bright and through the windows of the railway carriage he could see the plains of France. He wept. The train arrived at 9.35. An immense crowd was waiting. His reception was indescribable.

The daughter of Théophile Gautier, Judith, was there. It was on the arm of this beautiful young woman that he reached a small café opposite the station. There she barred the door with her outstretched leg against a "frenzied crowd." Hugo spoke to her with charming gallantry. Then Paul Meurice arrived and said that he must make a speech to the people.[17] A window was opened. First from the balcony on the first floor, then from his carriage, the Great Exile had to speak four separate times. There were cries of *"Vive Victor Hugo!"* Somebody recited a few lines from *Les Châtiments*. The crowd wanted to drag him to the Hôtel de Ville. He called out: "No, citizens! I have come not to shake the Provisional Government of the Republic, but to support it!" There were shouts, also, of *"Vive le petit Georges!"* When he reached the Avenue Frochot and the house belonging to Paul Meurice where he was to lodge, he said to the people: "You have repaid me in one hour for twenty years of exile!" A violent storm of thunder and lightning shattered the darkness. The heavens themselves were with him.

PART X

Death and Transfiguration

46

The Terrible Year

> I would I were not French, that I might say
> I choose thee, France, and in this thy day
> Of martyrdom, proclaim thee, torn by the vulture's claw,
> My country and my glory; my love for evermore.
>
> VICTOR HUGO

THERE is something frightening as well as sweet in returning to one's native land after a long exile. Sweet, in so far as one sees again persons and places that for years have filled the dreaming mind with a painful nostalgia. *"Que la terre de France était riante et blonde!"* Hugo had murmured in far-off Guernsey. Sweet indeed was it to see once more this land of France, this beloved city of Paris. But frightening, too, because he saw on his return how all had changed (*Où donc es-tu, foyer où je me réchauffais?*); because his native land seemed peopled now with more of the dead than the living; because he felt almost a stranger among so many new faces; especially since, now descended from the Olympus of exile where only untrammelled thought was king, he must mingle with the quarrels of the streets and the market place.

For twenty years Hugo had been the prophet of the Republic, the distant inspiration of resistance to the Empire. There can be no doubt that in September 1870 he was filled with the vague hope that he would hear himself acclaimed as the incontestable head of a Government of Union intent on continuing the fight against the enemy. But already the die had been cast. Very cleverly Jules Favre and his friends had occupied the Hôtel de Ville on September 4th, thus forestalling the establishment of a Commune of Paris. They had elected as President of the Provisional Government General Trochu, an anti-Bonapartist to be sure, but at heart a clerical and a monarchist. He appeared, however, to be master of the army, and to that extent necessary. The men who would have liked to establish a Commune—Flourens, Blanqui, Ledru-Rollin—were champing at the bit and in no way inclined to accept the new regime. They would have been glad enough to annex Hugo and the prestige that went with him, but he wisely held aloof. "I am an almost impossible mixer," he said. To be the poet of the Republic meant more to him than to be President of the Government, or head of the opposition. Nevertheless he felt to some extent discouraged. *"J'étais le vieux rôdeur sauvage de la mer."*[1] On his rock he had been a sea-god. In a Paris lodging he had once more dwindled into a vulnerable human being.

In the Avenue Frochot, at the house of Paul Meurice which had been his first asylum, he received innumerable visitors: little Louis Blanc; the writer Jules Claretie, who brought him a golden bee which had taken flight from the Imperial mantle; generals who were seeking commands; officials asking for posts. To all of them he said: "I am nothing," which was a polite way of saying, "I will do nothing." He met again Théophile Gautier, tender, affectionate, but embarrassed, for the good Théo had been "on the pay-roll of the Empire," one of the critics in the service of *Le Moniteur,* and librarian to the Princess Mathilde. "I embraced him," wrote Hugo. "He was just a little bit frightened. I asked him to dine with me." It would have been ungracious in him to treat Gautier with severity. In 1867, when *Hernani* was revived, he had shown himself to be as valiant and as faithful as in the days of the rose-pink doublet. The *Moniteur* had asked him to make cuts in an article judged to be over-enthusiastic. He had offered to resign. Now he was on the point of losing everything. "I was going to be an Academician, to be given a seat in the Senate . . . I was going to settle down in a comfortable little niche . . . and now, here I am, on the shelf! Brrr! the coming of the Republic has blown everything sky-high!"[2]

Edmond de Goncourt paid a call on the Old Man of the Sea, and took notes; that was his purpose in life. Meurice's apartment was chock-a-block with friends sprawling on the divans. Charles Hugo, dangerously fat, in National Guard uniform, started little Georges playing games. In the half-darkness Hugo's head, with the light full on it, had a noble look. All were struck by the "beautiful and rebellious white locks in his hair, such as one sees on Michelangelo's prophets, and on his face a curious look of placidity that was almost ecstatic. Yes, an *ecstaticism*, though now and again there were flashes, almost immediately extinguished, of a black, black, black eye."[3]

Goncourt asked him whether he felt glad to be back in Paris. "Yes, I like Paris as it is now," replied Hugo. "I should not have liked to see the Bois de Boulogne when it was filled with carriages, barouches and landaus. I find pleasure in it now that it is a morass, a ruin. It is beautiful! it is splendid!"

On the occasion of this visit Victor Hugo showed as "amiable, simple, companionable, not in the least grandiloquent or sibylline. His rare personality makes itself felt only in delicate hints, as when he speaks of the improvement made in Paris, and mentions Notre-Dame. One is grateful for his slightly cold, slightly haughty politeness, which it is a pleasure to come across in these days of banal effusiveness."[4] Democrat though he might be now, he still retained the aloof dignity of the young Levite of 1820, simple, but not familiar.

Goncourt, with his natural tendency to scepticism and discouragement, had already accepted the inevitability of defeat, and was genuinely astonished by Victor Hugo's bellicose enthusiasm. "We shall get on our feet again," said the Old Man: "we must not perish." In his intense patriotism he could not listen to the soldiers marching through the streets singing the "Marseillaise" and "Le Chant du Départ," without crying. "I hear those tremendous words: *'Un Français doit vivre pour Elle—Pour Elle, un Français doit mourir . . .'* I hear and I weep! . . . Forward, brave lads! Where you go, I will go, too!"[5] He wrote to General Trochu offering his services; but his friends managed to persuade him that he was of more use living than dead.

He had no sooner arrived than he issued an *Appeal to the Germans*: "Germans, I speak to you as a friend . . . What is this disastrous misunderstanding between us? Two nations have made Europe. Those two nations are France and Germany. Today Germany is trying to destroy Europe. How can such a thing be possible? This war was not of our making. It was willed by the Empire, and the Empire is dead. It is good that it should be. We have nothing in common with that corpse . . . Germans, if you persist, so be it; you have been warned. Go ahead, if you will; attack the walls of Paris. Under your shells and your bullets she will defend herself. Old as I am, I shall be there, unarmed. It is well for me that I should be with those who die; I pity you that you should be with the kings who kill . . ."[6] He had hoped that this appeal would fall on willing ears, and that if Victor Hugo stood forth between the two armies, the war would end. "It would be he who would end!" said an ill-conditioned joker.

When the Old Man saw the iron circle drawing tighter round Paris, he turned savage. "It seems that the Prussians have decreed that France shall be Germany, and Germany Prussia; that I, who am speaking to you, born of Lorraine, am a German; that noon shall be midnight; that the Eurotas, the Nile, the Tiber and the Seine are nothing but tributaries of the Spree; that the city which for four centuries has been the glory of the world is now a useless encumbrance; that Berlin is enough . . . that no proof has been advanced that the sun is a necessity; that, in any case, we gave a bad example to mankind; that we are of Gomorrha, and they, the Prussians, the fire fallen from Heaven; that the time has come to make an end; that from now onwards the human race is nothing but a second-rate Power . . . Make no mistake about it: Paris will defend herself victoriously. Citizens! forward into battle! . . . O Paris!

thou hast crowned the statue of Strasbourg with flowers: history shall crown thee with stars!"[7]

Already the besieged city was becoming transformed. Hatters were selling spiked Prussian helmets, brought back by the retreating soldiers, and Hugo displayed one of these to his astonished grandchildren. Butchers were exhibiting for sale the flayed carcasses of horses and donkeys. All round the city the forests were ablaze, and as, in the days of *Les Orientales,* Victor Hugo had gone to watch the setting sun, so now he gazed upon the distant flames, or at the captive balloon in mid-heaven. Juliette accompanied him on these pilgrimages. They travelled all round Paris by train on the Ceinture line. They found matter for amazement in Baron Haussmann's tall new houses. Juliette saw the piles of flowers at the base of the statue of Strasbourg which once, long ago, Pradier had designed, using her as his model. In a great many theatres *Les Châtiments* were declaimed, the receipts going to the purchase of cannon for the Army of Paris. So great was the success of these recitations that the committee was able to acquire three pieces of ordnance, which were named *Châteaudun, Châtiments,* and *Victor Hugo.* The actors came for rehearsal to the Avenue Frochot. In this way Victor Hugo acted as host to Frédérick Lemaître, Lia Félix, Marie Laurent. He was happy to be back again in the atmosphere of the stage which is so alive, so intoxicating, that no one who has breathed it once can ever forget it.

In the streets were to be seen soldiers of the line, men from the flying columns, irregulars, often loaded with vegetables collected under enemy fire. The shops were becoming empty. Workers in smocks and caps could be heard shouting: *"Vive la Commune!"* Men were being called to the colours. On October 31st the Commune (Blanqui, Flourens) attempted to overthrow the Provisional Government. *Victor Hugo's Diary*: "At midnight some National Guardsmen came to fetch me to the Hôtel de Ville, there, they said, to *preside* over the new Government. I replied that I was profoundly opposed to this attempt, and refused to go with them; at three o'clock in the morning Flourens and Blanqui left the Hôtel de Ville, and Trochu marched in."[8] The papers praised Hugo for holding aloof.

Like all Parisians, he had but little to eat. "Rats are being made into pâté; I am told it is quite good." The Jardin des Plantes sent him some joints of bear, deer and antelope. At the New Year he gave little Georges and little Jeanne a basketful of toys. Louis Koch had presented his aunt Juliette Drouet with two cabbages and a brace of live partridges, a royal gift. The grandfather made light of these privations, and pertinaciously turned them into matter for verse. To the lovely Judith Gautier,[9] who had refused an invitation to dinner, he wrote:

Si vous êtiez venue, ô belle que j'admire!
Je vous aurais offert un repas sans rival;
J'aurais tué Pégase et je l'aurais fait cuire.
Afin de vous servir une aile de cheval.[10]

He even turned his Will into quatrain:

Je lègue au pays, non ma cendre,
Mais mon bifteck, morceau de roi.
Belles, si vous mangez de moi,
Vous verrez combien je suis tendre![11]

The bombardment tore great holes in Paris. The quarter in which he had lived as a child, les Feuillantines, suffered. A shell breached the Chapel of the Virgin at Saint-Sulpice, in which he had been married. The friends of the Commune were becoming more and more insistent in their attempts to persuade the poet to give them his help in overturning the Government. He was more and more losing faith in Trochu, who kept on talking about his "sortie," but never made one. He formulated a definition of him as "Past participle of the verb *trop choir*" (to flop excessively). He wrote a very brutal couplet about him:

. . . Soldat brave, honnête, pieux, nul,
Bon canon, mais ayant un peu trop de recul . . .[12]

He thought, however, that there was greater danger for the country in an upheaval in face of the enemy than in maintaining its present impotent Government—"a pygmy that thinks it can get a child on this giantess, France." At first Paris had taken the siege with high-spirited courage, but later the heroic comedy turned to tragedy. Famine was in possession. Shells whistled overhead. In the distance the flushed walls of Saint-Cloud were burning. Sorties were made at Champagny and Montretout, but failed "owing to the incapacity of the commanders," said the Parisians. The journalist Henry Bauer called Trochu "an Émile Ollivier on horseback!"

On January 29th came the armistice. It was snowing. The flinty Bismarck said: "The creature is dead"; Paris saw the entry of poultry and butchers' meat, but also of spiked helmets.

Before peace could be made, a National Assembly must be elected. This sat at Bordeaux. Naturally Victor Hugo was one of the candidates in the Department of the Seine, and quite certain of being returned. He left for Bordeaux. Though the idea of making one in an assembly saddled with the duty of ratifying defeat was unpleasing to him, he could not stand aloof. In his diary he wrote: "I came to Paris hoping to find a grave: I shall go to Bordeaux with the intention of resuming my exile . . ."[13] He started from Paris on February 13th, 1871. The

Assembly just elected did not represent his own republican and patriotic feelings. The country, taken by surprise, wanted to have no more to do with the Bonapartists, whom it blamed for the defeat; nor had it any use for the republicans. Consequently it had voted for the old monarchist party, and for peace. Country squires, elderly legitimists who since 1830 had not shown their noses outside their châteaux, now met in the Allées de Tourny at Bordeaux. They got on the poet's nerves. *Victor Hugo to Paul Meurice, February 18th, 1871:* "Between ourselves, the situation is quite appalling. The Assembly is *une Chambre introuvable*; nothing like it has ever been seen. *We* are in the proportion of fifty to seven hundred. It may well be that, in view of the frightful blows to be anticipated from the majority, the only possible line of action will be a mass secession of the Left, carried out with a purpose, which will be to hang on the flank of the Assembly and deal sporadic blows which *might* end by killing it. . . ."[14]

In the city thus invaded by the deputies, it was difficult to find accommodation, more especially for Hugo who never moved without his tribe at his heels. Charles and his family managed to get hold of a small apartment at 13 rue Saint-Maur. Alice remarked that the number, 13, seemed to haunt them. They had left Paris on February 13th; there had been thirteen of them in the saloon-car. The poet, who was very superstitious, scented approaching misfortune. However that might be, he no sooner showed himself than the city gave itself up to a frenzy of welcome. The National Guardsmen waved their caps; the crowd shouted so loudly that the old man, moved to tears, had to take refuge in a café. On the 16th, the results from the Paris constituency were announced: Louis Blanc, 216,000; Victor Hugo, 214,000; Garibaldi, 200,000. Little Thiers was at once elected Head of the Executive by the Right Wing of the Assembly.

Gambetta, Louis Blanc, Brisson, Lockroy and Clemenceau rallied round Victor Hugo and made him president of the Left. He had little time now for leisure: sessions of the Assembly, meetings of the Left, personal work. In such free moments as he could find, he took out little Georges and little Jeanne for walks. "I might be described as Victor Hugo, people's representative and children's nurse." On February 26th he celebrated his sixty-ninth birthday. On the 28th Thiers laid before the Assembly, for ratification, a "hideous treaty": Alsace and Lorraine were sacrificed. Hugo announced in committee that he would not vote for disposing of the two provinces in this way:

"Paris," he said, "is resigned to her death, but not to our dishonour. Mark this: it is for Europe as well as for France that Paris has conferred on us the duty of speaking loud and clear. Paris is exercising her function as capital of the continent."[15] He said that even if France signed, Germany would not *have* the two provinces: "to take is not to possess

... conquest is pillage; it is nothing more. It may be a fact, but facts do not confer rights. Alsace and Lorraine want to remain part of France, and, no matter what happens, part of France they will be, because France has a twofold title: *Republic* and *Civilization*. France, on her side, will abandon not a jot or tittle of her duty towards Alsace and Lorraine, towards herself, towards the world. Gentlemen, there are in Strasbourg, in that glorious Strasbourg now lying crushed under Prussian shell-fire, two statues: one of Gutenberg and one of Kléber. There sounds within me a voice crying aloud and swearing to Gutenberg that we will never allow civilization to be stifled; swearing to Kléber that we will never allow the Republic to be strangled . . ." He prophesied revenge:

Oh! the hour will sound—I can feel already the coming of that immense revenge. At this very moment I can hear our triumphant future striding forward into history. Assuredly, it will begin tomorrow; from tomorrow France will have but a single thought—to withdraw into herself, to rest for a while in the formidable brooding of despair, to recover her strength, to bring up her children, nourishing on a sacred anger the little ones who, as time passes, will become grown men, to forge cannons and to drill her citizens, to build an army which shall be a people in arms, to call science to the aid of war, to study the methods of Prussia as Rome once studied those of Carthage, to grow in strength and firmness, to be regenerated, to become once more France the Great, the France of 1792, the France of the mind and of the sword. . . . Then, suddenly, a day will come when she will stand upright again! Oh! then will she be a power to reckon with. We shall see her, at a single stroke, resume possession of Alsace, resume possession of Lorraine! Is that all? No, we shall see her, at a single stroke, resume possession—mark my words well—of Trèves, Mayence, Cologne, Coblentz . . . of all the left bank of the Rhine. Then we shall hear France cry aloud: *Now it is my turn! Germany, here I am! Am I your enemy? No, I am your sister. I have taken back all, and all I will give again, on one condition— that we shall together make one people, one family, one Republic. . . .*[16]

On his way out he heard one simple-minded member of the Right say to another: "Louis Blanc is abominable, but Victor Hugo is worse." Hugo had wanted the whole of the Left to leave the Assembly at the same time as the representatives of Alsace and Lorraine. His advice was not followed. When the Assembly, which lived in terror of Paris, decided to establish itself at Versailles, he protested: "Gentlemen, let us not march on Paris. Let us not go further than Prussia. The Prussians have dismembered France: it is not for us to behead her . . ."[17] His advice was not followed.

On March 8th the Assembly debated the case of Garibaldi: it was proposed that the election (in Algeria) of the great Italian should be

declared null and void, though in the worst days he had put himself
at the service of France. Hugo protested, to the fury of the majority, in
a tumultuous session. What? One single foreigner had come forward to
fight for France. Among all the generals of the war he, alone, had not
been beaten, and it was now proposed to exclude him . . . The Vicomte
de Lorgeril persistently interrupted him, treating Garibaldi as an
"extra in a melodrama," and ending with these words: "The Assembly
refuses to listen to Monsieur Victor Hugo, on the grounds that he does
not speak French." To an accompaniment of cries of "Order!" the
president asked Hugo to explain himself. "I will give you satisfaction,
gentlemen," he replied: "I will go farther than you have done. Three
weeks ago you refused to listen to Garibaldi . . . Today you refuse to
listen to me. I ask no more. I tender you my resignation."[18]

It was in vain that the President voiced the regrets of the Assembly;
in vain that Louis Blanc spoke of the pain felt by so many Frenchmen
at seeing a man of genius forced into the position of having to leave
a French Assembly. "It is his own fault!" shouted a voice from the
Right. "The decision is his," added the Duc de Marmier. The Left,
to a man, made representations at the poet's lodgings. On March 11th
Hugo made ready to start for Arcachon. He was overjoyed at the
thought of leaving an Assembly which he despised, and slamming the
door behind him. All the same, he regretted the things that had been
left undone, and noted: "Proposals which my resignation has made it
impossible for me to put forward: abolition of the death-penalty; abolition of humiliating and excessive penalties; reform of the magistrature;
motions preparatory to the establishment of a United States of Europe;
free and obligatory education; women's rights . . ."[19] (A large enough
programme to fill a century.)

For some time he had been sleeping badly. He brooded over the
various odd concatenations of the number 13, and reflected that he
was once again to leave a temporary asylum on March 13th. A bad
omen. He heard knockings in the night as of a hammer on wood. He
spent a day wandering about Bordeaux, and visited the Palais Gallien.
That night he was to dine at the Restaurant Lanta with Alice, Charles
and three friends. Alice and the other guests were punctual to the hour
named. Charles was late. Suddenly a waiter came into the room where
they were sitting and said that somebody was outside, asking for him.
It was Monsieur Porte, the landlord of No. 13 rue Saint-Maur. "You
must be brave, sir. Monsieur Charles . . ." "What of him?" "He is
dead." Hugo leaned against the wall. "Yes," continued Porte, "he had
taken a cab. When the driver opened the door outside the Café de
Bordeaux, he found him lying with blood pouring from his mouth and
nose. It was a sudden attack of apoplexy . . ." Hugo told Alice that he
would be back soon, and hurried to the rue Saint-Maur, whither

Charles's body had been carried. The children were asleep. *Victor Hugo's Diary, March 14th, 1871:* "I consoled Alice, mingling my tears with hers. I spoke to her as *tu* for the first time. Paid the restaurant for yesterday's dinner—the one at which we were waiting for Charles, 27 fr. 75."[20]

Hugo decided that his son should be buried at Père Lachaise, in the tomb of General Hugo. He left Bordeaux on March 17th, at half-past six in the evening, heavy-hearted but courageous.

> Coup sur coup. Deuil sur deuil. Ah! l'épreuve redouble.
> Soit! Cet homme pensif l'acceptera sans trouble.[21]

47

Whose the Fault?

I have seen shipwrecked and helpless men plunge to their death
Unaided, and have leapt on the ship at its latest breath,
Holding their misery than all your joys more true,
Choosing to die with them than live and lord it with you.

VICTOR HUGO

THE funeral train arrived to find Paris in the middle of an up-
heaval. The Commune had seized power. Revolutionaries and
patriots were united in anger against the treaty and the Assembly.
Rumours were in the air; there was fighting at Montmartre; two generals had been shot. Victor Hugo, with his son's coffin, was at the Gare
d'Orléans. The father, wearing mourning, received his friends in the
stationmaster's office. To Goncourt he said: "You have had a no less
terrible blow . . . But my case is out of the ordinary: to be struck twice
by lightning in the space of a single life! . . ."[1] The procession started.
A motley concourse followed it: a few men of letters; François-Victor,
walking beside his father; and the people in arms. "Hugo's white head,
framed in a hood, behind the hearse, dominated the mixed throng. It
looked like the head of a warrior monk in the days of the Ligue."[2] In
the Place de la Bastille a guard of honour formed spontaneously, with
arms reversed. Over the whole distance, as far as Père Lachaise, battalions of the National Guard presented arms and saluted the flag.
Drums beat a tattoo and the bugles sounded. Barricades compelled
the cortège to go a long way round.

At the cemetery, Vacquerie delivered an oration. Flowers were
thrown on the coffin. It was too long for the vault, and it was found
necessary to cut into the masonry. This took a long time. Hugo looked
broodingly at his father's tomb, which he had not seen since his return
from exile; at the coffin of his eldest son; at the empty space which,
doubtless, he himself would soon occupy. Lines, unsought, formed in
his mind:

Le tambour bat aux champs et le drapeau s'incline.
De la Bastille au pied de la morne colline,

Où les siècles passés près du siècle vivant
Dorment sous les cyprès peu troublés par le vent.
Le peuple a l'arme au bras; le peuple est triste: il pense,
Et ses grands bataillons font la haie en silence.
Le fils mort et le père aspirant au tombeau
Passent, l'un hier encor vaillant, robuste et beau,
L'autre vieux et cachant les pleurs de son visage;
Et chaque légion les salue au passage. . . .[3]

Before the coffin was lowered into the vault Hugo kneeled down and kissed it. That was his ritual act. When he moved away, the crowd surrounded him. Strangers wrung his hand. "How truly this people loves me, and how deeply I love them!"

At once, with Juliette, Alice and the children, he left for Brussels, where Charles had lived since his marriage, where now his heirs faced a heavily encumbered future. There were those who blamed the poet, saying that he had clutched at a convenient excuse for clearing out and thus avoiding the necessity of making a difficult choice. Yet a stay in Belgium was, at this moment, an imperative necessity. Alice and Charles, devotees of Spa, had been cleaned out at the tables. They had lost heavily, and had borrowed on a large scale. *Victor Hugo's Diary, April 8th, 1871:* "Alice and the children had *déjeuner* with me . . . Together with Victor we went to see the lawyer, Van Halten. He informed me of the total amount of their common indebtedness. The acknowledged debts in Brussels amount to rather more than 30,000 francs . . . To this sum of 30,000 (jointly owed by Charles and Alice) must be added 41,125 francs due to *Le Rappel* and 8000 owing to Émile Allix. There are also the costs of the funeral in Paris, and the lawyer's fee in Brussels."[4] . . . *April 9th, 1871:* "I have informed Victor that Alice must send back the shawl for which she has not yet paid [a shawl embroidered with gold palm-leaves, valued at 1000 francs] about which I shall certainly do nothing, not wishing to saddle the two children, who are minors, with this additional responsibility. . . ."[5]

Hugo followed the happenings in Paris with close attention. Frenchmen were fighting Frenchmen under the very eyes of the enemy. Had he thought that he could be of any use, he would, he said, have gone back, in spite of his duty to the family. "Nothing should keep me from doing so, but I believe that I should only exacerbate the situation. My fault is that I always tell the truth, and what can be more unwelcome than that? . . . The Assembly will have none of me: the Commune does not know me. Obviously, I am to blame."[6] The news worsened. The Commune was killing and burning. Versailles was bombarding Paris. "In short, this Commune is as idiotic as the Assembly. Both sides are mad. But France, Paris and the Republic will find a way out . . ."[7] he added, confident, in the last analysis, in the wisdom of an old country. On August 20th he heard of the death of Émile Deschamps, that most charming of friends, who now, after appalling sufferings, had reached the end of his life at the age of eighty. He listened in the moonlight to a nightingale singing in the trees of the Place des Barricades, and wondered whether perhaps the voice might be that of one of his "dear dead." Jeanne, asleep and dreaming, suddenly cried out "Papa" but the father of whom she spoke was dead. Georges' grandfather taught the boy to read, and wrote a poem for *Le Rappel*. It was called "Un Cri," and was an appeal to the combatants to put an end to the dismal slaughter:

> Combattants! Combattants! Qu'est-ce que vous voulez?
> Vous êtes comme un feu qui dévore les blés,
> Et vous tuez l'honneur, la raison, l'espérance!
> Quoi? D'un côté la France et de l'autre la France!
> Arrêtez! C'est le deuil qui sort de vos succès
> Chaque coup de canon de Français à Français
> Jette—car l'attentat à sa source remonte—
> Devant lui le trépas, derrière lui la honte. . . .[8]

He did not condone the excesses of the Commune, but, all the same, implored the Government of Versailles not to answer violence with cruelty. There must be no reprisals.

> Je ne fais point fléchir les mots auxquels je crois:
> Raison, progrès, honneur, loyauté, devoirs, droits,
> On ne va point au vrai par une route oblique.
> Soit juste: c'est ainsi qu'on sert le république;
> Le devoir envers elle est l'équité pour tous;
> Pas de colère; nul n'est juste s'il n'est doux . . .
> J'ai payé de vingt ans d'exil ce droit austère
> D'opposer aux fureurs un refus solitaire
> Et de fermer mon âme aux aveugles courroux;
> Si je vois les cachots sinistres, les verrous,
> Les chaînes menacer mon ennemi, je l'aime;
> Et je donne un asile à mon proscripteur même,
> Ce qui fait qu'il est bon d'avoir été proscrit.
> Je sauverais Judas si j'étais Jésus-Christ.[9]

But in Paris, as in Versailles, the spirit of hatred was in control. Each day brought to Hugo news of the death or arrest of some old friend: Flourens killed, Chaudey shot by the Commune, Lockroy arrested by the Government of Versailles. Then, after troops from Versailles had entered Paris on May 21st, Rochefort and Henry Bauer were thrown into prison. Louise Michel, the "Red Virgin," whose "terrifying compassion" he had admired, was under sentence of death. The Commune had executed sixty-four hostages: the Assembly shot six thousand prisoners—a hundred for one. "These men," wrote Hugo, "say *All for the law, all by the law*. What have your actions been? Summary shootings, killings without trial, improvised courts-martial . . ."[10] The beaten Communards were flowing into Belgium. Hugo made it known that he would give shelter in his own house (Place des Barricades, No. 4) to these new exiles. "Let us not shut our doors against the fugitives, innocent perhaps, and most certainly unconscious, doers of evil. . . ."[11]

His declaration in favour of the right of sanctuary appeared in *L'Indépendance Belge*. He received many letters of congratulation, but was awakened in the night by shouts of *"À mort Victor Hugo! À mort le brigand! À la Lanterne!"* Stones shattered his windows and broke his crystal chandeliers. Little Georges, in a fit of terror, said: "It's the Prussians!" The mob tried to tear down the shutters. They were met with resistance. These assailants were young dandies, about fifty in number. The incident was not really serious, but a decree was issued by the Belgian Government enjoining "one Victor Hugo, man of letters, sixty-nine years of age, to leave this kingdom, without delay, never to return."[12]

To the honour of the Belgians be it said that there were vehement protests against this expulsion, in the Chamber of Representatives no less than in the country at large. Hugo wrote a noble letter:

Every lost cause becomes an object of attack by the processes of law. My own view has always been that we should examine before judging, especially before condemning, especially before carrying out the sentence. That, I have always thought, is a principle beyond question. It seems that I am wrong, and that to kill outright is a better one . . . Perhaps it is good for me that there should always be a modicum of exile in my life. I persist, however, in not confusing the Belgian people with the Belgian Government, and having been favoured with a long period of hospitality, forgive the Government, and thank the people. . . .[13]

A return to France at this moment would have exposed him to vain and violent scenes. He decided to go to Luxembourg. In the course of their summer trips he had, on four occasions, stayed with Juliette in the small town of Vianden. It had charmed him for two reasons. The inhabitants had recognized and serenaded him, and he had fallen in love with the ruins of an old castle, very Hugoesque in appearance, which dominated the valley. There he would find peace. Luxembourg gave him a great welcome. On the station platform men, as they passed him, murmured *"Vive la République!"* and several women, blessed with good looks, gazed at him with a tenderness in their eyes which it needed no words to express.

In Vianden he rented two houses: one of them old and with carved gables, leaning above the river. One for himself;[14] the other, opposite, for his family.[15] He at once settled down to work, glad to get back to his novel and his poems, but deeply distressed by the news which reached him from Paris. Meurice had been arrested; Vacquerie had been visited by the police. Rochefort seemed destined for deportation. Louise Michel, that "savage little dreamer," had shouted, when brought before the War Council: "If you're not a lot of cowards, kill me!" He wrote a beautiful poem for her,[16] and protested against the excessive lengths to which reprisals were being taken. Louis Blanc and Victor Schœlcher, both of them dangerously exposed, took the prudent line and dissociated themselves from him. *Victor Hugo's Diary, July 13th, 1871:* "I shall answer them: 'Frankness calls for frankness . . . I would have neither red crime nor white. You have remained silent: I have spoken. I have fought against the principle of *vae victis.*' . . ."[17]

Because it was being noised abroad that he was giving a warm welcome to refugees, a young woman of eighteen, Marie Mercier, wrote asking for asylum. She had been the companion of Maurice Garreau, a locksmith who, under the Commune, had accepted the position of governor of the Mazas prison. Though he had not, it appeared, acted with cruelty, he had been shot without trial by the Versailles authorities, and his mistress, like Sophie Hugo long ago, had followed, by noting the bloodstains on the road, a wagon loaded with corpses to the Bercy cemetery. This Marie Mercier, "the widow Garreau," was now seeking work. Hugo prevailed upon his daughter-in-law Alice to employ her as a maid. He himself took her as his mistress. She was a pretty creature, "dark-complexioned, with a round, high-coloured face, and full lips." She told him stories of the Commune: "O! the rivers of blood I have seen!" she said.

Marie had hesitated, in her profound grief, to embark upon a new love-affair, but Olympio was persuasive. "He had a faculty of pleasing that was all his own," she could still say thirty years later. She saw no harm in what she was doing. She was in great distress, and little more than a child—"with her grief, her loneliness, the melancholy charm of her eighteen years, and the tears which lay like pearls on her pink cheeks under her crape veil."[18] "He sang the praises of all that my husband and I had loved—liberty, justice, the Republic," said Marie[19] . . . As once to Juliette, so now to her, he spoke of God and Immortality, of flowers, trees, the Infinite and love. "She was deeply attached to him, admired him, adored him, and wanted to have a child by him."[20] Responsive to his wishes, she bathed naked in the Our, before the eyes of her old-young lover. No less active than she was, he took her for long expeditions up the nearby mountains. After returning from these lovers' climbs, alone in the little house where he wrote standing at a high desk, he worked at *L'Année terrible, Quatre-vingt-treize,* and at additional matter for a new *Légende des Siècles* in which, apropos of Mahomet, he spoke of himself:

> Par moments, il faisait mettre une femme nue
> Et la regardait, puis il contemplait la nue
> Et disait: "La beauté sur terre, au ciel le jour."[21]

The sanguinary recollections of Marie Mercier inspired some fine poems, mournful and generous, in which the voices of young girls sang as they went to their death with proud disdain. Untiringly Hugo repeated that those who were being struck down were his brothers; that he would defend, in defeat, those whom he had fought in the time of their triumph; that big guns solve no problems, but only love:

> Voici ce qui remue en l'âme du banni:
> —Hélas! tout n'est pas dit et tout n'est pas fini
> Parce qu'on a creusé dans la rue une fosse,
> Parce qu'un chef désigne un mur où l'on adosse
> Des pauvres gens devant les feut de pelotons,
> Parce qu'on exécute au hasard, à tatons,
> Sans choix, sous la mitraille et sous la fusillade,
> Pères, mères, le fou, le brigand, le malade,
> Et qu'on fait consumer en hâte, par la chaux,
> Des corps d'hommes sanglants et d'enfants encor chauds![22]

Between that prostitute, State interest, and mercy Hugo had made his choice. But was State interest a valid argument; was it even of use to the State? He turned to mockery, using once again the sour raillery of *Les Châtiments*:

> Quoi? Rester fraternel, c'est être chimérique!
> Rêver l'Europe libre autant que l'Amérique,
> Réclamer l'équité, l'examen, la raison,
> C'est faire du nuage et du vent sa maison. . . .[23]

Those two months were incredibly productive. The conquest of the young woman had given a feverish stimulus to his mind. Other women, too, had offered themselves, and them he took with an easy nonchalance. Towards the end of his stay he visited Thionville, to see the town which had been defended and made famous by his father, then went to Altwies, where he found Marie Mercier established (by him) as a dressmaker. His diary is full of triumphant entries. *September 3rd, 1871: Maria . . . parece amorosa. September 11th: Quiero que esta me haga uno niño. September 12th: Ahora, todos los dias y a toda hora, misma Maria. September 22nd: "Misma—toda . . ."*[24] The use of Spanish was intended to protect the intimacies of his diary from Juliette's jealous curiosity.

On October 1st he reached Paris. What sort of a welcome would he find? Xavier de Montépin had demanded his expulsion from the Société des Auteurs on the ground that he had given his support to a gang of murderers. Xavier de Montépin was a writer of newspaper serials, of a number of melodramas, and author of this remarkable aphorism: "Liberty of conscience is a phrase completely empty of meaning." *Victor Hugo's Diary, September 5th, 1871:* "It is just a year ago since I returned to Paris. How I was acclaimed then! How different now! What have I done?—my duty . . ." *September 16th, 1871:* "Received a telegram from Meurice. He has taken a year's lease for us of an apartment at No. 66 rue de la Rochefoucauld."[25]

It was a pretty gloomy return. He took a drive with Juliette and saw the ruins of the Tuileries, of the Hôtel de Ville. He was begged to intervene in favour of Rochefort. He asked Thiers to see him, but had no great hopes of the meeting. "I no longer count for anything." He took the train to Versailles. A man wearing yellow gloves recognized him in the carriage and glared. At the Prefecture he was shown into a large room draped with crimson silk. Thiers came in and showed more cordiality than Hugo had expected. "There are differences between us," said Hugo, "to which both you and I hold fast. But there is no reason why our two consciences should not come to terms."

It was agreed that Rochefort should not be put on board ship, that he should be free to see his children, and to write. Hugo pressed for an amnesty, and demanded that blind obedience to the "brass-hats" should cease. Thiers admitted that he was powerless: "I am nothing more than a poor devil of a dictator in a black coat . . . I am like you, a man who has been beaten but looks as though he had won. Like you, I have to force my way through a storm of insults." In the train, on the return journey, a young woman, pointing to something in a newspaper, said to her husband: "Victor Hugo is a hero." "Be careful," replied the man in a low voice, "that's him, over there." The poet's hat was lying on the seat. She took it and kissed the crape band. Then she said: "You have suffered much, sir: continue in your work of defending the defeated." He kissed her hand.

Next day he went to see Rochefort. "But for you I should be dead," said the prisoner. During the next few days Hugo felt that he would like to see something of *his* Paris. Very nearly all the houses in which he had lived were now demolished. *Le Rappel* had been authorized to resume publication. In the first number he inserted a "Lettre aux Rédacteurs":

At the present moment there is one thing, and one thing only, to be done. What is that? Raise France up! Raise France up for whom? For France? No, for the world. One does not rekindle a torch for the torch's sake . . . One rekindles a torch for him who extinguished it, who, by extinguishing it, made himself blind; and it is for Germany that we must raise France up. Yes, for Germany. Germany is a slave, and it is from France that liberty will return to her.[26]

The issue went to a premium. Hugo's old readers were faithful to him. But to the notables he was an object of hatred. The *salons*, all monarchist or Bonapartist, because they disliked his politics cried down his genius. One day, at the Princess Mathilde's (whose exile had lasted for only two years), Théophile Gautier had been the only person present who defended him. "Say what you will, he remains the great Hugo, the poet of mists and clouds and sea—the poet of the fluid elements . . ."[27] But the poet of mists had committed the crime of being also the poet of the poor.

The year 1872 was a gloomy time for him. In the January elections he was defeated. His attitude of indulgence towards the Communards frightened the voters. In February his unfortunate daughter returned to Paris. For some time now the family had entirely lost sight of Adèle. Pinson had been sent on garrison duty to the island of Barbados. She had followed him, but had given her address to nobody, and alone, completely without resources, had relapsed into a state of insanity which made it necessary for her to be shut away. She was finally identified and brought back to France by a Negress, "Madame Céline Alvarez Baà, an influential lady of the Colony." *Victor Hugo's Diary, February 23rd, 1872*: "*La primera negra de mi vida.*" *March 5th*: "I went to the house of Doctor Allix, to take to Madame Baà, who is leaving on the 17th for Trinidad (via Liverpool):

(1) A gift of money		500
(2) Her passage to Trinidad		800
(3) Her fare to Liverpool		100
(4) A sum for miscellaneous expenses		100
		1500 francs

"Madame Baà has handed me Adèle's jewelry. Everything of hers has been broken and ransacked. I found my wife's ring. I gave Madame Baà, as a reminder of Adèle, two gold bracelets, a brooch, and some ear-pendants, also of gold." *March 10th:* "She leaves on March 12th. I gave her the fifteen hundred francs in *notes,* also the gold ornaments. Jeanne was with me. She stared at Madame Baà, who is black."[28] Was it, one wonders, only as a reminder of her pitiable travelling-companion that "the first Negress of my life" received these gifts?

Adèle was admitted to Saint-Mandé. She did not leave it (after Victor Hugo's death) except to go to the Château de Suresnes, a former manor belonging to La Princesse de Vaudémont, which had been turned into a luxurious nursing-home, where she occupied a *pavillon*. She died there in 1915, at eighty years of age. She was gentle, and did not appear to be unhappy, though her mind often wandered. She had remained a good musician, a tireless pianist, and claimed as her own work all the most celebrated operas. Her sole distraction was being taken to the Horticultural Gardens and the Bon-Marché. A strange fear "of being without a penny"—the result of her memories of poverty at Barbados—led her to conceal, like a dog, everything that was given to her. As in the old days of Eugène, Hugo had this secret sore place in his life. "My poor daughter Adèle, more dead than any dead could be. There are emotions of which I would leave no trace. I visited my poor daughter yesterday: what a prostrating experience!"[29]

Only work, and the life of the senses, retained their power to tear him from his ghosts. Women continued to occupy a great place in his existence. "It is a great effort for me to talk," he said to Burty: "to make a speech is more exhausing for me than making love three times . . ."— then, after a moment's thought, "or even four!"[30] He was, at that time, seventy. A revival of *Ruy Blas* at the Odéon brought him once more into the company of actresses. Juliette was present when he read the play to the cast. "J. J. was there," Hugo noted on January 2nd: "what memories it brought back!"[31] The part of the queen, which Madame Hugo had once taken away from Mademoiselle Juliette, was allotted to Sarah Bernhardt, a lithe, feline young woman, with enormous eyes and a golden voice. At first she behaved intolerably, playing the spoiled child, refusing to put herself out in order to go and see Hugo, whom she treated as a "pardoned Communard." He had had others of her type to deal with and soon tamed her. When she came to know the "Monster" she became infatuated with him. "The Monster was charming, and so intelligent, so quick, and so gallant. His gallantry was of the kind that one feels as homage, not as an insult: so kind to the humble, too, and always gay. He was not, to be sure, a model of elegance, but there was in his gestures restraint, and in his speech a softness which reminded others that he had once been a peer of France. Often, when he had to rebuke one of the company, he would do so in verse. Once, at rehearsal, I sat on a table swinging my legs! He saw that I was impatient, and rising to his feet in the middle of the stalls exclaimed:

> Une reine d'Espagne, honnête et respectable
> Ne devrait pas ainsi s'asseoir sur une table!"[32]

By the time of the first performance, author and actress were on affectionate terms. *Victor Hugo's Diary, February 20th, 1872:* "House full. Saw and congratulated Sarah Bernhardt. *Bise de Boca . . .*"[33] *March 28th, 1872:* "Went to the Odéon. Saw Mademoiselle Sarah Bernhardt in her dressing-room. She was changing . . ."[34] At the supper given at Braibant's to celebrate the hundredth performance, he was surrounded by beauties. Sarah said to him: "Come on, give us women a kiss! Begin with me!" When he had embraced all those present, she added: "And end with me!"[35] On November 2nd, 1875, recording a visit from her, Hugo entered in his diary the words *"No sera el chico hecho!"* (There will be no child.) Are we to assume that Sarah, who already had a small boy as a result of her liaison with the Prince de Ligne,[36] made the same request as Marie Mercier had done? Did she perhaps consider that she was with child by the works of Victor Hugo? "As to England, the trip is put off," she wrote in that same year, 1875, to Doctor de Lambert, her medical attendant. "The *real* reason is fear that there might be trouble in connection with Victor Hugo. I am ill, and my nerves are on edge . . . the egotistic stupidity of the human race exasperates me. Tomorrow I shall make one more effort—SARAH."[37]

It was Sarah who, in 1872, went to see the "beloved Monster" in order to break to him the news that the Director of the Odéon, Charles de Chilly, was dead. At the funeral Hugo saw again the octogenarian Baron Taylor, who in the days of the *cénacle* and Vigny had been one of his earliest friends. The two men had not met for twenty-five years: "we have had time to become, he a Senator, I an outlaw."

Among the innumerable feminine admirers—actresses, authoresses, fashionable ladies—who at that time were proffering their charms and filling his private diaries with their photographs (carefully stuck on the verso of certain pages, and often accompanied with dried flowers), the reigning queen was Judith Gautier, very lovely, with black hair, "a white complexion faintly touched with pink and large eyes with something animal about the way the lashes grew, giving to the lethargic creature the indefinable and mysterious look of a female sphinx . . ."[38] He had known and paid court to her since the days in Brussels, whither she had gone with her husband, Catulle Mendès. In 1872 she frequently went to see Hugo, in order to talk with him about her father. The good Théo was, at that time, suffering from heart-trouble, and more than ever obliged to work for a living. Hugo, with brotherly affection, offered him the hospitality of his Guernsey home, and then, since the journey would have been dangerous for the invalid, obtained a pension for him. On July 12th he wrote a sonnet for Judith: "Ave, Dea, moriturus te saluta":

La mort et la beauté sont deux choses profondes
Qui contiennent tant d'ombre et d'azur qu'on dirait
Deux sœurs également terribles et fécondes
Ayant la même énigme et le même secret.

Ô femmes! voix, regards, cheveux noirs, tresses blondes,
Brillez, je meurs! Ayez l'éclat, l'amour, l'attrait,
Ô perles que la mer mêle à ses grandes ondes;
Ô lumineux oiseaux de la sombre forêt!

Judith, nos deux destins sont plus près l'un de l'autre
Qu'on ne croirait, à voir mon visage et le vôtre;
Tout le divin abîme apparait dans vos yeux,
Et moi, je sens le gouffre étoilé dans mon âme;
Nous sommes tous les deux voisins du ciel, madame,
Puisque vous êtes belle et puisque je suis vieux.[39]

He was seventy, she twenty-two, but to him she was *toda*. With
wit and grace she promised him herself, reminding him of a line in
Ruy Blas:

"Mon maître,
   Sous vos pieds, dans l'ombre, un homme est là.
   Il attend . . .

I have given the matter careful thought, and am decided. Thank you.
JUDITH M."[40]

An intoxicating conquest! He hoped that he might get Judith to
go to Hauteville House, for it was there that he meant to seek refuge.
The success of *Ruy Blas* had set all the theatrical directors of Paris on
tip-toe to get new plays from Victor Hugo. "But," said he, "having
to rehearse one piece makes it impossible for me to write another. So,
since I have no more than four or five years left me in which to produce,
I had rather concentrate on what I have in my head. What I really
need is to get away." Being, as a man, insatiably curious and only too
attractive, exhausted with politics and lovely listeners, he dreamed of
long hours of solitary work and reading. His honeymoon with the Paris
of 1870 had, by 1872, turned into what Byron would have called a
treacle-moon. *L'Année terrible,* an admirable collection, had been
received there with no very great excitement. The press blamed him
for having intervened in favour of Louise Michel, Henri Rochefort,
and all the vanquished Communards, and for his socialist tendencies.
"As I came down the stairs," wrote Goncourt after a visit to the rue de
la Rochefoucauld, "although I had been moved by the gracious good
manners of that great spirit, there was, deep down in me, a feeling of

irony, when I thought of all the mystical, sonorous, empty mumbo-jumbo by means of which men like Michelet and Hugo pontificate, seeking to impose themselves on their environment, as though they were Augurs having the ear of the Gods . . ."[41] Everything was conspiring to make an absence desirable. Juliette, moved by jealousy and a love of the open air, summoned up a vision of "that good and lovely Guernsey." Hugo himself played the echo:

> Puisque je suis étrange au milieu de la ville . . .
> Puisque je déraisonne à ce point de penser
> Que la victoire aimante est la seule victoire . . .

There being no room for him now among the fanatics of either side, he was once more eager for an honourable and redeeming exile. Gladly he left for Guernsey on August 7th, 1872, planning to call in at Jersey on the way.

48

Afterglow

The urchin Cupid into my poor old heart
Returns with trumpets and the blare of brass.

VICTOR HUGO

HAUTEVILLE HOUSE. It was joy for him to see again the look-out awash with sunlight, and the leaping waves. Juliette expanded like a flower: "Fire and flames, sunshine and love, on earth as in Heaven. In my heart and in my mind I adore you."[1] Once again she watched for the signal. Once again she was struck by the "fantastic beauty" of the house which her lord had decorated. Once again she caught her glimpse of the beloved body in the icy morning air. Once again she was happy in the knowledge that her "dear one" was making strides in his work. In the space of a few months he produced a number of drafts for *Le Théâtre en liberté*, poems for the new *Légende des Siècles*, and one of the best of all his novels, *Quatre-vingt-treize*.

At first the house was enlivened by the presence of Alice and her children, but it could not be expected that a very young widow should enjoy an island solitude under the wing of her father-in-law's old mistress. Madame Charles Hugo was sweet and good. Was it her fault that she grew bored? Juliette, when she spoke of Alice, became bitter. *September 8th, 1872:* "Not everyone shares our taste for calm and gentle walks round this enchanting island."[2] After no more than a month Alice decided to take the children back to Paris. *Juliette Drouet to Victor Hugo, September 27th, 1872:* "My heart is heavy when I think what pain their departure will cause you. I love you, but know only too well that that is not enough to keep you from being the most unhappy of fathers at this moment. . . ."[3]

On October 1st François-Victor (a sick man: he was suffering from tuberculosis), Alice, Georges and Jeanne took boat for France. *Diary:* "They got into the carriage. I embraced Jeanne, who seemed surprised, and said, 'Come on and get in, Papapa' . . . I shut the door. The carriage drove off. I followed it with my eyes as far as the corner. They disappeared. The wrench was terrible." *October 15th:* "No news of my little ones. This seeing them no more will shorten my life—though that

408

is not a very serious matter." *November 3rd:* "Letter from Alice. Victor is certainly very ill. I am crushed under a weight of sadness."[4]

Paul Meurice and Édouard Lockroy urged him strongly to return to Paris and exercise his influence in politics; but he knew that Guernsey was his salvation. "I get through more in a week here than I do in a month of Paris." The quality of the work he was now doing fell in no way short of its quantity. The good Théo was dead, and he wrote as an *in memoriam* one of the loveliest of all French poems:

> Ami, poète, esprit, tu fuis notre nuit noire,
> Tu sors de nos rumeurs pour entrer dans la gloire,
> Je te salue au seuil sévère du tombeau . . .
>
> J'y cours. Ne fermez pas la porte funéraire.
> Passons, car c'est la loi: nul ne peut s'y soustraire;
> Tout penche; et ce grand siècle avec tous ses rayons
> Entre en cette ombre immense, où, pâles, nous fuyons.
> Oh! quel farouche bruit font dans la crépuscule,
> Les chênes qu'on abat pour le-bâcher d'Hercule![5]

Absolute, unequalled mastery.

Judith Gautier to Victor Hugo: "My thanks to you, Master. Since he left us, this is the first pleasure I have known . . . How happy he would have been to see such homage given by the God to his disciple! But the poem is not in your dear handwriting. Won't you let me have the manuscript?" *Victor Hugo to Judith Gautier:* "Here, Madame, is the manuscript. That great and much-loved poet lives on in you. By dint of brooding on the ideal, he created you, who, both as woman and as spirit, are perfect Beauty. *I kiss your wings.*" The phrase has a familiar ring.[6]

Never had he worked so happily at any novel as he did at *Quatre-vingt-treize. November 21st, 1872:* "I started today on the book *Quatre-vingt-treize* (first draft). In my *crystal room* I have before my eyes the portrait of Charles, and the two portraits of Georges and Jeanne. I took the new crystal ink-pot, bought in Paris. I uncorked a fresh bottle of ink, and filled the new ink-pot. I took a ream of wove paper, purchased especially for this book. I took a trusty, well-tried pen, and settled down to write the first page . . ."[7] *December 16th:* "I shall now go straight ahead, writing every day, God willing."[8]

Going straight ahead had been his method in the days of *Notre-Dame de Paris* when he was thirty; now, in his seventies, he had no less vigour, no less constant a flow of inspiration. *Quatre-vingt-treize* deals with the struggle, which had been that of his youth, between the Whites and the Blues, not now, as with Marius in *Les Misérables*, confined to one man's soul, but in action. The setting, the Chouans' country, was familiar to him: Fougères, Dol, the forests of hollow trees, the Bocage and the farmsteads, all these he had visited in the old days with Juliette, whose native land it was. It was she who had put his travel-notes in order. Major Hugo had waged this war with mercy. His son had a right to the bird's-eye view of such a subject, to treat it from the point of view of a fair-minded judge, to display in either camp, royalist and republican alike, grandeur and savagery cheek by jowl. Gauvain, the young leader of the Blues (to whom Hugo gave Juliette Drouet's family name), is a pure-hearted and generous hero, but the Marquis de Lantenac, too, aristocrat and Chouan, sacrifices himself to save three children. The dialogue is theatrical, but the French Revolution had *been* theatrical and dramatic. Its heroes had struck sublime poses, and had held them to the gates of death. Hugo's very defects served him well in describing these supermen. Juliette copied the book with enthusiasm. "I am all aghast with admiration when I look at the multiplication-table of your masterpieces."

On January 1st, 1873, she repeated the prayer which he had once composed for her: "O God! let us live together for ever. May he be fulfilled in me, and I in him. So order it that he shall never be absent from any day of my life, or from one single moment of my eternity. Grant that I may be always, in this life and the next, beloved and useful: useful to my beloved, and loved by him. Save us, transfigure us, and make us one."[9] On the anniversary date of their love she reminded him, for the fortieth time, of that February morning in 1833, when she had blown him kisses from her window, and he, turning his head at every step, had sent them back to her. "The scene has changed, and I have put on the disguise of old age, but my heart and soul have both stayed young, and now adore you, as they did on the day when, for the first time, I gave myself to you."[10]

Ah! how much she needed these rites and these memories, if she were to stay brave enough to go on living! For her *divine master* (the sacrilegious phrase is her own) remained incorrigible. When on November 20th, 1872, Marie Mercier, the Undine of the "Our, with its limpid waters," put in an appearance in Guernsey, her lover of a single summer gave her a not very warm welcome. *Victor Hugo's Diary:* "I have persuaded her to go to London, and thence to Brussels. I will pay her passage."[11] The reason was that Juliette had committed the imprudence, in March 1872, of engaging a laundress of twenty-two, named Blanche, who was the possessor of a dangerous beauty. This newcomer was not without a modicum of education. Her spelling and her handwriting compared favourably with those of Julie Chenay. She knew a great deal of poetry by heart, especially of Hugo's. Madame Drouet, tired of secretarial labours, had it in mind to train her in the duties of a copyist. She was pure, and without a trace of coquetry.

Finding this wise virgin in the house of old friends who had remained faithful in the days of the *coup d'état,* Juliette had been moved by a desire to get her away from the wash-house in which she was working. She little knew that, by so acting, she was putting her own happiness in jeopardy.

Blanche had been brought up by the Lanvins, and was reputed to be either their daughter or their granddaughter. They themselves had never denied this fictive parenthood. In point of fact Blanche-Marie-Zélia had been born on November 4th, 1849, of a father and a mother unknown. In such cases, French law insists on *three* first names, one of which is held to take the place of a surname. Dark-haired, with brooding eyes and a fine figure, Blanche was of a type sure to appeal to Victor Hugo by reason of her majestic build and slow, harmonious movements. The Lanvins, who were utterly devoted to Juliette, and without any illusions about the Minotaur, had advised their adopted daughter to be very, very careful. In Paris she had had no advances to repulse. Judith Gautier, Sarah Bernhardt, Jane Essler, Eugénie Guinault, Zélie Robert, Albertine Séran and many others had provided sufficient food for the master's appetite.

At Hauteville House, on the contrary, Blanche found herself alone with the Old Man of the Sea, and he began at once to bring his powerful charm to bear on her. Fame, genius, intelligence, creative power—how should a mere girl, seeing a torrent of masterpieces emerging from that brain, not have been conquered? Admiration is one of the well-trodden ways that lead to love. King David was tempted. For a while he genuinely tried to do battle with his desires. The *Diary* proves this: *January 27th, 1873: "Alba. Peligro. Aguardarse. No quiero malo para ella, ni para la que tiene mi corazon . . .* (Blanche. Danger. Be careful. I wish no ill to her, nor to the one who holds my heart) . . ."[12] When he became pressing, the poor girl seemed to be so unhappy that the ogre's pity was aroused. *"Since she had never granted me anything . . . She stammered out 'Monsieur,' and I, 'Madame' . . . As yet, I had seen nothing but a tiny bit of her shoulder."*

> Nous nous sentions glisser vaguement sur la pente
> De l'idylle où l'amour, traître et divin, serpente,
> Et qui mène, à travers on ne sait quel jardin,
> Souvent à l'enfer, mais en passant par l'éden.
> Le printemps laisse faire; il permet; rien ne bouge.
> Nous marchions; elle était rose et devenait rouge,
> Et je ne savais rien, tremblant de mon succès,
> Sinon qu'elle pensait à ce que je pensais.[13]

He had given her a new name, "Alba," and brought to her the poems that he had written in her praise. She was dazzled, captivated, but fought a heroic rearguard action. Finally, after months of struggle, the poor girl yielded, and gave to the master, because she was so lovely, the same delight that Juliette once had done. He told her so, in perfect verse, as had always been his way with the obliging fair. Never had the old enchanter written more ardent poetry. His victory, following the pattern of its forerunners, stimulated his creative powers. His novel was sweet with the scents of the countryside, of flowering hedgerows, because his walks with Blanche gave all their beauty to the fields of ripening corn.

Unfortunately Juliette was only too close at hand in Hauteville Féerie. Trained by experience in tracking down unhappiness to its source, it was not long before she guessed what was going on at Hauteville House. All the same, on May 20th, Hugo remembered his habitual recital of love's litanies. "My wish is that our two spirits, on this blessed anniversary of your birth, should blend into one their sweet morning rays . . . My lips kiss your feet, my spirit embraces yours . . ."[14] Her spirit, however, was filled with mistrust. Juliette extorted a confession from Blanche. The girl cried, excused herself, declared that she was engaged to be married. It was agreed, with the full approval of the Lanvins, that she should leave Guernsey. There must be no scandal.

Victor Hugo's Diary: July 1st, 1873: Blanche is leaving J-J—She is to be replaced by Henriette [Morvan] who will arrive on July 15th . . . Blanche departed this morning for Paris, by way of Jersey. Suzanne accompanied her to the boat. There is no sailing, tomorrow, Wednesday, for Granville. Blanche will have to go to Saint-Malo.[15]

Juliette Drouet to Victor Hugo, July 1st, 1873: I have been helping poor Blanche with her preparations for departure, not without emotion, though I have (or think I have, which comes to the same thing) good reasons for not being unhappy at her leaving. It was she herself, if it comes to that, who was anxious to get away, and just now her face is radiant with joy. I hope sincerely, and with all my heart, that she will find happiness in Paris. If it were in my power to contribute to it, I would do so with pleasure, provided it were not to the detriment of my own. . . .[16]

Maybe the beautiful "Alba" was acting in strict good faith when she told Juliette that she was "going back to Paris in order to get married." Maybe Hugo was sincere when he swore never to see her again. But the power of pleasure to attract is stronger than the power of an oath to restrain. *Quatre-vingt-treize* was finished. The reports about François-Victor's health were becoming alarming. Guernsey, without "Alba," bored him. On July 31st, 1873, he took Juliette with him to France. MacMahon had just succeeded Thiers. The "brass-hats" had carried the day, and people were beginning to wonder whether, perhaps, another *coup d'état* might not be in preparation. However that might be, there was a stiffening in the policy of repression. Rochefort, whom Thiers, faithful to his promise, had kept in France, started for Nouméa in a convict ship. The Great Preacher of Amnesty was going to have his work cut out. Whenever he spoke of the Assembly or of MacMahon, "an implacable hardness showed in his face, and his black eyes flashed fire."[17]

He went to live at Auteuil in the Avenue des Sycomores[18] with his dying son, whom Madame Charles Hugo was devotedly nursing. Goncourt saw them there, François-Victor in an armchair, "his face the colour of wax, hugging himself as though he could not keep warm"; his father, "standing as stiff and rigid as a stage Huguenot." Hugo drank the wine of Suresnes, without water, recalling for the benefit of the company the dinners given by Abel, in the old days at mother Saguet's, with their vast omelettes and broiled chickens. "On those occasions," he said, "we drank a great deal of this thin wine which has such a lovely white-currant colour . . ."[19] Goncourt thought that his robust and vigorous good health made a very unpleasant contrast with the appearance of his dying son, who looked blue with cold.

In spite of the promises he had made to Juliette, Hugo lost no time in seeing Blanche, *toda*. He installed her on the Quai de la Tournelle. Almost every day, after *déjeuner*, he climbed to the top of the Batignolles–Jardin-des-Plantes omnibus, and went off to feast his eyes on his living statue.

> Elle me dit: "Veux-tu que je reste en chemise?"
> Et je lui dis: "Jamais la femme n'est mieux mise
> Que toute nue." Ô! jours du printemps passager!
> On commence par rire. On finit par songer.
> Joie! Astarte sans masque. Extase! Isis sans voile.
> Avez-vous vu parfois se lever une étoile?
> Ce fut superbe! "Et bien" dit elle, "me voici."
> Et devant Adonis Vénus était ainsi. . . .[20]

Sometimes they walked together in the Jardin-des-Plantes. She would take her work-basket, and sit there sewing, "silent and grave," or, suddenly, in a burst of happiness, "start to sing some childish song." It was an astonishing idyll: Philemon and Amaryllis. Sometimes, on their way home, they met a beggar, and Hugo gave him alms, in quittance of who knows what debt to the gods, and then carefully entered in his diary the sum thus spent on charity. Before passing judgment on him, "we should do well to remember how greatly physical love added vigour to his genius."[21] When the instinct of the male conspires with the feelings of a poet, who can be strong enough to resist? But there were times when Hugo passed sentence on himself. In the presence of the dying François-Victor, of Alice and the children, he was visited, on the subject of this double life, with a sense of regret, almost of remorse, by an awareness of degradation. His deeper self, his conscience, would have preferred a more chaste old age. His flesh drove him on to the omnibus and to the white statue of the Quai de la Tournelle:

> Ô triste esprit humain, par le corps possédé!
> Ô délire des sens! Ivresse, extase, fange!
> Noircissement du cygne! Abaissement de l'ange!
> La chair, voilà l'écueil le terme où s'amoindrit
> Et s'abat, frémissant, le plus superbe esprit!
>
> Pas un fort qui ne tombe ou qui ne soit tombé.
> Elle fait échouer David à Bethsabé,
> Et Socrate devant Aspasie, et limite
> Salomon au lit tiède où dort la Sunamite.[22]

These illustrious examples of over-vigorous age were powerless to console Juliette. In September she had him watched by a private detective, and by that means discovered what she called "these shameful adventures." *Diary, September 19th, 1873, 7.30:* "Catastrophe! Letter from Juliette J. J. Frightful anxiety. Horrible night . . ."[23] Leaving a letter of farewell, she had taken flight, as in the days of her youth. Hugo, overwhelmed, desperate, torn with anxiety, took steps to find her, and dispatched telegrams here, there and everywhere.

Diary, September 22nd-24th, 1873: "Three days of agony . . . Every kind of torment . . . The cold necessity of secrecy . . . I have got to say nothing and look as usual . . . I show nothing in my face, but my heart is broken . . ."[24] At last news came that she had been seen in Brussels: "A gleam of light. Run to earth." *Diary, September 26th, 1873:* "Did not attend the dress-rehearsal of *Marie Tudor* . . . so as not to miss the train which gets in at 9.5. Waited for an hour and a quarter. I had eaten nothing, I bought a penny roll and ate half of it. At 9.5 the train came in. We saw one another. Happiness and despair in equal parts . . ."[25] For he loved her tenderly. "My life and soul are gone," he had said when he thought that she was lost to him. But the old faun in him did not want to die, and Juliette was incapable of admitting, as it would have been wise of her to do, that a man of such incomparable virility was still young, though she was fading. She made him swear, "on the head of his dying son," that he would break with Blanche. The undertaking was not honoured, and a relapse, once the crisis was past, came quickly. The diary is thickly sown with notes of lovers' meetings:

Juliette Drouet to Victor Hugo, October 16th, 1873: All I know is that I cannot long endure this conflict, endlessly renewed, between my poor old love and the young temptations that come your way, even if they are not of your seeking, though of that I have my doubts. . . .[26]

November 18th, 1873: Dearest, I don't want to nag you about your little bits of nonsense, but I can't help feeling that my old love must cut a pretty poor figure among your crowd of tarts, all beak, feathers, and what-not, with their competing cluckings—*"pécopin, pécopin, pécopin"*—while my poor crested pigeon wears himself out with cooing: *"baldour, baldour, baldour* . . ."[27] The fantastic pursuit has been going on now for a long time, and you show no sign of being tired or discouraged. From today I am putting the key of my heart under the door, and leaving the rest in the hands of the good God. . . .[28]

François-Victor died on December 26th, 1873. *Victor Hugo's Diary:* "Another severance, and this time the last. Only Georges and Jeanne left . . ."[29] The funeral, as in the case of Charles, was a civil ceremony. "What a crowd!" wrote Flaubert to George Sand: "and not a cry, not the tiniest disturbance! The poor father, whom I could not keep from embracing, is broken but stoical . . ."[30] One of the newspapers blamed him for attending his son's funeral in a soft hat. Little Louis Blanc gave a most touching address.

The younger of Victor Hugo's two sons has rejoined the elder. Three years ago they were both of them full of life. Death, which had separated them for the last few years, has now once more united them. When their father wrote:

> Aujourdhui, je n'ai plus de tout ce que j'avais
> Qu'un fils et qu'une fille,
> Me voilà presque seul! Dans cette ombre où je vais
> Dieu m'ôte la famille!

—when, from his great and tortured heart the cry was wrung: *"Oh! demeurez, vous deux qui me restez!"* did he foresee that, towards him, nature would be so inexorable? Did he foresee that it would be *his* home that would be *la maison sans enfants?* It is as though destiny were proportioning his share of suffering to his glory, and giving him so much unhappiness as shall show equal with his genius. . . .[31]

On January 1st, 1874, he awoke about two o'clock in the morning, and started to write a poem which had just come to him: "Et maintenant à quoi suis-je bon? A mourir." But he knew that this was not true. In spite of destiny's repeated blows, the old oak still stood. In spite of "frequent hearses," Hugo was still finding happiness in work. Not for a moment did he tire "of finding fulfilment and strength in his art . . . What tremendous poetry," said Paul Valéry, "poetry with which no other body of poems can compare in extent, in structure, in resonance, in plenitude, did he not write in the last period of his life!"[32] Maurice Barrès loved "the surge of Hugo's last poems, standing out to sea, and displaying all their beauties on the strand," and admired the "sheer power of an old man weighed down with the treasures he so much longed to show, he who was to die so soon, and no longer played the goldsmith, but gave us the precious metal in its pure and virgin state. . . ."[33]

Of this final uprush of supreme and masterly vigour, Hugo was fully conscious. To Houssaye, who dined with him in January 1874, he said: "I am like a forest that has several times been felled; the young trees are increasingly strong and vigorous. For half a century now I have been setting down my thoughts in prose and verse, but feel that I have uttered only the thousandth part of all that is in me . . ."[34] The young poets searched despairingly for elbow room upon some height not yet already occupied by him, but, incapable of competing with him on his own ground, looked for fresh fields to conquer. Symbolism was born, but what Symbolist poem could be more beautiful, more mysterious, or more obscure than "L'Escalier"? Did not Mallarmé's "magic corridor lead straight to Hugo's cloakroom"? This, Mallarmé knew full well, and none talked better than he did of the old magician. Master-minstrel that he was, he found endless amusement in showing how this or that poem of the younger school might have been written by Hugo. "Do you know," he once asked, "what I think is the loveliest line that Hugo ever produced? It is *Le soleil s'est couché ce soir dans les nuées.*"[35]

With his contemporaries he no longer had any very close contact. His intimates were dead. He no longer attended the Academy. There had been a time when he had found much pleasure in the Dictionary "sessions," for he was curious in the matter of etymologies, and fascinated by the mystery of subjunctives. But politics now divided him from his colleagues. On January 29th, 1874, he went to the Quai Conti for the first time since December 1851. The occasion was an election at which he wanted to vote for the son of his old friend Alexandre Dumas. After twenty-five years of absence, the staff of the Institut no longer knew him by sight, and one of the ushers said to him: "You can't go through there!" His companion on duty exclaimed: "Why, if it isn't Monsieur Victor Hugo!" When the Director called the roll of names, he forgot to include his. Only five members shook him by the hand, but in the courtyard all the curious spontaneously uncovered as he passed.

49

21 Rue de Clichy

O N APRIL 29th, 1874, the family settled into No. 21 rue de Clichy. Hugo had rented two floors. One he kept for himself, Alice and the children. The other contained two reception rooms and Madame Drouet's apartment. Juliette had no peace. She was for ever going up to the bedroom floor. But Alice complained that there was not a room she could call her own, and threatened to leave with Georges and Jeanne. In this way she brought irresistible pressure to bear on the grandfather, and Juliette was asked to retire downstairs again. Madame Drouet chose to treat this trivial inconvenience as a tragedy.

May 7th, 1874: Dearest, the separation which I dreaded as nothing less than a cause of great unhappiness is now an accomplished fact . . . My heart is filled with the gloomiest forebodings. The floor which separates us is like a broken bridge between our two hearts. From this evening there will no longer be any intimacy between us . . . I am trying to draw a little courage from the thought that the happiness I have lost will be made up to you by the presence of your two dear grandchildren.[1]

Naturally, she considered the "cold and selfish demands of Madame Charles" to be the cause of all her ills. Already in the previous summer, when leaving Guernsey to return to the rue Pigalle, she had written: "Let us pray together that peace, unity and happiness may enter your family circle, never to leave it again."[2] She wrote to her Victor that he was "a permanent victim of ingratitude among his nearest and dearest . . . Madame Charles, badly served by her friends, and badly advised, is unknowingly subjected to the evil influence of those who are your enemies . . ."[3] But Hugo had a weakness for Alice, who was young and pretty. The two separate flats were situated on the third and fourth floors. Hugo climbed the stairs without ever getting out of breath. His eyesight was as good as a young man's, and he was staggered when, for the first time in his life, he had an attack of toothache. "What *is* all this?" he asked. Every evening he entertained to dinner twelve or fourteen guests. (The number 13 still filled him with a feeling of fear which he could not overcome.) He loved to surround himself with charming women, to kiss their hands, to load them with attentions. He received

417

his guests standing, and wearing a loosely knotted tie, white or black, hanging from beneath his turned-down collar. Madame Drouet stood on his right, "dressed with an old-fashioned and slightly theatrical elegance," in black velvet with a tucker of faded old lace. The meal was almost always the same, for Hugo did not like innovations: turbot with a not very thick sauce, or lobster; roast beef; *pâté-de-foie-gras;* ice. The master's appetite was still voracious. After dinner a move was made to the red drawing-room. Madame Drouet dozed quietly, "her lovely white hair lying about her head like the two wings of a dove, and the bows on her bodice rising and falling to the gentle, almost resigned, breathing of an old lady asleep."[4]

Poor Juliette was still fighting to defend her old love, but the infernal merry-go-round continued. *To Victor Hugo, January 13th, 1874:* "I followed you with my eyes, as I used to do, as far as the corner of the street. But you did not, as you used to do, turn round to give me a friendly wave of the hand. What does that prove? ? ? I would rather you did not answer those three marks of interrogation, which have the shape of tarts on the make . . . Quite apart from anything to do with me and you, I think it would be well if you gradually got rid of all these street-haunters, who prowl round you like so many bitches in heat."[5] As a heading to one of her letters she quoted Voltaire: *"Qui n'a pas le cœur de son âge—De son âge a tout le malheur."*

Though her beloved was taking, each day, the Batignolles–Jardin-des-Plantes omnibus, for the purpose, as he said, "of enjoying the sensation of being alone in a crowd," but really in order to visit Blanche, Juliette's jealousy was for a time concentrated on Judith Gautier. Hugo, who had promised to be from now on, if not faithful, at least frank, had shown her certain verses written for *Madame J . . .* his snow beauty; *Nivea non frigida.*[6] A cruel loyalty, that. But Juliette preferred a rival who was at least glorious, the daughter and wife of a poet, to the obscure Blanche. She begged Victor "to consider himself completely free to do what he liked," and declared that she had no objection to "the conjunction of a poet and his beautiful source of inspiration." He swore that his feelings were entirely platonic. It was time, indeed, that they were no more. Besides, Juliette pointed out, desire had already consummated infidelity. As consolation, he sent her a poem quite as lovely as any that he had offered to Judith:

> *A une Immortelle:*
> Quoi? vous, gloire, auréole, éblouissement, grâce,
> Vous qui ne passez pas, vous craignez ce qui passe? . . .
> Comment? Vous, la beauté céleste, vous craignez,
> Déesse, la beaute d'en-bas? Vous qui régnez,
> Vous redoutez l'éclat éphémère de celles

Qu'Avril jette et qui sont comme ces étincelles
Qui, comme la verveine et la sauge, et le thym,
Naissent dans la lueur fuyante d'un matin,
Embaument un moment les prés et les charmilles,
Et qui durent autant que l'aube, étant ses filles? . . .
Vous jalouse! De qui? Vous troublée! Et pourquoi?
Le jour sans nuit, c'est vous; l'amour sans fin, c'est toi . . .

Sois calme en ton azure. Qu'importe, à toi, flamme,
Clarté, splendeur, toujours présente comme une âme,
A toi l'enchantement de l'abîme vermeil,
Faite pour le baiser éternel du soleil,
Qu'un rayon en passant sur une fleur se pose?
L'étoile, au fond des cieux, n'a pas peur de la rose.[7]

She was "dazzled, moved to the depths" of her being . . . "though that does not prevent me from feeling that a sharp point has pierced right through my heart."[8] Still, if these various escapades could bring her old lover happiness . . . but they did not do that. *Juliette to Victor:* "You love philanderings—even casual ones—whence the disgust and nausea of your life, and of my heart. Though you cast your happiness and mine into the jar of the Danaïds, you will never succeed in filling it high enough to let you drink one single drop of that pleasure on which you would slake your thirst. You are not happy, my poor, too-much beloved, nor am I any happier than you. Women are like running sores in your side, which grow and grow because you lack the courage to cauterize them once and for all. *My* torment is to love you too well. So, you see, we both suffer from an incurable disease. Alas!"[9] In either case it was a disease of the heart and the will.

But the erotic frenzy never made inroads on his morning hours of work. The neighbours could see him, from dawn onwards, in his "Holy of Holies," standing at his desk, dressed in a red jersey and grey reefer-coat. In the evenings, surrounded by his friends, he was, said Flaubert, "adorable." Edmond de Goncourt, dining in the rue de Clichy on December 27th, 1875, found him in a frock-coat with a velvet collar, with a white silk scarf loosely festooned about his neck, reclining on a sofa and discoursing about the role of the conciliator, which he wished thence forward to play. The dinner might have been one "given by a village curé to his Bishop." The Banvilles, husband and wife, were there, Saint-Victor, Dalloz, Juliette Drouet and Alice Hugo—"prettily smiling and carelessly swathed in a black lace dress . . . with her little demon of a daughter, and her sweet little boy with the velvet eyes." In the low-ceilinged dining-room, above the heads of the guests, was a gas-burner, so hot that they almost felt their brains sizzle. Alice, inconvenienced by the heat, loudly complained, but Hugo went on drinking

champagne and holding forth—charming, fluent and quite insensitive
to other people's feelings. After dinner he read poetry aloud.

We found Hugo quite alone in the dining-room, standing by the table,
occupied with the preparations for his poetry reading: preparations which
were not unlike the preliminaries to a conjuring entertainment, with the
conjuror practising tricks in a corner. And then, later, there was Hugo with
his back to the drawing-room fireplace, holding in his hand the large sheet
of paper on which he had had some of his poems copied for America—a fragment of the manuscripts bequeathed by him to the Library, which, he told
us, were written on a specially strong wove paper to keep them from falling
to pieces.

Slowly he put on his spectacles—which vanity had long kept him from
using—with a sort of dreamy movement, wiping the beads of sweat from his
prominently veined forehead with his handkerchief. At last he began with a
species of exordium, as though to give us good warning that he still had
whole worlds stored away in his brain. "Gentlemen, I am seventy-four years
old, and I am on the threshold of my career." He read us *Le Soufflet du Père*,
and a sequence from *La Légende des Siècles*, which contained some lines so
beautiful that they seemed to be not of this world. It is a curious experience
to watch Hugo reading! The mantelpiece had been arranged like a theatre
back-drop for the occasion. Fourteen candles, reflected in the mirror, made,
at his back, a splash of light against which his face, like the face of darkness
—as he might have said—stood out, detached, aureoled with a radiance which
played in the rough texture of his cropped hair, and shone on his white
collar, giving a pink translucence to his pointed satyr's ears. . . .[10]

In 1875 Alice took the children to Italy. Their grandfather wrote
regularly. *September 5th, 1875:* "Dear Alice, here is my news. All goes
well, but ... on August 16th, as I was getting off the bus—listen Georges,
listen Jeanne—a toff fell bang on my head. It was so flabbergasting that
I was flabbergasted, but having nothing more wrong with me than my
ribs stove in, and a few teeth and eyes the fewer, I picked myself up
and ran all the way home without saying anything so as not to give
the church papers the happiness of announcing my death . . . PAPAPA
(O! I was forgetting: the poor little lady-parrot is dead. I have given
the widower a new wife [*cocotte*] for whom I paid twenty francs [price
of a *cocotte*]. I made a present of the lady-parrot to the little widowed
gentleman, and to you, dear Alice, a gift of twenty francs.)"[11] Careful
accounting is the basis of good housekeeping.

Political, as well as literary, friends went to see him in the rue de
Clichy: Louis Blanc, Jules Simon, Gambetta, Clemenceau. Time was
slowly having an effect, and a feeling was abroad that the Commune
had better be forgiven and forgotten. Hugo, who had always stood for
clemency, was now regarded as a precursor. Juliette, forever hungry

for popularity where he was concerned, wanted him to re-enter political life. In January 1876, as a result of a proposal made by Clemenceau, he came forward as a candidate for the Senate and was elected on the second ballot. *Juliette Drouet to Victor Hugo, January 19th, 1876:* "It seems to me that your mere presence there should cast, in this chaos of stupidities and basenesses, a flood of light; in other words, of the good, the beneficial, the beautiful and the just, like the *Fiat Lux* of God . . ."[12] But it was at once obvious to him that his influence would count for very little. In assemblies, cynicism has a way of getting the better of idealism, and this first Senate of the Third Republic had not much republicanism about it.

Hugo championed the granting of an amnesty, and denounced the scandalous contrast between the policy of repression, as applied to the men of March 18th (that is to say, of the Commune), and the indulgence extended to those of December 2nd. "It is time we stopped shocking the conscience of Humanity. It is time we abandoned the shameful system of two separate scales of weights and measures. I demand a full and complete amnesty for what happened on March 18th . . ."[13] The motion was put to the vote. For Hugo, 10: all the rest of the Senate, against. But the Parisian crowds gave him a better reception than the assemblies and applauded him. *Juliette Drouet to Victor Hugo, May 23rd, 1876:* "If the general public had been able to vote, the amnesty would be an accomplished fact, and you would be carried in triumph for having so generously and magnificently demanded it. But, sooner or later, whether they like it or not, this mob of savage imbeciles will have to toe the line. . . ."[14]

Disappointed by this defeat, she found herself regretting the days of exile and the happy isle. "The birds are already feeling the return of spring, to judge by the way they are chasing one another . . . I, personally, feel all the memories of our young love bursting into flower, and my old heart beats more strongly when I think of you at this moment. How delicious it must be to be in love in Guernsey . . . with my little garden filled with your favourite flowers, and the sea singing gently beneath my windows. How gladly would I trade Versailles and its Palace, and its heartless, brainless orators, for my little house of Hauteville Féerie, or for the honest barking of the 'Senate' of Hauteville House."[15]

Eighteen hundred and seventy-seven was a year of political battles. The President of the Council, Jules Simon, a Jew with the temperament of a Roman Cardinal, and a regular visitor to the rue de Clichy, tried in vain to come to terms with MacMahon, who could not put up with the anti-clericalism of Gambetta. "We can no longer move forward together," he said to Jules Simon; "I had rather be turned out than continue under the orders of Monsieur Gambetta." It was, for the marshal, a question of hierarchy. He declared that he would make use of the right, which he enjoyed under the Constitution, to dissolve the Chamber, should the Senate agree. Hugo called a meeting of the leaders of the Left at his house to oppose this project. *Victor Hugo's Diary, September 19th, 1877:* "MacMahon's manifesto. A single man throwing down the glove to France."[16]

Several days previously he had been visited by the Emperor of Brazil, Dom Pedro, who came to the rue de Clichy and treated him as, formerly, he had wanted the kings of France to treat him—as an equal. When he came into the room, the Emperor said to him: "I need your reassurance: I am rather shy"; then: "I have one particular ambition, and that is that you should introduce me to Mademoiselle Jeanne." Hugo said to the child: "Jeanne, allow me to present you to the Emperor of Brazil." She murmured, deeply disappointed: "But he's not dressed up!"[17] When the poet said: "Sire, may I be permitted to present my grandson to Your Majesty?" the Emperor replied: "There is only one majesty here, and that is Victor Hugo." Dom Pedro accepted an invitation to dinner for Tuesday, as a simple traveller, with such guests as turned up regularly on that day.

The Senate was like a hive at swarming-time. Victor Hugo, the spearpoint of MacMahon's enemies, put the essential question in committee: "If the president dissolves the Chamber, and if he is beaten, will he accept defeat?" A minister who was present did not dare to reply. On June 21st Victor Hugo made a fine and lengthy speech opposing the motion for dissolution:

I ask nothing better than to believe in loyalty, but I remember that we have believed in it before now. It is not my fault if I remember this. I see resemblances which make me uneasy, not on my own account, for I have nothing to lose in life, and much to gain in death, but on account of my country. Gentlemen, I beg you to listen to a white-haired man who has seen what you may be going to see again. His only interest on this earth is your interest. His advice, to friends and enemies alike, is given in all honesty. He can neither hate nor lie, being as he is so close to the eternal truth. You are about to embark on an adventure. Well, then, listen to one who has already travelled that road. You are face to face with the unknown. Listen to him who says to you: "This unknown is something that I know." You are about to go on board a ship, the sails of which are fluttering in the wind. It will soon set out on a long voyage, laden with promises. Listen to the man who says to you: "Stop while there is yet time. I have had experience of this particular type of shipwreck. . . ."[18]

He was applauded by the Left. Next day Jeanne (eight years old) asked, when she came into the room: "Did everything go well in the

Senate?" Yes, everything had gone well, but as always he had preached only to the converted.

The motion for dissolution was carried by a bare majority: 149 to 130. At the elections the republicans gained an overwhelming victory: 326 to 200. The marshal's position became impossible. "He must either submit or resign," said Gambetta. He first of all submitted, then resigned. The part played by Victor Hugo in the success of the Left had been limited by reason of his age and of his long absence from public life, but it was incontestable. From then on his position "in the Third Republic was that of a Patriarch and a Doctor."[19]

The patriarch had more than one Ruth. Every day after *déjeuner,* he left the rue de Clichy, "that infernal house," where Lockroy, beloved of Alice, exercised a cantankerous authority; where Juliette, a prey to "gloomy moods," rummaged through pockets and secret drawers for intimate letters. Sometimes he went to see Blanche, sometimes he met Marie the Bather, for "life had not been kind" to the Undine of Vianden, and she had written asking for further help. She was living in the rue de Crimée, not far from the Buttes-Chaumont Park and the Avenue d'Allemagne,[20] in a district served by the Étoile-Montholon—Place-du-Trône tramway. In the diaries for 1875-1878, the words "Crimée, Chaumont, Allemagne and Star-Month"[21] all stand for Marie Mercier. They are regularly prefaced by the words *assistance* or *secours,* followed by a set of figures. What an expense love is for old men! Erotic symbols, very easy to interpret, make obvious the prowess of Olympio. We know, from the diaries, that he went with Marie to the Buttes-Chaumont, to the gingerbread fair, and to the cemetery of Père Lachaise.

"I make regular use of the trams which run from Étoile to Trône, and of the Batignolles—Jardin-des-Plantes omnibuses," wrote Victor Hugo on New Year's Day 1878 to the Chairman of the General Omnibus Company. "Allow me, through you, to make a present to the conductors and the drivers on those two lines of the sum of five hundred francs."

At about the same time "Madame d'Aunet, 182 rue de Rivoli," reminded Victor Hugo of her existence and asked for money. "I am making her a present of two thousand francs. To be sent at once." He who breaks hearts has to pay for them.

50

The Art of Being a Grandfather

IN 1879 he published *L'Art d'être Grandpère*. He had always loved children; he understood them and found a lively enjoyment in what there is in them of the primitive, the natural, the poetic. Tragically deprived of his sons and his daughters, he had become devotedly attached to his grandchildren. Georges was good-looking and serious, Jeanne unruly and gay. Their grandfather played with them, drew their portraits, treasured their tiny shoes, as Jean Valjean had those of the child Cosette. He wrote down their sayings.

Jeanne said: "I was a little love with Papapa; I didn't say a word." *Victor Hugo's Diary, October 31st, 1873:* "Georges, having disobeyed his mother, who had told him that he must not touch a certain pot of jam, said to me: 'Papapa, will you give me permission to have eaten the jam this morning?' "[1] *October 29:* "Yesterday evening I found in my bed a doll which Jeanne had laid on my pillow—'to *seep* (sleep) with Papapa.' "[2]

Such lucky finds enchanted him. He allowed his grandchildren to spread their toys over his manuscripts. *November 12th, 1873:* "After *déjeuner* we went to Saint-Mandé, she (J. J.), I and little Jeanne. My poor girl is as well as she can be; she is quite calm and in good health. Jeanne kissed her aunt and talked a great deal about her on our way home.[3] We called in at the pastry-cook's." When Georges was four and a half (February 14th, 1873) he was taken to see a revival of *Marion de Lorme,* and spent the whole of the next day saying over and again, *"L'homme rouge qui passe!"* In front of Notre-Dame Georges said proudly, "Papapa's towers!" Hugo solemnly inscribed his books to them. On a copy of *L'Année terrible,* intended for his grandson, he wrote: "For Georges, in fifteen years from now."

> L'avenir me plaît, tel que mon cœur le comprend,
> Car, moi, je serai mort, et toi, tu seras grand.

And, on one meant for Jeanne:

> Ta petite ombre emplit cette épopée étrange.
> Lis, Jeanne, et deviens femme en restant toujours ange.[4]

424

He insisted, with his sister-in-law, that the children, young though they were, should always come down to dinner on great occasions. When this happened, their nurses could not get them to bed before eleven o'clock at night. But sometimes, according to Georges Hugo, "we fell asleep in the middle of the meal, lulled by the sound of voices. Edmond de Goncourt has told me that one evening Jeanne dropped off with a leg of chicken in her hand, and her head in her plate. . . ."[5]

On the full-dress anniversaries, the children drank Papapa's health. "I, the youngest, drink to you, the oldest," said Jeanne, on February 26th. For her own birthday she shyly demanded a "*tost*." If he scolded, Jeanne admonished him: "you ought not to scold those who love you." To little Marthe Féval (aged three), who was not very well behaved, Jeanne (aged six) said with much gravity: "Marthe! Monsieur Victor Hugo is looking at you." Their grandfather told them stories: *Le méchant garçon et le bon chien, Le mauvais roi et la bonne puce*. With a quill pen, on scraps of cardboard, he gave them good or bad marks. These they found under their napkins: "sometimes they took the form of cherubic children's faces with curly hair and a crown of stars; sometimes of fantastic birds, with their beaks open, perched on flowering branches, and singing."[6]

L'Art d'être Grandpère in part consisted of notes made by their "adoring and enchanted" elder. Several of the poems ("La Lune," "Jeanne était au pain sec dans le cabinet noir") are no more than children's sayings, versified. Others express the feelings of their grandfather, astonished that he, who had waged war against an Emperor, should find himself defeated by a little child.[7] But it was his belief that the poet should always pass from the level of daily life to that of mystery. At the Zoo he could look at the wild beasts with the eyes, simultaneously, of childhood and of wisdom. The tots trembled a little, and laughed much.

> Moi, je n'exige pas que Dieu toujours s'observe,
> Il faut bien tolérer quelques excès de verve
> Chez un si grand poète, et ne point se fâcher
> Si Celui qui nuance une fleur de pêcher
> Et courbe l'arc-en-ciel sur l'Ocèan qu'il dompte,
> Après un colibri, nous donne un mastodonte!
> C'est son humeur à lui d'être de mauvais goût,
> D'ajouter l'hydre au gouffre et le ver à l'égout,
> D'avoir, en toute chose, un stature étrange
> Et d'être un Rabelais d'où sort un Michel-Ange.
> C'est Dieu; moi, je l'accepte.[8]

These lines are a defence, not only of God, but of Hugo; a justification of the antitheses of nature and of poetry. Looking at the tiger the children said: "Oo, what a big cat!" The poet was troubled by the "*énorme bâillement du gouffre qui s'ennuie*," but found an intoxicating delight in seeing "*d'un côté l'épouvante et de l'autre l'amour.*" Since, too, the technical mastery of the artist never ceased to grow, he ended this book with poems made out of nothing, some of them strangely surrealist, like "Choses du Soir," others impressionistic, like the one on early morning sounds heard in Guernsey:

> J'entends des voix. Lueurs à travers ma paupière.
> Une cloche est en branle à l'église Saint-Pierre.
> Cris des baigneurs: "Plus près . . . plus loin . . . non, par ici!
> Non, par là! "Les oiseaux gazouillent. Jeanne aussi.
> Georges l'appelle. Chants des coqs. Une truelle
> Racle un toit. Des chevaux passent dans la ruelle.
> Grincement d'une faulx qui coupe le gazon.
> Chocs. Rumeurs. Des couvreurs marchent sur la maison.
> Bruits du port. Sifflements des machines chauffées.
> Music militaire arrivant par bouffées.
> Brouhaha sur le quai. Voix françaises: "Merci . . .
> Bonjour . . . Adieu. . . ." Sans doute il est tard, car voici
> Que vient, tout près de moi, chanter, mon rouge-gorge.
> Vacarme de marteaux lointains dans une forge.
> L'eau clapote. On entend haleter un steamer.
> Une mouche entre. Souffle immense de la mer.[9]

The book had an immediate success. Quiet and simple emotions make a wide appeal. A grandfather who accepts and loves his role will always please. What he had set out to do, to deify children as so many poets have deified their mistresses, was something new. "No one," wrote Théodore de Banville, "but the poet of *La Légende des Siècles* could have had the imagination necessary to effect this transposition, for it is true to say that the Child as a subject for art and poetry dates from him, and became a living reality only in his work."[10] The first edition was exhausted within a few days, and others followed in quick succession. Georges and Jeanne became almost legendary children, treated in Paris with that wondering affection which London gives to its royal princes.

51

The Devil and His Train

Even before the hearse drives up, the body says farewell.

VICTOR HUGO

THE delightful walks he took with Georges and Jeanne, the arch‐
angelic verses which he wrote for and about them, must not be
allowed to falsify the picture of Victor Hugo in his last years. The
adoration which he felt for the innocence of the very young had
not put an end to the old man's garnering of wild oats. On January
11th, 1877, Alice told him that after six years of widowhood she was
going to marry again. Her second husband was to be Édouard Lockroy,
the Deputy for the Bouches-du-Rhône, the former secretary of Renan,
the mordant and witty journalist. On the eve of ordering the cards
announcing the ceremony she expressed a wish that her famous
father-in-law's name should be associated with the event. This was
tantamount to asking Monsieur Victor Hugo to make a public an‐
nouncement to the effect that Madame Charles Hugo would soon
cease to bear "the sounding name." In order to maintain the fiction
of a solidly united family, the poet consented. *Victor Hugo to Alice,
March 27th, 1877:* "Dear Alice, you know that I never send out this
kind of announcement . . . still, for your sake, I will break my usual
habit. I do not wish to refuse what you have asked of me with such
tender graciousness and tact. Since, therefore, you want my name to
be included, included it shall be—you could not have chosen two
better persons than Louis Blanc and Vacquerie."[1] On another occasion
Alice thought that she had come across, in one of Hugo's poems, some
allusion to unfaithful widows, and told him that she felt profoundly
hurt. He, sensitive to the young woman's vexation, wrote: "Sweet, dear
and charming Alice, my daughter, my child, be reassured. Those lines
were written more than a year ago; I will show you the manuscript.
I know, as you do, that you are putting your future into the hands
of a good and generous man. I have no thought in my mind but to
give you my blessing."[2]

This marriage left Victor Hugo much greater freedom of action.
In spite of his seventy-five years he took full advantage of it. True, he

428 DEATH AND TRANSFIGURATION

was becoming more and more conscious of the unsavoury picture of
an old man in love. He had written a *Philémon perverti*, a comedy
which never got beyond the draft stage, in which he treated his own
character with great harshness. Philémon is not restrained by the
suffering of the gentle Baucis, but falls a victim to the charms of the
young Eglé:

> Prendre une jeune au lieu de la vieille qu'on a!
> Manger de la chair fraîche avec du bon pain tendre,
> Au lieu de chair salée avec de vieux biscuit!
> Ô fascination dont la splendeur me luit!
> Je romps avec la vieille. Il faut qu'elle s'en aille!
> Je sens que je vais être un horrible canaille![3]

Returning home after a debauch, Philémon finds Baucis dead of
want and suffering. In despair he flees for refuge to his mistress. But
Eglé cruelly mocks at her senile lover, who sighs out "I love you!"
between two fits of coughing. *End of the scenario:* "Darkness falls on
the old man. It was his devil—every man has a devil who leads him
to his doom—who had made him drunk with love personified by
Églé. Baucis was his angel. This is made clear in a scene set in the
deep blue of Heaven, after his death. . . ."[4]

In this severe little drama we see Philémon sitting in judgment on
himself. The spirit would not pardon "this act of bestial satisfaction."
Moreover, no matter how robust the body was, these indulgences
exhausted it. "First warning, *gravis cura*," he noted down in his diary[5]
. . . and, again, *June 30th, 1875*: "A very odd thing has happened. I
was suddenly struck with a complete failure of memory. It lasted for
about two hours."[6]

He wore himself out in other ways, too, publishing *L'Histoire d'un
Crime*, which he considered to be more topical than ever; supporting
the candidature of Jules Grévy; speaking eloquently at the celebration
of the Voltaire centenary; taking the chair at an International Literary
Congress. During the night of June 27th-28th, 1878, in very hot
weather, and after a rather too lavish dinner followed by a violent
discussion (about a joint Rousseau-Voltaire celebration), he had a
very slight stroke. His speech became thick, his movements uncertain.
But he seemed to recover and next day, in spite of protests from his
family, wanted to go and see "Alba" at the Quai de Tournelle. "Dear
beloved," Juliette wrote to him on the following evening (June 28th,
Friday evening, 7 P.M.), "I thought you seemed a trifle tired . . ."[7] The
two doctors, Allix and Sée, who had been sufficiently worried to keep
a careful eye on him, made it quite clear that, from now on, he "ought
to renounce all pleasures of the body." "But, doctor," he had artlessly
replied, "surely it is *nature's* duty to give that sort of warning!" Baucis-

Juliette begged him to leave as soon as possible for Guernsey, and this he agreed to do, on July 4th.

There he rapidly improved, but the ravening nymphs continued to write to him, using Paul Meurice as their letter-box. Juliette, who on this occasion was living at Hauteville House, noticed, when the post arrived, that he hid certain envelopes in his pocket. In one of her daily *scrawls*, she begged him to look after himself:

August 20th, 1878: The proud prostrations of my spirit before yours are addressed to the divine being that you are, and not to the vulgar, bestial idol of depraved and cynical passions that you are not. Your glory, which dazzles the whole world, illuminates your life as well. Your dawn was pure: your dusk must be venerable and sacred. I long, at the cost of what remains to me of life, to preserve you from certain faults which are unworthy of the majesty of your genius and your length of years. . . .[8]

In a fit of the sulks he snubbed her, calling her *school-teacher*. How, he asked, could she take the letters of "hysterical lunatics" seriously? "I am fully aware that my spirit is part and parcel of yours," he wrote to her. But Juliette, embittered, humiliated and disappointed, showed her "most aggressive self" . . . "She used everything as a pretext for quarrelling, even in Guernsey," said Juana Lesclide, the wife of Hugo's secretary. "This woman, who would gladly have given her life for the Master, delighted in starting a campaign of pin-pricks. The result of their endless bickering was a state of nervous prostration, in the course of which the illustrious patient inveighed against his nearest and dearest. One morning things came to a head over a letter written by a former servant-girl. Madame Drouet had opened it . . . there were tears and grinding of teeth . . . Scarcely had peace been restored, when a new storm burst, occasioned, this time, by a 'wallet,' discovered hidden away in the study, into which Madame Drouet frequently trespassed and turned everything upside-down."[9]

The wallet, stamped with the initials V. H., contained five thousand francs in gold. "For what 'kindnesses' were those five thousand francs going to pay? Such, with brutal frankness, was the question asked . . . On another occasion the house was thrown in confusion because of a number of diaries, dating from five years back, found in a corner, and all of them bearing women's names. Tears. Recriminations. Estrangement . . ."[10] One evening, when Hugo had decided to take a stroll down the rue des Cornets, which was the prostitutes' quarter, "Madame Drouet, after a scene of indescribable violence, told her impenitent friend that she had made up her mind to leave him, and that nothing would alter her determination."[11] She would end her days, she said, in Jéna, with her nephew Louis Koch and her three grand-nephews. In October she was still hesitating about following

Hugo to Paris, and offered to share the solitude of Julie Chenay, who was staying behind to look after Hauteville House. All the same, on November 9th, the old lovers embarked together on *Diana*.

Meurice had rented for them, at 130 Avenue d'Eylau, a small house belonging to the Princesse de Lusignan. The Lockroy couple, with Georges and Jeanne, settled down next door, at 132. Juliette, who was supposed in principle to occupy the first floor, soon made her home in the second, where she occupied a room next to the one in which Hugo slept. This was hung with cherry-coloured damask, and furnished with a Louis XIII fourposter with twisted columns, a chest of drawers carrying a bust of the Republic, and two tables, one on top of the other, at which he worked standing. Since his minor stroke he had, as a matter of fact, done very little work. Through the good offices of his disciples, each year now saw the publication of a handsome volume of his poems: in 1879 *La Pitié suprême, Religion et Religions* and *L'Âne;* in 1881 *Les Quatre Vents de L'Esprit;* in 1882 *Torquemada;* in 1883 the final version of *La Légende des Siècles.* The literary world, half-rebellious, half-admiring, was amazed by the spectacle of so productive an old age. In point of fact, all these poems were old.

Since the desertion of Alice Lockroy, Juliette, though far from well, had become the unquestioned ruler of his home. The part was a heavy one for an old and worn-out woman to play: bells constantly ringing, dinner-party after dinner-party, "to say nothing of declarations of love falling as thick as hail in March." Hugo had laid upon her and Richard Lesclide the task of opening all letters addressed to the Avenue d'Eylau, wishing to be freed from the necessity of doing it himself, and also in the hope of inspiring his anxious companion with confidence. But the more intimate missives reached him via Paul Meurice. Backed up by Lockroy, who sometimes ventured on a passage of arms with the Grand Old Man, Juliette had brought about a complete break, so far as Blanche was concerned. She was reduced to a state of panic by being told that Victor Hugo might die suddenly in her arms; she was warned that she might well kill him if she did not keep out of his way. Juliette persuaded Hugo to supply her with the capital sum needed for the purchase of a bookshop, advised her to get married, and promised to talk Madame Lanvin, who since the Guernsey adventure had refused to have anything to do with the guilty young woman, into forgiving her.

A clerk who knew Blanche's story and could not resist her beauty made a proposal that he should add his name to the three already possessed by her. Émile Rochereuil was handsome, with a romantic appearance and a sound intelligence. He had got to know "Alba" after her return from Guernsey. She had told him of her misfortunes. He offered both a civil and a church marriage. Abandoned, discouraged, disabused, she accepted the offer.

Their marriage took place on December 2nd, 1879, at the Mairie of the 20th arrondissement. The nuptial blessing was given at the church of Saint-Jean-Baptiste. Two of Blanche's neighbours (Pierre Moreau, a barber, and Basile Moreau, a pork-butcher) acted as witnesses for the bride; a relation (Constant Rochereuil) and a colleague (Adrien Bornet, clerk) for the groom. No member of the Lanvin family was present at the double ceremony, but Victoire Larcher, Émile's widowed mother, gave her consent to the marriage. *Victor Hugo's Diary, December 17th, 1879:* "B[lanche]'s wedding. She was married on December 2nd at Belleville. I was informed of this through the medium of an invitation." One daughter, Émilie, and two sons, Georges and Louis, were born of this union which brought "Alba" much unhappiness. "She gave way to profound discouragement, and let her home and her business go to rack and ruin."[12]

With Blanche out of the way, many eager candidates came forward to fill the empty place. At seventy-eight Hugo was still writing secretly to Jane Essler, to a young woman called Adèle Gallois, and to Léonie de Vitrac, the widow of a certain Lesage, "all of them willing to replace me for board and bed and no other emolument," wrote Juliette ironically. "She is a poet, she adores you, and so on and so on . . . I hope, my dear little man, that you will cease to attract imprudently this female under your roof . . . a burned child dreads the fire; a broken heart fears fresh wounds. My own are still so raw that I can scarcely be indifferent, and, whatever attraction this person may have for you, I do beg you to spare me the uneasiness all this is causing me. . . ."[13]

The great-hearted mistress had a few last moments of happiness. In September 1879 she accompanied her beloved to Villequier, and was proud to be received into the Vacquerie household. Nevertheless she did not accompany Victor Hugo to the cemetery. He had, in fact, never suggested that she should. Would Juliette herself, perhaps, in her fierce humility, have thought it indecent that they should have visited together the shade of Adèle? We may well have doubts on that point, and indeed a note of light and secret irony can be detected in her daily letter:

Juliette Drouet to Victor Hugo, September 13th, 1879: I did not dare ask to be allowed to go with you yesterday on your pious pilgrimage, but I should like to add to your prayer to God, and to your dear, great spirits, a tribute due from poor human respect. If you authorize me to do so, I will go, before leaving Villequier, to bow my knee before those venerated graves, and to give them, under the canopy of Heaven, the marks of my profound

respect and eternal blessing. But this I will do only if you consent, because
not for the world should I wish to deal a blow at *human propriety* by any
outward manifestation of the sublime feelings which I carry in my heart for
all your dear dead. . . .[14]

In his diary, Hugo wrote:

September 12th, 1879: After *déjeuner* I visited my daughter's grave. The
cemetery adjoins the church. Léopoldine's burial-place is in the middle of
a large family tomb, which contains separate vaults. Her husband lies next
to her, under an inscription recording their marriage and the circumstances
of their deaths. Below it is inscribed: *De profundis clamavi ad te.* In front is
the grave of my wife, with this inscription: ADÈLE, FEMME DE VICTOR HUGO.
All around are the graves of the Vacquerie family. Prayer. Love. I stayed
there until six o'clock in the evening. I went into the church. It dates from
the fifteenth century. Simple, but beautiful and well-kept.

September 18th, 1879: I went to the grave. Prayer. They can hear me, and
I them. . . .[15]

In 1881, Hugo's entry upon his eightieth year was celebrated as a
National Festival. A triumphal arch was erected in the Avenue d'Eylau.
The people of Paris were invited to march in procession under the
poet's windows on February 26th. The provincial cities sent numerous
delegations and gifts of flowers. The President of the Council, Jules
Ferry, had paid a visit on the previous evening in order to associate
the Government with this act of homage. All punishments were cancelled in the *lycées,* colleges and schools. Standing at the open window,
indifferent to the chill air of February, with Georges on one side of
him and Jeanne on the other, Victor Hugo watched the procession of
six hundred thousand admirers. It took all day to pass the house.
A heap of flowers, as high as a small hill, was piled in the roadway.
With a priestly movement of the head he expressed his thanks.

To Charles de Pomairols, who said what a magnificent sight he
had been with his white hair, his eyes filled with tears, and his grandchildren clinging to his arms, he replied, looking at Georges and
Jeanne: "Yes, they're dear children. Two good little republicans. . . ."[16]

The following week, when he entered the great hall of the Luxembourg, the Senate rose to its feet and applauded. Léon Say, who was
presiding, said no more than: "Genius has taken its seat: the Senate
has expressed its welcome." Nothing like it had ever been seen. He
who in the days of his ambitious maturity had been tight-laced in a
peer's gold-embroidered uniform now looked like "an old carpenter
or bricklayer." Wearing his black alpaca coat, and giving the impression of a rock battered by the white spume of the years, he had become
an object of veneration to the whole of France. In July the Avenue

d'Eylau was renamed Avenue Victor Hugo, and his friends could address their letters: *To Monsieur Victor Hugo, in his Avenue*. On July 14th there was another procession, with bands, fanfares, male-voice choirs, and the "Marseillaise," which he loved, a hundred times repeated. On July 21st the feast day of Saint-Victor was observed in the privacy of his family.

The inconsolable Blanche mingled, on each of these triumphal occasions, with the crowd in the Avenue. Again and again she walked past the house in the hope of getting a last glimpse of her old lover, now lost to her, but not forgotten. She was unhappy. She had found herself married to a scoundrel who took disgraceful advantage of the confidences she had made him, played fast and loose with her money,[17] and even went so far as to threaten Lockroy with his intention of publishing the love-letters and poems which Blanche had received from her illustrious seducer. At this glorious moment of Hugo's apotheosis, the scandal would have been still more serious than had been the case in 1845 when he had been caught *in flagrante delicto*. The poet's answer was a cry of despair: "A long and honourable life; eighty years; devotion; good actions in association with women, for women, by women . . . all now fallen by the basest, meanest, most infamous calumny into the muck-heap . . ."[18] The blackmailer sold the original documents to Lockroy for a very large sum of money. "Alba," who was entirely blameless, suffered deeply as a result of this shameful business.

"She used to make contact with the master's friends," says Madame Lesclide; "we often saw her in the cast-room at the Louvre" where she went to ask Lesclide for "news of Monsieur." "She listened with the greatest attention to everything that was said about him! Her serious face seemed to light up for a moment, then, almost immediately, relapsed into dejection, while warm tears flowed from her eyes." This unhappiness of hers was perfectly sincere. "She would stand for long periods on the pavement of the Avenue Victor Hugo, watching for the poet to leave the house, doing everything she could to catch sight of him. Paul Meurice was kind to the poor afflicted creature when he ran into her pacing up and down before the house . . . One day Juliette recognized her former lady's-maid. She flew into a furious rage and used the meeting as an excuse for picking a violent quarrel with the master . . ."[19] Woe to jealousy, the jaundice of the heart!

From August 21st to September 15th, 1882, Victor Hugo's honorary, but now at last openly acknowledged, mistress went with him on a visit to Paul Meurice at Veules-les-Roses. It was a matter of deep satisfaction to her to be welcomed to the house where Madame Paul Meurice had always refused to receive her. On returning home she was compelled to take to her bed. She was suffering from a malignant tumour in the digestive tract. In the face of the old woman, now wasted as a result of her cancer, no trace remained of the dazzling beauty of 1830, except, perhaps, the gentle sweetness of the eyes, and the fine modelling of the lips. On such occasions as she could sit huddled in the embrasure of her window, she could see on the other side of the avenue the quiet gardens of a convent, and, "so as not to have to think," watched the Sœurs de la Sagesse, who reminded her of her childhood at the Perpetual Adoration.

She knew that there was no hope for her, and expressed a wish that the question of a "double burial" should be settled. She was referring to hers and Claire's. For a long time she had wanted to have twin graves, but Hugo had neglected to take the necessary steps. *Juliette Drouet to Victor Hugo, October 18th, 1881:* "Unless you dislike the idea, I should very much like you to let me see to the arrangements for myself, one day soon. I should not be interfering with your habits, or those of the household. You can't, I think, refuse me that, and I want you to give me your permission immediately, since time presses . . . ."[20] A year later (*November 1st, 1882*), the sick woman asked the poet: "Let us look together through those sublime poems which you once dedicated to me, so that I may decide which lines had better be used for my epitaph, when I shall have ceased to be of this world. . . ."[21]

The old couple went for the last time to Saint-Mandé on June 21st, 1882; Juliette to visit her dead daughter, Hugo his daughter in confinement. At eight o'clock in the morning he had received a moving little note from her: "Dear beloved, I am grateful to you for going with me today to that sad but sweet place of meeting, Sainte-Mandé. I feel that my regrets will be less bitter when I stand at the grave of my child. I hope that you will find your dear daughter in good health, and that we shall both of us return from this pious pilgrimage, if not consoled—for we can have no consolation in this world—at least resigned to God's will. . . ."[22]

It will be remembered that the first performance of *Le Roi s'amuse* had taken place on November 22nd, 1832, and that the play, having been placed under an official ban, could not be given a second time. Now, in order to celebrate the fiftieth anniversary, Émile Perrin, the Director of the Théâtre-Français, put the play on again, and was particularly anxious that the revival should be presented on November 22nd, 1882. Juliette, already a dying woman, was present (supreme honour) at this performance, with Victor Hugo, in the Director's own box. The President of the Republic, Jules Grévy, was in the stage-box in his official capacity. After this final act of homage there was nothing for Juliette to do but to die of hunger.

5 2

Deepening Shadows

"Dear friend, when I have left this mortal me,
Let no one take my place!" said she,
"No other lover!" Then solemnly and with uplifted eyes
Added: "For then I'd die again—in Paradise."

VICTOR HUGO

SHE spoke as little as possible of her approaching death, although she was well aware of her condition, because Victor Hugo (like Goethe) insisted that "she should cleanse herself of all unhappiness," and "shake off all melancholy" before coming to see him.[1] At dinners in the Avenue d'Eylau, emaciated and scarcely recognizable, she carried through a sublime act of deception. She did not wish to be an object of solicitude during the meal, and would raise her empty glass when Victor Hugo drank to her health, saying, as he did so, how lucky he had been when he first met her fifty years ago; and then, when he protested that she was eating nothing, replied: "Monsieur, I am unable to."

"But she was still able, whenever she heard the least sound of coughing from Victor Hugo's room at night, to get up and prepare his infusion . . ."[2] On January 1st, 1883, she wrote her last letter: "Dear darling: I do not know where I shall be this time next year, but it makes me proud and happy to give my signature to your Life Certificate for that day, when it comes, in these three words—I love you . . . JULIETTE."[3]

The old man's New Year wishes—the last—were expressed as follows: "When I say *Bless you,* I speak of Heaven; when I say *Sleep well,* I speak of Earth; when I say *I love you,* I speak of myself."[4] She could no longer take any nourishment at all. Each evening Victor Hugo sat by her bed for an hour, "and she listened devotedly to the arguments with which he tried to prove that she was not really suffering at all."[5] She did her best to smile, and until the very end maintained this heroic attitude in his presence.

She died on May 11th, 1883, at the age of seventy-seven. Victor Hugo had her buried in the Saint-Mandé cemetery, next to Claire

Pradier, under the flagstone which Juliette herself had chosen.[6] So overcome was he that he could not leave the house where she had died to take his place in the funeral procession. Auguste Vacquerie, whose part it was to superintend the arrangements for all Hugo funerals, delivered an address: "She for whom we weep was a heroine . . ." He declared that she had "a right to her part in the poet's glory, having shown her loyalty in the time of testing."[7]

That, too, was what Victor Hugo felt. For the anniversary of February 1883, the date of their "golden wedding," he had given her a photograph of himself, with, on it, the words: *"Cinquante ans d'amour, c'est le plus beau mariage."* Well-deserved homage to her who, after a life of troubles, had given an example of complete sacrifice to a redeeming love. Had Hugo been worthy of such a sacrifice? Though desire had weakened, the sense of attachment had never grown less. By associating Juliette with his work, he had given her a matchless life. Much has been said of his "monstrous Hugoism," but, to inspire such feelings, a man must have, over and above his genius, a great many human qualities. "Nothing redounds more to the credit of Victor Hugo than the love of this wonderful woman." Of this he was well aware.

> Sur ma tombe on mettra, comme ma grande gloire,
> Le souvenir profond, adoré, combattu,
> D'un amour qui fut faute et qui devint vertu.[8]

Juliette left a will. She had had, for some time, what amounted to a fortune, Hugo having registered in her name seventy National Bank of Belgium Bonds (worth one hundred and twenty thousand francs in 1881, or more than twenty-four million in 1954). He had expected, at that time, to predecease her, and had wanted to provide for his companion. When he realized that she was beyond hope (and, especially, when the Koch family was exercising an increasing influence on her), he had made her sign a transfer. *Note by Juliette:* "This day, September 8th, 1881, Monsieur Victor Hugo came home with seventy National Bank of Belgium Bonds, thirty-five of them bearer bonds, and thirty-five registered in my name. These he had once, over-generously, given to me. I urged him to have a form of transfer prepared, and it was sent to him, this same day, by the National Bank—J. D."[9] In exchange for this restitution, and to recompense Juliette for her disinterested behaviour, Hugo guaranteed her an income of twenty thousand francs in the unexpected event of her surviving him.

There remained to Juliette Gauvain, known as Juliette Drouet, not only a number of shares, but jewellery, *objets d'art*, and a great many valuable papers. After her death it appeared that the furniture from Hauteville Féerie and the apartment in Paris, the plate, the jewels, the manuscripts, the letters and the portraits, were all to go to her nephew Louis Koch.

Juliette's Will, Article 3: In the event of Monsieur Victor Hugo wishing to buy back, as souvenirs, the property willed by me in the two preceding articles, it is my wish that my heirs should agree to such a sale, in consideration of the desire expressed by Monsieur Victor Hugo.

Article 4: As to monies, whether in cash or in banknotes, which may be found, to a considerable sum, in my possession, I declare that these all belong to Monsieur Victor Hugo, having been confided to me in trust for the administration of his personal fortune. Consequently, such monies should be handed over to him intact, as being his property.[10]

Victor Hugo bought in nothing. Had he examined the piles of papers in Juliette's possession, he would have found, among other souvenirs, the bundle of love-letters addressed by him to Madame Biard, and sent in a moment of spite by Léonie to her rival. But Léonie, attractive though no doubt she was, never occupied in the poet's life a place comparable to that filled by his great-hearted mistress. From the moment of Madame Drouet's death, Hugo's heart and spirit went into mourning.

> Oh! comment traverser sans elle des années?
> Ôtez moi de la vie, ô Dieu, reprenez moi,
> N'attendez pas un jour, n'attendez pas une heure!
> Que vais-je devenir jusqu'à ce que je meure?[11]

53

"Et Nos Soleils Couchants Sont des Apothéoses..."

Not easily does a man tear God out of his heart.

VICTOR HUGO

HE CONTINUED to entertain, in the Avenue Victor Hugo, with his customary courtesy, kissing ladies' hands, or, when they were wearing gloves, their bare wrists. His devoted secretary Richard Lesclide wrote his letters for him. Every Sunday the traditional "At Home" drew crowds of people. Hugo appeared to be completely remote. Camille Saint-Saëns, who dined at the house, described the occasion: "The Master sat at the head of the table, but said very little. With his sturdy appearance, his firm, sonorous voice, and his even temper, he did not give the impression of an old man, but, rather, of someone who was ageless, eternal, beyond the power of Time to touch. But, alas! nothing can stay Time's hand, and his fine intelligence began to show signs of wandering. . . ."[1]

Blanche Rochereuil had tried to see him again after Juliette's death. This thunder-and-lightning liaison remained the one great memory of her ruined life. The place left vacant by Madame Drouet was waiting to be filled. "She hoped that Victor Hugo, freed from a yoke which had hung heavy upon his life, would finally come back to her."[2] But octogenarians, though they may still remember the distant past, are untrustworthy where more recent events are concerned. When Hugo lost Juliette, he had not seen "Alba" for five years, and may even have forgotten her. She tried in vain to correspond with him. Her letters, which expressed, turn and turn about, anger and prayer, stiffness and humility, were all intercepted. Hugo's friends treated her now as an importunate nuisance. "Blanche has just left," wrote Lesclide in 1884; "she had to be turned out. She is miserably unhappy, and lives in a garret on the Île Saint-Louis. . . ."[3]

Hugo did not want any notice to be taken of his birthday: *"Me souhaiter ma fête! Amis renoncez-vous—Ma vie a tant de deuils qu'elle n'a plus de fêtes . . ."*[4] The vigorous body was at last wearing out.

438

He could no longer run after an omnibus and clamber to the top. All the same, he still went out. He had become a very regular attendant at the meetings of the Academy. Whenever a chair fell vacant, he always voted for Leconte de Lisle, because it bored him to have to make a choice between the candidates. The Permanent Secretary, Camille Doucet, said to him: "It is most irregular! You cannot vote for a man who has not offered himself for election." "I am perfectly well aware of that," replied Hugo, "but I find it more convenient."[5]

A good saying of his was long quoted in the Magny Dining-Club: "It is time I emptied the bottle." Then, sitting brooding in his chair, he came out with the line: *"J'aurai bientôt fini d'encombrer l'horizon."*

He frequently intervened in world affairs, to save some man condemned to death, to protect Jews from a pogrom, insurgents threatened with repression. Romain Rolland, as a young man, kept a number of *Don Quichotte* which contained a coloured cartoon representing *Le Vieux Orphée* with a halo of white hair, touching his lyre and raising his voice for victims of some sort or other. He was a species of French Tolstoy, "the self-appointed shepherd of the vast herd of mankind." "The old grandiloquent voice had become quavering," said Rolland; "it did not intimidate the executioners, but we, the millions, listened to its distant echoes with feelings of piety and pride." It was fine, it was necessary, that justice should be upheld. "The name of Hugo in old age was married with that of the Republic. His fame, among all the many famous names in art and letters, was the only one that was a living reality in the hearts of the French people. . . ."[6]

In August 1883 Romain Rolland set eyes on the living Victor Hugo for the first time. It was in Switzerland, whither Alice Lockroy had taken him for a rest. The garden of the Hôtel Byron had been invaded by a crowd of persons from both sides of Lake Geneva. The tricolour flag floated from the terrace. The grandfather made an appearance between his two grandchildren. "How old he was! White, lined, his eyes sunken, his brows knotted in a frown. I got the impression of somebody who had emerged from the deep-down gulf of all the ages. In reply to cries of *"Vive Hugo!"* he raised his hand, as though in protest, and cried, in his turn, *"Vive la République"* . . . The crowd devoured him with their eyes. Their curiosity seemed to be insatiable. A working man close to me said to his wife: "An ugly old buffer . . . but a damned good-looker all the same!"[7]

In Paris he was a familiar figure in the streets, even when it was snowing. He wore nothing over his frockcoat. "My youth is my protection," he said. He went with Alice to see Bartholdi working on his Statue of Liberty. He was frequently to be seen leaning on the arm of a young poetess, who had translated Shelley, and had once been reader to the Empress of Russia. Her name was Tola Dorian, who before her marriage had been Princess Mestchersky. On one occasion when he was with her he stopped on the Pont d'Iéna, and turned to face the setting sun. Drawing his companion's attention to the flaming sky, he said: "What a magnificent sight! You, my child, will often see its like, but I shall soon see something even more superb. I am old, I am going to die. I shall see God! What a tremendous thing to see God and to speak with Him! What shall I say? I often wonder. I am preparing for the occasion. . . ."[8]

He remained faithful to his belief in immortality. When somebody once said to him that the soul ended with death, he answered: "For your soul that may be true, but I know that mine is eternal . . ."[9] To his secretary, who had said "the weather is very cold today," he replied: "the weather is in other hands than ours." On the day after Juliette's death he went to speak of these things to a priest, Dom Bosco. "Yes, I saw him," said the latter, "and we had a chat. He is afraid of what people may say. And then, look at the folk by whom he is surrounded. Just look at them!"[10] It is true that when he prayed for himself and for his dead, his atheist friends blushed "at such a display of weakness," and did their best to cast a cloak round this "old Noah drunk on the Beyond."[11] A young man, an assiduous haunter of the Avenue d'Eylau Sundays, called Anatole France, wrote: "There is no use in blinking the fact that he dealt in words rather than in ideas. It is painful to find that what he presented to the world as the fine flower of philosophic thought was no more than a mass of commonplace and incoherent fancies."[12] Against this verdict should be set the words of the philosopher Renouvier: "Hugo's thought is precisely what philosophy should be when it is also poetry"; and those of Alain: "Intelligence is the guiding-light of the clever. But to predict what nobody has either hoped or wished, to do *that* is to have something which goes beyond mere intelligence. Whence the glory of being hooted at, a glory which, for our poet, still lives on."

The Old man of the Sea had long known what it was in which he believed. He believed that an Almighty Power created the world, maintains it in being, and will be our Judge. He believed that we outlive the body, and that we are responsible for our actions. In 1860 he had put his faith into words: "I believe in God, I believe in the soul, I believe that we shall be called upon to answer for our deeds. I commit myself to the universal Father. Since all existing religions have failed in their duty to Humanity and to God, no priest shall have a part in my funeral. I leave my heart to the dear ones whom I love.—V. H."

On August 31st, 1881, he had drawn up his will in a firm hand:

God. The soul. Responsibility. This threefold notion is sufficient for man. It has been sufficient for me. In it I have lived. In it I die. Truth, Light, Justice, Conscience—that is God, *Deus, Dies.*

I give forty thousand francs to the poor. I wish to be taken to the cemetery in a pauper's hearse.

I appoint as executors of my will Messieurs Jules Grévy, Léon Say, Léon Gambetta. They shall have full right to co-opt whomsoever they may wish.[13] I bequeath all my manuscripts and all writings and drawings by me which may be found among my possessions to the Bibliothèque nationale of Paris, which will, one day, be the Library of the United States of Europe.

I leave behind me a sick daughter and two grandchildren. May my blessing be on all three. Except for the eight thousand francs a year, necessary for the maintenance of my daughter, everything of which I die possessed shall be the property of my two grandchildren. Let me here state that the annual income for life which I give to their mother, Alice, should be assured, and that I raise this sum to twelve thousand francs.[14] This applies also to the annual income which I bequeath to the brave woman who, at the time of the *coup d'état,* more than once saved my life at the risk of her own, and who has since preserved the trunk containing my manuscripts.[15]

I am about to close my bodily eyes; but the eyes of my spirit will remain open, more widely open than ever. I refuse the prayers of the churches. I ask a prayer of all human spirits.

Victor Hugo[16]

He knew now that death was near at hand. In his diary for January 9th, 1884, he wrote:

> Triste, sourd, vieux,
> Silencieux,
> Ferme tes yeux
> Ouverts aux cieux.

A few days before his death he dined at the Lion d'Or with the Committee of the "Société des gens de lettres." Since he said nothing it was thought that he was dozing, but he heard perfectly clearly and responded with astonishing eloquence to the toast drunk in his honour. From time to time his eyes still showed black and terrifying. To his grandson he said: "Love . . . seek love . . . Give pleasure and take it in loving as fully as you can."[17] Even in his last days the faun in him was still avid of nymphs. "Until the very end his virility was demanding, and never completely satisfied . . . The diary which he began on January 1st, 1885, records eight sexual performances, the last one of all being dated April 5th, 1885."[18] But he knew that at his age neither pleasure nor fame could provide a refuge against death.

A l'heure où l'on remplit de son nom les deux pôles,
Voilà qu'on est poussé dehors par les épaules.

.   .   .   .   .   .

.   .   .   .   .   .

Il suffit d'un cheval emporté, d'un gravier
Dans le flanc, d'une porte entrouverte en janvier,
D'un rétrécissement du canal de l'urètre,
Pour qu'au lieur d'une fille on voie entrer un prêtre.[19]

In his case the mortal blow took the form of a congestion of the lungs, on May 18th. He felt that the end was at hand and said to Paul Meurice, in Spanish: "She will be very welcome." It is good to know that even in his final delirium he could still compose a perfect line: *"C'est ici le combat du jour et de la nuit"*—which sums up his own life, and the lives of all men.

On May 21st Cardinal Guibert, Archbishop of Paris, wrote to Madame Lockroy that he had "sincerely prayed for the illustrious invalid," adding that, should Victor Hugo wish to see a priest, he would take upon himself "the sweet duty of bringing to him the help and consolation needed by all at so cruel a testing-time,"[20] Édouard Lockroy replied to the Cardinal, thanking him for his letter, but refusing the offer. On receiving this answer, the Cardinal remarked that "Hugo was anxious to go to God, but did not want God to come to him."[21] It had not been possible to consult Hugo's wishes, for he was already at the point of death. He died on May 22nd, while saying goodbye to Georges and Jeanne. His last words, *"Je vois de la lumière noire,"* are reminiscent of one of his finest lines: *"Cet affreux soleil noir d'où rayonne la nuit."* His final death-rattle "was like the sound of pebbles dragged backwards by the sea."[22] "A storm of thunder and hail burst over Paris at the moment when the old god breathed his last."[23]

On hearing the news the Senate and the Chamber adjourned, as a mark of respect for an occasion of national mourning. It was decided that the Panthéon should, in his honour, be restored to the position which the Constituent Assembly had intended it to occupy, that the inscription *"Aux grands hommes, la patrie reconnaissante"* should be restored to its pediment, and that the body of Victor Hugo should be buried within its walls, after lying in state beneath the Arc de Triomphe.

The vigil of a whole great city took place on May 31st. "The scene had to be seen to be believed," wrote Barrès: "the coffin lifted in the black darkness, and the greenish glare of the street-lamps showing livid on the Imperial gateway, and reflected in the breast-plates of the cavalrymen who, torch in hand, were keeping back the crowd. A mass of people eddied and flowed from as far away as the Place de la Concorde, pressing forward against the barrier of terrified horses to within two hundred yards of the catafalque. There was, in them, a wild wonder at the knowledge that they had made a god. . . ."[24]

Twelve young French poets formed a guard of honour. All around the Arc de Triomphe, in the avenue and houses, was a multitudinous murmuring of verse, "words, words, words—for," said Barrès, "his power and his greatness lay in his mastery of French words." Yes, to have had that power was one of his supremacies, but there was another yet more dazzling, his mastery of universal feelings. Because he had, more completely than anybody else, voiced what all had felt—the piety with which a country honours its dead; the joys of young fatherhood; the charms of childhood; the intoxication of young love; the duty of all to the poor; the horror of defeat and the greatness of mercy— the voice of a whole people now cradled this great man in his grave.

That night, said Romain Rolland, was dionysiac. "On the Place de la Concorde the cities of France were in mourning, but at the Étoile, around the Arc de Triomphe, where the god lay sleeping, a conqueror in the field of glory snatched from his great rival, Napoleon—there was no question of either tears or prostrations . . . The scene resembled a Kermesse by Jordaens." The crowd might have been that of the Forum or the Suburra round the body of an emperor. Then, shortly before dawn, "in the middle of all this joy, this pomp of lictors and legionaries, of heaped flowers and wreaths and gleaming weapons," there appeared, in an empty space, "the pauper's hearse, black and unadorned, with only two small wreaths of white roses. The body of a dead man. The last antithesis . . ."[25] At this same hour, in the darkness of the Carmelite Convent of Tulle, Marie Hugo, the general's niece (in religion, Sister Marie-Joseph de Jésus), surrounded by her kneeling companions, was praying for the eternal rest of his soul.

Victor Hugo was escorted from the Étoile to the Panthéon by a funeral, and triumphal, procession. Two million Frenchmen followed the hearse. The avenues through which this tide of humanity surged were lined with masts bearing shields on which were inscribed: Les Misérables—Les Feuilles d'Automne—Les Contemplations—Quatre- vingt-treize. In the street, where lamps were lit in broad day and veiled in crape, there was a trembling of pallid flames. For the first time in the history of mankind a whole nation was rendering to a poet the honours usually reserved for sovereigns and military leaders. It was as though France, on this day of mourning and of glory, was determined to repeat, in honour of Victor Hugo, the words which he, fifty years earlier, had addressed to the dead Napoleon:

Ô! va, nous te ferons de belles funérailles!
Nous aurons bien aussi peut-être nos batailles.
Nous en ombragerons ton cercueil respecté.
Nous y convierons tout: Europe, Afrique, Asie,
Et nous t'amènerons la jeune poésie
Chantant la jeune liberté.[26]

This apotheosis had recalled the "great funeral ceremonies of the East." The crowds and the ministers departed. Like Napoleon's marshals after the leave-taking at Fontainebleau, writers, old and young alike, as they returned from the Panthéon gave vent to an *Ouf!*—a sigh of relief that the formalities were over. From Mallarmé no *Ouf* had come, but he regretted that Hugo, in the Panthéon, among scholars and men of politics accustomed to the domes of Institutes and Parliaments, should have been relegated to a crypt, whereas in the Luxembourg he might have slept "with the wide air about him, and in his ears the cooing of ring-doves."[27]

Men always grow weary in time, even of their admirations. During the half-century following his death Hugo's reputation encountered much rough weather. Other poets, Baudelaire, Mallarmé, Valéry, have been thought to attain to a greater perfection, and, indeed, because of the strict and novel standards which they set themselves, have frequently done so. But without Hugo they would never have existed at all, as they themselves have admitted. "When one considers," said Baudelaire, "the condition of French poetry before he appeared, and the new lease of life which it has enjoyed since his coming; when one thinks how narrowly restricted it would have been but for his example; it is impossible not to look on him as on one of those rare spirits sent by heaven into this world, there, in the field of literature, to bring us salvation . . ."[28]—and Valéry: "He was the very embodiment of power . . . To get a clear view of his stature, one has to realize what the poets born within the climate of his influence have had to invent in order to be able to compete with him at all."

The years passed. Time, which smothers hills and the lower slopes with undergrowth, has no effect upon the summits. Above the ocean of oblivion which has swallowed up so much literature of the nineteenth century, the Hugo archipelago proudly lifts its peaks with their crown of rich imagery. The monuments in which the great memories of France have found such a wealth of symbols are still linked indissolubly with his many writings. From the towers of Notre Dame, *forming the H of his name,* to the dome of the Invalides, under which the flags still quiver in that breath from his lips which first set them in motion; from the Arc de Triomphe to the Vendôme Column; Paris, whole and entire, sounds one great consistent Ode to Victor Hugo's honour, rears itself aloft, a poem in stone, each verse of which is one of the high spots of our national history.

The ceremonies which marked the one hundred and fiftieth anniversary of his birth were surrounded, in the Panthéon, with an aura of grateful and filial respect. Never has a nation been so closely knit with one single body of writing. For more than half a century our struggles had in him a point of reference, our murmurings an echo, our epic deeds a minstrel. Of this ancient and glorious community he had sounded forth the festivals and tocsins and passing bells. "Even today his poems, his cries, his furies and his laughter work on men's spirits in the quiet of libraries and within the stones of many tombs . . ."[29] On that June 10th, 1952, we saw the immense basilica filled with a silent, thoughtful crowd. From roof to floor great tricolour banners trembled like living flames in the beams of the searchlights, and, through the high doors opening on to one of the very old quarters of Paris could be seen, as once around the Arc de Triomphe, the swirls and eddies of a vast human concourse filling the wide square before Sainte-Geneviève.

"Ô l'herbe épaisse où sont les morts!" Some days after these official celebrations a few of us decided to make a pilgrimage to the graves of the two women whose names deserved to be included in them. Madame Drouet is buried beside her daughter Claire in the old cemetery of Saint-Mandé. It is now a piece of waste-land surrounded by suburban houses. Juliette had asked that these lines by Victor Hugo should be carved upon her tombstone:

> Quand je ne serai plus qu'une cendre glacée,
> Quand mes yeux fatigués seront fermés au jour,
> Dis-toi, si dans ton cœur ma mémoire est fixée:
> Le monde a sa pensée.
> Moi, j'avais son amour!

But neither Georges nor Jeanne, nor Louis Koch, Juliette's nephew, took the trouble to obey the wishes of the forgotten dead. For a long time there was, upon the bare and barren stone, no name, no date. Those had to wait until Juliette had found friends who came after she had vanished—Monsieur and Madame Louis Icart. A "Société des Amis de Juliette Drouet" has today taken upon itself to maintain the twin graves, and marble gleams white among the dilapidated and moss-grown tombs.

At Villequier, the small stone graveyard lies in the shadow of an ancient church, behind a wall half concealed by elder bushes. It is peopled by sailors and Seine pilots. Close by the entrance, the two families of Hugo and Vacquerie occupy a group of nineteen graves. There we may read:

CHARLES VACQUERIE

AGÉ DE 26 ANS

LÉOPOLDINE VACQUERIE

NÉE HUGO

MARIÉS LE 15 FÉVRIER ET MORTS

LE 4 SEPTEMBRE 1843

De profundis clamavi ad te, Domine

Thither went Hugo on a day in 1847, with a "bunch of green holly and flowering heather." There lie ADÈLE, FEMME DE VICTOR HUGO with, on her left hand, that other Adèle Hugo, the poor girl with her inoffensive manias (1830-1915). On her right, a space was long kept vacant for her lord, though there were doubts whether he might not prefer to rest in Père Lachaise, close to his son and to his father, the general. A "grateful country" solved the problem by admitting him to the Panthéon. It was Auguste Vacquerie who chose to be buried in this Normandy village with his parents, and side by side with the woman whom he had, all his life long, so chastely loved. He had composed his own epitaph:

> Je veux qu'à son tombeau, le mien soit ressemblant.
> Ainsi mourir n'aura pour moi rien de troublant.
> Et ce sera reprendre une habitude ancienne
> Que de ravoir ma chambre à côté de la sienne.

The intended reference was to his mother who rests beside the drowned pair, but when he wrote those lines was he not also thinking a little of his beloved friend? We could not help but ask that question. From the high and melancholy spot we gazed upon the grey, gloomy waters of the Seine, and the great ships moving up the river. Black clouds were piling above the horizon. A tatter of mist slowly enveloped us. Suddenly a storm broke with unbelievable violence. Flashes of lightning and crashes of thunder followed one another with terrifying rapidity. Torrents of water swirled among the tombs, and we were held there motionless by incessant zigzags striking from a riven sky. The close proximity of Hugo always breeds thoughts of mystery, and now it seemed to me that the old god, master of clouds and trailing vapours, had for the last time wished, by striking upon the walls of Heaven such monstrous blows, to show that though he might be absent in the flesh from this place of family buryings, he was there no less in spirit, and in the power and dread magnificence of genius.

Bibliography

MANUSCRIPT SOURCES

Bibliothèque nationale: département des manuscrits.

N.A.F. (Victor Hugo Collections), 13464, 13466, 13467, 13468, 13471, 13475, 13479: Victor Hugo's private diaries, in part unpublished.

N.A.F. 13414: unpublished letters from Adèle Foucher to Victor Hugo.

N.A.F. 23803-23807: holograph MS. in 5 vols. by Madame Victor Hugo: *Victor Hugo raconté par un témoin de sa vie*.

SPŒLBERCH DE LOVENJOUL COLLECTION

D. 571-D. 575: Sainte-Beuve's note-books, in part unpublished.

D. 525. Unpublished article by Sainte-Beuve on *Les Rayons et les Ombres* entitled "Des Gladiateurs en littérature."

D. 588: Letters from Victor Hugo to Sainte-Beuve.

D. 517: *Les Œuvres de Pierre Ronsard, gentilhomme vendômois prince des poètes français* (at Paris, at the shop of Nicolas Buonaumont Saint-Hilaire, à l'enseigne de Saint-Claude, 1609).

The copy given to Victor Hugo by Sainte-Beuve; enriched with autographs by Lamartine, Alfred de Vigny, Madame Amable Tastu, Alexandre Dumas the elder, Louis Boulanger, Antoine Fontaney, Ernest Fouinet, Ulric Guttinguer and Sainte-Beuve.

C. 495: Unpublished letters from Adèle Hugo to Théophile Gautier.

MAISON DE VICTOR HUGO

Two of Victor Hugo's private diaries, in part unpublished.

PRIVATE COLLECTIONS

MONSIEUR ALFRED DUPONT. An unpublished letter from Victor Hugo to his Trébuchet uncle; an unpublished letter from Léopoldine Hugo to Louise Bertin; unpublished letters from Victor Hugo to Colonel Charras, and to his daughter-in-law Alice Charles-Hugo.

MADAME ANDRÉ GAVEAU (before her marriage) LEFÈVRE-VACQUERIE. An unpublished letter from Madame Victor Hugo to Victor Hugo; unpublished letters from Charles Hugo to his brother François-Victor Hugo; unpublished letters from Alice Charles-Hugo to her brother-in-law François-Victor; Juliette Drouet's holograph will.

MONSIEUR JEAN MONTARGIS. Unpublished letters from Victor Hugo to Madame Biard (Léonie d'Aunet); numerous documents having to do with the Paul Meurice estate.

MONSIEUR GABRIEL FAURE. Letters from Victor Hugo to Paul-François Dubois, editor of *Le Globe*.

MADAME SIMONE ANDRÉ-MAUROIS. Unpublished letters from Émile Deschamps to Victor Hugo; Juliette Drouet's account-book; unpublished letters from Auguste

Vacquerie to Madame Victor Hugo; an article on James Pradier, dictated by Victor Hugo to Juliette Drouet; a letter from Victor Hugo to the Comte de Salvandy: unpublished notes on his mother by François-Victor Hugo; unpublished letters from Victor Hugo to Cuvillier-Fleury; unpublished letters from Sarah Bernhardt to various correspondents.

MONSIEUR GEORGES BLAIZOT. An unpublished letter from Sainte-Beuve to Madame Victor Hugo; unpublished correspondence between James Pradier and Juliette Drouet.

PRINTED SOURCES

ALAIN (pseud. of ÉMILE AUGUSTE CHARTIER). *Humanités* (Paris, éditions du Méridien, 1946).

ALLEM, MAURICE. *Sainte-Beuve et "Volupté"* (Paris, E. Malfère, 1935).

AMBRIÈRE, FRANCIS. "Du nouveau sur l'enfance de Victor Hugo" (*Les Nouvelles Littéraires,* March 30th, 1929); "La Bibliothèque de Louis Barthou; Hugo" (*Les Nouvelles Littéraires,* March 16th, 1935); "Les Cent Ans d' 'Angelo' " (*Mercure de France,* April 15th, 1935); "Hugophobes et huglâtres" (*Mercure de France,* June 1st, 1935); "Esther Guimont, courtisane des lettres" (*Minerve,* September 29th, 1935).

ANCELOT, VIRGINIE. *Un Salon de Paris* (Paris, E. Dentu, 1866).

ARAGON, LOUIS. *Avez-vous lu Victor Hugo?* An anthology with notes (Paris, Les Éditions Français, Réunis, 1952).

ARLAND, MARCEL. *Anthologie de la Poésie française* (Paris, Stock, 1941).

ASSELINE, ALFRED. *Victor Hugo intime* (Paris, G. Marpon and E. Flammarion, 1885).

AUDIAT, PIERRE. *Ainsi vécut Victor Hugo* (Paris, Hachette, 1947).

AYDA, ADILA. *L'influence de Victor Hugo sur Stéphane Mallarmé* (Istanbul, Dialogues, 1953).

BALZAC, HONORÉ DE. *Lettres à l'Étrangère,* vol. I (Paris, Calmann-Lévy, 1889); vol. II (ibid., 1906); vol. III (ibid., 1933); vol. IV (ibid., 1950); vol. V, still unpublished in 1954, the original MS. of which is in the Spœlberch de Lovenjoul Collection.

BANVILLE, THÉODORE DE. *Les Camées parisiens* (Paris, R. Pincebourde, 1866); "Châtiments" (*Le National,* November 30th, 1870); "Victor Hugo poète (*Revue générale,* Brussels, June 15th, 1885).

BARBEY D'AUREVILLY, JULES. *"Les Misérables" de M. Victor Hugo* (chez tous les libraires, Paris, 1862); *Les Œuvres et les Hommes: les Poètes,* III (Paris, Amyot, 1862); *Le Théâtre contemporain,* vols. III and IV (Paris, Quantin, 1889-92); "Quatre-vingt-treize" (*Le Constitutionnel,* March 19th, 1874); "La Légende des Siècles," second series (*Le Constitutionnel,* March 12th, 1877).

BARBIER, AUGUSTE. *Souvenirs personnels et Silhouettes contemporaines* (Paris, E. Dentu, 1883).

BARRÈRE, JEAN-BERTRAND. *La Fantaisie de Victor Hugo, 1802-1851* (Paris, José Corti, 1949); *La Fantaisie de Victor Hugo, thèmes et motifs* (Paris, José Corti, 1950); *Hugo, l'homme et l'œuvre* (Paris, Boivin et Cie, 1952).

BARRÈS, MAURICE. *Les Déracinés* (Paris, E. Fasquelle, 1897); *Mes Cahiers,* 12 vols. (Paris, Plon, 1929-49).

BARTHOU, LOUIS. *Les Amours d'un Poète* (Paris, Louis Conard, 1919); "Victor Hugo élève de Biscarrat" (*Revue de Paris,* February 1st, 1925); "Lettres d'Alfred de Vigny à Victor Hugo, 1826-1831" (*Revue des Deux Mondes,* February 1st, 1925); *Le Général Hugo* (Paris, Hachette, 1926).

BAUDELAIRE, CHARLES. *Théophile Gautier,* with a Prefatory Letter from Victor Hugo to Baudelaire (Paris, Poulet-Malassis et de Broise, 1859); "Les Misérables" (*Le Boulevard,* April 20th, 1862); "Notice sur Victor Hugo," vol. IV of *Les Poètes français,* by Eugène Crépet; *L'Art romantique* (Paris, Michel Levy, 1868); *Lettres inédites de Baudelaire à sa mère* (Paris, Louis Conard, 1918); *Correspondance,* 4 vols. (Louis Conard, 1947-48).

BAUDOUIN, CHARLES. *Psychanalyse de Victor Hugo* (Geneva, Éditions de Mont Blanc, 1943).

BAUER, GERARD. "Victor Hugo jugé par Barbey d'Aurevilly" (*L'Écho de Paris,* November 16th, 1922); "Une Interprétation d'Hernani" (*L'Opinion,* December 8th, 1922); "Le Centenaire d'Hernani à la Comédie-Française" (*Les Annales,* March 15th, 1930).

BEAUNIER, ANDRÉ. "Elle et Lui: Victor Hugo et Juliette Drouet" (*Revue des Deux Mondes,* September 1st, 1914).

BÉGUIN, ALBERT. *Gérard de Nerval* (Paris, Stock, 1936); "Le Songe de Jean-Paul et Victor Hugo" (*Revue de Littérature comparée,* October-December 1934); *L'Ame romantique et le Rêve* (Paris, José Corti, 1939).

BELLESORT, ANDRÉ. *Sainte-Beuve et le XIXe siècle* (Paris, Perrin, 1927); *Victor Hugo, essai sur son œuvre* (Paris, Perrin, 1929).

BENOÎT-LEVY, EDMOND. *Le Jeunesse de Victor Hugo* (Paris, Albin Michel, 1928); "Madame Victor Hugo et Juliette Drouet" (*Les Nouvelles Littéraires,* March 26th, 1927); "Après la mort de Gustave Simon. Les inédits de Victor Hugo" (*Les Nouvelles Littéraires,* February 4th, 1928); *"Les Misérables" de Victor Hugo* (Paris, Edgar Malfère, 1929).

BÉRARD, LÉON. "Discours prononcé au Luxembourg pour le cinquantenaire de la mort de Victor Hugo" (*Le Temps,* July 1st, 1935).

BERNHARDT, LYSIANE. *Sarah Barnhardt, ma grand-mère* (Paris, Éditions du Pavois, 1945).

BERNHARDT, SARAH. *Mémoires* (Paris, E. Fasquelle, 1907); "Comment Victor Hugo faisait répéter" (*Le Gaulois,* November 25th and 26th, 1911).

BERNOVILLE, GAÉTAN. "Victor Hugo et l'Allemagne" (*Les Lettres,* April 1st, 1919).

BERRET, PAUL. *La Philosophie de Victor Hugo et deux Mythes de "La Légende des Siècles"* (Paris, H. Paulin, 1910); *Le Moyen Age dans "la Légende des Siècles" et les sources de Victor Hugo* (Paris, H. Paulin, 1911); "La Légende des Siècles de 1859," introduction a l'édition des "Grands Écrivains de France" (Paris, Hachette, 1921); *Victor Hugo* (Paris, Garnier frères, 1927).

BERTAL, GEORGES. *Auguste Vacquerie, sa vie et son œuvre* (Paris, F. Andréol, 1889).

BERTAUT, JULES. *Victor Hugo* (Paris, Louis Michaud, 1910); "La Première de 'Le Roi s'amuse' " (*Revue des Deux Mondes,* November 15th, 1932); "Victor Hugo et la Réalité historique" (*Candide,* June 6th, 1935).

BILLY, ANDRÉ. *Sainte-Beuve,* 2 vols. (Paris, Flammarion, 1952); "Sainte-Beuve et Madame Victor Hugo" (*L'Œuvre,* May 25th, 1926); "Anniversaire de Victor Hugo" (*L'Œuvre,* February 27th, 1928); "Claudel et Hugo" (*L'Œuvre,* January 28th, 1930); "Les Tombes de Villequier" (*Le Figaro,* May 2nd, 1937); " 'William Shakespeare' de Victor Hugo" (*Le Figaro,* September 18th, 1937); "Victor Hugo" (*Le Figaro,* January 27th, 1940); "Les Jeunes Poètes aux Funérailles de Victor Hugo" (*Le Figaro Littéraire,* August 3rd, 1946).

BIRÉ, EDMOND. *Victor Hugo avant 1830,* new edition (Paris, Perrin, 1892); *Victor Hugo après 1830,* 2 vols. (Paris, Perrin, 1891); *Victor Hugo après 1852* (Paris, Perrin, 1894).

BLAIZOT, GEORGES. "Remarques nouvelles sur l'édition originale des 'Misérables'; Paris ou Bruxelles?" (*Bulletin du Bibliophile,* January 20th and February 20th, 1936); "Un livre qui n'est plus négligé: 'Victor Hugo raconté par un témoin de sa vie' " (*Bulletin du Bibliophile,* July 20th, 1936); "Hugo, Lamartine et la Statue d'Henri IV" (*Bulletin du Bibliophile,* December 20th, 1936).

BLUM, LÉON. *En lisant* (Paris, Ollendorff, 1906).

BONNEROT, JEAN. *Bibliographie de l'Œuvre de Sainte-Beuve,* 4 vols. (Paris, Giraud-Badin, 1937-52).

BORNEQUE, JACQUES-HENRY. "Les Leçons de Villequier" (*Le Monde,* October 4th, 1952).

BOUTERON, MARCEL. *Muses romantiques* (Paris, Le Goupy, 1926).

BOYÉ, MAURICE-PIERRE. "Victor Hugo et ses inconnues" (*Quo Vadis,* 1952); "Le Dernier Amour de Victor Hugo" (*Quo Vadis,* December, 1953).

BREMOND, HENRI. *Le Roman et l'Histoire d'une Conversion. Ulric Guttinguer et Sainte-Beuve* (Paris, Plon, 1925); *Pour le romantisme* (Bloud et Gay, 1923).

BRUNET, GEORGES. *Victor Hugo* (Paris, Éditions Rieder, Collection "Maîtres des Littératures," 1935).

BRUNETIÈRE, FERDINAND. *Victor Hugo* (Paris, Hachette, 1902); *L'Évolution de la Poésie lyrique en France au XIXe siècle,* 2 vols. (Paris, Hachette, 1894); *Histoire de la Littérature française,* vol. 4: *Le Dix-neuvième Siècle* (Paris, Delagrave, 1918).

CASTELNAU, JACQUES. *Adèle Hugo, l'épouse d'Olympio* (Paris, Tallandier, collection "Amantes et Égéries," 1941); *Catalogue de l'Exposition "Enfance et Jeunesse de Victor Hugo."* Préface de Jean Sergent. Maison de Victor Hugo, May 1952 (Ville de Paris, May, 1952); *Catalogue de l'Exposition organisée pour le 150e anniversaire de la naissance de Victor Hugo.* Bibliothèque nationale, June 1952. Introduction by Julien Cain. Articles by Suzanne Solente and de Jean Prinet; *Catalogue de l'Exposition "Maturité de Victor Hugo."* Preface by Jean Sergent. Maison de Victor Hugo, May-July 1953 (Ville de Paris, 1953).

CHARAVAY, ERNEST. *Histoire de'un Crime* (Paris, Charavay, 1877).

CHARAVAY, ÉTIENNE. " 'Hernani' et la Comédie-Française" (*L'Amateur d'Autographes,* June and July 1872).

CHARLIER, GUSTAVE. *Juliette Drouet à Bruxelles* (Brussels, M. Veissenbruch, 1919); *Victor Hugo à Bruxelles* (Brussels. Éditions de la Jeunesse nouvelle, 1922); *Une Amitié romantique: Saint-Valry et Victor Hugo* (Brussels, René Van Sulfer, 1927).

CHENAY, PAUL. *Victor Hugo à Guernesey* (Paris, Félix Juven, 1902).

CHESNIER, DU CHESNE, A. *Le "Ronsard" de Victor Hugo* (Paris, G. Crès, 1929).

CLARETIE, JULES. *Victor Hugo. Souvenirs intimes* (Paris, Librairie Molière, 1902); *La Vie à Paris, 1880-1885,* 6 vols. (Paris, V. Havard, 1881-85); *La Vie à Paris,* 15 vols. (Paris, E. Fasquelle, 1896-1914).

CLAUDEL, PAUL. *Positions et Propositions* (Paris, Gallimard, 1928); "Sur Victor Hugo" (*Les Nouvelles Littéraires,* June 8th, 1935).

CLÉMENT-JANIN, P. *Victor Hugo en exil, d'après sa correspondance avec Jules Janin* (Paris, Éditions du Monde nouveau, 1922); *Drames et Comédies romantiques* (Paris, Le Goupy, 1928).

CRÉPET, EUGÈNE. *Les Poètes français,* vol. IV (Paris, Gide et Hachette, 1863).

CUVILLIER-FLEURY, ALFRED-AUGUSTE. "Monsieur Victor Hugo (*Journal des Débats,* June 16th, 1850); "Les Misérables" (*Journal des Débats,* April 29th and May 6th, 1862).

DAUBRAY, CÉCILE. *Victor Hugo et ses Correspondants,* with a Foreword by Paul Valéry (Paris, Albin Michel, 1947).

DAUDET, JULIA ALLARD, MADAME ALPHONSE. *Souvenirs autour d'un groupe littéraire* (Paris, E. Faquelle, 1909).

DAUDET, LÉON. *La Tragique Existence de Victor Hugo* (Paris, Albin Michel, 1937).

D'ANGERS, DAVID. *Correspondance avec Victor Hugo, Lamartine, Chateaubriand, Vigny,* edited by H. Jouin (Paris, Plon, 1890).

DEFFOUX, LÉON. "Les Lettres de Madame Hugo à Sainte-Beuve." Procès-verbal de l'incinération de 334 lettres d'Adèle Hugo à Sainte-Beuve, November 29th, 1885 (*Mercure de France,* June 1st, 1937).

DEGUELDRE, J. "Un Illustre Actionnaire de la Banque: Victor Hugo" (*Revue de la Banque Nationale de Belgique,* February 1949).

DELACROIX, EUGÈNE. *Journal,* 3 vols., new edition, revised and enlarged. Introduction by André Joubin (Paris, Plon, 1850).

DELFORGE, LUCIENNE. "La Vie amoureuse de Victor Hugo et de Juliette Drouet" (Tangiers, Éditions internationales du *Journal de Tanger,* 1953).

DRESSE, PAUL. *Gœthe et Hugo* (Brussels, Editions Libris, 1942); "Une Viste à Falkenstein" (*La Grive,* July 1951).

DROUET, JULIETTE. *Mille et une lettres d'amour à Victor Hugo.* A selection, with Preface and Notes by Paul Souchon (Paris, Gallimard, 1951).

DUBUC, ANDRÉ. *Villequier dans la Vie et l'Œuvre de Victor Hugo* (Rouen, imprimerie Lainé, 1946).

DUFAY, PIERRE. *Eugène Hugo, sa vie, sa folie, ses œuvres* (Paris, Jean Fort, 1924).

DUMAS, ALEXANDRE. "Victor Hugo raconté par Alexandre Dumas" (*Revue encyclopédique,* vol. II, 1892, Nos. 33 and 34.)

DURRY, MARIE-JEANNE. "Centenaire romantique, 'Bug-Jargal' et Le Globe" (*Le Figaro,* literary supplement of March 27th, 1926).

ESCHOLIER, RAYMOND. *Victor Hugo artiste* (Paris, Éditions G. Crès, 1926); *La Vie glorieuse de Victor Hugo* (Paris, Plon, 1928); *Eugène Delacroix,* 3 vols. (Paris, H. Floury, 1926-29); *Victor Hugo raconté par ceux qui l'ont vu* (Paris, Stock, Delamain et Boutelleau, 1931); *La Place Royale et Victor Hugo* (Paris, Firmin-Didot, 1933); *Victor Hugo et les Femmes* (Paris, Flammarion, 1935); *Victor Hugo cet inconnu* (Paris, Plon, 1951); *Un Amant de Génie: Victor Hugo* (Paris, Arthème Fayard, 1953).

FAGUET, ÉMILE. *Dix-neuvième Siècle. Études littéraires* (Paris, Lecène et Oudin, 1887).

FARGUE, LÉON-PAUL. *Lanterne magique* (Marseilles, Laffont, 1944); "Le Vieux Dieu" (*Les Nouvelles littéraires,* April 20th, 1935).

FAYARD, JEAN. "Victor Hugo au Panthéon" (*Candide,* December 27th, 1928).

FLAUBERT, GUSTAVE. *Correspondance,* new and enlarged edition, vols. III, V, and IX (Paris, Louis Conard, 1926-33).

FONTANEY, ANTOINE. *Journal intime,* edited, with an Introduction and Notes, by René Jasinski (Paris, Les Presses françaises, 1925); "Les Romans de Victor Hugo" (*Revue des Deux Mondes,* May 1832).

FOUCHER, PAUL. *Entre cour et jardin* (Paris, Amyot, 1867); *Coulisses du Passé* (Paris, E. Dentu, 1873).

FOUCHER, PIERRE. *La Belle-Famille de Victor Hugo. Souvenirs de Pierre Foucher.* With an Introduction and Notes by Louis Guimbaud (Paris, 1929).

FRANCE, ANATOLE. *La Vie littéraire,* 5 vols. (Paris, Calmann-Lévy, 1888-1949); *Vers des temps meilleurs* (Paris, E. Pelletan, 1910); *Les Poèmes du Souvenir* (Paris, E. Pelletan, 1910); "Ernest Renan et Victor Hugo" (*Revue de Paris,* November 1st, 1924).

GAUTIER, JUDITH. *Le Collier des Jours, souvenirs de ma vie* (Paris, Félix Juven, 1902); *Le Second Rang du Collier* (Paris, Juven, 1903); *Le Troisième Rang du Collier* (Paris, Juven, 1909).

GAUTIER, THÉOPHILE. *Les Jeune-France* (Paris, Renduel, 1833); *Histoire de l'Art dramatique en France depuis vingt-cinq ans,* 6 vols. (Paris, Hetzel, Magnin, Blanchard et Cie, 1858-59); *Dessins de Victor Hugo,* engraved by Paul Chenay, text by Théophile Gautier (Paris, Castel, 1863); *Histoire de Romantisme* (Paris, Charpentier, 1874); *Souvenirs de théâtre, d'art et de critique* (Paris, Charpentier, 1883).

GIDE, ANDRÉ. *Divers* (Paris, Gallimard, 1931); *Journal 1889-1939* (Paris, Gallimard,

Bibliothèque de la Pléiade, 1939); *Anthologie de la Poésie française,* selected and with a Preface by André Gide (Paris, Gallimard, 1949).

GILLET, LOUIS. "Shakespeare et les Poètes romantiques" *(Les Nouvelles littéraires,* June 28th, 1930).

GIRARD, HENRI. *Émile Deschamps, 1791-1871:—Émile Deschamps dilettante,* 2 vols. (Paris, Honoré Champion, 1921).

GIRARDIN, DELPHINE GAY, MADAME ÉMILE DE. *Lettres parisiennes,* 4 vols. (Paris, Michel Lévy, 1857); "Election de Victor Hugo à l'Académie" *(La Presse,* January 8th, 1841); "Victor Hugo à l'Académie" *(La Presse,* June 4th, 1841); "Lettre à Victor Hugo" *(Paris Magazine,* November 24th, 1867); "Lettres inédites à Victor Hugo" *(Revue mondiale,* May 1st, 1922).

GIRAUD, VICTOR. *La Vie secrète de Sainte-Beuve* (Paris, Éditions Stock, 1935); "Chateaubriand et Victor Hugo" *(Revue latine,* vol. III, 1904); "La Légende de 'l'enfant sublime'" *(Revue d'Histoire littéraire de la France,* July-September 1926); Victor Hugo, non le poète, mais l'homme" *(Revue des Deux Mondes,* October 15th, 1929).

GLATIGNY, ALBERT. "Lettres à Victor Hugo et à Paul Meurice," edited by Gustave Simon *(Revue de Paris,* February 1st, 1906); *Lettres inédites à Madame Victor Hugo* (Rouen, A. Desvages, 1932).

GOETHE, J. W. VON. *Conversations de Gœthe pendant les dernières années de sa vie (1822-1832) recueillies par Eckermann,* 2 vols. (Paris, Charpentier, 1865).

GONCOURT, EDMOND ET JULES DE. *Journal. Mémoires de la vie littéraire,* definitive edition, 9 vols. (Paris, Flammarion et Fasquelle, 1935-36).

GREGH, FERNAND. *La Fenêtre ouverte* (Paris, E. Fasquelle, 1901); *Les Clartés humaines* (Paris, E. Fasquelle, 1904); *Étude sur Victor Hugo* (Paris, Charpentier, 1905); *L'Œuvre de Victor Hugo,* an address delivered to the Sorbonne on the occasion of the inauguration of the Victor Hugo Chair (Paris, Flammarion, 1933); "A-propos des Lettres à la Fiancée" *(Revue Bleue,* March 16th, 1901).

GRILLET, CLAUDIUS. *Victor Hugo spirite* (Lyons: Emmanuel Vitte, 1929).

GUEHENNO, JEAN. *Jeunesse de la France (A-propos de Victor Hugo)* (Paris, Bernard Grasset, 1936); "Appel au Poète d'aujourd'hui" *(Europe,* June 15th, 1935).

GUIARD, AMÉDÉE. *La Fonction du Poète,* a thesis on Victor Hugo (Paris, Bloud, 1910); *Virgile et Victor Hugo* (Paris, Bloud, 1910).

GUILLEMIN, HENRI. "Victor Hugo posthume" *(Journal de Genève,* January 22nd, 1944); "Un Carnet de Victor Hugo" *(Le Figaro Littéraire,* April 16th, 1946); *Le Coup du 2 Décembre* (Paris, Gallimard, 1951); *Victor Hugo par lui-même* (Éditions du Seuil, Collection "Écrivains de toujours," 1951); "Lettres inédites de Victor Hugo, de Madame Hugo et de leur fille Adèle" *(La Table Ronde,* April 1952).

GUIMBAUD, LOUIS. *Victor Hugo et Juliette Drouet* (Paris, Auguste Blaizot, 1914); *Victor Hugo et Madame Biard* (Paris, Auguste Blaizot, 1927); *Les "Orientales" de Victor Hugo* (Paris, Edgar Malfère, 1928); *La Mère de Victor Hugo* (Paris, Plon, 1930); "Juliette Drouet avant Victor Hugo" *(Europe,* special number, February-March 1952).

HANOTAUX, GABRIEL. *Discours prononcé au Panthéon pour le centenaire de Victor Hugo,* February 26th, 1902 (Paris, Firmin-Didot, 1902).

HAZARD, PAUL. "Avec Victor Hugo en exil" *(Revue des Deux Mondes,* November 15th, 1930).

HENRIOT, ÉMILE. *Courrier littéraire* (Paris, La Renaissance du Livre, 1922); *Livres et Portraits,* 2 vols. (Paris, Plon, 1923-27); *Esquisses et notes de Lecture* (Paris, Editions de la Nouvelle Revue critique,* 1928); *Romanesques et Romantiques* (Paris, Plon, 1930); *De Marie de France à Katherine Mansfield: Alice Ozy et ses Poètes* (Paris, Plon, 1937); *Poètes français,* vol. II: *De Lamartine à Valéry* (Lyons, H. Lardanchet, 1946); *Les Romantiques* (Paris, Albin Michel, 1953).

HERRIOT, EDOUARD. *Précis de l'Histoire des Lettres françaises* (Paris, E. Cornely, 1905); "Victor Hugo" (*Conferencia*, March 7th, 1919).

HEUGEL, JACQUES. *Essai sur la Philosophie de Victor Hugo*, followed by *Reflexions sur la même thème* (Paris, Calmann-Lévy, 1930); *Essai sur la Philosophie de Victor Hugo du point de vue gnostique* (Paris, Calmann-Lévy, 1922).

HOFMANNSTHAL, HUGO VON. *Essai sur Victor Hugo*, translated from the German by Marie Ley-Deutsch (Geneva-Paris, Librairie E. Droz, 1937).

HOUSSAYE, ARSÈNE. *Les Confessions. Souvenirs d'un demi-siècle*, 6 vols. (Paris, E. Dentu, 1885-91); *Souvenirs de Jeunnese*, 2 vols. (Paris, Flammarion, 1896).

For all the quotations from Victor Hugo printed in this book, the pagination (except where otherwise stated) is that of the edition in 45 volumes, known as the *Édition de l'Imprimerie Nationale* (Paris, Paul Ollendorff, and subsequently Albin Michel). It was edited first by Paul Meurice (1904-5), then after his death by Gustave Simon (1905-14), and finally, after an interruption of ten years (1924-28), completed by Madame Cécile Daubray (1933-52).

The four titles immediately following were published separately and do not appear in the *Édition de l'Imprimerie Nationale*.

HUGO, VICTOR. *Pierres*, verse and prose collected and edited by Henri Guillemin (Geneva, Milieu du Monde, 1951); *Trois Cahiers de Vers français, 1815-18*, edited by Gérauld Venzac (Paris, Jacques Damase, 1952); *Souvenirs personnels, 1848-1851*, collected and edited by Henri Guillemin (Paris, Gallimard, 1952); *Cris dans l'Ombre et Chansons loitaines*, collected and edited by Henri Guillemin (Paris, Albin Michel, 1953).

HUGO, ADÈLE FOUCHER, MADAME VICTOR. *Victor Hugo raconté par un témoin de sa vie* (Brussels, A. Lacroix, Verboeckhoven et Cie, 1863), 2 vols.

HUGO, CHARLES. *Les Hommes de l'exil* (Paris, A. Lemerre, 1875).

HUGO, GEORGES VICTOR. *Mon Grand-Père* (Paris, Calmann-Lévy, 1902).

HUGO, LÉOPOLD, GÉNÉRAL. *Mémoires*, with a Preface and Notes by Louis Guimbaud (Paris, Éditions Excelsior, in the Collection "Jadis et naguère," 1934).

JANIN, JULES. *Histoire de la Littérature dramatique*, 6 vols. (Paris, Michel Lévy, 1853-58).

JASINSKI, RENÉ. *Les Années romantiques de Théophile Gautier* (Paris, Vuibert, 1929).

KARR, ALPHONSE. *Les Guêpes* (Paris, Michel Lévy, 1862); *Le Livre de Bord*, 4 vols. (Paris, Calmann-Lévy, 1879-80).

KEMP, ROBERT. "Les Lettres d'Alfred de Vigny à Victor Hugo" (*La Liberté*, August 4th, 1925); "Sainte-Beuve et Madame Victor Hugo" (*La Liberté*, April 1st, 1926); "Le Général Hugo" (*La Liberté*, June 3rd, 1926); " 'Les Orientales' " (*La Liberté*, February 11th, 1929); " 'Les Misérables' " (*La Liberté*, September 23rd, 1929); "Victor Hugo" (*La Liberté*, January 20th, 1930); "La Mère de Victor Hugo" (*La Liberté*, October 9th, 1930); and numerous recent articles in *Les Nouvelles littéraires*.

LACRETELLE, JACQUES DE. *L'Écrivain public* (Paris, Gallimard, 1936).

LACRETELLE, PIERRE DE. *Vie politique de Victor Hugo* (Paris, Hachette, 1928); "La Véritable Édition originale des 'Châtiments' " (*Bulletin du Bibliophile*, January-April 1952); "Éditions originales des 'Odes et Ballades' " (*Bulletin du Bibliophile*, July-August 1922); "La Véritable Édition originale des 'Contemplations' " (*Bulletin du Bibliophile*, November 1922); "Victor Hugo et ses Éditeurs" (*Revue de France*, October 1st and November 1st, 1923).

LA FORCE, DUC DE. " 'Lucrèce Borgia' de Victor Hugo" (*Revue des Deux Mondes*, January 1st, 1936); "A-propos de 'Ruy Blas' " (*Revue des Deux Mondes*, January 15th, 1938).

LALOU, RENÉ. *Prosateurs romantiques* (Paris, Éditions du Trianon, 1930); *Histoire de la Littérature française contemporaine,* 2 vols. (Presses Universitaires de France, 1940-41).

LAMARTINE, ALPHONSE DE. *Cours familier de Littérature,* vols. 14 and 15 (Paris, chez l'auteur, rue de la Ville-l'Évêque, 1862-63); *Souvenirs et Portraits,* vol. 3 (Paris, Hachette, 1872); *Correspondance,* vol. 5 (Paris, Hachette, 1875).

LANSON, GUSTAVE. *Histoire de la Littérature française,* 2 vols. (Paris, Hachette, 1924).

LARROUMET, GUSTAVE. *La Maison de Victor Hugo. Impressions de Guernesey* (Paris, Honoré Champion, 1895).

LASSERRE, PIERRE. *Le Romantisme français* (Paris, Mercure de France, 1908).

LATOUCHE, HENRI DE. "La Camaraderie littéraire" *(Revue de Paris,* October 1829).

LECOMTE, GEORGES. "Discours prononcé à Guernesey July 7th, 1914 pour l'inauguration de la statue de Victor Hugo" *(Le Temps,* July 8th, 1914); *Gloire de l'Île-de-France: Victor Hugo dans la vallée de la Bièvre* (Paris, Renaissance de la Livre, 1934); "Juliette Drouet" *(Conferencia,* August 15th, 1935).

LECONTE DE LISLE, CHARLES. *Discours de reception à l'Académie française, prononcé March 31st, 1887* (Paris, Firmin Didot, 1887).

LEROY, MAXIME. *Vie de Sainte-Beuve* (Paris, J-B. Janin, 1947).

LESCLIDE, JUANA RICHARD. *Victor Hugo intime* (Paris, Félix Juven, 1902); "Les Correspondants de Victor Hugo" *(Les Annales,* June 28th, 1903); "Le Dernier Anniversaire et la Mort de Hugo" *(Les Annales,* May 25th, 1935).

LESCLIDE, RICHARD. *Propos de table de Victor Hugo* (Paris, E. Dentu, 1885).

LEVAILLANT, MAURICE. *La Tristesse d'Olympio,* together with a study of Victor Hugo (Paris, H. Champion, 1928); *Œuvre de Victor Hugo.* A selection, together with reviews and notes (Paris, Delagrave, 1937); *Victor Hugo, Juliette Drouet et la "Tristesse d'Olympio"* (Paris, Delagrave, 1945); "Sur un quatrain de Victor Hugo" *(Le Figaro,* October 13th, 1933); "Dans l'atelier de Victor Hugo *(Revue des Deux Mondes,* May 1st, 1930); "Le Vrai Victor Hugo" *(Europe,* special number, February-March 1952).

LOCKROY, EDOUARD. *Au hasard de la vie. Souvenirs sur Victor Hugo* (Paris, Bernard Grasset, 1913).

LŒWEL, PIERRE. "L'Œuvre de Victor Hugo" *(L'Ordre,* January 24th, 1934).

LOVENJOUL, CHARLES DE SPŒLBERCH DE. *Sainte-Beuve inconnu* (Paris, Plon, 1901); *Alfred de Musset et Victor Hugo* (Paris, E. Rouveyre, 1878).

LOVIOT, LOUIS. *Alice Ozy* (Paris, Dorbon ainé, 1910).

LYONNET, HENRY. *Les Premières de Victor Hugo* (Paris, Delagrave, 1930); *Dictionnaire des Comédiens français* (Geneva, Bibliothèque de la Revue internationale illustrée. Undated).

MABILLEAU, LÉOPOLD. *Victor Hugo* (Paris, Hachette, "Collection des Grands Écrivains français," 1893); "Le Sens de la Vue chez Victor Hugo" *(Revue des Deux Mondes,* October 15th, 1890).

MALO, HENRI. *Delphine Gay de Girardin* (Paris, Émile-Paul, 1924); *La Gloire du vicomte de Launay, Delphine de Girardin* (Paris, Émile-Paul, 1925).

MAULNIER, THIERRY. *Introduction à la Poésie française* (Paris, Gallimard, 1939); *Langages* (Lausanne, Marguerat, 1947).

MAYNIAL, ÉDOUARD. *Précis de Littérature française* (Paris, Delagrave, 1936); *Anthologie des Poètes du XIXe siècle* (Paris, Hachette, 1932).

MENESSIER, MARIE NODIER, MADAME. *Charles Nodier, épisodes et souvenirs de sa vie* (Paris, Didier, 1867).

MEURICE, PAUL. *Correspondance entre Victor Hugo et Paul Meurice* (Paris, E. Fasquelle, 1909).

MICHAUT, G. *Le "Livre d'Amour" de Sainte-Beuve* (Paris, Fontemoing, 1905); *Sainte-Beuve amoureux et poète* (Paris, Fontemoing, 1910).

MONDOR, HENRI. *Vie de Mallarmé,* one-volume edition (Paris, Gallimard, 1943).

MONTARGIS, JEAN. "La Première et la Dernière Œuvre dramatique de Victor Hugo . . ." (*Nouvelle Revue française,* March 1st, 1939).

MOREAU, PIERRE. *Le Romantisme* (Paris, J. de Gigord, 1932).

NOAILLES, ANNA, COMTESSE DE. "Apologie pour Victor Hugo" (*Les Nouvelles littéraires,* June 30th, 1923); "Soyons justes!" (*Les Nouvelles littéraires,* April 28th, 1927).

NODIER, CHARLES. *Souvenirs, Portraits et Épisodes,* 2 vols. (Paris, Levavasseur, 1831).

NOIR, VICTOR. "L'Enterrement de Madame Victor Hugo à Villequier" (*Journal de Rouen,* September 1st, 1868).

OLIVIER, JUSTE. *Paris en 1830, Journal,* edited by André Delattre and Marc Denkinger, with a Preface by Fernand Baldensperger (Paris, Mercure de France, 1951).

PAILLERON, MARIE-LOUISE. *François Buloz et ses Amis. La Vie littéraire sous Louis-Philippe* (Paris, Firmin-Didot, 1930); *La "Revue des Deux Mondes" et la Comédie-Française* (Paris, Firmin-Didot, 1930); *Les Derniers Romantiques* (Paris, Perrin, 1923);*Les Écrivains du Second Empire* (Paris, Perrin, 1924).

PARMÉNIE, A., and BONNIER DE LA CHAPELLE, C. *Histoire d'un Éditeur et de ses Auteurs: Pierre-Jules Hetzel* (Paris, Albin Michel, 1953).

PAVIE, THÉODORE. *Victor Pavie, sa jeunesse, ses relations littéraires* (Angers, P. Lachèse et Dolbeau, 1887).

PAVIE, VICTOR. *Les Revenants: Charles Nodier* (Angers, Germain et Grassin, 1883).

PÉGUY, CHARLES. *Victor-Marie, comte Hugo* (Paris, Gallimard, 1934).

PERCHE, LOUIS. *Victor Hugo* (Paris, Pierre Seghers, 1952).

PIA, PASCAL. *Baudelaire par lui-même* (Paris, Éditions du Seuil, Collection "Écrivains de toujours," 1952).

PLANCHE, GUSTAVE. *Portraits littéraires,* 2 vols. (Paris, Librairie de Werdet, 1836; enlarged edition, Paris, Charpentier, 1853); *Nouveaux Portraits littéraires,* 2 vols. (Paris, Amyot, 1854).

PONTMARTIN, ARMAND DE. *Causeries du Samedi* (Paris, Michel Lévy, 1857).

POTIN, ÉMILE. "La Maison de l'Avenue d'Eylau" (*Bulletin de la Société historique d'Auteuil et de Passy,* vol. IV, 1901-3).

POULET, GEORGES. *Études sur le Temps humain* (Paris, Plon, Collection "L'Épi," 1950); *La Distance intérieure* (Paris, Plon, Collection "L'Épi," 1952).

PRÉVOST, JEAN. "Le Cinquantenaire de la Mort de Victor Hugo" (*Revue des Vivants,* March 1935).

PROUST, MARCEL. "A-propos de Baudelaire" (*Nouvelle Revue française,* June 21st, 1921); *Chroniques* (Paris, Gallimard, 1927).

RAMUZ, C.-F. *Anthologie de la Poésie française,* vol. 2 (Paris, Éditions Corréa, 1943).

RECLUS, MAURICE. *Émile de Girardin* (Paris, Hachette, 1934); "Victor Hugo, poète maudit" (*La Renaissance,* February 1st, 1919).

REGNIER, HENRI DE. *Figures et Caractères* (Paris, Mercure de France, 1901); *Proses datées* (Paris, Mercure de France, 1925).

RENAN, ERNEST. *Dialogue des Morts* (Paris, Calmann-Lévy, 1886); *Feuilles détachées* (Paris, Calmann-Lévy, 1882).

RENARD, JULES. *Journal, 1887-1910,* 4 vols. (Paris, F. Bernouard, 1927).

RENOUVIER, CHARLES. *Victor Hugo le poète* (Paris, A. Colin, 1893); *Victor Hugo le philosophe* (Paris, A. Colin, 1900).

RIVET, GUSTAVE. *Victor Hugo chez lui* (Paris, Maurice Dreyfous, 1878).

ROCHEBLAVE, SAMUEL. "Madame Victor Hugo portraitiste" (*Journal des Débats,* August 1st, 1927); "Paul de Saint-Victor et la famille Hugo" (*Revue de Paris,* August 1st, 1933).

ROCHEFORT, HENRI. *Les Aventures de ma Vie,* 5 vols. (Paris, Paul Dupont, 1896).

ROLLAND, ROMAIN. *Campagnons de Route* (Paris, Éditions du Sablier, 1936); "Le Vieux Orphée" (*Europe,* special number, February-March 1952).

ROSTAND, EDMOND. "Un Soir à 'Hernani' " (*Le Gaulois,* March 4th, 1902).

ROY, CLAUDE. *La Vie de Victor Hugo racontée par Victor Hugo* (Paris, René Julliard, 1952); "Notes sur la lecture des poètes nommés Victor Hugo" (*Europe,* special number, February-March 1952).

SAINTE-BEUVE, CHARLES-AUGUSTIN. *Volupté* (Paris, Eugène Renduel, 1834); *Livre d'Amour* (Paris, 1843); *Portraits contemporains,* new and enlarged edition in 5 vols. (Paris, Michel Lévy, 1869-71); *Premiers Lundis,* new edition, edited by Maurice Allem (Paris, Garnier frères, 1934); *Vie, Poésies et Pensées de Joseph Delorme* (Paris, Delangle, 1829); *Les Consolations* (Paris, Urbain Canel, 1830); *Causeries du Lundi,* vol. XI (Paris, Garnier, 1881); *Nouveaux Lundis* (Paris, Calmann-Lévy, 1903); *Les Cahiers de Sainte-Beuve* (Paris, A. Lemerre, 1876); *Mes Poisons,* edited by Victor Giraud (Paris, Plon, 1926); *Correspondance générale,* edited and annotated by Jean Bonnerot, 6 volumes so far published (Éditions Stock, Delamain et Boutelleau, 1935-49).

SAINT-VICTOR, PAUL DE. *Victor Hugo* (Paris, Calmann-Lévy, 1892).

SAND, GEORGE. *Autour de la Table* (Paris, E. Dentu, 1862); *Nouvelles Lettres d'un Voyageur* (Paris, Michel Lévy, 1877); *Questions d'Art et de Littérature* (Paris, Michel Lévy, 1878); *Souvenirs et Idées* (Paris, Calmann-Lévy, 1904); "Correspondance inédite entre Victor Hugo et George Sand" (*Revue de France,* December 1st, 1922).

SAULNIER, V.-L. *La Littérature du Siècle romantique* (Paris, Presses Universitaires de France, 1925).

SAURAT, DENIS. *La Religion de Victor Hugo* (Paris, Hachette, 1929); *La Littérature et l'Occultisme,* vol. I: *Étude sur la Poésie philosophique moderne* (Paris, Rieder, 1929); *idem,* vol. II: *Victor-Hugo et les Dieux du Peuple* (Paris, Éditions du Vieux Colombier, 1948); *Modernes* (Paris, Denoel et Steele, 1935); *Perspectives* (Paris, Éditions Stock, 1938).

SCHERER, EDMOND. *Études sur la Littérature contemporaine,* vols. VIII and X (Paris, Calmann-Lévy, 1886-95).

SÉCHÉ, LÉON. *Sainte-Beuve,* 2 vols. (Paris, Mercure de France, 1904); *Le Cénacle de la Muse française, 1823-27* (Paris, Mercure de France, 1909); *Delphine Gay, Madame de Girardin* (Paris, Mercure de France, 1910); *Le Cénacle de Joseph Delorme:* vol. I, *Victor Hugo et les Poètes;* vol. II, *Victor Hugo et les Artistes* (Paris, Mercure de France, 1912).

SECRET, JEAN. *Madame de Solms-Rattazzi et son Groupe littéraire* (Aix-les-Bains, Armans, 1936).

SÉGU, FRÉDÉRIC. *Henri de Latouche, romantique républicain 1785-1851,* and *H. Latouche, journaliste dilettante* (Paris, Société d'édition "Les Belles Lettres," 1931).

SEILLIÈRE, ERNEST. *Le Romantisme* (Paris, Stock, 1925); *Romantisme et démocratie romantique* (Paris, Éditions de la Nouvelle Revue critique, 1930).

SERGENT, JEAN. *Description sommaire de "Hauteville House"* and *Notice historique* (Paris, direction des Beaux Arts, undated); Catalogue de l'Exposition, *Enfance et Jeunesse de Victor Hugo* (Maison de Victor Hugo, 1952); Catalogue de l'Exposition, *Maturité de Victor Hugo* (Maison de Victor Hugo, 1953); "Rythme poétique et Musique" (*Revue musicale,* September-October 1935).

SIMON, GUSTAVE. *Le Roman de Sainte-Beuve* (Paris, Ollendorff, 1906); *La Vie d'une Femme* (Paris, Ollendorff, 1914); *Les Tables tournantes de Jersey,* records of the séances (Paris, Louis Conard, 1923); *L'Enfance de Victor Hugo* (Paris, Hachette, 1904); "A-propos de 'Marion de Lorme' " (*Revue de Paris,* March 15th, 1907);

"Les Origines des 'Misérables'" (*Revue de Paris*, January 15th, 1909); "Dix Années de Collaboration" (*Revue de Paris*, May 1st and 15th, 1919).

SOUCHON, PAUL. *Olympio et Juliette* (Paris, Albin Michel, 1940); *La plus aimante, ou Victor Hugo entre Juliette et Madame Biard* (Paris, Albin Michel, 1941); *La Servitude amoureuse de Juliette Drouet* (Paris, Albin Michel, 1942); *Juliette Drouet* (Paris, Tallandier, 1942); *Les Prophéties de Victor Hugo* (Paris, Tallandier, 1945); *Les Deux Femmes de Victor Hugo* (Paris, Tallandier, 1948); *Mille et une lettres d'amour* [de Juliette Drouet] *à Victor Hugo* (Paris, Gallimard, 1951); *Claire Pradier* (posthumous and unpublished; shown to the author by Madame Lucienne Delforge).

STAPFER, PAUL. *Victor Hugo à Guernesey. Souvenirs personnels* (Société française d'Imprimerie et de Librairie, 1905).

STIEGLER, GASTON. "Une Inconnue de Victor Hugo" [Marie Mercier] (*Le Figaro*, May 3rd, 1893).

TALVART, HECTOR, and PLACE, JOSEPH. *Bibliographie des Auteurs Modernes de langue française*, vol. 9 (Paris, Éditions de la Chronique des Lettres françaises, aux Horizons de France, 1949).

THIBAUDET, ALBERT. *Histoire de la Littérature française, de 1789 à nos jours* (Paris, Éditions Stock, Delamain et Boutelleau, 1936); "Les Romantiques et les Parnassiens" (*Revue de Paris*, June 15th, 1933); "Victor Hugo était-il intelligent?" (*Nouvelle Revue française*, October 1st, 1934); "Situation de Victor Hugo" (*Revue de Paris*, May 15th, 1935).

TOUCHARD, PIERRE-AIMÉ. *Grands Écrivains français, de Rabelais à Hugo* (Paris, Presses Universitaires de France, 1941).

TRAZ, ROBERT DE. "Les Poètes en exil" (*Revue hebdomadaire*, June 19th, 1909).

TRESCH, MATHIAS. "Sur les pas de Victor Hugo à Vianden" (*La Grive*, July 1935).

UZANNE, OCTAVE. *Propos de table du poète en exil* (Paris, l'Art et l'Idée, 1892); "Le Journal d'Adèle Hugo" (*L'Écho de Paris*, January 10th, 1902).

VACQUERIE, AUGUSTE. *Profils et Grimaces* (Paris, Michel Lévy, 1856); *Les Miettes de l'Histoire (Trois Ans à Jersey)* (Paris, Pagnerre, 1863); "Guernesey" (*La Presse*, April 16th, 1856); "Madame de Girardin chez Victor Hugo" (*Le Gaulois*, February 8th, 1897); "Les Derniers Moments de Victor Hugo" (*Chronique médicale*, March 1st, 1902).

VAUDOYER, JEAN-LOUIS. *Alice Ozy ou l'Aspasie moderne* (Paris, Trémois, 1930); "Les Formes de la Nuit: Victor Hugo artiste" (*Le Gaulois*, October 4th, 1926).

VERLAINE, MATHILDE MAUTÉ, MADAME PAUL. *Mémoires de ma Vie*, edited by François Porché (Paris, Flammarion, 1935).

VERLAINE, PAUL. *Œuvres posthumes* (Paris, A. Messein, 1913); *Correspondance*, vol. 3 (Paris, Messein, 1929).

VERNEUIL, LOUIS. *La Vie merveilleuse de Sarah Bernhardt* (New York, Brentano's, 1942).

VEUILLOT, LOUIS. *Mélanges*, 14 vols. (Paris, P. Lethielleux, 1933-40); *Œuvres complètes* (Paris, P. Lethielleux, 1927-32); *Études sur Victor Hugo* (Paris, V. Palmé, 1886).

VIEL-CASTEL, COMTE HORACE DE. *Mémoires sur le règne de Napoléon III*, 6 vols. (Verne, imprimerie Haller, 1883-84).

VIENNET, GUILLAUME. *Épitre aux Muses sur les Romantiques* (Paris, Ladvocat, 1834).

VIGNAUD, JEAN. "Pour ou contre Victor Hugo" (*La Critique littéraire*, December 1934); "Victor Hugo" (*Le Petit Parisien*, November 13th, 1934).

VIGNY, ALFRED DE. *Correspondance 1822-1863*, 2 vols. (Paris, La Renaissance du Livre, 1913); *Correspondance générale*, vol. I, 1816-35 (Paris, Louis Conrad, 1933).

VOGÜÉ, EUGÈNE-MELCHIOR DE. *Spectacles contemporains (Les Funérailles de Victor Hugo)* (Paris, A. Colin, 1891).

WACK, HENRY WELLINGTON. *The Romance of Victor Hugo and Juliette Drouet*, with a Foreword by Jean de La Hire (New York and London, Putnam, 1905; Paris, Librairie Universelle, 1906).

WAILLY, LÉON DE. *Angelica Kauffman*, 2 vols. (Paris, Dupont, 1839).

Notes

CHAPTER 1

[1] Victor Hugo, "Un Soir que je regardais le ciel" (*Les Contemplations*, Book II, XXVIII, p. 116).

[2] Maurice Barrès, *Nos Maîtres.*

[3] Louis Guimbaud, *La Mère de Victor Hugo*, p. 6.

[4] Ibid., p. 68.

[5] *Victor Hugo raconté par un témoin de sa vie*, p. 13.

[6] Louis Barthou, *Le Général Hugo*, p. 19.

[7] Ibid., pp. 20-1.

[8] Ibid., p. 24.

[9] Ibid., p. 27.

[10] Louis-Joseph Hugo, born at Nancy on February 14th, 1777, died at Chameyrat (Corrèze) on December 18th, 1853.

[11] François-Juste Hugo born at Nancy on August 3rd, 1780, died at Valence in 1831.

[12] Albert Duruy, "Le Brigadier Muscat," an article published in the *Revue des Deux Mondes*, November 15th, 1885, p. 402.

[13] Ibid., p. 403.

[14] Louis Barthou, *Le Général Hugo*, pp. 29-30.

[15] Ibid., p. 31.

[16] Ibid., p. 32.

[17] Ibid., p. 35.

[18] Quoted by Louis Guimbaud in *La Mère de Victor Hugo*, pp. 133-4.

[19] *Victor Hugo raconté*, etc., vol. I, p. 31.

[20] Louis Barthou, *Le Général Hugo*, p. 43.

[21] Ibid., p. 47.

[22] Ibid., p. 53.

CHAPTER 2

[1] *Victor Hugo raconté*, etc., vol. I, pp. 31-2.

[2] Louis Guimbaud, *La Mère de Victor Hugo*, p. 175.

[3] *Victor Hugo raconté*, etc., vol. I, p. 50.

[4] Ibid., vol. I, p. 53.

[5] Sainte-Beuve, "L'Enfance d'Adèle" (*Livre d'Amour*, vol. IV, p. 13).

[6] Louis Barthou, *Le Général Hugo*, pp. 74-5.

[7] *Victor Hugo raconté*, etc., pp. 55-6.

[8] Victor Hugo, *Le Dernier Jour d'un Condamné*, p. 681.

[9] Victor Hugo, "Ce qui se passait aux Feuillantines" (*Les Rayons et les Ombres*, p. 590):

> Three masters had I in those golden years
> That passed, alas! too soon:
> A garden, an old priest, and that high boon,
> My mother.

[10] Victor Hugo, *Toute la Lyre*, vol. II, chap. v. p. 5.

[11] *Victor Hugo raconté*, etc., vol. I, p. 58.

[12] Victor Hugo, "La Forêt Noire" (*En Voyage*, vol. II, p. 469).

[13] Victor Hugo, "Le Droit et le Loi" (*Actes et Paroles*, vol. I, p. 14).

[14] Victor Hugo, "Pyrénées" (*En Voyage*, vol. II, p. 298).

[15] Léopold Mabilleau, *Victor Hugo*, p. 8.
[16] Louis Barthou, *Le Général Hugo*, p. 84.
[17] Louis Guimbaud, *La Mère de Victor Hugo*, p. 210.
[18] Hugo von Hoffmansthal, *Essei sur Victor Hugo*.
[19] Victor Hugo, *Le Dernier Jour d'un Condamné*, p. 681.
[20] Léopold Mabilleau, *Victor Hugo*, p. 8.

CHAPTER 3

[1] *Victor Hugo raconté*, etc., vol. I, p. 274.
[2] Sainte-Beuve, *Portraits contemporains*, vol. I, p. 391.
[3] Louis Barthou, *Le Général Hugo*, p. 88.
[4] Now rue du Cherche-Midi.
[5] Victor Hugo, *Le Dernier Jour d'un Condamné*, p. 682.
[6] Victor Hugo, *Correspondance*, vol. I, p. 291.
[7] Victor Hugo, *Cahiers de Vers français inédits* (1815-18), edited by Gérauld-Venzac (published by Jacques Damase, 1952), p. 29.
[8] Louis Barthou, *Le Général Hugo*, p. 100.
[9] Jean Bertrand Barrère, *La Fantaisie de Victor Hugo*, vol. I, p. 26.
[10] Victor Hugo, "Mon Enfance" (*Odes et Ballades*, p. 255):

> From distant journeyings I took my homeward road
> Bearing a bundled, fitfully gleaming load.
> I dreamed as though I had, upon my way,
> Been wandering where those magic sources glowed
> Whose waters steal men's hearts away.
>
> Then memories sprouted in my seething brains,
> And, as I walked the earth, I murmured strains
> Of poesy: and as, unseen, my mother watched me go,
> She wept and smiled, saying, "To him a fairy speaks
> Whom we cannot see plain."

[11] Marcel Proust, *Jean Santeuil*, vol. I, p. 42.

CHAPTER 4

[1] Maison de Victor Hugo: Catalogue, *Enfance et Jeunesse de Victor Hugo*, No. 158, p. 53.
[2] Victor Hugo, *Correspondance*, vol. I, p. 294.
[3] Ibid., vol. I, pp. 294-5.
[4] Victor Hugo, *Les Misérables*, Part I, Book III, chap. 1, pp. 121-3.
[5] Sainte-Beuve, *Nouveaux Lundis*, vol. XI, p. 2.
[6] Sainte-Beuve, *Vie de Joseph Delorme*, p. 4.
[7] Alfred de Vigny, *Servitude et Grandeur militaires*.
[8] Victor Hugo, *Correspondance*, vol. I, p. 297.
[9] The former Louis Barthou Collection.
[10] Victor Hugo, *Correspondance*, Vol. I, p. 300.
[11] Letter from General Hugo, dated August 6th, 1818.
[12] Now rue Bonaparte.
[13] Victor Hugo, "Mes Adieux à l'Enfance" (*Odes et Ballades*, p. 445):

> O time! what hast thou done with youth's demise?
> Or, rather, what hast thou now done with me?
> I look about to find myself, and see
> Only a madman longing to be wise.

[14] Victor Hugo, "Le Désir de la Gloire" (*Océan*, vol. VI, p. 31):

> O God of power, O Fame
> Grant him that calls upon thy name
> A place in days to be;
> Fame, 'tis to thee that I aspire,
> Ah, let thy name inspire
> Me to write verses that shall live with thee.

CHAPTER 5

¹ Raymond Escholier, *Un Amant de Génie*, p. 78.
² Maison de Victor Hugo: Catalogue, *Enfance et Jeunesse de Victor Hugo*, No. 173, pp. 59-60.
³ Edmond Benoît-Lévy, *La Jeunesse de Victor Hugo*, p. 249.
⁴ Victor Hugo, *Lettres à la Fiancée*, p. 42.
⁵ Victor Hugo, "Le Jeune Banni." "Essais et Poésies diverses" (*Odes et Ballades*, p. 489):

> These lines for which your maiden love
> Promised me kisses which shocked modesty
> Daily holds back . . . .

⁶ Victor Hugo, *Lettres à la Fiancée*, p. 12.
⁷ Bibliothèque nationale, département des manuscrits, N.A.F. 13414.
⁸ Victor Hugo, *Lettres à la Fiancée*, p. 14.
⁹ Ibid., p. 89.
¹⁰ Ibid., p. 22.
¹¹ Ibid., p. 23.
¹² Raymond Escholier, *Un Amant de Génie*, p. 80.
¹³ Victor Hugo, *Lettres à la Fiancée*, pp. 154-5.
¹⁴ Émile Henriot, *Les Romantiques*, p. 82.
¹⁵ Victor Hugo, *Lettres à la Fiancée*, p. 24.
¹⁶ Bibliothèque nationale, département des manuscrits, N.A.F. 13414.
¹⁷ Victor Hugo, *Lettres à la Fiancée*, p. 22.
¹⁸ Ibid., p. 23.
¹⁹ Ibid., p. 42.

CHAPTER 6

¹ Maison de Victor Hugo: Catalogue, *Enfance et Jeunesse de Victor Hugo*, No. 173, p. 60.
² Victor Hugo, "Fragments de critique—Journal d'un jeune Jacobite de 1819" (*Littérature et Philosophie mêlées*, pp. 26 and 38).
³ Ibid., p. 38.
⁴ Victor Hugo, "Reliquat," (*Littérature et Philosophie mêlées*, p. 45).
⁵ Ibid., p. 252.
⁶ Alfred de Vigny, *Journal d'un Poète*.
⁷ *Victor Hugo raconté*, etc., vol. II, p. 5.
⁸ Ibid., vol. II, p. 7.
⁹ Ibid., vol. II, p. 12.
¹⁰ Victor Hugo, "Le Jeune Banni" (*Odes et Ballades*, p. 487):

> Now greatly venturing I write. What aid
> Till now had this afforded?
> The whispered vows accorded
> By love to our young lips scarce made
> A fledgling's flight, but on a word subsided.

¹¹ Victor Hugo, *Lettres à la Fiancée*, p. 141.
¹² Sainte-Beuve.

CHAPTER 7

¹ Victor Hugo, *Lettres à la Fiancée*, p. 185.
² Ibid., p. 35, n. 1.
³ Ibid., p. 35.
⁴ Ibid., p. 36, n. 2.
⁵ Ibid., p. 36.
⁶ Raymond Escholier, *Un Amant de Génie*, pp. 90-1.
⁷ Ibid., pp. 90-1.
⁸ Victor Hugo, *Lettres à la Fiancée*, pp. 42-3.
⁹ Bibliothèque nationale, département des manuscrits, N.A.F. 13414.
¹⁰ The version given in *Victor Hugo raconté*, etc., is disproved by a contemporary letter written by Hugo himself.

[11] Maison de Victor Hugo: Catalogue, *Enfance et Jeunesse de Victor Hugo*, No. 257, p. 94.

[12] Ibid., No. 261, p. 95.

[13] Victor Hugo, *Correspondance*, vol. I, p. 327.

[14] Ibid.

[15] Jean-Bertrand Barrère, *La Fantaisie de Victor Hugo*, vol. I, p. 43.

[16] Bibliothèque nationale, départemente des manuscrits, N.A.F. 13414.

[17] Victor Hugo, *Correspondance*, vol. I, pp. 325-6.

[18] *Souvenirs de Pierre Foucher*, edited by Louis Guimbaud, p. 201.

[19] Victor Hugo, *Correspondance*, vol. I, p. 330.

[20] Unpublished letter in the Alfred Dupont Collection.

[21] *Victor Hugo raconté*, etc., vol. II, pp. 51-2.

[22] Victor Hugo, *Les Misérables*, Part III, Book V, chap. 1, pp. 391-2, and Book VI, chap. 1, p. 411.

[23] Victor Hugo, *Lettres à la Fiancée*, pp. 123-4.

[24] Ibid., p. 51, n. 1 and p. 55, n. 1.

[25] Ibid., p. 54.

[26] Ibid., p. 58, n. 1.

[27] Ibid., p. 79, n. 1.

[28] Ibid., pp. 84-5.

[29] Ibid., p. 64, n. 1.

[30] Ibid., p. 54.

[31] Ibid., p. 64.

[32] Ibid., p. 90, n. 1.

[33] Ibid., p. 90.

[34] Ibid., p. 153.

[35] Louis Barthou, *Le Général Hugo*, pp. 115-16.

[36] Victor Hugo, *Correspondance*, vol. I, p. 344.

[37] Victor Hugo, *Lettres à la Fiancée*, pp. 72-3.

CHAPTER 8

[1] Victor Hugo, *Lettres à la Fiancée*, p. 103, n. 1.

[2] Ibid., p. 103.

[3] Ibid., p. 107.

[4] Ibid., p. 106, n. 2.

[5] Bibliothèque nationale, département des manuscrits, N.A.F. 13414.

[6] Victor Hugo, *Lettres à la Fiancée*, pp. 99-101.

[7] Ibid., pp. 99 and 117-18.

[8] Ibid., p. 148.

[9] Ibid., p. 150.

[10] Ibid., p. 160, n. 1.

[11] Ibid., p. 163.

[12] Ibid., p. 202, n. 1.

[13] Ibid., p. 216, n. 1.

[14] Ibid., p. 232.

[15] *Victor Hugo raconté*, etc., vol. II, p. 63.

[16] Abbé P. Dubois, *Victor Hugo et ses Idées religieuses*, p. 318.

[17] Jean Hugo Collection.

[18] Henri Guillemin, *Victor Hugo par lui-même*, p. 50.

[19] Victor Hugo, *Les Misérables*, Part V, Book VI, "La Nuit blanche," chap. II, p. 215.

CHAPTER 9

[1] Victor Hugo, *Les Misérables*, Part V, Book VII, "La Dernière Gorgée du Calice—I. Le Septième et le Huitième Ciel," p. 233.

[2] *Victor Hugo raconté*, etc., vol. II, p. 87.

[3] Maison de Victor Hugo: Catalogue, *Enfance et Jeunesse de Victor Hugo*, No. 299, p. 110.

[4] See Baudouin, *Psychanalyse de Victor Hugo*.

[5] Victor Hugo, "Promontorium Somnii," in "Reliquat," *William Shakespeare*, pp. 304 and 310-11.

[6] Quoted by Louis Guimbaud in *Les Orientales de Victor Hugo*, p. 10.

[7] Jules Renard, *Journal,* vol. IV, p. 882.

[8] Jean-Bertrand Barrère, *La Fantaisie de Victor Hugo,* vol. I, pp. 56-7.

[9] Victor Hugo, Preface to *Han d'Islande,* p. 6.

[10] Gustave Simon, "Lamartine et Victor Hugo," an article published in *La Revue de Paris,* April 15th, 1904, p. 671.

[11] Louis Barthou, "Lettres inédites d'Alfred de Vigny à Victor Hugo" (*Revue des Deux Mondes,* February 1st, 1925, p. 516).

[12] Ibid., p. 520.

[13] Ibid., p. 516.

CHAPTER 10

[1] *Les Méditations poétiques,* the book which first established Lamartine's reputation [Translator].

[2] Sainte-Beuve, *Portraits contemporains,* vol. II, p. 179.

[3] Ibid., vol. I, p. 409.

[4] Letter quoted by Léon Séché in *Le Cénacle de La Muse française,* p. 60.

[5] Quoted from Guttinguer's *Mémoires* by Léon Séché in *Le Cénacle de La Muse française,* pp. 244-5.

[6] Arsène Ancelot: "Epître," published in *La Muse française,* September 1823.

> France, now all entranced, waits for your poetry
> And proudly leaves it to posterity.

[7] Quoted by Edmond Biré in *Victor Hugo avant 1830,* p. 341:

> On Bouvines glory shines as on Marengo:
> Win immortality with just one ode superb.
> Then it will matter not whether you're called Malherbe,
> Jean-Baptiste or Victor-Hugo.

[8] *La Muse française,* vol. II, issue dated May 12th, 1824, p. 286.

[9] Quoted by Edmond Biré in *Victor Hugo avant 1830,* p. 341:

> 'Twixt the two schools what difference should there be?
> They are two loving sisters, whose ages matter not.
> One is called hope, the other memory,
> And side by side in harness they should trot.

[10] Madame de Staël, *De l'Allemagne.*

[11] "Discours prononcé par Louis-Simon Auger, 24 avril, 1824, à la séance publique des Académies." Quoted by Léon Séché, in *Le Cénacle de La Muse française,* p. 79.

[12] Ibid., p. 82.

[13] Émile Deschamps, "La Guerre en temps de paix" (*La Muse française,* vol. II, p. 294).

[14] Paul Valéry.

[15] Émile Deschamps, "La Guerre en temps de paix" (*La Muse française,* vol. II, p. 301. The article in question is signed "Le Jeune Moraliste").

[16] Le Jeune Moraliste (Émile Deschamps), "La Guerre en temps de paix" (*La Muse française,* vol. II, p. 302).

CHAPTER 11

[1] Victor Hugo, *Correspondance,* vol. I, p. 397.

[2] Ibid., vol. I, p. 396.

[3] Jean-Bertrand Barrère, *Hugo, l'homme et l'œuvre,* p. 20.

[4] Louis Barthou, "Lettres d'Alfred de Vigny à Victor Hugo" (*Revue des Deux Mondes,* February 1st, 1925, pp. 523-5).

[5] Ibid., p. 527.

[6] Maison de Victor Hugo: Catalogue, *Enfance et Jeunesse de Victor Hugo,* No. 380, p. 144 (only a small part of this letter has been published).

[7] Letter printed by Cécile Daubray in *Victor Hugo et ses correspondants,* pp. 114-16.

[8] *Victor Hugo raconté,* etc., vol. I, p. 104.

[9] Victor Hugo, *Correspondance,* vol. I, p. 386.

[10] Ibid., vol. I, p. 388.

[11] Ibid., vol. I, p. 400. This letter is addressed to Alfred de Vigny.

[12] Ibid., vol. I, p. 402.

[13] Ibid., vol. I, p. 403.

[14] Ibid., vol. I, p. 406.

[15] Ibid., vol. I, p. 408.

[16] Ibid., vol. I, p. 413.

[17] Victor Hugo, "France et Belgique" (*En Voyage*, vol. II, p. 44).

[18] Victor Hugo, "À Rheims," in "Reliquat," *William Shakespeare*, p. 251.

[19] Ibid., p. 252.

[20] Ibid., p. 253.

[21] *Victor Hugo raconté*, etc., vol. II, p. 99.

[22] Victor Hugo, *Correspondance*, vol. I, p. 419, n. 2.

[23] Ibid., vol. I, p. 420.

[24] Ibid., vol. I, p. 429.

[25] Mary Ann Eliza Birch (1790-1863) had married Lamartine in 1820. In announcing the marriage to his friends, the author of *Les Méditations* had referred to his thirty-year-old fiancée in the following terms: "a good, sensible bargain . . . and a model of all the virtues— though I could have done with a bit more in the way of beauty. . . ."

[26] *Victor Hugo raconté*, etc., vol. II, p. 114.

[27] Ibid., vol. II, p. 138.

[28] Ibid., vol. II, p. 130.

CHAPTER 12

[1] See Gustave Simon, "Lamartine et Victor Hugo," an article published in the *Revue de Paris*, April 15th, 1904, p. 683.

[2] Louis Guimbaud, *"Les Orientales" de Victor Hugo*, p. 10.

[3] Sainte-Beuve, *Premiers Lundis*, vol. I, p. 179.

[4] Ibid.

[5] Victor Hugo, "Encore à toi" (*Odes et Ballades*, p. 262):

> I love you as some being out of reach,
> As some ancestress with far-seeing eyes,
> Some timid sister who can fondly teach
> A lesson of sweet service to my pain,
> A dear child of old age. My love's so deep
> That at mere mention of your name I weep.

[6] *Conversations de Gœthe pendant les dernières années de sa vie (1822-1832) receuillies par Eckermann*, vol. I, p. 262.

[7] Sainte-Beuve, "Recit à Adèle" (*Livre de l'Amour*, first, anonymous edition, printed in 1843 without publisher's name, vol. VIII, p. 23):

> In morning smock she artless art displays,
> And sets me blushing with her ardent gaze.
> From her to him my questing eyeballs rove,
> And in a glare of light with troubled shyness move,
> Intent upon the poet's spread of talk,
> Which, scarce begun, sweeps on and heeds no balk.
>
> Upright, his youthful spouse stands there, all ears;
> And all that deep accord a wonder bears,
> Uniting thunderous waves and near-by palm.
> Then soon she tires of the mere listening part,
> And lets her wandering thoughts from him depart;
> Her hands seem eager now for simple household things,
> But some wild chariot bears her up on wings,
> And when, as I take leave, I greet her thrice,
> She nothing hears till he does back entice
> Her truant mood. . . .

[8] Victor Hugo, *Correspondance*, vol. I, p. 441.

[9] Charles Bruneau, *Histoire de la Langue française*, vol. XII, pp. 199-204.

[10] Virginie Ancelot, *Les Salons de Paris*, pp. 125-6.

[11] Victor Hugo, *Correspondance*, vol. I, p. 440.

[12] Sainte-Beuve, *Correspondance générale*, vol. I, pp. 78-81.

[13] Stendhal, "Qu'est-ce que le romanticisme?" (*Racine et Shakespeare*, vol. II, p. 32).

[14] Victor Hugo, "A la Colonne de la Place Vendôme" (*Odes et Ballades*, pp. 170-1):

> Take heed! France, on whose fields was bred another age,
> Is not so dead as to endure outrage!
> Her parties for a while their hates undo.
> Faced by an insult now, all join, all stand upright,
> All rush to arms, and La Vendée her bright
> Sword sharpens on the stone of Waterloo!
>
> .   .   .   .
>
> Should I be silent, who in days of yore
> Grew drunk to hear my Saxon name sound in the din of war,
> I, who followed the streaming flag of Fate,
> Who to the trumpet's note added my childish voice,
> For whom a sword's gold knot was then my toy of choice,
> Who in my nurse's arms could feel a soldier's hate?

[15] Extract from an anonymous article published in *La Pandore* of February 10th, 1827.

CHAPTER 13

[1] Louis Guimbaud, *"Les Orientales" de Victor Hugo*, p. 11.

[2] Victor Hugo, *Correspondance*, p. 436 and pp. 437-45.

[3] *Souvenirs*, by Victor Pavie, *passim*.

[4] Quoted by André Billy in *Sainte-Beuve*, vol. I, p. 90.

[5] Alfred de Musset, "Mardoche," I:

> . . . always to that hour keeping
> When through the mist the cats go wandering and weeping,
> Comes Monsieur Hugo to see fair Phoebus die.

[6] Victor Hugo, "Soleils couchants" (*Les Feuilles d'Automne*, pp. 100-1):

> I love the fall of evenings still and fair,
> Touching with gold the storied manor there
>   Among the trees;
> Or turning mists to drawn-out banks of fire,
> Or in the blue of heaven breaking entire
>   On archipelagoes of cloud.

[7] Victor Hugo, "Extase" (*Les Orientales*, p. 744):

> I stood upon a beach one starry night,
> With not a cloud and not a sail in sight.
> My gaze was plunged beyond reality.
> Woods, mountains and all nature joined the fête,
> And, mingling murmurs, seemed to interrogate
>   The waves of Ocean and the fires on high.
>
> And golden stars in endless galaxies,
> Sang loud or soft in countless harmonies,
> As low they bowed their fiery crowns, o'erawed;
> And blue ungoverned waves that naught arrests,
> Sang too, as low they bowed their foaming crests;
>   "It is the Lord! it is the Lord our God!"
>   Translation by Alan Conder (*A Treasury of French Poetry*)

[8] Louis Guimbaud, *"Les Orientales" de Victor Hugo*, pp. 23-4.

[9] Published in *La Quotidienne*, November 2nd, 1829.

[10] Victor Hugo, *Correspondance*, vol. I, p. 459.

[11] Unpublished letter in the Simone André-Maurois Collection.

[12] Unpublished letters in the Simone André-Maurois Collection.

[13] Quoted by Georges Ascoli in his Sorbonne lectures on "Le Théâtre romantique."

[14] Letter printed by Louis Barthou in *La Revue des Deux Mondes*, February 1st, 1925, p. 530.

[15] Quoted by Georges Ascoli in his Sorbonne lectures on "Le Théâtre romantique."

[16] Alfred de Vigny, *Correspondance*, First Series (1816-35), p. 169 (édition Conard). Letter dated February 9th, 1829.

[17] Alfred de Vigny, *Journal d'un Poète*, pp. 892-3 of the Pléiade edition.

[18] Jules Janin, *Cours de la Littérature dramatique*, p. 357 et seq.

[19] See Raymond Escholier, *Un Amant de Génie*, p. 99.

[20] Victor Hugo, *Correspondance*, vol. I, p. 446.

[21] Baptized Victor at Saint-Sulpice on November 5th, 1828, this younger son decided, in 1849, to take the names François-Victor for two reasons: (1) because he was at that time writing in *L'Évènement* and had to find some way of distinguishing himself from Victor Hugo senior, and (2) because his letters were continually being opened by his father.

[22] Charles Baudelaire, *L'Art romantique*, XIX, "Reflexions sur quelques-uns de mes contemporains, p. 519 of the Pléiade edition.

[23] Victor Hugo, Preface to *Les Orientales*, pp. 615-22.

[24] Armand Hoog.

CHAPTER 14

[1] Alfred de Vigny, *Journal d'un Poète*, p. 892 of the Pléiade edition.

[2] Henri Bremond, *Le Roman et l'Histoire d'une Conversion*, p. 95.

[3] Sainte-Beuve, *Correspondance générale*, vol. I, p. 146.

[4] *Vie, Pensées et Poésies de Joseph Delorme*, original edition, p. 27.

[5] Victor Hugo, *Correspondance*, vol. I, p. 449.

[6] Spœlberch de Lovenjoul Collection.

CHAPTER 15

[1] Alfred de Vigny, "Lettre à Lord . . . sur la soirée du 24 octobre, 1829, et sur un système dramatique," p. 336 of the Pléiade edition (vol. I).

[2] Letter published in *La Revue hebdomadaire*, March 14th, 1903.

[3] Victor Hugo, *Correspondance*, vol. I, p. 446.

[4] Frédéric Saulnier, *Édouard Turquety*, p. 73.

[5] Alfred de Vigny, *Correspondance*, First Series, p. 182 of the Conard edition.

[6] Victor Hugo, *Correspondance*, vol. I, pp. 456-7.

[7] Jean-Bertrand Barrère, *Hugo, l'homme et l'œuvre*, p. 59.

[8] See Léon Séché, *Le Cénacle de Joseph Delorme*, vol. I, p. 276.

[9] Victor Hugo, *Correspondance*, vol. I, p. 458.

[10] See Pierre Jourda, "Les Souvenirs de Vienne," an article published in the *Revue des Deux Mondes*, July 1st, 1929, pp. 130-1.

CHAPTER 16

[1] Theodore Pavie, *Victor Pavie, sa jeunesse, ses relations littéraires*, p. 198.

[2] Sainte-Beuve, *Volupté*, vol. I, pp. 59-60.

[3] Quoted by André Billy in *Sainte-Beuve*, vol. I, p. 79.

[4] Sainte-Beuve, *Volupté*, vol. I, p. 190.

[5] Sainte-Beuve, *Correspondance générale*, vol. I, p. 146.

[6] Ibid., vol. I, p. 149.

[7] Sainte-Beuve, *Volupté*, vol. I, p. 108.

[8] Sainte-Beuve, "Notes et Remarques," printed by Ch. Pierrot in his *Table générale et analytique des "Causeries du Lundi,"* p. 41 in the Garnier edition.

[9] Victor Hugo, *Correspondance*, vol. I, p. 462.

[10] Gustave Simon, *Le Roman de Sainte-Beuve*, p. 44.

[11] Letter from Ulric Guttinguer to Sainte-Beuve, quoted by Henri Bremond in *Le Roman et l'Histoire d'une Conversion*, pp. 103-4.

[12] Sainte-Beuve, *Correspondance générale*, vol. I, pp 179-80.

[13] The *témoin* of *Victor Hugo raconté*, etc. (whose book was written thirty years after the battle of *Hernani*), says six thousand, but the contract, five.

[14] *Victor Hugo raconté*, etc., vol. II, p. 316.

[15] Quoted by Ernest Dupuy in *La Jeunesse des Romantiques*, p. 86.

[16] Sainte-Beuve, *Nouveaux Lundis*, vol. V, p. 456.

[17] Bibliothèque de l'Arsenal, Rondel Collection. This passage was reproduced in fac-

simile in the special number of *Arts et Métiers graphiques* devoted to Victor Hugo, June 1st, 1935.

[18] See Viennet, "Les Romantiques jugés par un Classique" (*Revue des Deux Mondes*, July 1st, 1929, pp. 134 and 141).

[19] Sainte-Beuve, *Correspondance générale*, vol. I, pp. 181-2.

[20] Victor Hugo, *Correspondance*, vol. I, p. 472.

[21] Sainte-Beuve, *Correspondance générale*, vol. I, p. 194.

[22] Ibid., vol. I, pp. 197-8.

[23] Sainte-Beuve, *Mes Poisons*, pp. 37-9.

[24] Unpublished.

CHAPTER 17

[1] Juste Olivier, *Paris en 1830*, pp. 188-97.

[2] Ibid., p. 211.

[3] Victor Hugo, "Où donc est le bonheur" (*Les Feuilles d'Automne*, vol. XVIII, pp. 61-2).

[4] Victor Hugo, "Journal des idées et des Opinions d'un Révolutionnaire de 1830" (*Littérature et Philosophie mêlées*, vol. I, p. 87).

[5] Victor Hugo, "Dicté après fuillet 1830" (*Les Chants du Crépuscule*, p. 190).

[6] "Historique," *Les Chants du Crépuscule*, p. 325.

[7] Sainte-Beuve, *Nouveaux Lundis*, vol. XIII, p. 10.

[8] Victor Hugo, "Journal des Idées et des Opinions d'un Révolutionnaire de 1830" (*Littérature et Philosophie mêlées*, vol. I, p. 87).

[9] *Victor Hugo raconté*, etc., vol. II, p. 345.

[10] Sainte-Beuve, *Correspondance générale*, vol. I, p. 203.

[11] Sainte-Beuve, *Premiers Lundis*, vol. I, p. 378.

[12] Ibid., vol. I, pp. 409 and 412.

[13] Spœlberch de Lovenjoul Collection, D. 588, fol. 26.

[14] Sainte-Beuve, *Volupté*, vol. I, p. 321.

[15] Sainte-Beuve, *Correspondance générale*, vol. I, pp. 209-10.

[16] Spœlberch de Lovenjoul Collection, D. 588, fol. 28.

[17] See André Billy, *Sainte-Beuve*, vol. I, p. 126.

[18] Spœlberch de Lovenjoul Collection, D. 588, fol. 34. This note is not printed in Victor Hugo's *Correspondance*, nor is it included in the *addenda* to vol. IV, published in 1952.

[19] Sainte-Beuve, *Portraits contemporains*, vol. I, p. 173 of the Garnier edition.

CHAPTER 18

[1] "Historique," *Notre-Dame de Paris*, p. 448.

[2] Victor Hugo, *Notre-Dame de Paris*.

[3] Émile Faguet, *Dix-neuvième siècle*, p. 201.

[4] Victor Hugo, *Notre-Dame de Paris*.

[5] "Historique," *Notre-Dame de Paris*, p. 449.

[6] Sainte-Beuve, *Correspondance générale*, vol. I, p. 222.

[7] Ibid., vol. I, pp. 222-3.

[8] Spœlberch de Lovenjoul Collection, D. 588, fol. 40.

[9] Gustave Simon, *Le Roman de Saint-Beuve*, p. 126.

[10] Letter published by J.-J. Weiss in *Le Livre du Centenaire du Journal des Débats* (1789-1889), p. 49. It is not included in Victor Hugo's *Correspondance*.

[11] Spœlberch de Lovenjoul Collection, D. 588, fols. 46-7. This letter is quoted in part by André Billy in his *Sainte-Beuve*, vol. I, pp. 140-1.

[12] Sainte-Beuve, *Correspondance générale*, vol. I, p. 244.

[13] Spœlberch de Lovenjoul Collection, D. 588, fols. 48-9.

[14] Sainte-Beuve, *Correspondance générale*, vol. I, pp. 246-7.

CHAPTER 19

[1] Sainte-Beuve, *Correspondance générale*, vol. I, p. 254.

[2] Sainte-Beuve, *Livre d'Amour*, vol. XI, p. 40.

[3] Sainte-Beuve, *Correspondance générale*, vol. I, p. 276.

[4] Victor Hugo, "Amour" (*Tas de Pierres*, p. 415).

[5] Victor Hugo, *Les Feuilles d'Automne*, Preface, pp. 7, 9-10.

⁶ Victor Hugo, "Soleils couchants" (*Les Feuilles d'Automne,* vol. VI, p. 105):

> Tonight clouds swallowed up the sinking sun.
> Tomorrow storm will come, the evening and the night;
> Then dawn, its brightness all by mists undone;
> Then nights, then days, time striding out of sight.

⁷ Victor Hugo, "Ce qu'on entend sur la montagne" (*Les Feuilles d'Automne,* vol. V, p. 26).

> I wonder wherefore are we here,
> And what the end to which we steer,
> What part the human spirit plays
> And why the Lord, who only can appraise
> His work, has linked in fatal marriage bond
> The song of nature, and the groans of all who know despond.

⁸ Sainte-Beuve, *Portraits contemporains,* vol. I, pp. 272-3 of the original edition.

CHAPTER 20

¹ Paul Bourget, *Études et Portraits,* vol. I, p. 113.
² Victor Hugo, *Marion de Lorme,* Preface, p. 9.
³ Antoine Fontaney, *Journal intime,* September 6th, 1832, p. 150.
⁴ Victor Hugo, "Moi" (*Tas de Pierres,* p. 245).
⁵ Sainte-Beuve, *Correspondance générale,* vol. I, pp. 281-2.
⁶ Jules Janin, *Contes fantastiques,* vol. II, p. 10.
⁷ Victor Hugo, *Correspondance,* vol. I, p. 511.
⁸ Sainte-Beuve, *Portraits de Femmes,* p. 35.
⁹ This is now the Place des Vosges. The Victor Hugo Museum is at No. 6.
¹⁰ Arsène Houssaye, *Confessions,* vol. I, p. 254.
¹¹ Antoine Fontaney, *Journal intime,* p. 10.
¹² Sainte-Beuve, *Correspondance générale,* vol. I, p. 314.
¹³ Spœlberch de Lovenjoul Collection. Unpublished.
¹⁴ See Adophe Jullien, "Le Romantisme et l'éditeur Renduel," an article published in the *Revue des Deux Mondes,* December 1st, 1895, p. 666.
¹⁵ Antoine Fontaney, *Journal intime,* p. 161.
¹⁶ Victor Hugo, Notes to *Marion de Lorme,* p. 507.

CHAPTER 21

¹ See Louis Guimbaud, "Juliette Drouet avant Victor Hugo," an article published in the special number of *Europe* (February-March, 1952), p. 57.
² Paul Souchon, "Claire Pradier" (unpublished manuscript).
³ Unpublished. Georges Blaizot Collection.
⁴ See Raymond Escholier, *Un Amant de Génie,* p. 118.
⁵ Théophile Gautier, *Portraits contemporain,* p. 379.
⁶ See Raymond Escholier, *Un Amant de Génie,* p. 123.
⁷ Juliette Drouet, *Mille et une lettres, d'amour à Victor Hugo,* p. 13.
⁸ Victor Hugo, *Le Livre de l'Anniversaire,* quoted by Louis Barthou in *Les Amours d'un Poète,* p. 139.
⁹ Théophile Gautier, "Mademoiselle Juliette," an article published in a symposium to which Balzac, Nerval, Gautier, Hugo, Sandeau, Roger de Beauvois, and others contributed, *Les Belles Femmes de Paris* (Paris, 10 rue Christine, 1840).
¹⁰ Spœlberch de Lovenjoul Collection. Unpublished.
¹¹ Victor Hugo, *Correspondance,* vol. I, p. 529.
¹² Unpublished letter. Alfred Dupont Collection.
¹³ Letter quoted by René Ternois in "Tristesse de Sainte-Beuve," an article published in *L'Éducation nationale.*
¹⁴ See Paul Souchon, *Les Deux Femmes de Victor Hugo,* p. 34.
¹⁵ See Raymond Escholier, *Un Amant de Génie,* pp. 137-8.
¹⁶ Louis Barthou, *Les Amours d'un Poète,* pp. 153-4.
¹⁷ Louis Guimbaud, *Victor Hugo et Juliette Drouet,* p. 266.
¹⁸ Louis Barthou, *Les Amours d'un Poète,* pp. 156-60.
¹⁹ Marguerite-Joséphine Ferrand, known as Ida Ferrier, married Dumas the elder on

February 5th, 1840. She left the stage and later ran away from her husband and lived in Italy with the Duke of Villafranca. She died at Genoa on March 11th, 1859.

[20] Raymond Escholier, *Un Amant de Génie*, pp. 148-9.

CHAPTER 22

[1] Alfred de Vigny, author of *Eloa*.
[2] Antony and Émile Deschamps.
[3] Spœlberch de Lovenjoul Collection, D. 2044, quoted by Maurice Allem in *Sainte-Beuve et Volupté*, pp. 94-5. Sainte-Beuve had scribbled this very private note on the back of a letter which Lamennais had written, asking him to come for a stay at La Chênaie.
[4] Victor Hugo, "Sur Mirabeau" (*Littérature et Philosophie mêlées*, p. 198).
[5] Ibid.
[6] Ibid., pp. 217-18.
[7] Spœlberch de Lovenjoul Collection, D. 588, fols. 97 and 98.
[8] Sainte-Beuve, *Correspondance générale*, vol. I, p. 425.
[9] Spœlberch de Lovenjoul Collection, D. 588, fol. 126.
[10] Spœlberch de Lovenjoul Collection, D. 588, fol. 101.
[11] Juliette Drouet, *Mille et une lettres*, etc., p. 34.
[12] Ibid., p. 39.
[13] Ibid., p. 41.
[14] Louis Guimbaud, *Victor Hugo et Juliette Drouet*, pp. 72-3.
[15] Jacques-Firmin Lanvin, born on the 11th germinal, Year XI (April 1st, 1803), had married, on June 21st, 1824, Antoinette-Eliza Véron, born on 2nd vendémiaire, Year XIII, an intimate companion of Juliette Drouet.
[16] Juliette Drouet, *Mille et une lettres*, etc., p. 40.
[17] Ibid., pp. 43-44.
[18] Raymond Escholier, *Un Amant de Génie*, p. 153.
[19] Juliette Drouet, *Mille et une lettres*, etc., p. 51.
[20] Louis Barthou, *Les Amours d'un Poète*, pp. 191-2.
[21] Ibid., p. 193.
[22] Raymond Escholier, *Un Amant de Génie*, p. 163.
[23] Louis Guimbaud, *Victor Hugo et Juliette Drouet*, p. 279.
[24] Raymond Escholier, *Un Amant de Génie*, p. 168.
[25] Victor Hugo, "Bretagne et Normandie" (*En Voyage*, vol. II, p. 18).
[26] Louis Barthou, *Les Amours d'un Poète*, p. 201.
[27] Ibid., p. 202.
[28] Louis Guimbaud, *Victor Hugo et Juliette Drouet*, p. 64.
[29] Victor Hugo, "Dans l'église de . . . (*Les Chants du Crépuscule*, p. 286):

> It was a humble church with ceiling low,
>   Where for three hundred years
> Many human hearts did go,
>   And dropped there many tears.
>
> Sad and calm in the fading light
>   Was that church apart,
> Unserved the altar, with no flames dight,
>   Like a loveless heart.

CHAPTER 23

[1] Simone André-Maurois Collection.
[2] Louis Barthou, *Les Amours d'un Poète*, p. 224.
[3] Louis Guimbaud, *Victor Hugo et Juliette Drouet*, p. 98.
[4] Juliette Drouet, *Mille et une lettres*, etc., p. 71.
[5] Ibid., p. 75.
[6] Victor Hugo, *Les Chants du Crépuscule*, XXV, p. 262:

> Since to thy brimming cup my lips I oft have set,
> Since often in thy hands I've laid my pallid brow,
> Since I have breathed thy soul's sweet breath which even now,
> Though that was long ago, perfumes the darkness yet,

> Since it was given me to hear the mysteries
> That dwelt within thy heart, where mortal secrets sleep,
> Since I have seen thee smile, since I have seen thee weep,
> Thy lips upon my lips, thine eyes upon my eyes. . . .
>
> I can defy the years in their impetuous flight:
> Flee on! I cannot age, though swift be your career!
> Flee on with all your flowers, that wither and grow sere;
> My soul enshrines a flower that none can pluck or blight.
>
> Your wing may smite my vase, yet not a drop be spilled.
> I slake my thirst there—yet, replenished, it brims o'er;
> Your ashes cannot quench my spirit's flame, nor your
> Oblivion quench the love with which my heart is filled!

> Translated by Alan Conder (*A Treasury of French Poetry*)

[7] Nearly nine million in 1954.
[8] Paul Souchon, *Les Deux Femmes de Victor Hugo*, pp. 64-5.
[9] Gustave Simon, *La Vie d'une Femme*, pp. 214-15.
[10] Paul Souchon, *Les Deux Femmes de Victor Hugo*, p. 64.
[11] Ibid., p. 65.
[12] Maison de Victor Hugo: Catalogue, *Maturité de Victor Hugo*, No. 324, p. 117.
[13] Jacques Castelnau, *Adèle Hugo*, p. 141.
[14] Maison de Victor Hugo: Catalogue, *Maturité de Victor Hugo*, No. 239, p. 118.
[15] Juliette Drouet, *Mille et une lettres*, etc., p. 615.
[16] Paul Souchon, *Olympio et Juliette*, p. 99.
[17] Ibid., pp. 105-6.
[18] Ibid., p. 179.
[19] On this theme, see Émile Henriot's *Les Romantiques*.
[20] Maurice Levaillant, *La Tristesse d'Olympio*, p. 50.
[21] Victor Hugo, "A Olympio" (*Les Voix intérieures*, XXX, p. 467):

> Young man, men quailed once at your eye severe,
>   Your calm and thunderous brow:
> Your name was such as men dread, revere,
>   Alas! but now
>
> The wicked swarm around to bite and tear
>   With murderous teeth,
> And those same men, with envious despair,
>   Seek to descry what secret lies beneath.

[22] Namely: XIV, XXI, XXII, XXIII, XXIV, XXVI, XXVII, XXVIII, XXIX, XXX, XXXI and XXXIII.
[23] Sainte-Beuve, *Portraits contemporains*, vol. I, p. 461.
[24] *Les Chants du Crépuscule*, XXXVI, p. 298:

> Be thou for ever blest
> Eve whom no fruit can tempt,
> And from all thoughts exempt
> Save those of virtue on the mountain crest.

[25] Adèle, at this time, was thirty-two!
[26] Jacques Castelnau, *Adèle Hugo*, pp. 141-2.
[27] Sainte-Beuve, *Correspondance générale*, vol. II, p. 52.
[28] Paul Souchon, *Les Deux Femmes de Victor Hugo*, p. 85.
[29] Louis Guimbaud, *Victor Hugo et Juliette Drouet*, p. 305.
[30] Ibid., p. 312.

CHAPTER 24

[1] Victor Hugo, "Fonction du Poète" (*Les Rayons et les Ombres*, vol. I, p. 539):

> Woe to him who takes his sandals
> When the hatreds and the scandals
> Fill the world with storm in spate!

> Shame to the thinker who crops his wings,
> Takes his way, and useless sings,
> Passing through the city gate. . . .

[2] Victor Hugo, "Le Monde et le Siècle" (*Les Rayons et les Ombres*, vol. VII, p. 567):

> What purpose in Thy work, O Lord? Wherefore the dash
> Of surging river waters, or of the lightning's flash?
> Why hast Thou set in motion this great globe
> With cities, mountains filled, and its encircling robe
> Of moving oceans? Why dost Thou lean it, turn and turn about
> To face the darkness, or when night is out,
> The day's gold face, now in obscurity, now bright with dawn?

[3] Sainte-Beuve, *Mes Poisons*, p. 44.
[4] Louis Barthou, *Les Amours d'un Poète*, p. 260.
[5] Paul Souchon, *Les Deux Femmes de Victor Hugo*, p. 135.
[6] See Alexandre Dumas, *Mémoires*, vol. IV, p. 53.

> [7] I've beat you to it through the portal,
> My only claim a dotard's state.
> You, who already are immortal,
> Can well afford to wait.

[8] Edmond Biré, *Victor Hugo après 1830*, vol. I, p. 199.
[9] Pierre Audiat, *Ainsi vécut Victor Hugo*, p. 179.
[10] *La Presse*, January 7th, 1837.
[11] André Billy, *Sainte-Beuve, sa vie et son temps*, vol. I, p. 253.
[12] Sainte-Beuve, *Mes Poisons*, p. 47.
[13] Spœlberch de Lovenjoul Collection.
[14] Antoine Fontaney, *Journal intime*, pp. 194-5.
[15] Maison de Victor Hugo: Catalogue, *Maturité de Victor Hugo*, No. 342, p. 123.
[16] Ibid., No. 349, p. 125.
[17] Ibid., No. 354, p. 127.
[18] Sainte-Beuve, *Correspondance générale*, vol. II, p. 179.
[19] Auguste Barbier, from whom this quotation is taken, was in error, Fontaney, having eloped with Gabrielle from the convent in which her mother had placed her, lived with her as her husband at No. 20 rue de l'Ouest. But, fearing that such a marriage might injure his career in the Diplomatic Service, he had constantly refused to marry his mistress. He was a consumptive, and survived her for barely two months.
[20] Auguste Barbier, *Souvenirs personnels, 1883*, p. 262
[21] Sainte-Beuve, *Correspondance générale*, vol. II, p. 205.
[22] Sainte-Beuve, "Madame de Pontivy," p. 203 in the Calmann-Lévy edition of the *Clou d'Or*, 1200 copies, printed in 1921.
[23] Sainte-Beuve, *Correspondance générale*, vol. II, p. 365.
[24] Ibid., vol. VI, p. 173.
[25] Paul Souchon, *Les Deux Femmes de Victor Hugo*, p. 100.
[26] Juliette Drouet, *Mille et une lettres*, etc., p. 91.
[27] Ibid.
[28] Ibid., p. 103.
[29] Her sister, Julie Foucher, at that time a girl of fifteen.
[30] Paul Souchon, *Les Deux Femmes de Victor Hugo*, pp. 77-8.
[31] Victor Hugo, "Dieppe" (*En Voyage*, vol. II, p. 136).
[32] Juliette Drouet, *Mille et une lettres*, etc., p. 127.
[33] Victor Hugo, "Tristesse d'Olympio" (*Les Rayons et les Ombres*, XXXIV, p. 631):

> He sought the well-loved scenes, the pool, the spring,
> The hut where alms meant purses' emptying,
>   The old ash bent and grey,
> Love's dim retreat in woods with shadowy boles,
> Wherein, in kisses, both their mingled souls
>   Forgot the world each day.

> The garden, orchard, and lone house he sought,
> The grating whence the eye enchanted caught
>   The sloping avenue . . .
> He paled: his footfalls echoed sombrely,
> And shadows from the past rose where each tree
>   Its own dark shadow threw.

Translated by Alan Conder (*A Treasury of French Poetry*)

[34] Victor Hugo, "Tristesse d'Olympio" (*Les Rayons et les Ombres*, XXXIV, p. 635):

> To change all things how short a time you take,
> Calm nature, weaver of forgetfulness!
> How cruelly your endless changes break
> The mystic threads that bind our hearts, alas!
>
> The things that we owned others will inherit.
> We came there once and others must come yet.
> They will resume the dream of our twin spirit,
> Yet even so they will not finish it.
>
> So be it! Garden, home, retreats, forget!
> Grass, hide our threshold, briar our footsteps, too!
> Sing, birds; flow, streams; grow, leaves, and live on yet!
> But those whom you forget forget not you.
>
> For you seem love's own ghost whom we entreat,
> Oasis on our journey through waste lands,
> O valley where we roamed, supreme retreat,
> Where once we wept and held each other's hands.
>
> All passions gently with the years take wing;
> One takes his mask, and one his knife, until,
> Like a singing troupe of players, journeying,
> The lessening group fades out behind the hill.

Translated by Alan Conder (*A Treasury of French Poetry*)

[35] Antoine Fontaney, *Journal intime*, p. 126.

[36] Victor Hugo, "A Eugène, vicomte H . . ." (*Les Voix intérieures*, XXIX, pp. 460-3):

> High on the hill you'll sleep where grasses grow,
> Where winter comes, and all the winds that blow,
>   Your roof the sky;
> Dust, you will sleep up there in earthy sheets,
> While I live on with those in city streets
>   Who talk on and pass by.
>
> I must stay on, suffer and live and do,
> Hearing my name swell ever louder through
>   Fame's brazen mouth;
> While with a Spartan smile I still must hide
> The fox that ceaselessly gnaws at my side
>   And leave untold the truth.

[37] Maison de Victor Hugo: Catalogue, *Maturité de Victor Hugo*, No. 364, p. 130.

CHAPTER 25

[1] Jean Sergent, *Catalogue de l'Exposition* "Maturité de Victor Hugo," p. 402.

[2] Juliette Drouet, *Mille et une lettres,* etc., p. 149.

[3] Ibid.

[4] Paul Souchon, *Les Deux Femmes de Victor Hugo,* p. 89.

[5] Ibid.

[6] Louis Guimbaud, *Victor Hugo et Juliette Drouet,* p. 357.

[7] Gustave Planche, " 'Ruy Blas,' drame de Monsieur Victor Hugo," an article published in the *Revue des Deux Mondes,* August 15th, 1838, pp. 532-48.

[8] Louis Guimbaud, *Victor Hugo et Juliette Drouet,* pp. 366-7.

9 "Au Roi Louis-Philippe, après l'arrêt prononcé le 12 juillet 1839" (*Les Rayons et les Ombres*, III, p. 555). Louis-Philippe had just lost his daughter, Marie, Princesse Alexandre de Württemberg, who had died at the age of twenty-six. The "royal enfant" is the little Comte de Paris, son of the Duke and Duchess of Orleans:

> In the name of your Angel now flown like a dove,
> Of that young, royal child, sweet and frail as a reed!
> Show thy mercy once more, in the name of the grave!
> In the name of the cradle, give mercy all heed!

10 Letter published in *L'Évènement*, August 29th, 1839.

11 Victor Hugo, *Les Misérables*, Part IV, Book LIV, chap. III, "Louis-Philippe," pp. 17-18.

12 Spœlberch de Lovenjoul Collection, D. 571, fol. iii. Victor Giraud, who printed this phrase in *Mes Poisons*, substituted the word "deflowered" for "raped."

13 Juliette Drouet, *Mille et une lettres*, etc., p. 201.

14 Ibid., p. 202.

15 Ibid., p. 212.

16 Ibid.

17 Charles Magnin, "Un Duel politique," an article published in the *Revue des Deux Mondes*, June 15th, 1841.

18 See, on the subject of Salvandy, a good article by Rosita, published in *Rolet*, July 11th, 18th and 25th, 1953.

19 "Discours prononcés dans la séance publique tenue par l'Académie française le 3 juin, 1841," pp. 36-7.

20 Juliette Drouet, *Mille et une lettres*, etc., p. 213.

21 Unpublished. Simone André-Maurois Collection.

22 Charles Magnin: article published in the *Revue des Deux Mondes*, June 15th, 1841, p. 843.

23 *La Mode*, 1841, vol. II, p. 843.

24 *Le Retour de l'Empereur*, par Victor Hugo (Paris, Delloye, 14 decembre, 1840), brochure in-8vo de 30 pages. Prix, 1 franc.

25 Factures de la *Laiterie Suisse*, rue de l'Echarpe, No. 1, sur le grand trottoir tenant aux arcades de place Royale, au Marais.

26 Madeleine Dubois et Patrice Roussel, *De quoi vivait Victor Hugo*, p. 107 (Éditions des Deux-Rives, 1952).

27 Ibid.

28 Paul Souchon, *Les Deux Femmes de Victor Hugo*, pp. 115-16.

29 Louis Barthou, *Les Amours d'un Poète*, p. 262.

30 Ibid., p. 264:

> What gifts come to us with the year that is new?
> I'm not less tender, nor less beautiful, you;
> In ten years our two hearts have not aged by a day.
> Complain not of time, nor sigh a reproach,
> For to Heaven, as he flies, he clears the approach,
> And from love never turns our faces away.

31 A novel by Théophile Gautier, published in 1837.

32 Spœlberch de Lovenjoul Collection, C. 495, fol. 325.

33 Spœlberch de Lovenjoul Collection, C. 495, fol. 329.

34 The painter, Louis Boulanger, was working at a portrait of Adèle Hugo, which was exhibited at the Salon of 1839. Célestin Nanteuil made an etching from this picture, which is now to be seen in the Maison de Victor Hugo, Place des Vosges.

35 Spœlberch de Lovenjoul Collection, C. 495, fol. 362.

36 *Une Larme du Diable*, which Théophile Gautier had just published with Desessart.

37 This certainly refers to *Ruy Blas*, which had just appeared in book form.

38 Spœlberch de Lovenjoul Collection, C. 495, fol. 333.

39 By Eugène Piot (1812-90).

40 Spœlberch de Lovenjoul Collection, C. 495, fol. 351.

41 Saint-James is one of the districts of Neuilly. Gautier was already occupying a garden-house, at 32 rue de Longchamp, in which he died in 1872. The architect Charles Robelin had built a house for himself at 4 rue Saint James adorned with "turrets, Gothic windows

filled with stained glass, faïence decorations, and two marble medallions, one representing Raphael, the other Michelangelo."

[42] Spœlberch de Lovenjoul Collection, C. 495, fol. 360.

[43] Spœlberch de Lovenjoul Collection, C. 495, fol. 367.

[44] Maison de Victor Hugo: Catalogue, *Maturité de Victor Hugo*, No. 377, p. 135.

[45] Ibid., No. 388, p. 135.

[46] Ibid., No. 388, p. 138.

CHAPTER 26

[1] Victor Hugo, "Le Rhin, lettres à un ami" (*En Voyage*, vol. I, p. 3).

[2] Ibid., vol. I, pp. 9-10.

[3] *Journal des Débats*, March 31st, 1842. Cuvillier-Fleury afterwards reprinted this article in a volume entitled *Voyages et Voyageurs*. He called it "Monsieur Victor Hugo sur les bords du Rhin."

[4] Léopold Mabilleau, *Victor Hugo*, p. 74.

[5] Henry Jouin, *David d'Angers et ses Relations littéraires*, p. 195.

[6] "This road," we read in *Choses vues* (p. 73), "is called *la route de la Révolte*. It owes its sinister name to the insurrection of the October 6th, which was fomented by Philippe-Égalité against Louis XVI. Just as they were turning into it, the horses which were drawing Égalité's grandson got out of hand, *revolted*, in fact . . . and, two-thirds of the way down that ill-omened thorough-fare, the Prince fell."

[7] Juliette Drouet, *Mille et une lettres*, etc., p. 244.

CHAPTER 27

[1] Juliette Drouet, *Mille et une lettres*, etc., p. 248.

[2] Paul Claudel, *Positions et Propositions*, p. 50.

[3] For the whole of this, see André Dubuc, *Villequier dans la vie et l'œuvre de Victor Hugo* (Rouen, Imprimerie Lainé, 1946).

[4] Simone André-Maurois Collection.

[5] André Dubuc, *Villequier dans la vie et l'œuvre de Victor Hugo*, p. 16.

[6] Simone André-Maurois Collection.

[7] Charles-Isidore Vacquerie died one month after his son's marriage, in March 1843.

[8] André Dubuc, *Villequier dans la vie et l'œuvre de Victor Hugo*, p. 17.

[9] Victor Hugo, "15 février, 1843" (*Les Contemplations*, Book IV, "Pauca Meae," p. 248):

> Love him who loves thee and in him find your gain.
> Farewell, be his treasure who once was our own!
> Go, darling child, to another now flown.
> To him carry bliss, and with us leave the pain.
>
> We cling to you here, but elsewhere a long while
> He has sought you: child, angel, and daughter and wife.
> Two duties you have: to give pain and new life.
> Leave us with a tear, and join him with a smile.

[10] Juliette Drouet, *Mille et une lettres*, etc., p. 248.

[11] André Dubuc, *Villequier dans la vie et l'œuvre de Victor Hugo*, p. 19.

[12] Juliette Drouet, *Mille et une lettres*, etc.

[13] Victor Hugo, "Le Rhin: lettre XIV" (*En Voyage*, vol. I, p. 120).

[14] On the subject of Hugo's recurrent themes and complexes, see Charles Baudouin, *Psychanalyse de Victor Hugo*, pp. 11-25.

[15] Jean-Bartrand Barrère, *Victor Hugo*.

[16] Théophile Gautier, *Histoire de Romantisme*, p. 59.

[17] Juliette Drouet, *Mille et une lettres*, etc., p. 258.

[18] Marie-Louise Pailleron, *Les Derniers Romantiques*, p. 143.

[19] Sainte-Beuve, *Chroniques parisiennes*, p. 13.

[20] *Le Charivari*, March 31st, 1843:

> Said Hugo scanning the blue
> To the Lord in a very low tone:
> "Why should a star have a *queue*
> And the *Burgraves* have none?"

[21] Heinrich Heine, *Lutèce*, p. 303.

[22] Honoré de Balzac, *Lettres à l'Étrangère*, vol. II, p. 158.

[23] Maurice Levaillant.

[24] Maison de Victor Hugo: Catalogue, *Maturité de Victor Hugo*, No. 452, p. 158.

[25] Victor Hugo, "Pyrénées. Bayonne" (*En Voyage*, vol. II, p. 298).

[26] Victor Hugo, "Pyrénées. La Charrette à Bœufs" (*En Voyage*, vol. II, p. 318). Poulet in his *Distance intérieure* quite rightly points out that this passage is an instance of Proust's "involuntary memory."

[27] Victor Hugo, "Pyrénées. Saint-Sébastien" (*En Voyage*, vol. II, p. 326).

[28] Victor Hugo, "Pyrénées. l'Ile d'Oléron" (*En Voyage*, vol. II, p. 437).

[29] Bibliothèque nationale, département des manuscrits. N.A.F. 24794, fols. 175 (verso) and 176. The weekly magazine, *Arts*, printed a fragment of this unpublished journal of Juliette Drouet in its issue of July 10th-16th, 1952, p. 12.

[30] André Dubuc, *Villequier dans la vie et l'œuvre de Victor Hugo*, p. 29.

[31] Jacques-Henry Bornecque, "Les Leçons de Villequier," an article published in *Le Monde*, October 4th, 1952, p. 9.

[32] Victor Hugo, *Correspondance*, vol. I, p. 612.

[33] Jacques-Henry Bornecque, *Les Leçons de Villequier*, p. 9.

[34] Letter published by Maurice Levaillant in the *Revue des Deux Mondes*, May 1st, 1930, p. 175.

[35] Victor Hugo, "Carnet de 1843—Alpes et Pyrénées" (*En Voyage*, vol. II, p. 592).

[36] Simone André-Maurois Collection.

[37] Edmond Biré, *Victor Hugo après 1830*, vol. II, p. 46.

[38] Sainte-Beuve, *Correspondance générale*, vol. V, p. 277.

[39] Honoré de Balzac, *Lettres à l'Étrangère*, vol. II, p. 245.

[40] Victor Hugo, "Pauca Meae," IX (*Les Contemplations*, Book IV, p. 229).

[41] Victor Hugo, "Pauca Meae," XIV (*Les Contemplations*, Book IV, p. 237).

[42] Ibid.

1844

I was thirty, she was ten,
And I was her world, her all.
How fragrant the grass was then
'Neath the trees so green and tall.

Sweet angel, with thoughts white as snow,
Prattling gaily, home once again . . .
All that passed away long ago
Like shadow and wind on the plain.

1846

Oh memories of dawn and spring!
And the warming sun so soft and mild!
—When she was still a tiny thing,
And her sister yet a child. . . .

Know you, set high upon the hill
Which links Montlignon with Saint-Leu,
A terraced place that slopes downhill
Between dark woods and the sky's blue?

'Twas there we lived—take thou the way,
My heart, into that distant memory!—
Under my window I heard her play
All through the morning, quietly.

1847

At dawn tomorrow, when the world grows pale
I'll leave. I know that thou awaitest me.
Through woods I'll go, and mountains I shall scale.
No longer can I live so far from thee.

And blind to evening's gold, I'll know not whether
Far sails glide harbourwards upon the wave;
And when I'm there, I'll place upon thy grave
Green holly and a spray of flowering heather.

The versions of the lines under the dates 1844 and 1847 are by Alan Conder (*Treasury of French Poetry*).

CHAPTER 28

[1] Louis Guimbaud, *Victor Hugo et Madame Biard*, p. 52.
[2] Juliette Drouet, *Mille et une lettres*, etc., pp. 260-1.
[3] Louis Guimbaud, *Victor Hugo et Madame Biard*, p. 58.
[4] Juliette Drouet, *Mille et une lettres*, etc., p. 250.
[5] Victor Hugo, "Soir d'Avril" (*Dernière Gerbe*, LXX, pp. 378-80):

It was the first of April's frail
    And lovely evenings that we knew:
Beloved, I recall it well,
    Do you recall it, too?

We wandered through the spreading town
    Silently, side by side,
At the hour when quietness settles down
    In darkness to abide.

Above the ancient winding ways
    Notre-Dame reared towards the sky
Twin ghosts that caught the enraptured gaze,
    The towers of her sanctuary.

The winding Seine had made its stream
    A geometric fantasy,
And set a bright and mirrored gleam
    Beneath the bridges' masonry.

"I am held still in calm and pride,"
    You said, "my love is true":
While I was all content to bide
    Entrancèd by the sense of you.

It was a blest and sacred time:
    Do you recall it still?
That evening of the young year's prime
    That first day of April.

[6] Unpublished letter. Jean Montargis Collection.
[7] Unpublished letter. Jean Montargis Collection.
[8] Louis Guimbaud, *Victor Hugo et Madame Biard*, p. 96.
[9] Fortunée Lormier-Lagrave, subsequently Madame Hamelin (1776-1851), had been born at Santo Domingo.
[10] Louis Guimbaud, *Victor Hugo et Madame Biard*, p. 101.
[11] Pierre Audiat, *Ainsi vécut Victor Hugo*, p. 212.
[12] "Discours prononcés dans la séance publique tenue par l'Académie française, 27 février, 1845," pp. 29-31.
[13] Spœlberch de Lovenjoul Collection.
[14] Louis Guimbaud, *Victor Hugo et Madame Biard*, p. 102.
[15] Victor Hugo, "Aux Tuileries, 1844. Le Roi Louis-Philippe" (*Choses vues*, vol. I, p. 124).
[16] *Le National*, April 17th, 1845.
[17] Charles Maurice, *Histoire anecdotique du Théâtre et de la Littérature*, vol. II, p. 260.
[18] Letter from Théodore Pavie to his brother Victor, quoted by Edmond Biré in *Victor Hugo après 1830*, vol. II, p. 81.
[19] Louis Guimbaud, *Victor Hugo et Madame Biard*, p. 106.

[20] *Correspondance de Lamartine,* edited by Valentine de Lamartine, vol. VI, pp. 168 and 170.

[21] Sainte-Beuve, *Correspondance générale,* vol. VI, p. 221.

CHAPTER 29

[1] Louis Guimbaud, *Victor Hugo et Madame Biard,* p. 127.

[2] Juliette Drouet, *Mille et une lettres,* etc., pp. 344 and 354.

[3] Ibid., p. 325.

[4] Victor Hugo, "Claire" (*Les Contemplations,* Book VI, pp. 352-4):

> What then? Yours too, yours that in her turn
> Has followed mine: deep-hearted mother, though you yet may leave
> The door wide open for her fond return,
> This stone, half buried in the grass, is still a grave.
>
> She has gone hence in dawn's first gleam,
> Light in the morning, virtue in the azure sky,
> Mouth which had nothing known but the kiss of dream,
> Soul which sleeps only 'neath God's canopy.

[5] Victor Hugo, "Discours du 14 juin, 1847, prononcé à la Chambre des Paris" (*Actes et Paroles,* vol. I, *Avant l'exil,* p. 95).

[6] Henri Guillemin, *Victor Hugo par lui-même,* p. 6.

[7] Victor Hugo, "Théâtre, Mademoiselle George" (*Choses vues,* vol. I, pp. 237-8).

[8] Victor Hugo, "Pauca Meae," XI (*Les Contemplations,* Book IV, p. 232):

> Before assemblies all sunk in gloom we have our say:
> Faced by the goal we strive to reach, and our appointed way,
> We feel both strong and weak, powerful yet small,
> Part of life's tide, in the storm a glittering ray.
> Things come, things pass; mourning and festal day;
> Forward we move, then back; hard grows the fight—
> Then, at the last, comes death's profound and silent night.

[9] Francis Ambrière, "Esther Guimont, courtisane des lettres," an article published in *Minerve,* September 29th, 1945.

[10] Raymond Escholier, *Un Amant de Génie,* p. 293.

[11] Victor Hugo, "L'Interpellation" (*Choses vues,* vol. I, p. 301).

CHAPTER 30

[1] Victor Hugo, "D'après nature" (*Choses vues,* vol. II, p. 27).

[2] Ibid., vol. II, pp. 28-9.

[3] Victor Hugo, "Lettre aux Électeurs" (*Actes et Paroles,* vol. I, *Avant l'exil,* p. 99) .

[4] Victor Hugo, "20 mai, 1848. Victor Hugo à ses concitoyens" (*Actes et Paroles,* vol. I, *Avant l'exil,* p. 106).

[5] Juliette Drouet, *Mille et une lettres, etc.,* p. 358.

[6] Ibid.

[7] Victor Hugo, "Assemblé constituante, 20th 1848. Ateliers nationaux" (*Actes et Paroles,* vol. I, *Avant l'exil,* pp. 122-3).

[8] Ibid., vol. I, p. 125.

[9] Victor Hugo, *Souvenirs personnels,* collected by Henri Guillemin, p. 68.

[10] Ibid.

[11] Ibid., p. 73.

[12] Victor Hugo, *Les Misérables,* Part V, Book I, chap. 1, p. 6.

[13] Henri Guillemin, *Victor Hugo par lui-même,* p. 40.

[14] Victor Hugo, "Les Journées de Juin" (*Choses vues,* vol. I, pp. 356-7).

[15] Victor Hugo, *Souvenirs personnels,* p. 99 (Gallimard, 1952).

[16] Ibid., p. 115.

[17] Honoré de Balzac, *Lettres à l'Étrangère,* vol. V (unpublished), fol. 529.

[18] Henri Guillemin, *Victor Hugo par lui-même,* p. 62.

[19] Honoré de Balzac, *Lettres à l'Étrangère,* vol. V (unpublished), fol. 461.

[20] Ibid., vol. V (unpublished), fol. 473.

CHAPTER 31

[1] Probably in October 1848. There is a deal of controversy about the date. See Pierre Audiat, *Ainsi vécut Victor Hugo*, p. 233.

[2] Victor Hugo, *Histoire d'un Crime*, "Première Journée: Le Guet-Apens—I Sécurité," p. 274.

[3] *L'Évènement*, November 6, 1848.

[4] Victor Hugo, "Le Premier Dîner" (*Choses vues*, vol. I, p. 413).

[5] Ibid.

[6] Victor Hugo, "Chez Lamartine" (*Choses vues*, vol. I, p. 42).

[7] Victor Hugo, "Mort de Chateaubriand" (*Choses vues*, vol. I, p. 363).

[8] Among the guests present on this occasion, whom Madame Victor Hugo did not mention, were the Duchesse de Maillé, the Princesse de Poix, the Duc de Valençay, the Comte Molé, General Changarnier, General Cavaignac, Messieurs Thiers and Armand Marrast, the Comte de Rémusat, the Comte de Montalembert, etc.

[9] Clément Janin, *Victor Hugo en exil*, p. 31.

[10] Unpublished letter. Georges Blaizot Collection.

[11] Barbey d'Aurevilly.

[12] Henri Guillemin, *Le Coup du 2 Décembre*.

[13] Victor Hugo, "Assemblée législative, discours du 9 juillet, 1849—La Misére" (*Actes et Paroles*, vol. I, *Avant l'exil*, p. 160).

[14] Ibid.

[15] *L'Évènement*, in its issue of October 17th, made mention of the dinner given the previous evening by the Prince-President. "Historique," *Avant l'exil* (*Actes et Paroles*, vol. I, p. 649) states categorically that this dinner took place on the 16th.

[16] Victor Hugo, "Assemblée législative, discours du 19 octobre, 1849—L'Expédition de Rome" (*Actes et Paroles*, vol. I, *Avant l'exil*, pp. 173-5).

[17] Victor Hugo, "Réponse à Monsieur de Montalembert, 20 octobre 1849" (*Actes et Paroles*, vol. I, *Avant l'exil*, p. 176).

[18] Victor Hugo, "Moi—Océan" (*Tas de Pierres*, p. 263).

[19] Victor Hugo, "Historique," *Avant l'exil* (*Actes et Paroles*, vol. I, p. 649).

[20] *L'Évènement*, October 26th, 1849.

CHAPTER 32

[1] Victor Hugo, *Avant l'exil* (*Actes et Paroles*, vol. I, p. 651).

[2] Victor Hugo, "Discours du 15 janvier, 1850, sur La Liberté de l'Enseignement" (*Actes et Paroles*, vol. I, *Avant l'exil*, p. 182).

[3] Victor Hugo, "Discours du 5 avril, 1850, sur La Déportation" (*Actes et Paroles*, vol. I, *Avant l'exil*, p. 193).

[4] Ibid., vol. I, p. 197.

[5] Victor Hugo, "Discours du 21 mai, 1850, sur Le Suffrage universel" (*Actes et Paroles*, vol. I, *Avant l'exil*, p. 212).

[6] Victor Hugo, "Historique," *Avant l'exil* (*Actes et Paroles*, vol. I, p. 656).

[7] Louis Guimbaud, *Victor Hugo et Juliette Drouet*, p. 167.

[8] Comte Horace de Viel-Castel, *Mémoires*, vol. I, p. 27.

[9] Victor Hugo, "Amour" (*Les Contemplations*, Book III, X, p. 142):

> Can one direct one's loving? Why do two persons love?
> Ask of the rippling stream, ask of the ambient air,
> Ask of the moth that flies into the candle's glare
> Ask of the golden sunbeam that plays on the ripening vine,
> Ask of all things that sing, and call to each other, and pine!
> Ask of the restless nests under the April sky!
> The heart in bewilderment says: "Who knows the answer? Not I!"

[10] Raymond Escholier, *Un Amant de Génie*, p. 351.

[11] Ibid., pp. 352-3.

[12] Louis Guimbaud, *Victor Hugo et Juliette Drouet*, p. 169.

[13] Juliette Drouet, *Mille et une lettres*, etc., p. 391.

[14] Ibid., p. 392.

[15] Ibid., p. 402.

16 Ibid., pp. 406-7.

17 Victor Hugo, "Discours du 6 février, 1851 prononcé à la réunion du douzième bureau de l'Assemblée législative" (*Actes et Paroles,* vol. I, *Avant l'exil,* pp. 351-2).

18 Satory, near Versailles, was where military manœuvres were carried out [Translator].

19 Victor Hugo, "Discours du 17 juillet, 1851 su La Révision de la Constitution" (*Actes et Paroles,* vol. I, *Avant l'exil,* pp. 255-7).

20 Charles Baudouin, *Psychanalyse de Victor Hugo,* p. 114.

21 Louis Guimbaud, *Victor Hugo et Juliette Drouet,* p. 171.

22 Ibid., p. 172.

23 Victor Hugo, *Les Contemplations,* Book II, XXIV, p. 107:

> Let in the dawn, after our times of weeping,
> Dawn that is daughter of night, love that is misery's heir
> All that glows in the shadows sleeping,
> All that smiles in the trembling tear.

24 Juliette Drouet, *Mille et une lettres,* etc., pp. 411-12.

CHAPTER 33

1 Victor Hugo, *Histoire d'un Crime,* "Première Journée: Le Guet-Apens," chap. XVI, p. 362.

2 Victor Hugo, *Carnet de 1856.* Eugène Planès Collection.

3 Raymond Escholier, *Victor Hugo, cet inconnu,* p. 259.

4 Ibid.

5 Ibid., pp. 258-9.

6 Victor Hugo, "Historique," *Pendant l'exil* (*Actes et Paroles,* vol. II, p. 482).

7 Unpublished letter. Simone André-Maurois Collection.

8 Gustave Simon, *La Vie d'une Femme,* p. 250.

9 Victor Hugo, *Correspondance,* vol. II, pp. 38-9.

CHAPTER 34

1 Victor Hugo, *William Shakespeare,* p. 476.

2 Victor Hugo, *Les Misérables,* Part II, Book VII, chap. VIII, p. 231.

3 Victor Hugo, *Correspondance,* vol. II, p. 33.

4 Luthereau was a French journalist, editor-in-chief of *La Renaissance,* a Brussels paper, and proprietor of a printing-house.

5 Victor Hugo, *Correspondance,* vol. II, p. 31.

6 Paul Claudel, *L'Otage,* Act III, Sc. 2.

7 Juliette Drouet, *Mille et une lettres,* etc., p. 415.

8 Ibid., pp. 416-17.

9 Ibid., p. 417.

10 Victor Hugo, *Correspondance,* vol. II, pp. 68-9.

11 Gustave Simon, *La Vie d'une Femme,* p. 252.

12 Ibid., p. 253.

13 Ibid., p. 264.

14 Victor Hugo, "Historique," *Pendant l'exil* (*Actes et Paroles,* vol. II, p. 486).

15 Victor Hugo, *Correspondance,* vol. II, p. 56.

16 Ibid., p. 42.

17 Louis Guimbaud, *Victor Hugo et Madame Biard,* p. 180.

18 Louis Guimbaud, *Les Amours d'un Poète,* p. 316.

19 Victor Hugo, *Correspondance,* vol. II, p. 29.

20 Raymond Escholier, *Victor Hugo, cet inconnu,* p. 262.

21 Victor Hugo, "Bruxelles" (*En Voyage,* vol. II, p. 86).

22 Gustave Simon, *La Vie d'une Femme,* p. 280.

23 Letter published in *Les Lettres françaises.*

24 Gustave Simon, *La Vie d'une Femme,* p. 273.

25 Ibid., p. 265.

26 Victor Hugo, *Napoléon le Petit,* Book VI, pp. 141-3.

27 Clément Janin, *Victor Hugo en exil,* pp. 39-40.

28 See A. Parménie and C. Bonnier de la Chapelle, *Histoire d'un Éditeur et de ses Auteurs: Pierre-Jules Hetzel,* p. 164.

[29] Victor Hugo, *Correspondance*, vol. II, p. 52.

[30] Juliette Drouet, *Mille et une lettres*, etc., p. 423.

[31] Ibid., p. 424.

[32] Ibid., p. 429.

[33] Ibid.

[34] Victor Hugo, *Correspondance*, vol. II, p. 55.

[35] *Voyage d'une Femme au Spitzberg*, par Léonie d'Aunet (Paris, Hachette, 1853).

[36] *La Revue de Paris*, which published the *Voyage d'une Femme au Spitzberg* in 1852, before its appearance in book form.

[37] Letter quoted in a note to Victor Hugo's *Correspondance*, vol. II, p. 55.

[38] Victor Hugo, *Correspondance*, vol. II, pp. 55-6.

[39] Ibid., vol. II, p. 68.

[40] Patrice Boussel and Madeleine Dubois, *De quoi vivait Victor Hugo*, p. 128.

[41] Gustave Simon, *La Vie d'une Femme*, pp. 294-5.

[42] Three years later (on April 14th, 1855) this *Ronsard* figured again in an auction. Maxime du Camp bought it for 900 francs and gave it to Valentine Delessert, who kept it until her death. On April 27th, 1895, when the library of the late Madame Gabriel Delessert was dispersed, a mysterious amateur, "whose name was not revealed," purchased the *Ronsard* through a third party, for 1100 francs. This amateur was the Vicomte de Spœlberch de Lovenjoul. Émile Henriot was the first person to reveal the identity of the purchaser in an article published in the *Revue des Bibliothèques*, January 1913.

[43] Jules Janin, *Histoire de la Littérature dramatique*, vol. IV, pp. 419-21. (The article appeared in the *Journal des Débats*, June 7th, 1852.)

[44] See Théophile Gautier, *Histoire du Romantisme*, the chapter entitled "La vente du mobilier de Victor Hugo." See also a poem by Adolphe Dumas, "La Maison vendue," quoted by Clément Janin in *Victor Hugo en exil*, p. 49.

[45] Victor Hugo, *Correspondance*, vol. II, pp. 108-9.

[46] Clément Janin, *Victor Hugo en exil*, pp. 52-3.

[47] Jules Janin, *Histoire de la Littérature dramatique*, vol. IV, pp. 401-23.

CHAPTER 35

[1] Unpublished letter. Alfred Dupont Collection.

[2] Juliette Drouet, *Mille et une lettres*, etc., p. 436.

[3] Jean-Bertrand Barrère, *Hugo, l'homme et l'œuvre*, p. 126.

[4] Victor Hugo, "Historique," *Châtiments*, p. 468.

[5] A. Parménie and C. Bonnier de la Chapelle, *Histoire d'un Éditeur et de ses Auteurs: Pierre-Jules Hetzel*, pp. 204-5.

[6] *Souvenirs de Pierre Foucher* (Paris, Plon, 1929).

[7] Gustave Simon, *La Vie d'une Femme*, p. 307.

[8] Louis Guimbaud, *Victor Hugo et Madame Biard*, p. 186.

[9] Paul Claudel, *Positions et Propositions*, p. 43.

[10] Clément Janin, *Victor Hugo en exil*, p. 61.

[11] Juliette Drouet, *Mille et une lettres*, etc., p. 444.

[12] Ibid., p. 446.

[13] Sainte-Beuve, *Mes Poisons*, p. 32.

[14] Victor Hugo, "Historique," *Pendant l'exil* (*Actes et Paroles*, vol. II, p. 496).

[15] C. Parménie and C. Bonnier de la Chapelle, *Histoire d'un Éditeur et de ses Auteurs: Pierre-Jules Hetzel*, p. 202.

CHAPTER 36

[1] *Napoléon le Petit*.

[2] "Historique," *Pendant l'exil* (*Actes et Paroles*, vol. II, p. 498).

[3] Paul Claudel, *Positions et Propositions*, p. 45.

[4] Auguste Vacquerie, *Les Miettes de l'Histoire*, p. 408.

[5] Gustave Simon, *La Vie d'une Femme*, p. 307.

[6] Juliette Drouet, *Mille et une lettres*, etc., p. 455.

[7] Ibid., p. 457.

[8] Paul Berret, "La Légende des Siècles de 1859" (Introduction to a series of "Grands Écrivains de France," p. xxv).

[9] Ibid., p. xxxiii.

[10] Denis Saurat, *Victor Hugo et les Dieux du Peuple*.

[11] Paul Berret, "Victor Hugo spirite," an article published in the *Revue des Deux Mondes*, August 1st, 1922, p. 558.

CHAPTER 37

[1] He, himself, gave a more complete list of these: see *Pierres*, p. 267 (Geneva, éditions du Milieu du Monde, 1951).

[2] Denis Saurat, *Victor Hugo et les Dieux du Peuple*, p. 20.

CHAPTER 38

[1] Victor Hugo, "Historique," *Pendant l'exil* (*Actes et Paroles*, vol. II, pp. 501-2).

[2] Victor Hugo, "Lettre à Louis Bonaparte" (*Actes et Paroles*, vol. II, *Pendant l'exil*, p. 116).

[3] Félix Pyat, "Lettre à la Reine d'Angleterre," published in *L'Homme*, October 10th, 1855.

[4] Victor Hugo, "Expulsion de Jersey" (*Actes et Paroles*, vol. II, *Pendant l'exil*, p. 128).

[5] Auguste Vacquerie, *Profils et Grimaces*, p. 419.

[6] Gustave Simon, *La Vie d'une Femme*, pp. 314-15.

[7] *Correspondance entre Victor Hugo et Paul Meurice*, p. 68 (Paris, Charpentier, 1909).

[8] Ibid., p. 74.

[9] Sainte-Beuve, *Pages choisies des grands écrivains*, p. 406 (Paris, Armand-Colin et Calmann-Lévy, 1924).

[10] Victor Hugo and his two sons.

[11] Gustave Simon, *La Vie d'une Femme*, pp. 325-6.

[12] *Ibid.*, pp. 326-8.

[13] A. Parménie and C. Bonnier de la Chapelle, *Histoire d'un Éditeur et de ses Auteurs: Pierre-Jules Hetzel*, p. 305.

[14] Raymond Escholier, *Un Amant de Génie*, pp. 376-8.

[15] Clément Janin, *Victor Hugo en exil*, p. 107.

[16] Juliette Drouet, *Mille et une lettres*, etc., p. 525.

[17] Gustave Simon, *La Vie d'une Femme*, pp. 320-1.

[18] Ibid., p. 322.

[19] Ibid., p. 324.

[20] "Lettres de Madame Victor Hugo à sa sœur Julie," published in the *Revue de Paris*, October 1st, 1912, p. 561.

CHAPTER 39

[1] Victor Hugo, *Correspondance*, vol. II, p. 248.

[2] Ibid., p. 281.

[3] *Le Livre du Centenaire du Journal des Débats*, p. 413.

[4] Victor Hugo, *La Légende des Siècles*, Preface, vol. I, pp. 5-6.

[5] See Maurice Barrès, *Mes Cahiers*, vol. III, pp. 81-2.

[6] "Lettres de Madame Victor Hugo à sa sœur, Julie," published in the *Revue de Paris*, October 1st, 1912, p. 554.

[7] Ibid., p. 542.

[8] Gustave Simon, *La Vie d'une Femme*, p. 331.

[9] Ibid., pp. 332-3.

[10] Ibid., p. 334.

[11] Juliette Drouet, *Mille et une lettres*, etc., p. 508.

[12] A. Parménie and C. Bonnier de la Chapelle, *Histoire d'un Éditeur et de ses Auteurs: Pierre-Jules Hetzel*, p. 292.

[13] Juliette Drouet, *Mille et une lettres*, etc., p. 513.

[14] Ibid., pp. 512-13.

[15] Ibid., p. 516.

[16] Victor Hugo, *Correspondance*, vol. II, p. 319.

[17] Gustave Flaubert, *Correspondance*, vol. IV, p. 333.

[18] Victor Hugo, "Déclaration" (*Actes et Paroles*, vol. II, *Pendant l'exil*, p. 141).

CHAPTER 40

[1] Victor Hugo, *Les Misérables*.

[2] Edmond de Goncourt, *Journal*, vol. III, p. 143.

[3] There was talk of a marriage for Julie Foucher, then thirty-six years of age, who was very anxious to leave Saint-Denis.

[4] Gustave Simon, *La Vie d'une Femme*, p. 332.

[5] Bibliothèque nationale: département des manuscrits, N.A.F.

[6] Aglaé Viénot, the daughter of a notary. Émile Deschamps had married her in 1817. She died in 1855.

[7] Unpublished letter. Simone André-Maurois Collection.

[8] Letter published by Henri Guillemin in *La Table Ronde*, April 1952, p. 385.

[9] Gustave Simon, *La Vie d'une Femme*, p. 385.

[10] A. Parménie and C. Bonnier de la Chapelle, *Histoire d'un Éditeur et de ses Auteurs: Pierre-Jules Hetzel*, pp. 411-12.

[11] Victor Hugo, *Correspondance*, vol. II, p. 453.

[12] Letter published by Henri Guillemin in *La Table Ronde*, April 1952, pp. 48-9.

[13] Gustave Simon, *La Vie d'une Femme*, p. 334.

[14] Letter published by Henri Guillemin in *La Table Ronde*, April 1953, pp. 44-5.

[15] Anne-Caroline-Alice Lehaene (1847-1928) was the daughter of Pierre-Jules Lehaene and Louise-Clémence Bois, both of whom were, at this time, dead.

[16] Victor Hugo, "LXIV: 22 septembre, 1854" (*Toute la lyre*, Book VI, p. 193):

> When two loving hearts have quietly grown old,
> For them what a joy, bliss not to be told!
> Love! Heaven's Hymen! which can claim only
> Their loyalty. His rays shine still, though not his flame.
> What once he joined as two are now but one at last,
> And from the memories they hold of a long mingled past,
> A life has flowered which cannot but be shared
> —Just such a life, Juliette, is ours; we have been spared
> To know the quiet evening after the blaze of day.
> Love that's still love can as sweet friendship stay.

[17] Hitherto unpublished. Simone André-Maurois Collection.

[18] Louis Barthou, *Les Amours d'un Poète*, p. 342.

[19] Ibid., p. 343.

[20] Juliette Drouet, *Mille et une lettres*, etc., p. 608.

CHAPTER 41

[1] Quoted by Edmond-Benoît Lévy in *Les Misérables de Victor Hugo*, p. 28.

[2] Ibid., p. 54.

[3] Juliette Drouet, *Mille et une lettres*, etc., p. 537.

[4] Ibid., p. 562.

[5] Victor Hugo, *Les Misérables*, vol. II, "Cosette," Book I, chap. II, p. 12.

[6] Victor Hugo, *Correspondance*, vol. II, p. 355.

[7] Victor Hugo, "Historique," *L'Homme qui rit*, p. 578.

[8] More than sixty million in 1954.

[9] *Correspondance entre Victor Hugo et Paul Meurice*, p. 158.

[10] Edmond-Benoît Lévy, *Les Misérables de Victor Hugo*, p. 141.

[11] *Les Misérables*, "Revue de la critique," vol. VI, pp. 373-4.

[12] Charles Baudelaire, *Correspondance générale*, vol. IV, pp. 89 and 100.

[13] Victor Hugo, Prefatory Letter, published as an introduction to Baudelaire's *Théophile Gautier*, p. 11.

[14] Pascal Pia, *Baudelaire par lui-même*, p. 138.

[15] Victor Hugo, *Les Misérables*, Part IV, Book I, chap. I, p. 6.

[16] Ibid., "Revue de la critique," vol. V, p. 366.

[17] Edmond and Jules de Goncourt, *Journal*, vol. II, p. 99.

CHAPTER 42

[1] Jean-Bertrand Barrère, *Hugo, l'homme et l'œuvre*, p. 197.

[2] "Historique," *William Shakespeare*, pp. 416-17.

[3] Ibid., p. 437.

[4] *Mondes,* p. 123.

[5] *William Shakespeare,* "Revue de la critique," p. 439.

[6] In Victor Hugo's notebooks, Hauteville II means Hauteville Féerie, the cottage in which the poet had installed Juliette Drouet, after making her leave La Fallue on the grounds that it was damp.

[7] Bibliothèque nationale, département des manuscrits, N.A.F. 13464, fols. 75-8.

CHAPTER 43

[1] Juliette Drouet, *Mille et une lettres,* etc., p. 628.

[2] Ibid., p. 633.

[3] Ibid., p. 641.

[4] Pascal Pia, *Baudelaire par lui-même,* p. 141.

[5] Georges-Charles-Victor-Léopold Hugo, born in Brussels on August 16th, 1868; died in Paris on February 5th, 1925. He married, first, Pauline Ménard-Dorian, and, second, Dora-Charlotte Dorian, the divorced wife of Jean Ajalbert.

[6] Léopoldine-Adèle-Jeanne, born in Brussels on September 29th, 1869; died in Paris on November 30th, 1941. She became Madame Léon Daudet, and later, first, Madame Jean Charcot, and, finally, Madame Michel Négreponte.

[7] Victor Hugo, *Correspondance,* vol. III, p. 256.

[8] Ibid., vol. III, p. 110.

[9] Juliette Drouet.

[10] Victor Hugo, *Correspondance,* vol. III, p. 105.

[11] Ibid., vol. III, p. 86.

[12] "Historique," *Travailleurs de la Mer,* p. 505.

[13] Ibid., p. 520.

[14] Ibid., p. 527.

[15] Ibid., p. 521.

[16] *Les Travailleurs de la Mer,* "Revue de la critique," p. 537.

[17] Victor Hugo, *Correspondance,* vol. II, p. 535.

[18] Gustave Simon, *La Vie d'une Femme,* p. 401.

CHAPTER 44

[1] Victor Hugo, *Correspondance,* vol. III, p. 33.

[2] Gustave Simon, *La Vie d'une Femme,* p. 412.

[3] Ibid., p. 420.

[4] Article by Théophile Gautier in the *Moniteur universel,* June 21st, 1867.

[5] Article by Jules Janin in the *Journal des Débats,* June 24th, 1867.

[6] Bibliothèque nationale, département des manuscrits, N.A.F. 13466, fol. 22.

[7] Unpublished letters, from the collection of Madame Gaveau, who, before her marriage, was a Lefèvre-Vacquerie.

[8] Unpublished letter in Madame Gaveau's collection.

[9] Marie-Henriette Biard, vicomtesse de Peyronny, was at this time 28 years old. After being left a widow, she took as her second husband the Baron Double (1848-95), and maintained a *salon* in the town-house belonging to him in the Avenue d'Antin. She was for a long time a contributor to the *Figaro* under the pen-name of "Étincelle." Her daughter by her first marriage became Madame Camille Bouisson.

[10] Unpublished letter in Madame Gaveau's collection.

[11] That is to say, to Paris, where Charles and Alice, whose stay was to be brief, had been settled for two months. They remained until the end of July, and then returned to Brussels by way of Spa, where they spent some days. Victor Hugo was in a discontented and sulky mood. "My father is going to send you my allowance, which I shall get at last, after *a delay of nine months!*" was Charles's bitter comment to his brother.

[12] Unpublished letters in Madame Gaveau's collection.

[13] Gustave Simon, *La Vie d'une Femme,* p. 429.

[14] Victor Hugo, "Extraits des Carnets" (*Choses vues,* vol. II, pp. 137-8).

[15] Bibliothèque nationale, département des manuscrits, N.A.F. 13467, fol. 98.

[16] By César Mitkievicz, 29 rue Neuve, Brussels.

[17] Collection formerly in the possession of Louis Barthou.

[18] Juliette Drouet, *Mille et une lettres,* etc., p. 652.

[19] Bibliothèque nationale, département des manuscrits, N.A.F. 13466, fol. 142.
[20] Victor Hugo, *Correspondance*, vol. III, p. 140.
[21] Victor Hugo, *L'Homme qui rit*, Part II, Book VII, chap. III, pp. 424-5.
[22] "Historique," *L'Homme qui rit*, p. 590.
[23] Bibliothèque nationale, département des manuscrits, N.A.F. 13466, fol. 175.
[24] Victor Hugo, *Correspondance*, vol. III, p. 156.

CHAPTER 45

[1] Victor Hugo, *Correspondance*, vol. III, pp. 192-3.
[2] Bibliothèque nationale, département des manuscrits, N.A.F. 13468, fol. 48.
[3] Victor Hugo, *Correspondance*, vol. III, p. 210.
[4] Unpublished. Bibliothèque nationale, département des manuscrits, N.A.F. 13467, fol. 149.
[5] Victor Hugo, "Congrès de la Paix à Lausanne," September 14th, 1869 (*Actes et Paroles*, vol. II, *Pendant l'exil*, p. 291).
[6] Abbreviation of *Juju* which, in the *Diaries*, always stands for Juliette.
[7] Bibliothèque nationale, département des manuscrits, N.A.F. 13467, fol. 171.
[8] Bibliothèque nationale, département des manuscrits, N.A.F. 13467, fol. 178.
[9] Victor Hugo, *Correspondance*, vol. III, p. 198.
[10] Ibid., vol. III, p. 256.
[11] Victor Hugo, "Les 7,500,000 oui," Prologue (*l'Année terrible*, p. 16).
[12] Victor Hugo, "Historique," *Pendant l'exil* (*Actes et Paroles*, vol. II, p. 581).
[13] Ibid.
[14] *Diaries*, made available by Monsieur Jean Montargis, III, p. 64.
[15] Victor Hugo, "Historique," *Pendant l'exil* (*Actes et Paroles*, vol. II, p. 582).
[16] Victor Hugo, *Correspondance*, vol. III, p. 267.
[17] Raymond Escholier, *Un Amant de Génie*, p. 453.

CHAPTER 46

[1] Victor Hugo, "Octobre, I" (*l'Année terrible*, p. 39).
[2] Edmond de Goncourt, *Journal*, vol. IV, p. 78.
[3] Ibid., vol. IV, p. 93.
[4] Ibid.
[5] Victor Hugo, "Extraits de ses Carnets, 1870-1871" (*Choses vues*, vol. II).
[6] Victor Hugo, "Aux Allemands" (*Actes et Paroles*, vol. III, *Depuis l'exil*, pp. 37-41).
[7] Victor Hugo, "Aux Parisiens" (*Actes et Paroles*, vol. III, *Depuis l'exil*, pp. 46-9).
[8] Victor Hugo, *Choses vues*, vol. II, p. 154.
[9] Judith (1850-1917) was the youngest daughter of Théophile Gautier and Ernesta Grisi. She became the first wife of Catulle Mendès.

[10] O had you been here whom I admire truly,
A meal you'd have had beyond all compare:
For Pegasus slaughtered and then roasted duly,
A wing of that steed should have fall'n to your share.

[11] No ashes I leave, dearest ma'am,
But a steak of me, fit for a king.
When you've eaten me, then you will sing
About how very tender I am!

[12] Victor Hugo, *L'Année terrible*, p. 221:

An honest soldier, loyal, brave and true,
A quite good gun, but with too much recoil.

[13] Victor Hugo, "Historique," *Depuis l'exil* (*Actes et Paroles*, vol. III, p. 550).
[14] Victor Hugo, *Correspondance*, vol. III, p. 275.
[15] Victor Hugo, "Discours sur la Guerre," Assemblée nationale, séance du 1er mars, 1871 (*Actes et Paroles*, vol. III, *Depuis l'exil*, p. 69).
[16] Ibid., pp. 70-3.
[17] Victor Hugo, "La Question de Paris," Onzième Bureau, séance du 6 mars, 1871 (*Actes et Paroles*, vol. III, *Depuis l'exil*, p. 83).

[18] Victor Hugo, "Assemblée nationale, séance du 8 mars, 1871" (*Actes et Paroles*, vol. III, *Depuis l'exil*, p. 86).

[19] Victor Hugo, "Reliquat," *Depuis l'exil* (*Actes et Paroles*, vol. III, pp. 436-7).

[20] Unpublished. Bibliothèque nationale, N.A.F. 13471, fol. 27.

[21] Victor Hugo, "Mars, V" (*L'Année terrible*, p. 137).

CHAPTER 47

[1] Edmond de Goncourt, *Journal*, vol. IV, p. 181.

[2] Ibid.

[3] Victor Hugo, "L'Enterrement" (*L'Année terrible*, p. 134):

> The drums roll, and the flag dips and hangs still.
> From the Bastille to the foot of the gloomy hill,
> Where years long past, beneath the cypress trees,
> Sleep with today, unvexed by any breeze.
> A people in arms, mourning and brooding, stay
> Silent, unmoving, guarding the funeral way.
> The dead son, and the father ripe for the grave
> Pass by, the one but yesterday strong, lovely, and brave,
> The other old, tears hidden, holds high his head.
> Legion by legion Paris salutes the dead.

[4] Bibliothèque nationale, département des manuscrits, N.A.F. 13471, fols. 175-7.

[5] Ibid., fol. 43.

[6] Victor Hugo, "Historique," *Depuis l'exil* (*Actes et Paroles*, vol. III, p. 555).

[7] Victor Hugo, "Carnet de 1871" (*Choses vues*, vol. II, p. 188).

[8] Victor Hugo, "Un Cri" (*L'Année terrible*, p. 144):

> O you furious fighters! To what end are you drawn?
> You are just like a fire devouring the corn,
> Your victims are honour and reason and hope,
> France here, and France there, on the slippery slope.
> Hold your hands! for success can breed nothing but death
> Between Frenchmen and Frenchmen the cannon's hot breath
> Spits forth, fratricidal, its stench and its flame,
> But slaughter before it, behind it but shame!

[9] Victor Hugo, "Pas de Représailles" (*L'Année terrible*, pp. 147-9):

> Of the words that I have lived by, I will not now lose sight:
> Progress and Reason, Honour, Duty, Right,
> No man can come to truth by twisting ways.
> Be just: and give your country length of days.
> The duty that we owe to her is equity for all;
> No malice: the ungentle we never just can call.
> Twenty long years of exile have given me the right
> To harden my face against fury, that terrible blight,
> To shut the doors of my spirit against all blinding ire.
> If gloomy dungeons and bars and bolts conspire
> To oppress my vanquished foe, then must I love him still,
> And even to my banisher I will
> Offer asylum—thus making banishment a gift from Heaven.
> Had I been Christ, Judas himself had been forgiven.

[10] Victor Hugo, "Historique," *Depuis l'exil* (*Actes et Paroles*, vol. III, p. 556).

[11] Victor Hugo, "Reliquat," *Depuis l'exil* (*Actes et Paroles*, vol. III, p. 438).

[12] Victor Hugo, "L'Incident belge" (*Actes et Paroles*, vol. III, *Depuis l'exil*, p. 123).

[13] Victor Hugo, "Lettre à cinq représentants du Peuple belge" (*Actes et Paroles*, vol. III, *Depuis l'exil*, p. 135).

[14] It now contains a Victor Hugo museum.

[15] This is now the Hôtel Victor-Hugo.

[16] Victor Hugo, "Virgo Major" (*Toute la Lyre*, vol. I, p. 82).

[17] Victor Hugo, "Carnet de 1871" (*Choses vues*, vol. II, p. 192).

[18] Raymond Escholier, *Victor Hugo, cet inconnu*, p. 313.

[19] Gaston Stiegler, "Une Inconnue de Victor Hugo," an article published in *Le Figaro*, May 5th, 1893.

[20] Henri Guillemin, *Victor Hugo par lui-même*, p. 58.

[21] Victor Hugo, "L'Islam" (*La Légende des Siècles*, vol. I, p. 161):

> Sometimes he made a woman strip nude
> Then looked at her and brooded on the nude
> And said: "On earth is beauty, in Heaven the light of day."

[22] Victor Hugo, "A Vianden" (*L'Année terrible*, p. 215):

> Here is what stirs within the exile's head:
> —Alas! all is not ended yet, all is not said
> Simply because a grave is dug in the eyes of all,
> Because a leader lines against a wall
> Poor folk to stand facing a firing squad,
> Because at random, fumblingly, to God
> Are sent the souls of men under a leaden hail,
> Fathers and mothers, madmen, scoundrels, those who ail,
> And bodies quickly are consumed in lime,
> Men dripping blood, children who've had no time
> Even to grow cold. . . .

[23] Victor Hugo, "Juin, II" (*L'Année terrible*, p. 189):

> What! Brotherhood? 'Tis but a chimera
> To hope a Europe free as America,
> To think that justice, conscience, sense will come
> Is to make cloudy vapours and the wind one's home.

[24] Raymond Escholier, *Un Amant de Génie*, pp. 495-6.

[25] Victor Hugo, "Carnet de 1871" (*Choses vues*, vol. II, p. 196).

[26] Victor Hugo, "Aux Rédacteurs du Rappel" (*Actes et Paroles*, vol. III, *Depuis l'exil*, p. 147).

[27] Edmond de Goncourt, *Journal*, vol. V, p. 18.

[28] Raymond Escholier, *Un Amant de Génie*, pp. 522-4.

[29] Henri Guillemin, *Victor Hugo par lui-même*, p. 68.

[30] Edmond de Goncourt, *Journal*, vol. V, p. 34.

[31] Raymond Escholier, *Un Amant de Génie*, p. 511.

[32] Ibid., pp. 513-14.

[33] Raymond Escholier, *Victor Hugo, cet inconnu*, p. 316.

[34] Raymond Escholier, *Un Amant de Génie*, p. 517.

[35] Victor Hugo, "La Centième de Ruy Blas" (*Choses vues*, vol. II, p. 207).

[36] Maurice Bernhardt.

[37] Unpublished letter. Simone André-Maurois Collection.

[38] Edmond de Goncourt, *Journal*, vol. V, p. 82.

[39] Victor Hugo, "Ave, Dea, moriturus te salutat" (*Toute la Lyre*, V, XXXIV, p. 64):

> Two deep-down things are death and loveliness,
> With much of dark in them, much of bright blue:
> Sisters they seem, with terror fraught, and fruitfulness,
> Having the same mystery, the same secret, too
>
> O women! Voices, looks, black hair, or golden tress
> Shine on, I die: be brilliant, lovely, and a lodestone true,
> Pearls that the sea doth mingle with the stress
> Of waters: luminous birds who with their light the forest strew.
>
> Judith, our destinies are closely knit,
> Though, seeing your face and mine, but few would credit it;
> All the divine abyss shows in your eye.
>
> But I am by the starry depths beset;
> Near neighbours of Heaven have we two been set:
> You a fair woman, and an old man, I.

[40] Raymond Escholier, *Un Amant de Génie*, p. 534.
[41] Edmond de Goncourt, *Journal*, vol. V, p. 36.

CHAPTER 48

[1] Juliette Drouet, *Mille et une lettres*, etc., p. 688.
[2] Ibid., p. 689.
[3] Ibid., p. 690.
[4] Victor Hugo, "Historique," *Depuis l'exil* (*Actes et Paroles*, vol. III, pp. 578-9).
[5] Victor Hugo, "A Théophile Gautier" (*Toute la Lyre*, IV, vol. I, p. 339):

> Friend, Poet, Spirit, you flee the darkness of our night,
> Winging from out our turmoil to live on in the light
> Of glory. You I salute upon the gloomy portal . . .
>
> Thither I hasten. Shut not the funerary door.
> We all must pass that way, none can escape, it is the law;
> All things shall fall, and this great age, so bright,
> Enter the vasty darkness, where, poor and pale we flicker through the night.
> Oh! what a fearful din at evening make the trees
> Felled for the funeral pyre of Hercules!

[6] Raymond Escholier, *Un Amant de Génie*, p. 537.
[7] Victor Hugo, "Historique," *Depuis l'exil* (*Actes et Paroles*, vol. III, p. 579).
[8] Ibid., vol. III, p. 580.
[9] Juliette Drouet, *Mille et une lettres*, etc., p. 696.
[10] Ibid., pp. 696-7.
[11] Victor Hugo, "Historique," *Depuis l'exil* (*Actes et Paroles*, vol. III, p. 579).
[12] Raymond Escholier, *Un Amant de Génie*, p. 554.
[13] Victor Hugo, "La Forêt" (*Toute la Lyre*, vol. II, VI, XL, pp. 146-7):

> Vaguely we felt ourselves slip on that steep incline
> Idyllic, where love—traitor and god—makes serpentine
> Descent, leading men on through who knows what fair glade
> Often to Hell, by way of paradise. Spring urges the escapade
> With sweet indulgence. Nothing stirs.
> Onward we went. Those pink cheeks that were hers
> Flooded to scarlet. Trembling with success, I nothing knew
> Save that what I was thinking, she was thinking too.

[14] Raymond Escholier, *Un Amant de Génie*, p. 561.
[15] Raymond Escholier, *Victor Hugo cet inconnu*, p. 321.
[16] Juliette Drouet, *Mille et une lettres*, etc., p. 700.
[17] Edmond de Goncourt, *Journal*, vol. V, p. 74.
[18] A private road belonging to the Villa Montmorency.
[19] Edmond de Goncourt, *Journal*, vol. V, pp. 71-3.
[20] Victor Hugo, "Nuda" (*Océan*, LIX, p. 96):

> She said: "Shall I keep on my shift?"
> I said: "Never can woman make lovelier gift
> Than utter nakedness." O! short-lived days of Spring!
> That start with laughter, and end in pondering.
> Joy! Ashtaroth unmasked: Ecstasy, Isis bare.
> Have you at times looked at a rising star?
> A gorgeous spectacle! "Well, here I am!" said she.
> And thus did Venus stand for Adonis to see.

[21] Maurice Barrès, *Mes Cahiers*, vol. XII, p. 28.
[22] Victor Hugo, "Soyez donc demi-dieu" (*Océan*, LVIII, p. 95):

> Sad human spirit in the body pent!
> Delirium of the senses, all ecstasy and crawling!
> The Swan besmirched with black, the Angel falling!
> The flesh, aye, that's the reef, the ultimate deep
> To which, diminished and abased, the noblest must creep!

> No man so strong but falls, or some time fell.
> David on Bathsheba foundered, so they tell:
> Before Aspasia Socrates did bite
> The dust, and Solomon shared the bed where slept the Shulamite.

[23] Maison de Victor Hugo, *Carnet de 1873*.

[24] Ibid.

[25] Ibid.

[26] Juliette Drouet, *Mille et une lettres*, etc., p. 701.

[27] The reference is to the handsome Pécopin and the beautiful Baldour in *Le Rhin*.

[28] Juliette Drouet, *Mille et une lettres*, etc., p. 701.

[29] Victor Hugo, "Historique," *Depuis l'exil* (*Actes et Paroles*, vol. III, p. 584).

[30] Gustave Flaubert, *Correspondance*, vol. VII, p. 108.

[31] Victor Hugo, *Depuis l'exil* (*Actes et Paroles*, vol. III, p. 201).

[32] Paul Valéry, "Situation de Baudelaire" (*Variété*, vol. II, p. 152).

[33] Maurice Barrès, *Mes Cahiers*, vol. IX, p. 50.

[34] Arsène Houssaye, *Confessions*, vol. V, p. 294.

[35] Henri Mondor, *Vie de Mallarmé*, p. 412 (in the one-volume edition published by Gallimard in 1943). See, too, Adila Ayda, "L'influence de Victor Hugo sur Stéphane Mallarmé" (Istanbul, *Dialogues*, 1953).

CHAPTER 49

[1] Juliette Drouet, *Mille et une lettres*, etc., pp. 714-15.

[2] Henri Guillemin, *Victor Hugo par lui-même*, p. 68.

[3] Juliette Drouet, *Mille et une lettres*, etc., p. 709.

[4] Madame Alphonse Daudet, "Souvenirs autour d'un groupe littéraire," an article published in the *Revue Bleue*, November 14th, 1908, p. 611.

[5] Juliette Drouet, *Mille et une lettres*, etc., pp. 707-8.

[6] See Victor Hugo, *Toute la Lyre*, VI, XXXV, p. 141.

[7] Victor Hugo, "A une Immortelle" (*Toute la Lyre*, VI, LI, p. 170).

> What? you, all glory, radiance and grace,
> That never fades, why should you fear what fades apace?
> How should a Goddess, a celestial beauty fear
> Earth's lower beauty? You who queen it here
> Dread but a fugitive brilliance which must pass,
> Shed by the breeze of April on the grass—
> And as verbena, sage and thyme,
> Born of the fleeting light of morning's clime,
> Scent for a moment fields and rustic glades,
> Not lasting out the dawn being her maids?
> You, jealous? Of whom? You, distressed! and how?
> Day without night are you: love without end art thou.
>
> Rest in your sky, serene. What boots it to a flame.
> A brightness and a light, ever the same,
> Whose realm the crimson deepness is,
> Made for the glowing sun's eternal kiss,
> —That a ray should on the flower its warmth dispose?
> The star in Heaven does not fear the rose.

[8] Juliette Drouet, *Mille et une lettres*, etc., p. 717.

[9] Ibid., pp. 719-20.

[10] Edmond de Goncourt, *Journal*, vol. V, pp. 186-7 and 201.

[11] Unpublished letter. Alfred Dupont Collection.

[12] Juliette Drouet, *Mille et une lettres*, etc., p. 743.

[13] Victor Hugo, "L'Amnistie au Sénat, séance du 22 mai, 1876" (*Actes et Paroles*, vol. III, *Depuis l'exil*, p. 253).

[14] Juliette Drouet, *Mille et une lettres*, etc., p. 751.

[15] Ibid., p. 745.

[16] Victor Hugo, *Choses vues*, vol. II, p. 231.

[17] Victor Hugo, "Historique," *Depuis l'exil* (*Actes et Paroles,* vol. III, p. 590).

[18] Victor Hugo, "Le 16 mai. La dissolution" (*Actes et Paroles,* vol. III, *Depuis l'exil,* p. 275).

[19] Pierre Audiat, *Ainsi vécut Victor Hugo,* p. 332.

[20] The name of Jean Jaurès was given to this avenue in 1914.

[21] Étoile-Montholon.

CHAPTER 50

[1] Bibliothèque nationale, département des manuscrits, N.A.F. 13475, fol. 29.

[2] Bibliothèque nationale, département des manuscrits, N.A.F. 13475, fol. 27.

[3] Bibliothèque nationale, département des manuscrits, N.A.F. 13475, fol. 37. Unpublished.

[4] "Historique," *L'Art d'être Grand-Père,* p. 624.

[5] Georges Hugo, *Mon Grand-Père,* p. 31.

[6] Ibid., p. 21.

[7] Victor Hugo, "Victor, sed victus" (*L'Art d'être Grand-Père,* Book I, IV, p. 411).

[8] Victor Hugo, "Poème du Jardin des Plantes" (*L'Art d'être Grand-Père,* Book I, XI, p. 424):

> I'd not demand that God should be for ever at His best,
> One must be patient with the extravagant zest
> In so great a poet, and not presume to teach
> His business to God, who having stained the peach,
> And bent the rainbow over His disciplined sea,
> Does, after dressing out with rapturous glee
> The gorgeous humming-bird, invent the mastodon.
> It is His will, and not for us to question,
> To show bad taste; to set the hydra in the deep-down den
> And the worm creeping along the drain;
> To be in all things unforeseeable, and so
> Choose to be Rabelais fathering Angelo.
> For He is God: and we must fain accept.

[9] Victor Hugo, "Fenêtres ouvertes. Le Matin. En dormant" (*L'Art d'être Grand-Père,* Book I, XI, p. 424):

> I can hear voices. Behind my lids the light begins to swell.
> In Saint Peter's church the din of a swinging bell.
> The cries of bathers: "Nearer . . . far out . . . by you . . .
> No, there!" The birds are twittering, and young Jeanne, too.
> Georges calls her. Cocks crow. A trowel rasps on a slate.
> Down in the lane horses are moving with a leisurely gait.
> Scream of a scythe as somebody starts to mow.
> Knocks. Noises. Tilers on the roof moving to and fro.
> Harbour sounds. Steam hissing. Now and then
> Come gusts of military music. Babble of working men
> Out on the pier. French voices: "How are you? . . .
> A thousand thanks—well, time to say adieu."
> It must be late, for, just now, robin sang.
> Din from a far-off smithy, and the clang
> Of hammers. Clop of water. A steamer puffing free.
> A fly comes through the window. Vast breathing of the sea.

[10] Victor Hugo, *L'Art d'être Grand-Père,* "Revue de la critique," p. 639.

CHAPTER 51

[1] As witnesses at Alice's wedding, which took place on April 3rd, 1877. Unpublished letter, Alfred Dupont Collection.

[2] Unpublished letter, Alfred Dupont Collection.

[3] Victor Hugo, "Philémon perverti" ("Comédies cassées," II, "Reliquat," *Théâtre en liberté,* p. 525).

> To take a girl and leave that fond, white head!
> Feast on young flesh with new and succulent bread,
> Instead of on stale meat with biscuit hard and mouldy!
> O fascination that has dazzled me!

> I'll break with the old wife, I'll her defy!
> Even though I know that I am wallowing in a sty.

4 Victor Hugo, "Philémon perverti" ("Comédies cassées," II, "Reliquat," *Théâtre en liberté*, p. 525).

5 Bibliothèque nationale, département des manuscrits, N.A.F. 13475, fol. 41 (November 19th, 1873).

6 Bibliothèque nationale, département des manuscrits, N.A.F. 13475, fol. 110.

7 Juliette Drouet, *Mille et une lettres*, etc., p. 873.

8 Ibid., p. 775.

9 Juana Richard-Lesclide, *Victor Hugo intime*, pp. 69-71.

10 Ibid., p. 72.

11 Ibid., p. 74.

12 Ibid., p. 203.

13 Juliette Drouet, *Mille et une lettres*, etc., pp. 793-5.

14 Ibid., p. 793.

15 Victor Hugo, *Choses vues*, vol. II, pp. 236-7.

16 Maurice Barrès, *Mes Cahiers*, vol. X, p. 275.

17 Juana Richard-Lesclide, *Victor Hugo intime*, p. 203.

18 Raymond Escholier, *Un Amant de Génie*, p. 615.

19 Juana Richard-Lesclide, *Victor Hugo intime*, pp. 203-4.

20 Juliette Drouet, *Mille et une lettres*, etc., p. 822.

21 Ibid., p. 823.

22 Ibid., p. 827.

CHAPTER 52

1 Louis Guimbaud, *Victor Hugo et Juliette Drouet*, p. 254.

2 Paul Souchon, *Juliette Drouet*, p. 243.

3 Juliette Drouet, *Mille et une lettres*, etc., p. 828.

4 Louis Barthou, *Les Amours d'un poète*, p. 385.

5 Louis Guimbaud, *Victor Hugo et Juliette Drouet*, p. 254.

6 On October 30th, 1881.

7 Paul Souchon, *Juliette Drouet*, p. 254.

8 Victor Hugo, "Moi" (*Tas de Pierres*, p. 271).

9 J. Degueldre, "Un illustre Actionnaire de la Banque, Victor Hugo," an article published in *La Revue de la Banque Nationale de Belgique*, February 1948. The delicate negotiations concerned with the transfer are all set out on pp. 3-5.

10 Collection of Madame André Gaveau.

11 Victor Hugo, "Vers faits en dormant" (*Tas de Pierres*, p. 491):

> Oh! how, without her, can I live through years?
> Take Thou my life, God, take me to Thyself,
> Let not a day, let not an hour go by!
> What will become of me until I die?

CHAPTER 53

1 Raymond Escholier, *Un Amant de Génie*, p. 617.

2 Juana Richard-Lesclide, *Victor Hugo intime*, p. 204.

3 See Maurice-Pierre Boyé, "Le Dernier Amour de Victor Hugo," an article published in *Quo Vadis*, December 1953, p. 85. To the unpublished texts supplied by Monsieur Boyé, who owns the Lesclide archives, may be added a detail from the Registry of Births and Deaths. Blanche, Rochereuil's widow, died on January 10th, 1909, at the Laënnec Hospital, where she held the post of superintendent.

4 Victor Hugo, "Moi" (*Tas de Pierres*, p. 271).

5 Maurice Barrès, *Mes Cahiers*, vol. III, p. 55.

6 Romain Rolland, "Le Vieux Orphée," an article published in *Europe*, special number, February-March 1952, pp. 18-19.

7 Ibid., p. 21.

8 Maurice Barrès, *Mes Cahiers*, vol. X, p. 276.

9 Ibid., p. 191.

[10] Paul Berret, "Victor Hugo et la Vie future," an article published in the *Revue des Deux Mondes,* May 15th, 1935, p. 348.

[11] Henri Guillemin, *Victor Hugo par lui-même,* p. 81.

[12] Anatole France, *La Vie Littéraire,* vol. I, p. 115.

[13] Hugo, in fact, survived Gambetta, who died in 1882. By a deed, registered on July 1st, 1885, Jules Grévy refused to act as executor of the will. Paul Meurice, Auguste Vacquerie and Ernest Lefèvre (Vacquerie's nephew) faithfully carried out the duties of literary executors.

[14] In an earlier version of the will (April 9th, 1875) the children's mother is several times referred to as *Madame Charles Hugo.* Does the substitution of the single Christian name *Alice* indicate the repugnance felt by Hugo for calling his son's remarried widow *Madame Simon, known as Lockroy?*

[15] This clause had become null and void owing to the death of Juliette Drouet in 1883.

[16] Victor Hugo, *Actes et Paroles,* vol. III, *Depuis l'exil,* p. 358.

[17] Georges Hugo, *Mon Grand-Père,* p. 53.

[18] Henri Guillemin, *Victor Hugo par lui-même,* p. 58.

[19] Victor Hugo, *Les Quatre Vents de l'Esprit,* Book I xli, pp. 99-100:

> Just when from pole to pole one's name is being sung
> Somebody gives a push in the back, and out one is flung.
>
> .   .   .   .
>
> It needs but a runaway horse, a speck of gravel or so,
> A door left open in winter weather, a bladder blockage, and lo
> Instead of a woman, a priest comes into the room.

[20] Paul Berret, "Victor Hugo et la Vie future," an article published in the *Revue des Deux Mondes,* May 15th, 1935, p. 349.

[21] Arsène Houssaye, *Confessions,* vol. V, p. 317.

[22] Raymond Escholier, *Victor Hugo, cet inconnu,* p. 336.

[23] Romain Rolland, "Le Vieux Orphée," an article published in *Europe,* special number, February-March, 1952, p. 23.

[24] Maurice Barrès, *Les Déracinés,* p. 216.

[25] Romain Rolland, "Le Vieux Orphée," *Europe,* special number, February-March 1952, pp. 25-6.

[26] Victor Hugo, "A la Colonne" (*Les Chants du Crépuscule,* vol. II, p. 201).

[27] Henri Mondor, *Vie de Mallarmé,* pp. 470-1.

[28] Charles Baudelaire, "Victor Hugo" (*L'Art romantique,* vol. XIX, p. 519) (in the Pléiade edition, vol. II).

[29] Léon-Paul Fargue.

Index